THE WAITE GROUP'S

Object-Oriented Programming in C++, Third Edition

Robert Lafore

SAMS

201 West 103rd St., Indianapolis, Indiana, 46290 USA

EXECUTIVE EDITOR: Tracy Dunkelberger
ACQUISITIONS EDITOR: Tracy Dunkelberger
DEVELOPMENT EDITOR: Jeff Durham
MANAGING EDITOR: Jodi Jensen
SENIOR EDITOR: Susan Ross Moore
COPY EDITOR: Howard A. Jones
INDEXER: Rebecca Salerno
PROOFREADER: Eddie Lushbaugh
TECHNICAL EDITOR: Andrei Kossorouko
SOFTWARE DEVELOPMENT SPECIALIST: Dan Scherf
TEAM COORDINATOR: Michelle Newcomb
INTERIOR DESIGN: Gary Adair
COVER DESIGN: Karen Ruggles
LAYOUT TECHNICIANS: Tim Osborn, Staci Somers, Mark Walchle

Copyright © 1999 by Sams Publishing

All rights reserved. No part of this book shall be reproduced, stored in a retrieval system, or transmitted by any means, electronic, mechanical, photocopying, recording, or otherwise, without written permission from the publisher. No patent liability is assumed with respect to the use of the information contained herein. Although every precaution has been taken in the preparation of this book, the publisher and author assume no responsibility for errors or omissions. Neither is any liability assumed for damages resulting from the use of the information contained herein.

International Standard Book Number: 0-57169-160-X

Library of Congress Catalog Card Number: 98-85905

Printed in the United States of America

First Printing: December 1998

00 99 98   4   3   2   1

Trademarks

All terms mentioned in this book that are known to be trademarks or service marks have been appropriately capitalized. Sams Publishing cannot attest to the accuracy of this information. Use of a term in this book should not be regarded as affecting the validity of any trademark or service mark.

Warning and Disclaimer

Every effort has been made to make this book as complete and as accurate as possible, but no warranty or fitness is implied. The information provided is on an "as is" basis. The authors and the publisher shall have neither liability or responsibility to any person or entity with respect to any loss or damages arising from the information contained in this book or from the use of programs accompanying it.

Dedication

This book is dedicated to GGL and her indomitable spirit.

About the Author

Robert Lafore has been writing books about computer programming since 1982. His best-selling titles include *Assembly Language Programming for the IBM PC*, *C Programming Using Turbo C++*, *C++ Interactive Course*, and *Data Structures and Algorithms in Java*. Mr. Lafore holds degrees in mathematics and electrical engineering, and has been active in programming since the days of the PDP-5, when 4K of main memory was considered luxurious. His interests include hiking, windsurfing, and recreational mathematics.

Contents at a Glance

Introduction 1
Chapter 1: The Big Picture 7
Chapter 2: C++ Programming Basics 23
Chapter 3: Loops and Decisions 67
Chapter 4: Structures 119
Chapter 5: Functions 147
Chapter 6: Objects and Classes 195
Chapter 7: Arrays and Strings 241
Chapter 8: Operator Overloading .291
Chapter 9: Inheritance 337
Chapter 10: Pointers 389
Chapter 11: Virtual Functions 453
Chapter 12: Streams and Files 513
Chapter 13: Multifile Programs 573
Chapter 14: Templates and Exceptions 615
Chapter 15: The Standard Template Library 653
Chapter 16: Object-Oriented Design 721

Appendix A: ASCII Table 777
Appendix B: C++ Keywords 787
Appendix C: Microsoft Visual C++ 791
Appendix D: Borland C++Builder 797
Appendix E: Console Graphics Lite 807
Appendix F: Debugging 813
Appendix G: Answers to Questions and Exercises 831
Appendix H: Bibliography 889
Index 891

Contents

Introduction 1

Chapter 1: The Big Picture 7

Why Do We Need Object-Oriented Programming? .7
    Procedural Languages 8
    The Object-Oriented Approach 11
Characteristics of Object-Oriented Languages 14
    Objects 14
    Classes 15
    Inheritance 16
    Reusability 18
    Creating New Data Types 18
    Polymorphism and Overloading 19
C++ and C 19
Laying the Groundwork 20
Summary 20
Questions 21

Chapter 2: C++ Programming Basics 23

Getting Started 23
Basic Program Construction 24
    Functions 24
    Program Statements 26
    Whitespace 26
Output Using oout 27
    String Constants 28
Directives 28
    Preprocessor Directives 28
    Header Files 29
    The using Directive 29
Comments 29
    Comment Syntax 30
    When to Use Comments 30
    Alternative Comment Syntax 30
Integer Variables 31
    Defining Integer Variables 31
    Declarations and Definitions 33
    Variable Names 33
    Assignment Statements 33

Integer Constants 34
Output Variations 34
The `endl` Manipulator 34
Other Integer Types 35
Character Variables 35
Character Constants 36
Initialization 37
Escape Sequences 37
Input with `cin` 38
Variables Defined at Point of Use .39
Cascading `<<` 39
Expressions 40
Precedence 40
Floating Point Types 40
Type `float` 41
Type `double` and `long double` 42
Floating-Point Constants 42
The `const` Qualifier 43
The `#define` Directive 43
Type `bool` 43
The `setw` Manipulator 44
Cascading the Insertion Operator .46
Multiple Definitions 46
The `iomanip` Header File 46
Variable Type Summary 46
`unsigned` Data Types 47
Type Conversion 48
Automatic Conversions 49
Casts 50
Arithmetic Operators 52
The Remainder Operator 52
Arithmetic Assignment Operators .53
Increment Operators 54
Library Functions 56
Header Files 58
Library Files 58
Header Files and Library Files 58
Two Ways to Use `#include` 59
Summary 60
Questions 61
Exercises 63

Chapter 3: Loops and Decisions   67

Relational Operators 67

Loops 70

    The `for` Loop 70

    Debugging Animation 75

    `for` Loop Variations 76

    The `while` Loop 77

    Precedence: Arithmetic and Relational Operators 80

    The `do` Loop 81

    When to Use Which Loop 84

Decisions 84

    The `if` Statement 84

    The `if...else` Statement 88

    The `else...if` Construction 95

    The `switch` Statement 96

    The Conditional Operator 100

Logical Operators 103

    Logical **and** Operator 103

    Logical **OR** Operator 105

    Logical **NOT** Operator 106

Precedence Summary 107

Other Control Statements 107

    The `break` Statement 107

    The `continue` Statement 110

    The `goto` Statement 111

Summary 112

Questions 112

Exercises 115

Chapter 4: Structures   119

Structures 119

    A Simple Structure 120

    Declaring the Structure 120

    Defining a Structure Variable 122

    Accessing Structure Members 123

    Other Structure Features 124

    A Measurement Example 127

    Structures Within Structures 129

    A Card Game Example 132

    Structures and Classes 134

Enumerations 135
   Days of the Week 135
   One Thing or Another 137
   Organizing the Cards 139
   Specifying Integer Values 141
   Not Perfect 141
   Other Examples 141
Summary 141
Questions 142
Exercises 144

Chapter 5: Functions   147

Simple Functions 148
   The Function Declaration 149
   Calling the Function 149
   The Function Definition 150
   Comparison with Library Functions 151
   Eliminating the Declaration 152
Passing Arguments to Functions 152
   Passing Constants 153
   Passing Variables 154
   Passing by Value 155
   Structures as Arguments 155
   Names in the Declaration 160
Returning Values from Functions 161
   The `return` Statement 162
   Returning Structure Variables .164
Reference Arguments 166
   Passing Simple Data Types by Reference 166
   A More Complex Pass by Reference 168
   Passing Structures by Reference 170
   Notes on Passing by Reference 172
Overloaded Functions 172
   Different Numbers of Arguments 172
   Different Kinds of Arguments 174
Inline Functions 176
Default Arguments 178
Variables and Storage Classes 179
   Automatic Variables 180
   External Variables 182
   Static Variables 183
   Storage 185

Returning by Reference 185
    Function Calls on the Left of the Equal Sign .186
    Don't Worry Yet 187
const Function Arguments 187
Summary 188
Questions 189
Exercises 191

Chapter 6: Objects and Classes   195

A Simple Class 195
    Classes and Objects 197
    Declaring the Class 197
    Using the Class 199
    Calling Member Functions 200
C++ Objects As Physical Objects 202
    Widget Parts as Objects 202
    Circles as Objects 203
C++ Objects As Data Types 205
Constructors 206
    A Counter Example 206
    A Graphics Example 209
    Destructors 210
Objects as Function Arguments 211
    Overloaded Constructors 212
    Member Functions Defined Outside the Class 213
    Objects As Arguments 214
The Default Copy Constructor 216
Returning Objects from Functions 217
    Arguments and Objects 218
A Card-Game Example 219
Structures and Classes 223
Classes, Objects, and Memory 224
Static Class Data 224
    Uses of Static Class Data 225
    An Example of Static Class Data 225
    Separate Declaration and Definition 227
const and Classes 228
    const Member Functions 228
    const Objects 230
What Does It All Mean? 231
Summary 232
Questions 233
Exercises 235

Chapter 7: Arrays and Strings   241

Array Fundamentals 242
   Defining Arrays 242
   Array Elements 243
   Accessing Array Elements 244
   Averaging Array Elements 244
   Initializing Arrays 245
   Multidimensional Arrays 246
   Passing Arrays to Functions .251
Function Declaration with Array Argument 252
   Arrays of Structures 253
Arrays As Class Member Data 255
Arrays of Objects 258
   Arrays of English Distances 258
   Arrays of Cards 261
C-Strings 264
   C-string Variables 265
   Avoiding Buffer Overflow 265
   String Constants 267
   Reading Embedded Blanks 267
   Reading Multiple Lines 268
   Copying a String the Hard Way 269
   Copying a String the Easy Way 270
   Arrays of Strings 270
   Strings As Class Members 272
   A User-Defined String Type .273
The Standard C++ `string` Class 275
   Defining and Assigning `string` Objects 276
   Input/Output with `string` Objects 277
   Finding `string` Objects 278
   Modifying `string` Objects .279
   Comparing `string` Objects .280
   Accessing Characters in `string` Objects 281
   Other `string` Functions 282
Summary 283
Questions 283
Exercises 286

Chapter 8: Operator Overloading   291

Overloading Unary Operators 292
   The `operator` Keyword 293
   Operator Arguments 294

Operator Return Values 294
Nameless Temporary Objects 296
Postfix Notation 297
Overloading Binary Operators 299
Arithmetic Operators 299
Concatenating Strings 302
Multiple Overloading 304
Comparison Operators 304
Arithmetic Assignment Operators 307
The Subscript Operator [] 309
Data Conversion 312
Conversions Between Basic Types 313
Conversions Between Objects and Basic Types 313
Conversions Between Objects of Different Classes 318
Conversions: When to Use What 324
Pitfalls of Operator Overloading and Conversion .325
Use Similar Meanings 325
Use Similar Syntax 325
Show Restraint 326
Avoid Ambiguity 326
Not All Operators Can Be Overloaded 326
Keywords `explicit` and `mutable` 326
Preventing Conversions with `explicit` 326
Changing `const` Object Data Using `mutable` 328
Summary 330
Questions 330
Exercises 333

Chapter 9: Inheritance   337
Derived Class and Base Class 338
Specifying the Derived Class 340
Accessing Base Class Members 341
The protected Access Specifier 342
Derived Class Constructors 345
Overriding Member Functions 347
Which Function Is Used? 348
Scope Resolution with Overridden Functions .349
Inheritance in the English Distance Class 349
Operation of `englen` 351
Constructors in `DistSign` 351
Member Functions in `DistSign` 352
Abetting Inheritance 352

Class Hierarchies 352
   "Abstract" Base Class 356
   Constructors and Member Functions 356
Inheritance and Graphics Shapes .357
Public and Private Inheritance 359
   Access Combinations 360
   Access Specifiers: When to Use What 362
Levels of Inheritance 362
Multiple Inheritance 365
   Member Functions in Multiple Inheritance 366
`private` Derivation in `empmult` 371
   Constructors in Multiple Inheritance 371
Ambiguity in Multiple Inheritance 374
Containership: Classes Within Classes 376
Inheritance and Program Development 380
Summary 381
Questions 381
Exercises 383

Chapter 10: Pointers   **389**
Addresses and Pointers 390
The Address-of Operator **&** 391
   Pointer Variables 392
   Syntax Quibbles 394
   Accessing the Variable Pointed To 395
   Pointer to **void** 398
Pointers and Arrays 399
   Pointer Constants and Pointer Variables 401
Pointers and Functions 402
   Passing Simple Variables 402
   Passing Arrays 404
   Sorting Array Elements 406
Pointers and C-type Strings 410
   Pointers to String Constants .410
   Strings As Function Arguments 411
   Copying a String Using Pointers 412
   Library String Functions 413
   The **const** Modifier and Pointers 413
   Arrays of Pointers to Strings .414
Memory Management: **new** and **delete** 416
   The **new** Operator 416
   The **delete** Operator 418
   A String Class Using **new** 419

Pointers to Objects 420
   Referring to Members 421
   Another Approach to new 422
   An Array of Pointers to Objects 423
A Linked List Example 425
   A Chain of Pointers 425
   Adding an Item to the List 427
   Displaying the List Contents 428
   Self-Containing Classes 429
   Augmenting linklist 429
Pointers to Pointers 429
   Sorting Pointers 431
   The person** Data Type 432
   Comparing Strings 433
A Parsing Example 434
   Parsing Arithmetic Expressions 434
   The parse Program 435
Simulation: A Horse Race 438
Debugging Pointers 443
Summary 443
Questions 444
Exercises 447

Chapter 11: Virtual Functions   **453**
Finding An Object's Class with typeid() 453
Virtual Functions 453
   Normal Member Functions Accessed with Pointers 454
   Virtual Member Functions Accessed with Pointers 456
   Late Binding 458
   Abstract Classes and Pure Virtual Functions 459
   Virtual Functions and the person Class 460
   Virtual Functions in a Graphics Example 463
   Virtual Destructors 465
   Virtual Base Classes 466
Friend Functions 468
   Friends As Bridges 468
   Breaching the Walls 469
   English Distance Example 469
   friends for Functional Notation 472
   friend Classes 475

Static Functions 476
    Accessing `static` Functions 477
    Numbering the Objects 478
    Investigating Destructors 478
Assignment and Copy Initialization 478
    Overloading the Assignment Operator 479
    The Copy Constructor 482
    A Memory-Efficient String Class 485
The `this` Pointer 492
    Accessing Member Data with `this` 493
    Using `this` for Returning Values 494
    Revised `strimem` Program 495
Dynamic Type Information 498
    Checking the Type of a Class with `dynamic_cast` 498
    Changing Pointer Types with `dynamic_cast` 499
    The `typeid` Operator 501
Summary 502
Questions 503
Exercises 506

Chapter 12: Streams and Files   **513**
Stream Classes 513
    Advantages of Streams 513
    The Stream Class Hierarchy 514
    The `ios` Class 515
    The `istream` Class 519
    The `ostream` Class 521
    The `iostream` and the `_withassign` Classes 521
Stream Errors 522
    Error-Status Bits 522
    Inputting Numbers 523
    Too Many Characters 524
    No-Input Input 524
    Inputting Strings and Characters 525
    Error-Free Distances 525
Disk File I/O with Streams 528
    Formatted File I/O 528
    Strings with Embedded Blanks 530
    Character I/O 532
    Binary I/O 533

The `reinterpret_cast` Operator 535
Closing Files 535
Object I/O 535
I/O with Multiple Objects 538
File Pointers 540
Specifying the Position 541
Specifying the Offset 541
The `tellg()` Function 543
Error Handling in File I/O 544
Reacting to Errors 544
Analyzing Errors 545
File I/O with Member Functions 546
Objects That Read and Write Themselves 546
Classes That Read and Write Themselves 549
Overloading the Extraction and Insertion Operators 557
Overloading for `cout` and `cin` 557
Overloading for Files 559
Memory As a Stream Object 561
Command-Line Arguments 562
Printer Output 565
Summary 566
Questions 567
Exercises 569

Chapter 13: Multifile Programs   **573**
Reasons for Multifile Programs 573
Class Libraries 573
Organization and Conceptualization .576
Creating a Multifile Program 576
Header Files 576
Directory 576
Projects 576
A Very Long Number Class 577
Numbers As Strings 577
The Class Specifier 578
The Member Functions 579
The Application Program 582
A High-Rise Elevator Simulation 583
Running the `elev` Program 583
Designing the System 584
Listings for `elev` 586
Elevator Strategy 597

A Water-Distribution System 598
   Components of a Water System 598
   Flow, Pressure, and Back Pressure 599
   Component Input and Output 600
   Making Connections 601
   Simplifying Assumptions 601
   Program Design 602
   Programming the Connections 606
   Base and Derived Classes 606
   The Component Base Class 607
   The Flows-Into Operator 607
   Derived Classes 608
   The `Switch` Class 608
   The pipe_app.cpp File 609
Summary 612
Questions 612
Projects 613

Chapter 14: Templates and Exceptions   **615**
Function Templates 615
   A Simple Function Template 616
   Function Templates with Multiple Arguments 619
Class Templates 622
   Class Name Depends on Context 625
   A Linked List Class Using Templates 628
   Storing User-Defined Data Types 630
Exceptions 633
   Why Do We Need Exceptions? 633
   Exception Syntax 634
   A Simple Exception Example 636
   Multiple Exceptions 639
   Exceptions with the Distance Class .641
   Exceptions with Arguments 642
   Extracting Data from the Exception Object 645
   The `bad_alloc` Class 646
   Exception Notes 646
Summary 648
Questions 648
Exercises 650

Chapter 15: The Standard Template Library   **653**
Introduction to the STL 653
   Containers 654
   Algorithms 659

Iterators 660
Potential Problems with the STL 661
Algorithms 661
The `find()` Algorithm 661
The `count()` Algorithm 662
The `sort()` Algorithm 663
The `search()` Algorithm 663
The `merge()` Algorithm 664
Function Objects 665
The `for_each()` Algorithm 667
The `transform()` Algorithm 668
Sequential Containers 669
Vectors 669
Lists 672
Deques 675
Iterators 676
Iterators as Smart Pointers 677
Iterators as an Interface 678
Matching Algorithms with Containers 680
Iterators at Work 683
Specialized Iterators 686
Iterator Adapters 687
Stream Iterators 690
Associative Containers 693
Sets and Multisets 694
Maps and Multimaps 697
Storing User-Defined Objects 700
A Set of `person` Objects 700
A List of `person` Objects 703
Function Objects 707
Predefined Function Objects 707
Writing Your Own Function Objects 710
Function `objects` Used to Modify Container Behavior 714
Summary 714
Questions 715
Exercises 718

Chapter 16: Object-Oriented Design   721
Our Approach to OOD 721
CRC Cards 722
Use Cases 722
Class Diagrams 722

The Programming Problem 722
   Hand-Written Forms 723
   Assumptions 724
The CRC Modeling Team 725
   Members of the Team 726
   The Problem Summary Statement 726
Constructing the CRC Cards 727
   Classes 728
   Responsibilities 729
   Collaborators 731
   The Tenant CRC Card 731
   The Expense CRC Card 732
   The Rent Input Screen CRC Card 732
   The Rent Record CRC Card 733
   The Expense Input Screen CRC Card 734
   The Expense Record CRC Card .734
   The Annual Report CRC Card .734
   The User Interface CRC Card 735
   The Scribe 736
Use Cases 737
   Use Case 1: User Inputs an Expense 737
   Use Case 2: The User Inputs a Rent 738
   Trouble with the "User Inputs a Rent" Use Case 738
   The Remaining Use Cases 742
   Simplifications 743
Class Relationships 744
   Attribute 744
   Association 745
   Navigability 745
   Aggregation 746
   Composition 746
   Objects and Classes 748
   Multiplicity 748
   Generalization 749
   Coupling and Cohesion 750
Class Diagrams 750
   Arranging the CRC Cards 751
   Associations in Landlord 752
   Aggregations in Landlord 753
Writing the Program 753
   The Header File 753
   The .cpp Files 759
   More Simplifications 768

Interacting with the Program 768
Prototyping 770
Final Thoughts 771
Summary 771
Questions 772
Projects 775

Appendix A: ASCII Chart   **777**

Appendix B: Standard C++ Keywords   **787**
A 787
B 787
C 787
D 787
E 788
F 788
G 788
I 788
L 788
M 788
N 788
O 789
P 789
R 789
S 789
T 789
U 789
V 790
W 790

Appendix C: Microsoft Visual C++   **791**
Screen Elements 791
Single-File Programs 792
    Building an Existing File 792
    Writing a New File 792
    Run-Time Type Information (RTTI) .793
Multifile Programs 793
    Projects and Workspaces 793
    Source Files Already Exist 793
    Saving, Closing, and Opening Projects 794
    Compiling and Linking 794
Building Console Graphics Lite Programs 794

Debugging 795
    Single Stepping 795
    Watching Variables 796
    Stepping Into Functions 796
    Breakpoints 796

Appendix D: Borland C++Builder   797

Running the Example Programs in C++Builder 797
Cleaning up the Screen 798
Creating a New Project 798
Saving a Project 799
Starting with Existing Files 800
Compiling, Linking, and Executing 800
    Executing from C++Builder 800
    Executing from MS-DOS 801
    Precompiled Header Files 801
    Closing and Opening Projects 801
Adding a Header File to Your Project 801
    Creating a New Header File 801
    Editing an Existing Header File 802
    Telling C++Builder the Header File's Location 802
Projects with Multiple Source Files 802
    Creating Additional Source Files 802
    Adding Additional Source Files to Your Project 803
    The Project Manager 803
    Weird New Lines in Your Program .803
Console Graphics Lite Programs 804
Debugging 804
    Single Stepping 804
    Watching Variables 805
    Tracing Into Functions 805
    Breakpoints 805

Appendix E: Console Graphics Lite   807

Using the Console Graphics Routines .808
The Console Graphics Functions 808
Implementations of the Console Graphics Lite functions 810
    Microsoft Compilers 811
    Borland Compilers 811

Appendix F: Debugging   813

Algorithms 813
Member Functions 825
Iterators 827

Appendix G: Answers to Questions and Exercises 831

Chapter 1 831
   Answers to Questions 831
Chapter 2 832
   Answers to Questions 832
   Solutions to Exercises 833
Chapter 3 834
   Answers to Questions 834
   Solutions to Exercises 836
Chapter 4 838
   Answers to Questions 838
   Solutions to Exercises 839
Chapter 5 841
   Answers to Questions 841
   Solutions to Exercises 842
Chapter 6 845
   Answers to Questions 845
   Solutions to Exercises 846
Chapter 7 849
   Answers to Questions 849
   Solutions to Exercises 850
Chapter 8 853
   Answers to Questions 853
   Solutions to Exercises 854
Chapter 9 859
   Solutions to Exercises 859
Chapter 10 864
   Answers to Questions 864
   Solutions to Exercises 865
Chapter 11 869
   Answers to Questions 869
   Solutions to Exercises 870
Chapter 12 874
   Answers to Questions 874
   Solutions to Exercises 875
Chapter 13 877
   Answers to Questions 877
Chapter 14 878
   Answers to Questions 878
   Solutions to Exercises 879

Chapter 15 882
   Answers to Questions 882
   Solutions to Exercises 883
Chapter 16 887
   Answers to Questions 887

Appendix H: Bibliography   889

   Books on Advanced C++ 889
   Defining Documents 889
   Books on Specific Topics 890
   Books on the History of C++ 890
   Books on Other Topics 890
   Learning C++ Online 890

Index   891

Acknowledgments to the Third Edition

I'd like to thank the entire team at Macmillan Computer Publishing. In particular, Tracy Dunkelberger ably spearheaded the entire project and exhibited great patience with what turned out to be a lengthy schedule. Jeff Durham handled the myriad details involved in interfacing between me and the editors with skill and good humor. Andrei Kossorouko lent his expertise in C++ to ensure that I didn't make this edition worse instead of better.

Acknowledgments to the Second Edition

My thanks to the following professors—users of this book as a text at their respective colleges and universities—for their help in planning the second edition: Dave Bridges, Frank Cioch, Jack Davidson, Terrence Fries, Jimmie Hattemer, Jack Van Luik, Kieran Mathieson, Bill McCarty, Anita Millspaugh, Ian Moraes, Jorge Prendes, Steve Silva, and Edward Wright.

I would like to thank the many readers of the first edition who wrote in with corrections and suggestions, many of which were invaluable.

At Waite Group Press, Joanne Miller has ably ridden herd on my errant scheduling and filled in as academic liaison, and Scott Calamar, as always, has made sure that everyone knew what they were doing. Deirdre Greene provided an uncannily sharp eye as copy editor.

Thanks, too, to Mike Radtke and Harry Henderson for their expert technical reviews.

Special thanks to Edward Wright, of Western Oregon State College, for reviewing and experimenting with the new exercises.

Acknowledgments to the First Edition

My primary thanks go to Mitch Waite, who poured over every inch of the manuscript with painstaking attention to detail and made a semi-infinite number of helpful suggestions.

Bill McCarty of Azusa Pacific University reviewed the content of the manuscript and its suitability for classroom use, suggested many excellent improvements, and attempted to correct my dyslexic spelling.

George Leach ran all the programs, and, to our horror, found several that didn't perform correctly in certain circumstances. I trust these problems have all been fixed; if not, the fault is entirely mine.

Scott Calamar of The Waite Group dealt with the myriad organizational aspects of writing and producing this book. His competence and unfailing good humor were an important ingredient in its completion.

I would also like to thank Nan Borreson of Borland for supplying the latest releases of the software (among other useful tidbits), Harry Henderson for reviewing the exercises, Louise Orlando of The Waite Group for ably shepherding the book through production, Merrill Peterson of Matrix Productions for coordinating the most trouble-free production run I've ever been involved with, Juan Vargas for the innovative design, and Frances Hasegawa for her uncanny ability to decipher my sketches and produce beautiful and effective art.

Preface

The major changes to this Third Edition are concerned with Standard C++ and object-oriented design. In addition, the book is no longer geared exclusively to Borland C++ compilers.

Standard C++, finalized in the fall of 1997, introduced many new features to C++. Some of these features, such as templates and exceptions, had already been adopted by compiler manufacturers. However, the Standard Template Library (STL) has only recently been included in compilers. This book adds a chapter on the STL.

We've also introduced other features from Standard C++, including new header files, the `string` class, new-style casts, namespaces, and so on.

The design of object-oriented programs has received increasing emphasis in recent years, so we've added a chapter on object-oriented design.

The advent of Standard C++ means that, at least to a greater extent than before, all compilers should treat source code in the same way. Accordingly, we've modified our emphasis on Borland compilers, and now focus on code that should work with any Standard C++ compiler. Of course, the reality seldom matches the ideal, so so the programs in this book have been tested with both Microsoft and Borland compilers, and modified when necessary to work with both of them.

Tell Us What You Think!

As the reader of this book, *you* are our most important critic and commentator. We value your opinion and want to know what we're doing right, what we could do better, what areas you'd like to see us publish in, and any other words of wisdom you're willing to pass our way.

As the Executive Editor for the Advanced Programming and Distributed Architectures team at Macmillan Computer Publishing, I welcome your comments. You can fax, email, or write me directly to let me know what you did or didn't like about this book—as well as what we can do to make our books stronger.

Please note that I cannot help you with technical problems related to the topic of this book, and that due to the high volume of mail I receive, I might not be able to reply to every message.

When you write, please be sure to include this book's title and author as well as your name and phone or fax number. I will carefully review your comments and share them with the author and editors who worked on the book.

Fax: 317-817-7070
Email: `programming@mcp.com`
Mail: Tracy Dunkelberger
        Executive Editor
        Advanced Programming and Distributed Architectures
        Macmillan Computer Publishing
        201 West 103rd Street
        Indianapolis, IN 46290 USA

INTRODUCTION

Object-oriented programming (OOP) is the most dramatic innovation in software development in the last decade. It ranks in importance with the development of the first higher-level languages at the dawn of the computer age. Sooner or later, every programmer will be affected by the object-oriented approach to program design.

Advantages of OOP

Why is everyone so excited about OOP? The chief problem with computer programs is complexity. Large programs are probably the most complicated entities ever created by humans. Because of this complexity, programs are prone to error, and software errors can be expensive and even life threatening (in air-traffic control, for example). Object-oriented programming offers a new and powerful way to cope with this complexity. Its goal is clearer, more reliable, more easily maintained programs.

Languages and Development Platforms

Of the object-oriented programming languages, C++ is by far the most widely used. (Java, a recent addition to the field of OO languages, lacks certain features, such as pointers, that make it less powerful and versatile than C++.)

In past years the standards for C++ have been in a state of evolution. This meant that each compiler vendor handled certain details differently. However, in November 1997, the ANSI/ISO C++ standards committee approved the final draft of what is now known as Standard C++. (ANSI stands for American National Standards Institute, and ISO stands for International Standards Institute.) Standard C++ adds many new features to the language, such as the Standard Template Library (STL). In this book we follow Standard C++ (except for a few places which we'll note as we go along).

The most popular development environments for C++ are manufactured by Microsoft and Borland and run on the various flavors of Microsoft Windows. In this book we've attempted in ensure that all example programs run on the current versions of both Borland and Microsoft compilers. (See Appendixes C and D for more on these compilers.)

What this Book Does

This book teaches object-oriented programming with the C++ programming language, using either Microsoft or Borland compilers. It is suitable for professional programmers, students, and kitchen-table enthusiasts.

New Concepts

OOP involves concepts that are new to programmers of traditional languages such as Pascal, Basic, and C. These ideas, such as classes, inheritance, and polymorphism, lie at the heart of object-oriented programming. But it's easy to lose sight of these concepts when discussing the specifics of an object-oriented language. Many books overwhelm the reader with the details of language features, while ignoring the reason these features exist. This book attempts to keep an eye on the big picture and relate the details to the larger concepts.

The Gradual Approach

We take a gradual approach in this book, starting with very simple programming examples and working up to full-fledged object-oriented applications. We introduce new concepts slowly so that you will have time to digest one idea before going on to the next. We use figures whenever possible to help clarify new ideas. There are questions and programming exercises at the end of most chapters to enhance the book's usefulness in the classroom. Answers to the questions and to the first few (starred) exercises can be found in Appendix D. The exercises vary in difficulty to pose a variety of challenges for the student.

What You Need to Know to Use this Book

You can use this book even if you have no previous programming experience. However, such experience, in BASIC or Pascal, for example, certainly won't hurt.

You do not need to know the C language to use this book. Many books on C++ assume that you already know C, but this one does not. It teaches C++ from the ground up. If you do know C, it won't hurt, but you may be surprised at how little overlap there is between C and C++.

You should be familiar with the basic operations of Microsoft Windows, such as starting applications and copying files.

Software and Hardware

You should have the latest version of either the Microsoft or the Borland C++ compiler. Both products come in low-priced "Learning Editions" suitable for students.

Appendix C provides detailed information on operating the Microsoft compiler, while Appendix D does the same for the Inprise (Borland) product. Other compilers will probably handle most of the programs in this book as written, if they adhere to Standard C++.

Your computer should have enough processor speed, memory, and hard disk space to run the compiler you've chosen. You can check the manufacturer's specifications to determine these requirements.

Console-Mode Programs

The example programs in this book are console-mode programs. They run in a character-mode window within the compiler environment, or directly within an MS-DOS box. This avoids the complexity of full-scale graphics-oriented Windows programs. Go for It!

You may have heard that C++ is difficult to learn. It's true that it might be a little more challenging than BASIC, but it's really quite similar to other languages, with two or three "grand ideas" thrown in. These new ideas are fascinating in themselves, and we think you'll have fun learning about them. They are also becoming part of the programming culture; they're something everyone should know a little bit about, like evolution and psychoanalysis. We hope this book will help you enjoy learning about these new ideas, at the same time that it teaches you the details of programming in C++.

A Note to Teachers

Teachers, and others who already know C, may be interested in some details of the approach we use in this book and how it's organized.

Standard C++

We've revised all the programs in this book to make them compatible with Standard C++. This involved, at a minimum, changes to header files, the addition of namespace designation, and making return type . Many programs received more extensive modifications, including the substitution in many places of the new class for the old C-style strings.

We devote a new chapter to the STL (Standard Template Library), which is now included in Standard C++.

Object-Oriented Design

Students are frequently mystified by the process of breaking a programming project into appropriate classes. For this reason we've added a chapter on object-oriented design. This chapter is placed near the end of the book, but we encourage students to skim it earlier to get the flavor of OOD. Of course, small programs don't require such a formal design approach, but it's helpful to know what's involved even when designing programs in your head. C++ is not the same as C.

Some institutions want their students to learn C before learning C++. In our view this is a mistake. C and C++ are entirely separate languages. It's true that their syntax is similar, and C is actually a subset of C++. But the similarity is largely a historical accident. In fact, the basic approach in a C++ program is radically different from that in a C program.

C++ has overtaken C as the preferred language for serious software development. Thus we don't believe it is necessary or advantageous to teach C before teaching C++. Students who don't know C are saved the time and trouble of learning C and then learning C++, an inefficient approach. Students who already know C may be able to skim parts of some chapters, but they will find that a remarkable percentage of the material is new.

Optimize Organization for OOP

We could have begun the book by teaching the procedural concepts common to C and C++, and moved on to the new OOP concepts once the procedural approach had been digested. That seemed counterproductive, however, because one of our goals is to begin true object-oriented programming as quickly as possible. Accordingly, we provide a minimum of procedural groundwork before getting to objects in Chapter 7. Even the initial chapters are heavily steeped in C++, as opposed to C, usage.

We introduce some concepts earlier than is traditional in books on C. For example, structures are a key feature for understanding C++ because classes are syntactically an extension of structures. For this reason, we introduce structures in Chapter 5 so that they will be familiar when we discuss classes.

Some concepts, such as pointers, are introduced later than in traditional C books. It's not necessary to understand pointers to follow the essentials of OOP, and pointers are usually a stumbling block for C and C++ students. Therefore, we defer a discussion of pointers until the main concepts of OOP have been thoroughly digested.

Substitute Superior C++ Features

Some features of C have been superseded by new approaches in C++. For instance, the and functions, input/output workhorses in C, are seldom used in C++ because and do a better job. Consequently, we leave out descriptions of these functions. Similarly, constants and macros in C have been largely superseded by the qualifier and inline functions in C++, and need be mentioned only briefly.

Minimize Irrelevant Capabilities

Because the focus in this book is on object-oriented programming, we can leave out some features of C that are seldom used and are not particularly relevant to OOP. For instance, it isn't necessary to understand the C bit-wise operators (used to operate on individual bits) to learn object-oriented programming. These and a few other features can be dropped from our discussion, or mentioned only briefly, with no loss in understanding of the major features of C++.

The result is a book that focuses on the fundamentals of OOP, moving the reader gently but briskly toward an understanding of new concepts and their application to real programming problems.

Programming Examples

There are numerous listings of code scattered throughout the book that you will want to try out for yourself. The program examples are available for download by going to Macmillan Computer Publishing's web site, `http://www.mcp.com/product_support`, and go to this book's page by entering the ISBN and clicking Search. To download the programming examples, just click the appropriate link on the page.

Programming Exercises

One of the major changes in the second edition was the addition of numerous exercises. Each of these involves the creation of a complete C++ program. There are roughly 12 exercises per chapter. Solutions to the first three or four exercises in each chapter are provided in Appendix D. For the remainder of the exercises, readers are on their own, although qualified instructors can suggested solutions. Please visit Macmillan Computer Publishing's Web site, `http://www.mcp.com/product_support`, and go to this book's page by entering the ISBN and clicking Search. Click on the appropriate link to receive instructions on downloading the encrypted files and decoding them.

The exercises vary considerably in their degree of difficulty. In each chapter the early exercises are fairly easy, while later ones are more challenging. Instructors will probably want to assign only those exercises suited to the level of a particular class.

CHAPTER 1

THE BIG PICTURE

You will learn about the following in this chapter:

- Procedural versus object-oriented languages

- Features of object-oriented languages

- Brief introduction to classes and objects

- Brief introduction to inheritance

- C++ and C

This book teaches you how to program in C++, a computer language that supports *object-oriented programming* (OOP). Why do we need OOP? What does it do that traditional languages like C, Pascal, and BASIC don't? What are the principles behind OOP? Two key concepts in OOP are *objects* and *classes*. What do these terms mean? What is the relationship between C++ and the older C language?

This chapter explores these questions and provides an overview of the features to be discussed in the balance of the book. What we say here will necessarily be rather general (although mercifully brief). If you find the discussion somewhat abstract, don't worry. The concepts we mention here will come into focus as we demonstrate them in detail in subsequent chapters.

Why Do We Need Object-Oriented Programming?

Object-oriented programming was developed because limitations were discovered in earlier approaches to programming. To appreciate what OOP does, we need to understand what these limitations are and how they arose from traditional programming languages.

Procedural Languages

C, Pascal, FORTRAN, and similar languages are *procedural languages*. That is, each statement in the language tells the computer to do something: Get some input, add these numbers, divide by 6, display that output. A program in a procedural language is a list of instructions.

For very small programs, no other organizing principle (often called a *paradigm*) is needed. The programmer creates the list of instructions, and the computer carries them out.

Division into Functions

When programs become larger, a single list of instructions becomes unwieldy. Few programmers can comprehend a program of more than a few hundred statements unless it is broken down into smaller units. For this reason the *function* was adopted as a way to make programs more comprehensible to their human creators. (The term function is used in C++ and C. In other languages the same concept may be referred to as a subroutine, a subprogram, or a procedure.) A procedural program is divided into functions, and (ideally, at least) each function has a clearly defined purpose and a clearly defined interface to the other functions in the program.

The idea of breaking a program into functions can be further extended by grouping a number of functions together into a larger entity called a *module* (which is often a file), but the principle is similar: a grouping of components that carries out specific tasks.

Dividing a program into functions and modules is one of the cornerstones of *structured programming*, the somewhat loosely defined discipline that influenced programming organization for several decades before the advent of object-oriented programming.

Problems with Structured Programming

As programs grow ever larger and more complex, even the structured programming approach begins to show signs of strain. You may have heard about, or been involved in, horror stories of program development. The project is too complex, the schedule slips, more programmers are added, complexity increases, costs skyrocket, the schedule slips further, and disaster ensues. (See *The Mythical Man-Month*, by Frederick P. Brooks, Jr., Addison-Wesley, 1982, for a vivid description of this process.)

Analyzing the reasons for these failures reveals that there are weaknesses in the procedural paradigm itself. No matter how well the structured programming approach is implemented, large programs become excessively complex.

What are the reasons for these problems with procedural languages? There are two related problems. First, functions have unrestricted access to global data. Second, unrelated functions and data, the basis of the procedural paradigm, provide a poor model of the real world.

Let's examine these problems in the context of an inventory program. One important global data item in such a program is the collection of items in the inventory. Various functions access this data to input a new item, display an item, modify an item, and so on.

Unrestricted Access

In a procedural program, one written in C for example, there are two kinds of data. *Local data* is hidden inside a function, and is used exclusively by the function. In the inventory program a display function might use local data to remember which item it was displaying. Local data is closely related to its function and is safe from modification by other functions.

However, when two or more functions must access the same data—and this is true of the most important data in a program—then the data must be made *global*, as our collection of inventory items is. Global data can be accessed by *any* function in the program. (We ignore the issue of grouping functions into modules, which doesn't materially affect our argument.) The arrangement of local and global variables in a procedural program is shown in Figure 1.1.

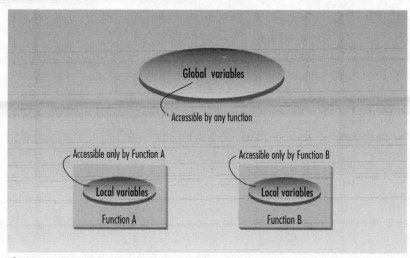

Figure 1.1   Global and local variables.

In a large program, there are many functions and many global data items. The problem with the procedural paradigm is that this leads to an even larger number of potential connections between functions and data, as shown in Figure 1.2.

This large number of connections causes problems in several ways. First, it makes a program's structure difficult to conceptualize. Second, it makes the program difficult to modify. A change made in a global data item may result in rewriting all the functions that access that item.

For example, in our inventory program, someone may decide that the product codes for the inventory items should be changed from five digits to 12 digits. This may necessitate a change from a **short** to a **long** data type.

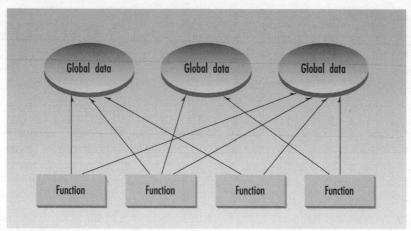

Figure 1.2 The procedural paradigm.

Now all the functions that operate on the data must be modified to deal with a **long** instead of a **short**. It's similar to what happens when your local supermarket moves the bread from aisle 4 to aisle 7. Everyone who patronizes the supermarket must then figure out where the bread has gone, and adjust their shopping habits accordingly.

When data items are modified in a large program it may not be easy to tell which functions access the data, and even when you figure this out, modifications to the functions may cause them to work incorrectly with other global data items. Everything is related to everything else, so a modification anywhere has far-reaching, and often unintended, consequences.

Real-World Modeling

The second—and more important—problem with the procedural paradigm is that its arrangement of separate data and functions does a poor job of modeling things in the real world. In the physical world we deal with objects such as people and cars. Such objects aren't like data and they aren't like functions. Complex real-world objects have both *attributes* and *behavior*.

Attributes

Examples of attributes (sometimes called *characteristics*) are, for people, eye color and job titles; and, for cars, horsepower and number of doors. As it turns out, attributes in the real world are equivalent to data in a program: they have a certain specific values, such as blue (for eye color) or four (for the number of doors).

Behavior

Behavior is something a real-world object does in response to some stimulus. If you ask your boss for a raise, she will generally say yes or no. If you apply the brakes in a car, it will generally stop. Saying something and stopping are examples of behavior. Behavior is like a function: you call a function to do something, like display the inventory, and it does it.

So neither data nor functions, by themselves, model real world objects effectively.

New Data Types

There are other problems with procedural languages. One is the difficulty of creating new data types. Computer languages typically have several built-in data types: integers, floating-point numbers, characters, and so on. What if you want to invent your own data type? Perhaps you want to work with complex numbers, or two-dimensional coordinates, or dates— quantities the built-in data types don't handle easily. Being able to create your own types is called *extensibility*; you can extend the capabilities of the language. Traditional languages are not usually extensible. Without unnatural convolutions, you can't bundle both x and y coordinates together into a single variable called *Point*, and then add and subtract values of this type. The result is that traditional programs are more complex to write and maintain.

The Object-Oriented Approach

The fundamental idea behind object-oriented languages is to combine into a single unit both *data* and the *functions that operate on that data*. Such a unit is called an *object*.

An object's functions, called *member functions* in C++, typically provide the only way to access its data. If you want to read a data item in an object, you call a member function in the object. It will access the data and return the value to you. You can't access the data directly. The data is *hidden*, so it is safe from accidental alteration. Data and its functions are said to be *encapsulated* into a single entity. *Data encapsulation* and *data hiding* are key terms in the description of object-oriented languages.

If you want to modify the data in an object, you know exactly what functions interact with it: the member functions in the object. No other functions can access the data. This simplifies writing, debugging, and maintaining the program.

A C++ program typically consists of a number of objects, which communicate with each other by calling one another's member functions. The organization of a C++ program is shown in Figure 1.3.

We should mention that what are called member functions in C++ are called *methods* in some other object-oriented (OO) languages (such as Smalltalk, one of the first OO languages). Also, data items are referred to as *attributes* or *instance variables*. Calling an object's member function is referred to as *sending a message* to the object. These terms are not official C++ terminology, but they are used with increasing frequency, especially in object-oriented design.

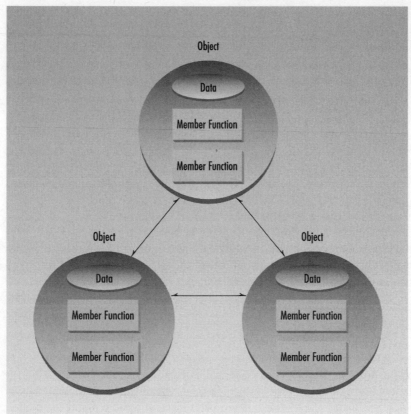

Figure 1.3   The object-oriented paradigm.

An Analogy

You might want to think of objects as departments—such as sales, accounting, personnel, and so on—in a company. Departments provide an important approach to corporate organization. In most companies (except very small ones), people don't work on personnel problems one day, the payroll the next, and then go out in the field as salespeople the week after. Each department has its own personnel, with clearly assigned duties. It also has its own data: the accounting department has payroll figures, the sales department has sales figures, the personnel department keeps records of each employee, and so on.

The people in each department control and operate on that department's data. Dividing the company into departments makes it easier to comprehend and control the company's activities, and helps maintain the integrity of the information used by the company. The accounting department, for instance, is responsible for the payroll data. If you're a sales manager, and you need to know the total of all the salaries paid in the southern region in July, you don't just walk into the accounting department and start rummaging through file cabinets. You send a memo to the appropriate person in the department, then wait for that person to access the data and send you a reply with the information you want. This ensures that the data is accessed accurately and that it is not corrupted by inept outsiders. This view of corporate organization is shown in Figure 1.4. In the same way, objects provide an approach to program organization while helping to maintain the integrity of the program's data.

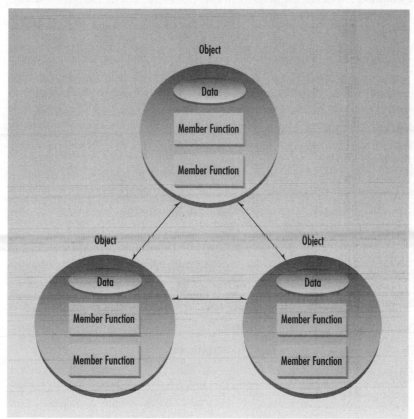

Figure 1.4   The corporate paradigm.

OOP: An Approach to Organization

Keep in mind that object-oriented programming is not primarily concerned with the details of program operation. Instead, it deals with the overall organization of the program. Most individual program statements in C++ are similar to statements in procedural languages, and many are identical to statements in C. Indeed, an entire member function in a C++ program may be very similar to a procedural function in C. It is only when you look at the larger context that you can determine whether a statement or a function is part of a procedural C program or an object-oriented C++ program.

Characteristics of Object-Oriented Languages

Let's briefly examine a few of the major elements of object-oriented languages in general, and C++ in particular.

Objects

When you approach a programming problem in an object-oriented language, you no longer ask how the problem will be divided into functions, but how it will be divided into objects. Thinking in terms of objects, rather than functions, has a surprisingly helpful effect on how easily programs can be designed. This results from the close match between objects in the programming sense and objects in the real world. This process is described in detail in Chapter 16, "Object-Oriented Design."

What kinds of things become objects in object-oriented programs? The answer to this is limited only by your imagination, but here are some typical categories to start you thinking:

- **Physical objects**

    Automobiles in a traffic-flow simulation

    Electrical components in a circuit-design program

    Countries in an economics model

    Aircraft in an air-traffic-control system

- **Elements of the computer-user environment**

    Windows

    Menus

    Graphics objects (lines, rectangles, circles)

    The mouse, keyboard, disk drives, printer

- **Data-storage constructs**

    Customized arrays

    Stacks

    Linked lists

    Binary trees

- **Human entities**

  Employees

  Students

  Customers

  Salespeople

- **Collections of data**

  An inventory

  A personnel file

  A dictionary

  A table of the latitudes and longitudes of world cities

- **User-defined data types**

  Time

  Angles

  Complex numbers

  Points on the plane

- **Components in computer games**

  Cars in an auto race

  Positions in a board game (chess, checkers)

  Animals in an ecological simulation

  Opponents and friends in adventure games

The match between programming objects and real-world objects is the happy result of combining data and functions: The resulting objects offer a revolution in program design. No such close match between programming constructs and the items being modeled exists in a procedural language.

Classes

In OOP we say that objects are members of *classes*. What does this mean? Let's look at an analogy. Almost all computer languages have built-in data types. For instance, a data type int, meaning integer, is predefined in C++ (as we'll see in Chapter 3, "Loops and Decisions"). You can declare as many variables of type int as you need in your program:

```
int day;
int count;
int divisor;
int answer;
```

In a similar way, you can define many objects of the same class, as shown in Figure 1.5. A class serves as a plan, or template. It specifies what data and what functions will be included in objects of that class. Defining the class doesn't create any objects, just as the mere existence of data type `int` doesn't create any variables.

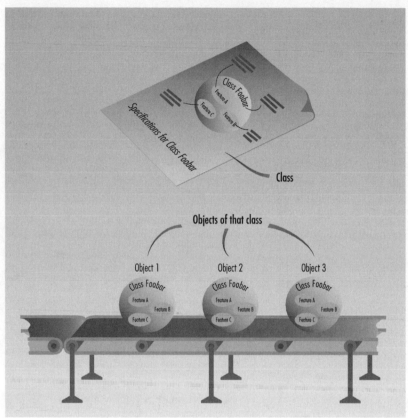

Figure 1.5   A class and its objects.

A class is thus a description of a number of similar objects. This fits our non-technical understanding of the word *class*. Prince, Sting, and Madonna are members of the class of rock musicians. There is no one person called "rock musician," but specific people with specific names are members of this class if they possess certain characteristics.

Inheritance

The idea of classes leads to the idea of *inheritance*. In our daily lives, we use the concept of classes as divided into subclasses. We know that the class of animals is divided into mammals, amphibians, insects, birds, and so on. The class of vehicles is divided into cars, trucks, buses, and motorcycles.

The principle in this sort of division is that each subclass shares common characteristics with the class from which it's derived. Cars, trucks, buses, and motorcycles all have wheels and a motor; these are the defining characteristics of vehicles. In addition to the characteristics shared with other members of the class, each subclass also has its own particular characteristics: Buses, for instance, have seats for many people, while trucks have space for hauling heavy loads.

This idea is shown in Figure 1.6. Notice in the figure that features A and B, which are part of the base class, are common to all the derived classes, but that each derived class also has features of its own.

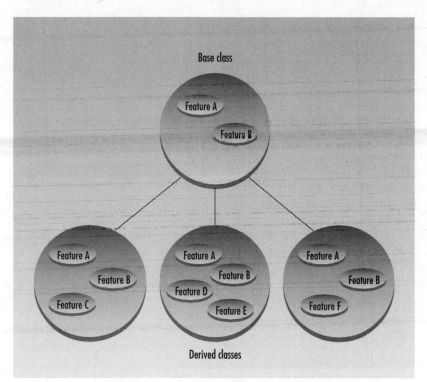

Figure 1.6 Inheritance.

In a similar way, an OOP class can be divided into subclasses. In C++ the original class is called the *base class*; other classes can be defined that share its characteristics, but add their own as well. These are called *derived classes*.

Don't confuse the relation of objects to classes, on the one hand, with the relation of a base class to derived classes, on the other. Objects, which exist in the computer's memory, each embody the exact characteristics of their class, which serves as a template. Derived classes inherit some characteristics from their base class, but add new ones of their own.

Inheritance is somewhat analogous to using functions to simplify a traditional procedural program. If we find that three different sections of a procedural program do almost exactly the same thing, we recognize an opportunity to extract the common elements of these three sections and put them into a single function. The three sections of the program can call the function to execute the common actions, and they can perform their own individual processing as well. Similarly, a base class contains elements common to a group of derived classes. As functions do in a procedural program, inheritance shortens an object-oriented program and clarifies the relationship among program elements.

Reusability

Once a class has been written, created, and debugged, it can be distributed to other programmers for use in their own programs. This is called *reusability*. It is similar to the way a library of functions in a procedural language can be incorporated into different programs.

However, in OOP, the concept of inheritance provides an important extension to the idea of reusability. A programmer can take an existing class and, without modifying it, add additional features and capabilities to it. This is done by deriving a new class from the existing one. The new class will inherit the capabilities of the old one, but is free to add new features of its own.

For example, you might have written (or purchased from someone else) a class that creates a menu system, such as that used in Windows or other Graphic User Interfaces (GUIs). This class works fine, and you don't want to change it, but you want to add the capability to make some menu entries flash on and off. To do this, you simply create a new class that inherits all the capabilities of the existing one but adds flashing menu entries.

The ease with which existing software can be reused is an important benefit of OOP. Many companies find that being able to reuse classes on a second project provides an increased return on their original programming investment. We'll have more to say about this in later chapters.

Creating New Data Types

One of the benefits of objects is that they give the programmer a convenient way to construct new data types. Suppose you work with two-dimensional positions (such as x and y coordinates, or latitude and longitude) in your program. You would like to express operations on these positional values with normal arithmetic operations, such as

```
position1 = position2 + origin
```

where the variables `position1`, `position2`, and `origin` each represent a pair of independent numerical quantities. By creating a class that incorporates these two values, and declaring `position1`, `position2`, and `origin` to be objects of this class, we can, in effect, create a new data type. Many features of C++ are intended to facilitate the creation of new data types in this manner.

Polymorphism and Overloading

Note that the = (equal) and + (plus) operators, used in the position arithmetic shown above, don't act the same way they do in operations on built-in types like `int`. The objects `position1` and so on are not predefined in C++, but are programmer-defined objects of class `Position`. How do the = and + operators know how to operate on objects? The answer is that we can define new operations for these operators. These operations will be member functions of the `Position` class.

Using operators or functions in different ways, depending on what they are operating on, is called *polymorphism* (one thing with several distinct forms). When an existing operator, such as + or =, is given the capability to operate on a new data type, it is said to be *overloaded*. Overloading is a kind of polymorphism; it is also an important feature of OOP.

C++ and C

C++ is derived from the C language. Strictly speaking, it is a superset of C: Almost every correct statement in C is also a correct statement in C++, although the reverse is not true. The most important elements added to C to create C++ are concerned with classes, objects, and object-oriented programming. (C++ was originally called "C with classes.") However, C++ has many other new features as well, including an improved approach to input/output (I/O) and a new way to write comments. Figure 1.7 shows the relationship of C and C++.

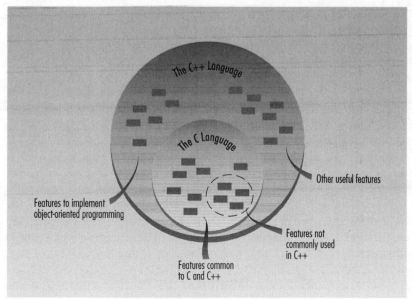

Figure 1.7   The relationship between C and C++.

In fact, the practical differences between C and C++ are larger than you might think. Although you can write a program in C++ that looks like a program in C, hardly anyone does. C++ programmers not only make use of the new features of C++, they also emphasize the traditional C features in different proportions than do C programmers.

If you already know C, you will have a head start in learning C++ (although you may also have some bad habits to unlearn), but much of the material will be new.

Laying the Groundwork

Our goal is to help you begin writing OOP programs as soon as possible. However, as we noted, much of C++ is inherited from C, so while the overall structure of a C++ program may be OOP, down in the trenches you need to know some old-fashioned procedural fundamentals. Chapters 2 through 5 therefore deal with the "traditional" aspects of C++, many of which are also found in C. You will learn about variables and I/O, about control structures like loops and decisions, and about functions themselves. You will also learn about structures, since the same syntax that's used for structures is used for classes.

If you already know C, you might be tempted to skip these chapters. However, you will find that there are many differences, some obvious and some rather subtle, between C and C++. Our advice is to read these chapters, skimming what you know, and concentrating on the ways C++ differs from C.

The specific discussion of OOP starts in Chapter 6, "Objects and Classes," when we begin to explore objects and classes. From then on the examples will be object oriented.

Summary

OOP is a way of organizing programs. The emphasis is on the way programs are designed, not on coding details. In particular, OOP programs are organized around objects, which contain both data and functions that act on that data. A class is a template for a number of objects.

Inheritance allows a class to be derived from an existing class without modifying it. The derived class has all the data and functions of the parent class, but adds new ones of its own. Inheritance makes possible reuseability, or using a class over and over in different programs.

C++ is a superset of C. It adds to the C language the capability to implement OOP. It also adds a variety of other features. In addition, the emphasis is changed in C++, so that some features common to C, although still available in C++, are seldom used, while others are used far more frequently. The result is a surprisingly different language.

The general concepts discussed in this chapter will become more concrete as you learn more about the details of C++. You may want to refer back to this chapter as you progress further into this book.

Questions

Answers to questions can be found in Appendix G, "Answers to Questions and Exercises."
Note that throughout this book, multiple-choice questions can have more than one correct answer.

1. Pascal, BASIC, and C are p___ languages, while C++ is an o ____.language.

2. A widget is to the blueprint for a widget as an object is to

    a. a member function.

    b. a class.

    c. an operator.

    d. a data item.

3. The two major components of an object are ___ and functions that _____.

4. In C++, a function contained within a class is called

    a. a member function.

    b. an operator.

    c. a class function.

    d. a method.

5. Protecting data from access by unauthorized functions is called ____.

6. Which of the following are good reasons to use an object-oriented language?

    a. You can define your own data types.

    b. Program statements are simpler than in procedural languages.

    c. An OO program can be taught to correct its own errors.

    d. It's easier to conceptualize an OO program.

7. _____ model entities in the real world more closely than do functions.

8. True or false: A C++ program is similar to a C program except for the details of coding.

9. Bundling data and functions together is called ____.

10. When a language has the capability to produce new data types, it is said to be

    a. reprehensible.

    b. encapsulated.

    c. overloaded.

    d. extensible.

11. True or false: You can easily tell, from any two lines of code, whether a program is written in C or C++.

12. The ability of a function or operator to act in different ways on different data types is called _____.

13. A normal C++ operator that acts in special ways on newly defined data types is said to be

    a. glorified.

    b. encapsulated.

    c. classified.

    d. overloaded.

14. Memorizing the new terms used in C++ is

    a. critically important.

    b. something you can return to later.

    c. the key to wealth and success.

    d. completely irrelevant.

CHAPTER 2

C++ PROGRAMMING BASICS

You will learn about the following in this chapter:

- C++ program structure
- Variables
- Input/output with cout and cin

- Arithmetic operators
- Assignment and increment operators

*I*n any language there are some fundamentals you need to know before you can write even the most elementary programs. This chapter introduces three such fundamentals: basic program construction, variables, and input/output (I/O). It also touches on a variety of other language features, including comments, arithmetic operators, the increment operator, data conversion, and library functions.

These topics are not conceptually difficult, but you may find that the style in C++ is a little austere compared with, say, BASIC or Pascal. Before you learn what it's all about, a C++ program may remind you more of a mathematics formula than a computer program. Don't worry about this. You'll find that as you gain familiarity with C++, it starts to look less forbidding, while other languages begin to seem unnecessarily fancy and verbose.

Getting Started

As we noted in the introduction, you can use either a Microsoft or an Inprise (formerly Borland) compiler with this book. Appendixes C and D provide details about their operation. The compilers take source code and transform it into executable files, which your computer can run as it does other programs. Source files are text files (extension .CPP) that correspond with the listings printed in this book. Executable files have the .EXE extension, and can be executed either from within your compiler, or, if you're familiar with MS-DOS, directly from a DOS window.

The programs run without modification on the Microsoft compiler or in an MS-DOS window. If you're using the Borland compiler, you'll need to modify the programs slightly before running them; otherwise the output won't remain on the screen long enough to see. Make sure to read Appendix D, "Borland C++," to see how this is done.

Basic Program Construction

Let's look at a very simple C++ program. This program is called FIRST, so its source file is FIRST.CPP. It simply prints a sentence on the screen. Here it is:

```
#include <iostream>
using namespace std;

int main()
   {
   cout << "Every age has a language of its own\n";
   return 0;
   }
```

Despite its small size, this program demonstrates a great deal about the construction of C++ programs. Let's examine it in detail.

Functions

Functions are one of the fundamental building blocks of C++. The FIRST program consists almost entirely of a single function called `main()`. The only parts of this program that are not part of the function are the first two lines—the ones that start with `#include` and `using`. (We'll see what these lines do in a moment.)

We noted in Chapter 1, "The Big Picture," that a function can be part of a class, in which case it is called a *member function*. However, functions can also exist independently of classes. We are not yet ready to talk about classes, so we will show functions that are separate standalone entities, as `main()` is here.

Function Name

The parentheses following the word `main` are the distinguishing feature of a function. Without the parentheses the compiler would think that `main` refers to a variable or to some other program element. When we discuss functions in the text, we'll follow the same convention that C++ uses: We'll put parentheses following the function name. Later on we'll see that the parentheses aren't always empty. They're used to hold function *arguments*: values passed from the calling program to the function.

The word `int` preceding the function name indicates that this particular function has a return value of type `int`. Don't worry about this now; we'll learn about data types later in this chapter and return values in Chapter 5, "Functions."

Braces and the Function Body

The *body* of a function is surrounded by *braces* (sometimes called *curly brackets*). These braces play the same role as the `BEGIN` and `END` keywords in some other languages: They surround or *delimit* a block of program statements. Every function must use this pair of braces around the function body. In this example there are only two statements in the function body: the line starting with `cout`, and the line starting with `return`. However, a function body can consist of many statements.

Always Start with `main()`

When you run a C++ program, the first statement executed will be at the beginning of a function called `main()`. The program may consist of many functions, classes, and other program elements, but on startup, control always goes to `main()`. If there is no function called `main()` in your program, an error will be signaled.

In most C++ programs, as we'll see later, `main()` calls member functions in various objects to carry out the program's real work. The `main()` function may also contain calls to other standalone functions. This is shown in Figure 2.1.

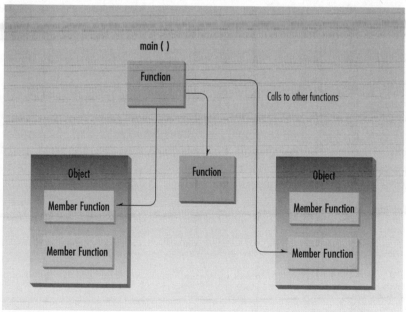

Figure 2.1   Objects, functions and `main()`.

Program Statements

The program *statement* is the fundamental unit of C++ programming. There are two statements in the FIRST program: the line

```
cout << "Every age has a language of its own\n";
```

and the return statement

```
return 0;
```

The first statement tells the computer to display the quoted phrase. Most statements tell the computer to do something. In this respect, statements in C++ are similar to statements in other languages. In fact, as we've noted, the majority of statements in C++ are identical to statements in C.

A semicolon signals the end of the statement. This is a crucial part of the syntax but easy to forget. In some languages (like BASIC), the end of a statement is signaled by the end of the line, but that's not true in C++. If you leave out the semicolon, the compiler will often (although not always) signal an error.

The last statement in the function body is `return 0;`. This tells `main()` to return the value 0 to whoever called it, in this case the operating system or compiler. In older versions of C++ you could give `main()` the return type of void and dispense with the return statement, but this is not considered correct in Standard C++. We'll learn more about `return` in Chapter 5.

Whitespace

We mentioned that the end of a line isn't important to a C++ compiler. Actually, the compiler ignores whitespace almost completely. *Whitespace* is defined as spaces, carriage returns, linefeeds, tabs, vertical tabs, and formfeeds. These characters are invisible to the compiler. You can put several statements on one line, separated by any number of spaces or tabs, or you can run a statement over two or more lines. It's all the same to the compiler. Thus the FIRST program could be written this way:

```
#include <iostream>
using
namespace std;

int main () { cout
<<
"Every age has a language of its own\n"
; return
0;}
```

We don't recommend this syntax—it's nonstandard and hard to read—but it does compile correctly.

There are several exceptions to the rule that whitespace is invisible to the compiler. The first line of the program, starting with `#include`, is a preprocessor directive, which must be written on one line. Also, string constants, such as `"Every age has a language of` `its own"`, cannot be broken into separate lines. (If you need a long string constant, you can insert a backslash (\\) at the line break, or divide the string into two separate strings, each surrounded by quotes.)

Output Using `cout`

As you have seen, the statement

```
cout << "Every age has a language of its own\n";
```

causes the phrase in quotation marks to be displayed on the screen. How does this work? A complete description of this statement requires an understanding of objects, operator overloading, and other topics we won't discuss until later in the book, but here's a brief preview.

The identifier **cout** (pronounced "C out") is actually an *object*. It is predefined in C++ to correspond to the *standard output stream*. A *stream* is an abstraction that refers to a flow of data. The standard output stream normally flows to the screen display—although it can be redirected to other output devices. We'll discuss streams (and redirection) in Chapter 12, "Streams and Files"

The operator << is called the *insertion* or *put to* operator. It directs the contents of the variable on its right to the object on its left. In FIRST it directs the string constant "Every age has a language of its own\n" to cout, which sends it to the display.

(If you know C, you'll recognize << as the *left-shift* bit-wise operator and wonder how it can also be used to direct output. In C++, operators can be overloaded. That is, they can perform different activities, depending on the context. We'll learn about overloading in Chapter 8, "Operator Overloading.")

Although the concepts behind the use of **cout** and << may be obscure at this point, using them is easy. They'll appear in almost every example program. Figure 2.2 shows the result of using **cout** and the insertion operator <<.

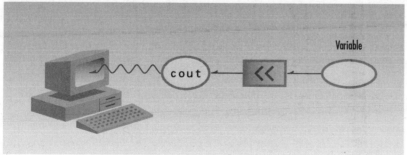

Figure 2.2   Output with `cout`.

String Constants

The phrase in quotation marks, `"Every age has a language of its own\n"`, is an example of a *string constant*. As you probably know, a constant, unlike a variable, cannot be given a new value as the program runs. Its value is set when the program is written, and it retains this value throughout the program's existence.

As we'll see later, the situation regarding strings is rather complicated in C++. Two ways of handling strings are commonly used. A string can be represented by an array of characters, or it can be represented as an object of a class. We'll learn more about both kinds of strings in Chapter 7, "Arrays and Strings."

The `'\n'` character at the end of string constant is an example of an *escape sequence*. It causes the next text output to be displayed on a new line. We use it here so that the phrases such as "Press any key to continue," inserted by some compilers for display after the program terminates, will appear on a new line. We'll discuss escape sequences later in this chapter.

Directives

The two lines that begin the FIRST program are directives. The first is a preprocessor directive, and the second is a using directive. They occupy a sort of gray area: They're not part of the basic C++ language, but they're necessary anyway.

Preprocessor Directives

The first line of the FIRST program,

```
#include <iostream>
```

might look like a program statement, but it's not. It isn't part of a function body and doesn't end with a semicolon, as program statements must. Instead, it starts with a number sign (#). It's called a *preprocessor directive*. Recall that program statements are instructions to the *computer* to do something, like adding two numbers or printing a sentence. A preprocessor directive, on the other hand, is an instruction to the *compiler*. A part of the compiler called the *preprocessor* deals with these directives before it begins the real compilation process.

The preprocessor directive `#include` tells the compiler to insert another file into your source file. In effect, the `#include` directive is replaced by the contents of the file indicated. Using an `#include` directive to insert another file into your source file is similar to pasting a block of text into a document with your word processor.

`#include` is only one of many preprocessor directives, all of which can be identified by the initial # sign. The use of preprocessor directives is not as common in C++ as it is in C, but we'll look at a few additional examples as we go along. The type file usually included by `#include` is called a *header file*.

Header Files

In the FIRST example, the preprocessor directive #include tells the compiler to add the source file IOSTREAM to the FIRST.CPP source file before compiling. Why do this? IOSTREAM is an example of a *header file* (sometimes called an *include file*). It's concerned with basic input/output operations, and contains declarations that are needed by the **cout** identifier and the << operator. Without these declarations, the compiler won't recognize **cout** and will think << is being used incorrectly. There are many such include files. The newer Standard C++ header files don't have a file extension, but some older header files, left over from the days of the C language, have the extension .H.

If you want to see what's in IOSTREAM, you can use your compiler to find the **include** directory for your compiler and display it as a source file in the edit window. Or you can look at it with the Wordpad or Notepad utilities. The contents won't make much sense at this point, but you will at least prove to yourself that IOSTREAM is a source file, written in normal ASCII characters.

We'll return to the topic of header files at the end of this chapter, when we introduce library functions.

The `using` Directive

A C++ program can be divided into different *namespaces*. A namespace is a part of the program in which certain names are recognized; outside of the namespace they're unknown. The directive

```
using namespace std;
```

says that all the program statements that follow are within the *std* namespace. Various program components such as **cout** are declared within this namespace. If we didn't use the **using** directive, we would need to append the **std** name to many program elements. For example, in the FIRST program we'd need to say

```
std::cout << "Every age has a language of its own.";
```

To avoid adding **std::** dozens of times in programs we use the **using** directive instead. We'll discuss namespaces further in Chapter 13, "Multifile Programs."

Comments

Comments are an important part of any program. They help the person writing a program, and anyone else who must read the source file, understand what's going on. The compiler ignores comments, so they do not add to the file size or execution time of the executable program.

Comment Syntax

Let's rewrite our FIRST program, incorporating comments into our source file. We'll call the new program COMMENTS:

```
// comments.cpp
// demonstrates comments
#include <iostream>              //preprocessor directive
using namespace std;            //"using" directive

int main()                      //function name "main"
   {                            //start function body
   cout << "Every age has a language of its own\n";  //statement
   return 0;                    //statement
   }                            //end function body
```

Comments start with a double slash symbol (//) and terminate at the end of the line. (This is one of the exceptions to the rule that the compiler ignores whitespace.) A comment can start at the beginning of the line or on the same line following a program statement. Both possibilities are shown in the COMMENTS example.

When to Use Comments

Comments are almost always a good thing. Most programmers don't use enough of them. If you're tempted to leave out comments, remember that not everyone is as smart as you; they may need more explanation than you do about what your program is doing. Also, you may not be as smart next month, when you've forgotten key details of your program's operation, as you are today.

Use comments to explain to the person looking at the listing what you're trying to do. The details are in the program statements themselves, so the comments should concentrate on the big picture, clarifying your reasons for using a certain statement or group of statements.

Alternative Comment Syntax

There's a second comment style available in C++:

```
/* this is an old-style comment */
```

This type of comment (the only comment originally available in C) begins with the /* character pair and ends with */ (not with the end of the line). These symbols are harder to type (since / is lowercase while * is uppercase) and take up more space on the line, so this style is not generally used in C++. However, it has advantages in special situations. You can write a multiline comment with only two comment symbols:

```
/* this
is a
potentially
very long
multiline
comment
*/
```

This is a good approach to making a comment out of a large text passage, since it saves inserting the // symbol on every line.

You can also insert a /* */ comment anywhere within the text of a program line:

```
func1()
   {  /* empty function body */  }
```

If you attempt to use the // style comment in this case, the closing brace won't be visible to the compiler—since a // style comment runs to the end of the line—and the code won't compile correctly.

Integer Variables

Variables are the most fundamental part of any language. A variable has a symbolic name and can be given a variety of values. Variables are located in particular places in the computer's memory. When a variable is given a value, that value is actually placed in the memory space assigned to the variable. Most popular languages use the same general variable types, such as integers, floating-point numbers, and characters, so you are probably already familiar with the ideas behind them.

Integer variables represent integer numbers like 1, 30,000, and –27. Such numbers are used for counting discrete numbers of objects, like 11 pencils or 99 bottles of beer. Unlike floating-point numbers, integers have no fractional part; you can express the idea of *four* using integers, but not *four and one-half*.

Defining Integer Variables

Integer variables exist in several sizes, but the most commonly used is type int. The amount of memory occupied by the integer types is system dependent. On a 32-bit system like Windows 98, an int occupies 4 bytes (which is 32 bits) of memory. This allows an int to hold numbers in the range from –2,147,483,648 to 2,147,483,647. Figure 2.3 shows an integer variable in memory.

While type int occupies 4 bytes on current Windows computers, it occupied only 2 bytes in MS-DOS and earlier versions of Windows. The ranges occupied by the various types are listed in the header file LIMITS; you can also look them up using your compiler's help system.

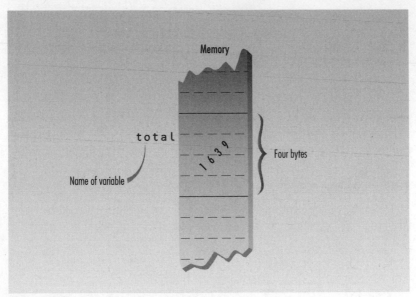

Figure 2.3 Variable of type int in memory.

Here's a program that defines and uses several variables of type int:

```
// intvars.cpp
// demonstrates integer variables
#include <iostream>
using namespace std;

int main()
   {
   int var1;                 //define var1
   int var2;                 //define var2

   var1 = 20;                //assign value to var1
   var2 = var1 + 10;         //assign value to var2
   cout << "var1+10 is ";    //output text
   cout << var2 << endl;     //output value of var2
   return 0;
   }
```

Type this program into your compiler's edit screen (or load it from the Web site), compile and link it, and then run it. Examine the output window. The statements

```
int var1;
int var2;
```

define two integer variables, var1 and var2. The keyword int signals the type of variable. These statements, which are called *declarations*, must terminate with a semicolon, like other program statements.

You must declare a variable before using it. However, you can place variable declarations anywhere in a program. It's not necessary to declare variables before the first executable statement (as was necessary in C). However, it's probably more readable if commonly used variables are located at the beginning of the program.

Declarations and Definitions

Let's digress for a moment to note a subtle distinction between the terms *definition* and *declaration* as applied to variables.

A *declaration* introduces a variable's name (such as var1) into a program and specifies its type (such as int). However, if a declaration also sets aside memory for the variable, it is also called a *definition*. The statements

```
int var1;
int var2;
```

in the INTVARS program are definitions because they set aside memory for var1 and var2. We'll be concerned mostly with declarations that are also definitions; but later on we'll see various kinds of declarations that are not definitions.

Variable Names

The program INTVARS uses variables named var1 and var2. The names given to variables (and other program features) are called *identifiers*. What are the rules for writing identifiers? You can use upper- and lowercase letters, and the digits from 1 to 9. You can also use the underscore (_). The first character must be a letter or underscore. Identifiers can be as long as you like, but only the first 247 characters (in Visual C++) or 250 characters (in C++ Builder) will be recognized. The compiler distinguishes between upper- and lowercase letters, so Var is not the same as var or VAR.

You can't use a C++ keyword as a variable name e. A *keyword* is a predefined word with a special meaning, like int, class, if, while, and so on. A complete list of keywords can be found in Appendix B, "C++ Keywords," and in your compiler's documentation.

Many C++ programmers follow the convention of using all lowercase letters for variable names. Other programmers use a mixture of upper- and lowercase, as in IntVar or dataCount. Still others make liberal use of underscores. Whichever approach you use, it's good to be consistent throughout a program. Names in all uppercase are sometimes reserved for constants (see the discussion of const that follows). These same conventions apply to naming other program elements such as classes and functions.

Assignment Statements

The statements

```
var1 = 20;
var2 = var1 + 10;
```

assign values to the two variables. The equal sign =, as you might guess, causes the value on the right to be assigned to the variable on the left. The = in C++ is equivalent to the :=

in Pascal or the = in BASIC. In the first line shown here, `var1`, which previously had no value, is given the value 20.

Integer Constants

The number 20 is an *integer constant*. Constants don't change during the course of the program. An integer constant consists of numerical digits. There must be no decimal point in an integer constant, and it must lie within the range of integers.

In the second program line shown here, the plus sign (+) adds the value of `var1` and 10, in which 10 is another constant. The result of this addition is then assigned to `var2`.

Output Variations

The statement

```
cout << "var1+10 is ";
```

displays a string constant, as we've seen before. The next statement,

```
cout << var2 << endl;
```

displays the value of the variable `var2`. As you can see in your console output window, the output of the program is

```
var1+10 is 30
```

Note that `cout` and the `<<` operator know how to treat an integer and a string differently. If we send them a string, they print it as text. If we send them an integer, they print it as a number. This may seem obvious, but it is another example of operator overloading, a key feature of C++. (C programmers will remember that such functions as `printf()` need to be told not only the variable to be displayed, but the type of the variable as well, which makes the syntax far less intuitive.)

As you can see, the output of the two `cout` statements appears on the same line on the output screen. No linefeed is inserted automatically. If you want to start on a new line, you must do it yourself. We've seen how to do this with the `'\n'` escape sequence; now we'll see another way: using something called a *manipulator*.

The `endl` Manipulator

The last `cout` statement in the INTVARS program ends with an unfamiliar word: `endl`. This causes a linefeed to be inserted into the stream, so that subsequent text is displayed on the next line. It has the same effect as sending the `'\n'` character, but is somewhat clearer. It's an example of a *manipulator*. Manipulators are instructions to the output stream that modify the output in various ways; we'll see more of them as we go along. Strictly speaking, `endl` (unlike '\n') also causes the output buffer to be flushed, but this happens invisibly so for most purposes the two are equivalent.

Other Integer Types

There are several numerical integer types besides type `int`. These are types `long` and `short`. (Strictly speaking type `char` is an integer type as well, but we'll cover it separately.) We noted that the size of type `int` is system dependent. In contrast, types `long` and `short` have fixed sizes no matter what system is used.

Type `long` always occupies four bytes, which is the same as type `int` on 32-bit Windows systems. Thus it has the same range, from −2,147,483,648 to 2,147,483,647. It can also be written as `long int`; this means the same as `long`. There's little point in using type `long` on 32-bit systems, since it's the same as `int`. However, if your program may need to run on a 16-bit system such as MS-DOS, or on older versions of Windows, then specifying type `long` will guarantee a four-bit integer type. In 16-bit systems, type `int` has the same range as type `short`.

On all systems type `short` occupies two bytes, giving it a range of −32,768 to 32,767. There's probably not much point using type `short` on modern Windows systems unless it's important to save memory. Type `int`, although twice as large, is accessed faster than type `short`.

If you want to create a constant of type `long`, use the letter `L` following the numerical value, as in

```
longvar = 7678L; // assigns long constant 7678 to longvar
```

Many compilers offer integer types that explicitly specify the number of bits used. (Remember there are 8 bits to a byte.) These type names are preceded by two underscores. They are `__int8`, `__int16`, `__int32`, and `__int64`. The `__int8` type corresponds to `char`, and (at least in 32-bit systems like the current version of Windows) The type name `__int16` corresponds to `short` and `__int32` corresponds to both `int` and `long`. The `__int64` type holds huge integers with up to 19 decimal digits. Using these type names has the advantage that the number of bytes used for a variable is not implementation dependent. However, this is not usually an issue, and these types are seldom used.

Character Variables

Type `char` stores integers that range in value from −128 to 127. Variables of this type occupy only 1 byte (eight bits) of memory. Character variables are sometimes used to store numbers that confine themselves to this limited range, but they are much more commonly used to store ASCII characters.

As you may already know, the ASCII character set is a way of representing characters such as `'a'`, `'B'`, `'$'`, `'3'`, and so on, as numbers. These numbers range from 0 to 127. Most Windows systems extend this range to 255 to accommodate various foreign-language and graphics characters. Appendix A, "ASCII Table," shows the ASCII character set.

Complexities arise when foreign languages are used, and even when programs are transferred between computer systems in the same language. This is because the characters in the range 128 to 255 aren't standardized and because the one-byte size of type `char` is too small to accommodate the number of characters in many languages, such as Japanese. Standard C++ provides a larger character type called `wchar_t` to handle foreign languages. This is important if you're writing programs for international distribution. However, in this book we'll ignore type `wchar_t` and assume that we're dealing with the ASCII character set found in current versions of Windows.

Character Constants

Character constants use single quotation marks around a character, like 'a' and 'b'. (Note that this differs from *string* constants, which use double quotation marks.) When the C++ compiler encounters such a character constant, it translates it into the corresponding ASCII code. The constant `'a'` appearing in a program, for example, will be translated into 97, as shown in Figure 2.4.

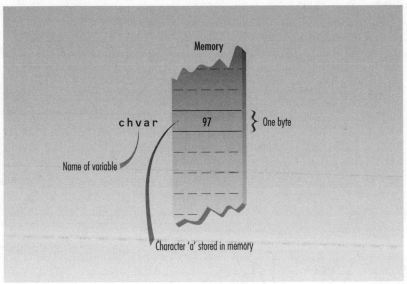

Figure 2.4 Variable of type `char` in memory.

Character variables can be assigned character constants as values. The following program shows some examples of character constants and variables.

```
// charvars.cpp
// demonstrates character variables
#include <iostream>          //for cout, etc.
using namespace std;

int main()
    {
```

```
char charvar1 = 'A';      //define char variable as character
char charvar2 = '\t';     //define char variable as tab

cout << charvar1;         //display character
cout << charvar2;         //display character
charvar1 = 'B';           //set char variable to char constant
cout << charvar1;         //display character
cout << '\n';             //display newline character
return 0;
}
```

Initialization

Variables can be initialized at the same time they are defined. In this program two variables of type char—charvar1 and charvar2—are initialized to the character constants 'A' and '\t'.

Escape Sequences

This second character constant, '\t', is an odd one. Like '\n' which we encountered earlier, it's an example of an *escape sequence*. The name reflects the fact that the backslash causes an "escape" from the normal way characters are interpreted. In this case the t is interpreted not as the character 't' but as the tab character. A tab causes printing to continue at the next tab stop. In console-mode programs, tab stops are positioned every eight spaces. Another character constant, '\n', is sent directly to cout in the last line of the program.

Escape sequences can be used both as separate characters and also embedded in string constants. Table 2.1 shows a list of common escape sequences.

Table 2.1 Common Escape Sequences

Escape Sequence	Character
\ a	Bell (beep)
\ b	Backspace
\ f	Formfeed
\ n	Newline
\ r	Return
\ t	Tab
\ \	Backslash
\ '	Single quotation mark
\ "	Double quotation marks
\ xdd	Hexadecimal notation

Since the backslash, the single quotation marks, and the double quotation marks all have specialized meanings when used in constants, they must be represented by escape sequences when we want to display them as characters. Here's an example of a quoted phrase in a string constant:

```
cout << "\"Run, Spot, run,\" she said.";
```

This translates to

```
"Run, Spot, run," she said.
```

Sometimes you need to represent a character constant that doesn't appear on the keyboard, such as the graphics characters above ASCII code 127. To do this, you can use the '\xdd' representation, where each **d** stands for a hexadecimal digit. If you want to print a solid rectangle, for example, you'll find such a character listed as decimal number 178, which is hexadecimal number **B2** in the ASCII table. This character would be represented by the character constant '\xB2'. We'll see some examples of this later.

The CHARVARS program prints the value of charvar1 ('A') and the value of charvar2 (a tab). It then sets charvar1 to a new value ('B'), prints that, and finally prints the newline. The output looks like this:

```
A       B
```

Input with cin

Now that we've seen some variable types in use, let's see how a program accomplishes input. The next example program asks the user for a temperature in degrees Fahrenheit, converts it to Celsius, and displays the result. It uses integer variables.

```cpp
// fahren.cpp
// demonstrates cin, newline
#include <iostream>
using namespace std;

int main()
    {
    int ftemp;  //for temperature in fahrenheit

    cout << "Enter temperature in fahrenheit: ";
    cin >> ftemp;
    int ctemp = (ftemp-32) * 5 / 9;
    cout << "Equivalent in Celsius is: " << ctemp << '\n';
    return 0;
    }
```

The statement

```
cin >> ftemp;
```

causes the program to wait for the user to type in a number. The resulting number is placed in the variable **ftemp**. The keyword **cin** (pronounced "C in") is an object, predefined in

C++ to correspond to the standard input stream. This stream represents data coming from the keyboard (unless it has been redirected). The >> is the *extraction* or *get from* operator. It takes the value from the stream object on its left and places it in the variable on its right.

Here's some sample interaction with the program:

```
Enter temperature in fahrenheit: 212
Equivalent in Celsius is: 100
```

Figure 2.5 shows input using `cin` and the extraction operator >>.

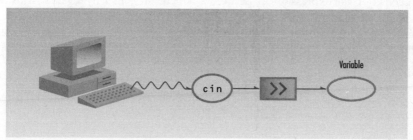

Figure 2.5   Input with cin.

Variables Defined at Point of Use

The FAHREN program has several new wrinkles besides its input capability. Look closely at the listing. Where is the variable `ctemp` defined? Not at the beginning of the program, but in the next-to-the-last line, where it's used to store the result of the arithmetic operation. As we noted earlier, you can define variables throughout a program, not just at the beginning. (Many languages, including C, require all variables to be defined before the first executable statement.)

Defining variables where they are used can make the listing easier to understand, since you don't need to refer repeatedly to the start of the listing to find the variable definitions. However, the practice should be used with discretion. Variables that are used in many places in a function are better defined at the start of the function.

Cascading <<

The insertion operator << is used repeatedly in the second `cout` statement in FAHREN. This is perfectly legal. The program first sends the phrase *Equivalent in celsius is:* to `cout`, then it sends the value of `ctemp`, and finally the newline character `'\n'`.

The extraction operator `>>` can be cascaded with `cin` in the same way, allowing the user to enter a series of values. However, this capability is not used so often, since it eliminates the opportunity to prompt the user between inputs.

Expressions

Any arrangement of variables, constants, and operators that specifies a computation is called an *expression*. Thus, `alpha+12` and `(alpha-37)*beta/2` are expressions. When the computations specified in the expression are performed, the result is usually a value. Thus if `alpha` is 7, the first expression shown has the value 19.

Parts of expressions may also be expressions. In the second example, `alpha-37` and `beta/2` are expressions. Even single variables and constants, like `alpha` and `37`, are considered to be expressions.

Note that expressions aren't the same as statements. Statements tell the compiler to do something and terminate with a semicolon, while expressions specify a computation. There can be several expressions in a statement.

Precedence

Note the parentheses in the expression

```
(ftemp-32) * 5 / 9
```

Without the parentheses, the multiplication would be carried out first, since `*` has higher priority than `-`. With the parentheses, the subtraction is done first, then the multiplication, since all operations inside parentheses are carried out first. What about the precedence of the `*` and `/` signs? When two arithmetic operators have the same precedence, the one on the left is executed first, so the multiplication will be carried out next; then the division. Precedence and parentheses are normally applied this same way in algebra and in other computer languages, so their use probably seems quite natural. However, precedence is an important topic in C++. We'll return to it later when we introduce different kinds of operators.

Floating Point Types

We've talked about type `int` and type `char`, both of which represent numbers as integers—that is, numbers without a fractional part. Now let's examine a different way of storing numbers—as floating-point variables.

Floating-point variables represent numbers with a decimal place—like 3.1415927, 0.0000625, and −10.2. They have both an integer part, to the left of the decimal point, and a fractional part, to the right. Floating-point variables represent what mathematicians call *real numbers*, which are used for measurable quantities like distance, area, and temperature and typically have a fractional part.

There are three kinds of floating-point variables in C++: type `float`, type `double`, and type `long double`. Let's start with the smallest of these, type `float`.

Type `float`

Type `float` stores numbers in the range of about 3.4×10^{-38} to 3.4×10^{38}, with a precision of seven digits. It occupies 4 bytes (32 bits) in memory, as shown in Figure 2.6. The following example program prompts the user to type in a floating-point number representing the radius of a circle. It then calculates and displays the circle's area.

```
// circarea.cpp
```

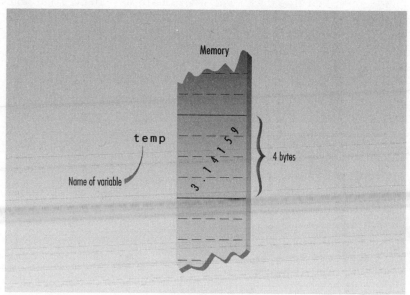

Figure 2.6   Variable of type `float` in memory.

```
// demonstrates floating point variables
#include <iostream>                        //for cout, etc.
using namespace std;

int main()
   {
   float rad;                             //variable of type float
   const float PI = 3.14159F;             //type const float

   cout << "Enter radius of circle: ";    //prompt
   cin >> rad;                            //get radius
   float area = PI * rad * rad;           //find area
   cout << "Area is " << area << endl;    //display answer
   return 0;
   }
```

Here's a sample interaction with the program:

```
Enter radius of circle: 0.5
Area is 0.785398
```

This is the area in square feet of a 12-inch LP record (which has a radius of 0.5 feet). At one time this was an important quantity for manufacturers of vinyl.

Type `double` and `long double`

The larger floating point types, `double` and `long double`, are similar to `float` except that they require more memory space and provide a wider range of values and more precision. Type `double` requires 8 bytes of storage and handles numbers in the range from 1.7×10^{-308} to 1.7×10^{308} with a precision of 15 digits. Type `long double` takes 16 bytes and stores numbers in the range of approximately 1.2×10^{-4932} to 1.2×10^{4932} with a precision of 19 digits. These types are shown in Figure 2.7.

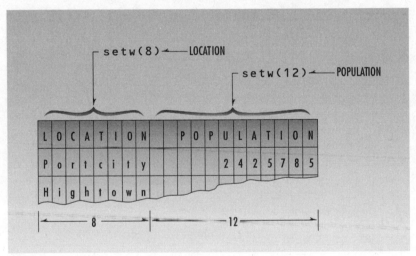

Figure 2.7   Variable of type `double` and `long double`.

Floating-Point Constants

The number 3.14159F in CIRCAREA is an example of a *floating-point constant*. The decimal point signals that it is a floating-point constant, and not an integer, and the F specifies that's it's type `float`, rather than `double` or `long double`. The number is written in normal decimal notation. You don't need a suffix letter with constants of type `double`; it's the default. With type `long double`, use the letter L.

You can also write floating-point constants using *exponential notation*. Exponential notation is a way of writing large numbers without having to write out a lot of zeros. For example, 1,000,000,000 can be written as 1.0E9 in exponential notation. Similarly, 1234.56 would be written 1.23456E3. (This is the same as 1.23456 times 10^3.) The number following the E is called the *exponent*. It indicates how many places the decimal point must be moved to change the number to ordinary decimal notation.

The exponent can be positive or negative. The exponential number 6.35239E–5 is equivalent to 0.0000635239 in decimal notation. This is the same as 6.35239 times 10^{-5}.

The `const` Qualifier

Besides demonstrating variables of type `float`, the CIRCAREA example also introduces the qualifier `const`. It's used in the statement

```
const float PI = 3.14159F;   //type const float
```

The keyword `const` (for constant) precedes the data type of a variable. It specifies that the value of a variable will not change throughout the program. Any attempt to alter the value of a variable defined with this qualifier will elicit an error message from the compiler.

The qualifier `const` ensures that your program does not inadvertently alter a variable that you intended to be a constant, such as the value of PI in CIRCAREA. It also reminds anyone reading the listing that the variable is not intended to change. The `const` modifier can apply to other entities besides simple variables. We'll learn more about this as we go along.

The `#define` Directive

Although the construction is not recommended in C++, constants can also be specified using the preprocessor directive `#define`. This directive sets up an equivalence between an identifier and a text phrase. For example, the line

```
#define PI 3.14159
```

appearing at the beginning of your program specifies that the identifier `PI` will be replaced by the text `3.14159` throughout the program. This construction has long been popular in C. However, you can't specify the data type of the constant using `#define`, which can lead to program bugs; so even in C `#define` has been superseded by `const` used with normal variables. However, you may encounter this construction in older programs.

Type `bool`

For completeness we should mention type `bool` here, although it won't be important until we discuss relational operators in the next chapter.

We've seen that variables of type `int` can have billions of possible values, and those of type `char` can have 256. Variables of type `bool` can have only two possible values: `true` and `false`. In theory a `bool` type requires only one bit (not byte) of storage, but in practice compilers often store them as integers because an integer can be quickly accessed, while an individual bit must be extracted from an integer, which requires additional time.

As we'll see, type **bool** is most commonly used to hold the results of comparisons. Is **alpha** less than **beta**? If so, a **bool** value is given the value **true**; if not, it's given the value **false**.

Type **bool** gets its name from George Boole, a 19th century English mathematician who invented the concept of using logical operators with true-or-false values. Thus such true/false values are often called *Boolean* values.

The **setw** Manipulator

We've mentioned that manipulators are operators used with the insertion operator << to modify—or manipulate—the way data is displayed. We've already seen the **endl** manipulator; now we'll look at another one: **setw**, which changes the field width of output.

You can think of each value displayed by **cout** as occupying a field: an imaginary box with a certain width. The default field is just wide enough to hold the value. That is, the integer 567 will occupy a field three characters wide, and the string **"pajamas"** will occupy a field seven characters wide. However, in certain situations this may not lead to optimal results. Here's an example. The WIDTH1 program prints the names of three cities in one column, and their populations in another.

```
// width1.cpp
// demonstrates need for setw manipulator
#include <iostream>
using namespace std;

int main()
   {
   long pop1=2425785, pop2=47, pop3=9761;

   cout << "LOCATION " << "POP." << endl
        << "Portcity " << pop1 << endl
        << "Hightown " << pop2 << endl
        << "Lowville " << pop3 << endl;
   return 0;
   }
```

Here's the output from this program:

```
LOCATION POP.
Portcity 2425785
Hightown 47
Lowville 9761
```

Unfortunately, this format makes it hard to compare the numbers; it would be better if they lined up to the right. Also, we had to insert spaces into the names of the cities to separate them from the numbers. This is an inconvenience.

Here's a variation of this program, WIDTH2, that uses the **setw** manipulator to eliminate these problems by specifying field widths for the names and the numbers:

```
// width2.cpp
// demonstrates setw manipulator
#include <iostream>
#include <iomanip>         // for setw
using namespace std;

int main()
   {
   long pop1=2425785, pop2=47, pop3=9761;

   cout << setw(8) << "LOCATION" << setw(12)
        << "POPULATION" << endl
        << setw(8) << "Portcity" << setw(12) << pop1 << endl
        << setw(8) << "Hightown" << setw(12) << pop2 << endl
        << setw(8) << "Lowville" << setw(12) << pop3 << endl;
   return 0;
   }
```

The **setw** manipulator causes the number (or string) that follows it in the stream to be printed within a field n characters wide, where n is the argument to **setw(n)**. The value is right-justified within the field. Figure 2.8 shows how this looks. Type **long** is used for the population figures, which prevents a potential overflow problem on systems that use 2-byte integer types, in which the largest integer value is 32,767.

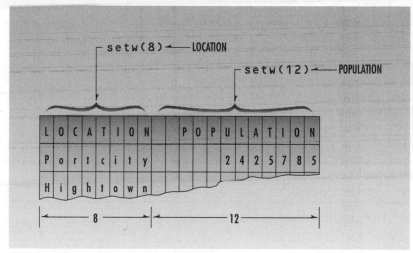

Figure 2.8   Field widths and setw.

Here's the output of WIDTH2:

```
LOCATION  POPULATION
Portcity    2425785
Hightown         47
Lowville       9761
```

Cascading the Insertion Operator

Note that there's only one **cout** statement in WIDTH1 and WIDTH2, although it's written on multiple lines. In doing this, we take advantage of the fact that the compiler ignores white-space, and that the insertion operator can be cascaded. The effect is the same as using four separate statements, each beginning with **cout**.

Multiple Definitions

We initialized the variables **pop1**, **pop2**, and **pop3** to specific values at the same time we defined them. This is similar to the way we initialized **char** variables in the CHARVARS example. Here, however, we've defined and initialized all three variables on one line, using the same **long** keyword and separating the variable names with commas. This saves space where a number of variables are all the same type.

The IOMANIP Header File

The declarations for the manipulators (except **endl**) are not in the usual IOSTREAM header file, but in a separate header file called IOMANIP. When you use these manipulators you must **#include** this header file in your program, as we do in the WIDTH2 example.

Variable Type Summary

Our program examples so far have used four data types—**int**, **char**, **float**, and **long**. In addition we've mentioned types **short**, **double**, and **long double**. Let's pause now to summarize these data types. Table 2.2 shows the keyword used to define the type, the numerical range the type can accommodate, the digits of precision (in the case of floating-point numbers), and the bytes of memory occupied in a 32-bit environment.

Table 2.2   Basic C++ Variable Types

| Keyword | Numerical Range | | Digits of Precision | Bytes of Memory |
	Low	High		
char	−128	127	n/a	1
short	−32,768	32,767	n/a	2
int	−2,147,483,648	2,147,483,647	n/a	4
long	−2,147,483,648	2,147,483,647	n/a	4
float	3.4×10^{-38}	3.4×10^{38}	7	4
double	1.7×10^{-308}	1.7×10^{308}	15	8
long double	3.4×10^{-4932}	1.1×10^{4932}	19	10

unsigned Data Types

By eliminating the sign of the character and integer types, you can change their range to start at 0 and include only positive numbers. This allows them to represent numbers twice as big as the signed type. Table 2.3 shows the unsigned versions.

Table 2.3   Unsigned Integer Types

Keyword	Numerical Range Low	High	Bytes of Memory
unsigned char	0	255	1
unsigned short	0	65,535	2
unsigned int	0	4,294,967,295	4
unsigned long	0	4,294,967,295	4

The unsigned types are used when the quantities represented are always positive—such as when representing a count of something—or when the positive range of the signed types is not quite large enough.

To change an integer type to an unsigned type, precede the data type keyword with the keyword unsigned. For example, an unsigned variable of type char would be defined as

```
unsigned char ucharvar;
```

Exceeding the range of signed types can lead to obscure program bugs. In certain (probably rare) situations such bugs can be eliminated by using unsigned types. For example, the following program stores the constant 1,500,000,000 (1.5 billion) both as an int in signedVar and as an unsigned int in unsignVar.

```cpp
// signtest.cpp
// tests signed and unsigned integers
#include <iostream>
using namespace std;

int main()
   {
   int signedVar = 1500000000;            //signed
   unsigned int unsignVar = 1500000000;   //unsigned

   signedVar = (signedVar * 2) / 3;   //calculation exceeds range
   unsignVar = (unsignVar * 2) / 3;   //calculation within range

   cout << "signedVar = " << signedVar << endl;   //wrong
   cout << "unsignVar = " << unsignVar << endl;   //OK
   return 0;
   }
```

The program multiplies both variables by 2, then divides them by 3. Although the result is smaller than the original number, the intermediate calculation is larger than the original number. This is a common situation, but it can lead to trouble. In SIGNTEST we expect that two-thirds the original value, or 1,000,000,000, will be restored to both variables. Unfortunately, in `signedVar` the multiplication created a result—3,000,000,000,000—that exceeded the range of the `int` variable (–2,147,483,648 to 2,147,483,647). Here's the output:

```
signedVar = -431,655,765
unsignVar = 1,000,000,000
```

The signed variable now displays an incorrect answer, while the unsigned variable, which is large enough to hold the intermediate result of the multiplication, records the result correctly. The moral is this: Be careful that all values generated in your program are within the range of the variables that hold them. (The results will be different on 16-bit or 64-bit computers, which use different numbers of bytes for type `int`.)

Type Conversion

C++, like C, is more forgiving than some languages in the way it treats expressions involving several different data types. As an example, consider the MIXED program:

```
// mixed.cpp
// shows mixed expressions
#include <iostream>
using namespace std;

int main()
    {
    int count = 7;
    float avgWeight = 155.5F;

    double totalWeight = count * avgWeight;
    cout << "totalWeight=" << totalWeight << endl;
    return 0;
    }
```

Here a variable of type `int` is multiplied by a variable of type `float` to yield a result of type `double`. This program compiles without error; the compiler considers it normal that you want to multiply (or perform any other arithmetic operation on) numbers of different types.

Not all languages are this relaxed. Some don't permit mixed expressions, and would flag the line that performs the arithmetic in MIXED as an error. Such languages assume that when you mix types you're making a mistake, and they try to save you from yourself. C++ and

C, however, assume that you must have a good reason for doing what you're doing, and they help carry out your intentions. This is one reason for the popularity of C++ and C. They give you more freedom. Of course, with more freedom, there's also more opportunity for you to make a mistake.

Automatic Conversions

Let's consider what happens when the compiler confronts such mixed-type expressions as that in MIXED. Types are considered "higher" or "lower," based roughly on the order shown in Table 2.4.

Table 2.4   Order of Data Types

Data Type	Order
long double	Highest
double	
float	
long	
int	
short	
char	Lowest

The arithmetic operators like + and * like to operate on two operands of the same type. When two operands of different types are encountered in the same expression, the lower-type variable is converted to the type of the higher-type variable. Thus in MIXED, the **int** value of **count** is converted to type **float** and stored in a temporary variable before being multiplied by the **float** variable **avgWeight**. The result (still of type **float**) is then converted to **double** so that it can be assigned to the **double** variable **totalWeight**. This process is shown in Figure 2.9.

These conversions take place invisibly, and ordinarily you don't need to think too much about them; C++ automatically does what you want. However, sometimes the compiler isn't so happy about conversions, as we'll see in a moment. Also, when we start to use objects, we will in effect be defining our own data types. We may want to use these new data types in mixed expressions, just as we use normal variables in mixed expressions. When this is the case, we must be careful to create our own conversion routines to change objects of one type into objects of another. The compiler won't do it for us, as it does here with the built-in data types.

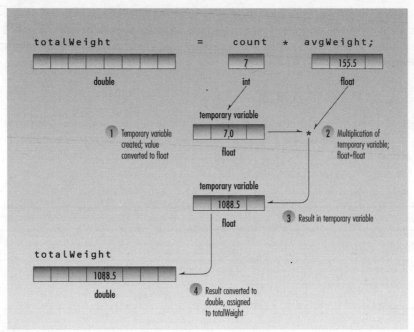

Figure 2.9   Data conversion.

Casts

Casts sounds like something to do with social classes in India, but in C++ the term applies to data conversions specified by the programmer, as opposed to the automatic data conversions we just described. Casts are also called *type casts*. What are casts for? Sometimes a programmer needs to convert a value from one type to another in a situation where the compiler will not do it automatically or without complaining.

There are several kinds of casts in Standard C++: static casts, dynamic casts, reinterpret casts, and **const** casts. Here we'll be concerned only with static casts; we'll learn about the others, which are used in more specialized situations, in later chapters.

C++ casts have a rather forbidding appearance. Here's a statement that uses a C++ cast to change a variable of type **int** into a variable of type **char**:

```
aCharVar = static_cast<char>(anIntVar);
```

Here the variable to be cast (**anIntVar**) is placed in parentheses and the type it's to be changed to (**char**) is placed in angle brackets. The result is that **anIntVar** is changed to type **char** before it's assigned to **aCharVar**. In this case the assignment statement would have carried out the cast itself, but there are situations where the cast is essential.

Recall that in the SIGNTEST example an intermediate result exceeded the capacity of the variable type, resulting in an erroneous result. We fixed the problem by using **unsigned int** instead of **int**. This worked because the intermediate result—3,000,000,000— would fit in the range of the unsigned variable.

But suppose an intermediate result won't fit the unsigned type either. In such a case we might be able to solve the problem by using a cast. Here's an example:

```
// cast.cpp
// tests signed and unsigned integers
#include <iostream>
using namespace std;

int main()
   {
   int intVar = 1500000000;                    //1,500,000,000
   intVar = (intVar * 10) / 10;                //result too large
   cout << "intVar = " << intVar << endl;      //wrong answer

   intVar = 1500000000;                        //cast to double
   intVar = (static_cast<double>(intVar) * 10) / 10;
   cout << "intVar = " << intVar << endl;      //right answer
   return 0;
   }
```

When we multiply the variable intVar by 10, the result—15,000,000,000—is far too large to fit in a variable of type int or unsigned int. This leads to the wrong answer, as shown by the output of the first part of the program.

We could redefine the data type of the variables to be **double**; this provides plenty of room, since this type holds numbers with up to 15 digits. But suppose that for some reason, such as keeping the program small, we don't want to change the variables to type **double**. In this case there's another solution: We can cast intVar to type **double** before multiplying. This is sometimes called *coercion*; the data is coerced into becoming another type. The expression

```
static_cast<double>(intVar)
```

casts intVar to type **double**. It generates a temporary variable of type **double** with the same value as intVar. It is this temporary variable that is multiplied by 10. Since it is type **double**, the result fits. This result is then divided by 10 and assigned to the normal **int** variable intVar. Here's the program's output:

```
intVar = 211509811
intVar = 1500000000
```

The first answer, without the cast, is wrong; but in the second answer, the cast produces the correct result.

Before Standard C++, casts were handled using quite a different format. Instead of

```
aCharVar = static_cast<char>(anIntVar);
```

you could say

```
aCharVar = (char)anIntVar;
```

or alternatively

```
aCharVar = char(anIntVar);
```

One trouble with these approaches is that they are hard to see; the syntax blends into the rest of the listing. They are also hard to search for using a Find operation with your source code editor. The new format solves this problem: `static_cast` is easy to see and easy to search for. These old casts still work, but their use is discouraged (or *depricated*, to use the technical term).

Casts should be used only when absolutely necessary. They are a controlled way of evading *type safety* (which means making sure that variables don't change types by mistake) and can lead to trouble because they make it impossible for the compiler to spot potential problems. However, sometimes casts can't be avoided. We'll see some examples as we go along of situations where casts are necessary.

Arithmetic Operators

As you have probably gathered by this time, C++ uses the four normal arithmetic operators +, -, *, and / for addition, subtraction, multiplication, and division. These operators work on all the data types, both integer and floating-point. They are used in much the same way that they are used in other languages, and are closely analogous to their use in algebra. However, there are some other arithmetic operators whose use is not so obvious.

The Remainder Operator

There is a fifth arithmetic operator that works only with integer variables (types `char`, `short`, `int`, and `long`). It's called the *remainder operator*, and is represented by `%`, the percent symbol. This operator (also called the *modulus operator*) finds the remainder when one number is divided by another. The REMAIND program demonstrates the effect.

```
// remaind.cpp
// demonstrates remainder operator
#include <iostream>
using namespace std;

int main()
   {
   cout <<  6 % 8 << endl      // 6
        <<  7 % 8 << endl      // 7
        <<  8 % 8 << endl      // 0
        <<  9 % 8 << endl      // 1
        << 10 % 8 << endl;     // 2
   return 0;
   }
```

Here the numbers 6 through 10 are divided by 8, using the remainder operator. The answers are 6, 7, 0, 1, and 2—the remainders of these divisions. The remainder operator is used in a wide variety of situations. We'll show examples as we go along.

A note about precedence: In the expression

```
cout << 6 % 8
```

the remainder operator is evaluated first because it has higher precedence than the << operator. If it did not, we would need to put parentheses around 6 % 8 to ensure it was evaluated before being acted on by <<.

Arithmetic Assignment Operators

C++ offers several ways to shorten and clarify your code. One of these is the *arithmetic assignment operator*. This operator helps to give C++ listings their distinctive appearance.

The following kind of statement is common in most languages.

```
total = total + item;   // adds "item" to "total"
```

In this situation you add something to an existing value (or you perform some other arithmetic operation on it). But the syntax of this statement offends those for whom brevity is important, because the name **total** appears twice. So C++ offers a condensed approach: the arithmetic assignment operator, which combines an arithmetic operator and an assignment operator and eliminates the repeated operand. Here's a statement that has exactly the same effect as the one above:

```
total += item;    // adds "item" to "total"
```

Figure 2.10 emphasizes the equivalence of the two forms.

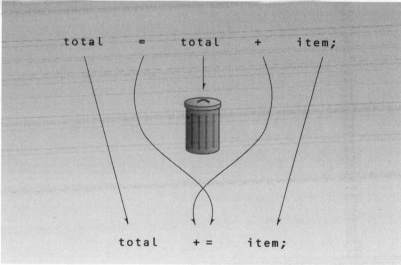

Figure 2.10   Arithmetic assignment operator.

There are arithmetic assignment operators corresponding to all the arithmetic operations: +=, -=, *=, /=, and %= (and some other operators as well). The following example shows the arithmetic assignment operators in use:

```
// assign.cpp
// demonstrates arithmetic assignment operators
#include <iostream>
using namespace std;

int main()
   {
   int ans = 27;

   ans += 10;              //same as: ans = ans + 10;
   cout << ans << ", ";
   ans -= 7;               //same as: ans = ans - 7;
   cout << ans << ", ";
   ans *= 2;               //same as: ans = ans * 2;
   cout << ans << ", ";
   ans /= 3;               //same as: ans = ans / 3;
   cout << ans << ", ";
   ans %= 3;               //same as: ans = ans % 3;
   cout << ans << endl;
   return 0;
   }
```

Here's the output from this program:

```
37, 30, 60, 20, 2
```

You don't need to use arithmetic assignment operators in your code, but they are a common feature of the language; they'll appear in numerous examples in this book.

Increment Operators

Here's an even more specialized operator. You often need to add 1 to the value of an existing variable. You can do this the "normal" way:

```
count = count + 1;    // adds 1 to "count"
```

Or you can use an arithmetic assignment operator:

```
count += 1;    // adds 1 to "count"
```

But there's an even more condensed approach:

```
++count;    // adds 1 to "count"
```

The ++ operator increments (adds 1 to) its argument.

Prefix and Postfix

As if this weren't weird enough, the increment operator can be used in two ways: as a *prefix*, meaning that the operator precedes the variable; and as a *postfix*, meaning that the operator follows the variable. What's the difference? Often a variable is incremented within a statement that performs some other operation on it. For example,

```
totalWeight = avgWeight * ++count;
```

The question here is this: Is the multiplication performed before or after **count** is incremented? In this case **count** is incremented first. How do we know that? Because prefix notation is used: **++count**. If we had used postfix notation, **count++**, the multiplication would have been performed first, then **count** would have been incremented. This is shown in Figure 2.11.

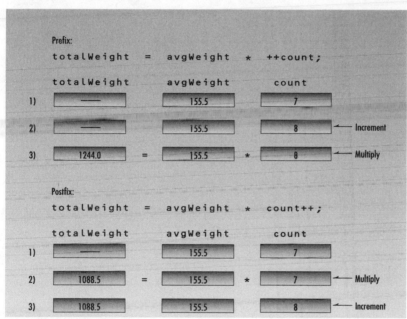

Figure 2.11   The increment operator.

Here's an example that shows both the prefix and postfix versions of the increment operator:

```
// increm.cpp
// demonstrates the increment operator
#include <iostream>
using namespace std;
```

```
int main()
   {
   int count = 10;

   cout << "count=" << count << endl;       //displays 10
   cout << "count=" << ++count << endl;      //displays 11 (prefix)
   cout << "count=" << count << endl;        //displays 11
   cout << "count=" << count++ << endl;      //displays 11 (postfix)
   cout << "count=" << count << endl;        //displays 12
   return 0;
   }
```

Here's the program's output:

```
count=10
count=11
count=11
count=11
count=12
```

The first time **count** is incremented, the prefix ++ operator is used. This causes the increment to happen at the beginning of the statement evaluation, before the output operation has been carried out. When the value of the expression ++**count** is displayed, it has already been incremented, and << sees the value 11. The second time **count** is incremented, the postfix ++ operator is used. When the expression **count**++ is displayed, it retains its unincremented value of 11. Following the completion of this statement, the increment takes effect, so that in the last statement of the program we see that **count** has acquired the value 12.

The Decrement (- -) Operator

The decrement operator, - -, behaves very much like the increment operator, except that it subtracts 1 from its operand. It too can be used in both prefix and postfix forms.

Library Functions

Many activities in C++ are carried out by *library functions*. These functions perform file access, mathematical computations, and data conversion, among other things. We don't want to dig too deeply into library functions before we explain how functions work (see Chapter 5), but you can use simple library functions without a thorough understanding of their operation.

The next example, SQRT, uses the library function **sqrt()** to calculate the square root of a number entered by the user.

```
// sqrt.cpp
// demonstrates sqrt() library function
#include <iostream>              //for cout, etc.
#include <cmath>                 //for sqrt()
using namespace std;

int main()
   {
   double number, answer;        //sqrt() requires type double

   cout << "Enter a number: ";
   cin >> number;                //get the number
   answer = sqrt(number);        //find square root
   cout << "Square root is "
    << answer << endl;           //display it
   return 0;
   }
```

The program first obtains a number from the user. This number is then used as an argument to the sqrt() function, in the statement

```
answer = sqrt(number);
```

An *argument* is the input to the function; it is placed inside the parentheses following the function name. The function then processes the argument and returns a value; this is the output from the function. In this case the return value is the square root of the original number. Returning a value means that the function expression takes on this value, which can then be assigned to another variable—in this case answer. The program then displays this value. Here's some output from the program:

```
Enter a number: 1000
Square root is 31.622777
```

Multiplying 31.622777 by itself on your pocket calculator will verify that this answer is pretty close.

The arguments to a function, and their return values, must be the correct data type. You can find what these data types are by looking at the description of the library function in your compiler's help file, which describes each of the hundreds of library functions. For sqrt(), the description specifies both an argument and a return value of type double, so we use variables of this type in the program.

Header Files

As with **cout** and other such objects, you must **#include** a header file that contains the declaration of any library functions you use. In the documentation for the **sqrt()** function, you'll see that the specified header file is CMATH. In SQRT the preprocessor directive

```
#include <cmath>
```

takes care of incorporating this header file into our source file.

If you don't include the appropriate header file when you use a library function, you'll get an error message like this from the compiler: *'sqrt' unidentified identifier*.

Library Files

We mentioned earlier that various files containing library functions and objects will be linked to your program to create an executable file. These files contain the actual machine-executable code for the functions. Such library files often have the extension .LIB. . The **sqrt()** function is found in such a file. It is automatically extracted from the file by the linker, and the proper connections are made so that it can be called (that is, invoked or accessed) from the SQRT program. Your compiler takes care of all these details for you, so ordinarily you don't need to worry about the process. However, you should understand what these files are for.

Header Files and Library Files

The relationship between library files and header files can be confusing, so let's review it. To use a library function like **sqrt()**, you must link the library file that contains it to your program. The appropriate functions from the library file are then connected to your program by the linker.

However, that's not the end of the story. The functions in your source file need to know the names and types of the functions and other elements in the library file. They are given this information in a header file. Each header file contains information for a particular group of functions. The functions themselves are grouped together in a library file, but the information about them is scattered throughout a number of header files. The IOSTREAM header file contains information for various I/O functions and objects, including **cout**, while the CMATH header file contains information for mathematics functions like **sqrt()**. If you were using string functions like **strcpy()**, you would include STRING.H, and so on.

Figure 2.12 shows the relationship of header files and library files to the other files used in program development.

The use of header files is common in C++. Whenever you use a library function or a predefined object or operator, you will need to use a header file that contains appropriate declarations.

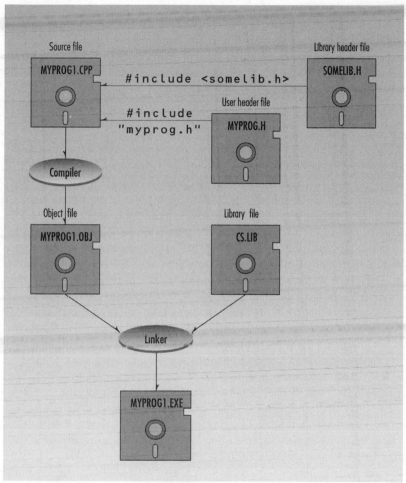

Figure 2.12 Header and library files.

Two Ways to Use `#include`

You can use `#include` in two ways. The angle brackets < and > surrounding the filenames IOSTREAM and CMATH in the SQRT example indicate that the compiler should begin searching for these files in the standard INCLUDE directory. This directory, which is traditionally called INCLUDE, holds the header files supplied by the compiler manufacturer for the system.

Instead of angle brackets around the filename, you can also use quotation marks, as in

```
#include "myheader.h"
```

Quotation marks instruct the compiler to begin its search for the header file in the current directory; this is usually the directory that contains the source file. You normally use quotation marks for header files you write yourself (a situation we'll explore in Chapter 13, "Multifile Programs"). Quotation marks or angle brackets work in any case, but making the appropriate choice speeds up the compilation process slightly by giving the compiler a hint about where to find the file.

Summary

In this chapter we've learned that a major building block of C++ programs is the *function*. A function named `main()` is always the first one executed when a program is executed.

A function is composed of *statements*, which tell the computer to do something. Each statement ends with a semicolon. A statement may contain one or more *expressions*, which are sequences of variables and operators that usually evaluate to a specific value.

Output is most commonly handled in C++ with the `cout` object and `<<` insertion operator, which together cause variables or constants to be sent to the standard output device—usually the screen. Input is handled with `cin` and the extraction operator `>>`, which cause values to be received from the standard input device—usually the keyboard.

Various data types are built into C++: `char`, `int`, and `long` and `short` are the integer types; and `float`, `double`, and `long double` are the floating-point types. All of these types are signed. Unsigned versions of the integer types, signaled by the keyword `unsigned`, don't hold negative numbers but hold positive ones twice as large. Type `bool` is used for Boolean variables and can hold only the constants `true` or `false`.

The `const` keyword stipulates that a variable's value will not change in the course of a program.

A variable is automatically converted from one type to another in mixed expressions (those involving different data types) and by casting, which allows the programmer to specify a conversion.

C++ employs the usual arithmetic operators `+`, `-`, `*`, and `/`. In addition, the remainder operator, `%`, returns the remainder of integer division.

The arithmetic assignment operators `+=`, `+-`, and so on perform an arithmetic operation and an assignment simultaneously. The increment and decrement operators `++` and `--` increase or decrease a variable by 1.

Preprocessor directives consist of instructions to the compiler, rather than to the computer. The `#include` directive tells the compiler to insert another file into the present source file, and the `#define` directive tells it to substitute one thing for another. The using directive tells the compiler to recognize names in a certain namespace.

If you use a library function in your program, the code for the function is in a library file, which is automatically linked to your program. A header file containing the function's declaration must be inserted into your source file with an `#include` statement.

Questions

Answers to questions can be found in Appendix G, "Answers to Questions and Exercises."

1. Dividing a program into functions

    a. is the key to object-oriented programming.

    b. makes the program easier to conceptualize.

    c. may reduce the size of the program.

    d. makes the program run faster.

2. A function name must be followed by _____.

3. A function body is delimited by _____.

4. Why is the `main()` function special?

5. A C++ instruction that tells the computer to do something is called a _____.

6. Write an example of a normal C++ comment and an example of an old-fashioned `/*` comment.

7. An expression

    a. usually evaluates to a numerical value.

    b. indicates the emotional state of the program.

    c. always occurs outside a function.

    d. may be part of a statement.

8. Specify how many bytes are occupied by the following data types in a 32-bit system:

    a. Type `int`

    b. Type `long double`

    c. Type `float`

    d. Type `long`

9. True or false: A variable of type `char` can hold the value 301.

10. What kind of program elements are the following?

   a. 12

   b. `'a'`

   c. 4.28915

   d. `JungleJim`

   e. `JungleJim()`

11. Write statements that display on the screen

   a. the character `'x'`.

   b. the name *Jim*.

   c. the number 509.

12. True or false: In an assignment statement, the value on the left of the equal sign is always equal to the value on the right.

13. Write a statement that displays the variable `george` in a field 10 characters wide.

14. What header file must you `#include` with your source file to use `cout` and `cin`?

15. Write a statement that gets a numerical value from the keyboard and places it in the variable `temp`.

16. What header file must you perform `#include` with your program to use `setw`?

17. Two exceptions to the rule that the compiler ignores whitespace are _____ and _____.

18. True or false: It's perfectly all right to use variables of different data types in the same arithmetic expression.

19. The expression 11%3 evaluates to _____.

20. An arithmetic assignment operator combines the effect of what two operators?

21. Write a statement that uses an arithmetic assignment operator to increase the value of the variable `temp` by 23. Write the same statement without the arithmetic assignment operator.

22. The increment operator increases the value of a variable by how much?

23. Assuming var1 starts with the value 20, what will the following code fragment print out?

```
cout << var1--;
cout << ++var1;
```

24. In the examples we've seen so far, header files have been used for what purpose?

25. The actual code for library functions is contained in a _____ file.

Exercises

Answers to the starred exercises can be found in Appendix G.

*1. Assuming there are 7.481 gallons in a cubic foot, write a program that asks the user to enter a number of gallons, and then displays the equivalent in cubic feet.

*2. Write a program that generates the following table:

```
1990      135
1991      7200
1992      11300
1993      16200
```

Use a single **cout** statement for all output.

*3. Write a program that generates the following output:

```
10
20
19
```

Use an integer constant for the 10, an arithmetic assignment operator to generate the 20, and a decrement operator to generate the 19.

4. Write a program that displays your favorite poem. Use an appropriate escape sequence for the line breaks. If you don't have a favorite poem, you can borrow this one by Ogden Nash:

```
Candy is dandy,
But liquor is quicker.
```

5. A library function, `islower()`, takes a single character (a letter) as an argument and returns a nonzero integer if the letter is lowercase, or zero if it is uppercase. This function requires the header file CTYPE.H. Write a program that allows the user to enter a letter, and then displays either zero or nonzero, depending on whether a lowercase or uppercase letter was entered. (See the SQRT program for clues.)

6. On a certain day the British pound was equivalent to $1.487 U.S., the French franc was $0.172, the German deutschemark was $0.584, and the Japanese yen was $0.00955. Write a program that allows the user to enter an amount in dollars, and then displays this value converted to these four other monetary units.

7. You can convert temperature from degrees Celsius to degrees Fahrenheit by multiplying by 9/5 and adding 32. Write a program that allows the user to enter a floating-point number representing degrees Celsius, and then displays the corresponding degrees Fahrenheit.

8. When a value is smaller than a field specified with `setw()`, the unused locations are, by default, filled in with spaces. The manipulator `setfill()` takes a single character as an argument and causes this character to be substituted for spaces in the empty parts of a field. Rewrite the WIDTH program so that the characters on each line between the location name and the population number are filled in with periods instead of spaces, as in

   ```
   Portcity.....2425785
   ```

9. If you have two fractions, a/b and c/d, their sum can be obtained from the formula

   ```
   a     c     a*d + b*c
   --- + --- = -----------
   b     d        b*d
   ```

   For example, 1/4 plus 2/3 is

   ```
   1     2     1*3 + 4*2     3 + 8        11
   --- + --- = ----------- = ------- = ----
   4     3        4*3          12          12
   ```

   Write a program that encourages the user to enter two fractions, and then displays their sum in fractional form. (You don't need to reduce it to lowest terms.) The interaction with the user might look like this:

   ```
   Enter first fraction: 1/2
      Enter second fraction: 2/5
      Sum = 9/10
   ```

You can take advantage of the fact that the extraction operator (>>) can be chained to read in more than one quantity at once:

```
cin >> a >> dummychar >> b;
```

10. In the heyday of the British empire, Great Britain used a monetary system based on pounds, shillings, and pence. There were 20 shillings to a pound, and 12 pence to a shilling. The notation for this old system used the pound sign, £, and two decimal points, so that, for example, £5.2.8 meant 5 pounds, 2 shillings, and 8 pence. (*Pence* is the plural of *penny*.) The new monetary system, introduced in the 1950s, consists of only pounds and pence, with 100 pence to a pound (like U.S. dollars and cents). We'll call this new system *decimal pounds*. Thus £5.2.8 in the old notation is £5.13 in decimal pounds (actually £5.1333333). Write a program to convert the old pounds-shillings-pence format to decimal pounds. An example of the user's interaction with the program would be

```
Enter pounds: 7
Enter shillings: 17
Enter pence: 9
Decimal pounds = £7.89
```

In both Borland C++ and Turbo C++, you can use the hex character constant '\x9c' to represent the pound sign (£). In Borland C++, you can put the pound sign into your program directly by pasting it from the Windows Character Map accessory.

11. By default, output is right-justified in its field. You can left-justify text output using the manipulator **setiosflags(ios::left)**. (For now, don't worry about what this new notation means.) Use this manipulator, along with **setw()**, to help generate the following output:

```
Last name    First name    Street address    Town      State
- - - - - - - - - - - - - - - - - - - - - - - - - - - - - - - - - - - -
    Jones      Bernard     109 Pine Lane    Littletown    MI
    O'Brian     Coleen     42 E. 99th Ave.    Bigcity      NY
    Wong       Harry      121-A Alabama St.   Lakeville    IL
```

12. Write the inverse of Exercise 10, so that the user enters an amount in Great Britain's new decimal-pounds notation (pounds and pence), and the program converts it to the old pounds-shillings-pence notation. An example of interaction with the program might be

```
Enter decimal pounds: 3.51
Equivalent in old notation = £3.10.2.
```

Make use of the fact that if you assign a floating-point value (say 12.34) to an integer variable, the decimal fraction (0.34) is lost; the integer value is simply 12. Use a cast to avoid a compiler warning. You can use statements like

```
float decpounds;      // input from user (new-style pounds)
int pounds;           // old-style (integer) pounds
float decfrac;        // decimal fraction (smaller than 1.0)

pounds = static_cast<int>(decpounds); // remove decimal fraction
   decfrac = decpounds - pounds;  // regain decimal fraction
```

You can then multiply `decfrac` by 20 to find shillings. A similar operation obtains pence.

CHAPTER 3

LOOPS AND DECISIONS

You will learn about the following in this chapter:

- Relational operators
- FOR, WHILE, and DO loops
- IF and IF...ELSE statements

- The SWITCH statement
- The conditional operator
- Logical operators

N ot many programs execute all their statements in strict order from beginning to end. Most programs (like many humans) decide what to do in response to changing circumstances. The flow of control jumps from one part of the program to another, depending on calculations performed in the program. Program statements that cause such jumps are called *control statements*. There are two major categories: loops and decisions.

How many times a loop is executed, or whether a decision results in the execution of a section of code, depends on whether certain expressions are true or false. These expressions typically involve a kind of operator called a *relational operator*, which compares two values. Since the operation of loops and decisions is so closely involved with these operators, we'll examine them first.

Relational Operators

A relational operator compares two values. The values can be any built-in C++ data type, such as char, int, and float, or—as we'll see later—they can be user-defined classes. The comparison involves such relationships as equal to, less than, and greater than. The result of the comparison is true or false; for example, either two values are equal (true), or they're not (false).

Our first program, RELAT, demonstrates relational operators in a comparison of integer variables and constants.

```
// relat.cpp
// demonstrates relational operators
#include <iostream>
using namespace std;

int main()
   {
   int numb;

   cout << "Enter a number: ";
   cin >> numb;
   cout << "numb<10  is " << (numb < 10)  << endl;
   cout << "numb>10  is " << (numb > 10)  << endl;
   cout << "numb==10 is " << (numb == 10) << endl;
   return 0;
   }
```

This program performs three kinds of comparisons between 10 and a number entered by the user. Here's the output when the user enters 20:

```
Enter a number: 20
numb<10  is 0
numb>10  is 1
numb==10 is 0
```

The first expression is true if numb is less than 10. The second expression is true if numb is greater than 10, and the third is true if numb is equal to 10. As you can see from the output, the C++ compiler considers that a true expression has the value 1, while a false expression has the value 0.

As we mentioned in the last chapter, Standard C++ includes a type bool, which can hold one of two constant values, true or false. You might think that results of relational expressions like numb<10 would be of type bool, and that the program would print false instead of 0 and true instead of 1. In fact C++ is rather schizophrenic on this point. Displaying the results of relational operations, or even the values of type bool variables, with cout<< yields 0 or 1, not false and true. Historically this is because C++ started out with no bool type. Before the advent of Standard C++, the *only* way to express false and true was with 0 and 1. Now false can be represented by either a bool value of false, or by an integer value of 0; and true can be represented by either a bool value of true or an integer value of 1.

In most simple situations the difference isn't apparent because we don't need to *display* true/false values; we just *use* them in loops and decisions to influence what the program will do next.

Here's the complete list of C++ relational operators:

Operator	Meaning
>	Greater than
<	Less than
==	Equal to
!=	Not equal to
>=	Greater than or equal to
<=	Less than or equal to

Now let's look at some expressions that use relational operators, and also look at the value of each expression. The first two lines are assignment statements that set the values of the variables harry and jane. You might want to hide the comments with your old Jose Canseco baseball card and see if you can predict which expressions evaluate to true and which to false.

```
jane = 44;          //assignment statement
harry = 12;         //assignment statement
(jane == harry)     //false
(harry <= 12)       //true
(jane > harry)      //true
(jane >= 44)        //true
(harry != 12)       //false
(7 < harry)         //true
(0)                 //false (by definition)
(44)                //true (since it's not 0)
```

Note that the equal operator, ==, uses two equal signs. A common mistake is to use a single equal sign—the assignment operator—as a relational operator. This is a nasty bug, since the compiler may not notice anything wrong. However, your program won't do what you want (unless you're very lucky).

Although C++ generates a 1 to indicate true, it assumes that any value other than 0 (such as −7 or 44) is true; only 0 is false. Thus, the last expression in the list is true.

Now let's see how these operators are used in typical situations. We'll examine loops first, then decisions.

Loops

Loops cause a section of your program to be repeated a certain number of times. The repetition continues while a condition is true. When the condition becomes false, the loop ends and control passes to the statements following the loop.

There are three kinds of loops in C++: the `for` loop, the `while` loop, and the `do` loop.

The `for` Loop

The `for` loop is (for many people, anyway) the easiest C++ loops to understand. All its loop-control elements are gathered in one place, while in the other loop constructions they are scattered about the program, which can make it harder to unravel how these loops work.

The `for` loop executes a section of code a fixed number of times. It's usually (although not always) used when you know, before entering the loop, how many times you want to execute the code.

Here's an example, FORDEMO, that displays the squares of the numbers from 0 to 14:

```
// fordemo.cpp
// demonstrates simple FOR loop
#include <iostream>
using namespace std;

int main()
   {
   int j;                       //define a loop variable

   for(j=0; j<15; j++)          //loop from 0 to 14,
      cout << j * j << "  ";    //displaying the square of j
   cout << endl;
   return 0;
   }
```

Here's the output:

```
0   1   4   9   16   25   36   49   64   81   100   121   144   169   196
```

How does this work? The `for` statement controls the loop. It consists of the keyword `for`, followed by parentheses that contain three expressions separated by semicolons:

```
for(j=0; j<15; j++)
```

These three expressions are the *initialization expression*, the *test expression*, and the *increment expression*, as shown in Figure 3.1.

These three expressions usually (but not always) involve the same variable, which we call the *loop variable*. In the FORDEMO example the loop variable is j. It's defined before the statements within the loop body start to execute.

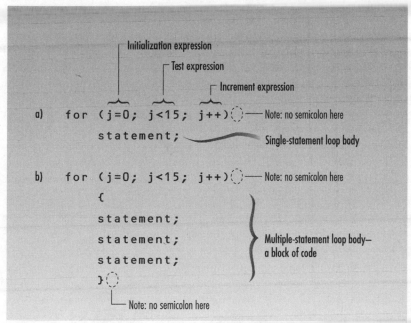

Figure 3.1 Syntax of the for loop.

The *body* of the loop is the code to be executed each time through the loop. Repeating this code is the raison d'être for the loop. In this example the loop body consists of a single statement:

```
cout << j * j << "  ";
```

This statement prints out the square of j, followed by two spaces. The square is found by multiplying j by itself. As the loop executes, j goes through the sequence 0, 1, 2, 3, and so on up to 14; so the squares of these numbers are displayed—0, 1, 4, 9, up to 196.

Note that the **for** statement is not followed by a semicolon. That's because the **for** statement and the loop body are together considered to be a program statement. This is an important detail. If you put a semicolon after the **for** statement, the compiler will think there is no loop body, and the program will do things you probably don't expect.

Let's see how the three expressions in the **for** statement control the loop.

The Initialization Expression

The initialization expression is executed only once, when the loop first starts. It gives the loop variable an initial value. In the FORDEMO example it sets j to 0.

The Test Expression

The test expression usually involves a relational operator. It is evaluated each time through the loop, just before the body of the loop is executed. It determines whether the loop will be executed again. If the test expression is true, the loop is executed one more time. If it's false, the loop ends, and control passes to the statements following the loop. In the FORDEMO example the statement

```
cout << endl;
```

is executed following the completion of the loop.

The Increment Expression

The increment expression changes the value of the loop variable, often by incrementing it. It is always executed at the end of the loop, after the loop body has been executed. Here the increment operator ++ adds 1 to j each time through the loop. Figure 3.2 shows a flowchart of a for loop's operation.

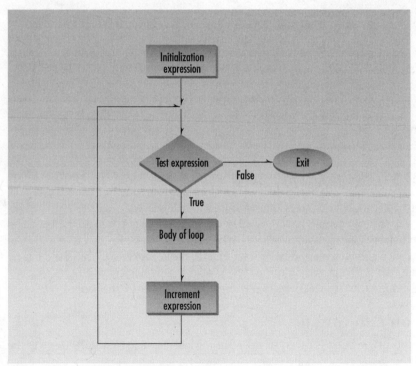

Figure 3.2   Operation of the for loop.

How Many Times?

The loop in the FORDEMO example executes exactly 15 times. The first time, j is 0. This is ensured in the initialization expression. The last time through the loop, j is 14. This is determined by the test expression j<15. When j becomes 15, the loop terminates; the loop body is not executed when j has this value. The arrangement shown is commonly used to do something a fixed number of times: start at 0, use a test expression with the less-than operator and a value equal to the desired number of iterations, and increment the loop variable after each iteration.

Here's another **for** loop example:

```
for(count=0; count<100; count++)
   // loop body
```

How many times will the loop body be repeated here? Exactly 100 times, with **count** going from 0 to 99.

Multiple Statements in Loop Body

Of course you may want to execute more than one statement in the loop body. Multiple statements are delimited by braces, just as functions are. Note that there is no semicolon following the final brace of the loop body, although there are semicolons following the individual statements in the loop body.

The next example, CUBELIST, uses three statements in the loop body. It prints out the cubes of the numbers from 1 to 10, using a two-column format.

```
// cubelist.cpp
// lists cubes from 1 to 10
#include <iostream>
#include <iomanip>                       //for setw
using namespace std;

int main()
   {
   int numb;                             //define loop variable

   for(numb=1; numb<=10; numb++)         //loop from 1 to 10
      {
      cout << setw(4) << numb;           //display 1st column
      int cube = numb*numb*numb;         //calculate cube
      cout << setw(6) << cube << endl;   //display 2nd column
      }
   return 0;
   }
```

Here's the output from the program:

```
 1     1
 2     8
 3    27
 4    64
 5   125
 6   216
 7   343
 8   512
 9   729
10  1000
```

We've made another change in the program to show there's nothing immutable about the format used in the last example. The loop variable is initialized to 1, not to 0, and it ends at 10, not at 9, by virtue of <=, the less-than-or-equal-to operator. The effect is that the loop body is executed 10 times, with the loop variable running from 1 to 10 (not from 0 to 9).

Blocks and Variable Visibility

The loop body, which consists of braces delimiting several statements, is called a *block* of code. One important aspect of a block is that a variable defined inside the block is not visible outside it. *Visible* means that program statements can access or "see" the variable. (We'll discuss visibility further in Chapter 5, "Functions.") In CUBELIST we define the variable **cube** inside the block, in the statement

```
int cube = numb*numb*numb;
```

You can't access this variable outside the block; it's only visible within the braces. Thus if you placed the statement

```
cube = 10;
```

after the loop body, the compiler would signal an error because the variable **cube** would be undefined outside the loop.

One advantage of restricting the visibility of variables is that the same variable name can be used within different blocks in the same program. (Defining variables inside a block, as we did in CUBELIST, is common in C++ but is not popular in C.)

Indentation and Loop Style

Good programming style dictates that the loop body be indented—that is, shifted right, relative to the loop statement (and to the rest of the program). In the FORDEMO example one line is indented, and in CUBELIST the entire block, including the braces, is indented. This indentation is an important visual aid to the programmer: It makes it easy to see where the loop body begins and ends. The compiler doesn't care whether you indent or not (at least there's no way to tell if it cares).

There is a common variation on the style we use for loops in this book. We show the braces aligned vertically, but some programmers prefer to place the opening brace just after the loop statement, like this:

```
for(numb=1; numb<=10; numb++)   {
   cout << setw(4) << numb;
   int cube = numb*numb*numb;
   cout << setw(6) << cube << endl;
   }
```

This saves a line in the listing but makes it more difficult to read, since the opening brace is harder to see and harder to match with the corresponding closing brace. Another style is to indent the body but not the braces:

```
for(numb=1; numb<=10; numb++)
{
   cout << setw(4) << numb;
   int cube = numb*numb*numb;
   cout << setw(6) << cube << endl;
}
```

This is a common approach, but at least for some people it makes it harder for the eye to connect the braces to the loop body. However, you can get used to almost anything. Whatever style you choose, use it consistently.

Debugging Animation

You can use the debugging features built into your compiler to create a dramatic animated display of loop operation. The key feature is *single-stepping*. Your compiler makes this easy. Start by opening a project for the program to be debugged, and an *Edit* window containing the source file. The exact instructions necessary to launch the debugger vary with different compilers, so consult Appendix C, "Microsoft Visual C++," or Appendix D, "Borland C++," as appropriate. By pressing a certain function key you can cause one line of your program to be executed at a time. This will show you the sequence of statements executed as the program proceeds. In a loop you'll see the statements within the loop executed; then control will jump back to the start of the loop and the cycle will be repeated.

You can also use the debugger to watch what happens to the values of different variables as you single step through the program. This is a powerful tool when you're debugging your program. You can experiment with this technique with the CUBELIST program by putting the numb and cube variables in a *Watch window* in your debugger and seeing how they change as the program proceeds. Again, consult the appropriate appendix for instructions on how to use Watch windows.

Single-stepping and the Watch window are powerful debugging tools. If your program doesn't behave as you think it should, you can use these features to monitor the values of key variables as you step through the program. Usually the source of the problem will become clear.

for Loop Variations

The increment expression doesn't need to increment the loop variable; it can perform any operation it likes. In the next example it *decrements* the loop variable. This program, FACTOR, asks the user to type in a number, and then calculates the factorial of this number. (The factorial is calculated by multiplying the original number by all the positive integers smaller than itself. Thus the factorial of 5 is 5*4*3*2*1, or 120.)

```cpp
// factor.cpp
// calculates factorials, demonstrates FOR loop
#include <iostream>
using namespace std;

int main()
   {
   unsigned int numb;
   unsigned long fact=1;                 //long for larger numbers

   cout << "Enter a number: ";
   cin >> numb;                          //get number

   for(int j=numb; j>0; j--)             //multiply 1 by
      fact *= j;                         //numb, numb-1, ..., 2, 1
   cout << "Factorial is " << fact << endl;
   return 0;
   }
```

In this example the initialization expression sets j to the value entered by the user. The test expression causes the loop to execute as long as j is greater than 0. The increment expression decrements j after each iteration.

We've used type `unsigned long` for the factorial, since the factorials of even small numbers are very large. On 32-bit systems like Windows `int` is the same as `long`, but `long` gives added capacity on 16-bit systems. The following output shows how large factorials can be, even for small input numbers:

```
Enter a number: 10
Factorial is 3628800
```

The largest number you can use for input is 12. You won't get an error message for larger inputs, but the results will be wrong, as the capacity of type `long` will be exceeded.

Variables Defined in for Statements

There's another wrinkle in this program: The loop variable j is defined inside the `for` statement:

```cpp
for(int j=numb; j>0; j--)
```

This is a common construction in C++. It defines the variable as closely as possible to its point of use in the listing. Variables defined in the loop statement this way are visible from the point of definition onward in the listing (unlike variables defined within a block, which are visible only within the block). It's best not to use this style if the variable will be used outside the loop.

Multiple Initialization and Test Expressions

You can put more than one expression in the initialization part of the **for** statement, separating the different expressions by commas. You can also have more than one increment expression. You can have only one test expression. Here's an example:

```
for( j=0, alpha=100; j<50; j++, beta-- )
   {
   // body of loop
   }
```

This example has a normal loop variable **j**, but it also initializes another variable, **alpha**, and decrements a third, **beta**. The variables **alpha** and **beta** don't need to have anything to do with each other, or with **j**. Multiple initialization expressions and multiple increment expressions are separated by commas.

Actually, you can leave out some or all of the expressions if you want to. The expression

```
for(;;)
```

is the same as a **while** loop with a test expression of **true**. We'll look at **while** loops next.

We'll avoid using such multiple or missing expressions. While these approaches can make the listing more concise, they also tend to decrease its readability. It's always possible to use standalone statements or a different form of loop to achieve the same effect.

The **while** Loop

The **for** loop does something a fixed number of times. What happens if you don't know how many times you want to do something before you start the loop? In this case a different kind of loop may be used: the **while** loop.

The next example, ENDON0, asks the user to enter a series of numbers. When the number entered is 0, the loop terminates. Notice that there's no way for the program to know in advance how many numbers will be typed before the 0 appears; that's up to the user.

```
// endon0.cpp
// demonstrates WHILE loop
#include <iostream>
using namespace std;

int main()
   {
   int n = 99;         // make sure n isn't initialized to 0

   while( n != 0 )     // loop until n is 0
      cin >> n;        // read a number into n
   cout << endl;
   return 0;
   }
```

Here's some sample output. The user enters numbers, and the loop continues until 0 is entered, at which point the loop and the program terminate.

```
1
27
33
144
9
0
```

The `while` loop looks like a simplified version of the `for` loop. It contains a test expression but no initialization or increment expressions. Figure 3.3 shows the syntax of the `while` loop.

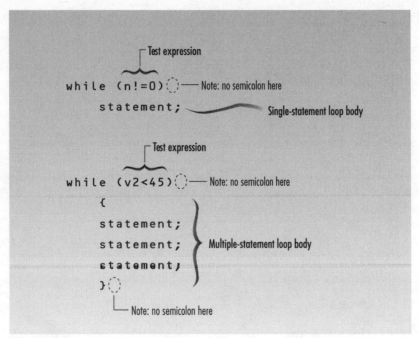

Figure 3.3 Syntax of the `while` loop.

As long as the test expression is true, the loop continues to be executed. In ENDON0, the text expression

```
n != 0
```

(n not equal to 0) is true until the user enters 0.

Figure 3.4 shows the operation of a `while` loop. The simplicity of the `while` loop is a bit illusory. Although there is no initialization expression, the loop variable (n in ENDON0) must be initialized before the loop begins. The loop body must also contain some statement that changes the value of the loop variable; otherwise the loop would never end. In ENDON0 it's `cin>>n;`.

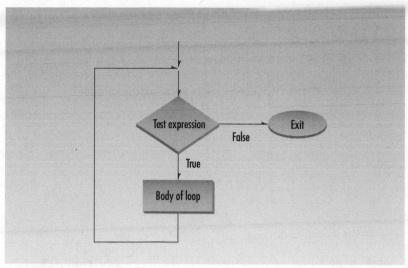

Figure 3.4   Operation of the `while` loop.

Multiple Statements in `while` Loop

The next example, WHILE4, uses multiple statements in a `while` loop. It's a variation of the CUBELIST program shown earlier with a `for` loop, but it calculates the fourth power, instead of the cube, of a series of integers. Let's assume that in this program it's important to put the results in a column four digits wide. To ensure that the results fit this column width, we must stop the loop before the results become larger than 9999. Without prior calculation we don't know what number will generate a result of this size, so we let the program figure it out. The test expression in the `while` statement terminates the program before the powers become too large.

```cpp
// while4.cpp
// prints numbers raised to fourth power
#include <iostream>
#include <iomanip>                  //for setw
using namespace std;

int main()
   {
   int pow=1;                       //power initially 1
   int numb=1;                      //numb goes from 1 to ???

   while( pow<9999 )                //loop while power <= 4 digits
      {
      cout << setw(2) << numb;      //display number
      cout << setw(5) << pow << endl; //display fourth power
      ++numb;                       //get ready for next power
      pow = numb*numb*numb*numb;    //calculate fourth power
      }
```

```
cout << endl;
return 0;
}
```

To find the fourth power of `numb`, we simply multiply it by itself four times. Each time through the loop we increment `numb`. But we don't use `numb` in the test expression in `while`; instead, the resulting value of `pow` determines when to terminate the loop. Here's the output:

```
1    1
2   16
3   81
4  256
5  625
6 1296
7 2401
8 4096
9 6561
```

The next number would be 10,000—too wide for our four-digit column; but by this time the loop has terminated.

Precedence: Arithmetic and Relational Operators

The next program touches on the question of operator precedence. It generates the famous sequence of numbers called *the Fibonacci series*. Here are the first few terms of the series:

```
1  1  2  3  5  8  13  21  34  55
```

Each term is found by adding the two previous ones: 1+1 is 2, 1+2 is 3, 2+3 is 5, 3+5 is 8, and so on. The Fibonacci series has applications in amazingly diverse fields, from sorting methods in computer science to the number of spirals in sunflowers.

One of the most interesting aspects of the Fibonacci series is its relation to the golden ratio. The golden ratio is supposed to be the ideal proportion in architecture and art, and was used in the design of ancient Greek temples. As the Fibonacci series is carried out further and further, the ratio of the last two terms approaches closer and closer to the golden ratio. Here's the listing for FIBO.CPP:

```
// fibo.cpp
// demonstrates WHILE loops using fibonacci series
#include <iostream>
using namespace std;

int main()
   {                                //largest unsigned long
   const unsigned long limit = 4294967295;
```

```
    unsigned long next=0;        //next-to-last term
    unsigned long last=1;        //last term

    while( next < limit / 2 )    //don't let results get too big
       {
       cout << last << "  ";     //display last term
       long sum = next + last;   //add last two terms
       next = last;              //variables move forward
       last = sum;               //   in the series
       }
    cout << endl;
    return 0;
    }
```

Here's the output:

```
1   1   2   3   5   8   13   21   34   55   89   144   233   377   610   987
1597   2584   4181   6765   10946   17711   28657   46368   75025   121393
196418   317811   514229   832040   1346269   2178309   3524578
5702887   9227465   14930352   24157817   39088169   63245986
102334155   165580141   267914296   433494437   701408733   1134903170
1836311903   2971215073
```

For you temple builders, the ratio of the last two terms gives an approximation of the golden ratio as 0.618033988—close enough for government work.

The FIBO program uses type unsigned long, the type that holds the largest positive integers. The test expression in the while statement terminates the loop before the numbers exceed the limit of this type. We define this limit as a const type, since it doesn't change. We must stop when next becomes larger than half the limit, otherwise sum would exceed the limit.

The test expression uses two operators:

```
(next < limit / 2)
```

Our intention is to compare next with the result of limit/2. That is, we want the division to be performed before the comparison. We could put parentheses around the division, to ensure that it's performed first.

```
(next < (limit/2) )
```

But we don't need the parentheses. Why not? Because arithmetic operators have a higher precedence than relational operators. This guarantees that limit/2 will be evaluated before the comparison is made, even without the parentheses. We'll summarize the precedence situation later in this chapter, when we look at logical operators.

The do Loop

In a while loop, the test expression is evaluated at the *beginning* of the loop. If the test expression is false when the loop is entered, the loop body won't be executed at all. In some situations this is what you want. But sometimes you want to guarantee that the loop body is executed at least once, no matter what the initial state of the test expression. When this is the case you should use the do loop, which places the test expression at the *end* of the loop.

Our example, DIVDO, invites the user to enter two numbers: a dividend (the top number in a division) and a divisor (the bottom number). It then calculates the quotient (the answer) and the remainder, using the / and % operators, and prints out the result.

```cpp
// divdo.cpp
// demonstrates DO loop
#include <iostream>
using namespace std;

int main()
   {
   long dividend, divisor;
   char ch;

   do                                    //start of do loop
      {                                  //do some processing
      cout << "Enter dividend: "; cin >> dividend;
      cout << "Enter divisor: ";  cin >> divisor;
      cout << "Quotient is " << dividend / divisor;
      cout << ", remainder is " << dividend % divisor;

      cout << "\nDo another? (y/n): ";   //do it again?
      cin >> ch;
      }
   while( ch != 'n' );                   //loop condition
   return 0;
   }
```

Most of this program resides within the **do** loop. First, the keyword **do** marks the beginning of the loop. Then, as with the other loops, braces delimit the body of the loop. Finally a **while** statement provides the test expression and terminates the loop. This **while** statement looks much like the one in a **while** loop, except for its position at the end of the loop and the fact that it ends with a semicolon (which is easy to forget!). The syntax of the **do** loop is shown in Figure 3.5.

Following each computation, DIVDO asks if the user wants to do another. If so, the user enters a 'y' character, and the test expression

```cpp
ch != 'n'
```

remains true. If the user enters 'n', the test expression becomes false and the loop terminates. Figure 3.6 charts the operation of the **do** loop. Here's an example of DIVDO's output:

```
Enter dividend: 11
Enter divisor: 3
Quotient is 3, remainder is 2
Do another? (y/n): y
Enter dividend: 222
Enter divisor: 17
Quotient is 13, remainder is 1
Do another? (y/n): n
```

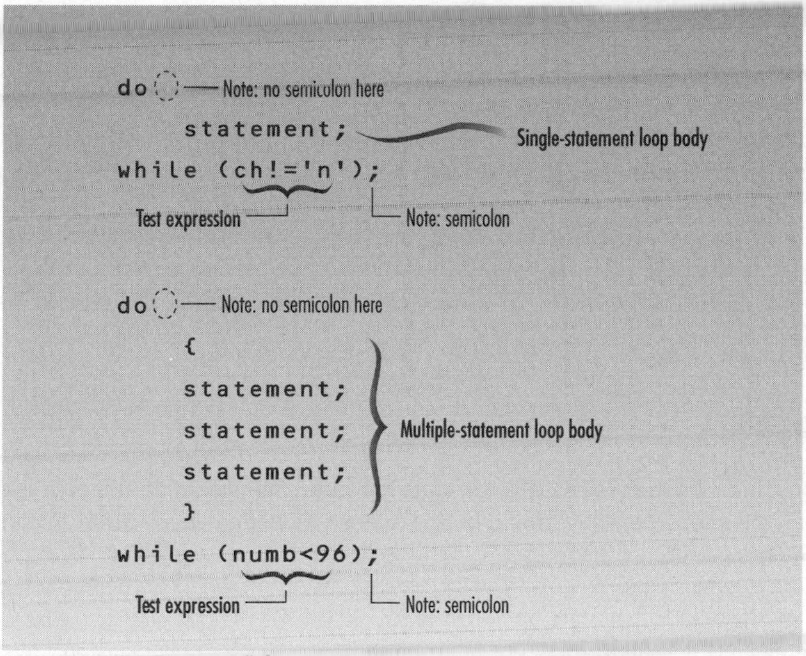

do
Note: no semicolon here
statement;
Single-statement loop body
while (ch!='n');
Test expression
Note: semicolon
do
Note: no semicolon here
{
statement;
statement;
statement;
}
Multiple-statement loop body
while (numb<96);
Test expression
Note: semicolon

Figure 3.5 Syntax of the do loop.

Body of loop
Test expression
Exit
False
True

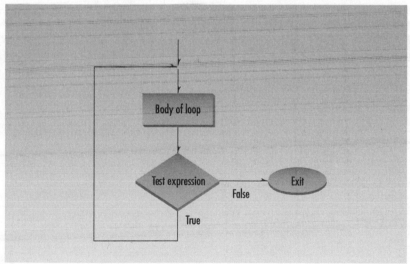

Figure 3.6 Operation of the do loop.

When to Use Which Loop

We've made some general statements about how loops are used. The `for` loop is appropriate when you know in advance how many times the loop will be executed. The `while` and `do` loops are used when you don't know in advance when the loop will terminate; the `while` loop when you may not want to execute the loop body even once, and the `do` loop when you're sure you want to execute the loop body at least once.

These criteria are somewhat arbitrary. Which loop type to use is more a matter of style than of hard-and-fast rules. You can actually make any of the loop types work in almost any situation. You should choose the type that makes your program the clearest and easiest to follow.

Decisions

The decisions in a loop always relate to the same question: Should we do this (the loop body) again? As humans we would find it boring to be so limited in our decision-making processes. We need to decide, not only whether to go to work again today (continuing the loop), but also whether to buy a red shirt or a green one (or no shirt at all), whether to take a vacation, and if so, in the mountains or by the sea.

Programs also need to make these one-time decisions. In a program a decision causes a one-time jump to a different part of the program, depending on the value of an expression. Decisions can be made in C++ in several ways. The most important is with the `if...else` statement, which chooses between two alternatives. This statement can be used without the `else`, as a simple `if` statement. Another decision statement, `switch`, creates branches for multiple alternative sections of code, depending on the value of a single variable. Finally the conditional operator is used in specialized situations. We'll examine each of these constructions.

The `if` Statement

The `if` statement is the simplest of the decision statements. Our next program, IFDEMO, provides an example.

```
// ifdemo.cpp
// demonstrates IF statement
#include <iostream>
using namespace std;

int main()
    {
    int x;

    cout << "Enter a number: ";
    cin >> x;
```

```
if( x > 100 )
    cout << "That number is greater than 100\n";
return 0;
}
```

The `if` keyword is followed by a test expression in parentheses. The syntax of the `if` statement is shown in Figure 3.7. As you can see, the syntax of `if` is very much like that of `while`. The difference is that the statements following the `if` are executed only once if the test expression is true; the statements following `while` are executed repeatedly until the test expression becomes false. Figure 3.8 shows the operation of the `if` statement.

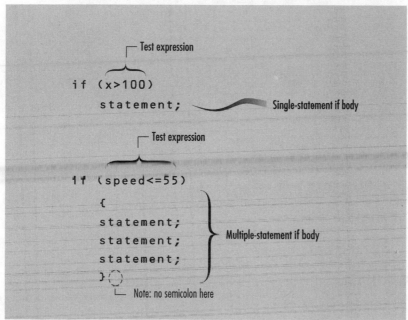

Figure 3.7   Syntax of the `if` statement.

Here's an example of the IFDEMO program's output when the number entered by the user is greater than 100:

```
Enter a number: 2000
That number is greater than 100
```

If the number entered is not greater than 100, the program will terminate without printing the second line.

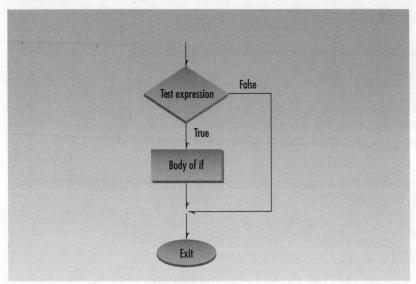

Figure 3.8   Operation of the `if` statement.

Multiple Statements in the `if` Body

As in loops, the code in an `if` body can consist of a single statement—as shown in the IFDEMO example—or a block of statements delimited by braces. This variation on IFDEMO, called IF2, shows how that looks.

```cpp
// if2.cpp
// demonstrates IF with multiline body
#include <iostream>
using namespace std;

int main()
   {
   int x;

   cout << "Enter a number: ";
   cin >> x;
   if( x > 100 )
      {
      cout << "The number " << x;
      cout << " is greater than 100\n";
      }
   return 0;
   }
```

Here's some output from IF2:

```
Enter a number: 12345
The number 12345 is greater than 100
```

Nesting ifs Inside Loops

The loop and decision structures we've seen so far can be nested inside one another. You can nest ifs inside loops, loops inside ifs, ifs inside ifs, and so on. Here's an example, PRIME, that nests an if within a for loop. This example tells you if a number you enter is a prime number. (Prime numbers are integers divisible only by themselves and 1. The first few primes are 1, 2, 3, 5, 7, 11, 13, 17.)

```cpp
// prime.cpp
// demonstrates IF statement with prime numbers
#include <iostream>
using namespace std;
#include <process.h>            //for exit()

int main()
   {
   unsigned long n, j;

   cout << "Enter a number: ";
   cin >> n;                    //get number to test
   for(j=2; j <= n/2; j++)      //divide by every integer from
      if(n%j == 0)              //2 on up; if remainder is 0,
         {                      //it's divisible by j
         cout << "It's not prime; divisible by " << j << endl;
         exit(0);              //exit from the program
         }
   cout << "It's prime\n";
   return 0;
   }
```

In this example the user enters a number that is assigned to n. The program then uses a for loop to divide n by all the numbers from 2 up to n/2. The divisor is j, the loop variable. If any value of j divides evenly into n, then n is not prime. When a number divides evenly into another, the remainder is 0; we use the remainder operator % in the if statement to test for this condition with each value of j. If the number is not prime, we tell the user and we exit from the program.

Here's output from three separate invocations of the program:

```
Enter a number: 13
It's prime
Enter a number: 22229
It's prime
Enter a number: 22231
It's not prime; divisible by 11
```

Notice that there are no braces around the loop body. This is because the if statement, and the statements in its body, are considered to be a single statement. If you like you can insert braces for readability, even though the compiler doesn't need them.

Library Function `exit()`

When PRIME discovers that a number is not prime, it exits immediately, since there's no use proving more than once that a number isn't prime. This is accomplished with the library function `exit()`. This function causes the program to terminate, no matter where it is in the listing. It has no return value. Its single argument, 0 in our example, is returned to the operating system when the program exits. (This value is useful in batch files, where you can use the ERRORLEVEL value to query the return value provided by `exit()`. The value 0 is normally used for a successful termination; other numbers indicate errors.)

The `if...else` Statement

The `if` statement lets you do something if a condition is true. If it isn't true, nothing happens. But suppose we want to do one thing if a condition is true, and do something else if it's false. That's where the `if...else` statement comes in. It consists of an `if` statement, followed by a statement or block of statements, followed by the keyword `else`, followed by *another* statement or block of statements. The syntax is shown in Figure 3.9.

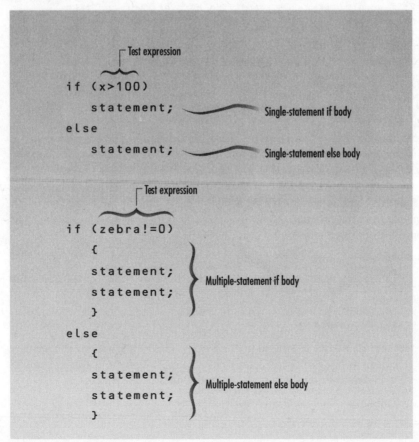

Figure 3.9 Syntax of the `if...else` statement

Here's a variation of our if example, with an else added to the if:

```cpp
// ifelse.cpp
// demonstrates IF...ELSE statememt
#include <iostream>
using namespace std;

int main()
    {
    int x;

    cout << "\nEnter a number: ";
    cin >> x;
    if( x > 100 )
       cout << "That number is greater than 100\n";
    else
       cout << "That number is not greater than 100\n";
    return 0;
    }
```

If the test expression in the if statement is true, the program prints one message; if it isn't, it prints the other.

Here's output from two different invocations of the program:

```
Enter a number: 300
That number is greater than 100
Enter a number: 3
That number is not greater than 100
```

The operation of the if...else statement is shown in Figure 3.10.

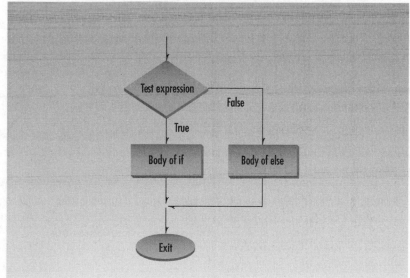

Figure 3.10   Operation of the if...else statement.

The `getche()` Library Function

Our next example shows an `if...else` statement embedded in a `while` loop. It also introduces a new library function: `getche()`. This program, CHCOUNT, counts the number of words and the number of characters in a phrase typed in by the user.

```
// chcount.cpp
// counts characters and words typed in
#include <iostream>
using namespace std;
#include <conio.h>            //for getche()

int main()
   {
   int chcount=0;             //counts non-space characters
   int wdcount=1;             //counts spaces between words
   char ch = 'a';             //ensure it isn't '\r'

   cout << "Enter a phrase: ";
   while( ch != '\r' )        //loop until Enter typed
      {
      ch = getche();          //read one character
      if( ch==' ' )           //if it's a space
      wdcount++;              //count a word
      else                    //otherwise,
      chcount++;              //count a character
      }                       //display results
   cout << "\nWords=" << wdcount << endl
        << "Letters=" << (chcount-1) << endl;
   return 0;
   }
```

So far we've used only `cin` and `>>` for input. That approach requires that the user always press the Enter key to inform the program that the input is complete. This is true even for single characters: The user must type the character, then press Enter. However, as in the present example, a program often needs to process each character typed by the user without waiting for an Enter. The `getche()` library function performs this service. It returns each character typed, as soon as it's typed. It takes no arguments, and requires the CONIO.H header file. In CHCOUNT the value of the character returned from `getche()` is assigned to `ch`. (The `getche()` function echoes the character to the screen. That's why there's an `e` at the end of `getche`. Another function, `getch()`, is similar to `getche()` but doesn't echo the character to the screen.)

The `if...else` statement causes the word count `wdcount` to be incremented if the character is a space, and the character count `chcount` to be incremented if the character is anything *but* a space. Thus anything that isn't a space is assumed to count as a character. (Note that this program is fairly naïve; it will be fooled by multiple spaces between words.)

Here's some sample interaction with CHCOUNT:

```
For while and do

Words=4
Letters=13
```

The test expression in the `while` statement checks to see if ch is the '\r' character, which is the character received from the keyboard when the Enter key is pressed. If so, the loop and the program terminate.

Assignment Expressions

The CHCOUNT program can be rewritten to save a line of code and demonstrate some important points about assignment expressions and precedence. The result is a construction that looks rather peculiar but is commonly used in C++ (and in C).

Here's the rewritten version, called CHCNT2:

```
// chcnt2.cpp
// counts characters and words typed in
#include <iostream>
using namespace std;
#include <conio.h>              // for getche()

int main()
   {
   int chcount=0;
   int wdcount=1;               // space between two words
   char ch;

   while( (ch=getche()) != '\r' )  // loop until Enter typed
      {
      if( ch==' ' )            // if it's a space
         wdcount++;            // count a word
      else                     // otherwise,
         chcount++;            // count a character
      }                        // display results
   cout << "\nWords=" << wdcount << endl
        << "Letters=" << chcount << endl;
   return 0;
   }
```

The value returned by `getche()` is assigned to `ch` as before, but this entire assignment expression has been moved inside the test expression for `while`. The assignment expression is compared with '\r' to see if the loop should terminate. This works because the entire assignment expression takes on the value used in the assignment. That is, if `getche()` returns 'a', then not only does `ch` take on the value 'a', but the expression

`(ch=getche())`

also takes on the value 'a'. This is then compared with '\r'.

The fact that assignment expressions have a value is also used in statements such as

`x = y = z = 0;`

This is perfectly legal in C++. First, `z` takes on the value 0, then `z = 0` takes on the value 0, which is assigned to `y`. Then the expression `y = z = 0` likewise takes on the value 0, which is assigned to `x`.

The parentheses around the assignment expression in

```
(ch=getche())
```

are necessary because the assignment operator = has a lower precedence than the relational operator !=. Without the parentheses the expression would be evaluated as

```
while( ch = (getche() != '\r') )    // not what we want
```

which would assign a true or false value to ch; not what we want.

The while statement in CHCNT2 provides a lot of power in a small space. It is not only a test expression (checking ch to see if it's '\r'); it also gets a character from the keyboard and assigns it to ch. It's also not easy to unravel the first time you see it.

Nested if...else Statements

You're probably too young to remember adventure games on early character-mode MS-DOS systems, but let's resurrect the concept here. You moved your "character" around an imaginary landscape, and discovered castles, sorcerers, treasure, and so on, using text—not pictures—for input and output. The next program, ADIFELSE, models a small part of such an adventure game.

```
''''''''''''''
// adifelse.cpp
// demonstrates IF...ELSE with adventure program
#include <iostream>
using namespace std;
#include <conio.h>              //for getche()

int main()
   {
   char dir='a';
   int x=10, y=10;

   cout << "Type Enter to quit\n";
   while( dir != '\r' )         //until Enter is typed
      {
      cout << "\nYour location is " << x << ", " << y;
      cout << "\nPress direction key (n, s, e, w): ";
      dir = getche();           //get character
      if( dir=='n')             //go north
         y--;
      else
         if( dir=='s' )         //go south
            y++;
         else
            if( dir=='e' )      //go east
               x++;
            else
               if( dir=='w' )   //go west
                  x--;
      } //end while
   return 0;
   } //end main
```

When the game starts, you find yourself on a barren moor. You can go one "unit" north, south, east, or west, while the program keeps track of where you are and reports your position, which starts at coordinates 10,10. Unfortunately, nothing exciting happens to your character, no matter where you go; the moor stretches almost limitlessly in all directions, as shown in Figure 3.11. We'll try to provide a little more excitement to this game later on.

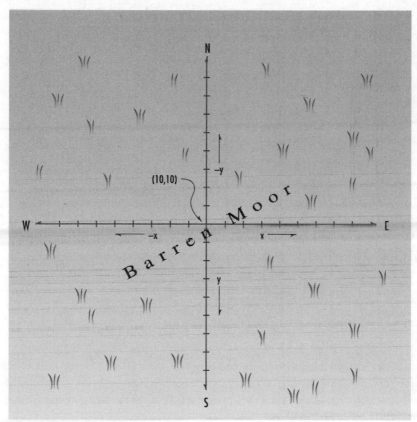

Figure 3.11   The barren moor.

Here's some sample interaction with ADIFELSE:

```
Your location is 10, 10
Press direction key (n, s, e, w): n
Your location is 10, 9
Press direction key (n, s, e, w): e
Your location is 11, 9
Press direction key (n, s, e, w):
```

You can press the [Enter] key to exit from the program.

This program may not cause a sensation in the video arcades, but it does demonstrate one way to handle multiple branches. It uses an `if` statement nested inside an `if...else` statement, which is nested inside another `if...else` statement, which is nested inside yet another `if...else` statement. If the first test condition is false, the second one is examined, and so on until all four have been checked. If any one proves true, the appropriate action is taken—changing the x or y coordinate—and the program exits from all the nested decisions. Such a nested group of `if...else` statements is called a *decision tree*.

Matching the `else`

There's a potential problem in nested `if...else` statements: You can inadvertently match an `else` with the wrong `if`. BADELSE provides an example:

```
// badelse.cpp
// demonstrates ELSE matched with wrong IF
#include <iostream>
using namespace std;

int main()
   {
   int a, b, c;
   cout << "Enter three numbers, a, b, and c:\n";
   cin >> a >> b >> c;

   if( a==b )
      if( b==c )
         cout << "a, b, and c are the same\n";
   else
      cout << "a and b are different\n";
   return 0;
   }
```

We've used multiple values with a single `cin`. Press Enter following each value you type in; the three values will be assigned to a, b, and c.

What happens if you enter **2**, then **3**, and then **3**? Variable **a** is 2, and **b** is 3. They're different, so the first test expression is false, and you would expect the `else` to be invoked, printing *a and b are different*. But in fact nothing is printed. Why not? Because the `else` is matched with the wrong `if`. The indentation would lead you to believe that the `else` is matched with the first `if`, but in fact it goes with the second `if`. Here's the rule: An `else` is matched with the last `if` that doesn't have its own `else`.

Here's a corrected version:

```
if(a==b)
   if(b==c)
      cout << "a, b, and c are the same\n";
   else
      cout << "b and c are different\n";
```

We changed the indentation and also the phrase printed by the `else` body. Now if you enter **2**, **3**, **3**, nothing will be printed. But entering **2**, **2**, **3** will cause the output

```
b and c are different
```

If you really want to pair an `else` with an earlier `if`, you can use braces around the inner `if`:

```
if(a==b)
   {
   if(b==c)
      cout << "a, b, and c are the same";
   }
else
   cout << "a and b are different";
```

Here the `else` is paired with the first `if`, as the indentation indicates. The braces make the `if` within them invisible to the following `else`.

The `else...if` Construction

The nested `if...else` statements in the ADIFELSE program look clumsy and can be hard—for humans—to interpret, especially if they are nested more deeply than shown. However there's another approach to writing the same statements. We need only reformat the program, obtaining the next example, ADELSEIF.

```
// adelseif.cpp
// demonstrates ELSE...IF with adventure program
#include <iostream>
using namespace std;
#include <conio.h>                 //for getche()

int main()
   {
   char dir='a';
   int x=10, y=10;

   cout << "Type Enter to quit\n";
   while( dir != '\r' )           //until Enter is typed
      {
      cout << "\nYour location is " << x << ", " << y;
      cout << "\nPress direction key (n, s, e, w): ";
      dir = getche();             //get character
      if( dir=='n')               //go north
         y--;
      else if( dir=='s' )         //go south
         y++;
      else if( dir=='e' )         //go east
         x++;
      else if( dir=='w' )         //go west
         x--;
      }  //end while
   return 0;
   }  //end main
```

The compiler sees this as identical to ADIFELSE, but we've rearranged the `if`s so they directly follow the `else`s. The result looks almost like a new keyword: `else if`. The program goes down the ladder of `else...if`s until one of the test expressions is true. It then executes the following statement and exits from the ladder. This format is clearer and easier to follow than the `if...else` approach.

The `switch` Statement

If you have a large decision tree, and all the decisions depend on the value of the same variable, you will probably want to consider a `switch` statement instead of a ladder of `if...else` or `else...if` constructions. Here's a simple example called PLATTERS that will appeal to nostalgia buffs:

```
// platters.cpp
// demonstrates SWITCH statement
#include <iostream>
using namespace std;

int main()
   {
   int speed;                          //turntable speed

   cout << "\nEnter 33, 45, or 78: ";
   cin >> speed;                       //user enters speed
   switch(speed)                       //selection based on speed
      {
      case 33:                         //user entered 33
         cout << "LP album\n";
         break;
      case 45:                         //user entered 45
         cout << "Single selection\n";
         break;
      case 78:                         //user entered 78
         cout << "Obsolete format\n";
         break;
      }
   return 0;
   }
```

This program prints one of three possible messages, depending on whether the user inputs the number **33**, **45**, or **78**. As you may recall, long-playing records (LPs) contained many songs and turned at 33 rpm, the smaller 45s held only a single song, and 78s were the format that preceded LPs and 45s.

The keyword `switch` is followed by a switch variable in parentheses.

```
switch(speed)
```

Braces then delimit a number of `case` statements. Each `case` keyword is followed by a constant, which is not in parentheses but is followed by a colon.

```
case 33:
```

The data type of the case constants should match that of the switch variable. Figure 3.12 shows the syntax of the switch statement.

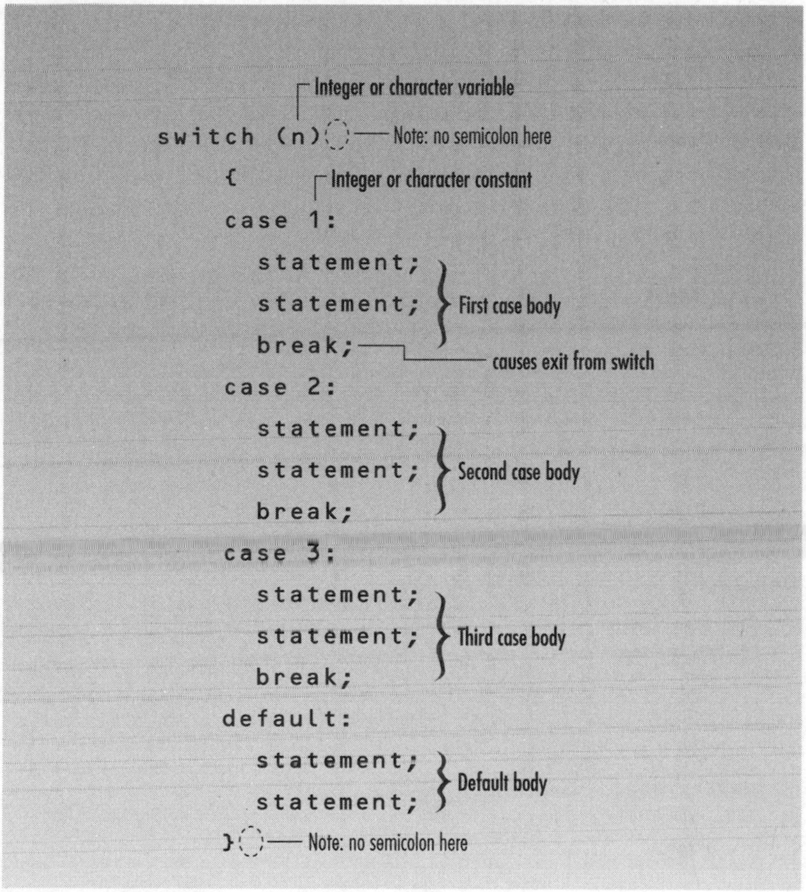

Figure 3.12 Syntax of the switch statement.

Before entering the switch, the program should assign a value to the switch variable. This value will usually match a constant in one of the case statements. When this is the case (pun intended!), the statements immediately following the keyword case will be executed, until a break is reached.

Here's an example of PLATTER's output:

```
Enter 33, 45, or 78: 45
Single selection
```

The break Statement

PLATTERS has a **break** statement at the end of each **case** section. The **break** keyword causes the entire **switch** statement to exit. Control goes to the first statement following the end of the **switch** construction, which in PLATTERS is the end of the program. Don't forget the **break**; without it, control passes down (or "falls through") to the statements for the next **case**, which is usually not what you want (although sometimes it's useful).

If the value of the switch variable doesn't match any of the **case** constants, then control passes to the end of the switch without doing anything. The operation of the **switch** statement is shown in Figure 3.13. The **break** keyword is also used to escape from loops; we'll discuss this soon.

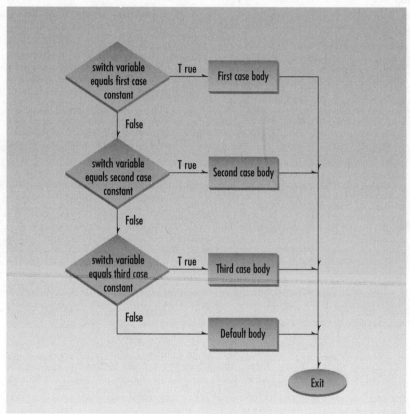

Figure 3.13 Operation of the **switch** statement.

switch Statement with Character Variables

The PLATTERS example shows a **switch** statement based on a variable of type **int**. You can also use type **char**. Here's our ADELSEIF program rewritten as ADSWITCH:

'''''''''''''''

```cpp
// adswitch.cpp
// demonstrates SWITCH with adventure program
#include <iostream>
using namespace std;
#include <conio.h>                              //for getche()

int main()
   {
   char dir='a';
   int x=10, y=10;

   while( dir != '\r' )
      {
      cout << "\nYour location is " << x << ", " << y;
      cout << "\nEnter direction (n, s, e, w): ";
      dir = getche();                           //get character
      switch(dir)                               //switch on it
         {
         case 'n':  y--; break;                 //go north
         case 's':  y++; break;                 //go south
         case 'e':  x++; break;                 //go east
         case 'w':  x--; break;                 //go west
         case '\r': cout << "Exiting\n"; break; //Enter key
         default:   cout << "Try again\n";      //unknown char
         } //end switch
      } //end while
   return 0;
   } //end main
```

A character variable **dir** is used as the switch variable, and character constants 'n', 's', and so on are used as the case constants. (Note that you can use integers and characters as switch variables, as shown in the last two examples, but you can't use floating-point numbers.)

Since they are so short, the statements following each **case** keyword have been written on one line, which makes for a more compact listing. We've also added a **case** to print an exit message when [Enter] is pressed.

The **default** Keyword

In the ADSWITCH program, where you expect to see the last **case** at the bottom of the **switch** construction, you instead see the keyword **default**. This keyword gives the **switch** construction a way to take an action if the value of the loop variable doesn't match any of the **case** constants. Here we use it to print **Try again** if the user types an unknown character. No **break** is necessary after **default**, since we're at the end of the **switch** anyway.

A `switch` statement is a common approach to analyzing input entered by the user. Each of the possible characters is represented by a `case`.

It's a good idea to use a `default` statement in all `switch` statements, even if you don't think you need it. A construction such as

```
default:
    cout << "Error: incorrect input to switch"; break;
```

alerts the programmer (or the user) that something has gone wrong in the operation of the program. In the interest of brevity we don't always include such a `default` statement, but you should, especially in serious programs.

`switch` Versus `if...else`

When do you use a series of `if...else` (or `else...if`) statements, and when do you use a `switch` statement? In an `if...else` construction you can use a series of expressions that involve unrelated variables and are as complex as you like. For example:

```
if( SteamPressure*Factor > 56 )
    // statements
else if( VoltageIn + VoltageOut < 23000)
    // statements
else if( day==Thursday )
    // statements
else
    // statements
```

In a `switch` statement, however, all the branches are selected by the same variable; the only thing distinguishing one branch from another is the value of this variable. You can't say

```
case a<3:
    // do something
    break;
```

The case constant must be an integer or character constant, like `3` or `'a'`, or an expression that evaluates to a constant, like `'a'+32`.

When these conditions are met, the `switch` statement is very clean—easy to write and to understand. It should be used whenever possible, especially when the decision tree has more than a few possibilities.

The Conditional Operator

Here's a strange sort of decision operator. It exists because of a common programming situation: A variable is given one value if something is true and another value if it's false. For example, here's an `if...else` statement that gives the variable `min` the value of `alpha` or the value of `beta`, depending on which is smaller:

```
if( alpha < beta )
    min = alpha;
else
    min = beta;
```

This sort of construction is so common that the designers of C++ (actually the designers of C, long ago) invented a compressed way to express it: the *conditional operator*. This operator consists of two symbols, which operate on three operands. It's the only such operator in C++; other operators operate on one or two operands. Here's the equivalent of the same program fragment, using a conditional operator:

```
min = (alpha<beta) ? alpha : beta;
```

The part of this statement to the right of the equal sign is called the *conditional expression*:

```
(alpha<beta) ? alpha : beta    // conditional expression
```

The question mark and the colon make up the conditional operator. The expression before the question mark,

```
(alpha<beta)
```

is the test expression. It and `alpha` and `beta` are the three operands.

If the test expression is true, then the entire conditional expression takes on the value of the operand following the question mark: `alpha` in this example. If the test expression is false, the conditional expression takes on the value of the operand following the colon: `beta`. The parentheses around the test expression aren't needed for the compiler, but they're customary; they make the statement easier to read (and it needs all the help it can get). Figure 3.14 shows the syntax of the conditional statement, and Figure 3.15 shows its operation.

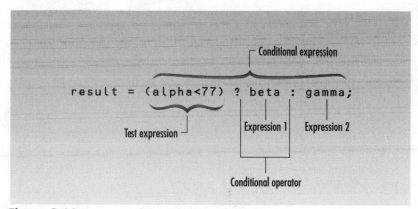

Figure 3.14   Syntax of the conditional operator.

The conditional expression can be assigned to another variable, or used anywhere a value can be. In this example it's assigned to the variable `min`.

Here's another example: a statement that uses a conditional operator to find the absolute value of a variable n. (The absolute value of a number is the number with any negative sign removed, so it's always positive.)

```
absvalue = n<0 ? -n : n;
```

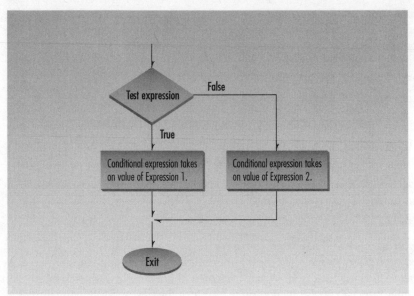

Figure 3.15   Operation of the conditional operator.

If n is less than 0, the expression becomes -n, a positive number. If n is not less than 0, the expression remains n. The result is the absolute value of n, which is assigned to absvalue.

Here's a program, CONDI.CPP, that uses the conditional operator to print an x every eight spaces in a line of text. You might use this to see where the tab stops are on your screen.

```
// condi.cpp
// prints 'x' every 8 columns
// demonstrates conditional operator
#include <iostream>
using namespace std;

int main()
   {
   for(int j=0; j<80; j++)         //for every column,
      {                            //ch is 'x' if column is
      char ch = (j%8) ? ' ' : 'x'; //multiple of 8, and
      cout << ch;                  //' ' (space) otherwise
      }
   return 0;
   }
```

Some of the right side of the output is lost because of the page width, but you can probably imagine it:

```
x       x       x       x       x       x       x       x       x
```

As j cycles through the numbers from 0 to 79, the remainder operator causes the expression (j % 8) to become false—that is, 0—only when j is a multiple of 8. So the conditional expression

```
(j%8) ? ' ' : 'x'
```

has the value ' ' (the space character) when j is not a multiple of 8, and the value 'x' when it is.

You may think this is terse, but we could have combined the two statements in the loop body into one, eliminating the ch variable:

```
cout << ( (j%8) ? ' ' : 'x' );
```

Hotshot C++ (and C) programmers love this sort of thing—getting a lot of bang from very little code. But you don't need to strive for concise code if you don't want to. Sometimes it becomes so obscure it's not worth the effort. Even using the conditional operator is optional: An if...else statement and a few extra program lines will accomplish the same thing.

Logical Operators

So far we've seen two families of operators (besides the oddball conditional operator). First are the arithmetic operators +, -, *, /, and %. Second are the relational operators <, >, <=, >=, ==, and !=.

Let's examine a third family of operators, called *logical operators*. These operators allow you to logically combine Boolean variables (that is, variables of type bool, with true or false values). For example, *today is a weekday* has a Boolean value, since it's either true or false. Another Boolean expression is *Maria took the car*. We can connect these expressions logically: If today is a weekday, and Maria took the car, then I'll have to take the bus. The logical connection here is the word *and*, which provides a true or false value to the combination of the two phrases. Only if they are *both* true will I have to take the bus.

Logical AND Operator

Let's see how logical operators combine Boolean expressions in C++. Here's an example, ADVENAND, that uses a logical operator to spruce up the adventure game from the ADSWITCH example. We'll bury some treasure at coordinates (7,11) and see if the player can find it.

```
''''''''''''
// advenand.cpp
// demonstrates AND logical operator
#include <iostream>
using namespace std;
#include <process.h>          //for exit()
#include <conio.h>            //for getche()

int main()
   {
```

```
  char dir='a';
  int x=10, y=10;

  while( dir != '\r' )
     {
     cout << "\nYour location is " << x << ", " << y;
     cout << "\nEnter direction (n, s, e, w): ";
     dir = getche();            //get direction
     switch(dir)
        {
        case 'n': y--; break;    //update coordinates
        case 's': y++; break;
        case 'e': x++; break;
        case 'w': x--; break;
        }
     if( x==7 && y==11 )         //if x is 7 and y is 11
        {
        cout << "\nYou found the treasure!\n";
        exit(0);                 //exit from program
        }
     } //end switch
  return 0;
  } //end main
```

The key to this program is the **if** statement

```
if( x==7 && y==11 )
```

The test expression will be true only if *both* x is 7 *and* y is 11. The logical **AND** operator && joins the two relational expressions to achieve this result. (A *relational expression* is one that uses a relational operator.)

Notice that parentheses are not necessary around the relational expressions.

```
( (x==7) && (y==11) )   // inner parentheses not necessary
```

This is because the relational operators have higher precedence than the logical operators.

Here's some interaction as the user arrives at these coordinates:

```
Your location is 7, 10
Enter direction (n, s, e, w): s
You found the treasure!
```

There are three logical operators in C++:

Operator	Effect
&&	Logical AND
!!	Logical OR
!	Logical NOT

There is no logical XOR (exclusive OR) operator in C++.

Let's look at examples of the `||` and `!` operators.

Logical OR Operator

Suppose in the adventure game you decide there will be dragons if the user goes too far east or too far west. Here's an example, ADVENOR, that uses the logical OR operator to implement this frightening impediment to free adventuring. It's a variation on the ADVENAND program.

```
// advenor.cpp
// demonstrates OR logical operator
#include <iostream>
using namespace std;
#include <process.h>            //for exit()
#include <conio.h>             //for getche()

int main()
   {
   char dir='a';
   int x=10, y=10;

   while( dir != '\r' )          //quit on Enter key
      {
      cout << "\n\nYour location is " << x << ", " << y;

      if( x<5 || x>15 )          //if x west of 5 OR east of 15
         cout << "\nBeware: dragons lurk here";

      cout << "\nEnter direction (n, s, e, w): ";
      dir = getche();           //get direction
      switch(dir)
         {
         case 'n': y--; break;   //update coordinates
         case 's': y++; break;
         case 'e': x++; break;
         case 'w': x--; break;
         } //end switch
      } //end while
   return 0;
   } //end main()
```

The expression

```
x<5 || x>15
```

is true whenever either x is less than 5 (the player is too far west), or x is greater than 15 (the player is too far east). Again, the `||` operator has lower precedence than the relational operators < and >, so no parentheses are needed in this expression.

Logical NOT Operator

The logical **NOT** operator ! is a *unary* operator—that is, it takes only one operand. (Almost all the operators we've seen thus far are *binary* operators; they take two operands. The conditional operator is the only *ternary* operator in C++.) The effect of the ! is that the logical value of its operand is reversed: If something is true, ! makes it false; if it is false, ! makes it true. (It would be nice if life were so easily manipulated.)

For example, (x==7) is true if x is equal to 7, but !(x==7) is true if x is not equal to 7. (In this situation you could use the relational *not equals* operator, x != 7, to achieve the same effect.)

A True/False Value for Every Integer Variable

We may have given you the impression that for an expression to have a true/false value, it must involve a relational operator. But in fact, every integer expression has a true/false value, even if it is only a single variable. The expression x is true whenever x is not 0, and false when x is 0. Applying the ! operator to this situation, we can see that the !x is true whenever x is 0, since it reverses the truth value of x.

Let's put these ideas to work. Imagine in your adventure game that you want to place a mushroom on all the locations where both x and y are a multiple of 7. (As you probably know, mushrooms, when consumed by the player, confer magical powers.) The remainder when x is divided by 7, which can be calculated by x%7, is 0 only when x is a multiple of 7. So to specify the mushroom locations, we can write

```
if( x%7==0 && y%7==0 )
   cout << "There's a mushroom here.\n";
```

However, remembering that expressions are true or false even if they don't involve relational operators, you can use the ! operator to provide a more concise format.

```
if( !(x%7) && !(y%7) )    // if not x%7 and not y%7
```

This has exactly the same effect.

We've said that the logical operators && and || have lower precedence than the relational operators. Why then do we need parentheses around x%7 and y%7? Because, even though it is a logical operator, ! is a unary operator, which has higher precedence than relational operators.

Precedence Summary

Let's summarize the precedence situation for the operators we've seen so far. The operators higher on the list have higher precedence than those lower down. Operators with higher precedence are evaluated before those with lower precedence. Operators on the same row have equal precedence. You can force an expression to be evaluated first by placing parentheses around it.

Operator type	Operators
Unary	!, ++, --, --
Arithmetic	Multiplicative *, /, %
	Additive +, --
Relational	inequality <, >, <=, >=
	equality ==, !=
Logical	and &&
	or ¦¦
Conditional	?:
Assignment	=, +=, ñ=, *=, /=, %=

Other Control Statements

There are several other control statements in C++. We've already seen one, **break**, used in **switch** statements, but it can be used other places as well. Another statement, **continue**, is used only in loops, and a third, **goto**, should be avoided. Let's look at these statements in turn.

The **break** Statement

The **break** statement causes an exit from a loop, just as it does from a **switch** statement. The next statement after the **break** is executed is the statement following the loop. Figure 3.16 shows the operation of the **break** statement.

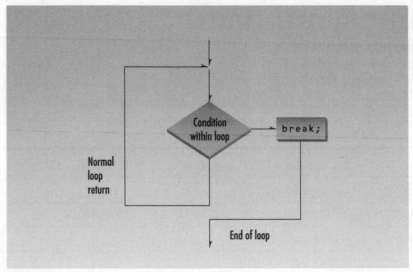

Figure 3.16   Operation of the **break** statement.

To demonstrate **break**, here's a program, SHOWPRIM, that displays the distribution of prime numbers in graphical form:

```
// showprim.cpp
// displays prime number distribution
#include <iostream>
using namespace std;
#include <conio.h>                    //for getche()

int main()
   {
   const unsigned char WHITE = 219;  //solid color (primes)
   const unsigned char GRAY  = 176;  //gray (non primes)
   unsigned char ch;
                                     //for each screen position
   for(int count=0; count<80*25-1; count++)
      {
      ch = WHITE;                    //assume it's prime
      for(int j=2; j<count; j++)     //divide by every integer from
      if(count%j == 0)               //2 on up; if remainder is 0,
         {
         ch = GRAY;                  //it's not prime
         break;                      //break out of inner loop
         }
      cout << ch;                    //display the character
      }
   getch();                          //freeze screen until keypress
   return 0;
   }
```

In effect every position on an 80-column by 25-line console screen is numbered, from 0 to 1999 (which is 80*25–1). If the number at a particular position is prime, the position is colored white; if it's not prime, it's colored gray.

Figure 3.17 shows the display. Strictly speaking, 0 is not considered a prime, but it's shown as white to avoid complicating the program. Think of the columns across the top as being numbered from 0 to 79. Notice that no primes (except 2) appear in even-numbered columns, since they're all divisible by 2. Is there a pattern to the other numbers? The world of mathematics will be very excited if you find a pattern that allows you to predict whether any given number is prime.

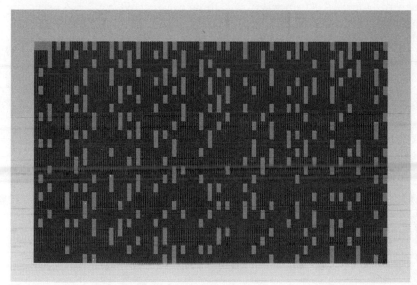

Figure 3.17   Output of SHOWPRIM program.

When the inner **for** loop determines that a number is not prime, it sets the character **ch** to GRAY, and then executes **break** to escape from the inner loop. (We don't want to exit from the entire program, as in the PRIME example, since we have a whole series of numbers to work on.)

Notice that **break** only takes you out of the innermost loop. This is true no matter what constructions are nested inside each other: **break** only takes you out of the construction in which it's embedded. If there were a **switch** within a loop, a **break** in the **switch** would only take you out of the **switch**, not out of the loop.

The last **cout** statement prints the graphics character, and then the loop continues, testing the next number for primeness.

ASCII Extended Character Set

This program uses two characters from the *extended ASCII character set*, the characters represented by the numbers from 128 to 255, as shown in Appendix A, "ASCII Table." The value 219 represents a solid-colored block (white on a black-and-white monitor), while 176 represents a gray block.

The SHOWPRIM example uses `getch()` in the last line, to keep the DOS prompt from scrolling the screen up when the program terminates. It freezes the screen until you press a key.

We use type `unsigned char` for the character variables in SHOWPRIM, since it goes up to 255. Type `char` only goes up to `127`.

The `continue` Statement

The `break` statement takes you out of the bottom of a loop. Sometimes, however, you want to go back to the top of the loop when something unexpected happens. Executing `continue` has this effect. (Strictly speaking, the `continue` takes you to the closing brace of the loop body, from which you may jump back to the top.) Figure 3.18 shows the operation of `continue`.

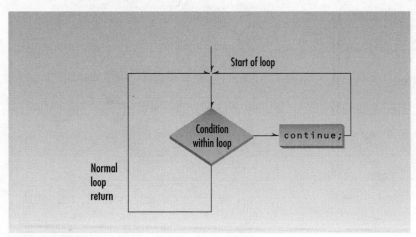

Figure 3.18 Operation of the continue statement.

Here's a variation on the DIVDO example. This program, which we saw earlier in this chapter, does division, but it has a fatal flaw: If the user inputs **0** as the divisor, the program undergoes catastrophic failure and terminates with the runtime error message *Divide Error*. The revised version of the program, DIVDO2, deals with this situation more gracefully.

```
// divdo2.cpp
// demonstrates CONTINUE statement
#include <iostream>
using namespace std;

int main()
    {
```

```
long dividend, divisor;
char ch;

do {
    cout << "Enter dividend: "; cin >> dividend;
    cout << "Enter divisor: ";  cin >> divisor;
    if( divisor == 0 )                  //if attempt to
        {                               //divide by 0,
        cout << "Illegal divisor\n";    //display message
        continue;                       //go to top of loop
        }
    cout << "Quotient is " << dividend / divisor;
    cout << ", remainder is " << dividend % divisor;

    cout << "\nDo another? (y/n): ";
    cin >> ch;
    } while( ch != 'n' );
return 0;
}
```

If the user inputs **0** for the divisor, the program prints an error message and, using **con-tinue**, returns to the top of the loop to issue the prompts again. Here's some sample output:

```
Enter dividend: 10
Enter divisor: 0
Illegal divisor
Enter dividend:
```

A **break** statement in this situation would cause an exit from the **do** loop and the program, an unnecessarily harsh response.

Notice that we've made the format of the **do** loop a little more compact. The **do** is on the same line as the opening brace, and the **while** is on the same line as the closing brace.

The goto Statement

We'll mention the **goto** statement here for the sake of completeness—not because it's a good idea to use it. If you've had any exposure to structured programming principles, you know that **goto**s can quickly lead to "spaghetti" code that is difficult to understand and debug. There is almost never any need to use **goto**, as is demonstrated by its absence in the program examples in this book.

With that lecture out of the way, here's the syntax. You insert a label in your code at the desired destination for the **goto**. The label is always terminated by a colon. The keyword **goto**, followed by this label name, then takes you to the label. The following code fragment demonstrates this approach.

```
goto SystemCrash;
// other statements
SystemCrash:
// control will begin here following goto
```

Summary

Relational operators compare two values to see if they're equal, if one is larger than the other, and so on. The result is a logical or Boolean (type `bool`) value, which is true or false. False is indicated by 0, and true by 1 or any other non-zero number.

There are three kinds of loops in C++. The `for` loop is most often used when you know in advance how many times you want to execute the loop. The `while` loop and `do` loops are used when the condition causing the loop to terminate arises within the loop, with the `while` loop not necessarily executing at all, and the `do` loop always executing at least once.

A loop body can be a single statement or a block of multiple statements delimited by braces. A variable defined within a block is visible only within that block.

There are four kinds of decision-making statements. The `if` statement does something if a test expression is true. The `if...else` statement does one thing if the test expression is true, and another thing if it isn't. The `else...if` construction is a way of rewriting a ladder of nested `if...else` statements to make it more readable. The `switch` statement branches to multiple sections of code, depending on the value of a single variable. The conditional operator simplifies returning one value if a test expression is true, and another if it's false.

The logical `AND` and `OR` operators combine two Boolean expressions to yield another one, and the logical `NOT` operator changes a Boolean value from true to false, or from false to true.

The `break` statement sends control to the end of the innermost loop or switch in which it occurs. The `continue` statement sends control to the top of the loop in which it occurs. The `goto` statement sends control to a label.

Precedence specifies which kinds of operations will be carried out first. The order is unary, arithmetic, relational, logical, conditional, assignment.

Questions

Answers to questions can be found in Appendix G, "Answers to Questions and Exercises."

1. A relational operator

    a. assigns one operand to another.

    b. yields a Boolean result.

    c. compares two operands.

    d. logically combines two operands.

2. Write an expression that uses a relational operator to return true if the variable `george` is not equal to `sally`.

3. Is −1 true or false?

4. Name and describe the usual purpose of three expressions in a `for` statement.

5. In a `for` loop with a multistatement loop body, semicolons should appear following

   a. the `for` statement itself.

   b. the closing brace in a multistatement loop body.

   c. each statement within the loop body.

   d. the test expression.

6. True or false: The increment expression in a `for` loop can decrement the loop variable.

7. Write a `for` loop that displays the numbers from 100 to 110.

8. A block of code is delimited by _____.

9. A variable defined within a block is visible

   a. from the point of definition onward in the program.

   b. from the point of definition onward in the function.

   c. from the point of definition onward in the block.

   d. throughout the function.

10. Write a `while` loop that displays the numbers from 100 to 110.

11. True or false: Relational operators have a higher precedence than arithmetic operators.

12. How many times is the loop body executed in a `do` loop?

13. Write a `do` loop that displays the numbers from 100 to 110.

14. Write an `if` statement that prints `Yes` if a variable `age` is greater than 21.

15. The library function `exit()` causes an exit from

   a. the loop in which it occurs.

   b. the block in which it occurs.

   c. the function in which it occurs.

   d. the program in which it occurs.

16. Write an `if...else` statement that displays `Yes` if a variable `age` is greater than 21, and displays `No` otherwise.

17. The `getche()` library function

    a. returns a character when any key is pressed.

    b. returns a character when [Enter] is pressed.

    c. displays a character on the screen when any key is pressed.

    d. does not display a character on the screen.

18. What is the character obtained from `cin` when the user presses the [Enter] key?

19. An `else` always matches the _____ `if`, unless the `if` is _____.

20. The `else...if` construction is obtained from a nested `if...else` by _____.

21. Write a `switch` statement that prints `Yes` if a variable `ch` is `'y'`, prints `No` if `ch` is `'n'`, and prints `Unknown response` otherwise.

22. Write a statement that uses a conditional operator to set `ticket` to 1 if `speed` is greater than 55, and to 0 otherwise.

23. The `&&` and `||` operators

    a. compare two numeric values.

    b. combine two numeric values.

    c. compare two Boolean values.

    d. combine two Boolean values.

24. Write an expression involving a logical operator that is true if `limit` is 55 and `speed` is greater than 55.

25. Arrange in order of precedence (highest first) the following kinds of operators: logical, unary, arithmetic, assignment, relational, conditional.

26. The `break` statement causes an exit

    a. only from the innermost loop.

    b. only from the innermost switch.

    c. from all loops and switches.

    d. from the innermost loop or switch.

27. Executing the `continue` operator from within a loop causes control to go to _____.

28. The `goto` statement causes control to go to

    a. an operator.

    b. a label.

    c. a variable.

    d. a function.

Exercises

Answers to the starred exercises can be found in Appendix G.

*1. Assume you want to generate a table of multiples of any given number. Write a program that allows the user to enter the number, and then generates the table, formatting it into 10 columns and 20 lines. Interaction with the program should look like this (only the first three lines are shown):

```
Enter a number: 7
    7   14   21   28   35   42   49   56   63   70
   77   84   91   98  105  112  119  126  133  140
  147  154  161  168  175  182  189  196  203  210
```

*2. Write a temperature-conversion program that gives the user the option of converting Fahrenheit to Celsius or Celsius to Fahrenheit. Then carry out the conversion. Use floating-point numbers. Interaction with the program might look like this:

```
Type 1 to convert Fahrenheit to Celsius,
     2 to convert Celsius to Fahrenheit: 1
Enter temperature in Fahrenheit: 70
In Celsius that's 21.111111
```

*3. Operators such as >>, which read input from the keyboard, must be able to convert a series of digits into a number. Write a program that does the same thing. It should allow the user to type up to six digits, and then display the resulting number as a type `long` integer. The digits should be read individually, as characters, using `getche()`. Constructing the number involves multiplying the existing value by 10 and then adding the new digit. (Hint: Subtract 48 or '0' to go from ASCII to a numerical digit.)

Here's some sample interaction:

```
Enter a number: 123456
Number is: 123456
```

*4. Create the equivalent of a four-function calculator. The program should request the user to enter a number, an operator, and another number. (Use floating point.) It should then carry out the specified arithmetical operation: adding, subtracting, multiplying, or dividing the two numbers. Use a `switch` statement to select the operation. Finally, display the result.

When it finishes the calculation, the program should ask if the user wants to do another calculation. The response can be `'y'` or `'n'`. Some sample interaction with the program might look like this:

```
Enter first number, operator, second number: 10 / 3
Answer = 3.333333
Do another (y/n)? y
Enter first number, operator, second number: 12 + 100
Answer = 112
Do another (y/n)? n
```

5. Use `for` loops to construct a program that displays a pyramid of Xs on the screen. The pyramid should look like this

```
    X
   XXX
  XXXXX
 XXXXXXX
XXXXXXXXX
```

except that it should be 20 lines high, instead of the 5 lines shown here. One way to do this is to nest two inner loops, one to print spaces and one to print Xs, inside an outer loop that steps down the screen from line to line.

6. Modify the FACTOR program in this chapter so that it repeatedly asks for a number and calculates its factorial, until the user enters 0, at which point it terminates. You can enclose the relevant statements in FACTOR in a `while` loop or a `do` loop to achieve this effect.

7. Write a program that calculates how much money you'll end up with if you invest an amount of money at a fixed interest rate, compounded yearly. Have the user furnish the initial amount, the number of years, and the yearly interest rate in percent. Some interaction with the program might look like this:

```
Enter initial amount: 3000
Enter number of years: 10
Enter interest rate (percent per year): 5.5
At the end of 10 years, you will have 5124.43 dollars.
```

At the end of the first year you have 3000 + (3000 * 0.055), which is 3165. At the end of the second year you have 3165 + (3165 * 0.055), which is 3339.08. Do this as many times as there are years. A `for` loop makes the calculation easy.

8. Write a program that repeatedly asks the user to enter two money amounts expressed in old-style British currency: pounds, shillings, and pence. (See Exercises 10 and 12 in Chapter 2, "C++ Programming Basics.") The program should then add the two amounts and display the answer, again in pounds, shillings, and pence. Use a `do` loop that asks the user if the program should be terminated. Typical interaction might be

    ```
    Enter first amount: £5.10.6
    Enter second amount: £3.2.6
    Total is £8.13.0
    Do you wish to continue (y/n)?
    ```

    To add the two amounts, you'll need to carry 1 shilling when the pence value is greater than 11, and carry 1 pound when there are more than 19 shillings.

9. Suppose you give a dinner party for six guests, but your table seats only four. In how many ways can four of the six guests arrange themselves at the table? Any of the six guests can sit in the first chair. Any of the remaining five can sit in the second chair. Any of the remaining four can sit in the third chair, and any of the remaining three can sit in the fourth chair. (The last two will have to stand.) So the number of possible arrangements of six guests in four chairs is 6*5*4*3, which is 360. Write a program that calculates the number of possible arrangements for any number of guests and any number of chairs. (Assume there will never be fewer guests than chairs.) Don't let this get too complicated. A simple `for` loop should do it.

10. Write another version of the program from Exercise 7 so that, instead of finding the final amount of your investment, you tell the program the final amount and it figures out how many years it will take, at a fixed rate of interest compounded yearly, to reach this amount. What sort of loop is appropriate for this problem? (Don't worry about fractional years; use an integer value for the year.)

11. Create a three-function calculator for old-style English currency, where money amounts are specified in pounds, shillings, and pence. (See Exercises 10 and 12 in Chapter 2.) The calculator should allow the user to add or subtract two money amounts, or to multiply a money amount by a floating-point number. (It doesn't make sense to multiply two money amounts; there is no such thing as square money. We'll ignore division. Use the general style of the ordinary four-function calculator in Exercise 4 in this chapter.)

12. Create a four-function calculator for fractions. (See Exercise 9 in Chapter 2, and Exercise 4 in this chapter.) Here are the formulas for the four arithmetic operations applied to fractions:

Addition:	a/b + c/d = (a*d + b*c) / (b*d)
Subtraction:	a/b - c/d = (a*d - b*c) / (b*d)
Multiplication:	a/b * c/d = (a*c) / (b*d)
Division:	a/b / c/d = (a*d) / (b*c)

The user should type the first fraction, an operator, and a second fraction. The program should then display the result and ask if the user wants to continue.

CHAPTER 4

STRUCTURES

You will learn about the following in this chapter:

- Structure declarations and definitions
- Accessing structure members
- Nested structures
- Structures as objects and data types
- Enumerations

W e've seen variables of simple data types, such as `float`, `char`, and `int`. Variables of such types represent one item of information: a height, an amount, a count, and so on. But just as groceries are organized into bags, employees into departments, and words into sentences, it's often convenient to organize simple variables into more complex entities. The C++ construction called the *structure* is one way to do this.

The first part of this chapter is devoted to structures. In the second part we'll look at a related topic: the enumerations.

Structures

A structure is a collection of simple variables. The variables in a structure can be of different types: Some can be `int`, some can be `float`, and so on. (This is unlike the array, which we'll meet later, in which all the variables must be the same type.) The data items in a structure are called the *members* of the structure.

In books on C programming, structures are often considered an advanced feature and are introduced toward the end of the book. However, for C++ programmers, structures are one of the two important building blocks in the understanding of objects and classes. In fact, the syntax of a structure is almost identical to that of a class. A structure (as typically used) is a collection of data, while a class is a collection of both data and functions. So by learning about structures we'll be paving the way for an understanding of classes and objects. Structures in C++ (and C) serve a similar purpose to *records* in some other languages such as Pascal.

A Simple Structure

Let's start off with a structure that contains three variables: two integers and a floating-point number. This structure represents an item in a widget company's parts inventory. (We assume that a widget is composed of several parts.) The structure is a kind of blueprint specifying what information is necessary for a single part. The company makes several kinds of widgets, so the widget model number is the first member of the structure. The number of the part itself is the next member, and the final member is the part's cost. (Those of you who consider part numbers unexciting need to open your eyes to the romance of commerce.)

The program PARTS declares the structure **part**, defines a structure variable of that type called **part1**, assigns values to its members, and then displays these values.

```
// parts.cpp
// uses parts inventory to demonstrate structures
#include <iostream>
using namespace std;
///////////////////////////////////////////////////////////
struct part                     //declare a structure
   {
   int modelnumber;             //ID number of widget
   int partnumber;              //ID number of widget part
   float cost;                  //cost of part
   };
///////////////////////////////////////////////////////////
int main()
   {
   part part1;                  //define a structure variable

   part1.modelnumber = 6244;  //give values to structure members
   part1.partnumber = 373;
   part1.cost = 217.55F;
                                //display structure members
   cout << "Model "    << part1.modelnumber;
   cout << ", part "   << part1.partnumber;
   cout << ", costs $" << part1.cost << endl;
   return 0;
   }
```

The program's output looks like this:

```
Model 6244, part 373, costs $217.55
```

The PARTS program has three main aspects: declaring the structure, defining a structure variable, and accessing the members of the structure. Let's look at each of these.

Declaring the Structure

The structure declaration tells how the structure is organized: It specifies what members the structure will have. Here it is:

```
struct part
   {
   int modelnumber;
   int partnumber;
   float cost;
   };
```

Syntax of the Structure Declaration

The keyword **struct** introduces the structure declaration. Next comes the *structure name* or *tag*, which is **part**. The declarations of the structure members—**modelnumber**, **partnumber**, and **cost**—are enclosed in braces. A semicolon follows the closing brace, terminating the entire structure. Note that this use of the semicolon for structures is unlike the usage for a block of code. As we've seen, blocks of code, which are used in loops, decisions, and functions, are also delimited by braces. However, they don't use a semicolon following the final brace. Figure 4.1 shows the syntax of the structure declaration.

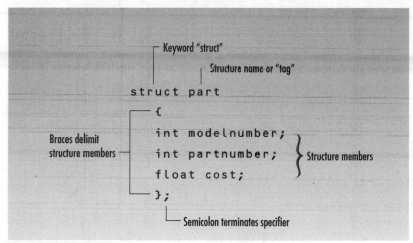

Figure 4.1 Syntax of the structure specifier.

Use of the Structure Declaration

The structure declaration serves only as a blueprint for the creation of variables of type **part**. The declaration does not itself define any variables; that is, it does not set aside any space in memory or even name any variables. It's merely a specification for how such structure variables will look when they are defined. This is shown in Figure 4.2.

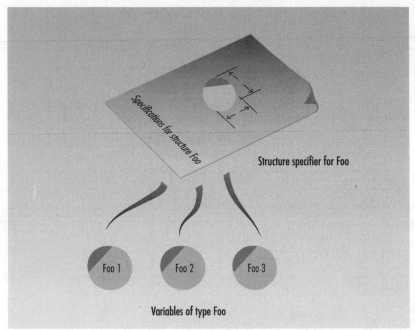

Figure 4.2   Structures and structure variables.

It's not accidental that this description sounds like the distinction we noted between classes and objects in Chapter 1, "The Big Picture." As we'll see, an object has the same relationship to its class that a variable of a structure type has to the structure declaration.

Defining a Structure Variable

The first statement in `main()`,

```
part part1;
```

defines a variable, called `part1`, of type structure `part`. This definition reserves space in memory for `part1`. How much space? Enough to hold all the members of `part1`—namely `modelnumber`, `partnumber`, and `cost`. In this case there will be 4 bytes for each of the two `int`s (assuming a 32-bit system), and 4 bytes for the `float`. Figure 4.3 shows how `part1` looks in memory. (The figure shows 2-byte integers.)

In some ways we can think of the `part` structure as the specification for a new data type. This will become more clear as we go along, but notice that the format for defining a structure variable is the same as that for defining a basic built-in data type such as `int`:

```
part part1;
int var1;
```

This similarity is not accidental. One of the aims of C++ is to make the syntax and the operation of user-defined data types as similar as possible to that of built-in data types. (In

C you need to include the keyword **struct** in structure definitions, as in **struct part part1;**. In C++ the keyword is not necessary.)

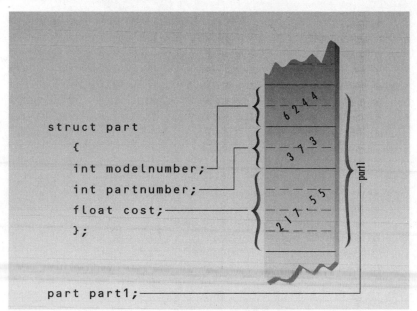

Figure 4.3   Structure members in memory.

Accessing Structure Members

Once a structure variable has been defined, its members can be accessed using something called the *dot operator*. Here's how the first member is given a value:

```
part1.modelnumber = 6244;
```

The structure member is written in three parts: the name of the structure variable (**part1**); the dot operator, which consists of a period (**.**); and the member name (**modelnumber**). This means "the **modelnumber** member of **part1**." The real name of the dot operator is *member access* operator, but of course no one wants to use such a lengthy term.

Remember that the first component of an expression involving the dot operator is the name of the specific structure variable (**part1** in this case), not the name of the structure declaration (**part**). The variable name must be used to distinguish one variable from another when there is more than one, such as **part1**, **part2**, and so on, as shown in Figure 4.4.

Structure members are treated just like other variables. In the statement **part1.modelnumber = 6244;**, the member is given the value 6244 using a normal assignment operator. The program also shows members used in **cout** statements such as:

```
cout << "\nModel " << part1.modelnumber;
```

These statements output the values of the structure members.

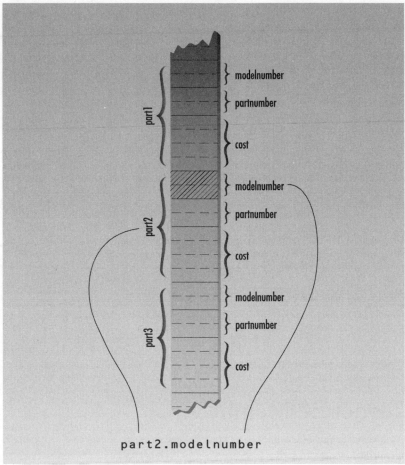

Figure 4.4 The dot operator.

Other Structure Features

Structures are surprisingly versatile. Let's look at some additional features of structure syntax and usage.

Combining Declaration and Definition

In the PARTS example we showed the structure declaration and the definition as two separate statements. These two statements can also be combined into a single statement, as shown in the next example, PARTSCOM.

```
// partscom.cpp
// uses parts inventory to demonstrate structures
#include <iostream>
using namespace std;
```

```
//////////////////////////////////////////////////////////////////
struct                          //no tag needed
   {
   int modelnumber;             //ID number of widget
   int partnumber;              //ID number of widget part
   float cost;                  //cost of part
   } part1;                     //definition goes here
//////////////////////////////////////////////////////////////////
int main()
   {
   part1.modelnumber = 6244;  //give values to structure members
   part1.partnumber = 373;
   part1.cost = 217.55F;
                              //display structure members
   cout << "Model "    << part1.modelnumber;
   cout << ", part "   << part1.partnumber;
   cout << ", costs $" << part1.cost << endl;
   return 0;
   }
```

In this program there is no separate statement for the structure definition:

```
part part1;
```

Instead, the variable name **part1** is placed at the end of the declaration:

```
struct
   {
   int modelnumber;
   int partnumber;
   float cost;
   } part1;
```

Notice that the tag name in the structure declaration can be removed, as we show here, if no more variables of this structure type will be defined later in the listing.

Merging the structure declaration and definition this way is a shorthand approach that can save a few program lines. Generally it is less clear and less flexible than using separate declarations and definitions.

Initializing Structure Members

The next example shows how structure members can be initialized when the structure variable is defined. It also demonstrates that you can have more than one variable of a given structure type (we hope you suspected this all along).

Here's the listing for PARTINIT:

```
// partinit.cpp
// shows initialization of structure variables
#include <iostream>
using namespace std;
//////////////////////////////////////////////////////////////////
struct part                     //specify a structure
   {
   int modelnumber;             //ID number of widget
```

```
    int partnumber;            //ID number of widget part
    float cost;                //cost of part
    };
/////////////////////////////////////////////////////////////
int main()
    {                          //initialize variable
    part part1 = { 6244, 373, 217.55F };
    part part2;                //define variable
                               //display first variable
    cout << "Model "    << part1.modelnumber;
    cout << ", part "   << part1.partnumber;
    cout << ", costs $" << part1.cost << endl;

    part2 = part1;             //assign first variable to second
                               //display second variable
    cout << "Model "    << part2.modelnumber;
    cout << ", part "   << part2.partnumber;
    cout << ", costs $" << part2.cost << endl;
    return 0;
    }
```

This program defines two variables of type part: part1 and part2. It initializes part1, prints out the values of its members, assigns part1 to part2, and prints out its members.

Here's the output:

```
Model 6244, part 373, costs $217.55
Model 6244, part 373, costs $217.55
```

Not surprisingly the same output is repeated, since one variable is made equal to the other.

Initializing Structure Variables

The part1 structure variable's members are initialized when the variable is defined:

```
part part1 = { 6244, 373, 217.55 };
```

The values to be assigned to the structure members are surrounded by braces and separated by commas. The first value in the list is assigned to the first member, the second to the second member, and so on.

Structure Variables in Assignment Statements

As can be seen in PARTINIT, one structure variable can be assigned to another:

```
part2 = part1;
```

The value of each member of part1 is assigned to the corresponding member of part2. Since a large structure can have dozens of members, such an assignment statement can require the computer to do a considerable amount of work.

Note that one structure variable can be assigned to another only when they are of the same structure type. If you try to assign a variable of one structure type to a variable of another type, the compiler will complain.

A Measurement Example

Let's see how a structure can be used to group a different kind of information. If you've ever looked at an architectural drawing, you know that (at least in the United States) distances are measured in feet and inches. (As you probably know, there are 12 inches in a foot.) The length of a living room, for example, might be given as 15′–8′, meaning 15 feet plus 8 inches. The hyphen isn't a negative sign; it merely separates the feet from the inches. This is part of the English system of measurement. (We'll make no judgment here on the merits of English versus metric.) Figure 4.5 shows typical length measurements in the English system.

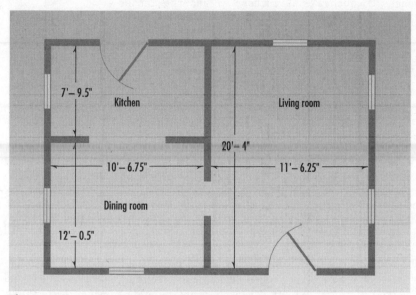

Figure 4.5 Measurements in the English system.

Suppose you want to create a drawing or architectural program that uses the English system. It will be convenient to store distances as two numbers, representing feet and inches. The next example, ENGLSTRC, gives an idea of how this could be done using a structure. This program will show how two measurements of type **Distance** can be added together.

```
// englstrc.cpp
// demonstrates structures using English measurements
#include <iostream>
using namespace std;
/////////////////////////////////////////////////////////////////
struct Distance                 //English distance
    {
    int feet;
```

```
    float inches;
    };
//////////////////////////////////////////////////////////////////
int main()
    {
    Distance d1, d3;                //define two lengths
    Distance d2 = { 11, 6.25 }; //define & initialize one length

                                    //get length d1 from user
    cout << "\nEnter feet: ";  cin >> d1.feet;
    cout << "Enter inches: ";  cin >> d1.inches;

                                    //add lengths d1 and d2 to get d3
    d3.inches = d1.inches + d2.inches;  //add the inches
    d3.feet = 0;                    //(for possible carry)
    if(d3.inches >= 12.0)           //if total exceeds 12.0,
        {                           //then decrease inches by 12.0
        d3.inches -= 12.0;          //and
        d3.feet++;                  //increase feet by 1
        }
    d3.feet += d1.feet + d2.feet;  //add the feet

                                    //display all lengths
    cout << d1.feet << "\'-" << d1.inches << "\" + ";
    cout << d2.feet << "\'-" << d2.inches << "\" = ";
    cout << d3.feet << "\'-" << d3.inches << "\"\n";
    return 0;
    }
```

Here the structure **Distance** has two members: **feet** and **inches**. The **inches** variable may have a fractional part, so we'll use type **float** for it. Feet are always integers, so we'll use type **int** for them.

We define two such distances, **d1** and **d3**, without initializing them, while we initialize another, **d2**, to 11′–6.25″. The program asks the user to enter a distance in feet and inches, and assigns this distance to **d1**. (The inches value should be smaller than 12.0.) It then adds the distance **d1** to **d2**, obtaining the total distance **d3**. Finally the program displays the two initial distances and the newly calculated total distance. Here's some output:

```
Enter feet: 10
Enter inches: 6.75
10'-6.75" + 11'-6.25" = 22'-1"
```

Notice that we can't add the two distances with a program statement like

```
d3 = d1 + d2;    // can't do this in ENGLSTRC
```

Why not? Because there is no routine built into C++ that knows how to add variables of type **Distance**. The + operator works with built-in types like **float**, but not with types we define ourselves, like **Distance**. (However, one of the benefits of using classes, as we'll see later, is the ability to add and perform other operations on user-defined data types.)

Structures Within Structures

You can nest structures within other structures. Here's a variation on the ENGLSTRC program that shows how this looks. In this program we want to create a data structure that stores the dimensions of a typical room: its length and width. Since we're working with English distances, we'll use two variables of type **Distance** as the length and width variables.

```
struct Room
   {
   Distance length;
   Distance width;
   }
```

Here's a program, ENGLAREA, that uses the **Room** structure to represent a room.

```cpp
// englarea.cpp
// demonstrates nested structures
#include <iostream>
using namespace std;
//////////////////////////////////////////////////////////////
struct Distance                 //English distance
   {
   int feet;
   float inches;
   };
//////////////////////////////////////////////////////////////
struct Room                     //rectangular area
   {
   Distance length;             //length of rectangle
   Distance width;              //width of rectangle
   };
//////////////////////////////////////////////////////////////
int main()
   {
   Room dining;                 //define a room

   dining.length.feet = 13;     //assign values to room
   dining.length.inches = 6.5;
   dining.width.feet = 10;
   dining.width.inches = 0.0;
                                //convert length & width
   float l = dining.length.feet + dining.length.inches/12;
   float w = dining.width.feet  + dining.width.inches/12;
                                //find area and display it
   cout << "Dining room area is " << l * w
        << " square feet\n" ;
   return 0;
   }
```

This program defines a single variable—**dining**—of type **Room**, in the line

```cpp
Room dining;  // variable dining of type Room
```

It then assigns values to the various members of this structure.

Accessing Nested Structure Members

Because one structure is nested inside another, we must apply the dot operator twice to access the structure members.

```
dining.length.feet = 13;
```

In this statement, `dining` is the name of the structure variable, as before; `length` is the name of a member in the outer structure (`Room`); and `feet` is the name of a member of the inner structure (`Distance`). The statement means "take the `feet` member of the `length` member of the variable `dining` and assign it the value 13." Figure 4.6 shows how this works.

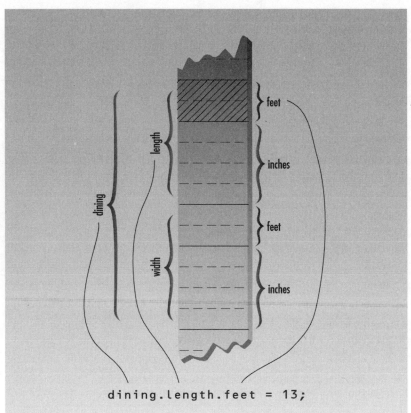

Figure 4.6 Dot operator and nested structures.

Once values have been assigned to members of `dining`, the program calculates the floor area of the room, as shown in Figure 4.7.

To find the area, the program converts the length and width from variables of type `Distance` to variables of type `float`, `1`, and `w`, representing distances in feet. The values of `1` and `w` are found by adding the `feet` member of `Distance` to the `inches` member divided by 12.

The feet member is converted to type float automatically before the addition is performed, and the result is type float. The l and w variables are then multiplied together to obtain the area.

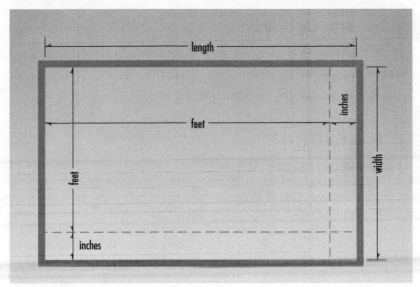

Figure 4.7   Area in feet and inches.

User-Defined Type Conversions

Note that the program converts two distances of type **Distance** to two distances of type **float**: the variables l and w. In effect it also converts the room's area, which is stored as a structure of type **Room** (which is defined as two structures of type **Distance**), to a single floating-point number representing the area in square feet. Here's the output:

```
Dining room area is 135.416672 square feet
```

Converting a value of one type to a value of another is an important aspect of programs that employ user-defined data types.

Initializing Nested Structures

How do you initialize a structure variable that itself contains structures? The following statement initializes the variable **dining** to the same values it is given in the ENGLAREA program:

```
Room dining = { {13, 6.5}, {10, 0.0} };
```

Each structure of type **Distance**, which is embedded in **Room**, is initialized separately. Remember that this involves surrounding the values with braces and separating them with commas. The first **Distance** is initialized to

```
{13, 6.5}
```

and the second to

```
{10, 0.0}
```

These two `Distance` values are then used to initialize the `Room` variable, again surrounding them with braces and separating them by commas.

Depth of Nesting

In theory, structures can be nested to any depth. In a program that designs apartment buildings, you might find yourself with statements like this one:

```
apartment1.laundry_room.washing_machine.width.feet
```

A Card Game Example

Let's examine a different kind of example. This one uses a structure to model a playing card. The program imitates a game played by cardsharps (professional gamblers) at carnivals. The cardsharp shows you three cards, then places them face down on the table and interchanges their positions several times. If you can guess correctly where a particular card is, you win. Everything is in plain sight, yet the cardsharp switches the cards so rapidly and confusingly that the player (the *mark*) almost always loses track of the card and loses the game which is, of course, played for money.

Here's the structure the program uses to represent a playing card:

```
struct card
   {
   int number;
   int suit;
   };
```

This structure uses separate members to hold the number of the card and the suit. The `number` runs from 2 to 14, where 11, 12, 13, and 14 represent the jack, queen, king, and ace, respectively (this is the order used in poker). The `suit` runs from 0 to 3, where these four numbers represent clubs, diamonds, hearts, and spades.

Here's the listing for CARDS:

```
// cards.cpp
// demonstrates structures using playing cards
#include <iostream>
using namespace std;

const int clubs = 0;                        //suits
const int diamonds = 1;
const int hearts = 2;
const int spades = 3;

const int jack = 11;                        //face cards
const int queen = 12;
const int king = 13;
const int ace = 14;
```

```
/////////////////////////////////////////////////////////////
struct card
    {
    int number;    //2 to 10, jack, queen, king, ace
    int suit;      //clubs, diamonds, hearts, spades
    };
/////////////////////////////////////////////////////////////
int main()
    {
    card temp, chosen, prize;                //define cards
    int position;

    card card1 = { 7, clubs };               //initialize card1
    cout << "Card 1 is the 7 of clubs\n";

    card card2 = { jack, hearts };           //initialize card2
    cout << "Card 2 is the jack of hearts\n";

    card card3 = { ace, spades };            //initialize card3
    cout << "Card 3 is the ace of spades\n";

    prize = card3;              //copy this card, to remember it

    cout << "I'm swapping card 1 and card 3\n";
    temp = card3; card3 = card1; card1 = temp;

    cout << "I'm swapping card 2 and card 3\n";
    temp = card3; card3 = card2; card2 = temp;

    cout << "I'm swapping card 1 and card 2\n";
    temp = card2; card2 = oard1; card1 = temp;

    cout << "Now, where (1, 2, or 3) is the ace of spades? ";
    cin >> position;

    switch (position)
        {
        case 1: chosen = card1; break;
        case 2: chosen = card2; break;
        case 3: chosen = card3; break;
        }
    if(chosen.number == prize.number &&       // compare cards
        chosen.suit == prize.suit)
        cout << "That's right!  You win!\n";
    else
        cout << "Sorry. You lose.\n";
    return 0;
    }
```

Here's some sample interaction with the program:

```
Card 1 is the 7 of clubs
Card 2 is the jack of hearts
Card 3 is the ace of spades
```

```
I'm swapping card 1 and card 3
I'm swapping card 2 and card 3
I'm swapping card 1 and card 2
Now, where (1, 2, or 3) is the ace of spades? 3
Sorry. You lose.
```

In this case, the hapless mark chose the wrong card (the right answer is 2).

The program begins by defining a number of variables of type `const int` for the face card and suit values. (Not all these variables are used in the program; they're included for completeness.) Next the `card` structure is specified. The program then defines three uninitialized variables of type `card`: `temp`, `chosen`, and `prize`. It also defines three cards—`card1`, `card2`, and `card3`—which it initializes to three arbitrary card values. It prints out the values of these cards for the user's information. It then sets a card variable, `prize`, to one of these card values as a way of remembering it. This card is the one whose location the player will be asked to guess at the end of the game.

Next the program rearranges the cards. It swaps the first and third cards, the second and third cards, and the first and second cards. Each time it tells the user what it's doing. (If you find the program too easy, you can add more such statements to further shuffle the cards. Flashing the statements on the screen for a limited time would also increase the challenge.)

Finally, the program asks the player what position a particular card is in. It sets a card variable, `chosen`, to the card in this position, and then compares `chosen` with the `prize` card. If they match, it's a win for the player; if not, it's a loss.

Notice how easy swapping cards is.

```
temp = card3;  card3 = card1;  card1 = temp;
```

Although the cards represent structures, they can be moved around very naturally, thanks to the ability of the assignment operator = to work with structures.

Unfortunately, just as structures can't be added, they also can't be compared. You can't say

```
if( chosen == prize )                    //not legal yet
```

because there's no routine built into the == operator that knows about the `card` structure. But, as with addition, this problem can be solved with operator overloading, as we'll see later.

Structures and Classes

We must confess to having misled you slightly on the capabilities of structures. It's true that structures are usually used to hold data only, and classes are used to hold both data and functions. However, in C++, structures can in fact hold both data and functions. (In C they can hold only data.) The syntactical distinction between structures and classes in C++ is minimal, so they can in theory be used almost interchangeably. But most C++ programmers use structures as we have in this chapter, exclusively for data. Classes are usually used to hold both data and functions, as we'll see in Chapter 6, "Objects and Classes."

Enumerations

As we've seen, structures can be looked at as a way to provide user-defined data types. A different approach to defining your own data type is the *enumeration*. This feature of C++ is less crucial than structures. You can write perfectly good object-oriented programs in C++ without knowing anything about enumerations. However, they are very much in the spirit of C++, in that, by allowing you to define your own data types, they can simplify and clarify your programming.

Days of the Week

Enumerated types work when you know in advance a finite (usually short) list of values that a data type can take on. Here's an example program, DAYENUM, that uses an enumeration for the days of the week:

```
// dayenum.cpp
// demonstrates enum types
#include <iostream>
using namespace std;
                            //specify enum type
enum days_of_week { Sun, Mon, Tue, Wed, Thu, Fri, Sat };

int main()
    {
    days_of_week day1, day2;    //define variables
                                //of type days_of_week
    day1 = Mon;                 //give values to
    day2 = Thu;                 //variables

    int diff = day2 - day1;     //can do integer arithmetic
    cout << "Days between = " << diff << endl;

    if(day1 < day2)             //can do comparisons
        cout << "day1 comes before day2\n";
    return 0;
    }
```

An **enum** declaration defines the set of all names that will be permissible values of the type. These permissible values are called *enumerators*. The **enum** type **days_of_week** has seven enumerators: **Sun**, **Mon**, **Tue**, and so on, up to **Sat**. Figure 4.8 shows the syntax of an **enum** declaration.

An *enumeration* is a list of all possible values. This is unlike the specification of an **int**, for example, which is given in terms of a range of values. In an **enum** you must give a specific name to every possible value. Figure 4.9 shows the difference between an **int** and an **enum**.

Once you've declared the **enum** type **days_of_week** as shown, you can define variables of this type. DAYENUM has two such variables, **day1** and **day2**, defined in the statement

```
days_of_week  day1, day2;
```

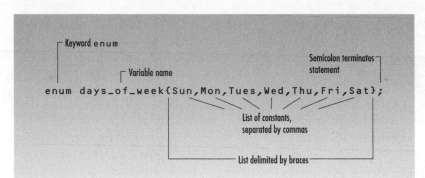

Figure 4.8   Syntax of **enum** specifier.

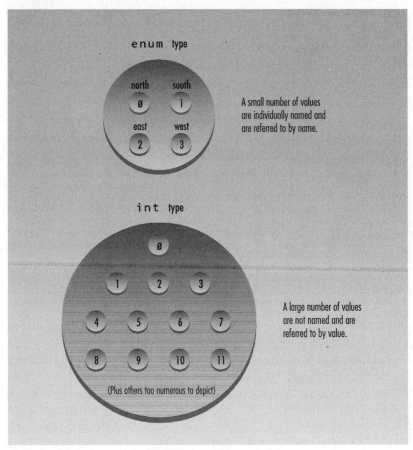

Figure 4.9   Usage of **ints** and **enums**.

(In C you must use the keyword **enum** before the type name.

```
enum days_of_week day1, day2;
```

In C++ this isn't necessary.)

Variables of an enumerated type, like **day1** and **day2**, can be given any of the values listed in the **enum** declaration. In the example we give them the values **Mon** and **Thu**. You can't use values that weren't listed in the declaration. Such statements as

```
day1 = halloween;
```

are illegal.

You can use the standard arithmetic operators on **enum** types. In the program we subtract two values. You can also use the comparison operators, as we show. Here's the program's output:

```
Days between = 3
day1 comes before day2
```

The use of arithmetic and relational operators doesn't make much sense with some **enum** types. For example, if you have the declaration

```
enum pets { cat, dog, hamster, canary, ocelot };
```

then it may not be clear what expressions like **dog + canary** or (**cat < hamster**) mean.

Enumerations are treated internally as integers. This explains why you can perform arithmetic and relational operations on them. Ordinarily the first name in the list is given the value 0, the next name is given the value 1, and so on. In the DAYENUM example, the values **Sun** through **Sat** are stored as the integer values 0 through 6.

Arithmetic operations on **enum** types take place on the integer values. However, although the compiler knows that your **enum** variables are really integers, you must be careful of trying to take advantage of this fact. If you say

```
day1 = 5;
```

the compiler will issue a warning (although it will compile). It's better to forget—whenever possible—that **enums** are really integers.

One Thing or Another

Our next example counts the words in a phrase typed in by the user. Unlike the earlier CHCOUNT example, however, it doesn't simply count spaces to determine the number of words. Instead it counts the places where a string of nonspace characters changes to a space, as shown in Figure 4.10.

This way you don't get a false count if you type multiple spaces between words. (It still doesn't handle tabs and other whitespace characters.) Here's the listing for WDCOUNT: This example shows an enumeration with only two enumerators.

```
// wdcount.cpp
// demonstrates enums, counts words in phrase
#include <iostream>
using namespace std;
```

```
#include <conio.h>              //for getche()

enum itsaWord { NO, YES };      //NO=0, YES=1

int main()
   {
   itsaWord isWord = NO;        //YES when in a word,
                                //NO when in whitespace
   char ch = 'a';               //character read from keyboard
   int wordcount = 0;           //number of words read

   cout << "Enter a phrase:\n";
   do {
      ch = getche();            //get character
      if(ch==' ' || ch=='\r')   //if white space,
         {
         if( isWord == YES )    //and doing a word,
            {                   //then it's end of word
            wordcount++;        //count the word
            isWord = NO;        //reset flag
            }
         }                      //otherwise, it's
      else                      //normal character
         if( isWord == NO )     //if start of word,
            isWord = YES;       //then set flag
      } while( ch != '\r' );    //quit on Enter key
   cout << "\n---Word count is " << wordcount << "---\n";
   return 0;
   }
```

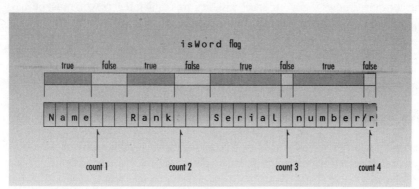

Figure 4.10 Operation of the WDCOUNT program.

The program cycles in a **do** loop, reading characters from the keyboard. It passes over (nonspace) characters until it finds a space. At this point it counts a word. Then it passes over spaces until it finds a character, and again counts characters until it finds a space. Doing this requires the program to remember whether it's in the middle of a word, or in the middle of a string of spaces. It remembers this with the **enum** variable **isWord**. This variable is defined to be of type **itsaWord**. This type is specified in the statement

```
enum itsaWord { NO, YES };
```

Variables of type **itsaWord** have only two possible values: **NO** and **YES**. Notice that the list starts with **NO**, so this value will be given the value 0—the value that indicates false. (We could also use a variable of type **bool** for this purpose.)

The **isWord** variable is set to **NO** when the program starts. When the program encounters the first nonspace character, it sets **isWord** to **YES** to indicate that it's in the middle of a word. It keeps this value until the next space is found, at which point it's set back to **NO**. Behind the scenes, **NO** has the value 0 and **YES** has the value 1, but we avoid making use of this fact. We could have used **if(isWord)** instead of **if(isWord == YES)**, and **if(!isWord)** instead of **if(isWord==NO)**, but this is not good style.

Note also that we need an extra set of braces around the second **if** statement in the program, so that the **else** will match with the first **if**.

Organizing the Cards

Here's our final example of **enum** types. Remember that in the CARDS program earlier in this chapter we defined a group of constants of type **const int** to represent a card's suits.

```
const int clubs = 0;
const int diamonds = 1;
const int hearts = 2;
const int spades = 3;
```

This sort of list is somewhat clumsy. Let's revise the CARDS program to use enumerations instead. Here's the listing for CARDENUM:

```
// cardenum.cpp
// demonstrates enumerations
#include <iostream>
using namespace std;

const int jack = 11;           //2 through 10 are unnamed integers
const int queen = 12;
const int king = 13;
const int ace = 14;

enum Suit { clubs, diamonds, hearts, spades };
/////////////////////////////////////////////////////////////////
struct card
   {
   int number;                 //2 to 10, jack, queen, king, ace
   Suit suit;                  //clubs, diamonds, hearts, spades
   };
/////////////////////////////////////////////////////////////////
```

```
int main()
   {
   card temp, chosen, prize;                //define cards
   int position;

   card card1 = { 7, clubs };               //initialize card1
   cout << "Card 1 is the seven of clubs\n";

   card card2 = { jack, hearts };           //initialize card2
   cout << "Card 2 is the jack of hearts\n";

   card card3 = { ace, spades };            //initialize card3
   cout << "Card 3 is the ace of spades\n";

   prize = card3;               //copy this card, to remember it

   cout << "I'm swapping card 1 and card 3\n";
   temp = card3; card3 = card1; card1 = temp;

   cout << "I'm swapping card 2 and card 3\n";
   temp = card3; card3 = card2; card2 = temp;

   cout << "I'm swapping card 1 and card 2\n";
   temp = card2; card2 = card1; card1 = temp;

   cout << "Now, where (1, 2, or 3) is the ace of spades? ";
   cin >> position;

   switch (position)
      {
      case 1: chosen = card1; break;
      case 2: chosen = card2; break;
      case 3: chosen = card3; break;
      }
   if(chosen.number == prize.number &&         //compare cards
         chosen.suit == prize.suit)
      cout << "That's right!  You win!\n";
   else
      cout << "Sorry. You lose.\n";
   return 0;
   }
```

Here the set of definitions for suits used in the CARDS program has been replaced by an **enum** declaration:

```
enum Suit { clubs, diamonds, hearts, spades };
```

This is a cleaner approach than using **const** variables. We know exactly what the possible values of the **suit** are; attempts to use other values, as in

```
card1.suit = 5;
```

result in warnings from the compiler.

Specifying Integer Values

We said that in an **enum** declaration the first enumerator was given the integer value 0, the second the value 1, and so on. This ordering can be altered by using an equal sign to specify a starting point other than 0. For example, if you want the suits to start with 1 instead of 0, you can say

```
enum Suit { clubs=1, diamonds, hearts, spades };
```

Subsequent names are given values starting at this point, so **diamonds** is 2, **hearts** is 3, and **spades** is 4. Actually you can use an equal sign to give a specified value to any enumerator.

Not Perfect

One annoying aspect of **enum** types is that they are not recognized by C++ input/output (I/O) statements. As an example, what do you think the following code fragment will cause to be displayed?

```
enum direction { north, south, east, west };
direction dir1 = south;
cout << dir1;
```

Did you guess the output would be **south**? That would be nice, but C++ I/O treats variables of **enum** types as integers, so the output would be **1**.

Other Examples

Here are some other examples of enumerated data declarations, to give you a feeling for possible uses of this feature:

```
enum months { Jan, Feb, Mar, Apr, May, Jun,
              Jul, Aug, Sep, Oct, Nov, Dec };

enum switch { off, on };

enum meridian { am, pm };

enum chess { pawn, knight, bishop, rook, queen, king };

enum coins { penny, nickel, dime, quarter, half-dollar, dollar };
```

We'll see other examples in future programs.

Summary

We've covered two topics in this chapter: structures and enumerations. *Structures* are an important component of C++, since their syntax is the same as that of classes. In fact, classes are (syntactically, at least) nothing more than structures that include functions.

Structures are typically used to group several data items together to form a single entity. A structure declaration lists the variables that make up the structure. Definitions then set aside memory for structure variables. Structure variables are treated as indivisible units in some situations (such as setting one structure variable equal to another), but in other situations their members are accessed individually (often using the dot operator).

An *enumeration* is a programmer-defined type that is limited to a fixed list of values. A declaration gives the type a name and specifies the permissible values, which are called *enumerators*. Definitions can then create variables of this type. Internally the compiler treats enumeration variables as integers.

Structures should not be confused with enumerations. Structures are a powerful and flexible way of grouping a diverse collection of data into a single entity. An enumeration allows the definition of variables that can take on a fixed set of values that are listed (enumerated) in the type's declaration.

Questions

Answers to questions can be found in Appendix G, "Answers to Questions and Exercises."

1. A structure brings together a group of

    a. items of the same data type.

    b. related data items.

    c. integers with user-defined names.

    d. variables.

2. True or false: A structure and a class use similar syntax.

3. The closing brace of a structure is followed by a _____.

4. Write a structure specification that includes three variables—all of type `int`—called `hrs`, `mins`, and `secs`. Call this structure `time`.

5. True or false: A structure declaration creates space in memory for a variable.

6. When accessing a structure member, the identifier to the left of the dot operator is the name of

    a. a structure member.

    b. a structure tag.

    c. a structure variable.

    d. the keyword `struct`.

7. Write a statement that sets the **hrs** member of the **time2** structure variable equal to 11.

8. If you have three variables defined to be of type **struct time**, and this
structure contains three **int** members, how many bytes of memory do
the variables use together?

9. Write a definition that initializes the members of **time1**—which is a variable of type **struct time**, as defined in Question 4—to **hrs** = 11, **mins** =
10, **secs** = 59.

10. True or false: You can assign one structure variable to another, provided
they are of the same type.

11. Write a statement that sets the variable **temp** equal to the **paw** member of
the **dogs** member of the **fido** variable.

12. An enumeration brings together a group of

    a. items of different data types.

    b. related data variables.

    c. integers with user-defined names.

    d. constant values.

13. Write a statement that declares an enumeration called **players** with the
values B1, B2, SS, B3, RF, CF, LF, P, and C.

14. Assuming the **enum** type **players** as declared in Question 13, define two
variables **joe** and **tom**, and assign them the values LF and P, respectively.

15. Assuming the statements of Questions 13 and 14, state whether each of
the following statements is legal.

    a. `joe = QB;`

    b. `tom = SS;`

    c. `LF = tom;`

    d. `difference = joe - tom;`

16. The first three enumerators of an **enum** type are normally represented by
the values _____, _____, and _____.

17. Write a statement that declares an enumeration called **speeds** with the
enumerators **obsolete**, **single**, and **album**. Give these three names the
integer values 78, 45, and 33.

18. State the reason why

```
enum isWord{ NO, YES };
```

is better than

```
enum isWord{ YES, NO };
```

Exercises

Answers to the starred exercises can be found in Appendix G.

*1. A phone number, such as (212) 767-8900, can be thought of as having three parts: the area code (212), the exchange (767), and the number (8900). Write a program that uses a structure to store these three parts of a phone number separately. Call the structure **phone**. Create two structure variables of type **phone**. Initialize one, and have the user input a number for the other one. Then display both numbers. The interchange might look like this:

```
Enter your area code, exchange, and number: 415 555 1212
My number is (212) 767-8900
Your number is (415) 555-1212
```

*2. A point on the two-dimensional plane can be represented by two numbers: an x coordinate and a y coordinate. For example, (4,5) represents a point 4 units to the right of the vertical axis, and 5 units up the horizontal axis. The sum of two points can be defined as a new point whose x coordinate is the sum of the x coordinates of the two points, and whose y coordinate is the sum of the y coordinates.

Write a program that uses a structure called **point** to model a point. Define three points, and have the user input values to two of them. Then set the third point equal to the sum of the other two, and display the value of the new point. Interaction with the program might look like this:

```
Enter coordinates for p1: 3 4
Enter coordinates for p2: 5 7
Coordinates of p1+p2 are: 8, 11
```

*3. Create a structure called **Volume** that uses three variables of type **Distance** (from the ENGLSTRC example) to model the volume of a room. Initialize a variable of type **Volume** to specific dimensions, then calculate the volume it represents, and print out the result. To calculate the volume, convert each dimension from a **Distance** variable to a variable of type **float** representing feet and fractions of a foot, and then multiply the resulting three numbers.

4. Create a structure called `employee` that contains two members: an employee number (type `int`) and the employee's compensation (in dollars; type `float`). Ask the user to fill in this data for three employees, store it in three variables of type `struct employee`, and then display the information for each employee.

5. Create a structure of type `date` that contains three members: the month, the day of the month, and the year, all of type int. (Or use day-month-year order if you prefer.) Have the user enter a date in the format 12/31/2001, store it in a variable of type `struct date`, then retrieve the values from the variable and print them out in the same format.

6. We said earlier that C++ I/O statements don't automatically understand the data types of enumerations. Instead, the (>>) and (<<) operators think of such variables simply as integers. You can overcome this limitation by using `switch` statements to translate between the user's way of expressing an enumerated variable and the actual values of the enumerated variable. For example, imagine an enumerated type with values that indicate an employee type within an organization:

```
enum etype { laborer, secretary, manager, accountant, executive,
researcher };
```

Write a program that first allows the user to specify a type by entering its first letter (`'l'`, `'s'`, `'m'`, and so on), then stores the type chosen as a value of a variable of type `enum etype`, and finally displays the complete word for this type.

```
Enter employee type (first letter only)
   laborer, secretary, manager,
   accountant, executive, researcher): a
Employee type is accountant.
```

You'll probably need two `switch` statements: one for input and one for output.

7. Add a variable of type `enum etype` (see Exercise 5), and another variable of type `struct date` (see Exercise 3) to the `employee` class of Exercise 4. Organize the resulting program so that the user enters four items of information for each of three employees: an employee number, the employee's compensation, the employee type, and the date of first employment. The program should store this information in three variables of type `employee`, and then display their contents.

8. Start with the fraction—adding program of Exercise 9 in Chapter 2, "C++ Programming Basics." This program stores the numerator and denominator of two fractions before adding them, and may also store the answer, which is also a fraction. Modify the program so that all fractions are

stored in variables of type `struct fraction`, whose two members are the fraction's numerator and denominator (both type `int`). All fraction-related data should be stored in structures of this type.

9. Create a structure called `time`. Its three members, all type `int`, should be called `hours`, `minutes`, and `seconds`. Write a program that prompts the user to enter a time value in hours, minutes, and seconds. This can be in 12:59:59 format, or each number can be entered at a separate prompt ("Enter hours:", and so forth). The program should then store the time in a variable of type `struct time`, and finally print out the total number of seconds represented by this time value:

```
long totalsecs = t1.hours*3600 + t1.minutes*60 + t1.seconds
```

10. Create a structure called `sterling` that stores money amounts in the old-style British system discussed in Exercises 8 and 11 in Chapter 3, "Loops and Decisions." The members could be called `pounds`, `shillings`, and `pence`, all of type `int`. The program should request the user to enter a money amount in new-style decimal pounds (type `double`), convert it to the old-style system, store it in a variable of type `struct sterling`, and then display this amount in pounds-shillings-pence format.

11. Use the `time` structure from Exercise 9, and write a program that obtains two `time` values from the user in 12:59:59 format, stores them in `struct time` variables, converts each one to seconds (type `int`), adds these quantities, converts the result back to hours-minutes-seconds, stores the result in a `time` structure, and finally displays the result in 12:59:59 format.

12. Revise the four-function fraction calculator program of Exercise 12 in Chapter 3 so that each fraction is stored internally as a variable of type `struct fraction`, as discussed in Exercise 8 in this chapter.

CHAPTER 5

FUNCTIONS

You will learn about the following in this chapter:

- Function definitions and declarations

- Arguments and return values

- Reference arguments

- Overloaded functions

- Default arguments

- Storage classes

A function groups a number of program statements into a unit and gives it a name. This unit can then be invoked from other parts of the program.

The most important reason to use functions is to aid in the conceptual organization of a program. Dividing a program into functions is, as we discussed in Chapter 1, "The Big Picture," one of the major principles of structured programming. (However, object-oriented programming provides other, more powerful ways to organize programs.)

Another reason to use functions (and the reason they were invented, long ago) is to reduce program size. Any sequence of instructions that appears in a program more than once is a candidate for being made into a function. The function's code is stored in only one place in memory, even though the function is executed many times in the course of the program. Figure 5.1 shows how a function is invoked from different sections of a program.

Functions in C++ (and C) are similar to subroutines and procedures in various other languages.

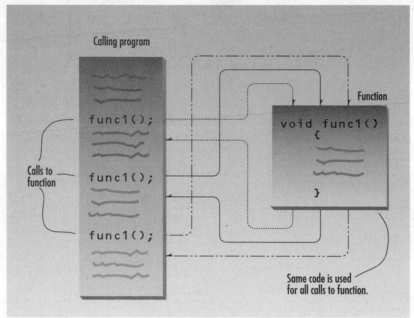

Figure 5.1   Flow of control to function.

Simple Functions

Our first example demonstrates a simple function whose purpose is to print a line of 45 asterisks. The example program generates a table, and lines of asterisks are used to make the table more readable. Here's the listing for TABLE:

```
// table.cpp
// demonstrates simple function
#include <iostream>
using namespace std;

void starline();                              //function declaration
                                              //   (prototype)

int main()
   {
   starline();                                //call to function
   cout << "Data type    Range" << endl;
   starline();                                //call to function
   cout << "char         -128 to 127" << endl
        << "short        -32,768 to 32,767" << endl
        << "int          System dependent" << endl
        << "long         -2,147,483,648 to 2,147,483,647" << endl;
   starline();                                //call to function
   return 0;
   }
//------------------------------------------------------------
```

```
// starline()
// function definition
void starline()                          //function declarator
   {
   for(int j=0; j<45; j++)               //function body
      cout << '*';
   cout << endl;
   }
```

The output from the program looks like this:

```
*********************************************
Data type    Range
*********************************************
char         -128 to 127
short        -32,768 to 32,767
int          System dependent
double       -2,147,483,648 to 2,147,483,647
```

The program consists of two functions: main() and starline(). You've already seen many programs that use main() alone. What other components are necessary to add a function to the program? There are three: the function *declaration*, the *calls* to the function, and the function *definition*.

The Function Declaration

Just as you can't use a variable without first telling the compiler what it is, you also can't use a function without telling the compiler about it. There are two ways to do this. The approach we show here is to *declare* the function before it is called. (The other approach is to *define* it before it's called; we'll examine that next.). In the TABLE program, the function starline() is declared in the line

```
void starline();
```

The declaration tells the compiler that at some later point we plan to present a function called *starline*. The keyword void specifies that the function has no return value, and the empty parentheses indicate that it takes no arguments. (You can also use the keyword void in parentheses to indicate that the function takes no arguments, as is often done in C, but leaving them empty is the more common practice in C++.) We'll have more to say about arguments and return values soon.

Notice that the function declaration is terminated with a semicolon. It is a complete statement in itself.

Function declarations are also called *prototypes*, since they provide a model or blueprint for the function. They tell the compiler, "a function that looks like this is coming up later in the program, so it's all right if you see references to it before you see the function itself."

Calling the Function

The function is *called* (or *invoked*, or *executed*) three times from main(). Each of the three calls looks like this:

```
starline();
```

This is all we need to call the function: the function name, followed by parentheses. The syntax of the call is very similar to that of the declaration, except that the return type is not used. The call is terminated by a semicolon. Executing the call statement causes the function to execute; that is, control is transferred to the function, the statements in the function definition (which we'll examine in a moment) are executed, and then control returns to the statement following the function call.

The Function Definition

Finally, we come to the function itself, which is referred to as the function *definition*. The definition contains the actual code for the function. Here's the definition for `starline()`:

```
void starline()            //declarator
   {
   for(int j=0; j<45; j++)  //function body
      cout << '*';
   cout << endl;
   }
```

The definition consists of a line called the *declarator*, followed by the function *body*. The function body is composed of the statements that make up the function, delimited by braces.

The declarator must agree with the declaration: It must use the same function name, have the same argument types in the same order (if there are arguments), and have the same return type.

Notice that the declarator is *not* terminated by a semicolon. Figure 5.2 shows the syntax of the function declaration, function call, and function definition.

When the function is called, control is transferred to the first statement in the function body. The other statements in the function body are then executed, and when the closing brace is encountered, control returns to the calling program.

Table 5.1 summarizes the different function components.

Table 5.1   Function Components

Component	Purpose	Example
Declaration (prototype)	Specifies function name, argument types, and return value. Alerts compiler (and programmer) that function is coming up later.	`void func();`
Call	Causes the function to be executed.	`func();`
Definition	The function itself. Contains the lines of code that constitute the function. `{` `// lines of code` `}`	`void func()`
Declarator	First line of definition.	`void func()`

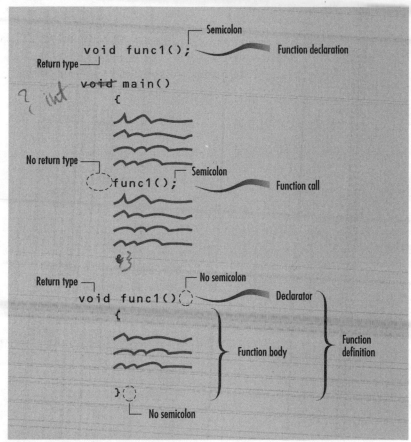

Figure 5.2   Function syntax.

Comparison with Library Functions

We've already seen some library functions in use. We have embedded calls to library functions, such as

```
ch = getche();
```

in our program code. Where are the declaration and definition for this library function? The declaration is in the header file specified at the beginning of the program (CONIO.H, for getche()). The definition (compiled into executable code) is in a library file that's linked automatically to your program when you build it.

When we use a library function we don't need to write the declaration or definition. But when we write our own functions, the declaration and definition are part of our source file, as we've shown in the TABLE example. (Things get more complicated in multifile programs, as we'll discuss in Chapter 13, "Multifile Programs.")

Eliminating the Declaration

The second approach to inserting a function into a program is to eliminate the function declaration and place the function definition (the function itself) in the listing before the first call to the function. For example, we could rewrite TABLE to produce TABLE2, in which the definition for `starline()` appears first.

```
// table2.cpp
// demonstrates function definition preceding function calls
#include <iostream>
using namespace std;                  //no function declaration
//--------------------------------------------------------------
// starline()                         //function definition
void starline()
   {
   for(int j=0; j<45; j++)
      cout << '*';
   cout << endl;
   }
//--------------------------------------------------------------
int main()                            //main() follows function
   {
   starline();                        //call to function
   cout << "Data type   Range" << endl;
   starline();                        //call to function
   cout << "char        -128 to 127" << endl
        << "short       -32,768 to 32,767" << endl
        << "int         System dependent" << endl
        << "long        -2,147,483,648 to 2,147,483,647" << endl;
   starline();                        //call to function
   return 0;
   }
```

This approach is simpler for short programs, in that it removes the declaration, but it is less flexible. To use this technique when there are more than a few functions, the programmer must give considerable thought to arranging the functions so that each one appears before it is called by any other. Sometimes this is impossible. Also, many programmers prefer to place `main()` first in the listing, since it is where execution begins. In general we'll stick with the first approach, using declarations and starting the listing with `main()`.

Passing Arguments to Functions

An *argument* is a piece of data (an `int` value, for example) passed from a program to the function. Arguments allow a function to operate with different values, or even to do different things, depending on the requirements of the program calling it.

Passing Constants

As an example, let's suppose we decide that the `starline()` function in the last example is too rigid. Instead of a function that always prints 45 asterisks, we want a function that will print any character any number of times.

Here's a program, TABLEARG, that incorporates just such a function. We use arguments to pass the character to be printed and the number of times to print it.

```
// tablearg.cpp
// demonstrates function arguments
#include <iostream>
using namespace std;
void repchar(char, int);                    //function declaration

int main()
   {
   repchar('-', 43);                        //call to function
   cout << "Data type    Range" << endl;
   repchar('=', 23);                        //call to function
   cout << "char         -128 to 127" << endl
        << "short        -32,768 to 32,767" << endl
        << "int          System dependent" << endl
        << "double       -2,147,400,040 to 0,147,483,647" << endl;
   repchar('-', 43);                        //oall to function
   return 0;
   }
//-----------------------------------------------------------
// repchar()
// function definition
void repchar(char ch, int n)                //function declarator
   {
   for(int j=0; j<n; j++)                   //function body
      cout << ch;
   cout << endl;
   }
```

The new function is called `repchar()`. Its declaration looks like this:

```
void repchar(char, int);    // declaration specifies data types
```

The items in the parentheses are the data types of the arguments that will be sent to `repchar()`: `char` and `int`.

In a function call, specific values—constants in this case—are inserted in the appropriate place in the parentheses:

```
repchar('-', 43);    // function call specifies actual values
```

This statement instructs `repchar()` to print a line of 43 dashes. The values supplied in the call must be of the types specified in the declaration: the first argument, the '-' character, must be of type `char`; and the second argument, the number 43, must be of type `int`. The types in the declaration and the definition must also agree.

The next call to `repchar()`,

```
repchar('=', 23);
```

tells it to print a line of 23 equal signs. The third call again prints 43 dashes. Here's the output from TABLEARG:

```
- - - - - - - - - - - - - - - - - - - - - - - - - - - - - - - - - - - - - - - - -
Data type    Range
=======================
char         -128 to 127
short        -32,768 to 32,767
int          System dependent
long         -2,147,483,648 to 2,147,483,647
```

The calling program supplies *arguments*, such as '-' and 43, to the function. The variables used within the function to hold the argument values are called *parameters*; in `repchar()` they are `ch` and `n`. (We should note that many programmers use the terms argument and parameter somewhat interchangeably.) The declarator in the function definition specifies both the data types and the names of the parameters:

```
void repchar(char ch, int n)   //declarator specifies parameter
                               //names and data types
```

These parameter names, `ch` and `n`, are used in the function as if they were normal variables. Placing them in the declarator is equivalent to defining them with statements like

```
char ch;
int n;
```

When the function is called, its parameters are automatically initialized to the values passed by the calling program.

Passing Variables

In the TABLEARG example the arguments were constants: '-', 43, and so on. Let's look at an example where variables, instead of constants, are passed as arguments. This program, VARARG, incorporates the same `repchar()` function as did TABLEARG, but lets the user specify the character and the number of times it should be repeated.

```
// vararg.cpp
// demonstrates variable arguments
#include <iostream>
using namespace std;
void repchar(char, int);                    //function declaration

int main()
   {
   char chin;
   int nin;
```

```
    cout << "Enter a character: ";
    cin >> chin;
    cout << "Enter number of times to repeat it: ";
    cin >> nin;
    repchar(chin, nin);
    return 0;
    }
//-------------------------------------------------------------
// repchar()
// function definition
void repchar(char ch, int n)              //function declarator
    {
    for(int j=0; j<n; j++)                //function body
        cout << ch;
    cout << endl;
    }
```

Here's some sample interaction with VARARG:

```
Enter a character: +
Enter number of times to repeat it: 20
++++++++++++++++++++
```

Here chin and nin in main() are used as arguments to repchar():

```
repchar(chin, nin);    // function call
```

The data types of variables used as arguments must match those specified in the function declaration and definition, just as they must for constants. That is, chin must be a char, and nin must be an int.

Passing by Value

In VARARG the particular values possessed by chin and nin when the function call is executed will be passed to the function. As it did when constants were passed to it, the function creates new variables to hold the values of these variable arguments. The function gives these new variables the names and data types of the parameters specified in the declarator: ch of type char and n of type int. It initializes these parameters to the values passed. They are then accessed like other variables by statements in the function body.

Passing arguments in this way, where the function creates copies of the arguments passed to it, is called *passing by value*. We'll explore another approach, *passing by reference*, later in this chapter. Figure 5.3 shows how new variables are created in the function when arguments are passed by value.

Structures as Arguments

Entire structures can be passed as arguments to functions. We'll show two examples, one with the Distance structure, and one with a structure representing a graphics shape.

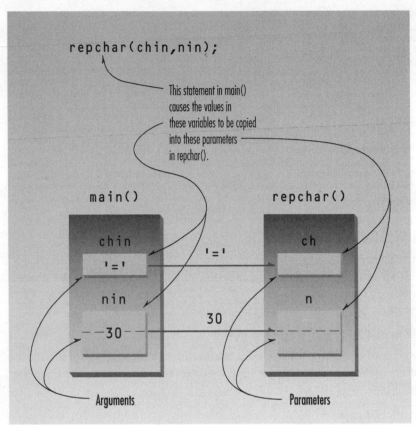

Figure 5.3 Passing by value.

Passing a Distance Structure

This example features a function that uses an argument of type **Distance**, the same structure type we saw in several programs in Chapter 4, "Structures." Here's the listing for ENGLDISP:

```
// engldisp.cpp
// demonstrates passing structure as argument
#include <iostream>
using namespace std;
//////////////////////////////////////////////////////////////
struct Distance                 //English distance
   {
   int feet;
   float inches;
   };
//////////////////////////////////////////////////////////////
void engldisp( Distance );      //declaration
```

```
int main()
   {
   Distance d1, d2;                //define two lengths

                                   //get length d1 from user
   cout << "Enter feet: ";  cin >> d1.feet;
   cout << "Enter inches: ";  cin >> d1.inches;

                                   //get length d2 from user
   cout << "\nEnter feet: ";  cin >> d2.feet;
   cout << "Enter inches: ";  cin >> d2.inches;

   cout << "\nd1 = ";
   engldisp(d1);                   //display length 1
   cout << "\nd2 = ";
   engldisp(d2);                   //display length 2
   cout << endl;
   return 0;
   }
//--------------------------------------------------------------
// engldisp()
// display structure of type Distance in feet and inches
void engldisp( Distance dd )    //parameter dd of type Distance
   {
   cout << dd.feet << "\'-" << dd.inches << "\"";
   }
```

The `main()` part of this program accepts two distances in feet-and-inches format from the user, and places these values in two structures, `d1` and `d2`. It then calls a function, `engldisp()`, that takes a `Distance` structure variable as an argument. The purpose of the function is to display the distance passed to it in the standard format, such as $10'-2.25''$. Here's some sample interaction with the program:

```
Enter feet: 6
Enter inches: 4

Enter feet: 5
Enter inches: 4.25

d1 = 6'-4"
d2 = 5'-4.25"
```

The function declaration and the function calls in `main()`, and the declarator in the function body, treat the structure variables just as they would any other variable used as an argument; this one just happens to be type `Distance`, rather than a basic type like `char` or `int`.

In `main()` there are two calls to the function `engldisp()`. The first passes the structure `d1`; the second passes `d2`. The function `engldisp()` uses a parameter that is a structure of type `Distance`, which it names `dd`. As with simple variables, this structure variable is automatically initialized to the value of the structure passed from `main()`. Statements in `engldisp()` can then access the members of `dd` in the usual way, with the expressions `dd.feet` and `dd.inches`. Figure 5.4 shows a structure being passed as an argument to a function.

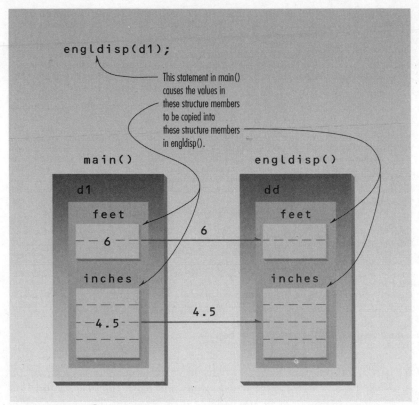

Figure 5.4 Structure passed as argument.

As with simple variables, the structure parameter `dd` in `engldisp()` is not the same as the arguments passed to it (`d1` and `d2`). Thus, `engldisp()` could (although it doesn't do so here) modify `dd` without affecting `d1` and `d2`. That is, if `engldisp()` contained statements like

```
dd.feet = 2;
dd.inches = 3.25;
```

this would have no effect on `d1` or `d2` in `main()`.

Passing a `circle` Structure

The next example of passing a structure to a function makes use of our Console Graphics Lite functions. You'll need to include the appropriate header file (MSOFTCON.H or BORLACON.H, depending on your compiler), and add the source file for Console Graphics (MSOFTCON.CPP or BORLACON.CPP) to your project. The Console Graphics Lite functions are described in Appendix E, "Console Graphics Lite," and how to use the Microsoft and Borland compilers is described in Appendix C, "Microsoft Visual C++," and Appendix D, "Borland C++Builder."

In this example a structure called circle represents a circular shape. Circles are positioned at a certain place on the console screen, and have a certain radius (size). They also have a color and a fill pattern. Possible values for the colors and fill patterns can be found in Appendix E. Here's the listing for CIRCSTRC:

```cpp
// circstrc.cpp
// circles as graphics objects
#include "msoftcon.h"          // for graphics functions
/////////////////////////////////////////////////////////////////
struct circle                  //graphics circle
   {
   int xCo, yCo;               //coordinates of center
   int radius;
   color fillcolor;            //color
   fstyle fillstyle;           //fill pattern
   };
/////////////////////////////////////////////////////////////////
void circ_draw(circle c)
   {
   set_color(c.fillcolor);                 //set color
   set_fill_style(c.fillstyle);            //set fill pattern
   draw_circle(c.xCo, c.yCo, c.radius);    //draw solid circle
   }
//-----------------------------------------------------------------
int main()
   {
   init_graphics();            //initialize graphics system
                               //create circles
   circle c1 = { 15, 7, 5, cBLUE, X_FILL };
   circle c2 = { 41, 12, 7, cRED, O_FILL };
   circle c3 = { 65, 18, 4, cGREEN, MEDIUM_FILL };

   circ_draw(c1);              //draw circles
   circ_draw(c2);
   circ_draw(c3);
   set_cursor_pos(1, 25);      //cursor to lower left corner
   return 0;
   }
```

The variables of type circle, which are c1, c2, and c3, are initialized to different sets of values. Here's how that looks for c1:

```cpp
circle c1 = { 15, 7, 5, cBLUE, X_FILL };
```

We assume that your console screen has 80 columns and 25 rows. The first value in this definition, 15, is the *column number* (the x coordinate) and the 7 is the *row number* (the y coordinate, starting at the top of the screen) where the center of the circle will be located. The 5 is the radius of the circle, the cBLUE is its color, and the X_FILL constant means it will be filled with the letter X. The two other circles are initialized similarly.

Once all the circles are created and initialized, we draw them by calling the circ_draw() function three times, once for each circle. Figure 5.5 shows the output of the CIRCSTRC program. Admittedly the circles are a bit ragged; a result of the limited number of pixels in console-mode graphics.

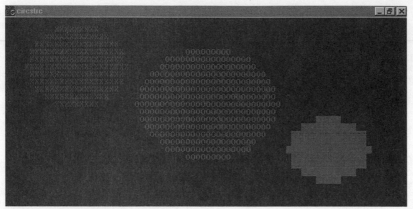

Figure 5.5 Output of the CIRCSTRC program.

Notice how the structure holds the characteristics of the circles, while the `circ_draw()` function causes them to actually do something (draw themselves). As we'll see in Chapter 6, "Objects and Classes," objects are formed by combining structures and functions to create entities that both possess characteristics and perform actions.

Names in the Declaration

Here's a way to increase the clarity of your function declarations. The idea is to insert meaningful names in the declaration, along with the data types. For example, suppose you were using a function that displayed a point on the screen. You could use a declaration with only data types,

```
void display_point(int, int);  //declaration
```

but a better approach is

```
void display_point(int horiz, int vert);  //declaration
```

These two declarations mean exactly the same thing to the compiler. However, the first approach, with (`int`, `int`), doesn't contain any hint about which argument is for the vertical coordinate and which is for the horizontal coordinate. The advantage of the second approach is clarity for the programmer: Anyone seeing this declaration is more likely to use the correct arguments when calling the function.

Note that the names in the declaration have no effect on the names you use when calling the function. You are perfectly free to use any argument names you want:

```
display_point(x, y);  // function call
```

We'll use this name-plus-datatype approach when it seems to make the listing clearer.

Returning Values from Functions

When a function completes its execution, it can return a single value to the calling program. Usually this return value consists of an answer to the problem the function has solved. The next example demonstrates a function that returns a weight in kilograms after being given a weight in pounds. Here's the listing for CONVERT:

```cpp
// convert.cpp
// demonstrates return values, converts pounds to kg
#include <iostream>
using namespace std;
float lbstokg(float);    //declaration

int main()
   {
   float lbs, kgs;

   cout << "\nEnter your weight in pounds: ";
   cin >> lbs;
   kgs = lbstokg(lbs);
   cout << "Your weight in kilograms is " << kgs << endl;
   return 0;
   }
//----------------------------------------------------------
// lbstokg()
// converts pounds to kilograms
float lbstokg(float pounds)
   {
   float kilograms =  0.453592 * pounds;
   return kilograms;
   }
```

Here's some sample interaction with this program:

```
Enter your weight in pounds: 182
Your weight in kilograms is 82.553741
```

When a function returns a value, the data type of this value must be specified. The function declaration does this by placing the data type, **float** in this case, before the function name in the declaration and the definition. Functions in earlier program examples returned no value, so the return type was **void**. In the CONVERT program, the function **lbstokg()** (*pounds to kilograms*, where **lbs** means pounds) returns type **float**, so the declaration is

```cpp
float lbstokg(float);
```

The first **float** specifies the return type. The **float** in parentheses specifies that an argument to be passed to **lbstokg()** is also of type **float**.

When a function returns a value, the call to the function

```cpp
lbstokg(lbs)
```

is considered to be an expression that takes on the value returned by the function. We can treat this expression like any other variable; in this case we use it in an assignment statement:

```
kgs = lbstokg(lbs);
```

This causes the variable `kgs` to be assigned the value returned by `lbstokg()`.

The return Statement

The function `lbstokg()` is passed an argument representing a weight in pounds, which it stores in the parameter pounds. It calculates the corresponding weight in kilograms by multiplying this pounds value by a constant; the result is stored in the variable kilograms. The value of this variable is then returned to the calling program using a return statement:

```
return kilograms;
```

Notice that both `main()` and `lbstokg()` have a place to store the kilogram variable: `kgs` in `main()`, and `kilograms` in `lbstokg()`. When the function returns, the value in kilograms is *copied into* `kgs`. The calling program does not access the kilograms variable in the function; only the value is returned. This process is shown in Figure 5.6.

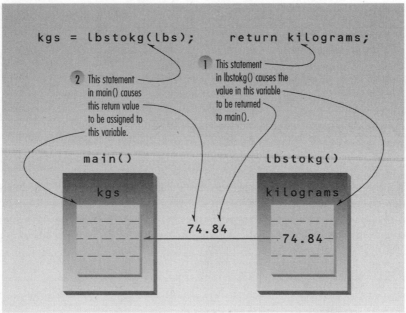

Figure 5.6 Returning a value.

While many arguments may be sent to a function, only one argument may be returned from it. This is a limitation when you need to return more information. However, there are other approaches to returning multiple variables from functions. One is to pass arguments by reference, which we'll look at later in this chapter.

You should always include a function's return type in the function declaration. If the function doesn't return anything, use the keyword **void** to indicate this fact. If you don't use a return type in the declaration, the compiler will assume that the function returns an **int** value. For example, the declaration

```
somefunc();    // declaration -- assumes return type is int
```

tells the compiler that **somefunc()** has a return type of **int**.

The reason for this is historical, based on usage in early versions of C. In practice you shouldn't take advantage of this default type. Always specify the return type explicitly, even if it actually is **int**. This keeps the listing consistent and readable.

Eliminating Unnecessary Variables

The CONVERT program contains several variables that are used in the interest of clarity but are not really necessary. A variation of this program, CONVERT2, shows how expressions containing functions can often be used in place of variables.

```cpp
// convert2.cpp
// eliminates unnecessary variables
#include <iostream>
using namespace std;
float lbstokg(float);    //declaration

int main()
   {
   float lbs;

   cout << "\nEnter your weight in pounds: ";
   cin >> lbs;
   cout << "Your weight in kilograms is " << lbstokg(lbs)
        << endl;
   return 0;
   }
//--------------------------------------------------------------
// lbstokg()
// converts pounds to kilograms
float lbstokg(float pounds)
   {
   return 0.453592 * pounds;
   }
```

In main() the variable **kgs** from the CONVERT program has been eliminated. Instead the function **lbstokg(lbs)** is inserted directly into the **cout** statement:

```cpp
cout << "Your weight in kilograms is " << lbstokg(lbs);
```

Also in the `lbstokg()` function, the variable `kilograms` is no longer used. The expression `0.453592*pounds` is inserted directly into the `return` statement:

```
return 0.453592 * pounds;
```

The calculation is carried out and the resulting value is returned to the calling program, just as the value of a variable would be.

For clarity, programmers often put parentheses around the expression used in a return statement:

```
return (0.453592 * pounds);
```

Even when not required by the compiler, extra parentheses in an expression don't do any harm, and they may help make the listing easier for us poor humans to read.

Experienced C++ (and C) programmers will probably prefer the concise form of CONVERT2 to the more verbose CONVERT. However, CONVERT2 is not so easy to understand, especially for the non-expert. The brevity-versus-clarity issue is a question of style, depending on your personal preference and on the expectations of those who will be reading your listing.

Returning Structure Variables

We've seen that structures can be used as arguments to functions. You can also use them as return values. Here's a program, RETSTRC, that incorporates a function that adds variables of type **Distance** and returns a value of this same type:

```
// retstrc.cpp
// demonstrates returning a structure
#include <iostream>
using namespace std;
////////////////////////////////////////////////////////////
struct Distance                         //English distance
   {
   int feet;
   float inches;
   };
////////////////////////////////////////////////////////////
Distance addengl(Distance, Distance);  //declarations
void engldisp(Distance);

int main()
   {
   Distance d1, d2, d3;                //define three lengths
                                       //get length d1 from user
   cout << "\nEnter feet: ";  cin >> d1.feet;
   cout << "Enter inches: ";  cin >> d1.inches;
                                       //get length d2 from user
   cout << "\nEnter feet: ";  cin >> d2.feet;
   cout << "Enter inches: ";  cin >> d2.inches;

   d3 = addengl(d1, d2);               //d3 is sum of d1 and d2
   cout << endl;
```

```
     engldisp(d1); cout << " + ";         //display all lengths
     engldisp(d2); cout << " = ";
     engldisp(d3); cout << endl;
     return 0;
     }
//------------------------------------------------------------
// addengl()
// adds two structures of type Distance, returns sum
Distance addengl( Distance dd1, Distance dd2 )
     {
     Distance dd3;                     //define a new structure for sum

     dd3.inches = dd1.inches + dd2.inches;  //add the inches
     dd3.feet = 0;                          //(for possible carry)
     if(dd3.inches >= 12.0)                 //if inches >= 12.0,
        {                                   //then decrease inches
        dd3.inches -= 12.0;                 //by 12.0 and
        dd3.feet++;                         //increase feet
        }                                   //by 1
     dd3.feet += dd1.feet + dd2.feet;    //add the feet
     return dd3;                         //return structure
     }
//------------------------------------------------------------
// engldisp()
// display structure of type Distance in feet and inches
void engldisp( Distance dd )
     {
     cout << dd.feet << "\'-" << dd.inches << "\"";
     }
```

The program asks the user for two lengths, in feet-and-inches format, adds them together by calling the function addengl(), and displays the results using the engldisp() function introduced in the ENGLDISP program. Here's some output from the program:

```
Enter feet: 4
Enter inches: 5.5

Enter feet: 5
Enter inches: 6.5

4'-5.5" + 5'-6.5" = 10'-0"
```

The main() part of the program adds the two lengths, each represented by a structure of type Distance, by calling the function addengl():

```
d3 = addengl(d1, d2);
```

This function returns the sum of d1 and d2, and in main() the result is assigned to the structure d3.

Internally, the addengl() function must create a new variable of type Distance to hold the results of its calculation. It can't simply return an expression, as in

```
return dd1+dd2;   // doesn't make sense here
```

because the process of adding the two structures actually takes several steps. The values of the individual members of **dd3** must be calculated, and then **dd3** is returned to the calling program with the statement

```
return dd3;
```

The result is assigned to **d3** in the calling program.

Besides showing how structures are used as return values, this program also shows two functions (three if you count **main()**) used in the same program. You can arrange the functions in any order. The only rule is that the function declarations must appear in the listing before any calls are made to the functions.

Reference Arguments

A *reference* provides an *alias*—a different name—for a variable. One of the most important uses for references is in passing arguments to functions.

We've seen examples of function arguments passed by value. When arguments are passed by value, the called function creates a new variable of the same type as the argument and copies the argument's value into it. As we noted, the function cannot access the original variable in the calling program, only the copy it created. Passing arguments by value is useful when the function does not need to modify the original variable in the calling program. In fact, it offers insurance that the function cannot harm the original variable.

Passing arguments by reference uses a different mechanism. Instead of a value being passed to the function, a *reference to* the original variable, in the calling program, is passed. (It's actually the *memory* address of the variable that is passed, although you don't need to know this.)

An important advantage of passing by reference is that the function can access the actual variables in the calling program. Among other benefits, this provides a mechanism for passing more than one value from the function back to the calling program.

Passing Simple Data Types by Reference

The next example, REF, shows a simple variable passed by reference.

```cpp
// ref.cpp
// demonstrates passing by reference
#include <iostream>
using namespace std;

int main()
   {
   void intfrac(float, float&, float&);      //declaration
   float number, intpart, fracpart;          //float variables

   do {
      cout << "\nEnter a real number: ";     //number from user
      cin >> number;
      intfrac(number, intpart, fracpart);    //find int and frac
```

```
        cout << "Integer part is " << intpart   //print them
             << ", fraction part is " << fracpart << endl;
     } while( number != 0.0 );                  //exit loop on 0.0
  return 0;
  }
//-------------------------------------------------------------
// intfrac()
// finds integer and fractional parts of real number
void intfrac(float n, float& intp, float& fracp)
  {
  long temp = static_cast<long>(n);   //convert to long,
  intp = static_cast<float>(temp);    //back to float
  fracp = n - intp;                   //subtract integer part
  }
```

The `main()` part of this program asks the user to enter a number of type `float`. The program will separate this number into an integer and a fractional part. That is, if the user's number is 12.456, the program should report that the integer part is 12.0 and the fractional part is 0.456. To find these two values, `main()` calls the function `intfrac()`. Here's some sample interaction:

```
Enter a real number: 99.44
Integer part is 99, fractional part is 0.44
```

Some compilers may generate spurious digits in the fractional part, such as 0.440002. This is an error in the compiler's conversion routine and can be ignored.

The `intfrac()` function finds the integer part by converting the number (which was passed to the parameter n) into a variable of type `long` with a cast, using the expression

```
long temp = static_cast<long>(n);
```

This effectively chops off the fractional part of the number, since integer types (of course) store only the integer part. The result is then converted back to type `float` with another cast:

```
intp = static_cast<float>(temp);
```

The fractional part is simply the original number less the integer part. (We should note that a library function, `fmod()`, performs a similar task for type `double`.)

The `intfrac()` function can find the integer and fractional parts, but how does it pass them back to `main()`? It could use a return statement to return one value, but not both. The problem is solved using reference arguments. Here's the declarator for the function:

```
void intfrac(float n, float& intp, float& fracp)
```

Reference arguments are indicated by the ampersand (&) following the data type:

```
float& intp
```

The & indicates that `intp` is an *alias*—another name—for whatever variable is passed as an argument. In other words, when you use the name `intp` in the `intfrac()` function, you are really referring to `intpart` in `main()`. The & can be taken to mean *reference to*, so

```
float& intp
```

means `intp` is a reference to the `float` variable passed to it. Similarly, `fracp` is an alias for—or a reference to—`fracpart`.

The function declaration echoes the usage of the ampersand in the definition:

```
void intfrac(float, float&, float&);   // ampersands
```

As in the definition, the ampersand follows those arguments that are passed by reference.

The ampersand is not used in the function call:

```
intfrac(number, intpart, fracpart);   // no ampersands
```

From the function call alone, there's no way to tell whether an argument will be passed by reference or by value.

While `intpart` and `fracpart` are passed by reference, the variable `number` is passed by value. `intp` and `intpart` are different names for the same place in memory, as are `fracp` and `fracpart`. On the other hand, since it is passed by value, the parameter `n` in `intfrac()` is a separate variable into which the value of `number` is copied. It can be passed by value because the `intfrac()` function doesn't need to modify `number`. Figure 5.7 shows how reference arguments work.

(C programmers should not confuse the ampersand that is used to mean *reference to* with the same symbol used to mean *address of*. These are different usages. We'll discuss the *address of* meaning of **&** in Chapter 10, "Pointers.")

A More Complex Pass by Reference

Here's a somewhat more complex example of passing simple arguments by reference. Suppose you have pairs of numbers in your program and you want to be sure that the smaller one always precedes the larger one. To do this you call a function, `order()`, which checks two numbers passed to it by reference and swaps the originals if the first is larger than the second. Here's the listing for REFORDER:

```
// reorder.cpp
// orders two arguments passed by reference
#include <iostream>
using namespace std;

int main()
   {
   void order(int&, int&);          //prototype

   int n1=99, n2=11;                //this pair not ordered
   int n3=22, n4=88;                //this pair ordered

   order(n1, n2);                   //order each pair of numbers
   order(n3, n4);

   cout << "n1=" << n1 << endl;     //print out all numbers
   cout << "n2=" << n2 << endl;
```

```
      cout << "n3=" << n3 << endl;
      cout << "n4=" << n4 << endl;
      return 0;
      }
//------------------------------------------------------------
void order(int& numb1, int& numb2)    //orders two numbers
   {
   if(numb1 > numb2)                   //if 1st larger than 2nd,
      {
      int temp = numb1;                //swap them
      numb1 = numb2;
      numb2 = temp;
      }
   }
```

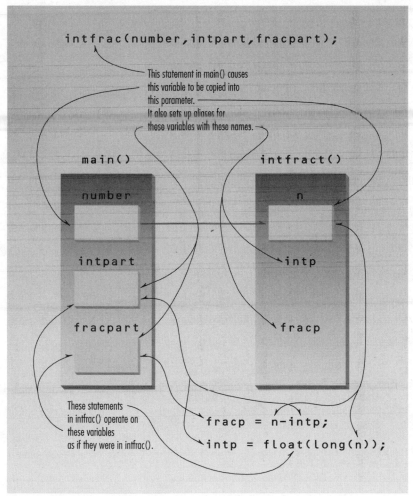

Figure 5.7   Passing by reference.

In main() there are two pairs of numbers—the first pair is not ordered and the second pair is ordered. The order() function is called once for each pair, and then all the numbers are printed out. The output reveals that the first pair has been swapped while the second pair hasn't. Here it is:

```
n1=11
n2=99
n3=22
n4=88
```

In the order() function, the first variable is called numb1 and the second is numb2. If numb1 is greater than numb2 the function stores numb1 in temp, puts numb2 in numb1, and finally puts temp back in numb2. Remember that numb1 and numb2 are simply different names for whatever arguments were passed; in this case, n1 and n2 on the first call to the function, and n2 and n3 on the second call. The effect is to check the ordering of the original arguments in the calling program and swap them if necessary.

Using reference arguments in this way is a sort of remote-control operation. The calling program tells the function what variables in the calling program to operate on, and the function modifies these variables without ever knowing their real names. It's as if you called the house painters and, although they never left their office, you sat back and watched as your dining room walls mysteriously changed color.

Passing Structures by Reference

You can pass structures by reference just as you can simple data types. Here's a program, REFERST, that performs scale conversions on values of type **Distance**. A scale conversion involves multiplying a group of distances by a factor. If a distance is 6′–8″, and a scale factor is 0.5, the new distance is 3′–4″. Such a conversion might be applied to all the dimensions of a building to make the building shrink but remain in proportion.

```cpp
// referst.cpp
// demonstrates passing structure by reference
#include <iostream>
using namespace std;
/////////////////////////////////////////////////////////////////
struct Distance                        //English distance
    {
    int feet;
    float inches;
    };
/////////////////////////////////////////////////////////////////
void scale( Distance&, float );        //function
void engldisp( Distance );             //declarations

int main()
    {
    Distance d1 = { 12, 6.5 };         //initialize d1 and d2
    Distance d2 = { 10, 5.5 };
```

```
   cout << "d1 = "; engldisp(d1);      //display old d1 and d2
   cout << "\nd2 = "; engldisp(d2);

   scale(d1, 0.5);                     //scale d1 and d2
   scale(d2, 0.25);

   cout << "\nd1 = "; engldisp(d1);    //display new d1 and d2
   cout << "\nd2 = "; engldisp(d2);
   cout << endl;
   return 0;
   }
//-----------------------------------------------------------
// scale()
// scales value of type Distance by factor
void scale( Distance& dd, float factor)
   {
   float inches = (dd.feet*12 + dd.inches) * factor;
   dd.feet = static_cast<int>(inches / 12);
   dd.inches = inches - dd.feet * 12;
   }
//-----------------------------------------------------------
// engldisp()
// display structure of type Distance in feet and inches
void engldisp( Distance dd )   //parameter dd of type Distance
   {
   cout << dd.feet << "\' " << dd.inches << "\"";
   }
```

REFERST initializes two **Distance** variables—**d1** and **d2**—to specific values, and displays them. Then it calls the **scale()** function to multiply **d1** by 0.5 and **d2** by 0.25. Finally, it displays the resulting values of the distances. Here's the program's output:

```
d1 = 12'-6.5"
d2 = 10'-5.5"
d1 = 6'-3.25"
d2 = 2'-7.375"
```

Here are the two calls to the function **scale()**:

```
scale(d1, 0.5);
scale(d2, 0.25);
```

The first call causes **d1** to be multiplied by 0.5 and the second causes **d2** to be multiplied by 0.25. Notice that these changes take place directly to **d1** and **d2**. The function doesn't return anything; the operation is performed directly on the **Distance** argument, which is passed by reference to **scale()**. (Since only one value is changed in the calling program, you could rewrite the function to pass the argument by value and return the scaled value. Calling such a function would look like this:

```
d1 = scale(d1, 0.5);
```

However, this is unnecessarily verbose.)

Notes on Passing by Reference

Passing arguments by reference is also possible in Pascal and newer versions of BASIC. References don't exist in C, where pointers serve a somewhat similar purpose, although often less conveniently. Reference arguments were introduced into C++ to provide flexibility in a variety of situations involving objects as well as simple variables.

The third way to pass arguments to functions, besides by value and by reference, is to use pointers. We'll explore this in Chapter 10, "Pointers."

Overloaded Functions

An overloaded function appears to perform different activities depending on the kind of data sent to it. Overloading is like the joke about the famous scientist who insisted that the thermos bottle was the greatest invention of all time. Why? "It's a miracle device," he said. "It keeps hot things hot, but cold things it keeps cold. How does it know?"

It may seem equally mysterious how an overloaded function knows what to do. It performs one operation on one kind of data but another operation on a different kind. Let's clarify matters with some examples.

Different Numbers of Arguments

Recall the `starline()` function in the TABLE example and the `repchar()` function from the TABLEARG example, both shown earlier in this chapter. The `starline()` function printed a line using 45 asterisks, while `repchar()` used a character and a line length that were both specified when the function was called. We might imagine a third function, `charline()`, that always prints 45 characters but that allows the calling program to specify the character to be printed. These three functions—`starline()`, `repchar()`, and `charline()`—perform similar activities but have different names. For programmers using these functions, that means three names to remember and three places to look them up if they are listed alphabetically in an application's *Function Reference* documentation.

It would be far more convenient to use the same name for all three functions, even though they each have different arguments. Here's a program, OVERLOAD, that makes this possible:

```
// overload.cpp
// demonstrates function overloading
#include <iostream>
using namespace std;

void repchar();                 //declarations
void repchar(char);
void repchar(char, int);

int main()
   {
   repchar();
   repchar('=');
   repchar('+', 30);
```

```
      return 0;
      }
//------------------------------------------------------------
// repchar()
// displays 45 asterisks
void repchar()
   {
   for(int j=0; j<45; j++)   // always loops 45 times
      cout << '*';           // always prints asterisk
   cout << endl;
   }
//------------------------------------------------------------
// repchar()
// displays 45 copies of specified character
void repchar(char ch)
   {
   for(int j=0; j<45; j++)   // always loops 45 times
      cout << ch;            // prints specified character
   cout << endl;
   }
//------------------------------------------------------------
// repchar()
// displays specified number of copies of specified character
void repchar(char ch, int n)
   {
   for(int j=0; j<n; j++)    // loops n times
      cout << ch;            // prints specified character
   cout << endl;
   }
```

This program prints out three lines of characters. Here's the output:

```
*********************************************
=============================================
++++++++++++++++++++++++++++++
```

The first two lines are 45 characters long, and the third is 30.

The program contains three functions with the same name. There are three declarations, three function calls, and three function definitions. What keeps the compiler from becoming hopelessly confused? It uses the number of arguments, and their data types, to distinguish one function from another. In other words, the declaration

```
void repchar();
```

which takes no arguments, describes an entirely different function than the declaration

```
void repchar(char);
```

which takes one argument of type char, or the declaration

```
void repchar(char, int);
```

which takes one argument of type char and another of type int.

The compiler, seeing several functions with the same name but different numbers of arguments, could decide the programmer had made a mistake (which is what it would do in C). Instead, it very tolerantly sets up a separate function for every such definition. Which one of these functions will be called depends on the number of arguments supplied in the call. Figure 5.8 shows this process.

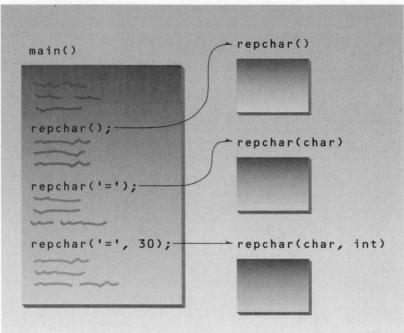

Figure 5.8   Overloaded functions.

Different Kinds of Arguments

In the OVERLOAD example we created several functions with the same name but different numbers of arguments. The compiler can also distinguish between overloaded functions with the same number of arguments, provided their type is different. Here's a program, OVERENGL, that uses an overloaded function to display a quantity in feet-and-inches format. The single argument to the function can be either a structure of type **Distance** (as used in the ENGLDISP example) or a simple variable of type **float**. Different functions are used depending on the type of argument.

```
// overengl.cpp
// demonstrates overloaded functions
#include <iostream>
using namespace std;
////////////////////////////////////////////////////////////////
struct Distance                    //English distance
   {
   int feet;
```

```
    float inches;
    };
//////////////////////////////////////////////////////////////////
void engldisp( Distance );      //declarations
void engldisp( float );

int main()
    {
    Distance d1;                    //distance of type Distance
    float d2;                       //distance of type float
                                    //get length d1 from user
    cout << "\nEnter feet: ";  cin >> d1.feet;
    cout << "Enter inches: ";  cin >> d1.inches;
                                    //get length d2 from user
    cout << "Enter entire distance in inches: "; cin >> d2;

    cout << "\nd1 = ";
    engldisp(d1);                   //display length 1
    cout << "\nd2 = ";
    engldisp(d2);                   //display length 2
    cout << endl;
    return 0;
    }
//--------------------------------------------------------------
// engldisp()
// display structure of type Distance in feet and inches
void engldisp( Distance dd )    //parameter dd of type Distance
    {
    cout << dd.feet << "\'-" << dd.inches << "\"";
    }
//--------------------------------------------------------------
// engldisp()
// display variable of type float in feet and inches
void engldisp( float dd )        //parameter dd of type float
    {
    int feet = static_cast<int>(dd / 12);
    float inches = dd - feet*12;
    cout << feet << "\'-" << inches << "\"";
    }
```

The user is invited to enter two distances, the first with separate feet and inches inputs, the second with a single large number for inches (109.5 inches, for example, instead of 9′–1.5″). The program calls the overloaded function engldisp() to display a value of type Distance for the first distance and of type float for the second. Here's some sample interaction with the program:

```
Enter feet: 5
Enter inches: 10.5
Enter entire distance in inches: 76.5
d1 = 5'-10.5"
d2 = 6'-4.5"
```

Notice that, while the different versions of `engldisp()` do similar things, the code is quite different. The version that accepts the all-inches input has to convert to feet and inches before displaying the result.

Overloaded functions can simplify the programmer's life by reducing the number of function names to be remembered. As an example of the complexity that arises when overloading is not used, consider the C++ library routines for finding the absolute value of a number. Because these routines must work with C (which does not allow overloading) as well as with C++, there must be separate versions of the absolute value routine for each data type. There are four of them: `abs()` for type `int`, `cabs()` for complex numbers, `fabs()` for type `double`, and `labs()` for type `long`. In C++, a single name, `abs()`, would suffice for all these data types.

As we'll see later, overloaded functions are also useful for handling different types of objects.

Inline Functions

We mentioned that functions save memory space because all the calls to the function cause the same code to be executed; the function body need not be duplicated in memory. When the compiler sees a function call, it normally generates a jump to the function. At the end of the function it jumps back to the instruction following the call, as shown in Figure 5.1 earlier in this chapter.

While this sequence of events may save memory space, it takes some extra time. There must be an instruction for the jump to the function (actually the assembly-language instruction CALL or something similar), instructions for saving registers, instructions for pushing arguments onto the stack in the calling program and removing them from the stack in the function (if there are arguments), instructions for restoring registers, and an instruction to return to the calling program. The return value (if any) must also be dealt with. All these instructions slow down the program.

To save execution time in short functions, you may elect to put the code in the function body directly in line with the code in the calling program. That is, each time there's a function call in the source file, the actual code from the function is inserted, instead of a jump to the function. The difference between a function and inline code is shown in Figure 5.9.

Long sections of repeated code are generally better off as normal functions: The savings in memory space is worth the comparatively small sacrifice in execution speed. But making a short section of code into an ordinary function may result in little savings in memory space, while imposing just as much time penalty as a larger function. In fact, if a function is very short, the instructions necessary to call it may take up as much space as the instructions within the function body, so that there is not only a time penalty but a space penalty as well.

In such cases you could simply repeat the necessary code in your program, inserting the same group of statements wherever it was needed. The trouble with repeatedly inserting the same code is that you lose the benefits of program organization and clarity that come with using functions. The program may run faster and take less space, but the listing is longer and more complex.

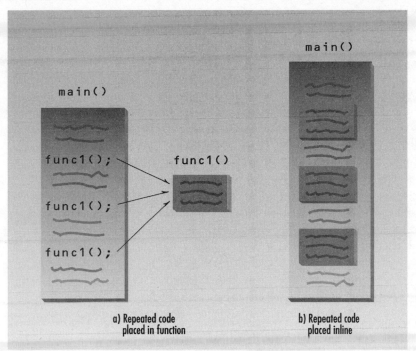

Figure 5.9   Functions versus inline code.

The solution to this quandary is the *inline function*. This kind of function is written like a normal function in the source file but compiles into inline code instead of into a function. The source file remains well organized and easy to read, since the function is shown as a separate entity. However, when the program is compiled, the function body is actually inserted into the program wherever a function call occurs.

Functions that are very short, say one or two statements, are candidates to be inlined. Here's INLINE, a variation on the CONVERT2 program. It inlines the **lbstokg()** function.

```
// inliner.cpp
// demonstrates inline functions
#include <iostream>
using namespace std;

// lbstokg()
// converts pounds to kilograms
inline float lbstokg(float pounds)
    {
    return 0.453592 * pounds;
    }
//------------------------------------------------------------
int main()
    {
    float lbs;
```

```
cout << "\nEnter your weight in pounds: ";
cin >> lbs;
cout << "Your weight in kilograms is " << lbstokg(lbs)
    << endl;
return 0;
}
```

It's easy to make a function inline: All you need is the keyword `inline` in the function definition:

```
inline float lbstokg(float pounds)
```

You should be aware that the inline keyword is actually just a *request* to the compiler. Sometimes the compiler will ignore the request and compile the function as a normal function. It might decide the function is too long to be inline, for instance.

(C programmers should note that inline functions largely take the place of `#define` macros in C. They serve the same purpose but provide better type checking and do not need special care with parentheses, as macros do.)

Default Arguments

Surprisingly, a function can be called without specifying all its arguments. This won't work on just any function: The function declaration must provide default values for those arguments that are not specified.

Here's an example, a variation on the OVERLOAD program that demonstrates this effect. In OVERLOAD we used three different functions with the same name to handle different numbers of arguments. The present example, MISSARG, achieves the same effect in a different way.

```
// missarg.cpp
// demonstrates missing and default arguments
#include <iostream>
using namespace std;

void repchar(char='*', int=45);     //declaration with
                                    //default arguments

int main()
   {
   repchar();                       //prints 45 asterisks
   repchar('=');                    //prints 45 equal signs
   repchar('+', 30);                //prints 30 plus signs
   return 0;
   }
//--------------------------------------------------------------
// repchar()
// displays line of characters
void repchar(char ch, int n)        //defaults supplied
```

```
{                          //    if necessary
for(int j=0; j<n; j++)     //loops n times
   cout << ch;             //prints ch
cout << endl;
}
```

In this program the function `repchar()` takes two arguments. It's called three times from `main()`. The first time it's called with no arguments, the second time with one, and the third time with two. Why do the first two calls work? Because the called function provides default arguments, which will be used if the calling program doesn't supply them. The default arguments are specified in the declaration for `repchar()`:

```
void repchar(char='*', int=45);  //declaration
```

The default argument follows an equal sign, which is placed directly after the type name. You can also use variable names, as in

```
void repchar(char reptChar='*', int numberReps=45);
```

If one argument is missing when the function is called, it is assumed to be the last argument. The `repchar()` function assigns the value of the single argument to the `ch` parameter and uses the default value 45 for the `n` parameter.

If both arguments are missing, the function assigns the default value `'*'` to `ch` and the default value 45 to `n`. Thus the three calls to the function all work, even though each has a different number of arguments.

Remember that missing arguments must be the trailing arguments—those at the end of the argument list. You can leave out the last three arguments, but you can't leave out the next-to-last and then put in the last. This is reasonable; how would the compiler know which arguments you meant, if you left out some in the middle? (Missing arguments could have been indicated with commas, but commas are notoriously subject to misprints, so the designers of C++ ignored this possibility.) Not surprisingly, the compiler will flag an error if you leave out arguments for which the function does not provide default values.

Default arguments are useful if you don't want to go to the trouble of writing arguments that, for example, almost always have the same value. They are also useful in cases where, after a program is written, the programmer decides to increase the capability of a function by adding another argument. Using default arguments means that the existing function calls can continue to use the old number of arguments, while new function calls can use more.

Variables and Storage Classes

Now that we know about functions, we can explore a feature of C++ that's related to the interaction of variables and functions: the *storage class*. The storage class of a variable determines which parts of the program can access it and how long it stays in existence. We'll look at variables with three storage classes—automatic, external, and static.

Automatic Variables

So far almost all the variables we've used in example programs have been defined inside the function in which they are used. That is, the definition occurs inside the braces that delimit the function body:

```
void somefunc()
   {
   int somevar;          //variables defined within
   float othervar;       //the function body
   // other statements
   }
```

Variables may be defined inside `main()` or inside other functions; the effect is similar, since `main()` is a function. Variables defined within a function body are called *automatic variables*. Actually, a keyword, `auto`, can be used to specify an automatic variable. You would say

```
void somefunc()
   {
   auto int somevar;          //same as int somevar
   auto float othervar;       //same as float othervar
   // other statements
   }
```

However, since this is the default, there is seldom any need to use the `auto` keyword. Variables defined within a function are automatic anyway.

Let's look at the two important characteristics of automatic variables—lifetime and visibility.

Lifetime

An automatic variable is not created until the function in which it is defined is called. (More accurately, we can say that variables defined within *any* block of code are not created until the block is executed.) In the program fragment just given, the variables `somevar` and `othervar` don't exist until the `somefunc()` function is called. That is, there is no place in memory where their values are stored; they are undefined. When control is transferred to `somefunc()`, the variables are created and memory space is set aside for them. Later, when `somefunc()` returns and control is passed back to the calling program, the variables are destroyed and their values are lost. The name *automatic* is used because the variables are automatically created when a function is called and automatically destroyed when it returns.

The time period between the creation and destruction of a variable is called its *lifetime* (or sometimes its *duration*). The lifetime of an automatic variable coincides with the time when the function in which it is defined is executing.

The idea behind limiting the lifetime of variables is to save memory space. If a function is not executing, the variables it uses during execution are presumably not needed. Removing them frees up memory that can then be used by other functions.

Visibility

A variable's *visibility* describes the locations within a program from which it can be accessed. It can be referred to in statements in some parts of the program; but in others, attempts to access it lead to an *unknown variable* error message. The word *scope* is also used to describe visibility. The scope of a variable is that part of the program where the variable is visible.

Automatic variables are only `visible`, meaning they can only be accessed, within the function in which they are defined. Suppose you have two functions in a program:

```
void somefunc()
   {
   int somevar;     //automatic variables
   float othervar;

   somevar = 10;    //OK
   othervar = 11;   //OK
   nextvar = 12;    //illegal: not visible in somefunc()
   }

void otherfunc()
   {
   int nextvar;     //automatic variable

   somevar = 20;    //illegal: not visible in otherfunc()
   othervar = 21;   //illegal: not visible in otherfunc()
   nextvar = 22;    //OK
   }
```

The variable `nextvar` is invisible in function `somefunc()`, and the variables `somevar` and `othervar` are invisible in `otherfunc()`.

Limiting the visibility of variables helps organize and modularize the program. You can be confident that the variables in one function are safe from accidental alteration by other functions because the other functions can't see them. This is an important part of *structured programming*, the methodology for organizing old-fashioned procedural programs. Limiting visibility is also an important part of object-oriented programming.

In the case of automatic variables, lifetime and visibility coincide: These variables exist only while the function in which they are defined is executing, and are only visible within that function. For some storage classes, however, lifetime and visibility are not the same.

Initialization

When an automatic variable is created, the compiler does not try to initialize it. Thus it will start off with an arbitrary value, which may be 0 but probably will be something else. If you want it initialized, you must do it explicitly, as in

```
int n = 33;
```

then it will start off with this value.

Automatic variables are sometimes called *local variables*, since they are visible only locally, in the function where they are defined.

External Variables

The next major storage class is *external*. While automatic variables are defined within functions, external variables are defined outside of (external to) any function. An external variable is visible to all the functions in a program. More precisely, it is visible to all those functions that follow the variable's definition in the listing. Usually you want external variables to be visible to all functions, so you put their declarations at the beginning of the listing. External variables are also called *global variables*, since they are known by all the functions in a program.

Here's a program, EXTERN, in which three functions all access an external variable.

```
// extern.cpp
// demonstrates external variables
#include <iostream>
using namespace std;
#include <conio.h>          //for getch()

char ch = 'a';              //exteral variable ch

void getachar();            //function declarations
void putachar();

int main()
   {
   while( ch != '\r' )      //main() accesses ch
      {
      getachar();
      putachar();
      }
   cout << endl;
   return 0;
   }
//------------------------------------------------------------
void getachar()             //getachar() accesses ch
   {
   ch = getch();
   }
//------------------------------------------------------------
void putachar()             //putachar() accesses ch
   {
   cout << ch;
   }
```

One function in EXTERN, `getachar()`, reads characters from the keyboard. It uses the library function `getch()`, which is like `getche()` except that it doesn't echo the character typed to the screen (hence the absence of the final **e** in the name). A second EXTERN function, `putachar()`, displays each character on the screen. The effect is that what you type is displayed in the normal way:

```
I'm typing in this line of text
```

The significant thing about this program is that the variable ch is not defined in any of the functions. Instead it is defined at the beginning of the file, before the first function. It is an external variable. Any function that follows the definition of ch in the listing can access it—in this case all the functions in EXTERN: main(), getachar(), and putachar(). Thus the visibility of ch is the entire source file.

Role of External Variables

The external storage class is used when a variable must be accessible to more than one function in a program. In procedural programs, external variables are often the most important variables in the program. However, as we noted in Chapter 1, external variables create organizational problems for the very reason that they can be accessed by any function. The wrong functions may access them, or functions may access them incorrectly. In an object-oriented program, there is less necessity for external variables.

Initialization

If an external variable is initialized, as in

```
int exvar = 199;
```

this initialization takes place when the file is first loaded. If an external variable is not initialized explicitly by the program; for example, if it is defined as

```
int exvar;
```

then it is initialized automatically to 0 when it is created. (This is unlike automatic variables, which are not initialized and probably contain random or *garbage* values when they are created.)

Lifetime and Visibility

External variables exist for the life of the program. That is, memory space is set aside for them when the program begins, and continues in existence until the program ends.

As we noted, external variables are visible in the file in which they are defined, starting at the point where they are defined. If ch were defined following main() but before getachar(), it would be visible in getachar() and putachar(), but not in main().

Static Variables

We'll touch on another storage class: *static*. Here we are concerned with static automatic variables. There are static external variables, but they are meaningful only in multifile programs, which we don't examine until Chapter 13.

A static automatic variable has the visibility of a local variable (that is, inside the function containing it). Its lifetime is similar to that of an external variable, except that it doesn't come into existence until the first call to the function containing it. Thereafter it remains in existence for the life of the program.

Static automatic variables are used when it's necessary for a function to remember a value when it is not being executed; that is, between calls to the function. In the next example, a function, `getavg()`, calculates a running average. It remembers the total of the numbers it has averaged before, and how many there were. Each time it receives a new number, sent as an argument from the calling program, it adds this number to the total, adds 1 to a count, and returns the new average by dividing the total by the count. Here's the listing for STATIC:

```cpp
// static.cpp
// demonstrates static variables
#include <iostream>
using namespace std;
float getavg(float);          //declaration

int main()
    {
    float data=1, avg;

    while( data != 0 )
        {
        cout << "Enter a number: ";
        cin >> data;
        avg = getavg(data);
        cout << "New average is " << avg << endl;
        }
    return 0;
    }
//-------------------------------------------------------------
// getavg()
// finds average of old plus new data
float getavg(float newdata)
    {
    static float total = 0;   //static variables are initialized
    static int count = 0;     //    only once per program

    count++;                  //increment count
    total += newdata;         //add new data to total
    return total / count;     //return the new average
    }
```

Here's some sample interaction:

```
Enter a number: 10
New average is 10        ←——————— total is 10, count is 1
Enter a number: 20
New average is 15        ←——————— total is 30, count is 2
Enter a number: 30
New average is 20        ←——————— total is 60, count is 3
```

The static variables `total` and `count` in `getavg()` retain their values after `getavg()` returns, so they're available the next time it's called.

Initialization

When static variables are initialized, as `total` and `count` are in `getavg()`, the initialization takes place only once—the first time their function is called. They are not reinitialized on subsequent calls to the function, as ordinary automatic variables are.

Storage

If you're familiar with operating system architecture, you might be interested to know that automatic variables are stored on the stack, while external and static variables are stored on the heap.

Table 5.2 summarizes the lifetime, visibility, and some other aspects of automatic, static automatic, and external variables.

Table 5.2 Storage Types

	Automatic	Static Auto	External
Visibility	function	function	file
Lifetime	function	program	program
Initialized value	not initialized	0	0
Storage	stack	heap	heap
Purpose	Variables used by a single function.	Same as auto, but must retain value when function terminates.	Variables used by several functions

Returning by Reference

Now that we know about external variables, we can examine a rather odd-looking C++ feature. Besides passing values by reference, you can also return a value by reference. Why you would want to do this may seem obscure. The primary reason is to allow you to use a function call on the left side of the equal sign. This is a somewhat bizarre concept, so let's look at an example. The RETREF program shows the mechanism.

```
// retref.cpp
// returning reference values
#include <iostream>
using namespace std;
int x;                  // global variable
int& setx();            // function declaration

int main()
   {                    // set x to a value, using
   setx() = 92;         // function call on left side
```

```
    cout << "x=" << x << endl;  // display new value in x
    return 0;
    }
//------------------------------------------------------------
int& setx()
    {
    return x;                    // returns the value to be modified
    }
```

In this program, the function `setx()` is declared with a reference type, `int&`, as the return type:

```
int& setx();
```

This function contains the statement

```
return x;
```

where x has been defined as an external variable. Now—and this is what looks so strange—you can put a call to this function on the left side of the equal sign:

```
setx() = 92;
```

The result is that the variable returned by the function is assigned the value on the right side of the equal sign. That is, x is given the value 92. The output from the program,

```
x=92
```

verifies that this assignment has taken place.

Function Calls on the Left of the Equal Sign

Does this still sound obscure? Remember that an ordinary function—one that returns a value—can be used as if it were a value:

```
y=squareroot(x);
```

Here whatever value `squareroot(x)` has (like 27.2) is assigned to y. The function is treated as if it were a value. A function that returns a reference, on the other hand, is treated as if it were a variable. It returns an *alias* to a variable, namely the variable in the function's return statement. In RETREF.C the function `setx()` returns a reference to the variable x. When this function is called, it's treated as if it were the variable x. Thus it can be used on the left side of an equal sign.

There are two corollaries to this. One is that you can't return a constant from a function that returns by reference. In `setx()`, you can't say

```
int& setx()
    {
    return 3;

    }
```

If you try this the compiler will complain that you need an "*lvalue*," that is, something that can go on the left side of the equal sign: a variable and not a constant.

More subtly, you can't return a reference to an automatic variable:

```
int& setx()
   {
   int x = 3;
   return x;     // error
   }
```

What's wrong with this? The problem is that a function's automatic variables are (probably) destroyed when the function returns, and it doesn't make sense to return a reference to something that no longer exists.

Don't Worry Yet

Of course, the question remains why one would ever want to use a function call on the left of an equal sign. In procedural programming there probably isn't too much use for this technique. As in the above example, there are easier ways to achieve the same result. However, in Chapter 8, "Operator Overloading," we'll find that returning by reference is an indispensable technique. Until then, keep it in the back of your mind.

const Function Arguments

We've seen that passing an argument by reference can be used to allow a function to modify a variable in the calling program. However, there are other reasons to pass by reference. One is efficiency. Some variables used for function arguments can be very large; a large structure would be an example. If an argument is large, then passing by reference is more efficient because, behind the scenes, only an address is really passed, not the entire variable.

Suppose you want to pass an argument by reference for efficiency, but not only do you want the function not to modify it, you want a guarantee that the function *cannot* modify it.

To obtain such a guarantee, you can apply the **const** modifier to the variable in the function declaration. The CONSTARG program shows how this looks.

```
//constarg.cpp
//demonstrates constant function arguments

void aFunc(int& a, const int& b);  //declaration

int main()
   {
   int alpha = 7;
   int beta = 11;
   aFunc(alpha, beta);
   return 0;
   }
//----------------------------------------------------------------
void aFunc(int& a, const int& b)    //definition
   {
   a = 107;    //OK
   b = 111;    //error: can't modify constant argument
   }
```

Here we want to be sure that `aFunc()` can't modify the variable `beta`. (We don't care if it modifies `alpha`.) So we use the `const` modifier with `beta` in the function declaration (and definition):

```
void aFunc(int& alpha, const int& beta);
```

Now the attempt to modify the `beta` in `aFunc()` is flagged as an error by the compiler. One of the design philosophies in C++ is that it's better for the compiler to find errors than to wait for them to surface at run time. The use of `const` function arguments is an example of this approach in action.

If you want to pass a `const` variable to a function as a reference argument, then you don't have a choice: It *must* be declared `const` in the function declaration. (There's no problem passing a `const` argument by value, because the function can't modify the original variable anyway.)

Many library functions use constant arguments in a similar way. We'll see examples as we go along.

Summary

Functions provide a way to help organize programs, and to reduce program size, by giving a block of code a name and allowing it to be executed from other parts of the program. Function *declarations* (prototypes) specify what the function looks like, function *calls* transfer control to the function, and function *definitions* contain the statements that make up the function. The function *declarator* is the first line of the definition.

Arguments can be sent to functions either *by value*, where the function works with a copy of the argument, or *by reference*, where the function works with the original argument in the calling program.

Functions can return only one value. Functions ordinarily return by value, but they can also return by reference, which allows the function call to be used on the left side of an assignment statement. Arguments and return values can be either simple data types or structures.

An *overloaded* function is actually a group of functions with the same name. Which of them is executed when the function is called depends on the type and number of arguments supplied in the call.

An *inline* function looks like a normal function in the source file but inserts the function's code directly into the calling program. Inline functions execute faster but may require more memory than normal functions unless they are very small.

If a function uses default arguments, calls to it need not include all the arguments shown in the declaration. Default values supplied by the function are used for the missing arguments.

Variables possess a characteristic called the *storage class*. The most common storage class is *automatic*. Variables of this class exist only while the function in which they are defined is executing, and are visible only within that function. *External* variables exist for the life of a program and can be visible throughout an entire file. *Static* automatic variables exist for the life of a program but are visible only in their own function.

A function cannot modify any of its arguments that are given the `const` modifier. A variable already defined as `const` in the calling program must be passed as a `const` argument.

In Chapter 4 we examined one of the two major parts of objects: structures, which are collections of data. In this chapter we explored the second part: functions. Now we're ready to put these two components together to create objects, the subject of Chapter 6.

Questions

Answers to questions can be found in Appendix G, "Answers to Questions and Exercises."

1. A function's single most important role is to

   a. give a name to a block of code.

   b. reduce program size.

   c. accept arguments and provide a return value.

   d. help organize a program into conceptual units.

2. A function itself is called the function d_____.

3. Write a function called `foo()` that displays the word `too`.

4. A one-statement description of a function is referred to as a function d_____ or a p_____.

5. The statements that carry out the work of the function constitute the function _____.

6. A program statement that invokes a function is a function _____.

7. The first line of a function definition is referred to as the _____.

8. A function argument is

   a. a variable in the function that receives a value from the calling program.

   b. a way that functions resist accepting the calling program's values.

   c. a value sent to the function by the calling program.

   d. a value returned by the function to the calling program.

9. True or false: When arguments are passed by value, the function works with the original arguments in the calling program.

10. What is the purpose of using argument names in a function declaration?

11. Which of the following can legitimately be passed to a function?

    a. A constant

    b. A variable

    c. A structure

    d. A header file

12. What is the significance of empty parentheses in a function declaration?

13. How many values can be returned from a function?

14. True or false: When a function returns a value, the entire function call can appear on the right side of the equal sign and be assigned to another variable.

15. Where is a function's return type specified?

16. A function that doesn't return anything has return type _____.

17. Here's a function:

```
int times2(int a)
   {
   return (a*2);
   }
```

Write a `main()` program that includes everything necessary to call this function.

18. When an argument is passed by reference,

    a. a variable is created in the function to hold the argument's value.

    b. the function cannot access the argument's value.

    c. a temporary variable is created in the calling program to hold the argument's value.

    d. the function accesses the argument's original value in the calling program.

19. What is a principle reason for passing arguments by reference?

20. Overloaded functions

    a. are a group of functions with the same name.

    b. all have the same number and types of arguments.

    c. make life simpler for programmers.

    d. may fail unexpectedly due to stress.

21. Write declarations for two overloaded functions named `bar()`. They both return type `int`. The first takes one argument of type `char`, and the second takes two arguments of type `char`. If this is impossible, say why.

22. In general, an inline function executes _____ than a normal function, but requires _____ memory.

23. Write the declarator for an inline function named `foobar()` that takes one argument of type `float` and returns type `float`.

24. A default argument has a value that

    a. may be supplied by the calling program.

    b. may be supplied by the function.

    c. must have a constant value.

    d. must have a variable value.

25. Write a declaration for a function called `blyth()` that takes two arguments and returns type `char`. The first argument is type `int`, and the second is type `float` with a default value of 3.14159.

26. Storage class is concerned with the _____ and _____ of a variable.

27. What functions can access an external variable that appears in the same file with them?

28. What functions can access an automatic variable?

29. A static automatic variable is used to

    a. make a variable visible to several functions.

    b. make a variable visible to only one function.

    c. conserve memory when a function is not executing.

    d. retain a value when a function is not executing.

30. In what unusual place can you use a function call when a function returns a value by reference?

Exercises

Answers to the starred exercises can be found in Appendix G.

*1. Refer to the CIRCAREA program in Chapter 2, "C++ Programming Basics." Write a function called `circarea()` that finds the area of a circle in a similar way. It should take an argument of type `float` and return an argument of the same type. Write a `main()` function that gets a radius value from the user, calls `circarea()`, and displays the result.

*2. Raising a number n to a power p is the same as multiplying n by itself p times. Write a function called `power()` that takes a `double` value for n and an `int` value for p, and returns the result as a `double` value. Use a default argument of 2 for p, so that if this argument is omitted, the number n will be squared. Write a `main()` function that gets values from the user to test this function.

*3. Write a function called `zeroSmaller()` that is passed two `int` arguments by reference and then sets the smaller of the two numbers to 0. Write a `main()` program to exercise this function.

*4. Write a function that takes two `Distance` values as arguments and returns the larger one. Include a `main()` program that accepts two `Distance` values from the user, compares them, and displays the larger. (See the RET-STRC program for hints.)

5. Write a function called `hms_to_secs()` that takes three `int` values—for hours, minutes, and seconds—as arguments, and returns the equivalent time in seconds (type `long`). Create a program that exercises this function by repeatedly obtaining a time value in hours, minutes, and seconds from the user (format 12:59:59), calling the function, and displaying the value of seconds it returns.

6. Start with the program from Exercise 11, Chapter 4, "Structures," which adds two `struct time` values. Keep the same functionality, but modify the program so that it uses two functions. The first, `time_to_secs()`, takes as its only argument a structure of type `time`, and returns the equivalent in seconds (type `long`). The second function, `secs_to_time()`, takes as its only argument a time in seconds (type `long`), and returns a structure of type `time`.

7. Start with the `power ()` function of Exercise 2, which works only with type `double`. Create a series of overloaded functions with the same name that, in addition to `double`, also work with types `char`, `int`, `long`, and `float`. Write a `main()` program that exercises these overloaded functions with all argument types.

8. Write a function called `swap()` that interchanges two `int` values passed to it by the calling program. (Note that this function swaps the values of the variables in the calling program, not those in the function.) You'll need to decide how to pass the arguments. Create a `main()` program to exercise the function.

9. This exercise is similar to Exercise 8, except that instead of two **int** variables, have the **swap()** function interchange two **struct time** values (see Exercise 6).

10. Write a function that, when you call it, displays a message telling how many times it has been called: "I have been called 3 times", or whatever. Write a **main()** program that calls this function at least 10 times. Try implementing this function in two different ways. First, use an external variable to store the count. Second, use a local **static** variable. Which is more appropriate? Why can't you use an automatic variable?

11. Write a program, based on the **sterling** structure of Exercise 10 in Chapter 4, "Structures," that obtains from the user two money amounts in old-style British format (£9:19:11), adds them, and displays the result, again in old-style format. Use three functions. The first should obtain a pounds-shillings-pence value from the user and return the value as a structure of type sterling. The second should take two arguments of type sterling and return a value of the same type, which is the sum of the arguments. The third should take a sterling structure as its argument and display its value.

12. Revise the four-function fraction calculator from Exercise 12, Chapter 4, so that it uses functions for each of the four arithmetic operations. They can be called **fadd()**, **fsub()**, **fmul()**, and **fdiv()**. Each of these functions should take two arguments of type **struct fraction**, and return an argument of the same type.

CHAPTER 6

OBJECTS AND CLASSES

You will learn about the following in this chapter:

- Member functions and data
- private and public
- Constructors and destructors
- Objects in the real world
- When to use objects

And now, the topics you've all been waiting for: objects and classes. The preliminaries are out of the way. We've learned about structures, which provide a way to group data elements. We've examined functions, which organize program actions into named entities. In this chapter we'll put these ideas together. We'll introduce several classes, starting with simple ones and working toward more complicated examples. We'll focus first on the details of classes and objects. At the end of the chapter we'll take a wider view, discussing what is to be gained by using the OOP approach.

As you read this chapter you may want to refer back to the concepts introduced in Chapter 1, "The Big Picture."

A Simple Class

Our first program contains a class and two objects of that class. Although it's simple, the program demonstrates the syntax and general features of classes in C++. Here's the listing for the SMALLOBJ program:

```
// smallobj.cpp
// demonstrates a small, simple object
#include <iostream>
using namespace std;
/////////////////////////////////////////////////////////////////
class smallobj                //declare a class
   {
   private:
      int somedata;           //class data
   public:
      void setdata(int d)     //member function to set data
```

```
                { somedata = d; }
        void showdata()          //member function to display data
            { cout << "Data is " << somedata << endl; }
    };
/////////////////////////////////////////////////////////////////
int main()
    {
    smallobj s1, s2;    //define two objects of class smallobj

    s1.setdata(1066);  //call member function to set data
    s2.setdata(1776);

    s1.showdata();      //call member function to display data
    s2.showdata();
    return 0;
    }
```

The class **smallobj** declared in this program contains one data item and two member functions. The two member functions provide the only access to the data item from outside the class. The first member function sets the data item to a value, and the second displays the value. (This may sound like Greek, but we'll see what these terms mean as we go along.)

Placing data and functions together into a single entity is the central idea of object-oriented programming. This is shown in Figure 6.1.

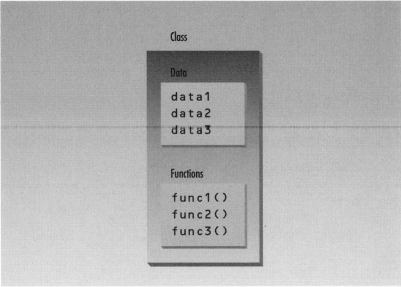

Figure 6.1   Classes contain data and functions.

Classes and Objects

Recall from Chapter 1 that an object has the same relationship to a class that a variable has to a data type. An object is said to be an *instance of* a class, in the same way my 1954 Chevrolet is an instance of a vehicle. In SMALLOBJ, the class—whose name is **smallobj**—is *declared* in the first part of the program. Later, in **main()**, we *define* two objects—**s1** and **s2**—that are instances of that class.

Each of the two objects is given a value, and each displays its value. Here's the output of the program:

```
Data is 1066     ←——————— object s1 displayed this
Data is 1776     ←——————— object s2 displayed this
```

We'll begin by looking in detail at the first part of the program—the declaration for the class **smallobj**. Later we'll focus on what **main()** does with objects of this class.

Declaring the Class

Here's the declaration (sometimes called a *specifier*) for the class **smallobj**, copied from the SMALLOBJ listing:

```
class smallobj              //declare a class
   {
 private:
      int somedata;         //class data
   public:
      void setdata(int d)   //member function to set data
         { somedata = d; }
      void showdata()       //member function to display data
         { cout << "\nData is " << somedata; }
   };
```

The declaration starts with the keyword **class**, followed by the class name—**smallobj** in this example. Like a structure, the body of the class is delimited by braces and terminated by a semicolon. (Don't forget the semicolon. Remember, data constructs like structures and classes end with a semicolon, while control constructs like functions and loops do not.)

private and public

The body of the class contains two unfamiliar keywords: **private** and **public**. What is their purpose?

A key feature of object-oriented programming is *data hiding*. This term does not refer to the activities of particularly paranoid programmers; rather it means that data is concealed within a class, so that it cannot be accessed mistakenly by functions outside the class. The primary mechanism for hiding data is to put it in a class and make it private. Private data or functions can only be accessed from within the class. Public data or functions, on the other hand, are accessible from outside the class. This is shown in Figure 6.2.

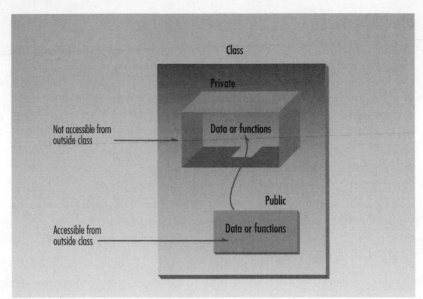

Figure 6.2 Private and public.

Hidden from Whom?

Don't confuse data hiding with the security techniques used to protect computer databases. To provide a security measure you might, for example, require a user to supply a password before granting access to a database. The password is meant to keep unauthorized or malevolent users from altering (or often even reading) the data.

Data hiding, on the other hand, means hiding data from parts of the program that don't need to access it. More specifically, one class's data is hidden from other classes. Data hiding is designed to protect well-intentioned programmers from honest mistakes. Programmers who really want to can figure out a way to access private data, but they will find it hard to do so by accident.

Class Data

The `smallobj` class contains one data item: `somedata`, which is of type `int`. The data items within a class are called *data members* (or sometimes *member data*). There can be any number of data members in a class, just as there can be any number of data items in a structure. The data member `somedata` follows the keyword `private`, so it can be accessed from within the class, but not from outside.

Member Functions

Member functions are functions that are included within a class. (In some object-oriented languages, such as Smalltalk, member functions are called *methods*; some writers use this term in C++ as well.) There are two member functions in smallobj: setdata() and showdata(). The function bodies of these functions have been written on the same line as the braces that delimit them. You could also use the more traditional format for these function definitions:

```
void setdata(int d)
   {
   somedata = d;
   }
```

and

```
void showdata()
   {
   cout << "\nData is " << somedata;
   }
```

However, when member functions are small, it is common to compress their definitions this way to save space.

Because setdata() and showdata() follow the keyword public, they can be accessed from outside the class. We'll see how this is done in a moment. Figure 6.3 shows the syntax of a class declaration.

Functions are Public, Data is Private

Usually the data within a class is private and the functions are public. This is a result of how classes are used. The data is hidden so it will be safe from accidental manipulation, while the functions that operate on the data are public so they can be accessed from outside the class. However, there is no rule that data must be private and functions public; in some circumstances you may find you'll need to use private functions and public data.

Member Functions Within Class Declaration

The member functions in the smallobj class perform operations that are quite common in classes: setting and retrieving the data stored in the class. The setdata() function accepts a value as a parameter and sets the somedata variable to this value. The showdata() function displays the value stored in somedata.

Note that the member functions setdata() and showdata() are *definitions* in that the actual code for the function is contained within the class declaration. (The functions are not definitions in the sense that memory is set aside for the function code; this doesn't happen until an object of the class is created.) Member functions defined inside a class this way are created as inline functions by default. (Inline functions were discussed in Chapter 5, "Functions.") We'll see later that it is also possible to *declare* a function within a class but to *define* it elsewhere. Functions defined outside the class are not normally inline.

Using the Class

Now that the class is declared, let's see how main() makes use of it. We'll see how objects are defined, and, once defined, how their member functions are accessed.

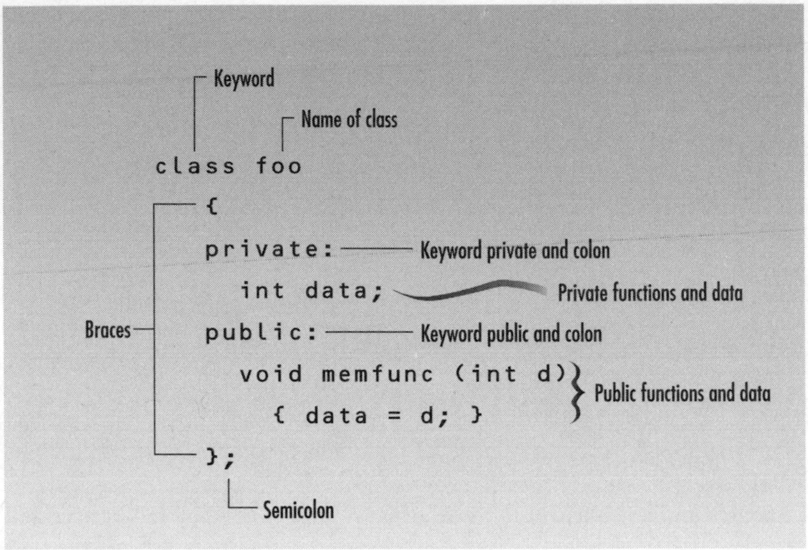

Figure 6.3 Syntax of a class specifier.

Defining Objects

The first statement in `main()`,

```
smallobj s1, s2;
```

defines two objects, **s1** and **s2**, of class **smallobj**. Remember that the declaration for the class **smallobj** does not create any objects. It only describes how they will look when they are created, just as a structure declaration describes how a structure will look but doesn't create any structure variables. It is the *definition* that actually creates objects that can be used by the program. Defining an object is similar to defining a variable of any data type: Space is set aside for it in memory.

Defining objects in this way means creating them. This is also called *instantiating* them. The term *instantiating* arises because an *instance* of the class is created. An object is an instance (that is, a specific example) of a class. Objects are sometimes called *instance variables*.

Calling Member Functions

The next two statements in `main()` call the member function `setdata()`:

```
s1.setdata(1066);
s2.setdata(1776);
```

These statements don't look like normal function calls. Why are the object names **s1** and **s2** connected to the function names with a period? This strange syntax is used to call a member function that is *associated with a specific object*. Because `setdata()` is a member function of the `smallobj` class, it must always be called in connection with an object of this class. It doesn't make sense to say

```
setdata(1066);
```

by itself, because a member function is always called to act on a specific object, not on the class in general. Attempting to access the class this way would be like trying to drive the blueprint of a car. Not only does this statement not make sense, but the compiler will issue an error message if you attempt it. Member functions of a class can be accessed only by an object of that class.

To use a member function, the dot operator (the period) connects the object name and the member function. The syntax is similar to the way we refer to structure members, but the parentheses signal that we're executing a member function rather than referring to a data item. (The dot operator is also called the *class member access* operator.)

The first call to `setdata()`,

```
s1.setdata(1066);
```

executes the `setdata()` member function of the `s1` object. This function sets the variable `somedata` in object `s1` to the value 1066. The second call,

```
s2.setdata(1776);
```

causes the variable `somedata` in `s2` to be set to 1776. Now we have two objects whose `somedata` variables have different values, as shown in Figure 6.4.

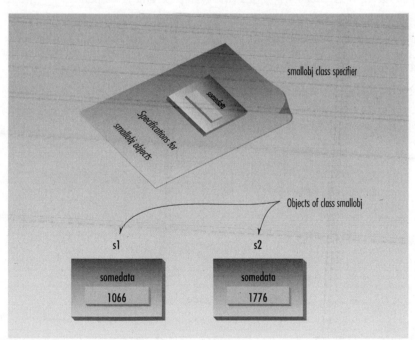

Figure 6.4   Two objects of class `smallobj`.

Similarly, the following two calls to the `showdata()` function will cause the two objects to display their values:

```
s1.showdata();
s2.showdata();
```

Messages

Some object-oriented languages refer to calls to member functions as *messages*. Thus the call

```
s1.showdata();
```

can be thought of as *sending a message* to `s1` telling it to show its data. The term *message* is not a formal term in C++, but it is a useful idea to keep in mind as we discuss member functions. Talking about messages emphasizes that objects are discrete entities and that we communicate with them by calling their member functions. Referring to the analogy with company organization in Chapter 1, it's like sending a message to the secretary in the sales department asking for a list of products sold in the southwest distribution area.

C++ Objects As Physical Objects

In many programming situations, objects in programs represent physical objects: things that can be felt or seen. These situations provide vivid examples of the correspondence between the program and the real world. We'll look at two such situations: widget parts and graphics circles.

Widget Parts as Objects

The `smallobj` class in the last example had only one data item. Let's examine an example of a somewhat more ambitious class. (These are not the same ambitious classes discussed in political science courses.) We'll create a class based on the structure for the widget parts inventory, last seen in such examples as PARTS in Chapter 4, "Structures." Here's the listing for OBJPART:

```cpp
// objpart.cpp
// widget part as an object
#include <iostream>
using namespace std;
///////////////////////////////////////////////////////////////////
class part                   //declare an object
   {
   private:
      int modelnumber;    //ID number of widget
      int partnumber;     //ID number of widget part
      float cost;         //cost of part
   public:
      void setpart(int mn, int pn, float c)  //set data
         {
```

```
               modelnumber = mn;
               partnumber = pn;
               cost = c;
               }
          void showpart()                      //display data
               {
               cout << "Model "     << modelnumber;
               cout << ", part "    << partnumber;
               cout << ", costs $" << cost << endl;
               }
     };
//////////////////////////////////////////////////////////////////
int main()
     {
     part part1;                               //define object
                                               //   of class part
     part1.setpart(6244, 373, 217.55F);  //call member function
     part1.showpart();                   //call member function
     return 0;
     }
```

This program features the class part. Instead of one data item, as SMALLOBJ had, this class has three: modelnumber, partnumber, and cost. A single member function, setpart(), supplies values to all three data items at once. Another function, showpart(), displays the values stored in all three items.

In this example, only one object of type part is created: part1. The member function setpart() sets the three data items in this part to the values 6244, 373, and 217.55. The member function showpart() then displays these values. Here's the output:

```
Model 6244, part 373, costs $217.55
```

This is a somewhat more realistic example than SMALLOBJ. If you were designing an inventory program you might actually want to create a class something like part. It's an example of a C++ object representing a physical object in the real world—a widget part.

Circles as Objects

In our next example, we'll examine an object used to represent a circle: the kind of circle displayed on your computer screen. An image isn't quite as physical an object as a widget part, which you can presumably hold in your hand, but you can certainly see such a circle when your program runs.

Our example is an object-oriented version of the CIRCSTRC program from Chapter 5. (As in that program, you'll need to add the appropriate Console Graphics Lite files to your project. See Appendix E, "Console Graphics Lite," and also the appendix for your particular compiler.) The program creates three circles with various characteristics and displays them. Here's the listing for CIRCLES:

```
// circles.cpp
// circles as graphics objects
#include "msoftcon.h"          // for graphics functions
//////////////////////////////////////////////////////////////////
```

```
class circle                   //graphics circle
    {
protected:
    int xCo, yCo;              //coordinates of center
    int radius;
    color fillcolor;           //color
    fstyle fillstyle;          //fill pattern
public:                        //sets circle attributes
    void set(int x, int y, int r, color fc, fstyle fs)
        {
        xCo = x;
        yCo = y;
        radius = r;
        fillcolor = fc;
        fillstyle = fs;
        }
    void draw()                //draws the circle
        {
        set_color(fillcolor);                //set color
        set_fill_style(fillstyle);           //set fill
        draw_circle(xCo, yCo, radius);       //draw solid circle
        }
    };
///////////////////////////////////////////////////////////////
int main()
    {
    init_graphics();           //initialize graphics system

    circle c1;                 //create circles
    circle c2;
    circle c3;
                               //set circle attributes
    c1.set(15, 7, 5, cBLUE, X_FILL);
    c2.set(41, 12, 7, cRED, O_FILL);
    c3.set(65, 18, 4, cGRFEN, MEDIUM_FILL);

    c1.draw();                 //draw circles
    c2.draw();
    c3.draw();
    set_cursor_pos(1, 25);     //lower left corner
    return 0;
    }
```

The output of this program is the same as that of the CIRCSTRC program in Chapter 5, shown in Figure 5.5 in that chapter. You may find it interesting to compare the two programs. In CIRCLES each circle is represented as a C++ object rather than as a combination of a structure variable and an unrelated `circ_draw()` function, as it was in CIRCSTRC. Notice in CIRCLES how everything connected with a circle—attributes, and functions—is brought together in the class declaration.

In CIRCLES, besides the **draw()** function, the circle class also requires the five-argument **set()** function to set its attributes. We'll see later that it's advantageous to dispense with this function and use a constructor instead.

C++ Objects As Data Types

Here's another kind of entity C++ objects can represent: variables of a user-defined data type. We'll use objects to represent distances measured in the English system, as discussed in Chapter 4. Here's the listing for ENGLOBJ:

```cpp
// englobj.cpp
// objects using English measurements
#include <iostream>
using namespace std;
//////////////////////////////////////////////////////////////
class Distance                      //English Distance class
   {
   private:
      int feet;
      float inches;
   public:
      void setdist(int ft, float in)  //set Distance to args
         { feet = ft; inches = in; }

      void getdist()                 //get length from user
         {
         cout << "\nEnter feet: ";  cin >> feet;
         cout << "Enter inches: ";  cin >> inches;
         }

      void showdist()               //display distance
         { cout << feet << "\'-" << inches << '\"'; }
   };
//////////////////////////////////////////////////////////////
int main()
   {
   Distance dist1, dist2;           //define two lengths

   dist1.setdist(11, 6.25);         //set dist1
   dist2.getdist();                 //get dist2 from user

                                    //display lengths
   cout << "\ndist1 = ";  dist1.showdist();
   cout << "\ndist2 = ";  dist2.showdist();
   cout << endl;
   return 0;
   }
```

In this program, the class **Distance** contains two data items, **feet** and **inches**. This is similar to the **Distance** structure seen in examples in Chapter 4, but here the class **Distance** also has three member functions: **setdist()**, which uses arguments to set feet and inches; **getdist()**, which gets values for feet and inches from the user at the keyboard; and **showdist()**, which displays the distance in feet-and-inches format.

The value of an object of class **Distance** can thus be set in either of two ways. In **main()** we define two objects of class **Distance**: **dist1** and **dist2**. The first is given a value using the `setdist()` member function with the arguments 11 and 6.25, and the second is given a value that is supplied by the user. Here's a sample interaction with the program:

```
Enter feet: 10
Enter inches: 4.75

dist1 = 11'-6.25"     ←—————— provided by arguments
dist2 = 10'-4.75"     ←—————— input by the user
```

Constructors

The ENGLOBJ example shows two ways that member functions can be used to give values to the data items in an object. Sometimes, however, it's convenient if an object can initialize itself when it's first created, without the need to make a separate call to a member function. Automatic initialization is carried out using a special member function called a *constructor*. A constructor is a member function that is executed automatically whenever an object is created. (The term *constructor* is sometimes abbreviated *ctor*, especially in program listings.)

A Counter Example

As an example, we'll create a class of objects that might be useful as a general-purpose programming element. A **counter** is a variable that counts things. Maybe it counts file accesses, or the number of times the user presses the Enter key, or the number of customers entering a bank. Each time such an event takes place, the counter is incremented (1 is added to it). The counter can also be accessed to find the current count.

Let's assume that this counter is important in the program and must be accessed by many different functions. In procedural languages such as C, a counter would probably be implemented as an external variable. However, as we noted in Chapter 1, external variables complicate the program's design and may be modified accidentally. This example, COUNTER, provides a counter variable that can be modified only through its member functions.

```cpp
// counter.cpp
// object represents a counter variable
#include <iostream>
using namespace std;
/////////////////////////////////////////////////////////////////
class Counter
   {
   private:
      unsigned int count;                 //count
   public:
      Counter() : count(0)                //constructor
         { /*empty body*/ }
      void inc_count()                    //increment count
         { count++; }
      int get_count()                     //return count
         { return count; }
   };
```

```
/////////////////////////////////////////////////////////////////
int main()
    {
    Counter c1, c2;                         //define and initialize

    cout << "\nc1=" << c1.get_count();      //display
    cout << "\nc2=" << c2.get_count();

    c1.inc_count();                         //increment c1
    c2.inc_count();                         //increment c2
    c2.inc_count();                         //increment c2

    cout << "\nc1=" << c1.get_count();      //display again
    cout << "\nc2=" << c2.get_count();
    cout << endl;
    return 0;
    }
```

The Counter class has one data member: count, of type unsigned int (since the count is always positive). It has three member functions: the constructor Counter(), which we'll look at in a moment; inc_count(), which adds 1 to count; and get_count(), which returns the current value of count.

Automatic Initialization

When an object of type Counter is first created, we want its count to be initialized to 0. After all, most counts start at 0. We could provide a set_count() function to do this and call it with an argument of 0, or we could provide a zero_count() function, which would always set count to 0. However, such functions would need to be executed every time we created a Counter object.

```
Counter c1;          //every time we do this,
c1.zero_count();     //we must do this too
```

This is mistake prone, because the programmer may forget to initialize the object after creating it. It's more reliable and convenient, especially when there are a great many objects of a given class, to cause each object to initialize itself when it's created. In the Counter class, the constructor Counter() does this. This function is called automatically whenever a new object of type Counter is created. Thus in main(), the statement

```
Counter c1, c2;
```

creates two objects of type Counter. As each is created, its constructor, Counter(), is executed. This function sets the count variable to 0. So the effect of this single statement is to not only create two objects, but also to initialize their count variables to 0.

Same Name As the Class

There are some unusual aspects of constructor functions. First, it is no accident that they have exactly the same name (Counter in this example) as the class of which they are members. This is one way the compiler knows they are constructors.

Second, no return type is used for constructors. Why not? Since the constructor is called automatically by the system, there's no program for it to return anything to; a return value wouldn't make sense. This is the second way the compiler knows they are constructors.

Initializer List

One of the most common tasks a constructor carries out is initializing data members. In the `Counter` class the constructor must initialize the `count` member to 0. You might think that this would be done in the constructor's function body, like this:

```
count()
   { count = 0; }
```

However, this is not the preferred approach (although it does work). Here's how you should initialize a data member:

```
count() : count(0)
   { }
```

The initialization takes place following the member function declarator but before the function body. It's preceded by a colon. The value is placed in parentheses following the member data.

If multiple members must be initialized, they're separated by commas. The result is the *initializer list* (sometimes called by other names, such as the *member-initialization list*).

```
someClass() : m1(7), m2(33), m2(4)  ←——— initializer list
   { }
```

Why not initialize members in the body of the constructor? The reasons are complex, but have to do with the fact that members initialized in the initializer list are given a value before the constructor even starts to execute. This is important in some situations. For example, the initializer list is the only way to initialize `const` member data and references.

Actions more complicated than simple initialization must be carried out in the constructor body, as with ordinary functions.

Messing with the Format

Note that, in writing the functions in this example, we've compressed them so they occupy only two lines each:

```
Counter()

   { count = 0; }
```

This is just the same (as far as the compiler is concerned) as the normal function syntax

```
Counter()
   {
   count = 0;
   }
```

The `main()` part of this program exercises the `Counter` class by creating two counters, `c1` and `c2`. It causes the counters to display their initial values, which—as arranged by the constructor—are 0. It then increments `c1` once and `c2` twice, and again causes the counters to display themselves (non-criminal behavior in this context). Here's the output:

```
c1=0
c2=0
c1=1
c2=2
```

If this isn't enough proof that the constructor is operating as advertised, we can rewrite the constructor to print a message when it executes.

```
Counter() : count(0)

   { cout << "I'm the constructor\n";  }
```

Now the program's output looks like this:

```
I'm the constructor
I'm the constructor
c1=0
c2=0
c1=1
c2=2
```

As you can see, the constructor is executed twice—once for `c1` and once for `c2`—when the statement

```
Counter c1, c2;
```

is executed in `main()`.

Do-It-Yourself Data

Constructors are pretty amazing when you think about it. Whoever writes language compilers (for C or BASIC or even for C++) must execute the equivalent of a constructor when the user defines a variable. If you define an `int`, for example, somewhere there's a constructor allocating four bytes of memory for it. If we can write our own constructors we can start to take over some of the tasks of a compiler writer. This is one step on the path to creating our own data types, as we'll see later.

A Graphics Example

Let's rewrite our earlier CIRCLES example to use a constructor instead of a `set()` function. To handle the initialization of the five attributes of `circles`, this constructor will have five arguments and five items in its initialization list. Here's the listing for CIRCTOR:

```
// circtor.cpp
// circles use constructor for initialization
#include "msoftcon.h"          // for graphics functions
/////////////////////////////////////////////////////////////
```

```
class circle                        //graphics circle
   {
   protected:
      int xCo, yCo;                 //coordinates of center
      int radius;
      color fillcolor;              //color
      fstyle fillstyle;             //fill pattern
   public:
                                    //constructor
      circle(int x, int y, int r, color fc, fstyle fs) :
         xCo(x), yCo(y), radius(r), fillcolor(fc), fillstyle(fs)
         { }

      void draw()                   //draws the circle
         {
         set_color(fillcolor);              //set color
         set_fill_style(fillstyle);         //set fill
         draw_circle(xCo, yCo, radius);     //draw solid circle
         }
   };
////////////////////////////////////////////////////////////////
int main()
   {
   init_graphics();                //initialize graphics system
                                   //create circles
   circle c1(15, 7, 5, cBLUE, X_FILL);
   circle c2(41, 12, 7, cRED, O_FILL);
   circle c3(65, 18, 4, cGREEN, MEDIUM_FILL);

   c1.draw();                      //draw circles
   c2.draw();
   c3.draw();
   set_cursor_pos(1, 25);          //lower left corner
   return 0;
   }
```

This program is similar to CIRCLES, except that `set()` has been replaced by the constructor. Note how this simplifies `main()`. Instead of two separate statements for each object, one to create it and one to set its attributes, now one statement both creates the object and sets its attributes at the same time.

Destructors

We've seen that a special member function—the constructor—is called automatically when an object is first created. You might guess that another function is called automatically when an object is destroyed. This is indeed the case. Such a function is called a *destructor*. A destructor has the same name as the constructor (which is the same as the class name) but is preceded by a tilde:

```
class Foo
   {
   private:
```

```
    int data;
public:
    Foo() : data(0)        //constructor (same name as class)
        {  }
    ~Foo()                 //destructor (same name with tilde)
        {  }
};
```

Like constructors, destructors do not have a return value. They also take no arguments (the assumption being that there's only one way to destroy an object).

The most common use of destructors is to deallocate memory that was allocated for the object by the constructor. We'll investigate these activities in Chapter 10, "Pointers." Until then we won't have much use for destructors.

Objects as Function Arguments

Our next program adds some embellishments to the ENGLOBJ example. It also demonstrates some new aspects of classes: constructor overloading, defining member functions outside the class, and—perhaps most importantly—objects as function arguments. Here's the listing for ENGLCON:

```
// englcon.cpp
// constructors, adds objects using member function
#include <iostream>
using namespace std;
/////////////////////////////////////////////////////////////////
class Distance                      //English Distance class
   {
   private:
      int feet;
      float inches;
   public:                          //constructor (no args)
      Distance() : feet(0), inches(0.0)
         {  }
                                     //constructor (two args)
      Distance(int ft, float in)  : feet(ft), inches(in)
         {  }

      void getdist()                //get length from user
         {
         cout << "\nEnter feet: ";  cin >> feet;
         cout << "Enter inches: ";  cin >> inches;
         }

      void showdist()               //display distance
         { cout << feet << "\'-" << inches << '\"'; }

      void add_dist( Distance, Distance );   //declaration
   };
//-------------------------------------------------------------
                                    //add lengths d2 and d3
```

will be defined outside class

```
void Distance::add_dist(Distance d2, Distance d3)
    {
    inches = d2.inches + d3.inches; //add the inches
    feet = 0;                        //(for possible carry)
    if(inches >= 12.0)               //if total exceeds 12.0,
        {                            //then decrease inches
        inches -= 12.0;              //by 12.0 and
        feet++;                      //increase feet
        }                            //by 1
    feet += d2.feet + d3.feet;       //add the feet
    }
///////////////////////////////////////////////////////////////
int main()
    {
    Distance dist1, dist3;           //define two lengths
    Distance dist2(11, 6.25);        //define and initialize dist2

    dist1.getdist();                 //get dist1 from user
    dist3.add_dist(dist1, dist2);    //dist3 = dist1 + dist2

                                     //display all lengths
    cout << "\ndist1 = ";  dist1.showdist();
    cout << "\ndist2 = ";  dist2.showdist();
    cout << "\ndist3 = ";  dist3.showdist();
    cout << endl;
    return 0;
    }
```

This program starts with a distance `dist2` set to an initial value and adds to it a distance `dist1`, whose value is supplied by the user, to obtain the sum of the distances. It then displays all three distances:

```
Enter feet: 17
Enter inches: 5.75


dist1 = 17'·5.75"
dist2 = 11'·6.25"
dist3 = 29'·0"
```

Let's see how the new features in this program are implemented.

Overloaded Constructors

It's convenient to be able to give variables of type `Distance` a value when they are first created. That is, we would like to use definitions like

```
Distance width(5, 6.25);
```

which defines an object, `width`, and simultaneously initializes it to a value of 5 for **feet** and 6.25 for **inches**.

To do this we write a constructor like this:

```
Distance(int ft, float in) : feet(ft), inches(in)
    {  }
```

This sets the member data `feet` and `inches` to whatever values are passed as arguments to the constructor. So far so good.

However, we also want to define variables of type `Distance` without initializing them, as we did in ENGLOBJ.

```
Distance dist1, dist2;
```

In that program there was no constructor, but our definitions worked just fine. How could they work without a constructor? Because an implicit no-argument constructor is built into the program automatically by the compiler, and it's this constructor that created the objects, even though we didn't define it in the class. This no-argument constructor is called the *default constructor*. If it weren't created automatically by the constructor, you wouldn't be able to create objects of a class for which no constructor was defined.

Often we want to initialize data members in the default (no-argument) constructor as well. If we let the default constructor do it, we don't really know what values the data members may be given. If we care what values they may be given, we need to explicitly define the constructor. In ENGLECON we show how this looks:

```
Distance() : feet(0), inches(0.0)    //default constructor
   { }          //no function body, doesn't do anything
```

The data members are initialized to constant values, in this case the integer value 0 and the `float` value 0.0, for `feet` and `inches` respectively. Now we can use objects initialized with the no-argument constructor and be confident they represent no distance (0 feet plus 0.0 inches) rather than some arbitrary value.

Since there are now two explicit constructors with the same name, `Distance()`, we say the constructor is *overloaded*. Which of the two constructors is executed when an object is created depends on how many arguments are used in the definition:

```
Distance length;        // calls first constructor
Distance width(11, 6.0);  // calls second constructor
```

Member Functions Defined Outside the Class

So far we've seen member functions that were defined inside the class declaration. This need not always be the case. ENGLCON shows a member function, `add_dist()`, that is not defined within the `Distance` class declaration. It is only *declared* inside the class, with the statement

```
void add_dist( Distance, Distance );
```

This tells the compiler that this function is a member of the class but that it will be defined outside the class declaration, someplace else in the listing.

In ENGLCON the `add_dist()` function is defined following the class declaration. It is adapted from the ENGLSTRC program in Chapter 4:

```
                        //add lengths d2 and d3
void Distance::add_dist(Distance d2, Distance d3)
   {
   inches = d2.inches + d3.inches;  //add the inches
```

```
feet = 0;                   //(for possible carry)
if(inches >= 12.0)          //if total exceeds 12.0,
   {                        //then decrease inches
   inches -= 12.0;          //by 12.0 and
   feet++;                  //increase feet
   }                        //by 1
feet += d2.feet + d3.feet;  //add the feet
}
```

The declarator in this definition contains some unfamiliar syntax. The function name, add_dist(), is preceded by the class name, Distance, and a new symbol—the double colon (::). This symbol is called the *scope resolution operator*. It is a way of specifying what class something is associated with. In this situation Distance::add_dist() means "the add_dist() member function of the Distance class." Figure 6.5 shows its usage.

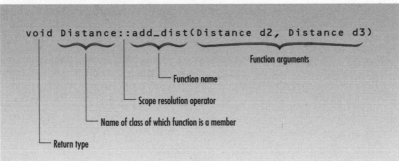

Figure 6.5   The scope resolution operator.

Objects As Arguments

Now we can see how ENGLCON works. The distances **dist1** and **dist3** are created using the default constructor (the one that takes no arguments). The distance **dist2** is created with the constructor that takes two arguments, and is initialized to the values passed in these arguments. A value is obtained for **dist1** by calling the member function **getdist()**, which obtains values from the user.

Now we want to add **dist1** and **dist2** to obtain **dist3**. The function call in **main()**,

```
dist3.add_dist(dist1, dist2);
```

does this. The two distances to be added, **dist1** and **dist2**, are supplied as arguments to **add_dist()**. The syntax for arguments that are objects is the same as that for arguments that are simple data types like **int**: The object name is supplied as the argument. Since **add_dist()** is a member function of the **Distance** class, it can access the private data in any object of class **Distance** supplied to it as an argument, using names like **dist1.inches** and **dist2.feet**.

Close examination of `add_dist()` emphasizes some important truths about member functions. A member function is always given access to the object for which it was called: the object connected to it with the dot operator. But it may be able to access other objects. In the following statement in ENGLCON, what objects can `add_dist()` access?

```
dist3.add_dist(dist1, dist2);
```

Besides `dist3`, the object for which it was called, it can also access `dist1` and `dist2`, because they are supplied as arguments. You might think of `dist3` as a sort of phantom argument; the member function always has access to it, even though it is not supplied as an argument. That's what this statement means: "Execute the `add_dist()` member function of `dist3`." When the variables `feet` and `inches` are referred to within this function, they refer to `dist3.feet` and `dist3.inches`

Notice that the result is not returned by the function. The return type of `add_dist()` is `void`. The result is stored automatically in the `dist3` object. Figure 6.6 shows the two distances `dist1` and `dist2` being added together, with the result stored in `dist3`.

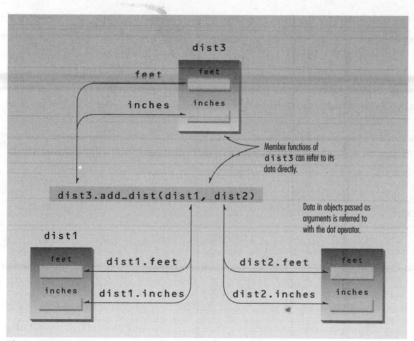

Figure 6.6   Result in this object.

To summarize: every call to a member function is associated with a particular object (unless it's a static function; we'll get to that later). The function has direct access using the member names alone (`feet` and `inches`) to all the members, whether private or public, of that object. It also has indirect access, using the object name and the member name, connected with the dot operator (`dist1.inches` or `dist2.feet`) to other objects of the same class that are passed as arguments.

The Default Copy Constructor

We've seen two ways to initialize objects. A no-argument constructor can initialize data members to constant values, and a multi-argument constructor can initialize data members to values passed as arguments. Let's mention another way to initialize an object: you can initialize it with *another object of the same type*. Surprisingly, you don't need to create a special constructor for this; one is already built into all classes. It's called the *default copy constructor*. It's a one-argument constructor whose argument is an object of the same class as the constructor. The ECOPYCON program shows how this constructor is used.

```cpp
// ecopycon.cpp
// initialize objects using default copy constructor
#include <iostream>
using namespace std;
//////////////////////////////////////////////////////////////////
class Distance                     //English Distance class
   {
   private:
      int feet;
      float inches;
   public:
                                       //constructor (no args)
      Distance() : feet(0), inches(0.0)
         {  }
      //Note: no one-arg constructor
                                       //constructor (two args)
      Distance(int ft, float in)  : feet(ft), inches(in)
         {  }

      void getdist()                //get length from user
         {
         cout << "\nEnter feet: ";  cin >> feet;
         cout << "Enter inches: ";  cin >> inches;
         }
      void showdist()               //display distance
         { cout << feet << "\'-" << inches << '\"'; }
   };
//////////////////////////////////////////////////////////////////
int main()
   {
   Distance dist1(11, 6.25);       //two-arg constructor
   Distance dist2(dist1);          //one-arg constructor
   Distance dist3 = dist1;         //also one-arg constructor

                                   //display all lengths
   cout << "\ndist1 = ";  dist1.showdist();
   cout << "\ndist2 = ";  dist2.showdist();
   cout << "\ndist3 = ";  dist3.showdist();
   cout << endl;
   return 0;
   }
```

We initialize dist1 to the value of 11'-6.25" using the two-argument constructor. Then we define two more objects of type Distance, dist2 and dist3, initializing both to the value of dist1. You might think this would require us to define a one-argument constructor, but initializing an object with another object of the same type is a special case. These definitions both use the default copy constructor. The object dist2 is initialized in the statement

```
Distance dist2(dist1);
```

This causes the default copy constructor for the Distance class to perform a member-by-member copy of dist1 into dist2. Surprisingly, a different format has exactly the same effect, causing dist1 to be copied member-by-member into dist3:

```
Distance dist3 = dist1;
```

Although this looks like an assignment statement, it is not. Both formats invoke the default copy constructor, and can be used interchangeably. Here's the output from the program:

```
dist1 = 11'-6.25"
dist2 = 11'-6.25"
dist3 = 11'-6.25"
```

This shows that the dist2 and dist3 objects have been initialized to the same value as dist1. In Chapter 11, "Virtual Functions and Other Subtleties," we discuss how to create your own custom copy constructor by overloading the default.

Returning Objects from Functions

In the ENGLCON example, we saw objects being passed as arguments to functions. Now we'll see an example of a function that returns an object. We'll modify the ENGLCON program to produce ENGLRET:

```cpp
// englret.cpp
// function returns value of type Distance
#include <iostream>
using namespace std;
/////////////////////////////////////////////////////////////////
class Distance                        //English Distance class
   {
   private:
      int feet;
      float inches;
   public:                            //constructor (no args)
      Distance() : feet(0), inches(0.0)
         { }                          //constructor (two args)
      Distance(int ft, float in) : feet(ft), inches(in)
         { }
```

```
        void getdist()                     //get length from user
           {
           cout << "\nEnter feet: ";  cin >> feet;
           cout << "Enter inches: ";  cin >> inches;
           }
        void showdist()                    //display distance
           { cout << feet << "\'-" << inches << '\"'; }

     Distance add_dist(Distance);     //add
   };
//------------------------------------------------------------
//add this distance to d2, return the sum
Distance Distance::add_dist(Distance d2)
   {
   Distance temp;                     //temporary variable
   temp.inches = inches + d2.inches;  //add the inches
   if(temp.inches >= 12.0)            //if total exceeds 12.0,
      {                               //then decrease inches
      temp.inches -= 12.0;            //by 12.0 and
      temp.feet = 1;                  //increase feet
      }                               //by 1
   temp.feet += feet + d2.feet;       //add the feet
   return temp;
   }
////////////////////////////////////////////////////////////////
int main()
   {
   Distance dist1, dist3;             //define two lengths
   Distance dist2(11, 6.25);          //define, initialize dist2

   dist1.getdist();                   //get dist1 from user
   dist3 = dist1.add_dist(dist2);     //dist3 = dist1 + dist2

                                      //display all lengths
   cout << "\ndist1 = ";  dist1.showdist();
   cout << "\ndist2 = ";  dist2.showdist();
   cout << "\ndist3 = ";  dist3.showdist();
   cout << endl;
   return 0;
   }
```

The ENGLRET program is very similar to ENGLCON, but the differences reveal important aspects of how functions work with objects.

Arguments and Objects

In ENGLCON, two distances were passed to **add_dist()** as arguments, and the result was stored in the object of which **add_dist()** was a member, namely **dist3**. In ENGLRET, one distance, **dist2**, is passed to **add_dist()** as an argument. It is added to the object,

dist1, of which **add_dist()** is a member, and the result is returned from the function. In **main()** the result is assigned to **dist3**, in the statement

```
dist3 = dist1.add_dist(dist2);
```

The effect is the same as the corresponding statement in ENGLCON, but it is somewhat more natural looking, since the assignment operator, =, is used in a natural way. In Chapter 8, "Operator Overloading," we'll see how to use the arithmetic + operator to achieve the even more obvious expression

```
dist3 = dist1 + dist2;
```

Here's the **add_dist()** function from ENGLRET:

```
//add this distance to d2, return the sum
Distance Distance::add_dist(Distance d2)
   {
   Distance temp;                       //temporary variable
   temp.inches = inches + d2.inches;    //add the inches
   if(temp.inches >= 12.0)              //if total exceeds 12.0,
      {                                 //then decrease inches
      temp.inches -= 12.0;              //by 12.0 and
      temp.feet = 1;                    //increase feet
      }                                 //by 1
   temp.feet += feet + d2.feet;         //add the feet
   return temp;
   }
```

Compare this with the same function in ENGLCON. As you can see, there are some subtle differences. In the ENGLRET version, a temporary object of class **Distance** is created. This object holds the sum until it can be returned to the calling program. The sum is calculated by adding two distances. The first is the object of which **add_dist()** is a member, **dist1**. Its member data is accessed in the function as **feet** and **inches**. The second is the object passed as an argument, **dist2**. Its member data is accessed as **d2.feet** and **d2.inches**. The result is stored in **temp** and accessed as **temp.feet** and **temp.inches**. The **temp** object is then returned by the function using the statement

```
return temp;
```

and the statement in **main()** assigns it to **dist3**. Notice that **dist1** is not modified; it simply supplies data to **add_dist()**. Figure 6.7 shows how this looks.

A Card-Game Example

As a larger example of objects modeling the real world, let's look at a variation of the CARDS program from Chapter 4. This program, CARDOBJ, has been rewritten to use objects. It does not introduce any new concepts, but it does use almost all the programming ideas we've discussed up to this point.

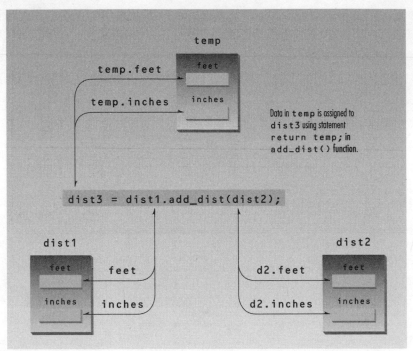

Figure 6.7   Result returned from the temporary object.

As the CARDS example did, CARDOBJ creates three cards with fixed values and switches them around in an attempt to confuse the user about their location. But in CARDOBJ each card is an object of class card. Here's the listing:

```
// cardobj.cpp
// cards as objects
#include <iostream>
using namespace std;

enum Suit { clubs, diamonds, hearts, spades };
const int jack = 11;        //from 2 to 10 are
const int queen = 12;       //integers without names
const int king = 13;
const int ace = 14;
/////////////////////////////////////////////////////////////////
class card
   {
   private:
      int number;           //2 to 10, jack, queen, king, ace
      Suit suit;            //clubs, diamonds, hearts, spades
   public:
      card ()               //constructor (no args)
         { }

                            //constructor (two args)
```

```
          card (int n, Suit s) : number(n), suit(s)
             {  }
          void display();            //display card
          bool isEqual(card);        //same as another card?
       };
//-------------------------------------------------------------
void card::display()                 //display the card
   {
   if( number >= 2 && number <= 10 )
      cout << number << " of ";
   else
      switch(number)
         {
         case jack:  cout << "jack of ";   break;
         case queen: cout << "queen of ";  break;
         case king:  cout << "king of ";   break;
         case ace:   cout << "ace of ";    break;
         }
   switch(suit)
      {
      case clubs:    cout << "clubs"; break;
      case diamonds: cout << "diamonds"; break;
      case hearts:   cout << "hearts"; break;
      case spades:   cout << "spades"; break;
      }
   }
//-------------------------------------------------------------
bool card::isEqual(card c2)          //return true if cards equal
   {
   return ( number==c2.number && suit==c2.suit ) ? true : false;
   }
////////////////////////////////////////////////////////////////
int main()
   {
   card temp, chosen, prize;         //define various cards
   int position;

   card card1( 7, clubs );           //define & initialize card1
   cout << "\nCard 1 is the ";
   card1.display();                  //display card1

   card card2( jack, hearts );       //define & initialize card2
   cout << "\nCard 2 is the ";
   card2.display();                  //display card2

   card card3( ace, spades );        //define & initialize card3
   cout << "\nCard 3 is the ";
   card3.display();                  //display card3

   prize = card3;                    //prize is the card to guess

   cout << "\nI'm swapping card 1 and card 3";
   temp = card3; card3 = card1; card1 = temp;
```

```
   cout << "\nI'm swapping card 2 and card 3";
   temp = card3; card3 = card2; card2 = temp;

   cout << "\nI'm swapping card 1 and card 2";
   temp = card2; card2 = card1; card1 = temp;

   cout << "\nNow, where (1, 2, or 3) is the ";
   prize.display();              //display prize card
   cout << "? ";
   cin >> position;              //get user's guess of position

   switch (position)
      {                          //set chosen to user's choice
      case 1: chosen = card1; break;
      case 2: chosen = card2; break;
      case 3: chosen = card3; break;
      }
   if( chosen.isEqual(prize) )   //is chosen card the prize?
      cout << "That's right!  You win!";
   else
      cout << "Sorry. You lose.";
   cout << "  You chose the ";
   chosen.display();             //display chosen card
   cout << endl;
   return 0;
   }
```

There are two constructors in class **card**. The first, which takes no arguments, is used in **main()** to create the cards **temp**, **chosen**, and **prize**, which are not initialized. The second constructor, which takes two arguments, is used to create **card1**, **card2**, and **card3** and to initialize them to specific values. Besides the constructors, **card** has two other member functions, both defined outside the class.

The **display()** function takes no arguments; it simply displays the card object of which it is a member, using the number and suit data items in the card. The statement in **main()**

```
chosen.display();
```

displays the card chosen by the user.

The **isEqual()** function checks whether the card is equal to a card supplied as an argument. It uses the conditional operator to compare the card of which it is a member with a card supplied as an argument. This function could also have been written with an **if...else** statement,

```
if( number==c2.number && suit==c2.suit )
   return true;
else
   return false;
```

but the conditional operator is more compact.

In **isEqual()** the argument is called **c2** as a reminder that there are two cards in the comparison: The first card is the object of which **isEqual()** is a member. The expression

```
if( chosen.isEqual(prize) )
```

in `main()` compares the card `chosen` with the card `prize`.

Here's the output when the user guesses an incorrect card:

```
Card 1 is the 7 of clubs
Card 2 is the jack of hearts
Card 3 is the ace of spades
I'm swapping card 1 and card 3
I'm swapping card 2 and card 3
I'm swapping card 1 and card 2
Now, where (1, 2, or 3) is the ace of spades? 1
Sorry, you lose. You chose the 7 of clubs
```

Structures and Classes

The examples so far in this book have portrayed structures as a way to group data and classes as a way to group both data and functions. In fact, you can use structures in almost exactly the same way that you use classes. The only formal difference between `class` and `struct` is that in a class the members are private by default, while in a structure they are public by default.

Here's the format we've been using for classes:

```
class foo
   {
   private:
      int data1;
   public:
      void func();
   };
```

Because private is the default in classes, this keyword is unnecessary. You can just as well write

```
class foo
   {
      int data1;
   public:
      void func();
   };
```

and the `data1` will still be private. Many programmers prefer this style. We like to include the `private` keyword because it offers an increase in clarity.

If you want to use a structure to accomplish the same thing as this class, you can dispense with the keyword `public`, provided you put the public members before the private ones:

```
struct foo
   {
      void func();
   private:
```

```
    int data1;
};
```

since public is the default. However, in most situations programmers don't use a `struct` this way. They use structures to group only data, and classes to group both data and functions.

Classes, Objects, and Memory

We've probably given you the impression that each object created from a class contains separate copies of that class's data and member functions. This is a good first approximation, since it emphasizes that objects are complete, self-contained entities, designed using the class declaration. The mental image here is of cars (objects) rolling off an assembly line, each one made according to a blueprint (the class declaration).

Things are not quite so simple. It's true that each object has its own separate data items. On the other hand, contrary to what you may have been led to believe, all the objects in a given class use the same member functions. The member functions are created and placed in memory only once—when they are defined in the class declaration. This makes sense; there's really no point in duplicating all the member functions in a class every time you create another object of that class, since the functions for each object are identical. The data items, however, will hold different values, so there must be a separate instance of each data item for each object. Data is therefore placed in memory when each object is defined, so there is a separate set of data for each object. Figure 6.8 shows how this looks.

In the SMALLOBJ example there are two objects of type `smallobj`, so there are two instances of `somedata` in memory. However, there is only one instance of the functions `setdata()` and `showdata()`. These functions are shared by all the objects of the class. There is no conflict because (at least in a single-threaded system) only one function is executed at a time.

In most situations you don't need to know that there is only one member function for an entire class. It's simpler to visualize each object as containing both its own data and its own member functions. But in some situations, such as in estimating the size of an executing program, it's helpful to know what's happening behind the scenes.

Static Class Data

Having said that each object contains its own separate data, we must now amend that slightly. If a data item in a class is declared as `static`, then only one such item is created for the entire class, no matter how many objects there are. A static data item is useful when all objects of the same class must share a common item of information. A member variable defined as `static` has characteristics similar to a normal static variable: It is visible only within the class, but its lifetime is the entire program. It continues to exist even if there are no items of the class. (See Chapter 5 for a discussion of static variables.) However, while a normal static variable is used to retain information between calls to a function, static class member data is used to share information among the objects of a class.

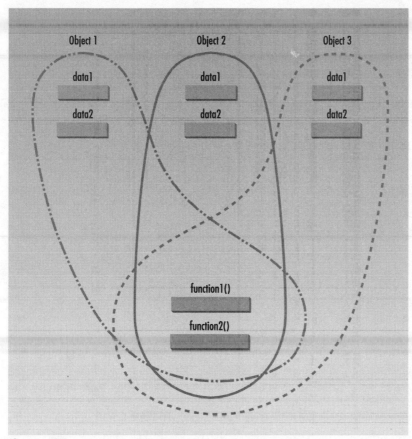

Figure 6.8   Objects, data, functions, and memory.

Uses of Static Class Data

Why would you want to use static member data? As an example, suppose an object need-ed to know how many other objects of its class were in the program. In a road-racing game, for example, a race car might want to know how many other cars were still in the race. In this case a static variable **count** could be included as a member of the class. All the objects would have access to this variable. It would be the same variable for all of them; they would all see the same count.

An Example of Static Class Data

Here's an example, STATDATA, that demonstrates a simple static data member:

```
// statdata.cpp
// static class data
#include <iostream>
```

```
using namespace std;
//////////////////////////////////////////////////////////////
class foo
   {
   private:
      static int count;     //only one data item for all objects
                            //note: *declaration* only!
   public:
      foo()                 //increments count when object created
         { count++; }
      int getcount()        //returns count
         { return count; }
   };
//--------------------------------------------------------------
int foo::count = 0;         //*definition* of count
//////////////////////////////////////////////////////////////
int main()
   {
   foo f1, f2, f3;          //create three objects

   cout << "count is " << f1.getcount() << endl;  //each object
   cout << "count is " << f2.getcount() << endl;  //sees the
   cout << "count is " << f3.getcount() << endl;  //same value
   return 0;
   }
```

The class `foo` in this example has one data item, `count`, which is type `static int`. The constructor for this class causes `count` to be incremented. In `main()` we define three objects of class `foo`. Since the constructor is called three times, `count` is incremented three times. Another member function, `getcount()`, returns the value in count. We call this function from all three objects, and—as we expected—each prints the same value. Here's the output:

```
count is 3     ←——————— static data
count is 3
count is 3
```

If we had used an ordinary automatic variable—as opposed to a static variable—for `count`, each constructor would have incremented its own private copy of `count` once, and the output would have been

```
count is 1     ←——————— automatic data
count is 1
count is 1
```

Static class variables are not used as often as ordinary non-static variables, but they are important in many situations. Figure 6.9 shows how static variables compare with automatic variables.

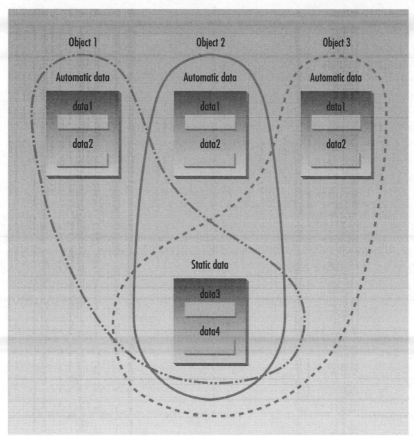

Figure 6.9   Static versus automatic member variables.

Separate Declaration and Definition

Static member data requires an unusual format. Ordinary variables are declared (the compiler is told about their name and type) and defined (the compiler sets aside memory to hold the variable) in the same statement. Static member data, on the other hand, requires two separate statements. The variable's declaration appears in the class declaration, but the variable is actually defined outside the class, in much the same way as an external variable.

Why is this two-part approach used? If static member data were defined inside the class declaration (as it actually was in early versions of C++), it would violate the idea that a class declaration is only a blueprint and does not set aside any memory. Putting the definition of static member data outside of the class also serves to emphasize that the memory space for such data is allocated only once, before the program starts to execute, and that one static member variable is accessed by an entire class; each object does not have its own version of the variable, as it would with ordinary member data. In this way a static member variable is more like a global variable.

It's easy to handle static data incorrectly, and the compiler is not helpful about such errors. If you include the declaration of a static variable but forget its definition, there will be no warning from the compiler. Everything looks fine until you get to the linker, which will tell you that you're trying to reference an undeclared external variable. This happens even if you include the definition, but forget the class name (the `foo::` in the STATDATA example).

const and Classes

We've seen several examples of `const` used on normal variables to prevent them from being modified, and in Chapter 5 we saw that `const` can be used with function arguments to keep a function from modifying a variable passed to it by reference. Now that we know about classes, we can introduce some other uses of `const`: on member functions, on member function arguments, and on objects. These concepts work together to provide some surprising benefits.

const Member Functions

A `const` member function guarantees that it will never modify any of its class's member data. The CONSTFU program shows how this works.

```
//constfu.cpp
//demonstrates const member functions
/
class aClass
   {
   private:
      int alpha;
   public:
      void nonFunc()        //non-const member function
         { alpha = 99; }    //OK

      void conFunc() const  //const member function
         { alpha = 99; }    //ERROR: can't modify a member
   };
```

The non-const function `nonFunc()` can modify member data alpha, but the constant function `conFunc()` can't. If it tries to, a compiler error results.

A function is made into a constant function by placing the keyword `const` after the declarator but before the function body. If there is a separate function declaration, `const` must be used in both declaration and definition. Member functions that do nothing but acquire data from an object are obvious candidates for being made `const`, because they don't need to modify any data.

Making a function const helps the compiler flag errors, and tells anyone looking at the listing that you intended the function not to modify anything in its object. It also makes possible the creation and use of const objects, which we'll discuss soon.

A Distance Example

To avoid raising too many subjects at once we have, up to now, avoided using const member functions in the example programs. However, there are many places where const member functions should be used. For example, in the Distance class, shown in several programs, the showdist() member function could be made const because it doesn't (or certainly shouldn't!) modify any of the data in the object for which it was called. It should simply display the data.

Also, in ENGLRET, the add_dist() function should not modify any of the data in the object for which it was called. This object should simply be added to the object passed as an argument, and the resulting sum is returned. We've modified the ENGLRET program to show how these two constant functions look. Here's the listing for ENGCONST:

```cpp
// engConst.cpp
// const member functions and const arguments to member functions
#include <iostream>
using namespace std;
////////////////////////////////////////////////////////////////
class Distance                          //English Distance class
   {
   private:
      int feet;
      float inches;
   public:                              //constructor (no args)
      Distance() : feet(0), inches(0.0)
         { }                            //constructor (two args)
      Distance(int ft, float in) : feet(ft), inches(in)
         { }

      void getdist()                    //get length from user
         {
         cout << "\nEnter feet: ";  cin >> feet;
         cout << "Enter inches: ";  cin >> inches;
         }
      void showdist() const             //display distance
         { cout << feet << "\'-" << inches << '\"'; }

      Distance add_dist(const Distance&) const;    //add
   };
//------------------------------------------------------------
//add this distance to d2, return the sum
Distance Distance::add_dist(const Distance& d2) const
   {
   Distance temp;                       //temporary variable

// feet = 0;                            //ERROR: can't modify this
// d2.feet = 0;                         //ERROR: can't modify d2
```

```
        temp.inches = inches + d2.inches;  //add the inches
        if(temp.inches >= 12.0)            //if total exceeds 12.0,
            {                              //then decrease inches
            temp.inches -= 12.0;           //by 12.0 and
            temp.feet = 1;                 //increase feet
            }                              //by 1
        temp.feet += feet + d2.feet;       //add the feet
        return temp;
        }
//////////////////////////////////////////////////////////////
int main()
    {
    Distance dist1, dist3;          //define two lengths
    Distance dist2(11, 6.25);       //define, initialize dist2

    dist1.getdist();                //get dist1 from user
    dist3 = dist1.add_dist(dist2);  //dist3 = dist1 + dist2

                                    //display all lengths
    cout << "\ndist1 = ";   dist1.showdist();
    cout << "\ndist2 = ";   dist2.showdist();
    cout << "\ndist3 = ";   dist3.showdist();
    cout << endl;
    return 0;
    }
```

Here `showdist()` and `add_dist()` are both constant member functions. In `add_dist()` we show in the first commented statement, `feet = 0`, that a compiler error is generated if you attempt to modify any of the data in the object for which this constant function was called.

const Member Function Arguments

We mentioned in Chapter 5 that if an argument is passed to an ordinary function by reference, and you don't want the function to modify it, then the argument should be made `const` in the function declaration (and definition). This is true of member functions as well. In ENGCONST the argument to `add_dist()` is passed by reference, and we want to make sure that ENGCONST won't modify this variable, which is `dist2` in `main()` Therefore we make the argument `d2` to `add_dist()` `const` in both declaration and definition. The second commented statement shows that the compiler will flag as an error any attempt by `add_dist()` to modify any member data of its argument `dist2`.

const Objects

In several example programs we've seen that we can apply `const` to variables of basic types like `int` to keep them from being modified. In a similar way we can apply `const` to objects of classes. When an object is declared as `const`, you can't modify it. It follows that you can use only `const` member functions with it, because they're the only ones that guarantee not to modify it. The CONSTOBJ program shows an example.

```
// constObj.cpp
// constant Distance objects
#include <iostream>
using namespace std;
/////////////////////////////////////////////////////////////
class Distance                          //English Distance class
   {
   private:
      int feet;
      float inches;
   public:                              //2-arg constructor
      Distance(int ft, float in) : feet(ft), inches(in)
         {  }
      void getdist()                    //user input; non-const func
         {
         cout << "\nEnter feet: ";  cin >> feet;
         cout << "Enter inches: ";  cin >> inches;
         }
      void showdist() const            //display distance; const func
         { cout << feet << "\'-" << inches << '\"'; }
   };
/////////////////////////////////////////////////////////////
int main()
   {
   const Distance football(300, 0);

// football.getdist();                  //ERROR: getdist() not const
   cout << "football = ";
   football.showdist();                 //OK
   cout << endl;
   return 0;
   }
```

A football field (for American-style football) is exactly 300 feet long. If we were to use the length of a football field in a program, it would make sense to make it const, because changing it would represent the end of the world for football fans. The CONSTOBJ program makes football a const variable. Now only const functions, such as showdist(), can be called for this object. Non-const functions, such as getdist(), which gives the object a new value obtained from the user, are illegal. In this way the compiler enforces the const value of football.

When you're designing classes it's a good idea to make const any function that does not modify any of the data in its object. This allows the user of the class to create const objects. These objects can use any const function, but cannot use any non-const function. Remember, using const helps the compiler to help you.

What Does It All Mean?

Now that you've been introduced to classes and objects, you may wonder what benefit they really offer. After all, as you can see by comparing several of the programs in this chapter with those in Chapter 4, it's possible to do the same sorts of things with a procedural approach as it is with objects.

One benefit of OOP that you may have glimpsed already is the close correspondence between the real-world things being modeled *by* the program and the C++ objects *in* the program. A widget part object in a program represents a widget part in the real world, a card object represents a card, a circle object represents a graphics circle, and so on. In C++ everything about a widget part is included in its class description—the part number and other data items, and the functions necessary to access and operate on this data. This makes it easy to conceptualize a programming problem. You figure out what parts of the problem can be most usefully represented as objects, and then put all the data and functions connected with that object into the class. If you're using a C++ class to represent a playing card, you put into this class the data items that represent the value of the card, and also the functions to set value, retrieve it, display it, compare it, and so on.

In a procedural program, by contrast, the external variables and functions connected with a real-world object are distributed all over the listing; they don't form a single, easily grasped unit.

In some situations it may not be obvious what parts of a real-life situation should be made into objects. If you're writing a program that plays chess, for instance, what are the objects? The chessmen, the squares on the board, or possibly entire board positions?

In small programs, such as many of those in this book, you can often proceed by trial and error. You break a problem into objects in one way and write trial class declarations for these objects. If the classes seem to match reality in a useful way, you continue. If they don't, you may need to start over, selecting different entities to be classes. The more experience you have with OOP, the easier it will be to break a programming problem into classes.

Larger programs may prove too complex for this trial and error approach. A new field, Object-Oriented Design (OOD) is increasingly applied to analyzing a programming problem and figuring out what classes and objects should be used to represent the real-world situation (which is often called the *problem domain*). We'll discuss this methodology in detail in Chapter 16, "Object-Oriented Design."

Some of the benefits of object-oriented programming are probably not apparent at this point. Remember that OOP was devised to cope with the complexity of large programs. Smaller programs, such as the examples in this chapter, have less need for the organizational power that OOP provides. The larger the program, the greater the benefit. But even for small programs, once you start thinking in object-oriented terms, the OO design approach becomes natural and surprisingly helpful. One advantage is that in an OO program the compiler can find many more conceptual errors than in a procedural program.

Summary

A class is a specification or blueprint for a number of objects. Objects consist of both data and functions that operate on that data. In a class declaration, the members—whether data or functions—can be `private`, meaning they can be accessed only by member functions of that class, or `public`, meaning they can be accessed by any function in the program.

A member function is a function that is a member of a class. Member functions have access to an object's private data, while non-member functions do not.

A constructor is a member function, with the same name as its class, that is executed every time an object of the class is created. A constructor has no return type but can take arguments. It is often used to give initial values to object data members. Constructors can be overloaded, so an object can be initialized in different ways.

A destructor is a member function with the same name as its class but preceded by a tilde (~). It is called when an object is destroyed. A destructor takes no arguments and has no return value.

In the computer's memory there is a separate copy of the data members for each object that is created from a class, but there is only one copy of a class's member functions. A data item can be restricted to a single instance for all objects of a class by making it `static`.

One reason to use OOP is the close correspondence between real-world objects and OOP classes. Deciding what objects and classes to use in a program can be complicated. For small programs, trial and error may be sufficient. For large programs a more systematic approach is usually needed.

Questions

Answers to questions can be found in Appendix G, "Answers to Questions and Exercises."

1. What is the purpose of a class declaration?

2. A _____ has the same relation to an _____ that a basic data type has to a variable of that type.

3. In a class declaration, data or functions designated `private` are accessible

    a. to any function in the program.

    b. only if you know the password.

    c. to member functions of that class.

    d. only to public members of the class.

4. Write a class declaration that creates a class called `leverage` with one private data member, `crowbar`, of type `int` and one public function whose declaration is `void pry()`.

5. True or false: Data items in a class must be private.

6. Write a statement that defines an object called `lever1` of the `leverage` class described in Question 4.

7. The dot operator (or class member access operator) connects the following two entities (reading from left to right):

   a. A class member and a class object

   b. A class object and a class

   c. A class and a member of that class

   d. A class object and a member of that class

8. Write a statement that executes the `pry()` function in the `lever1` object, as described in Questions 4 and 6.

9. Member functions defined inside a class declaration are _____ by default.

10. Write a member function called `getcrow()` for the `leverage` class described in Question 4. This function should return the value of the `crowbar` data. Assume the function is defined within the class declaration.

11. A constructor is executed automatically when an object is _____.

12. A constructor's name is the same as _____.

13. Write a constructor that initializes to 0 the `crowbar` data, a member of the `leverage` class described in Question 4. Assume the constructor is defined within the class declaration.

14. True or false: In a class you can have more than one constructor with the same name.

15. A member function can always access the data

    a. in the object of which it is a member.

    b. in the class of which it is a member.

    c. in any object of the class of which it is a member.

    d. in the public part of its class.

16. Assume the member function `getcrow()` described in Question 10 is defined outside the class declaration. Write the declaration that goes inside the class declaration.

17. Write a revised version of the `getcrow()` member function from Question 10 that is defined outside the class declaration.

18. The only technical difference between structures and classes in C++ is that _____.

19. If three objects of a class are defined, how many copies of that class's data items are stored in memory? How many copies of its member functions?

20. Sending a message to an object is the same as _____.

21. Classes are useful because they

    a. are removed from memory when not in use.

    b. permit data to be hidden from other classes.

    c. bring together all aspects of an entity in one place.

    d. can closely model objects in the real world.

22. True or false: There is a simple but precise methodology for dividing a real-world programming problem into classes.

23. For the object for which it was called, a **const** member function

    a. can modify both **const** and non-**const** member data.

    b. can modify only **const** member data.

    c. can modify only non-**const** member data.

    d. can modify neither **const** nor non-**const** member data.

24. True or false: If you declare a **const** object, it can only be used with **const** member functions.

25. Write a declaration (not a definition) for a **const void** function called **aFunc()** that takes one **const** argument called **jerry** of type **float**.

Exercises

Answers to the starred exercises can be found in Appendix G.

*1. Create a class that imitates part of the functionality of the basic data type **int**. Call the class **Int** (note different spelling). The only data in this class is an **int** variable. Include member functions to initialize an **Int** to 0, to initialize it to an **int** value, to display it (it looks just like an **int**), and to add two **Int** values.

Write a program that exercises this class by creating two initialized and one uninitialized **Int** values, adding these two initialized values and placing the response in the uninitialized value, and then displaying this result.

*2. Imagine a tollbooth at a bridge. Cars passing by the booth are expected to pay a 50 cent toll. Mostly they do, but sometimes a car goes by without paying. The tollbooth keeps track of the number of cars that have gone by, and of the total amount of money collected.

Model this tollbooth with a class called **tollBooth**. The two data items are a type **unsigned int** to hold the total number of cars, and a type **double** to hold the total amount of money collected. A constructor initializes both of these to 0. A member function called **payingCar()** increments the car total and adds 0.50 to the cash total. Another function, called **nopayCar()**, increments the car total but adds nothing to the cash total. Finally, a member function called **display()** displays the two totals. Make appropriate member functions **const**.

Include a program to test this class. This program should allow the user to push one key to count a paying car, and another to count a nonpaying car. Pushing the [Escape] key should cause the program to print out the total cars and total cash and then exit.

*3. Create a class called **time** that has separate **int** member data for hours, minutes, and seconds. One constructor should initialize this data to 0, and another should initialize it to fixed values. Another member function should display it, in 11:59:59 format. The final member function should add two objects of type **time** passed as arguments.

A **main()** program should create two initialized **time** objects (should they be **const**?) and one that isn't initialized. Then it should add the two initialized values together, leaving the result in the third **time** variable. Finally it should display the value of this third variable. Make appropriate member functions **const**.

4. Create an **employee** class, basing it on Exercise 4 of Chapter 4. The member data should comprise an **int** for storing the employee number, and a **float** for storing the employee's compensation. Member functions should allow the user to enter this data and display it. Write a **main()** that allows the user to enter data for three employees and display it.

5. Start with the **date** structure in Exercise 5 in Chapter 4 and transform it into a **date** class. Its member data should consist of three **int**s: **month**, **day**, and **year**. It should also have two member functions: **getdate()**, which allows the user to enter a date in 12/31/97 format, and **showdate()**, which displays the date.

6. Extend the **employee** class of Exercise 4 to include a **date** class (see Exercise 5) and an **etype enum** (see Exercise 6 in Chapter 4). An object of the **date** class should be used to hold the date of first employment; that is, the date when the employee was hired. The **etype** variable should hold the employee's type: laborer, secretary, manager, and so on. These two items will be private member data in the **employee** declaration, just like the employee number and salary. You'll need to extend the **getemploy()** and **putemploy()** functions to obtain this new information from the user and display it. These functions will probably need **switch** statements to handle the **etype** variable. Write a **main()** program that

allows the user to enter data for three employee variables, which then displays this data.

7. In ocean navigation, locations are measured in degrees and minutes of latitude and longitude. Thus if you're lying off the mouth of Papeete Harbor in Tahiti, your location is 149 degrees 34.8 minutes west longitude, and 17 degrees 31.5 minutes south latitude. This is written as 149834.8' W, 17831.5' S. There are 60 minutes in a degree. (An older system also divided a minute into 60 seconds, but the modern approach is to use decimal minutes instead.) Longitude is measured from 0 to 180 degrees, east or west from Greenwich, England, to the international dateline in the Pacific. Latitude is measured from 0 to 90 degrees, north or south from the equator to the poles.

   Create a class `angle` that includes three member variables: an `int` for degrees, a `float` for minutes, and a `char` for the direction letter (N, S, E, or W). This class can hold either a latitude variable or a longitude variable. Write one member function to obtain an angle value (in degrees and minutes) and a direction from the user, and a second to display the angle value in 179859.9' E format. Also write a three-argument constructor. Write a `main()` program that displays an angle initialized with the constructor, and then, within a loop, allows the user to input any angle value, and then displays the value. You can use the hex character constant `'\xF8'` which usually prints a degree (°) symbol.

8. Create a class that includes a data member that holds a "serial number" for each object created from the class. That is, the first object created will be numbered 1, the second 2, and so on.

   To do this, you'll need another data member that records a count of how many objects have been created so far. (This member should apply to the class as a whole; not to individual objects. What keyword specifies this?) Then, as each object is created, its constructor can examine this count member variable to determine the appropriate serial number for the new object.

   Add a member function that permits an object to report its own serial number. Then write a `main()` program that creates three objects and queries each one about its serial number. They should respond I am object number 2, and so on.

9. Transform the `fraction` structure from Exercise 8, Chapter 4 into a `fraction` class. Member data is the fraction's numerator and denominator. Member functions should accept input from the user in the form `3/5`, and output the fraction's value in the same format. Another member function should add two fraction values. Write a `main()` program that allows the user to repeatedly input two fractions, and which then displays their sum. After each operation ask if the user wants to continue.

10. Create a class called `ship` that incorporates a ship's number and location. Use the approach of Exercise 8 to number each `ship` object as it is created. Use two variables of the `angle` class from Exercise 7 to represent the ship's latitude and longitude. A member function of the `ship` class should get a position from the user and store it in the object; another should report the serial number and position. Write a `main()` program that creates three ships, asks the user to input the position of each, and then displays each ship's number and position.

11. Modify the four-function fraction calculator of Exercise 12, Chapter 5 to use a `fraction` class rather than a structure. There should be member functions for input and output, as well as for the four arithmetical operations. While you're at it, you might as well install the capability to reduce fractions to lowest terms. Here's a member function that will reduce the `fraction` object of which it is a member to lowest terms. It finds the greatest common divisor (gcd) of the fraction's numerator and denominator, and uses this gcd to divide both numbers.

```
void fraction::lowterms()     // change ourself to lowest terms
   {
   long tnum, tden, temp, gcd;

   tnum = labs(num);          // use non-negative copies
   tden = labs(den);          //     (needs cmath)
   if(tden==0 )    // check for n/0
      { cout << "Illegal fraction: division by 0"; exit(1); }
   else if( tnum==0 )         // check for 0/n
      { num=0; den = 1; return; }

   // this 'while' loop finds the gcd of tnum and tden
   while(tnum != 0)
      {
      if(tnum < tden)         // ensure numerator larger
         { temp=tnum; tnum=tden; tden=temp; }  // swap them
      tnum = tnum - tden;     // subtract them
      }
   gcd = tden;                // this is greatest common divisor
   num = num / gcd;           // divide both num and den by gcd
   den = den / gcd;           // to reduce frac to lowest terms
   }
```

You can call this function at the end of each arithmetic function, or just before you perform output. You'll also need the usual member functions: four arithmetic operations, input, and display. You may find a two-argument constructor useful.

12. Note that one advantage of the OOP approach is that an entire class can be used, without modification, in a different program. Use the `fraction` class from Exercise 11 in a program that generates a multiplication table for fractions. Let the user input a denominator, and then generate all

combinations of two such fractions that are between 0 and 1, and multiply them together. Here's an example of the output if the denominator is 6:

	1/6	1/3	1/2	2/3	5/6
1/6	1/36	1/18	1/12	1/9	5/36
1/3	1/18	1/9	1/6	2/9	5/18
1/2	1/12	1/6	1/4	1/3	5/12
2/3	1/9	2/9	1/3	4/9	5/9
5/6	5/36	5/18	5/12	5/9	25/36

CHAPTER 7

ARRAYS AND STRINGS

You will learn about the following in this chapter:

- Array definitions
- Accessing array elements
- Arrays as class members

- Arrays of objects
- Strings
- String input/output

In everyday life we commonly group similar objects into units. We buy peas by the can and eggs by the carton. In computer languages we also need to group together data items of the same type. The most basic mechanism that accomplishes this in C++ is the *array*. Arrays can hold a few data items or tens of thousands. The data items grouped in an array can be simple types like `int` or `float`, or they can be user-defined types like structures and objects.

Arrays are like structures in that they both group a number of items into a larger unit. But while a structure usually groups items of different types, an array groups items of the same type. More importantly, the items in a structure are accessed by name, while those in an array are accessed by an index number. Using an index number to specify an item allows easy access to a large number of items.

Arrays exist in almost every computer language. Arrays in C++ are similar to those in other languages, and identical to those in C.

In this chapter we'll look first at arrays of basic data types like `int` and `char`. Then we'll examine arrays used as data members in classes, and arrays used to hold objects. Thus this chapter is intended not only to introduce arrays, but to increase your understanding of object-oriented programming.

In Standard C++ the array is not the only way to group elements of the same type. A *vector*, which is part of the Standard Template library, is another approach. We'll look at vectors in Chapter 15, "The Standard Template Library."

In this chapter we'll also look at two different approaches to strings, which are used to store and manipulate text. The first kind of string is an array of type `char`, and the second is a member of the Standard C++ `string` class.

Array Fundamentals

A simple example program will serve to introduce arrays. This program, REPLAY, creates an array of four integers representing the ages of four people. It then asks the user to enter four values, which it places in the array. Finally, it displays all four values.

```cpp
// replay.cpp
// gets four ages from user, displays them
#include <iostream>
using namespace std;

int main()
   {
   int age[4];                      //array 'age' of 4 ints

   for(int j=0; j<4; j++)           //get 4 ages
      {
      cout << "Enter an age: ";
      cin >> age[j];                //access array element
      }
   for(j=0; j<4; j++)               //display 4 ages
      cout << "You entered " << age[j] << endl;
   return 0;
   }
```

Here's a sample interaction with the program:

```
Enter an age: 44
Enter an age: 16
Enter an age: 23
Enter an age: 68

You entered 44
You entered 16
You entered 23
You entered 68
```

The first `for` loop gets the ages from the user and places them in the array, while the second reads them from the array and displays them.

Defining Arrays

Like other variables in C++, an array must be defined before it can be used to store information. And, like other definitions, an array definition specifies a variable type and a name. But it includes another feature: a size. The size specifies how many data items the array will contain. It immediately follows the name, and is surrounded by square brackets. Figure 7.1 shows the syntax of an array definition.

In the REPLAY example, the array is type `int`. The name of the array comes next, followed immediately by an opening bracket, the array size, and a closing bracket. The number in brackets must be a constant or an expression that evaluates to a constant, and should also be an integer. In the example we use the value 4.

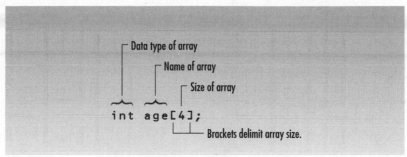

Figure 7.1   Syntax of array definition.

Array Elements

The items in an array are called *elements* (in contrast to the items in a structure, which are called *members*). As we noted, all the elements in an array are of the same type; only the values vary. Figure 7.2 shows the elements of the array **age**. (In the figure type **int** is assumed to occupy two bytes, as in 16-bit systems.)

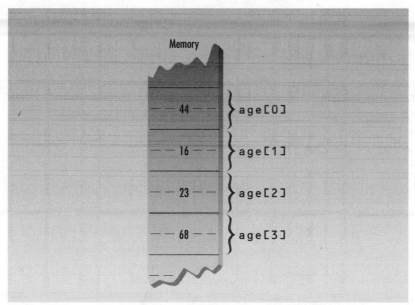

Figure 7.2   Array elements.

Following the conventional (although in some ways backward) approach, memory grows downward in the figure. That is, the first array elements are on the top of the page; later elements extend downward.

Since each element in **age** is an integer, it occupies four bytes (on 32-bit systems). As specified in the definition, the array has exactly four elements.

Notice that the first array element is numbered 0. Thus, since there are four elements, the last one is number 3. This is a potentially confusing situation; you might think the last element in a four-element array would be number 4, but it's not.

Accessing Array Elements

In the REPLAY example we access each array element twice. The first time, we insert a value into the array, with the line

```
cin >> age[j];
```

The second time, we read it out with the line

```
cout << "\nYou entered " << age[j];
```

In both cases, the expression for the array element is

```
age[j]
```

This consists of the name of the array, followed by brackets delimiting a variable j. Which of the four array elements is specified by this expression depends on the value of j; **age[0]** refers to the first element, **age[1]** to the second, **age[2]** to the third, and **age[3]** to the fourth. The variable (or constant) in the brackets is called the *array index*.

Since j is the loop variable in both **for** loops, it starts at 0 and is incremented until it reaches 3, thereby accessing each of the array elements in turn.

Averaging Array Elements

Here's another example of an array at work. This one, SALES, invites the user to enter a series of six values representing widget sales for each day of the week (excluding Sunday), and then calculates the average of these values. We use an array of type **double** so that monetary values can be entered.

```
// sales.cpp
// averages a weeks's widget sales (6 days)
#include <iostream>
using namespace std;

int main()
   {
   const int SIZE = 6;                //size of array
   double sales[SIZE];                //array of 6 variables

   cout << "Enter widget sales for 6 days\n";
   for(int j=0; j<SIZE; j++)          //put figures in array
      cin >> sales[j];

   double total = 0;
   for(j=0; j<SIZE; j++)              //read figures from array
      total += sales[j];             //to find total
```

```
double average = total / SIZE;  // find average
cout << "Average = " << average << endl;
return 0;
}
```

Here's some sample interaction with SALES:

```
Enter widget sales for 6 days
352.64
867.70
781.32
867.35
746.21
189.45
Average = 634.11
```

A new detail in this program is the use of a **const** variable for the array size and loop limits. This variable is defined at the start of the listing:

```
const int SIZE = 6;
```

Using a variable (instead of a number, such as the 4 used in the last example) makes it easier to change the array size: Only one program line needs to be changed to change the array size, loop limits, and anywhere else the array size appears. The all-uppercase name reminds us that the variable cannot be modified in the program.

Initializing Arrays

You can give values to each array element when the array is first defined. Here's an example, DAYS, that sets 12 array elements in the array **days_per_month** to the number of days in each month.

```
// days.cpp
// shows days from start of year to date specified
#include <iostream>
using namespace std;

int main()
    {
    int month, day, total_days;
    int days_per_month[12] = { 31, 28, 31, 30, 31, 30,
                               31, 31, 30, 31, 30, 31 };

    cout << "\nEnter month (1 to 12): ";  //get date
    cin >> month;
    cout << "Enter day (1 to 31): ";
    cin >> day;
    total_days = day;                      //separate days
    for(int j=0; j<month-1; j++)           //add days each month
       total_days += days_per_month[j];
    cout << "Total days from start of year is: " << total_days
         << endl;
    return 0;
    }
```

The program calculates the number of days from the beginning of the year to a date specified by the user. (Beware: It doesn't work for leap years.) Here's some sample interaction:

```
Enter month (1 to 12): 3
Enter day (1 to 31): 11
Total days from start of year is: 70
```

Once it gets the month and day values, the program first assigns the day value to the `total_days` variable. Then it cycles through a loop, where it adds values from the `days_per_month` array to `total_days`. The number of such values to add is one less than the number of months. For instance, if the user enters month 5, the values of the first four array elements (31, 28, 31, and 30) are added to the total.

The values to which `days_per_month` is initialized are surrounded by braces and separated by commas. They are connected to the array expression by an equal sign. Figure 7.3 shows the syntax.

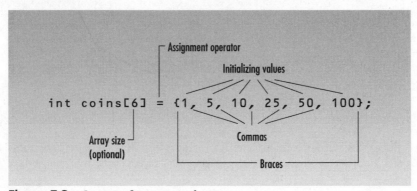

Figure 7.3 Syntax of array initialization.

Actually, we don't need to use the array size when we initialize all the array elements, since the compiler can figure it out by counting the initializing variables. Thus we can write

```
int days_per_month[] = { 31, 28, 31, 30, 31, 30,
                         31, 31, 30, 31, 30, 31 };
```

What happens if you do use an explicit array size, but it doesn't agree with the number of initializers? If there are too few initializers, the missing elements will be set to 0. If there are too many, an error is signaled.

Multidimensional Arrays

So far we've looked at arrays of one dimension: A single variable specifies each array element. But arrays can have higher dimensions. Here's a program, SALEMON, that uses a two-dimensional array to store sales figures for several districts and several months:

```
// salemon.cpp
// displays sales chart using 2-d array
```

```cpp
#include <iostream>
#include <iomanip>                      //for setprecision, etc.
using namespace std;

const int DISTRICTS = 4;                //array dimensions
const int MONTHS = 3;

int main()
   {
   int d, m;
   double sales[DISTRICTS][MONTHS];  //two-dimensional array
                                     //definition
   cout << endl;
   for(d=0; d<DISTRICTS; d++)         //get array values
      for(m=0; m<MONTHS; m++)
         {
         cout << "Enter sales for district " << d+1;
         cout << ", month " << m+1 << ": ";
         cin >> sales[d][m];          //put number in array
         }

   cout << "\n\n";
   cout << "                         Month\n";
   cout << "                  1         2         3";
   for(d=0; d<DISTRICTS; d++)
      {
      cout <<"\nDistrict " << d+1;
      for(m=0; m<MONTHS; m++)          //display array values
         cout << setiosflags(ios::fixed)      //not exponential
              << setiosflags(ios::showpoint)  //always use point
              << setprecision(2)              //digits to right
              << setw(10)                     //field width
              << sales[d][m];        //get number from array
      }  //end for(d)
   cout << endl;
   return 0;
   }  //end main
```

This program accepts the sales figures from the user and then displays them in a table.

```
Enter sales for district 1, month 1: 3964.23
Enter sales for district 1, month 2: 4135.87
Enter sales for district 1, month 3: 4397.98
Enter sales for district 2, month 1: 867.75
Enter sales for district 2, month 2: 923.59
Enter sales for district 2, month 3: 1037.01
Enter sales for district 3, month 1: 12.77
Enter sales for district 3, month 2: 378.32
Enter sales for district 3, month 3: 798.22
Enter sales for district 4, month 1: 2983.53
Enter sales for district 4, month 2: 3983.73
Enter sales for district 4, month 3: 9494.98
```

	Month		
	1	2	3
District 1	3964.23	4135.87	4397.98
District 2	867.75	923.59	1037.01
District 3	12.77	378.32	798.22
District 4	2983.53	3983.73	9494.98

Defining Multidimensional Arrays

The array is defined with two size specifiers, each enclosed in brackets:

```
double sales[DISTRICTS][MONTHS];
```

You can think about **sales** as a two-dimensional array, laid out like a checkerboard. Another way to think about it is that **sales** is an array of arrays. It is an array of **DISTRICTS** elements, each of which is an array of **MONTHS** elements. Figure 7.4 shows how this looks.

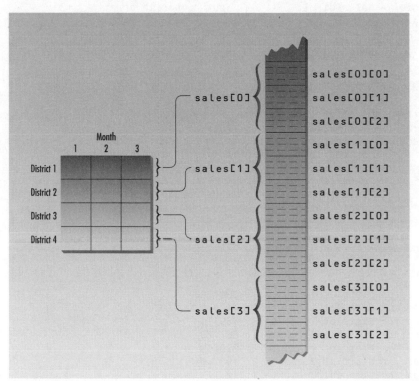

Figure 7.4   Two-dimensional array.

Of course there can be arrays of dimensions higher than two. A three-dimensional array is an array of arrays of arrays. It is accessed with three indexes:

```
elem = dimen3[x][y][z];
```

This is entirely analogous to one- and two-dimensional arrays.

Accessing Multidimensional Array Elements

Array elements in two-dimensional arrays require two indexes:

```
sales[d][m]
```

Notice that each index has its own set of brackets. Commas are not used. Don't write `sales[d,m]`; this works in some languages, but not in C++.

Formatting Numbers

The SALEMON program displays a table of dollar values. It's important that such values be formatted properly, so let's digress to see how this is done in C++. With dollar values you normally want to have exactly two digits to the right of the decimal point, and you want the decimal points of all the numbers in a column to line up. It's also nice if trailing zeros are displayed; you want 79.50, not 79.5.

Convincing the C++ I/O streams to do all this requires a little work. You've already seen the manipulator `setw()`, used to set the output field width. Formatting decimal numbers requires several additional manipulators.

Here's a statement that prints a floating-point number called `fpn` in a field 10 characters wide, with two digits to the right of the decimal point:

```
cout << setiosflags(ios::fixed)        //fixed (not exponential)
     << setiosflags(ios::showpoint)    //always show decimal point
     << setprecision(2)                //two decimal places
     << setw(10)                       //field width 10
     << fpn;                           //finally, the number
```

A group of one-bit **formatting flags** in a **long int** in the **ios** class determines how formatting will be carried out. At this point we don't need to know what the **ios** class is, or the reasons for the exact syntax used with this class, to make the manipulators work.

We're concerned with two of the **ios** flags: **fixed** and **showpoint**. To set the flags, use the manipulator **setiosflags**, with the name of the flag as an argument. The name must be preceded by the class name, **ios**, and the scope resolution operator (**::**).

The first two lines of the **cout** statement set the **ios** flags. (If you need to unset—that is, clear—the flags at some later point in your program, you can use the **resetiosflags** manipulator.) The **fixed** flag prevents numbers from being printed in exponential format, such as 3.45e3. The **showpoint** flag specifies that there will always be a decimal point, even if the number has no fractional part: 123.00, instead of 123.

To set the precision to two digits to the right of the decimal place, use the **setprecision** manipulator, with the number of digits as an argument. We've already seen how to set the field width by using the **setw** manipulator. Once all these manipulators have been sent to **cout**, you can send the number itself; it will be displayed in the desired format.

We'll talk more about the **ios** formatting flags in Chapter 12, "Streams and Files."

Initializing Multidimensional Arrays

As you might expect, you can initialize multidimensional arrays. The only prerequisite is a willingness to type a lot of braces and commas. Here's a variation of the SALEMON program that uses an initialized array instead of asking for input from the user. This program is called SALEINIT.

```cpp
// saleinit.cpp
// displays sales chart, initializes 2-d array
#include <iostream>
#include <iomanip>              //for setprecision, etc.
using namespace std;
const int DISTRICTS = 4;        //array dimensions
const int MONTHS = 3;

int main()
   {
   int d, m;
                                //initialize array elements
   double sales[DISTRICTS][MONTHS]
          = {   {  1432.07,    234.50,    654.01 },
                {   322.00, 13838.32, 17589.88 },
                {  9328.34,    934.00,   4492.30 },
                { 12838.29,   2332.63,     32.93 }  };
   cout << "\n\n";
   cout << "                            Month\n";
   cout << "              1           2          3";
   for(d=0; d<DISTRICTS; d++)
      {
      cout <<"\nDistrict " << d+1;
      for(m=0; m<MONTHS; m++)
         cout << setw(10) << setiosflags(ios::fixed)
              << setiosflags(ios::showpoint) << setprecision(2)
              << sales[d][m];  //access array element
      }
   cout << endl;
   return 0;
   }
```

Remember that a two-dimensional array is really an array of arrays. The format for initializing such an array is based on this fact. The initializing values for each subarray are enclosed in braces and separated by commas,

```cpp
{ 1432.07, 234.50, 654.01 }
```

and then all four of these subarrays, each of which is an element in the main array, is likewise enclosed by braces and separated by commas, as can be seen in the listing.

Passing Arrays to Functions

Arrays can be used as arguments to functions. Here's an example, a variation of the SALEINIT program, that passes the array of sales figures to a function whose purpose is to display the data as a table. Here's the listing for SALEFUNC:

```cpp
// salefunc.cpp
// passes array as argument
#include <iostream>
#include <iomanip>              //for setprecision, etc.
using namespace std;
const int DISTRICTS = 4;        //array dimensions
const int MONTHS = 3;
void display( double[DISTRICTS][MONTHS] );  //declaration
//-------------------------------------------------------------
int main()
    {                           //initialize two-dimensional array
    double sales[DISTRICTS][MONTHS]
        = { {  1432.07,   234.50,   654.01 },
            {   322.00, 13838.32, 17589.88 },
            {  9328.34,   934.00,  4492.30 },
            { 12838.29,  2332.63,    32.93 }  };

    display(sales);             //call function; array as argument
    cout << endl;
    return 0;
    } //end main
//-------------------------------------------------------------
//display()
//function to display 2-d array passed as argument
void display( double funsales[DISTRICTS][MONTHS] )
    {
    int d, m;

    cout << "\n\n";
    cout << "                     Month\n";
    cout << "             1        2        3";

    for(d=0; d<DISTRICTS; d++)
        {
        cout <<"\nDistrict " << d+1;
        for(m=0; m<MONTHS; m++)
            cout << setiosflags(ios::fixed) << setw(10)
                 << setiosflags(ios::showpoint) << setprecision(2)
                 << funsales[d][m];   //array element
        } //end for(d)
    } //end display
```

Function Declaration with Array Argument

In a function declaration, array arguments are represented by the data type and sizes of the array. Here's the declaration of the `display()` function:

```
void display( float[DISTRICTS][MONTHS] );  // declaration
```

Actually, there is one unnecessary piece of information here. The following statement works just as well:

```
void display( float[][MONTHS] );  // declaration
```

Why doesn't the function need the size of the first dimension? Again, remember that a two-dimensional array is an array of arrays. The function first thinks of the argument as an array of districts. It doesn't need to know how many districts there are, but it does need to know how big each district element is, so it can calculate where a particular element is (by multiplying the bytes per element times the index). So we must tell it the size of each element, which is MONTHS, but not how many there are, which is DISTRICTS.

It follows that if we were declaring a function that used a one-dimensional array as an argument, we would not need to use the array size:

```
void somefunc( int elem[] );   // declaration
```

Function Call with Array Argument

When the function is called, only the name of the array is used as an argument.

```
display(sales);   // function call
```

This name (`sales` in this case) actually represents the memory address of the array. We aren't going to explore addresses in detail until Chapter 10, "Pointers," but here are a few preliminary points about them.

Using an address for an array argument is similar to using a reference argument, in that the values of the array elements are not duplicated (copied) into the function. (See the discussion of reference arguments in Chapter 5, "Functions.") Instead, the function works with the original array, although it refers to it by a different name. This system is used for arrays because they can be very large; duplicating an entire array in every function that called it would be both time-consuming and wasteful of memory.

However, an address is not the same as a reference. No ampersand (`&`) is used with the array name in the function declaration. Until we discuss pointers, take it on faith that arrays are passed using their name alone, and that the function accesses the original array, not a duplicate.

Function Definition with Array Argument

In the function definition the declarator looks like this:

```
void display( double funsales[DISTRICTS][MONTHS] )
```

The array argument uses the data type, a name, and the sizes of the array dimensions. The array name used by the function (`funsales` in this example) can be different from the name that defines the array (`sales`), but they both refer to the same array. All the array dimensions must be specified (except in some cases the first one); the function needs them to access the array elements properly.

References to array elements in the function use the function's name for the array:

```
funsales[d][m]
```

But in all other ways the function can access array elements as if the array had been defined in the function.

Arrays of Structures

Arrays can contain structures as well as simple data types. Here's an example based on the `part` structure from Chapter 4, "Structures."

```cpp
// partaray.cpp
// structure variables as array elements
#include <iostream>
using namespace std;
const int SIZE = 4;                 //number of parts in array
/////////////////////////////////////////////////////////////////
struct part                         //specify a structure
   {
   int modelnumber;                 //ID number of widget
   int partnumber;                  //ID number of widget part
   float cost;                      //cost of part
   };
/////////////////////////////////////////////////////////////////
int main()
   {
   int n;
   part apart[SIZE];                //define array of structures

   for(n=0; n<SIZE; n++)            //get values for all members
      {
      cout << endl;
      cout << "Enter model number: ";
      cin >> apart[n].modelnumber;       //get model number
      cout << "Enter part number: ";
      cin >> apart[n].partnumber;        //get part number
      cout << "Enter cost: ";
      cin >> apart[n].cost;              //get cost
      }
   cout << endl;
   for(n=0; n<SIZE; n++)            //show values for all members
      {
      cout << "Model " << apart[n].modelnumber;
      cout << "  Part " << apart[n].partnumber;
      cout << "  Cost " << apart[n].cost << endl;
```

```
        }
    return 0;
    }
```

The user types in the model number, part number, and cost of a part. The program records this data in a structure. However, this structure is only one element in an array of structures. The program asks for the data for four different parts, and stores it in the four elements of the `apart` array. It then displays the information. Here's some sample input:

```
Enter model number: 44
Enter part number: 4954
Enter cost: 133.45

Enter model number: 44
Enter part number: 8431
Enter cost: 97.59

Enter model number: 77
Enter part number: 9343
Enter cost: 109.99

Enter model number: 77
Enter part number: 4297
Enter cost: 3456.55

Model 44  Part 4954  Cost 133.45
Model 44  Part 8431  Cost 97.59
Model 77  Part 9343  Cost 109.99
Model 77  Part 4297  Cost 3456.55
```

The array of structures is defined in the statement

```
part apart[SIZE];
```

This has the same syntax as that of arrays of simple data types. Only the type name, **part**, shows that this is an array of a more complex type.

Accessing a data item that is a member of a structure that is itself an element of an array involves a new syntax. For example,

```
apart[n].modelnumber
```

refers to the **modelnumber** member of the structure that is element **n** of the **apart** array. Figure 7.5 shows how this looks.

Arrays of structures are a useful data type in a variety of situations. We've shown an array of car parts, but we could also store an array of personnel data (name, age, salary), an array of geographical data about cities (name, population, elevation), and many other types of data.

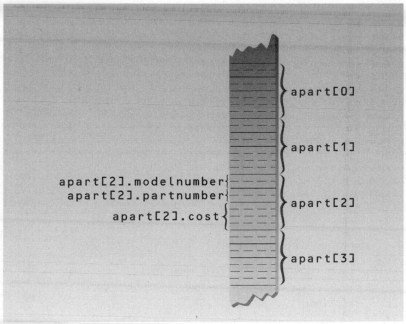

Figure 7.5   Array of structures.

Arrays As Class Member Data

Arrays can be used as data items in classes. Let's look at an example that models a common computer data structure: the stack.

A stack works like the spring-loaded devices that hold trays in cafeterias. When you put a tray on top, the stack sinks down a little; when you take a tray off, it pops up. The last tray placed on the stack is always the first tray removed.

Stacks are one of the cornerstones of the architecture of the microprocessors used in most modern computers. As we mentioned earlier, functions pass their arguments and store their return address on the stack. This kind of stack is implemented partly in hardware and is most conveniently accessed in assembly language. However, stacks can also be created completely in software. Software stacks offer a useful storage device in certain programming situations, such as in parsing (analyzing) algebraic expressions.

Our example program, STAKARAY, creates a simple stack class.

```
// stakaray.cpp
// a stack as a class
#include <iostream>
using namespace std;
/////////////////////////////////////////////////////////////////
```

```
class Stack
    {
    private:
        enum { MAX = 10 };           //(non-standard syntax)
        int st[MAX];                 //stack: array of integers
        int top;                     //number of top of stack
    public:
        Stack()                      //constructor
            { top = 0; }
        void push(int var)           //put number on stack
            { st[++top] = var; }
        int pop()                    //take number off stack
            { return st[top--]; }
    };
////////////////////////////////////////////////////////////////
int main()
    {
    Stack s1;

    s1.push(11);
    s1.push(22);
    cout << "1: " << s1.pop() << endl;   //22
    cout << "2: " << s1.pop() << endl;   //11
    s1.push(33);
    s1.push(44);
    s1.push(55);
    s1.push(66);
    cout << "3: " << s1.pop() << endl;   //66
    cout << "4: " << s1.pop() << endl;   //55
    cout << "5: " << s1.pop() << endl;   //44
    cout << "6: " << s1.pop() << endl;   //33
    return 0;
    }
```

The important member of the stack is the array st. An int variable, top, indicates the index of the last item placed on the stack; the location of this item is the *top* of the stack.

The size of the array used for the stack is specified by MAX, in the statement

```
enum { MAX = 10 };
```

This definition of MAX is unusual. In keeping with the philosophy of encapsulation, it's preferable to define constants that will be used entirely within a class, as MAX is here, within the class. Thus the use of global const variables for this purpose is non-optimal. Standard C++ mandates that we should be able to declare MAX within the class as

```
static const int MAX = 10;
```

This means that MAX is constant and applies to all objects in the class. Unfortunately, some compilers, including the current version of Microsoft Visual C++, do not allow this newly-approved construction.

As a workaround we can define such constants to be enumerators (described in Chapter 4). We don't need to name the enumeration, and we need only the one enumerator:

```
enum { MAX = 10 };
```

This defines MAX as an integer with the value 10, and the definition is contained entirely within the class. This approach works, but it's awkward. If your compiler supports the static const approach, you should use it instead to define constants within the class.

Figure 7.6 shows a stack. Since memory grows downward in the figure, the top of the stack is at the bottom in the figure. When an item is added to the stack, the address in top is incremented to point to the new top of the stack. When an item is removed, the value in top is decremented. (We don't need to erase the old value left in memory when an item is removed; it just becomes irrelevant.)

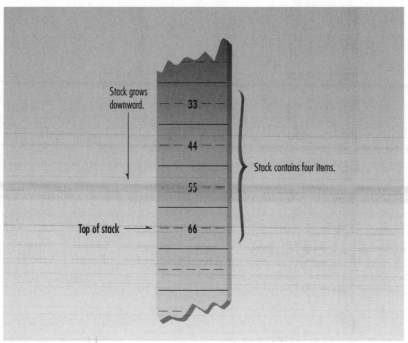

Figure 7.6   A stack.

To place an item on the stack—a process called *pushing* the item—you call the push() member function with the value to be stored as an argument. To retrieve (or *pop*) an item from the stack, you use the pop() member function, which returns the value of the item.

The main() program in STAKARAY exercises the stack class by creating an object, s1, of the class. It pushes two items onto the stack, and pops them off and displays them. Then it pushes four more items onto the stack, and pops them off and displays them. Here's the output:

```
1: 22
2: 11
3: 66
```

```
4: 55
5: 44
6: 33
```

As you can see, items are popped off the stack in reverse order; the last thing pushed is the first thing popped.

Notice the subtle use of prefix and postfix notation in the increment and decrement operators. The statement

```
st[++top] = var;
```

in the `push()` member function first increments `top` so that it points to the next available array element—one past the last element. It then assigns `var` to this element, which becomes the new top of the stack. The statement

```
return st[top--];
```

first returns the value it finds at the top of the stack, then decrements `top` so that it points to the preceding element.

The `stack` class is an example of an important feature of object-oriented programming: using a class to implement a *container* or data-storage mechanism. In Chapter 15, we'll see that a stack is only one of a number of ways to store data. There are also queues, sets, linked lists, and so on. A data-storage scheme is chosen that matches the specific requirements of the program. Using a preexisting class to provide data storage means that the programmer does not need to waste time duplicating the details of the data-storage mechanism.

Arrays of Objects

We've seen how an object can contain an array. We can also reverse that situation and create an array of objects. We'll look at two situations: an array of English distances and a deck of cards.

Arrays of English Distances

In Chapter 6, "Objects and Classes," we showed several examples of an English `Distance` class that incorporated feet and inches into an object representing a new data type. The next program, ENGLARAY, demonstrates an array of such objects.

```
// englaray.cpp
// objects using English measurements
#include <iostream>
using namespace std;
/////////////////////////////////////////////////////////////////
class Distance                        //English Distance class
   {
   private:
      int feet;
      float inches;
   public:
      void getdist()                  //get length from user
```

```
         {
         cout << "\n   Enter feet: "; cin >> feet;
         cout << "   Enter inches: "; cin >> inches;
         }
      void showdist() const        //display distance
         { cout << feet << "\'-" << inches << '\"'; }
   };
///////////////////////////////////////////////////////////////
int main()
   {
   Distance dist[100];             //array of distances
   int n=0;                        //count the entries
   char ans;                       //user response ('y' or 'n')

   cout << endl;

   do {                            //get distances from user
      cout << "Enter distance number " << n+1;
      dist[n++].getdist();         //store distance in array
      cout << "Enter another (y/n)?: ";
      cin >> ans;
      } while( ans != 'n' );       //quit if user types 'n'

   for(int j=0; j<n; j++)          //display all distances
      {
      cout << "\nDistance number " << j+1 << " is ";
      dist[j].showdist();
      }
   cout << endl;
   return 0;
   }
```

In this program the user types in as many distances as desired. After each distance is entered, the program asks if the user desires to enter another. If not, it terminates, and displays all the distances entered so far. Here's a sample interaction when the user enters three distances:

```
Enter distance number 1
   Enter feet: 5
   Enter inches: 4
Enter another (y/n)? y
Enter distance number 2
   Enter feet: 6
   Enter inches: 2.5
Enter another (y/n)? y
Enter distance number 3
   Enter feet: 5
   Enter inches: 10.75
Enter another (y/n)? n

Distance number 1 is 5'-4"
Distance number 2 is 6'-2.5"
Distance number 3 is 5'-10.75"
```

Of course, instead of simply displaying the distances already entered, the program could have averaged them, written them to disk, or operated on them in other ways.

Array Bounds

This program uses a **do** loop to get input from the user. This way the user can input data for as many structures of type **part** as seems desirable, up to **MAX**, the size of the array (which is set to 100).

Although it's hard to imagine anyone having the patience, what would happen if the user entered more than 100 distances? The answer is, something unpredictable but almost certainly bad. There is no bounds checking in C++ arrays. If the program inserts something beyond the end of the array, neither the compiler nor the runtime system will object. However, the renegade data will probably be written on top of other data or the program code itself. This may cause bizarre effects or crash the system completely.

The moral is that it is up to the programmer to deal with the array bounds checking. If it seems possible that the user will insert too much data for an array to hold, then the array should be made larger or some means of warning the user should be devised. For example, you could insert the following code at the beginning of the **do** loop in ENGLARAY:

```
if( n >= MAX )
   {
   cout << "\nThe array is full!!!";
   break;
   }
```

This causes a **break** out of the loop and prevents the array from overflowing.

Accessing Objects in an Array

The declaration of the **Distance** class in this program is similar to that used in previous programs. However, in the **main()** program we define an array of such objects:

```
Distance dist[MAX];
```

Here the data type of the **dist** array is **Distance**, and it has **MAX** elements. Figure 7.7 shows what this looks like.

A class member function that is an array element is accessed similarly to a structure member that is an array element, as in the PARTARAY example. Here's how the **showdist()** member function of the **j**th element of the array **dist** is invoked:

```
dist[j].showdist();
```

As you can see, a member function of an object that is an array element is accessed using the dot operator: The array name followed by the index in brackets is joined, using the dot operator, to the member function name followed by parentheses. This is similar to accessing a structure (or class) data member, except that the function name and parentheses are used instead of the data name.

Notice that when we call the **getdist()** member function to put a distance into the array, we take the opportunity to increment the array index **n**:

```
dist[n++].getdist();
```

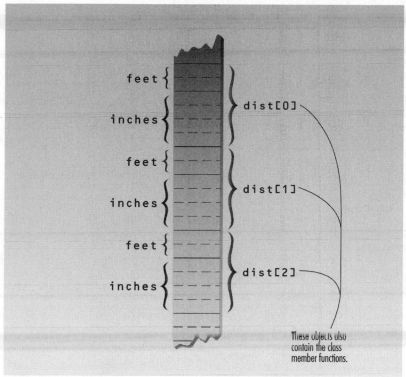

These objects also contain the class member functions.

Figure 7.7   Array of objects.

This way the next group of data obtained from the user will be placed in the structure in the next array element in **dist**. The n variable must be incremented manually like this because we use a **do** loop instead of a **for** loop. In the **for** loop, the loop variable—which is incremented automatically—can serve as the array index.

Arrays of Cards

Here's another, somewhat longer, example of an array of objects. You will no doubt remember the CARDOBJ example from Chapter 6. We'll borrow the **card** class from that example, and group an array of 52 such objects together in an array, thus creating a deck of cards. Here's the listing for CARDARAY:

```
// cardaray.cpp
// cards as objects
#include <iostream>
#include <cstdlib>              //for srand(), rand()
#include <ctime>               //for time for srand()
using namespace std;

enum Suit { clubs, diamonds, hearts, spades };
//from 2 to 10 are integers without names
```

```cpp
const int jack = 11;
const int queen = 12;
const int king = 13;
const int ace = 14;
///////////////////////////////////////////////////////////////
class card
   {
   private:
      int number;          //2 to 10, jack, queen, king, ace
      Suit suit;           //clubs, diamonds, hearts, spades
   public:
      card()                        //constructor
         { }
      void set(int n, Suit s)     //set card
         { suit = s; number = n; }
      void display();              //display card
   };
//-------------------------------------------------------------
void card::display()                //display the card
   {
   if( number >= 2 && number <= 10 )
      cout << number;
   else
      switch(number)
         {
         case jack:  cout << "J"; break;
         case queen: cout << "Q"; break;
         case king:  cout << "K"; break;
         case ace:   cout << "A"; break;
         }
   switch(suit)
      {
      case clubs:    cout << char(5); break;
      case diamonds: cout << char(4); break;
      case hearts:   cout << char(3); break;
      case spades:   cout << char(6); break;
      }
   }
///////////////////////////////////////////////////////////////
int main()
   {
   card deck[52];
   int j;

   cout << endl;
   for(j=0; j<52; j++)             //make an ordered deck
      {
      int num = (j % 13) + 2;   //cycles through 2 to 14, 4 times
      Suit su = Suit(j / 13);   //cycles through 0 to 3, 13 times
      deck[j].set(num, su);     //set card
      }
   cout << "\nOrdered deck:\n";
   for(j=0; j<52; j++)             //display ordered deck
```

```
      {
      deck[j].display();
      cout << "   ";
      if( !( (j+1) % 13) )         //newline every 13 cards
         cout << endl;
      }
   srand( time(NULL) );           //seed random numbers with time
   for(j=0; j<52; j++)            //for each card in the deck,
      {
      int k = rand() % 52;        //pick another card at random
      card temp = deck[j];        //and swap them
      deck[j] = deck[k];
      deck[k] = temp;
      }
   cout << "\nShuffled deck:\n";
   for(j=0; j<52; j++)            //display shuffled deck
      {
      deck[j].display();
      cout << ", ";
      if( !( (j+1) % 13) )         //newline every 13 cards
         cout << endl;
      }
   return 0;
   }  //end main
```

Once we've created a deck, it's hard to resist the temptation to shuffle it. We display the cards in the deck, shuffle it, and then display it again. To conserve space we use graphics characters for the club, diamond, heart, and spade. Figure 7.8 shows the output from the program. This program incorporates several new ideas, so let's look at them in turn.

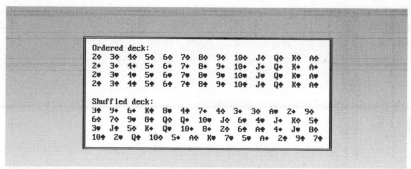

Figure 7.8   Output of the CARDARAY program.

Graphics Characters

There are several special graphics characters in the range below ASCII code 32. (See Appendix A, "ASCII Table," for a list of ASCII codes.) In the **display()** member function of **card** we use codes 5, 4, 3, and 6 to access the characters for a club, a diamond, a heart, and a spade, respectively. Casting these numbers to type **char**, as in

```
static_cast<char>(5)
```

causes the << operator to print them as characters rather than as numbers.

The Card Deck

The array of structures that constitutes the deck of cards is defined in the statement

```
card deck[52];
```

which creates an array called **deck**, consisting of 52 objects of type **card**. To display the jth card in the deck, we call the **display()** member function:

```
deck[j].display();
```

Random Numbers

It's always fun and sometimes even useful to generate random numbers. In this program we use them to shuffle the deck. Two steps are necessary to obtain random numbers. First the random-number generator must be *seeded* or initialized. To do this, we call the **srand()** library function. This function uses the system time as the seed, so it requires two header files, CSTDLIB and CTIME.

To actually generate a random number, we call the **rand()** library function. This function returns a random integer. To get a number in the range from 0 to 51, we apply the remainder operator and 52 to the result of **rand()**.

```
int k = rand() % 52;
```

The resulting random number **k** is then used as an index to swap two cards. We go through the **for** loop, swapping one card, whose index points to each card in 0-to-51 order, with another card, whose index is the random number. When all 52 cards have been exchanged with a random card, the deck is considered to be shuffled. This program could form the basis for a card-playing program, but we'll leave these details for the reader.

Arrays of objects are widely used in C++ programming. We'll see other examples as we go along.

C-Strings

We noted at the beginning of this chapter that two kinds of strings are commonly used in C++: C-strings, and strings that are objects of the **string** class. In this section, we'll describe the first kind, which fits the theme of the chapter in that C-strings are arrays of type **char**. We call these strings *C-strings*, or *C-style strings*, because they were the only kind of strings available in the C language (and in the early days of C++, for that matter). They may also be called **char*** strings, because they can be represented as pointers to type **char**. (The * indicates a pointer, as we'll learn in Chapter 10.)

Although strings created with the **string** class, which we'll examine in the next section, have superceded C-strings in many situations, C-strings are still important, for a variety of reasons. First, they are used in many C library functions. Second, they will continue to appear in legacy code for years to come. And third, for students of C++, C-strings are more primitive and therefore easier to understand on a fundamental level.

C-string Variables

As with other data types, strings can be variables or constants. We'll look at these two entities before going on to examine more complex string operations. Here's an example that defines a single string variable. (In the section we'll assume the word string means a C-string.) It asks the user to enter a string, and places this string in the string variable. Then it displays the string. Here's the listing for STRINGIN:

```
// stringin.cpp
// simple string variable
#include <iostream>
using namespace std;

int main()
   {
   const int MAX = 80;                //max characters in string
   char str[MAX];                     //string variable str

   cout << "Enter a string: ";
   cin >> str;                        //put string in str
                                      //display string from str
   cout << "You entered: " << str << endl;
   return 0;
   }
```

The definition of the string variable str looks like (and is) the definition of an array of type char:

```
char str[MAX];
```

We use the extraction operator >> to read a string from the keyboard and place it in the string variable str. This operator knows how to deal with strings; it understands that they are arrays of characters. If the user enters the string "Amanuensis" (one employed to copy manuscripts) in this program, the array str will look something like Figure 7.9.

Each character occupies 1 byte of memory. An important aspect of C-strings is that they must terminate with a byte containing 0. This is often represented by the character constant '\0', which is a character with an ASCII value of 0. This terminating zero is called the *null character*. When the << operator displays the string, it displays characters until it encounters the null character.

Avoiding Buffer Overflow

The STRINGIN program invites the user to type in a string. What happens if the user enters a string that is longer than the array used to hold it? As we mentioned earlier, there is no built-in mechanism in C++ to keep a program from inserting array elements outside an array. So an overly enthusiastic typist could end up crashing the system.

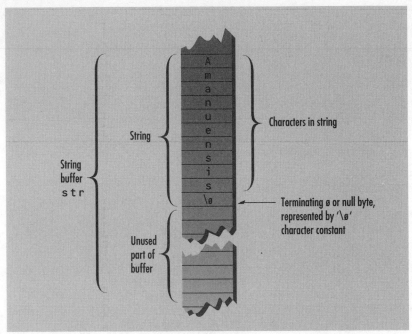

Figure 7.9 String stored in string variable.

However, it is possible to tell the **>>** operator to limit the number of characters it places in an array. The SAFETYIN program demonstrates this approach.

```
// safetyin.cpp
// avoids buffer overflow with cin.width
#include <iostream>
#include <iomanip>                    //for setw
using namespace std;

int main()
   {
   const int MAX = 20;               //max characters in string
   char str[MAX];                    //string variable str

   cout << "\nEnter a string: ";
   cin >> setw(MAX) >> str;          //put string in str,
                                     // no more than MAX chars
   cout << "You entered: " << str << endl;
   return 0;
   }
```

This program uses the **setw** manipulator to specify the maximum number of characters the input buffer can accept. The user may type more characters, but the **>>** operator won't insert them into the array. Actually, one character fewer than the number specified is inserted, so there is room in the buffer for the terminating null character. Thus, in SAFETYIN, a maximum of 19 characters are inserted.

String Constants

You can initialize a string to a constant value when you define it. Here's an example, STRINIT, that does just that (with the first line of a Shakespearean sonnet):

```
// strinit.cpp
// initialized string
#include <iostream>
using namespace std;

int main()
    {
    char str[] = "Farewell! thou art too dear for my possessing.";
    cout << str << endl;
    return 0;
    }
```

Here the string constant is written as a normal English phrase, delimited by quotes. This may seem surprising, since a string is an array of type `char`. In past examples you've seen arrays initialized to a series of values delimited by braces and separated by commas. Why isn't `str` initialized the same way? In fact you could use such a sequence of character constants:

```
char str[] = { 'F', 'a', 'r', 'e', 'w', 'e', 'l', 'l', '!',' ', 't', 'h',
```

and so on. Fortunately, the designers of C++ (and C) took pity on us and provided the short-cut approach shown in STRINIT. The effect is the same: The characters are placed one after the other in the array. As with all C-strings, the last character is a null (zero).

Reading Embedded Blanks

If you tried the STRINGIN program with strings that contained more than one word, you may have had an unpleasant surprise. Here's an example:
Enter a string: Law is a bottomless pit.
You entered: Law

Where did the rest of the phrase (a quotation from the Scottish writer John Arbuthnot, 1667ñ1735) go? It turns out that the extraction operator >> considers a space to be a terminating character. Thus it will read strings consisting of a single word, but anything typed after a space is thrown away.

To read text containing blanks we use another function, `cin::get()`. This syntax means a member function `get()` of the stream class of which `cin` is an object. The following example, BLANKSIN, shows how it's used.

```
// blanksin.cpp
// reads string with embedded blanks
#include <iostream>
using namespace std;

int main()
    {
    const int MAX = 80;                 //max characters in string
```

```
    char str[MAX];                          //string variable str

    cout << "\nEnter a string: ";
    cin.get(str, MAX);                      //put string in str
    cout << "You entered: " << str << endl;
    return 0;
    }
```

The first argument to `cin::get()` is the array address where the string being input will be placed. The second argument specifies the maximum size of the array, thus automatically avoiding buffer overrun.

Using this function, the input string is now stored in its entirety.

```
Enter a string: Law is a bottomless pit.
You entered: Law is a bottomless pit.
```

There's a potential problem when you mix `cin.get()` with `cin` and the extraction operator (>>). We'll discuss the use of the `ignore()` member function of `cin` to solve this problem in Chapter 12, "Streams and Files."

Reading Multiple Lines

We may have solved the problem of reading strings with embedded blanks, but what about strings with multiple lines? It turns out that the `cin::get()` function can take a third argument to help out in this situation. This argument specifies the character that tells the function to stop reading. The default value for this argument is the newline (`'\n'`) character, but if you call the function with some other character for this argument, the default will be overridden by the specified character.

In the next example, LINESIN, we call the function with a dollar sign (`'$'`) as the third argument:

```
// linesin.cpp
// reads multiple lines, terminates on '$' character
#include <iostream>
using namespace std;

const int MAX = 2000;                   //max characters in string
char str[MAX];                          //string variable str

int main()
    {
    cout << "\nEnter a string:\n";
    cin.get(str, MAX, '$');             //terminate with $
    cout << "You entered:\n" << str << endl;
    return 0;
    }
```

Now you can type as many lines of input as you want. The function will continue to accept characters until you enter the terminating character (or until you exceed the size of the array). Remember, you must still press ⏎Enter after typing the `'$'` character. Here's a sample interaction with a poem from Thomas Carew, 1595–1639:

```
Enter a string:
Ask me no more where Jove bestows
When June is past, the fading rose;
For in your beauty's orient deep
These flowers, as in their causes, sleep.
$
You entered:
Ask me no more where Jove bestows
When June is past, the fading rose;
For in your beauty's orient deep
These flowers, as in their causes, sleep.
```

We terminate each line with ⌨Enter⌨, but the program continues to accept input until we enter '$'.

Copying a String the Hard Way

The best way to understand the true nature of strings is to deal with them character by character. The following program does this.

```cpp
// strcopy1.cpp
// copies a string using a for loop
#include <iostream>
#include <cstring>                         //for strlen()
using namespace std;

int main()
   {                                       //initialized string
   char str1[] = "Oh, Captain, my Captain! "
        "our fearful trip is done";

   const int MAX = 80;                  //size of str2 buffer
   char str2[MAX];                      //empty string

   for(int j=0; j<strlen(str1); j++)    //copy strlen characters
      str2[j] = str1[j];                //   from str1 to str2
   str2[j] = '\0';                      //insert NULL at end
   cout << str2 << endl;                //display str2
   return 0;
   }
```

This program creates a string constant, str1, and a string variable, str2. It then uses a for loop to copy the string constant to the string variable. The copying is done one character at a time, in the statement

```cpp
str2[j] = str1[j];
```

Recall that the compiler concatenates two adjacent string constants into a single one, which allows us to write the quotation on two lines.

This program also introduces C-string library functions. Because there are no string operators built into C++, C-strings must usually be manipulated using library functions. Fortunately there are many such functions. The one we use in this program, strlen(), finds the length of a C-string (that is, how many characters are in it). We use this length as the limit in the `for` loop so that the right number of characters will be copied. When string functions are used, the header file CSTRING (or STRING.H) must be included (with `#include`) in the program.

The copied version of the string must be terminated with a null. However, the string length returned by `strlen()` does not include the null. We could copy one additional character, but it's safer to insert the null explicitly. We do this with the line

```
str2[j] = '\0';
```

If you don't insert this character, you'll find that the string printed by the program includes all sorts of weird characters following the string you want. The `<<` just keeps on printing characters, whatever they are, until by chance it encounters a `'\0'`.

Copying a String the Easy Way

Of course you don't need to use a `for` loop to copy a string. As you might have guessed, a library function will do it for you. Here's a revised version of the program, STRCOPY2, that uses the `strcpy()` function.

```cpp
// strcopy2.cpp
// copies a string using strcpy() function
#include <iostream>
#include <cstring>                          //for strcpy()
using namespace std;

int main()
   {
   char str1[] = "Tiger, tiger, burning bright\n"
                 "In the forests of the night";
   const int MAX = 80;                      //size of str2 buffer
   char str2[MAX];                          //empty string

   strcpy(str2, str1);                      //copy str1 to str2
   cout << str2 << endl;                    //display str2
   return 0;
   }
```

Note that you call this function like this:

```
strcpy(destination, source)
```

with the destination first. The right-to-left order is reminiscent of the format of normal assignment statements: The variable on the right is copied to the variable on the left.

Arrays of Strings

If there are arrays of arrays, of course there can be arrays of strings. This is actually quite a useful construction. Here's an example, STRARAY, that puts the names of the days of the week in an array:

```cpp
// straray.cpp
// array of strings
```

```
#include <iostream>
using namespace std;

int main()
   {
   const int DAYS = 7;                //number of strings in array
   const int MAX = 10;                //maximum size of each string
                                      //array of strings
   char star[DAYS][MAX] = { "Sunday", "Monday", "Tuesday",
                            "Wednesday", "Thursday",
                            "Friday", "Saturday"  };
   for(int j=0; j<DAYS; j++)          //display every string
      cout << star[j] << endl;
   return 0;
   }
```

The program prints out each string from the array:

```
Sunday
Monday
Tuesday
Wednesday
Thursday
Friday
Saturday
```

Since a string is an array, it must be true that star—an array of strings—is really a two-dimensional array. The first dimension of this array, DAYS, tells how many strings are in the array. The second dimension, MAX, specifies the maximum length of the strings (9 characters for "Wednesday" plus the terminating null makes 10). Figure 7.10 shows how this looks.

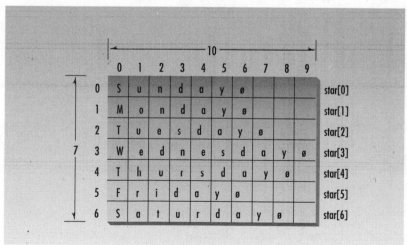

Figure 7.10 Array of strings.

Notice that some bytes are wasted following strings that are less than the maximum length. We'll learn how to remove this inefficiency when we talk about pointers.

The syntax for accessing a particular string may look surprising:

```
star[j];
```

If we're dealing with a two-dimensional array, where's the second index? Since a two-dimensional array is an array of arrays, we can access elements of the "outer" array, each of which is an array (in this case a string), individually. To do this we don't need the second index. So star[j] is string number j in the array of strings.

Strings As Class Members

Strings frequently appear as members of classes. The next example, a variation of the OBJPART program in Chapter 6, uses a C-string to hold the name of the widget part.

```cpp
// strpart.cpp
// string used in widget part object
#include <iostream>
#include <cstring>              //for strcpy()
using namespace std;
/////////////////////////////////////////////////////////////////
class part
    {
    private:
        char partname[30];   //name of widget part
        int partnumber;      //ID number of widget part
        double cost;         //cost of part
    public:
        void setpart(char pname[], int pn, double c)
            {
            strcpy(partname, pname);
            partnumber = pn;
            cost = c;
            }
        void showpart()      //display data
            {
            cout << "\nName="   << partname;
            cout << ", number=" << partnumber;
            cout << ", cost=$"  << cost;
            }
    };
/////////////////////////////////////////////////////////////////
int main()
    {
    part part1, part2;

    part1.setpart("handle bolt", 4473, 217.55);    //set parts
    part2.setpart("start lever", 9924, 419.25);
    cout << "\nFirst part: ";  part1.showpart();    //show parts
    cout << "\nSecond part: "; part2.showpart();
    cout << endl;
    return 0;
    }
```

This program defines two objects of class **part** and gives them values with the **setpart()** member function. Then it displays them with the **showpart()** member function. Here's the output:

```
First part:
Name=handle bolt, number=4473, cost=$217.55
Second part:
Name=start lever, number=9924, cost=$419.25
```

To reduce the size of the program, we've dropped the model number from the class members.

In the **setpart()** member function, we use the **strcpy()** string library function to copy the string from the argument **pname** to the class data member **partname**. Thus this function serves the same purpose with string variables that an assignment statement does with simple variables.

Besides those we've seen, there are library functions to add a string to another, compare strings, search for specific characters in strings, and perform many other actions. Descriptions of these functions can be found in your compiler's documentation.

A User-Defined String Type

There are some problems with C-strings as they are normally used in C++. For one thing, you can't use the perfectly reasonable expression

```
strDest = strSrc;
```

to set one string equal to another. (In some languages, like BASIC, this is perfectly all right.) The Standard C++ **string** class we'll examine in the next section will take care of this problem, but for the moment let's see if we can use object-oriented technology to solve the problem ourselves. Creating our own string class will give us an insight into representing strings as objects of a class, which will illuminate the operation of Standard C++ **string** class.

If we define our own string type, using a C++ class, we can use assignment statements. (Many other C-string operations, such as concatenation, can be simplified this way as well, but we'll have to wait until Chapter 8, "Operator Overloading," to see how this is done.)

The STROBJ program creates a class called **String**. (Don't confuse this homemade class **String** with the Standard C++ built-in class **string**, which has a lowercase 's'.) Here's the listing:

```
// strobj.cpp
// a string as a class
#include <iostream>
#include <cstring>          // for strcpy(), strcat()
using namespace std;
//////////////////////////////////////////////////////////////
class String
   {
   private:
      enum { SZ = 80; };                //max size of Strings
      char str[SZ];                     //array
   public:
```

```cpp
        String()                            //constructor, no args
            { str[0] = '\0'; }
        String( char s[] )                  //constructor, one arg
            { strcpy(str, s); }
        void display()                      //display string
            { cout << str; }
        void concat(String s2)              //add arg string to
            {                               //this string
            if( strlen(str)+strlen(s2.str) < SZ )
                strcat(str, s2.str);
            else
                cout << "\nString too long";
            }
    };
/////////////////////////////////////////////////////////////////
int main()
    {
    String s1("Merry Christmas!  ");        //uses constructor 2
    String s2 = "Season's Greetings!";      //alternate form of 2
    String s3;                              //uses constructor 1

    cout << "\ns1="; s1.display();          //display them all
    cout << "\ns2="; s2.display();
    cout << "\ns3="; s3.display();

    s3 = s1;                                //assignment
    cout << "\ns3="; s3.display();          //display s3

    s3.concat(s2);                          //concatenation
    cout << "\ns3="; s3.display();          //display s3
    cout << endl;
    return 0;
    }
```

The `String` class contains an array of type `char`. It may seem that our newly defined class is just the same as the original definition of a string: an array of type `char`. But, by wrapping the array in a class, we have achieved some interesting benefits. Since an object can be assigned the value of another object of the same class using the = operator, we can use statements like

```cpp
s3 = s1;
```

as we do in `main()`, to set one `String` object equal to another. We can also define our own member functions to deal with `Strings` (objects of class `String`).

In the STROBJ program, all `Strings` have the same length: SZ characters (which we set to 80). There are two constructors. The first sets the first character in `str` to the null character, `'\0'`, so the string has a length of 0. This constructor is called with statements like

```cpp
String s3;
```

The second constructor sets the `String` object to a "normal" (that is, a C-string) string constant. It uses the `strcpy()` library function to copy the string constant into the object's data. It's called with statements like

```
String s1("Merry Christmas! ");
```

The alternative format for calling this constructor, which works with any one-argument constructor, is

```
String s1 = "Merry Christmas! ");
```

Whichever format is used, this constructor effectively converts a C-string to a `String`—that is, a normal string constant to an object of class `String`. A member function, `display()`, displays the `String`.

Another member function of our `String` class, `concat()`, *concatenates* (adds) one `String` to another. The original `String` is the object of which `concat()` is a member. To this `String` will be added the `String` passed as an argument. Thus the statement in `main()`,

```
s3.concat(s2);
```

causes `s2` to be added to the existing `s3`. Since `s2` has been initialized to "Season's Greetings!" and `s3` has been assigned the value of `s1`, which was "Merry Christmas!" the resulting value of `s3` is "Merry Christmas! Season's Greetings!"

The `concat()` function uses the `strcat()` C library function to do the concatenation. This library function adds the string specified in the second argument to the string specified in the first argument. The output from the program is

```
s1=Merry Christmas!
s2=Season's Greetings!
s3=          ←———— nothing here yet
s3=Merry Christmas!     ←———— set equal to s1
s3=Merry Christmas! Season's Greetings!     ←———— s2 concatenated
```

If the two `String`s given to the `concat()` function together exceed the maximum `String` length, then the concatenation is not carried out, and a message is sent to the user.

We've just examined a simple string class. Now we'll see a far more sophisticated version of the same approach.

The Standard C++ `string` Class

Standard C++ includes a new class called `string`. This class improves on the traditional C-string in many ways. For one thing, you no longer need to worry about creating an array of the right size to hold string variables. The `string` class assumes all the responsibility for memory management. Also, the `string` class allows the use of overloaded operators, so you can concatenate string objects with the + operator: `s3 = s1 + s2`.

There are other benefits as well. This new class is more efficient and safer to use than C-strings were. In most situations it is the preferred approach. (However, as we noted earlier, there are still many situations in which C-strings must be used.) In this section we'll examine the `string` class and its various member functions and operators.

Defining and Assigning `string` Objects

You can define a `string` object in several ways. You can use a constructor with no arguments, creating an empty string. You can also use a one-argument constructor, where the argument is a C-string constant; that is, characters delimited by double quotes. As in our home-made `String` class, objects of class `string` can be assigned to one another with a simple assignment operator. The SSTRASS example shows how this looks.

```
//sstrass.cpp
//defining and assigning string objects
#include <iostream>
#include <string>
using namespace std;

int main()
   {
   string s1("Man");                  //initialize
   string s2 = "Beast";               //initialize
   string s3;

   s3 = s1;                           //assign
   cout << "s3 = " << s3 << endl;

   s3 = "Neither " + s1 + " nor ";    //concatenate
   s3 += s2;                          //concatenate
   cout << "s3 = " << s3 << endl;

   s1.swap(s2);                       //swap s1 and s2
   cout << s1 << " nor " << s2 << endl;
   return 0;
   }
```

Here the first three lines of code show three ways to define `string` objects. The first two initialize `strings`, and the second creates an empty `string` variable. The next line shows simple assignment with the = operator.

The `string` class uses a number of overloaded operators. We won't learn about the inner workings of operator overloading until the next chapter, but you can use these operators without knowing how they're constructed.

The overloaded + operator concatenates one string object with another. The statement

```
s3 = "Neither " + s1 + " nor ";
```

places the string `"Neither Man nor "` in the variable `s3`.

You can also use the += operator to append a string to the end of an existing string. The statement

```
s3 += s2;
```

appends `s2`, which is `"Beast"`, to the end of `s3`, producing the string `"Neither Man nor Beast"` and assigning it to `s3`.

This example also introduces our first `string` class member function: `swap()`, which exchanges the values of two string objects. It's called for one object with the other as an

argument. We apply it to **s1** ("Man") and **s2** ("Beast"), and then display their values to show that **s1** is now "Beast" and **s2** is now "Man".

Here's the output of SSTRASS:

```
s3 = Man
s3 = Neither Man nor Beast
Beast nor Man
```

Input/Output with `string` Objects

Input and output are handled in a similar way to that of C-strings. The `<<` and `>>` operators are overloaded to handle **string** objects, and a function `getline()` handles input that contains embedded blanks or multiple lines. The SSTRIO example shows how this looks.

```cpp
// sstrio.cpp
// string class input/output
#include <iostream>
#include <string>                    //for string class
using namespace std;

int main()
   {                                 //objects of string class
   string full_name, nickname, address;
   string greeting("Hello, ");

   cout << "Enter your full name: ";
   getline(cin, full_name);          //reads embedded blanks
   cout << "Your full name is: " << full_name << endl;

   cout << "Enter your nickname: ";
   cin >> nickname;                  //input to string object

   greeting += nickname;             //append name to greeting
   cout << greeting << endl;         //output: "Hello, Jim"

   cout << "Enter your address on separate lines\n";
   cout << "Terminate with '$'\n";
   getline(cin, address, '$');       //reads multiple lines
   cout << "Your address is: " << address << endl;
   return 0;
   }
```

The program reads the user's name, which presumably contains embedded blanks, using `getline()`. This function is similar to the `get()` function used with C-strings, but is not a member function. Instead, its first argument is the stream object from which the input will come (here it's `cin`), and the second is the **string** object where the text will be placed, `full_name`. This variable is then displayed using the `cout` and `<<`.

The program then reads the user's nickname, which is assumed to be one word, using `cin` and the `>>` operator. Finally the program uses a variation of `getline()`, with three arguments, to read the user's address, which may require multiple lines. The third argument specifies the character to be used to terminate the input. In the program we use the `'$'`

character, which the user must input as the last character before pressing the Enter key. If no third argument is supplied to `getline()`, the delimiter is assumed to be `'\n'`, which represents the Enter key. Here's some interaction with SSTRIO:

```
Enter your full name: F. Scott Fitzgerald
Your full name is: F. Scott Fitzgerald
Enter your nickname: Scotty
Hello, Scotty
Enter your address on separate lines:
Terminate with '$'
1922 Zelda Lane
East Egg, New York$
Your address is:
1922 Zelda Lane
East Egg, New York
```

Finding `string` Objects

The `string` class includes a variety of member functions for finding strings and substrings in `string` objects. The SSTRFIND example shows some of them.

```cpp
//sstrfind.cpp
//finding substrings in string objects
#include <iostream>
#include <string>
using namespace std;

int main()
   {
   string s1 =
      "In Xanadu did Kubla Kahn a stately pleasure dome decree";
   int n;

   n = s1.find("Kubla");
   oout << "Found Kubla at " << n << endl;

   n = s1.find_first_of("spde");
   cout << "First of spde at " << n << endl;

   n = s1.find_first_not_of("aeiouAEIOU");
   cout << "First consonant at " << n << endl;
   return 0;
   }
```

The `find()` function looks for the string used as its argument in the string for which it was called. Here it finds `"Kubla"` in `s1`, which holds the first line of the poem *Kubla Kahn* by Samuel Taylor Coleridge. It finds it at position 14. As with C-strings, the leftmost character position is numbered 0.

The `find_first_of()` function looks for any of a group of characters, and returns the position of the first one it finds. Here it looks for any of the group `'s'`, `'p'`, `'d'`, or `'e'`. The first of these it finds is the `'d'` in `Xanadu`, at position 7.

A similar function `find_first_not_of()` finds the first character in its string that is *not* one of a specified group. Here the group consists of all the vowels, both upper- and lowercase, so the function finds the first consonant, which is the second letter. The output of SSTRFIND is

```
Found Kubla at 14
First of spde at 7
First consonent at 1
```

There are variations on many of these functions that we don't demonstrate here, such as `rfind()`, which scans its string backward; `find_last_of()`, which finds the last character matching one of a group of characters, and `find_last_not_of()`.

Modifying `string` Objects

There are various ways to modify **string** objects. Our next example shows the member functions `erase()`, `replace()`, and `insert()` at work.

```cpp
//sstrchng.cpp
//changing parts of string objects
#include <iostream>
#include <string>
using namespace std;

int main()
   {
   string s1("Quick! Send for Count Graystone.");
   string s2("Lord");
   string s3("Don't ");

   s1.erase(0, 7);              //remove "Quick! "
   s1.replace(9, 5, s2);        //replace "Count" with "Lord"
   s1.replace(0, 1, "s");       //replace 'S' with 's'
   s1.insert(0, s3);            //insert "Don't " at beginning
   s1.erase(s1.size()-1, 1);    //remove '.'
   s1.append(3, '!');           //append "!!!"

   int x = s1.find(' ');        //find a space
   while( x < s1.size() )       //loop while spaces remain
      {
      s1.replace(x, 1, "/");    //replace with slash
      x = s1.find(' ');         //find next space
      }
   cout << "s1: " << s1 << endl;
   return 0;
   }
```

The `erase()` function removes a substring from a string. Its first argument is the position of the first character in the substring, and the second is the length of the substring. In the example it removes a **"Quick "** from the beginning of the string. The `replace()` function replaces part of the string with another string. The first argument is the position where the replacement should begin, the second is the number of characters in the original string to be replaced, and the third is the replacement string. Here `"Count"` is replaced by `"Lord"`.

The `insert()` function inserts the string specified by its second argument at the location specified by its first argument. Here it inserts `"Don't "` at the beginning of `s1`. The second use of `erase()` employs the `size()` member function, which returns the number of characters in the `string` object. The expression `size()-1` is the position of the last character, the period, which is erased. The `append()` function installs three exclamation points at the end of the sentence. In this version of the function the first argument is the number of characters to append, and the second is the character to be appended.

At the end of the program we show an idiom you can use to replace multiple instances of a substring with another string. Here, in a `while` loop, we look for the space character `' '` using `find()`, and replace each one with a slash using `replace()`.

We start with `s1` containing the string `"Quick! Send for Count Graystone."` After these changes, the output of SSTRCHNG is

```
s1: Don't/send/for/Lord/Graystone!!!
```

Comparing `string` Objects

You can use overloaded operators or the `compare()` function to compare string objects. These discover whether strings are the same, or whether they precede or follow one another alphabetically. The SSTRCOM program shows some of the possibilities.

```cpp
//sstrcom.cpp
//comparing string objects
#include <iostream>
#include <string>
using namespace std;

int main()
    {
    string aName = "George";
    string userName;

    cout << "Enter your first name: ";
    cin >> userName;
    if(userName==aName)                    //operator ==
        cout << "Greetings, George\n";
    else if(userName < aName)              //operator <
        cout << "You come before George\n";
    else
        cout << "You come after George\n";
                                           //compare() function
    int n = userName.compare(0, 2, aName, 0, 2);
    cout << "The first two letters of your name ";
    if(n==0)
        cout << "match ";
    else if(n < 0)
        cout << "come before ";
    else
```

```
         cout << "come after ";
      cout << aName.substr(0, 2) << endl;
      return 0;
      }
```

In the first part of the program the == and < operators are used to determine whether a name typed by the user is equal to, or precedes or follows alphabetically, the name George. In the second part of the program the compare() function compares only the first two letters of "George" with the first two letters of the name typed by the user (userName). The arguments to this version of compare() are the starting position in userName and the number of characters to compare, the string used for comparison (aName), and the starting position and number of characters in aName. Here's some interaction with SSTRCOM:

```
Enter your first name: Alfred
You come before George
The first two letters of your name come before Ge
```

The first two letters of "George" are obtained using the substr() member function. It returns a substring of the string for which it was called. Its first argument is the position of the substring, and the second is the number of characters.

Accessing Characters in string Objects

You can access individual characters within a string object in several ways. In our next example we'll show access using the at() member function. You can also use the overloaded [ ] operator, which makes the string object look like an array. However, the [ ] operator doesn't warn you if you attempt to access a character that's out of bounds (beyond the end of the string, for example). The [ ] operator behaves this way with real arrays, and it's more efficient. However, it can lead to hard-to-diagnose program bugs. It's safer to use the at()() function, which causes the program to stop if you use an out-of-bounds index. (It actually throws an exception; we'll discuss exceptions in Chapter 14, "Templates and Exceptions.")

```
//sstrchar.cpp
//accessing characters in string objects
#include <iostream>
#include <string>
using namespace std;

int main()
   {
   char charray[80];
   string word;

   cout << "Enter a word: ";
   cin >> word;
   int wlen = word.length();       //length of string object

   cout << "One character at a time: ";
   for(int j=0; j<wlen; j++)
      cout << word.at(j);          //exception if out-of-bounds
//    cout << word[j];             //no warning if out-of-bounds
```

```
word.copy(charray, wlen, 0);  //copy string object to array
charray[wlen] = 0;            //terminate with '\0'
cout << "\nArray contains: " << charray << endl;
return 0;
}
```

In this program we use `at()` to ()display all the characters in a `string` object, character by character. The argument to `at()` is the location of the character in the string.

We then show how you can use the `copy()` member ()function to copy a `string` object into an array of type `char`, effectively transforming it into a C-string. Following the copy, a null character (`'\0'`) must be inserted after the last character in the array to complete the transformation to a C-string. The `length()` member function ()of `string` returns the same number as() `size()`. Here's the output of `sstrchar`:

```
Enter a word: symbiosis
One character at a time: symbiosis
Array contains: symbiosis
```

(You can also convert `string` objects to C-strings using the `c_str()` or `data()` member functions. However, to use these functions you need to know about pointers, which we'll examine in Chapter 10.)

Other `string` Functions

We've seen that `size()` and `length()` both return the number of characters currently in a `string` object. The amount of memory occupied by a string is usually somewhat larger than that actually needed for the characters. (Although if it hasn't been initialized it uses 0 bytes for characters.) The `capacity()` member ()function returns the actual memory occupied. You can add characters to the string without causing it to expand its memory until this limit is reached. The `max_size()` member() function returns the maximum possible size of a string object. This amount corresponds to the size of `int` variables on your system, less 3 bytes. In 32-bit Windows systems this is 4,294,967,293 bytes, but the size of your memory will probably restrict this ()amount.

Most of the `string` member functions we've discussed have numerous variations in the numbers and types of arguments they take. Consult your compiler's documentation for details.

You should be aware that `string` objects are not terminated with a null or zero as C-strings are. Instead, the length of the string is a member of the class. So if you're stepping along the string, don't rely on finding a null to tell you when you've reached the end.

The `string` class is actually only one of many possible string-like classes, all derived from the template class `basic_string`. The `string` class is based on type `char`, but a common variant is to use type `wchar_t` instead. This allows `basic_string` to be used for foreign languages with many more characters than English. Your compiler's help file may list the `string` member functions under `basic_string`.

Summary

Arrays contain a number of data items of the same type. This type can be a simple data type, a structure, or a class. The items in an array are called *elements*. Elements are accessed by number; this number is called an *index*. Elements can be initialized to specific values when the array is defined. Arrays can have multiple dimensions. A two-dimensional array is an array of arrays. The address of an array can be used as an argument to a function; the array itself is not copied. Arrays can be used as member data in classes. Care must be taken to prevent data from being placed in memory outside an array.

C-strings are arrays of type `char`. The last character in a C-string must be the null character, `'\0'`. C-string constants take a special form so that they can be written conveniently: the text is surrounded by double quotes. A variety of library functions are used to manipulate C-strings. An array of C-strings is an array of arrays of type `char`. The creator of a C-string variable must ensure that the array is large enough to hold any text placed in it. C-strings are used as arguments to C-style library functions and will be found in older programs. They are not normally recommended for general use in new programs.

The preferred approach to strings is to use objects of the `string` class. These strings can be manipulated with numerous overloaded operators and member functions. The user need not worry about memory management with `string` objects.

Questions

Answers to questions can be found in Appendix G, "Answers to Questions and Exercises."

1. An array element is accessed using

   a. a first-in-first-out approach.

   b. the dot operator.

   c. a member name.

   d. an index number.

2. All the elements in an array must be the _____ data type.

3. Write a statement that defines a one-dimensional array called `doubleArray` of type `double` that holds 100 elements.

4. The elements of a 10-element array are numbered from _____ to _____.

5. Write a statement that takes element `j` of array `doubleArray` and writes it to `cout` with the insertion operator.

6. Element `doubleArray[7]` is which element of the array?

    a. The sixth

    b. The seventh

    c. The eighth

    d. Impossible to tell

7. Write a statement that defines an array `coins` of type `int` and initializes it to the values of the penny, nickel, dime, quarter, half-dollar, and dollar.

8. When a multidimensional array is accessed, each array index is

    a. separated by commas.

    b. surrounded by brackets and separated by commas.

    c. separated by commas and surrounded by brackets.

    d. surrounded by brackets.

9. Write an expression that accesses element 4 in subarray 2 in a two-dimensional array called `twoD`.

10. True or false: In C++ there can be an array of four dimensions.

11. For a two-dimensional array of type `float`, called `flarr`, write a statement that declares the array and initializes the first subarray to 52, 27, 83; the second to 94, 73, 49; and the third to 3, 6, 1.

12. An array name, used in the source file, represents the _____ of the array.

13. When an array name is passed to a function, the function

    a. accesses exactly the same array as the calling program.

    b. accesses a copy of the array passed by the program.

    c. refers to the array using the same name as that used by the calling program.

    d. refers to the array using a different name than that used by the calling program.

14. Tell what this statement defines:

```
employee emplist[1000];
```

15. Write an expression that accesses a structure member called `salary` in a structure variable that is the 17th element in an array called `emplist`.

16. In a stack, the data item placed on the stack first is

    a. not given an index number.

    b. given the index number 0.

    c. the first data item to be removed.

    d. the last data item to be removed.

17. Write a statement that defines an array called `manybirds` that holds 50 objects of type `bird`.

18. True or false: The compiler will complain if you try to access array element 14 in a 10-element array.

19. Write a statement that executes the member function `cheep()` in an object of class `bird` that is the 27th element in the array `manybirds`.

20. A string in C++ is an _____ of type _____.

21. Write a statement that defines a string variable called `city` that can hold a string of up to 20 characters (this is slightly tricky).

22. Write a statement that defines a string constant, called `dextrose`, that has the value "C6H12O6-H2O".

23. True or false: The extraction operator (>>) stops reading a string when it encounters a space.

24. You can read input that consists of multiple lines of text using

    a. the normal `cout <<` combination.

    b. the `cin.get()` function with one argument.

    c. the `cin.get()` function with two arguments.

    d. the `cin.get()` function with three arguments.

25. Write a statement that uses a string library function to copy the string `name` to the string `blank`.

26. Write the declaration for a class called `dog` that contains two data members: a string called `breed` and an `int` called `age`. (Don't include any member functions.)

27. True or false: You should prefer C-strings to the Standard C++ `string` class in new programs.

28. Objects of the **string** class

    a. are zero-terminated.

    b. can be copied with the assignment operator.

    c. do not require memory management.

    d. have no member functions.

29. Write a statement that finds where the string **"cat"** occurs in the string **s1**.

30. Write a statement that inserts the string **"cat"** into string **s1** at position 12.

Exercises

Answers to the starred exercises can be found in Appendix G.

*1. Write a function called **reversit()** that reverses a C-string (an array of **char**). Use a **for** loop that swaps the first and last characters, then the second and next-to-last characters, and so on. The string should be passed to **reversit()** as an argument.

Write a program to exercise **reversit()**. The program should get a string from the user, call **reversit()**, and print out the result. Use an input method that allows embedded blanks. Test the program with Napoleon's famous phrase, "Able was I ere I saw Elba."

*2. Create a class called **employee** that contains a name (an object of class **string**) and an employee number (type **long**). Include a member function called **getdata()** to get data from the user for insertion into the object, and another function called **putdata()** to display the data. Assume the name has no embedded blanks.

Write a **main()** program to exercise this class. It should create an array of type **employee**, and then invite the user to input data for up to 100 employees. Finally, it should print out the data for all the employees.

*3. Write a program that calculates the average of up to 100 English distances input by the user. Create an array of objects of the **Distance** class, as in the ENGLARAY example in this chapter. To calculate the average, you can borrow the **add_dist()** member function from the ENGLCON example in Chapter 6. You'll also need a member function that divides a **Distance** value by an integer. Here's one possibility:

```
void Distance::div_dist(Distance d2, int divisor)
   {
   float fltfeet = d2.feet + d2.inches/12.0;
   fltfeet /= divisor;
```

```
feet = int(fltfeet);
inches = (fltfeet-feet) * 12.0;
}
```

4. Start with a program that allows the user to input a number of integers, and then stores them in an `int` array. Write a function called `maxint()` that goes through the array, element by element, looking for the largest one. The function should take as arguments the address of the array and the number of elements in it, and return the index number of the largest element. The program should call this function and then display the largest element and its index number. (See the SALES program in this chapter.)

5. Start with the `fraction` class from Exercises 11 and 12 in Chapter 6. Write a `main()` program that obtains an arbitrary number of fractions from the user, stores them in an array of type `fraction`, averages them, and displays the result.

6. In the game of contract bridge, each of four players is dealt 13 cards, thus exhausting the entire deck. Modify the CARDARAY program in this chapter so that, after shuffling the deck, it deals four hands of 13 cards each. Each of the four players' hands should then be displayed.

7. One of the weaknesses of C++ for writing business programs is that it does not contain a built-in type for monetary values such as $173,698,001.32. Such a money type should be able to store a number with a fixed decimal point and about 17 digits of precision, which is enough to handle the national debt in dollars and cents. Fortunately, the built-in C++ type `long double` has 19 digits of precision, so we can use it as the basis of a money class, even though it uses a floating decimal. However, we'll need to add the capability to input and output money amounts preceded by a dollar sign and divided by commas into groups of three digits; this makes it much easier to read large numbers. As a first step toward developing such a class, write a function called `mstold()` that takes a *money string*, a string representing a money amount like

   `"$1,234,567,890,123.99"`

   as an argument, and returns the equivalent `long double`.

   You'll need to treat the money string as an array of characters, and go through it character by character, copying only digits (1 to 9) and the decimal point into another string. Ignore everything else, including the dollar sign and the commas. You can then use the `_atold()` library function (note the initial underscore; header file STDLIB.H or MATH.H) to convert the resulting pure string to a `long double`. Assume that money values will never be negative. Write a `main()` program to test `mstold()` by repeatedly obtaining a money string from the user and displaying the corresponding `long double`.

8. Another weakness of C++ is that it does not automatically check array indexes to see if they are in bounds. (This makes array operations faster but less safe.) We can use a class to create a safe array that checks the index of all array accesses.

   Write a class called `safearay` that uses an `int` array of fixed size (call it `LIMIT`) as its only data member. There will be two member functions. The first, `putel()`, takes an index number and an `int` value as arguments and inserts the `int` value into the array at the index. The second, `getel()`, takes an index number as an argument and returns the `int` value of the element with that index.

   ```
   safearay sa1;           // define a safearay object
   int temp = 12345;       // define an int value
   sa1.putel(7, temp);     // insert value of temp into array at index 7
   temp = sa1.getel(7);    // obtain value from array at index 7
   ```

   Both functions should check the index argument to make sure it is not less than 0 or greater than `LIMIT-1`. You can use this array without fear of writing over other parts of memory.

   Using functions to access array elements doesn't look as eloquent as using the `[]` operator. In Chapter 8 we'll see how to overload this operator to make our `safearay` class work more like built-in arrays.

9. A queue is a data storage device much like a stack. The difference is that in a stack the last data item stored is the first one retrieved, while in a queue the first data item stored is the first one retrieved. That is, a stack uses a last-in-first-out (LIFO) approach, while a queue uses first-in-first-out (FIFO). A queue is like a line of customers in a bank: The first one to join the queue is the first one served.

   Rewrite the STAKARAY program from this chapter to incorporate a class called `queue` instead of a class called `stack`. Besides a constructor, it should have two functions: one called `put()` to put a data item on the queue, and one called `get()` to get data from the queue. These are equivalent to `push()` and `pop()` in the `stack` class.

   Both a queue and a stack use an array to hold the data. However, instead of a single `int` variable called `top`, as the stack has, you'll need two variables for a queue: one called `head`, to point to the head of the queue, and one called `tail` to point to the tail. Items are placed on the queue at the tail (like the last customer getting in line at the bank) and removed from the queue at the head. The tail will follow the head along the array as items are added and removed from the queue. This results in an added complexity: When either the tail or the head gets to the end of the array, it must wrap around to the beginning. Thus you'll need a statement like

   ```
   if(tail == MAX-1)
      tail = -1;
   ```

to wrap the tail, and a similar one for the head. The array used in the queue is sometimes called a circular buffer, because the head and tail circle around it, with the data between them.

10. A matrix is a two-dimensional array. Create a class `matrix` that provides the same safety feature as the array class in Exercise 7; that is, it checks to be sure no array index is out of bounds. Make the member data in the `matrix` class a 10-by-10 array. A constructor should allow the programmer to specify the actual dimensions of the matrix (provided they're less than 10 by 10). The member functions that access data in the matrix will now need two index numbers: one for each dimension of the array. Here's what a fragment of a `main()` program that operates on such a class might look like:

```
matrix m1(3, 4);          // define a matrix object
int temp = 12345;         // define an int value
m1.putel(7, 4, temp);     // insert value of temp into matrix at 7,4
temp = m1.getel(7, 4);    // obtain value from matrix at 7,4
```

11. Refer back to the discussion of money strings in Exercise 6. Write a function called `ldtoms()` to convert a number represented as type `long double` to the same value represented as a money string. First you should check that the value of the original long double is not too large. We suggest that you don't try to convert any number greater than 9,999,999,999,999,990.00. Then convert the `long double` to a pure string (no dollar sign or commas) stored in memory, using an `ostrstream` object, as discussed earlier in this chapter. The resulting formatted string can go in a buffer called `ustring`.

You'll then need to start another string with a dollar sign; copy one digit from `ustring` at a time, starting from the left, and inserting a comma into the new string every three digits. Also, you'll need to suppress leading zeros. You want to display $3,124.95, for example, not $0,000,000,000,003,124.95. Don't forget to terminate the string with a '\0' character.

Write a `main()` program to exercise this function by having the user repeatedly input numbers in type `long double` format, and printing out the result as a money string.

12. Create a class called `bMoney`. It should store money amounts as a `long double`. Use the function `mstold()` to convert a money string entered as input into a `long double`, and the function `ldtoms()` to convert the `long double` to a money string for display. (See Exercises 6 and 10.) You can call the input and output member functions `getmoney()` and `putmoney()`. Write another member function that adds two `bMoney` amounts; you can call it `madd()`. Adding `bMoney` objects is easy: Just add the `long double` member data amounts in two `bMoney` objects. Write a

`main()` program that repeatedly requests the user to enter two money strings, and then displays the sum as a money string. Here's how the class `specifier` might look:

```cpp
class bMoney
    {
    private:
        long double money;
    public:
        bMoney();
        bMoney(char s[]);
        void madd(bMoney m1, bMoney m2);
        void getmoney();
        void putmoney();
    };
```

CHAPTER 8

OPERATOR OVERLOADING

You will learn about the following in this chapter:

- The operator keyword
- Overloading unary operators
- Overloading binary operators
- Constructors as conversion routines
- Converting between basic and user-defined types
- Thoughts on overloading

A Operator overloading is one of the most exciting features of object-oriented programming. It can transform complex, obscure program listings into intuitively obvious ones. For example, statements like

```
d3.addobjects(d1, d2);
```

or the similar but equally obscure

```
d3 = d1.addobjects(d2);
```

can be changed to the much more readable

```
d3 = d1 + d2;
```

The rather forbidding term *operator overloading* refers to giving the normal C++ operators, such as +, *, <=, and +=, additional meanings when they are applied to user-defined data types. Normally

```
a = b + c;
```

works only with basic types like int and float, and attempting to apply it when a, b, and c are objects of a user-defined class will cause complaints from the compiler. However, using overloading, you can make this statement legal even when a, b, and c are user-defined types.

In effect, operator overloading gives you the opportunity to redefine the C++ language. If you find yourself limited by the way the C++ operators work, you can change them to do whatever you want. By using classes to create new kinds of variables, and operator overloading to create new definitions for operators, you can extend C++ to be, in many ways, a new language of your own design.

Another kind of operation, *data type conversion*, is closely connected with operator overloading. C++ handles the conversion of simple types, like `int` and `float`, automatically; but conversions involving user-defined types require some work on the programmer's part. We'll look at data conversions in the second part of this chapter.

Overloaded operators are not all beer and skittles. We'll discuss some of the dangers of their use at the end of the chapter.

Overloading Unary Operators

Let's start off by overloading a *unary operator*. As you may recall from Chapter 2, unary operators act on only one operand. (An operand is simply a variable acted on by an operator.) Examples of unary operators are the increment and decrement operators ++ and --, and the unary minus, as in -33.

In the COUNTER example in Chapter 6, "Objects and Classes," we created a class `Counter` to keep track of a count. Objects of that class were incremented by calling a member function.

```
c1.inc_count();
```

That did the job, but the listing would have been more readable if we could have used the increment operator ++ instead:

```
++c1;
```

All dyed-in-the-wool C++ (and C) programmers would guess immediately that this expression increments `c1`.

Let's rewrite COUNTER to make this possible. Here's the listing for COUNTPP1:

```
// countpp1.cpp
// increment counter variable with ++ operator
#include <iostream>
using namespace std;
/////////////////////////////////////////////////////////////
class Counter
    {
    private:
        unsigned int count;                //count
    public:
        Counter() : count(0)               //constructor
            {  }
        unsigned int get_count()           //return count
            { return count; }
        void operator ++ ()                 //increment (prefix)
            {
            ++count;
            }
    };
/////////////////////////////////////////////////////////////
int main()
    {
```

```
   Counter c1, c2;                      //define and initialize

   cout << "\nc1=" << c1.get_count();   //display
   cout << "\nc2=" << c2.get_count();

   ++c1;                      //increment c1
   ++c2;                      //increment c2
   ++c2;                      //increment c2

   cout << "\nc1=" << c1.get_count();   //display again
   cout << "\nc2=" << c2.get_count() << endl;
   return 0;
   }
```

In this program we create two objects of class `Counter`: `c1` and `c2`. The counts in the objects are displayed; they are initially 0. Then, using the overloaded ++ operator, we increment `c1` once and `c2` twice, and display the resulting values. Here's the program's output:

```
c1=0     ←——————— counts are initially 0
c2=0
c1=1     ←——————— incremented once
c2=2     ←——————— incremented twice
```

The statements responsible for these operations are

```
++c1;
++c2;
++c2;
```

The ++ operator is applied once to `c1` and twice to `c2`. We use prefix notation in this example; we'll explore postfix later.

The `operator` Keyword

How do we teach a normal C++ operator to act on a user-defined operand? The keyword operator is used to overload the ++ operator in this declarator:

```
void operator ++ ()
```

The return type (`void` in this case) comes first, followed by the keyword `operator`, followed by the operator itself (++), and finally the argument list enclosed in parentheses (which are empty here). This declarator syntax tells the compiler to call this member function whenever the ++ operator is encountered, provided the operand (the variable operated on by the ++) is of type `Counter`.

We saw in Chapter 5, "Functions," that the only way the compiler can distinguish between overloaded functions is by looking at the data types and number of their arguments. In the same way, the only way it can distinguish between overloaded operators is by looking at the data type of their operands. If the operand is a basic type like an `int`, as in

```
++intvar;
```

then the compiler will use its built-in routine to increment an `int`. But if the operand is a `Counter` variable, then the compiler will know to use our user-written `operator++()` instead.

Operator Arguments

In `main()` the `++` operator is applied to a specific object, as in the expression `++c1`. Yet `operator++()` takes no arguments. What does this operator increment? It increments the `count` data in the object of which it is a member. Since member functions can always access the particular object for which they've been invoked, this operator requires no arguments. This is shown in Figure 8.1.

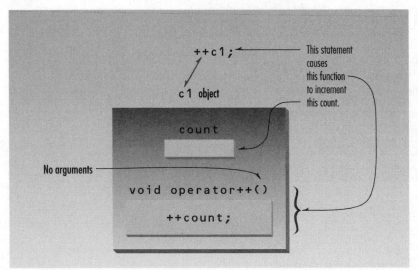

Figure 8.1   Overloaded unary operator: no arguments.

Operator Return Values

The `operator++()` function in the COUNTPP1 program has a subtle defect. You will discover it if you use a statement like this in `main()`:

```
c1 = ++c2;
```

The compiler will complain. Why? Because we have defined the `++` operator to have a return type of `void` in the `operator++()` function, while in the assignment statement it is being asked to return a variable of type `Counter`. That is, the compiler is being asked to return whatever value `c2` has after being operated on by the `++` operator, and assign this value to `c1`. So as defined in COUNTPP1, we can't use `++` to increment `Counter` objects in assignments; it must always stand alone with its operand. Of course the normal `++` operator, applied to basic data types like `int`, would not have this problem.

To make it possible to use our homemade `operator++()` in assignment expressions, we must provide a way for it to return a value. The next program, COUNTPP2, does just that.

```
// countpp2.cpp
// increment counter variable with ++ operator, return value
```

```
#include <iostream>
using namespace std;
/////////////////////////////////////////////////////////////////
class Counter
    {
    private:
        unsigned int count;         //count
    public:
        Counter() : count(0)        //constructor
            {  }
        unsigned int get_count()    //return count
            { return count; }
        Counter operator ++ ()      //increment count
            {
            ++count;                //increment count
            Counter temp;           //make a temporary Counter
            temp.count = count;     //give it same value as this obj
            return temp;            //return the copy
            }
    };
/////////////////////////////////////////////////////////////////
int main()
    {
    Counter c1, c2;                            //c1=0, c2=0

    cout << "\nc1=" << c1.get_count();         //display
    cout << "\nc2=" << c2.get_count();

    ++c1;                                      //c1=1
    c2 = ++c1;                                 //c1=2, c2=2

    cout << "\nc1=" << c1.get_count();    //display again
    cout << "\nc2=" << c2.get_count() << endl;
    return 0;
    }
```

Here the operator++() function creates a new object of type Counter, called temp, to use as a return value. It increments the count data in its own object as before, then creates the new temp object and assigns count in the new object as the same value as in its own object. Finally it returns the temp object. This has the desired effect. Expressions like

++c1

now return a value, so they can be used in other expressions, such as

c2 = ++c1;

as shown in main(), where the value returned from c1++ is assigned to c2. The output from this program is

```
c1=0
c2=0
c1=2
c2=2
```

Nameless Temporary Objects

In COUNTPP2 we created a temporary object of type **Counter**, named **temp**, whose sole purpose was to provide a return value for the ++ operator. This required three statements.

```
Counter temp;          // make a temporary Counter object
temp.count = count;    // give it same value as this object
return temp;           // return it
```

There are more convenient ways to return temporary objects from functions and overloaded operators. Let's examine another approach, as shown in the program COUNTPP3:

```cpp
// countpp3.cpp
// increment counter variable with ++ operator
// uses unnamed temporary object
#include <iostream>
using namespace std;
/////////////////////////////////////////////////////////////////
class Counter
    {
    private:
        unsigned int count;        //count
    public:
        Counter() : count(0)       //constructor  no args
            {  }
        Counter(int c) : count(c)  //constructor, one arg
            {  }
        unsigned int get_count()   //return count
            { return count; }
        Counter operator ++ ()     //increment count
            {
            ++count;                   //  increment count, then return
            return Counter(count);     //  an unnamed temporary object
            }                          //  initialized to this count
    };
/////////////////////////////////////////////////////////////////
int main()
    {
    Counter c1, c2;                        //c1=0, c2=0

    cout << "\nc1=" << c1.get_count();     //display
    cout << "\nc2=" << c2.get_count();

    ++c1;                                  //c1=1
    c2 = ++c1;                             //c1=2, c2=2

    cout << "\nc1=" << c1.get_count();     //display again
    cout << "\nc2=" << c2.get_count() << endl;
    return 0;
    }
```

In this program a single statement,

```
return Counter(count);
```

does what all three statements did in COUNTPP2. This statement creates an object of type **Counter**. This object has no name; it won't be around long enough to need one. This unnamed object is initialized to the value provided by the argument **count**.

But wait: Doesn't this require a constructor that takes one argument? It does, and to make this statement work we sneakily inserted just such a constructor into the member function list in COUNTPP3.

```
Counter(int c) : count(c)//constructor, one arg
   { }
```

Once the unnamed object is initialized to the value of **count**, it can then be returned. The output of this program is the same as that of COUNTPP2.

The approaches in both COUNTPP2 and COUNTPP3 involve making a copy of the original object (the object of which the function is a member), and returning the copy. (Another approach, as we'll see in Chapter 11, "Virtual Functions," is to return the value of the original object using the **this** pointer.)

Postfix Notation

So far we've shown the increment operator used only in its prefix form.

```
++c1
```

What about postfix, where the variable is incremented after its value is used in the expression?

```
c1++
```

To make both versions of the increment operator work, we define two overloaded ++ operators, as shown in the POSTFIX program:

```
// postfix.cpp
// overloaded ++ operator in both prefix and postfix
#include <iostream>
using namespace std;
//////////////////////////////////////////////////////////////
class Counter
   {
   private:
      unsigned int count;            //count
   public:
      Counter() : count(0)           //constructor  no args
         { }
      Counter(int c) : count(c)      //constructor, one arg
         { }
      unsigned int get_count() const //return count
        { return count; }

      Counter operator ++ ()         //increment count (prefix)
         {                           //increment count, then return
         return Counter(++count);    //an unnamed temporary object
         }                           //initialized to this count
```

```
            Counter operator ++ (int)    //increment count (postfix)
               {                         //return an unnamed temporary
            return Counter(count++); //object initialized to this
               }                         //count, then increment count
         };
//////////////////////////////////////////////////////////////
int main()
   {
   Counter c1, c2;                              //c1=0, c2=0

   cout << "\nc1=" << c1.get_count();     //display
   cout << "\nc2=" << c2.get_count();

   ++c1;                                        //c1=1
   c2 = ++c1;                                   //c1=2, c2=2 (prefix)

   cout << "\nc1=" << c1.get_count();     //display
   cout << "\nc2=" << c2.get_count();

   c2 = c1++;                                   //c1=3, c2=2 (postfix)

   cout << "\nc1=" << c1.get_count();     //display again
   cout << "\nc2=" << c2.get_count() << endl;
   return 0;
   }
```

Now there are two different declarators for overloading the ++ operator. The one we've seen before, for prefix notation, is

```
Counter operator ++ ()
```

The new one, for postfix notation, is

```
Counter operator ++ (int)
```

The only difference is the **int** in the parentheses. This **int** isn't really an argument, and it doesn't mean integer. It's simply a signal to the compiler to create the postfix version of the operator. The designers of C++ are fond of recycling existing operators and keywords to play multiple roles, and **int** is the one they chose to indicate postfix. (Well, can you think of a better syntax?) Here's the output from the program:

```
c1=0
c2=0
c1=2
c2=2
c1=3
c2=2
```

We saw the first four of these output lines in COUNTPP2 and COUNTPP3. But in the last two lines we see the results of the statement

```
c2=c1++;
```

Here **c1** is incremented to 3, but **c2** is assigned the value of **c1** before it is incremented, so **c2** retains the value 2.

Of course you can use this same approach with the decrement operator, (- -).

Overloading Binary Operators

Binary operators can be overloaded just as easily as unary operators. We'll look at examples that overload arithmetic operators, comparison operators, and arithmetic assignment operators.

Arithmetic Operators

In the ENGLCON program in Chapter 6 we showed how two English **Distance** objects could be added using a member function **add_dist()**:

```
dist3.add_dist(dist1, dist2);
```

By overloading the + operator we can reduce this dense-looking expression to

```
dist3 = dist1 + dist2;
```

Here's the listing for ENGLPLUS, which does just this:

```
// englplus.cpp
// overloaded '+' operator adds two Distances
#include <iostream>
using namespace std;
////////////////////////////////////////////////////////////////
class Distance                     //English Distance class
   {
   private:
      int feet;
      float inches;
   public:                         //constructor (no args)
      Distance() : feet(0), inches(0.0)
         {  }                      //constructor (two args)
      Distance(int ft, float in) : feet(ft), inches(in)
         {  }
      void getdist()               //get length from user
         {
         cout << "\nEnter feet: ";  cin >> feet;
         cout << "Enter inches: ";  cin >> inches;
         }
      void showdist() const        //display distance
         { cout << feet << "\'-" << inches << '\"'; }

      Distance operator + ( Distance ) const;  //add 2 distances
   };
//--------------------------------------------------------------
                                   //add this distance to d2
Distance Distance::operator + (Distance d2) const  //return sum
   {
   int f = feet + d2.feet;         //add the feet
   float i = inches + d2.inches;   //add the inches
   if(i >= 12.0)                   //if total exceeds 12.0,
      {                            //then decrease inches
      i -= 12.0;                   //by 12.0 and
```

```
      f++;                      //increase feet by 1
   }                           //return a temporary Distance
   return Distance(f,i);       //initialized to sum
}
////////////////////////////////////////////////////////////////
int main()
{
   Distance dist1, dist3, dist4;   //define distances
   dist1.getdist();                //get dist1 from user

   Distance dist2(11, 6.25);       //define, initialize dist2

   dist3 = dist1 + dist2;          //single '+' operator

   dist4 = dist1 + dist2 + dist3;  //multiple '+' operators
                                   //display all lengths
   cout << "dist1 = ";  dist1.showdist(); cout << endl;
   cout << "dist2 = ";  dist2.showdist(); cout << endl;
   cout << "dist3 = ";  dist3.showdist(); cout << endl;
   cout << "dist4 = ";  dist4.showdist(); cout << endl;
   return 0;
}
```

To show that the result of an addition can be used in another addition as well as in an assignment, another addition is performed in `main()`. We add `dist1`, `dist2`, and `dist3` to obtain `dist4` (which should be double the value of `dist3`), in the statement

```
dist4 = dist1 + dist2 + dist3;
```

Here's the output from the program:

```
Enter feet: 10
Enter inches: 6.5

dist1 = 10'-6.5"      ←———— from user
dist2 = 11'-6.25"     ←———— initialized in program
dist3 = 22'-0.75"     ←———— dist1+dist2
dist4 = 44'-1.5"      ←———— dist1+dist2+dist3
```

In class `Distance` the declaration for the `operator+()` function looks like this:

```
Distance operator + ( Distance );
```

This function has a return type of `Distance`, and takes one argument of type `Distance`.
   In expressions like

```
dist3 = dist1 + dist2;
```

it's important to understand how the return value and arguments of the operator relate to the objects. When the compiler sees this expression it looks at the argument types, and finding only type `Distance`, it realizes it must use the `Distance` member function `operator+()`. But what does this function use as its argument—`dist1` or `dist2`? And doesn't it need two arguments, since there are two numbers to be added?

Here's the key: The argument on the *left side* of the operator (**dist1** in this case) is the object of which the operator is a member. The object on the *right side* of the operator (**dist2**) must be furnished as an argument to the operator. The operator returns a value, which can be assigned or used in other ways; in this case it is assigned to **dist3**. Figure 8.2 shows how this looks.

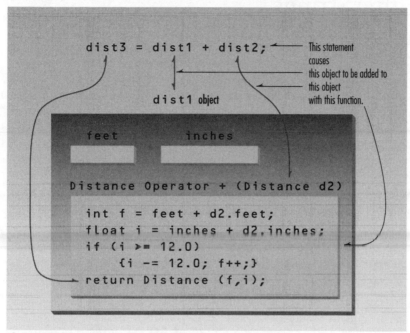

```
dist3 = dist1 + dist2;        This statement
                              causes
                              this object to be added to
                              this object
         dist1 object         with this function.


    feet            inches
  [        ]      [          ]

Distance Operator + (Distance d2)

  int f = feet + d2.feet;
  float i = inches + d2.inches;
  if (i >= 12.0)
      {i -= 12.0; f++;}
  return Distance (f,i);
```

Figure 8.2   Overloaded binary operator: one argument.

In the **operator+()** function, the left operand is accessed directly—since this is the object of which the operator is a member—using **feet** and **inches**. The right operand is accessed as function's argument, as **d2.feet** and **d2.inches**.

We can generalize and say that an overloaded operator always requires one less argument than its number of operands, since one operand is the object of which the operator is a member. That's why unary operators require no arguments. (This rule does not apply to friend functions and operators, a C++ feature we'll discuss in Chapter 11.)

To calculate the return value of **operator+()** in ENGLPLUS, we first add the **feet** and **inches** from the two operands (adjusting for a carry if necessary). The resulting values, **f** and **i**, are then used to initialize a nameless **Distance** object, which is returned in the statement

```
return Distance(f, i);
```

This is similar to the arrangement used in COUNTPP3, except that the constructor takes two arguments instead of one. The statement

```
dist3 = dist1 + dist2;
```

in `main()` then assigns the value of the nameless `Distance` object to `dist3`. Compare this intuitively obvious statement with the use of a function call to perform the same task, as in the ENGLCON example in Chapter 6.

Similar functions could be created to overload other operators in the `Distance` class, so you could subtract, multiply, and divide objects of this class in natural-looking ways.

Concatenating Strings

The + operator cannot be used to concatenate C-strings. That is, you can't say

```
str3 = str1 + str2;
```

where `str1`, `str2`, and `str3` are C-string variables (arrays of type `char`), as in "cat" plus "bird" equals "catbird." However, if we use our own `String` class, as shown in the STROBJ program in Chapter 6, then we can overload the + operator to perform such concatenation. This is what the Standard C++ `string` class does, but it's easier to see how it works in our less ambitious `String` class. Overloading the + operator to do something that isn't strictly addition is another example of redefining the C++ language. Here's the listing for STRPLUS:

```
// strplus.cpp
// overloaded '+' operator concatenates strings
#include <iostream>
using namespace std;
#include <string.h>        //for strcpy(), strcat()
#include <stdlib.h>        //for exit()
/////////////////////////////////////////////////////////////////
class String                //user-defined string type
   {
   private:
      enum { SZ=80 };               //size of String objects
      char str[SZ];                 //holds a string
   public:
      String()                      //constructor, no args
         { strcpy(str, ""); }
      String( char s[] )            //constructor, one arg
         { strcpy(str, s); }
      void display() const          //display the String
         { cout << str; }
      String operator + (String ss) const  //add Strings
         {
         String temp;               //make a temporary String
         if( strlen(str) + strlen(ss.str) < SZ )
            {
            strcpy(temp.str, str);    //copy this string to temp
            strcat(temp.str, ss.str); //add the argument string
            }
         else
            { cout << "\nString overflow"; exit(1); }
         return temp;               //return temp String
         }
   };
```

```
///////////////////////////////////////////////////////////
int main()
   {
   String s1 = "\nMerry Christmas!  ";    //uses constructor 2
   String s2 = "Happy new year!";         //uses constructor 2
   String s3;                             //uses constructor 1

   s1.display();                          //display strings
   s2.display();
   s3.display();

   s3 = s1 + s2;                          //add s2 to s1,
                                          //assign to s3
   s3.display();                          //display s3
   cout << endl;
   return 0;
   }
```

The program first displays three strings separately. (The third is empty at this point, so nothing is printed when it displays itself.) Then the first two strings are concatenated and placed in the third, and the third string is displayed again. Here's the output:

```
Merry Christmas!  Happy new year!    ←———— s1, s2, and s3 (empty)
Merry Christmas!  Happy new year!    ←———— s3 after concatenation
```

By now the basics of overloading the + operator should be somewhat familiar. The declarator

```
String operator + (String ss)
```

shows that the + operator takes one argument of type **String** and returns an object of the same type. The concatenation process in **operator+()** involves creating a temporary object of type **String**, copying the string from our own **String** object into it, concatenating the argument string using the library function **strcat()**, and returning the resulting temporary string. Note that we can't use the

```
return String(string);
```

approach, where a nameless temporary **String** is created, because we need access to the temporary **String** not only to initialize it, but to concatenate the argument string to it.

We must be careful that we don't overflow the fixed-length strings used in the **String** class. To prevent such accidents in the **operator+()** function, we check that the combined length of the two strings to be concatenated will not exceed the maximum string length. If they do, we print an error message instead of carrying out the concatenation operation. (We could handle errors in other ways, like returning a 0 if an error occurred, or better yet, throwing an exception, as discussed in Chapter 14, "Templates and Exceptions.")

Remember that using an **enum** to set the constant value **SZ** is a temporary fix. When all compilers comply with Standard C++ you can change it to:

```
static const int SZ = 80;
```

Multiple Overloading

We've seen several different uses of the + operator: to add English distances, and to concatenate strings. You could put both these classes together in the same program, and C++ would still know how to interpret the + operator: It selects the correct function to carry out the "addition" based on the type of operand.

Comparison Operators

Let's see how to overload a different kind of C++ operator: comparison operators.

Comparing Distances

In our first example we'll overload the *less than* operator < in the **Distance** class, so that we can compare two distances. Here's the listing for ENGLESS:

```cpp
// engless.cpp
// overloaded '<' operator compares two Distances
#include <iostream>
using namespace std;
//////////////////////////////////////////////////////////////
class Distance                      //English Distance class
   {
   private:
      int feet;
      float inches;
   public:                          //constructor (no args)
      Distance() : feet(0), inches(0.0)
         {  }                       //constructor (two args)
      Distance(int ft, float in) : feet(ft), inches(in)
         {  }
      void getdist()                //get length from user
         {
         cout << "\nEnter feet: ";  cin >> feet;
         cout << "Enter inches: ";  cin >> inches;
         }
      void showdist() const        //display distance
         { cout << feet << "\'-" << inches << '\"'; }
      bool operator < (Distance) const;  //compare distances
   };
//-------------------------------------------------------------
                                   //compare this distance with d2
bool Distance::operator < (Distance d2) const  //return the sum
   {
   float bf1 = feet + inches/12;
   float bf2 = d2.feet + d2.inches/12;
   return (bf1 < bf2) ? true : false;
   }
//////////////////////////////////////////////////////////////
int main()
   {
   Distance dist1;                  //define Distance dist1
```

```
   dist1.getdist();                    //get dist1 from user

   Distance dist2(6, 2.5);             //define and initialize dist2
                                       //display distances
   cout << "\ndist1 = ";   dist1.showdist();
   cout << "\ndist2 = ";   dist2.showdist();

   if( dist1 < dist2 )                 //overloaded '<' operator
      cout << "\ndist1 is less than dist2";
   else
      cout << "\ndist1 is greater than (or equal to) dist2";
   cout << endl;
   return 0;
   }
```

This program compares a distance entered by the user with a distance, 6'-2.5", initialized by the program. Depending on the result, it then prints one of two possible sentences. Here's some typical output:

```
Enter feet: 5
Enter inches: 11.5
dist1 = 5'-11.5"
dist2 = 6'-2.5"
dist1 is less than dist2
```

The approach used in the operator<() function in ENGLESS is similar to overloading the + operator in the ENGLPLUS program, except that here the operator<() function has a return type of bool. The return value is false or true, depending on the comparison of the two distances. The comparison is made by converting both distances to floating-point feet, and comparing them using the normal < operator. Remember that the use of the conditional operator

```
return (bf1 < bf2) ? true : false;
```

is the same as

```
if(bf1 < bf2)
   return true;
else
   return false;
```

Comparing Strings

Here's another example of overloading an operator, this time the *equal* (==) operator. We'll use it to compare two of our home-made String objects, returning true if they're the same and false if they're different. Here's the listing for STREQUAL:

```
//strequal.cpp
//overloaded '==' operator compares strings
#include <iostream>
using namespace std;
#include <string.h>        //for strcmp()
/////////////////////////////////////////////////////////////////////
```

```
class String                 //user-defined string type
   {
   private:
      enum { SZ = 80 };                 //size of String objects
      char str[SZ];                     //holds a string
   public:
      String()                          //constructor, no args
         { strcpy(str, ""); }
      String( char s[] )                //constructor, one arg
         { strcpy(str, s); }
      void display() const              //display a String
         { cout << str; }
      void getstr()                     //read a string
         { cin.get(str, SZ); }
      bool operator == (String ss) const  //check for equality
         {
         return ( strcmp(str, ss.str)==0 ) ? true : false;
         }
   };
/////////////////////////////////////////////////////////////////
int main()
   {
   String s1 = "yes";
   String s2 = "no";
   String s3;

   cout << "\nEnter 'yes' or 'no': ";
   s3.getstr();                         //get String from user

   if(s3==s1)                           //compare with "yes"
      cout << "You typed yes\n";
   else if(s3==s2)                      //compare with "no"
      cout << "You typed no\n";
   else
      cout << "You didn't follow instructions\n";
   return 0;
   }
```

The `main()` part of this program uses the == operator twice, once to see if a string input by the user is "yes" and once to see if it's "no." Here's the output when the user types "yes":

```
Enter 'yes' or 'no': yes
You typed yes
```

The `operator==()` function uses the library function `strcmp()` to compare the two C-strings. This function returns 0 if the strings are equal, a negative number if the first is less than the second, and a positive number if the first is greater than the second. Here *less than* and *greater than* are used in their lexicographical sense to indicate whether the first string appears before or after the second in an alphabetized listing.

Other comparison operators, such as < and >, could also be used to compare the lexicographical value of strings. Or, alternatively, these comparison operators could be redefined to compare string lengths. Since you're the one defining how the operators are used, you can use any definition that seems appropriate to your situation.

Arithmetic Assignment Operators

Let's finish up our exploration of overloaded binary operators with an arithmetic assignment operator: the += operator. Recall that this operator combines assignment and addition into one step. We'll use this operator to add one English distance to a second, leaving the result in the first. This is similar to the ENGLPLUS example shown earlier, but there is a subtle difference. Here's the listing for ENGLPLEQ:

```cpp
// englpleq.cpp
// overloaded '+=' assignment operator
#include <iostream>
using namespace std;
/////////////////////////////////////////////////////////////////
class Distance                        //English Distance class
   {
   private:
      int feet;
      float inches;
   public:                            //constructor (no args)
      Distance() : feet(0), inches(0.0)
         {  }                         //constructor (two args)
      Distance(int ft, float in) : feet(ft), inches(in)
         {  }
      void getdist()                  //get length from user
         {
         cout << "\nEnter feet: ";  cin >> feet;
         cout << "Enter inches: ";  cin >> inches;
         }
      void showdist() const          //display distance
         { cout << feet << "\'-" << inches << '\"'; }
      void operator += ( Distance );
   };
//---------------------------------------------------------------
                                      //add distance to this one
void Distance::operator += (Distance d2)
   {
   feet += d2.feet;                   //add the feet
   inches += d2.inches;               //add the inches
   if(inches >= 12.0)                 //if total exceeds 12.0,
      {                               //then decrease inches
      inches -= 12.0;                 //by 12.0 and
      feet++;                         //increase feet
      }                               //by 1
   }
/////////////////////////////////////////////////////////////////
int main()
   {
   Distance dist1;                    //define dist1
   dist1.getdist();                   //get dist1 from user
   cout << "\ndist1 = ";  dist1.showdist();

   Distance dist2(11, 6.25);          //define, initialize dist2
```

```
cout << "\ndist2 = ";  dist2.showdist();

dist1 += dist2;                      //dist1 = dist1 + dist2
cout << "\nAfter addition,";
cout << "\ndist1 = ";  dist1.showdist();
cout << endl;
return 0;
}
```

In this program we obtain a distance from the user and add to it a second distance, initialized to 11[sp]-6.25[dp] by the program. Here's a sample of interaction with the program:

```
Enter feet: 3
Enter inches: 5.75
dist1 = 3'-5.75"
dist2 = 11'-6.25"
After addition,
dist1 = 15'-0"
```

In this program the addition is carried out in `main()` with the statement

```
dist1 += dist2;
```

This causes the sum of `dist1` and `dist2` to be placed in `dist1`.

Notice the difference between the function used here, `operator+=()`, and that used in ENGLPLUS, `operator+()`. In the earlier `operator+()` function, a new object of type `Distance` had to be created and returned by the function so it could be assigned to a third `Distance` object, as in

```
dist3 = dist1 + dist2;
```

In the `operator+=()` function in ENGLPLEQ, the object that takes on the value of the sum is the object of which the function is a member. Thus it is `feet` and `inches` that are given values, not temporary variables used only to return an object. The `operator+=()` function has no return value; it returns type `void`. A return value is not necessary with arithmetic assignment operators like +=, because the result of the assignment operator is not assigned to anything. The operator is used alone, in expressions like the one in the program.

```
dist1 += dist2;
```

If you wanted to use this operator in more complex expressions, like

```
dist3 = dist1 += dist2;
```

then you would need to provide a return value. This can be done by ending the `operator+=()` function with a statement like

```
return Distance(feet, inches);
```

in which a nameless object is initialized to the same values as this object, and returned.

The Subscript Operator [ ]

The subscript operator, [ ], which is normally used to access array elements, can be overloaded. This is useful if you want to modify the way arrays work in C++. For example, you might want to make a "safe" array: One that automatically checks the index numbers you use to access the array, to ensure they are not out of bounds. (You can also use the **vector** class, described in Chapter 15, "The Standard Template Library.")

To demonstrate the overloaded subscript operator, we must return to another topic, first mentioned in Chapter 5: returning values from functions by reference. To be useful, the overloaded subscript operator must return by reference. To see why this is true, we'll show three example programs that implement a safe array, each one using a different approach to inserting and reading the array elements:

- Separate **put()** and **get()** functions

- A single **access()** function using return by reference

- The overloaded [ ] operator using return by reference

All three programs create a class called **safearay**, whose only member data is an array of 100 **int** values, and all three check to ensure that all array accesses are within bounds. The **main()** program in each program tests the class by filling the safe array with values (each one equal to 10 times its array index) and then displaying them all to assure the user that everything is working as it should.

Separate **get()** and **put()** Functions

The first program provides two functions to access the array elements: **putel()** to insert a value into the array, and **getel()** to find the value of an array element. Both functions check the value of the index number supplied to ensure it's not out of bounds; that is, less than 0 or larger than the array size (minus 1). Here's the listing for ARROVER1:

```
// arrover1.cpp
// creates safe array (index values are checked before access)
// uses separate put and get functions
#include <iostream>
using namespace std;
#include <process.h>                    // for exit()
const int LIMIT = 100;
/////////////////////////////////////////////////////////////////
class safearay
    {
    private:
        int arr[LIMIT];
    public:
        void putel(int n, int elvalue)  //set value of element
            {
            if( n< 0 || n>=LIMIT )
                { cout << "\nIndex out of bounds"; exit(1); }
            arr[n] = elvalue;
            }
```

```
        int getel(int n) const          //get value of element
            {
            if( n< 0 || n>=LIMIT )
                { cout << "\nIndex out of bounds"; exit(1); }
            return arr[n];
            }
    };
////////////////////////////////////////////////////////////////
int main()
    {
    safearay sa1;

    for(int j=0; j<LIMIT; j++)   // insert elements
        sa1.putel(j, j*10);

    for(j=0; j<LIMIT; j++)       // display elements
        {
        int temp = sa1.getel(j);
        cout << "Element " << j << " is " << temp << endl;
        }
    return 0;
    }
```

The data is inserted into the safe array with the `putel()` member function, and then displayed with `getel()`. This implements a safe array; you'll receive an error message if you attempt to use an out-of-bounds index. However, the format is a bit crude.

Single `access()` Function Returning by Reference

As it turns out, we can use the same member function both to insert data into the safe array and to read it out. The secret is to return the value from the function by reference. This means we can place the function on the left side of the equal sign, and the value on the right side will be assigned to the variable returned by the function, as explained in Chapter 5. Here's the listing for ARROVER2:

```
// arrover2.cpp
// creates safe array (index values are checked before access)
// uses one access() function for both put and get
#include <iostream>
using namespace std;
#include <process.h>           //for exit()
const int LIMIT = 100;         //array size
////////////////////////////////////////////////////////////////
class safearay
    {
    private:
        int arr[LIMIT];
    public:
        int& access(int n)         //note: return by reference
            {
            if( n< 0 || n>=LIMIT )
                { cout << "\nIndex out of bounds"; exit(1); }
            return arr[n];
```

```
            }
        };
//////////////////////////////////////////////////////////////
int main()
    {
    safearay sa1;

    for(int j=0; j<LIMIT; j++)      //insert elements
        sa1.access(j) = j*10;       //*left* side of equal sign

    for(j=0; j<LIMIT; j++)          //display elements
        {
        int temp = sa1.access(j); //*right* side of equal sign
        cout << "Element " << j << " is " << temp << endl;
        }
    return 0;
    }
```

The statement

```
sa1.access(j) = j*10;      // *left* side of equal sign
```

causes the value j*10 to be placed in arr[j], the return value of the function.

It's perhaps slightly more convenient to use the same function for input and output of the safe array than using separate functions; there's one less name to remember. But there's an even better way, with no names to remember at all.

Overloaded [ ] Operator Returning by Reference

To access the safe array using the same subscript ([ ]) operator that's used for normal C++ arrays, we overload the subscript operator in the safearay class. However, since this operator is commonly used on the left side of the equal sign, this overloaded function must return by reference, as we showed in the previous program. Here's the listing for ARROVER3:

```
// arrover3.cpp
// creates safe array (index values are checked before access)
// uses overloaded [] operator for both put and get

#include <iostream>
using namespace std;
#include <process.h>           //for exit()
const int LIMIT = 100;         //array size
//////////////////////////////////////////////////////////////
class safearay
    {
    private:
        int arr[LIMIT];
    public:
        int& operator [](int n)  //note: return by reference
            {
            if( n< 0 || n>=LIMIT )
                { cout << "\nIndex out of bounds"; exit(1); }
            return arr[n];
```

```
            }
    };
/////////////////////////////////////////////////////////////////
int main()
    {
    safearay sa1;

    for(int j=0; j<LIMIT; j++)   //insert elements
        sa1[j] = j*10;           //*left* side of equal sign

    for(j=0; j<LIMIT; j++)       //display elements
        {
        int temp = sa1[j];       //*right* side of equal sign
        cout << "Element " << j << " is " << temp << endl;
        }
    return 0;
    }
```

In this program we can use the natural subscript expressions

```
sa1[j] = j*10;
```

and

```
temp = sa1[j];
```

for input and output to the safe array.

Data Conversion

You already know that the = operator will assign a value from one variable to another, in statements like

```
intvar1 = intvar2;
```

where `intvar1` and `intvar2` are integer variables. You may also have noticed that = assigns the value of one user-defined object to another, provided they are of the same type, in statements like

```
dist3 = dist1 + dist2;
```

where the result of the addition, which is type `Distance`, is assigned to another object of type `Distance`, `dist3`. Normally, when the value of one object is assigned to another of the same type, the values of all the member data items are simply copied into the new object. The compiler doesn't need any special instructions to use = for the assignment of user-defined objects such as `Distance` objects.

Thus, assignments between types, whether they are basic types or user-defined types, are handled by the compiler with no effort on our part, provided that the same data type is used on both sides of the equal sign. But what happens when the variables on different sides of the = are of different types? This is a more thorny question, to which we will devote the balance of this chapter. We'll first review how the compiler handles the conversion of basic types, which it does automatically. Then we'll explore several situations where the compiler doesn't handle things automatically and we need to tell it what to do. These include conversions between basic types and user-defined types, and conversions between different user-defined types.

You might think it represents poor programming practice to convert routinely from one type to another. After all, languages such as Pascal go to considerable trouble to keep you from doing such conversions. However, the philosophy in C++ (and C) is that the flexibility provided by allowing conversions outweighs the dangers. This is a controversial issue; we'll return to it at the end of this chapter.

Conversions Between Basic Types

When we write a statement like

```
intvar = floatvar;
```

where `intvar` is of type `int` and `floatvar` is of type `float`, we are assuming that the compiler will call a special routine to convert the value of `floatvar`, which is expressed in floating-point format, to an integer format so that it can be assigned to `intvar`. There are of course many such conversions: from `float` to `double`, `char` to `float`, and so on. Each such conversion has its own routine, built into the compiler and called up when the data types on different sides of the = sign so dictate. We say such conversions are *implicit* because they aren't apparent in the listing.

Sometimes we want to force the compiler to convert one type to another. To do this we use the cast operator. For instance, to convert `float` to `int`, we can say

```
intvar = static_cast<int>(floatvar);
```

Casting provides *explicit* conversion: It's obvious in the listing that `static_cast<int>()` is intended to convert from `float` to `int`. However, such explicit conversions use the same built-in routines as implicit conversions.

Conversions Between Objects and Basic Types

When we want to convert between user-defined data types and basic types, we can't rely on built-in conversion routines, since the compiler doesn't know anything about user-defined types besides what we tell it. Instead, we must write these routines ourselves.

Our next example shows how to convert between a basic type and a user-defined type. In this example the user-defined type is (surprise!) the English `Distance` class from previous examples, and the basic type is `float`, which we use to represent meters, a unit of length in the metric measurement system.

The example shows conversion both from `Distance` to `float`, and from `float` to `Distance`. Here's the listing for ENGLCONV:

```
// englconv.cpp
// conversions: Distance to meters, meters to Distance
#include <iostream>
using namespace std;
/////////////////////////////////////////////////////////////
class Distance                      //English Distance class
```

```
       {
    private:
       const float MTF;                //meters to feet
       int feet;
       float inches;
    public:                            //constructor (no args)
       Distance() : feet(0), inches(0.0), MTF(3.280833F)
          {  }                         //constructor (one arg)
       Distance(float meters) : MTF(3.280833F)
          {                            //convert meters to Distance
          float fltfeet = MTF * meters;  //convert to float feet
          feet = int(fltfeet);         //feet is integer part
          inches = 12*(fltfeet-feet);  //inches is what's left
          }                            //constructor (two args)
       Distance(int ft, float in) : feet(ft),
                                     inches(in), MTF(3.280833F)
          {  }
       void getdist()                  //get length from user
          {
          cout << "\nEnter feet: ";  cin >> feet;
          cout << "Enter inches: ";  cin >> inches;
          }
       void showdist() const          //display distance
          { cout << feet << "\'-" << inches << '\"'; }

       operator float() const         //conversion operator
          {                           //converts Distance to meters
          float fracfeet = inches/12;     //convert the inches
          fracfeet += static_cast<float>(feet); //add the feet
          return fracfeet/MTF;            //convert to meters
          }
    };
////////////////////////////////////////////////////////////////
int main()
    {
    float mtrs;
    Distance dist1 = 2.35F;          //uses 1-arg constructor to
                                     //convert meters to Distance
    cout << "\ndist1 = "; dist1.showdist();

    mtrs = static_cast<float>(dist1); //uses conversion operator
                                      //for Distance to meters
    cout << "\ndist1 = " << mtrs << " meters\n";

    Distance dist2(5, 10.25);        //uses 2-arg constructor

    mtrs = dist2;                    //also uses conversion op
    cout << "\ndist2 = " << mtrs << " meters\n";

//  dist2 = mtrs;                    //error, = won't convert
    return 0;
    }
```

In `main()` the program first converts a fixed `float` quantity—2.35, representing meters—to feet and inches, using the one-argument constructor:

```
Distance dist1 = 2.35F;
```

Going in the other direction, it converts a `Distance` to meters in the statements

```
mtrs = static_cast<float>(dist2);
```

and

```
mtrs = dist2;
```

Here's the output:

```
dist1 = 7'-8.51949"     ←——— this is 2.35 meters
dist1 = 2.35 meters     ←——— this is 3'-3.369996"
dist2 = 1.78435 meters  ←——— this is 5'-10.25"
```

We've seen how conversions are performed using simple assignment statements in `main()`. Now let's see what goes on behind the scenes, in the `Distance` member functions. Converting a user-defined type to a basic type requires a different approach than converting a basic type to a user-defined type. We'll see how both types of conversions are carried out in ENGLCONV.

From Basic to User-Defined

To go from a basic type—`float` in this case—to a user-defined type such as `Distance`, we use a constructor with one argument. These are sometimes called *conversion constructors*. Here's how this constructor looks in ENGLCONV:

```
Distance(float meters)
   {
   float fltfeet = MTF * meters;
   feet = int(fltfeet);
   inches = 12 * (fltfeet-feet);
   }
```

This function is called when an object of type `Distance` is created with a single argument. The function assumes this argument represents meters. It converts the argument to feet and inches, and assigns the resulting values to the object. Thus the conversion from meters to `Distance` is carried out along with the creation of an object in the statement

```
Distance dist1 = 2.35;
```

From User-Defined to Basic

What about going the other way, from a user-defined type to a basic type? The trick here is to create something called a *conversion operator*. Here's where we do that in ENGLCONV:

```
operator float()
   {
   float fracfeet = inches/12;
   fracfeet += float(feet);
```

```
    return fracfeet/MTF;
    }
```

This operator takes the value of the **Distance** object of which it is a member, converts this value to a **float** value representing meters, and returns this value.

This operator can be called with an explicit cast:

```
mtrs = static_cast<float>(dist1);
```

or with a simple assignment:

```
mtrs = dist2;
```

Both forms convert the **Distance** object to its equivalent **float** value in meters.

Conversion Between C-Strings and **String** Objects

Here's another example that uses a one-argument constructor and a conversion operator. It operates on the **String** class that we saw in the STRPLUS example earlier in this chapter.

```
// strconv.cpp
// convert between ordinary strings and class String
#include <iostream>
using namespace std;
#include <string.h>             //for strcpy(), etc.
/////////////////////////////////////////////////////////////////
class String                    //user-defined string type
    {
    private:
        enum { SZ = 80 };       //size of all String objects
        char str[SZ];           //holds a string
    public:
        String()                //no-arg constructor
            { str[0] = '\0'; }
        String( char s[] )      //1-arg constructor
            { strcpy(str, s); } //   convert C-string to String
        void display() const    //display the String
            { cout << str; }
        operator char*()        //conversion operator
            { return str; }     //convert String to C-string
    };
/////////////////////////////////////////////////////////////////
int main()
    {
    String s1;                  //use no-arg constructor
                                //create and initialize C-string
    char xstr[] = "Joyeux Noel! ";

    s1 = xstr;                  //use 1-arg constructor
                                //   to convert C-string to String
    s1.display();               //display String

    String s2 = "Bonne Annee!"; //uses 1-arg constructor
                                //to initialize String
```

```
cout << static_cast<char*>(s2);  //use conversion operator
 cout << endl;                    //to convert String to C-string
 return 0;                        //before sending to << op
}
```

The one-argument constructor converts a normal string (an array of `char`) to an object of class `String`:

```
String(char s[])
  { strcpy(str, s); }
```

The C-string `s` is passed as an argument, and copied into the `str` data member in a newly created `String` object, using the `strcpy()` library function.

This conversion will be applied when a `String` is created, as in

```
String s2 = "Bonne Annee!";
```

or it will be applied in assignment statements, as in

```
s1 = xstr;
```

where `s1` is type `String` and `xstr` is a C-string.

A conversion operator is used to convert from a `String` type to a C-string:

```
operator char*()
  { return str; }
```

The use of the asterisk in this expression means *pointer to*. We won't explore pointers until Chapter 10, but its use here is not hard to figure out. It means *pointer to char*, which is very similar to *array of type char*. Thus `char*` is similar to `char[]`. It's another way of specifying a C-string data type.

The conversion operator is used by the compiler in the statement

```
cout << static_cast<char*>(s2);
```

Here the `s2` variable is an argument supplied to the overloaded operator `<<`. Since the `<<` operator doesn't know anything about our user-defined `String` type, the compiler looks for a way to convert `s2` to a type that `<<` does know about. We specify the type we want to convert it to with the `char*` cast, so it looks for a conversion from `String` to C-string, finds our operator `char*()` function, and uses it to generate a C-string, which is then sent on to `<<` to be displayed. (The effect is similar to calling the `String::display()` function, but given the ease and intuitive clarity of displaying with `<<`, the `display()` function is redundant and could be removed.)

Here's the output from STRCONV:

`Joyeux Noel! Bonne Annee!`

The STRCONV example demonstrates that conversions take place automatically not only in assignment statements but in other appropriate places, such as in arguments sent to operators (like `<<`) or functions. If you supply an operator or a function with arguments of the wrong type, they will be converted to arguments of an acceptable type, provided you have defined such a conversion.

Note that you can't use an explicit assignment statement to convert a `String` to a C-string:

```
xstr = s2;
```

The C-string `xstr` is an array, and you can't normally assign to arrays (although, as we'll see in Chapter 11, when you overload the assignment operator, all sorts of things are possible).

Conversions Between Objects of Different Classes

What about converting between objects of different user-defined classes? The same two methods just shown for conversions between basic types and user-defined types also apply to conversions between two user-defined types. That is, you can use a one-argument constructor or you can use a conversion operator. The choice depends on whether you want to put the conversion routine in the class declaration of the source object or of the destination object. For example, suppose you say

```
objecta = objectb;
```

where `objecta` is a member of class `A` and `objectb` is a member of class `B`. Is the conversion routine located in class `A` (the destination class, since `objecta` receives the value) or class `B` (the source class)? We'll look at both cases.

Two Kinds of Time

Our example programs will convert between two ways of measuring time: 12-hour time and 24-hour time. These methods of telling time are sometimes called *civilian time* and *military time*. Our `time12` class will represent civilian time, as used in digital clocks and airport flight departure displays. We'll assume that in this context there is no need for seconds, so `time12` uses only hours (from 1 to 12), minutes, and an "a.m." or "p.m." designation. Our `time24` class, which is for more exacting applications such as air navigation, uses hours (from 00 to 23), minutes, and seconds. Table 8.1 shows the differences.

Table 8.1 12-Hour and 24-Hour Time

12-hour Time	24-hour Time
12:00 a.m. (midnight)	00:00:00
12:01 a.m.	00:01:00
1:00 a.m.	01:00:00
6:00 a.m.	06:00:00
11:59 a.m	11:59:00
12:00 p.m. (noon)	12:00:00

12-hour Time	24-hour Time
12:01 p.m.	12:01:00
6:00 p.m.	18:00:00
11:59 p.m.	23:59:00

Note that 12 a.m. (midnight) in civilian time is 00 hours in military time. There is no 0 hours in civilian time. (In written works, noon is formally designated 12:00 m. and midnight is 12:00 p.m., but these aren't used in digital displays.)

Routine in Source Object

The first example program shows a conversion routine located in the source class. When the conversion routine is in the source class, it is commonly implemented as a conversion operator. Here's the listing for TIMES1:

```
//times1.cpp
//converts from time24 to time12 using operator in time24
#include <iostream>
#include <string>
using namespace std;
/////////////////////////////////////////////////////////////////
class time12
   {
   private:
      bool pm;                       //true = pm, false = am
      int hrs;                       //1 to 12
      int mins;                      //0 to 59
   public:                           //no-arg constructor
      time12() : pm(true), hrs(0), mins(0)
         {  }
                                     //3-arg constructor
      time12(bool ap, int h, int m) : pm(ap), hrs(h), mins(m)
         {  }
      void display() const          //format: 11:59 p.m.
         {
         cout << hrs << ':';
         if(mins < 10)
            cout << '0';             //extra zero for "01"
         cout << mins << ' ';
         string am_pm = pm ? "p.m." : "a.m.";
         cout << am_pm;
         }
   };
/////////////////////////////////////////////////////////////////
class time24
   {
   private:
      int hours;                     //0 to 23
      int minutes;                   //0 to 59
```

```
        int seconds;                    //0 to 59
    public:                             //no-arg constructor
        time24() : hours(0), minutes(0), seconds(0)
            {  }
        time24(int h, int m, int s) :   //3-arg constructor
                hours(h), minutes(m), seconds(s)
            {  }
        void display() const            //format: 23:15:01
            {
            if(hours < 10)    cout << '0';
            cout << hours << ':';
            if(minutes < 10)  cout << '0';
            cout << minutes << ':';
            if(seconds < 10)  cout << '0';
            cout << seconds;
            }
        operator time12(); const        //conversion operator
    };
//----------------------------------------------------------------
time24::operator time12() const              //conversion operator
    {
    int hrs24 = hours;
    bool pm = hours < 12 ? false : true;    //find am/pm
                                            //round secs
    int roundMins = seconds < 30 ? minutes : minutes+1;
    if(roundMins == 60)                     //carry mins?
        {
        roundMins=0;
        ++hrs24;
        if(hrs24 == 12 || hrs24 == 24)      //carry hrs?
            pm = (pm==true) ? false : true; //toggle am/pm
        }
    int hrs12 = (hrs24 < 13) ? hrs24 : hrs24-12;
    if(hrs12==0)                            //00 is 12 a.m.
        { hrs12=12; pm=false; }
    return time12(pm, hrs12, roundMins);
    }
/////////////////////////////////////////////////////////////////
int main()
    {
    int h, m, s;

    while(true)
        {                                   //get 24-hr time from user
        cout << "Enter 24-hour time: \n";
        cout << "   Hours (0 to 23): "; cin >> h;
        if(h > 23)                          //quit if hours > 23
            return(1);
        cout << "   Minutes: ";  cin >> m;
        cout << "   Seconds: ";  cin >> s;

        time24 t24(h, m, s);                //make a time24
        cout << "You entered: ";            //display the time24
```

```
    t24.display();

    time12 t12 = t24;                //convert time24 to time12

    cout << "\n12-hour time: ";      //display equivalent time12
    t12.display();
    cout << "\n\n";
    }
  return 0;
  }
```

In the `main()` part of TIMES1, we define an object of type **time24**, called **t24**, and give it values for hours, minutes, and seconds obtained from the user. We also define an object of type **time12**, called **t12**, and initialize it to **t24** in the statement

```
time 12 t12 = t24;
```

Since these objects are from different classes, the assignment involves a conversion, and—as we specified—in this program the conversion operator is a member of the **time24** class. Here's what it looks like:

```
time24::operator time12() const             //conversion operator
    {
    int hrs24 = hours;
    bool pm = hours < 12 ? false : true;   //find am/pm
                                           //round secs
    int roundMins = seconds < 30 ? minutes : minutes+1;
    if(roundMins == 60)                    //carry mins?
        {
        roundMins=0;
        ++hrs24;
        if(hrs24 == 12 || hrs24 == 24)     //carry hrs?
            pm = (pm==true) ? false : true; //toggle am/pm
        }
    int hrs12 = (hrs24 < 13) ? hrs24 : hrs24-12;
    if(hrs12==0)                           //00 is 12 a.m.
        { hrs12=12; pm=false; }
    return time12(pm, hrs12, roundMins);
    }
```

This function transforms the object of which it is a member to a **time12** object, and returns this object, which `main()` then assigns to **t12**. Here's some interaction with TIMES1:

```
Enter 24-hour time:
   Hours (0 to 23): 17
   Minutes: 59
   Seconds: 45
You entered: 17:59:45
12-hour time: 6:00 p.m.
```

The seconds value is rounded up, pushing the 12-hour time from 5:59 p.m. to 6:00 p.m. Entering an hours value greater than 23 causes the program to exit.

Routine in Destination Object

Let's see how the same conversion is carried out when the conversion routine is in the destination class. In this situation it's common to use a one-argument constructor. However, things are complicated by the fact that the constructor in the destination class must be able to access the data in the source class to perform the conversion. The data in time24—hours, minutes and seconds—is private, so we must provide special member functions in time24 to allow direct access to it. These are called getHrs(), getMins(), and getSecs().

Here's the listing for TIMES2:

```cpp
//times2.cpp
//converts from time24 to time12 using constructor in time12
#include <iostream>
#include <string>
using namespace std;
/////////////////////////////////////////////////////////////////
class time24
   {
   private:
      int hours;                        //0 to 23
      int minutes;                      //0 to 59
      int seconds;                      //0 to 59
   public:                              //no-arg constructor
      time24() : hours(0), minutes(0), seconds(0)
         { }
      time24(int h, int m, int s) :  //3-arg constructor
             hours(h), minutes(m), seconds(s)
         { }
      void display() const             //format 23:15:01
         {
         if(hours < 10)    cout << '0';
         cout << hours << ':';
         if(minutes < 10)  cout << '0';
         cout << minutes << ':';
         if(seconds < 10)  cout << '0';
         cout << seconds;
         }
      int getHrs() const    { return hours; }
      int getMins() const   { return minutes; }
      int getSecs() const   { return seconds; }
   };
/////////////////////////////////////////////////////////////////
class time12
   {
   private:
      bool pm;                          //true = pm, false = am
      int hrs;                          //1 to 12
      int mins;                         //0 to 59
   public:                              //no-arg constructor
      time12() : pm(true), hrs(0), mins(0)
         { }
```

```
      time12(time24);                  //1-arg constructor
                                       //3-arg constructor
      time12(bool ap, int h, int m) : pm(ap), hrs(h), mins(m)
         { }
      void display() const
         {
         cout << hrs << ':';
         if(mins < 10)  cout << '0';  //extra zero for "01"
         cout << mins << ' ';
         string am_pm = pm ? "p.m." : "a.m.";
         cout << am_pm;
         }
   };
//-------------------------------------------------------------
time12::time12( time24 t24 )          //1-arg constructor
   {                                  //converts time24 to time12
   int hrs24 = t24.getHrs();          //get hours
                                      //find am/pm
   pm = t24.getHrs() < 12 ? false : true;

   mins = (t24.getSecs() < 30) ?      //round secs
                     t24.getMins() : t24.getMins()+1;
   if(mins == 60)                     //carry mins?
      {
      mins=0;
      ++hrs24;
      if(hrs24 == 12 || hrs24 == 24)     //carry hrs?
         pm = (pm==true) ? false : true;  //toggle am/pm
      }
   hrs = (hrs24 < 13) ? hrs24 : hrs24-12; //convert hrs
   if(hrs==0)                         //00 is 12 a.m.
      { hrs=12; pm=false; }
   }
////////////////////////////////////////////////////////////////
int main()
   {
   int h, m, s;

   while(true)
      {                               //get 24-hour time from user
      cout << "Enter 24-hour time: \n";
      cout << "   Hours (0 to 23): "; cin >> h;
      if(h > 23)                      //quit if hours > 23
         return(1);
      cout << "   Minutes: ";  cin >> m;
      cout << "   Seconds: ";  cin >> s;

      time24 t24(h, m, s);            //make a time24
      cout << "You entered: ";        //display the time24
      t24.display();

      time12 t12 = t24;               //convert time24 to time12
```

```
            cout << "\n12-hour time: ";    //display equivalent time12
            t12.display();
            cout << "\n\n";
            }
        return 0;
        }
```

Here's the conversion routine, a one-argument constructor from the time12 class:

```
time12::time12( time24 t24 )             //1-arg constructor
    {                                    //converts time24 to time12
    int hrs24 = t24.getHrs();            //get hours
                                         //find am/pm
    pm = t24.getHrs() < 12 ? false : true;

    mins = (t24.getSecs() < 30) ?        //round secs
                        t24.getMins() : t24.getMins()+1;
    if(mins == 60)                       //carry mins?
        {
        mins=0;
        ++hrs24;
        if(hrs24 == 12 || hrs24 == 24)       //carry hrs?
            pm = (pm==true) ? false : true;  //toggle am/pm
        }
    hrs = (hrs24 < 13) ? hrs24 : hrs24-12; //convert hrs
    if(hrs==0)                           //00 is 12 a.m.
        { hrs=12; pm=false; }
    }
```

This function sets the object of which it is a member to values that correspond to the time24 values of the object received as an argument. It works in much the same way as the conversion operator in TIMES1, except that it must work a little harder to access the data in the time24 object, using getHrs() and similar functions.

The main() part of TIMES2 is the same as that in TIMES1. The one-argument constructor again allows the time24 to time12 conversion to take place in the statement

```
time12 t12 = t24;
```

The output is similar as well. The difference is behind the scenes, where the conversion is handled by a constructor in the destination object rather than a conversion operator in the source object.

Conversions: When to Use What

When should you use the one-argument constructor in the destination class, as opposed to the conversion operator in the source class? Mostly you can take your pick. However, sometimes the choice is made for you. If you have purchased a library of classes, you may not have access to their source code. If you use an object of such a class as the source in a conversion, then you'll have access only to the destination class, and you'll need to use a one-argument constructor. If the library class object is the destination, then you must use a conversion operator in the source.

Pitfalls of Operator Overloading and Conversion

Operator overloading and type conversions give you the opportunity to create what amounts to an entirely new language. When **a**, **b**, and **c** are objects from user-defined classes, and + is overloaded, the statement

```
a = b + c;
```

means something quite different than it does when **a**, **b**, and **c** are variables of basic data types. The ability to redefine the building blocks of the language can be a blessing in that it can make your listing more intuitive and readable. It can also have the opposite effect, making your listing more obscure and hard to understand. Here are some guidelines.

Use Similar Meanings

Use overloaded operators to perform operations that are as similar as possible to those performed on basic data types. You could overload the + sign to perform subtraction, for example, but that would hardly make your listings more comprehensible.

Overloading an operator assumes that it makes sense to perform a particular operation on objects of a certain class. If we're going to overload the + operator in class **X**, then the result of adding two objects of class **X** should have a meaning at least somewhat similar to addition. For example, in this chapter we showed how to overload the + operator for the English **Distance** class. Adding two distances is clearly meaningful. We also overloaded + for the **String** class. Here we interpret the addition of two strings to mean placing one string after another to form a third. This also has an intuitively satisfying interpretation. But for many classes it may not be reasonable to talk about "adding" their objects. You probably wouldn't want to add two objects of a class called **employee** that held personal data, for example.

Use Similar Syntax

Use overloaded operators in the same way you use basic types. For example, if **alpha** and **beta** are basic types, the assignment operator in the statement

```
alpha += beta;
```

sets **alpha** to the sum of **alpha** and **beta**. Any overloaded version of this operator should do something analogous. It should probably do the same thing as

```
alpha = alpha + beta;
```

where the + is overloaded.

Some syntactical characteristics of operators can't be changed even if you want them to. As you may have discovered, you can't overload a binary operator to be a unary operator, or vice versa.

Show Restraint

Remember that if you have overloaded the + operator, anyone unfamiliar with your listing will need to do considerable research to find out what a statement like

```
a = b + c;
```

really means. If the number of overloaded operators grows too large, and if they are used in non-intuitive ways, then the whole point of using them is lost, and the listing becomes less readable instead of more. Use overloaded operators sparingly, and only when the usage is obvious. When in doubt, use a function instead of an overloaded operator, since a function name can state its own purpose. If you write a function to find the left side of a string, for example, you're better off calling it `getleft()` than trying to overload some operator like `&&` to do the same thing.

Avoid Ambiguity

Suppose you use both a one-argument constructor and a conversion operator to perform the same conversion (`time24` to `time12`, for example). How will the compiler know which conversion to use? It won't. The compiler does not like to be placed in a situation where it doesn't know what to do, and it will signal an error. So avoid doing the same conversion in more than one way.

Not All Operators Can Be Overloaded

The following operators cannot be overloaded: the member access or dot operator (`.`), the scope resolution operator (`::`), and the conditional operator (`?:`). Also, the pointer-to-member operator (`->`), which we have not yet encountered, cannot be overloaded. In case you wondered, no, you can't create new operators (like `*&`) and try to overload them; only existing operators can be overloaded.

Keywords `explicit` and `mutable`

Let's look at two unusual keywords: `explicit` and `mutable`. They have quite different effects, but are grouped together here because they both modify class members. The `explicit` keyword relates to data conversion, but `mutable` has a more subtle purpose.

Preventing Conversions with `explicit`

There may be some specific conversions you have decided are a good thing, and you've taken steps to make them possible by installing appropriate conversion operators and one-argument constructors, as shown in the TIME1 and TIME2 examples. However, there may be other conversions that you don't want to happen. You should actively discourage any conversion that you don't want. This prevents unpleasant surprises.

It's easy to prevent a conversion performed by a conversion operator: just don't define the operator. However, things aren't so easy with constructors. You may want to construct objects using a single value of another type, but you may not want the implicit conversions a one-argument constructor makes possible in other situations. What to do?

Standard C++ includes a keyword, **explicit**, to solve this problem. It's placed just before the declaration of a one-argument constructor. The EXPLICIT example program (based on the ENGLCON program) shows how this looks.

```cpp
//explicit.cpp
#include <iostream>
using namespace std;
////////////////////////////////////////////////////////////////
class Distance                     //English Distance class
   {
   private:
      const float MTF;             //meters to feet
      int feet;
      float inches;
   public:                         //no-args constructor
      Distance() : feet(0), inches(0.0), MTF(3.280833F)
         { }
                                   //EXPLICIT one-arg constructor
      explicit Distance(float meters) : MTF(3.280833F)
         {
         float fltfeet = MTF * meters;
         feet = int(fltfeet);
         inches = 12*(fltfeet-feet);
         }
      void showdist()              //display distance
         { cout << feet << "\'-" << inches << '\"'; }
   };
////////////////////////////////////////////////////////////////
int main()
   {
   void fancyDist(Distance);       //declaration
   Distance dist1(2.35F);          //uses 1-arg constructor to
                                   //convert meters to Distance

// Distance dist1 = 2.35F;         //ERROR if ctor is explicit
   cout << "\ndist1 = "; dist1.showdist();

   float mtrs = 3.0F;
   cout << "\ndist1 ";
// fancyDist(mtrs);                //ERROR if ctor is explicit

   return 0;
   }
//-------------------------------------------------------------
void fancyDist(Distance d)
   {
```

```
cout << "(in feet and inches) = ";
d.showdist();
cout << endl;
}
```

This program includes a function (`fancyDist()`) that embellishes the output of a `Distance` object by printing the phrase "(in feet and inches)" before the feet and inches figures. The argument to this function is a `Distance` variable, and you can call `fancyDist()` with such a variable with no problem.

The tricky part is that, unless you take some action to prevent it, you can also call `fancyDist()` with a variable of type `float` as the argument:

```
fancyDist(mtrs);
```

The compiler will realize it's the wrong type and look for a conversion operator. Finding a `Distance` constructor that takes type `float` as an argument, it will arrange for this constructor to convert `float` to `Distance` and pass the `Distance` value to the function. This is an implicit conversion, one which you may not have intended to make possible.

However, if we make the constructor explicit, we prevent implicit conversions. You can check this by removing the comment symbol from the call to `fancyDist()` in the program: the compiler will tell you it can't perform the conversion. Without the explicit keyword, this call is perfectly legal.

As a side effect of the explicit constructor, note that you can't use the form of object initialization that uses an equal sign:

```
Distance dist1 = 2.35F;
```

Whereas the form with parentheses,

```
Distance dist1(2.35F);
```

works as it always has.

Changing `const` Object Data Using `mutable`

Ordinarily, when you create a `const` object (as described in Chapter 6), you want a guarantee that none of its member data can be changed. However, a situation occasionally arises where you want to create `const` objects that have some specific member data item that needs to be modified despite the object's `const`ness.

As an example, let's imagine a window, such as Windows' programs commonly draw on the screen. It may be that some of the features of the window, such as its scrollbars and menus, are *owned* by the window. Ownership is common in various programming situations, and indicates a greater degree of independence than when one object is an attribute of another. In such a situation an object may remain unchanged, except that its owner may change. A scrollbar retains the same size, color, and orientation, but its ownership may be transferred from one window to another. It's like what happens when your bank sells your mortgage to another bank; all the terms of the mortgage are the same, only the owner is different.

Let's say we want to be able to create **const** scrollbars in which attributes remain unchanged, except for their ownership. That's where the **mutable** keyword comes in. The MUTABLE program shows how this looks.

```cpp
//mutable.cpp
#include <iostream>
#include <string>
using namespace std;
/////////////////////////////////////////////////////////////
class scrollbar
   {
   private:
      int size;                    //related to constness
      mutable string owner;        //not relevant to constness
   public:
      scrollbar(int sz, string own) : size(sz), owner(own)
         {  }
      void setSize(int sz)              //changes size
         { size = sz; }
      void setOwner(string own) const  //changes owner
         { owner = own; }
      int getSize() const              //returns size
         { return size; }
      string getOwner() const          //returns owner
         { return owner; }
   };
/////////////////////////////////////////////////////////////
int main()
   {
   const scrollbar sbar(60, "Window1");

// sbar.setSize(100);                 //can't do this to const obj
   sbar.setOwner("Window2");          //this is OK
                                      //these are OK too
   cout << sbar.getSize() << ", " << sbar.getOwner() << endl;
   return 0;
   }
```

The **size** attribute represents the various scrollbar data that cannot be modified in **const** objects. The **owner** attribute, however, can change, even if the object is **const**. To permit this, it's made **mutable**. In **main()** we create a **const** object **sbar**. Its size cannot be modified, but its owner can, using the **setOwner()** function. (In a non-**const** object, of course, both attributes could be modified.) In this situation **sbar** is said to have *logical constness*. That means that in theory it can't be modified, but in practice it can, in a limited way.

Summary

In this chapter we've seen how the normal C++ operators can be given new meanings when applied to user-defined data types. The keyword *operator* is used to *overload* an operator, and the resulting operator will adopt the meaning supplied by the programmer.

Closely related to operator overloading is the issue of *type conversion*. Some conversions take place between user-defined types and basic types. Two approaches are used in such conversions: A one-argument constructor changes a basic type to a user-defined type, and a conversion operator converts a user-defined type to a basic type. When one user-defined type is converted to another, either approach can be used.

Table 8.2 summarizes these conversions.

Table 8.2   Type Conversions

	Routine In Destination	Routine In Source
Basic to basic	**(Built-In Conversion Operators)**	
Basic to class	Constructor	NA
Class to basic	NA	Conversion operator
Class to class	Constructor	Conversion operator

A constructor given the keyword `explicit` cannot be used in implicit data conversion situations. A data member given the keyword `mutable` can be changed, even if its object is `const`.

Questions

Answers to questions can be found in Appendix G, "Answers to Questions and Exercises."

1. Operator overloading is

   a. making C++ operators work with objects.

   b. giving C++ operators more than they can handle.

   c. giving new meanings to existing C++ operators.

   d. making new C++ operators.

2. Assuming that class X does not use any overloaded operators, write a statement that subtracts an object of class X, x1, from another such object, x2, and places the result in x3.

3. Assuming that class X includes a routine to overload the - operator, write a statement that would perform the same task as that specified in Question 2.

4. True or false: The >= operator can be overloaded.

5. Write a complete definition for an overloaded operator for the `Counter` class of the COUNTPP1 example that, instead of incrementing the count, decrements it.

6. How many arguments are required in the definition of an overloaded unary operator?

7. Assume a class `C` with objects `obj1`, `obj2`, and `obj3`. For the statement `obj3 = obj1 - obj2` to work correctly, the overloaded - operator must

    a. take two arguments.

    b. return a value.

    c. create a named temporary object.

    d. use the object of which it is a member as an operand.

8. Write a complete definition for an overloaded ++ operator for the `Distance` class from the ENGLPLUS example. It should add 1 to the `feet` member data, and make possible statements like:

```
dist1++;
```

9. Repeat Question 8, except statements like the following should be allowed:

```
dist2 = dist1++;
```

10. When used in prefix form, what does the overloaded ++ operator do differently from what it does in postfix form?

11. Here are two declarators that describe ways to add two string objects:

```
void add(String s1, String s2)
String operator + (String s)
```

Match the following from the first declarator with the appropriate selection from the second:

function name (**add**) matches _____.

return value (type **void**) matches _____.

first argument (**s1**) matches _____.

second argument (**s2**) matches _____.

object of which function is a member matches _____.

    a. argument (**s**)

    b. object of which operator is a member

    c. operator (**+**)

    d. return value (type **String**)

    e. no match for this item

12. True or false: An overloaded operator always requires one less argument than its number of operands.

13. When you overload an arithmetic assignment operator, the result

    a. goes in the object to the right of the operator.

    b. goes in the object to the left of the operator.

    c. goes in the object of which the operator is a member.

    d. must be returned.

14. Write the complete definition of an overloaded **++** operator that works with the **String** class from the STRPLUS example and has the effect of changing its operand to uppercase. You can use the library function **toupper()** (header file CCTYPE), which takes as its only argument the character to be changed and returns the changed character (or the same character if no change is necessary).

15. To convert from a user-defined class to a basic type, you would most likely use

    a. a built-in conversion operator.

    b. a one-argument constructor.

    c. an overloaded **=** operator.

    d. a conversion operator that's a member of the class.

16. True or false: The statement **objA=objB;** will cause a compiler error if the objects are of different classes.

17. To convert from a basic type to a user-defined class, you would most likely use

    a. a built-in conversion operator.

    b. a one-argument constructor.

    c. an overloaded = operator.

    d. a conversion operator that's a member of the class.

18. True or false: If you've defined a constructor to handle definitions like `aclass obj = intvar;` you can also make statements like `obj = intvar;`.

19. If `objA` is in class `A`, and `objB` is in class `B`, and you want to say `objA = objB;`, and you want the conversion routine to go in class `A`, what type of conversion routine might you use?

20. True or false: The compiler won't object if you overload the `*` operator to perform division.

Exercises

Answers to starred exercises can be found in Appendix G.

*1. To the `Distance` class in the ENGLPLUS program in this chapter, add an overloaded - operator that subtracts two distances. It should allow statements like `dist3=dist1-dist2;`. Assume the operator will never be used to subtract a larger number from a smaller one (that is, negative distances are not allowed).

*2. Write a program that substitutes an overloaded += operator for the overloaded + operator in the STRPLUS program in this chapter. This operator should allow statements like

```
s1 += s2;
```

where `s2` is added (concatenated) to `s1` and the result is left in `s1`. The operator should also permit the results of the operation to be used in other calculations, as in

```
s3 = s1 += s2;
```

*3. Modify the `time` class from Exercise 3 in Chapter 6 so that instead of a function `add_time()` it uses the overloaded + operator to add two times. Write a program to test this class.

*4. Create a class `Int` based on Exercise 1 in Chapter 6. Overload four integer arithmetic operators (+, -, *, and /) so that they operate on objects of type `Int`. If the result of any such arithmetic operation exceeds the normal range of `ints` (in a 32-bit environment)—from 2,147,483,648 to -2,147,483,647—have the operator print a warning and terminate the program. Such a data type might be useful where mistakes caused by arithmetic overflow are unacceptable. Hint: To facilitate checking for overflow, perform the calculations using type `long double`. Write a program to test this class.

5. Augment the `time` class referred to in Exercise 3 to include overloaded increment (++) and decrement (--) operators that operate in both prefix and postfix notation and return values. Add statements to `main()` to test these operators.

6. Add to the `time` class of Exercise 5 the ability to subtract two time values using the overloaded (-) operator, and to multiply a time value by a number of type `float`, using the overloaded (*) operator.

7. Modify the `fraction` class in the four-function fraction calculator from Exercise 11 in Chapter 6 so that it uses overloaded operators for addition, subtraction, multiplication, and division. (Remember the rules for fraction arithmetic in Exercise 12 in Chapter 3, "Loops and Decisions.") Also overload the == and != comparison operators, and use them to exit from the loop if the user enters 0/1, 0/1 for the values of the two input fractions. You may want to modify the `lowterms()` function so that it returns the value of its argument reduced to lowest terms. This makes it more useful in the arithmetic functions, where it can be applied just before the answer is returned.

8. Modify the `bMoney` class from Exercise 12 in Chapter 7, "Arrays and Strings," to include the following arithmetic operations, performed with overloaded operators:

```
bMoney = bMoney + bMoney
bMoney = bMoney - bMoney
bMoney = bMoney * long double  (price per widget times number of
widgets)
long double = bMoney / bMoney  (total price divided by price per
widget)
bMoney = bMoney / long double  (total price divided by number of
widgets)
```

Notice that the / operator is overloaded twice. The compiler can distinguish between the two usages because the arguments are different. Remember that it's easy to perform arithmetic operations on `bMoney` objects by performing the same operation on their `long double` data.

Make sure the `main()` program asks the user to enter two money strings and a floating-point number. It should then carry out all five operations and display the results. This should happen in a loop, so the user can enter more numbers if desired.

Some money operations don't make sense: `bMoney * bMoney` doesn't represent anything real, since there is no such thing as square money; and you can't add `bMoney` to `long double` (what's dollars plus widgets?). To make it impossible to compile such illegal operations, don't include conversion operators for `bMoney` to `long double` or `long double` to `bMoney`. If you do, and you write an expression like

```
bmon2 = bmon1 + widgets;  // doesn't make sense
```

then the compiler will automatically convert widgets to **bMoney** and carry out the addition. Without them, the compiler will flag such conversions as an error, making it easier to catch conceptual mistakes. Also, make any conversion constructors explicit.

There are some other plausible money operations that we don't yet know how to perform with overloaded operators, since they require an object on the right side of the operator but not the left:

```
long double * bMoney  // can't do this yet: bMoney only on right
long double / bMoney  // can't do this yet: bMoney only on right
```

We'll learn how to handle this situation when we discuss friend functions in Chapter 11.

9. Augment the **safearay** class in the ARROVER3 program in this chapter so that the user can specify both the upper and lower bound of the array (indexes running from 100 to 200, for example). Have the overloaded subscript operator check the index each time the array is accessed to ensure it is not out of bounds. You'll need to add a two-argument constructor that specifies the upper and lower bounds. Since we have not yet learned how to allocate memory dynamically, the member data will still be an array that starts at 0 and runs up to 99, but perhaps you can map the indexes for the **safearay** into different indexes in the real **int** array. For example, if the client selects a range from 100 to 175, you could map this into the range from **arr[0]** to **arr[75]**.

10. For math buffs only: Create a class **Polar** that represents the points on the plain as polar coordinates (radius and angle). Create an overloaded **+operator** for addition of two **Polar** quantities. "Adding" two points on the plain can be accomplished by adding their X coordinates and then adding their Y coordinates. This gives the X and Y coordinates of the "answer." Thus you'll need to convert two sets of polar coordinates to rectangular coordinates, add them, then convert the resulting rectangular representation back to polar.

11. Remember the **sterling** structure? We saw it in Exercise 10 in Chapter 2, "C++ Programming Basics," and in Exercise 11 in Chapter 5, among other places. Turn it into a class, with pounds (type **long**), shillings (type **int**), and pence (type **int**) data items. Create the following member functions:

- no-argument constructor
- one-argument constructor, taking type **double** (for converting from decimal pounds)

- three-argument constructor, taking pounds, shillings, and pence

- `getSterling()` to get an amount in pounds, shillings, and pence from the user, format £9.19.11

- `putSterling()` to display an amount in pounds, shillings, and pence, format £9.19.11

- addition (`sterling + sterling`) using overloaded + operator

- subtraction (`sterling - sterling`) using overloaded - operator

- multiplication (`sterling * double`) using overloaded * operator

- division (`sterling / sterling`) using overloaded / operator

- division (`sterling / double`) using overloaded / operator

- operator `double` (to convert to `double`)

To perform arithmetic, you could (for example) add each object's data separately: Add the pence, carry, add the shillings, carry, and so on. However, it's easier to use the conversion operator to convert both `sterling` objects to type `double`, perform the arithmetic on the doubles, and convert back to `sterling`. Thus the overloaded + operator looks like this:

```
sterling sterling::operator + (sterling s2)
   {
   return sterling( double(sterling(pounds, shillings, pence))
                 + double(s2) );
   }
```

This creates two temporary `double` variables, one derived from the object of which the function is a member, and one derived from the argument `s2`. These `double` variables are then added, and the result is converted back to `sterling` and returned.

Notice that we use a different philosophy with the `sterling` class than with the `bMoney` class. With sterling we use conversion operators, thus giving up the ability to catch illegal math operations but gaining simplicity in writing the overloaded math operators.

12. Write a program that incorporates both the `bMoney` class from Exercise 8 and the `sterling` class from Exercise 11. Write conversion operators to convert between `bMoney` and `sterling`, assuming that one pound (£1.0.0) equals fifty dollars ($50.00). This was the approximate exchange rate in the 19th century when the British Empire was at its height and the pounds-shillings-pence format was in use. Write a `main()` program that allows the user to enter an amount in either currency, and that then converts it to the other currency and displays the result. Minimize any modifications to the existing `bMoney` and `sterling` classes.

CHAPTER 9

INHERITANCE

You will learn about the following in this chapter:

- Reasons for inheritance
- Base and derived classes
- Access control
- Class hierarchies
- Multiple inheritance
- Inheritance and program development

*I*nheritance is probably the most powerful feature of object-oriented programming, after classes themselves. Inheritance is the process of creating new classes, called *derived classes*, from existing or *base classes*. The derived class inherits all the capabilities of the base class but can add embellishments and refinements of its own. The base class is unchanged by this process. The inheritance relationship is shown in Figure 9.1.

The arrow in Figure 9.1 goes in the opposite direction of what you might expect. If it pointed down we would label it *inheritance*. However, the more common approach is to point the arrow up, from the derived class to the base class, and to think of it as a "derived from" arrow.

Inheritance is an essential part of OOP. Its big payoff is that it permits code *reusability*. Once a base class is written and debugged, it need not be touched again, but, using inheritance, can nevertheless be adapted to work in different situations. Reusing existing code saves time and money and increases a program's reliability. Inheritance can also help in the original conceptualization of a programming problem, and in the overall design of the program.

An important result of reusability is the ease of distributing class libraries. A programmer can use a class created by another person or company, and, without modifying it, derive other classes from it that are suited to particular situations.

We'll examine these features of inheritance in more detail after we've seen some specific instances of inheritance at work.

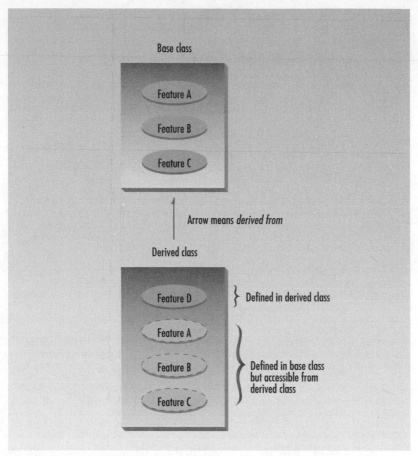

Figure 9.1 Inheritance.

Derived Class and Base Class

Remember the COUNTPP3 example from Chapter 8, "Operator Overloading?" This program used a class **Counter** as a general-purpose counter variable. A count could be initialized to 0 or to a specified number with constructors, incremented with the ++ operator, and read with the **get_count()** operator.

Let's suppose that we have worked long and hard to make the Counter class operate just the way we want, and we're pleased with the results, except for one thing. We really need a way to decrement the count. Perhaps we're counting people entering a bank, and we want to increment the count when they come in and decrement it when they go out, so that the count represents the number of people in the bank at any moment.

We could insert a decrement routine directly into the source code of the Counter class. However, there are several reasons why we might not want to do this. First, the Counter class works very well and has undergone many hours of testing and debugging. (Of course that's an exaggeration in this case, but it would be true in a larger and more complex class.) If we start fooling around with the source code for Counter, the testing process will need to be carried out again, and of course we may foul something up and spend hours debugging code that worked fine before we modified it.

In some situations there might be another reason for not modifying the Counter class: We might not have access to its source code, especially if it had been distributed as part of a class library. (We'll discuss this issue further in Chapter 13, "Multifile Programs.")

To avoid these problems we can use inheritance to create a new class based on Counter, without modifying Counter itself. Here's the listing for COUNTEN, which includes a new class, CountDn, that adds a decrement operator to the Counter class:

```cpp
// counten.cpp
// inheritance with Counter class
#include <iostream>
using namespace std;
/////////////////////////////////////////////////////////////////
class Counter                               //base class
   {
   protected:                               //NOTE: not private
      unsigned int count;                   //count
   public:
      Counter() : count(0)                  //no-arg constructor
         { }
      Counter(int c) : count(c)             //1-arg constructor
         { }
      unsigned int get_count() const        //return count
         { return count; }
      Counter operator ++ ()                //incr count (prefix)
         { return Counter(++count); }
   };
/////////////////////////////////////////////////////////////////
class CountDn : public Counter              //derived class
   {
   public:
      Counter operator -- ()                //decr count (prefix)
```

```
                { return Counter(--count); }
   };
//////////////////////////////////////////////////////////////////
int main()
   {
   CountDn c1;                          //c1 of class CountDn

   cout << "\nc1=" << c1.get_count();   //display c1

   ++c1; ++c1; ++c1;                    //increment c1, 3 times
   cout << "\nc1=" << c1.get_count();   //display it

   --c1; --c1;                          //decrement c1, twice
   cout << "\nc1=" << c1.get_count();   //display it
   cout << endl;
   return 0;
   }
```

The listing starts off with the `Counter` class, which (with one small exception, which we'll look at later) has not changed since its appearance in COUNTPP3. Notice that, for simplicity we haven't modeled this program on the POSTFIX program, which incorporated the second overloaded ++ operator to provide postfix notation.

Specifying the Derived Class

Following the `Counter` class in the listing is the specification for a new class, `CountDn`. This class incorporates a new function, `operator--()`, which decrements the count. However—and here's the key point—the new `CountDn` class inherits all the features of the `Counter` class. `CountDn` doesn't need a constructor or the `get_count()` or `operator++()` functions, because these already exist in `Counter`.

The first line of `CountDn` specifies that it is derived from `Counter`:

```
class CountDn : public Counter
```

Here we use a single colon (not the double colon used for the scope resolution operator), followed by the keyword `public` and the name of the base class `Counter`. This sets up the relationship between the classes. This line says `CountDn` *is derived from the base class* `Counter`. (We'll explore the effect of the keyword `public` later.) The relationship is shown in Figure 9.2.

Remember that the arrow in diagrams like this means *derived from*. The arrows point this way to emphasize that the derived class *refers to* functions and data in the base class, while the base class has no access to the derived class. Mathematicians call this kind of diagram a *directed acyclic graph*, or DAG (as in "DAGonnit, I drew the arrow the wrong way"). They are also called *inheritance trees*.

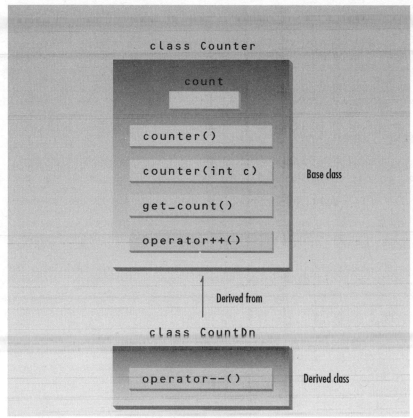

Figure 9.2 Class hierarchy in COUNTEN.

Accessing Base Class Members

An important topic in inheritance is knowing when a member function in the base class can be used by objects of the derived class. This is called *accessibility*. Let's see how the compiler handles the accessibility issue in the COUNTEN example.

Substituting Base Class Constructors

In the `main()` part of COUNTEN we create an object of class `CountDn`:

```
CountDn c1;
```

This causes `c1` to be created as an object of class `CountDn` and initialized to 0. But wait— how is this possible? There is no constructor in the `CountDn` class specifier, so what entity carries out the initialization? It turns out that—at least under certain circumstances—if you don't specify a constructor, the derived class will use an appropriate constructor from the base class. In COUNTEN there's no constructor in `CountDn`, so the compiler uses the no-argument constructor from `Count`.

This flexibility on the part of the compiler—using one function because another isn't available—appears regularly in inheritance situations. Generally, the substitution is what you want, but sometimes it can be unnerving.

Substituting Base Class Member Functions

The object `c1` of the `CountDn` class also uses the `operator++()` and `get_count()` functions from the `Counter` class. The first is used to increment `c1`:

```
++c1;
```

and the second is used to display the count in `c1`:

```
cout << "\nc1=" << c1.get_count();
```

Again the compiler, not finding these functions in the class of which `c1` is a member, uses member functions from the base class.

Output of COUNTEN

In `main()` we increment `c1` three times, print out the resulting value, decrement `c1` twice, and finally print out its value again. Here's the output:

```
c1=0    ???? after initialization
c1=3    ???? after ++c1, ++c1, ++c1
c1=1    ???? after --c1, --c1
```

The ++ operator, the constructors, the `get_count()` function in the `Counter` class, and the -- operator in the `CountDn` class all work with objects of type `CountDn`.

The `protected` Access Specifier

We have increased the functionality of a class without modifying it. Well, almost without modifying it. Let's look at the single change we made to the `Counter` class.

The data in the classes we've looked at so far, including `count` in the `Counter` class in the earlier COUNTPP3 program, have used the **private** access specifier.

In the `Counter` class in COUNTEN, `count` is given a new specifier: **protected**. What does this do?

Let's first review what we know about the access specifiers **private** and **public**. Class members (which can be data or functions) can always be accessed by functions *within their own class*, whether the members are private or public. But objects of a class defined *outside the class* can access class members only if the members are public. For instance, suppose an object `objA` is an instance of class `A`, and function `funcA()` is a member function of `A`. Then in `main()` (or any other function that is not a member of `A`) the statement

```
objA.funcA();
```

will not be legal unless `func()` is public. The object `objA` cannot access private members of class A. Private members are, well, *private*. This is shown in Figure 9.3.

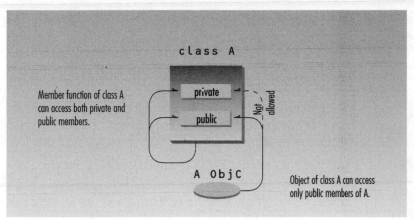

Figure 9.3   Access specifiers without inheritance.

This is all we need to know if we don't use inheritance. With inheritance, however, there is a whole raft of additional possibilities. The question that concerns us at the moment is, can member functions of the derived class access members of the base class? In other words, can `operator--()` in `CountDn` access `count` in `Counter`? The answer is that member functions can access members of the base class if the members are `public`, or if they are `protected`. They can't access `private` members.

We don't want to make `count public`, since that would allow it to be accessed by any function anywhere in the program and eliminate the advantages of data hiding. A `protected` member, on the other hand, can be accessed by member functions in its own class or—and here's the key—in any class derived from its own class. It can't be accessed from functions outside these classes, such as `main()`. This is just what we want. The situation is shown in Figure 9.4.

Table 9.1 summarizes the situation in a different way.

Table 9.1   Inheritance and Accessibility

Access Specifier	Accessible from Own Class	Accessible from Derived Class	Accessible from Objects Outside Class
public	yes	yes	yes
protected	yes	yes	no
private	yes	no	no

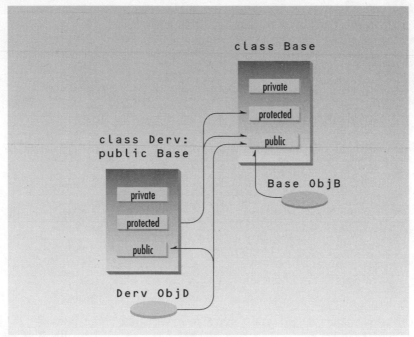

Figure 9.4   Access specifiers with inheritance.

The moral is that if you are writing a class that you suspect might be used, at any point in the future, as a base class for other classes, then any member data that the derived classes might need to access should be made `protected` rather than `private`. This ensures that the class is "inheritance ready."

Dangers of `protected`

You should know that there's a disadvantage to making class members `protected`. Say you've written a class library, which you're distributing to the public. Any programmer who buys this library can access protected members of your classes simply by deriving other classes from them. This makes protected members considerably less secure than private members. To avoid corrupted data, it's often safer to force derived classes to access data in the base class using only public functions in the base class, just as ordinary `main()` programs must do. Using the `protected` specifier leads to simpler programming, so we rely on it—perhaps a bit too much—in the examples in this book. You'll need to weigh the advantages of `protected` against its disadvantages in your own programs.

Base Class Unchanged

Remember that, even if other classes have been derived from it, the base class remains unchanged. In the `main()` part of COUNTEN, we could define objects of type `Counter`:

```
Counter c2;    ???? object of base class
```

Such objects would behave just as they would if `CountDn` didn't exist.

Note also that inheritance doesn't work in reverse. The base class and its objects don't know anything about any classes derived from the base class. In this example that means that objects of class `Counter`, such as `c2` defined here, can't use the `operator--()` function in `CountDn`. If you want a counter that you can decrement, it must be of class `CountDn`, not `Counter`.

Other Terms

In some languages the base class is called the *superclass* and the derived class is called the *subclass*. Some writers also refer to the base class as the *parent* and the derived class as the *child*.

Derived Class Constructors

There's a potential glitch in the COUNTEN program. What happens if we want to initialize a `CountDn` object to a value? Can the one-argument constructor in `Counter` be used? The answer is no. As we saw in COUNTEN, the compiler will substitute a no-argument constructor from the base class, but it draws the line at more complex constructors. To make such a definition work we must write a new set of constructors for the derived class. This is shown in the COUNTEN2 program.

```
// counten2.cpp
// constructors in derived class
#include <iostream>
using namespace std;
/////////////////////////////////////////////////////////////////
class Counter
    {
    protected:                          //NOTE: not private
        unsigned int count;             //count
    public:
        Counter() : count()             //constructor, no args
            { }
        Counter(int c) : count(c)       //constructor, one arg
            { }
        unsigned int get_count() const  //return count
            { return count; }
        Counter operator ++ ()          //incr count (prefix)
            { return Counter(++count); }
    };
/////////////////////////////////////////////////////////////////
class CountDn : public Counter
    {
    public:
        CountDn() : Counter()           //constructor, no args
            { }
        CountDn(int c) : Counter(c)     //constructor, 1 arg
            { }
```

```
            CountDn operator -- ()            //decr count (prefix)
                { return CountDn(--count); }
        };
//////////////////////////////////////////////////////////////////
int main()
    {
    CountDn c1;                              //class CountDn
    CountDn c2(100);

    cout << "\nc1=" << c1.get_count();       //display
    cout << "\nc2=" << c2.get_count();       //display

    ++c1; ++c1; ++c1;                        //increment c1
    cout << "\nc1=" << c1.get_count();       //display it

    --c2; --c2;                              //decrement c2
    cout << "\nc2=" << c2.get_count();       //display it

    CountDn c3 = --c2;                       //create c3 from c2
    cout << "\nc3=" << c3.get_count();       //display c3
    cout << endl;
    return 0;
    }
```

This program uses two new constructors in the **CountDn** class. Here is the one-argument constructor:

```
CountDn() : Counter()
    { }
```

This constructor has an unfamiliar feature: the function name following the colon. This construction causes the **CountDn()** constructor to call the **Counter()** constructor in the base class. In **main()**, when we say

```
CountDn c1;
```

the compiler will create an object of type **CountDn** and then call the **CountDn** constructor to initialize it. This constructor will in turn call the **Counter** constructor, which carries out the work. The **CountDn()** constructor could add additional statements of its own, but in this case it doesn't need to, so the function body between the braces is empty.

Calling a constructor from the initialization list may seem odd, but it makes sense. You want to initialize any variables, whether they're in the derived class or the base class, before any statements in either the derived or base-class constructors are executed. By calling the base-class constructor before the derived-class constructor starts to execute, we accomplish this.

The statement

```
CountDn c2(100);
```

in **main()** uses the one-argument constructor in **CountDn**. This constructor also calls the corresponding one-argument constructor in the base class:

```
CountDn(int c) : Counter(c)    ???? argument c is passed to Counter
    { }
```

This construction causes the argument **c** to be passed from **CountDn()** to **Counter()**, where it is used to initialize the object.

In **main()**, after initializing the **c1** and **c2** objects, we increment one and decrement the other and then print the results. The one-argument constructor is also used in an assignment statement.

```
CountDn c3 = --c2;
```

Overriding Member Functions

You can use member functions in a derived class that override—that is, have the same name as—those in the base class. You might want to do this so that calls in your program work the same way for objects of both base and derived classes.

Here's an example based on the STAKARAY program from Chapter 7, "Arrays and Strings." That program modeled a stack, a simple data storage device. It allowed you to push integers onto the stack and pop them off. However, STAKARAY had a potential flaw. If you tried to push too many items onto the stack, the program might bomb, since data would be placed in memory beyond the end of the **st[]** array. Or if you tried to pop too many items, the results would be meaningless, since you would be reading data from memory locations outside the array.

To cure these defects we've created a new class, **Stack2**, derived from **Stack**. Objects of **Stack2** behave in exactly the same way as those of **Stack**, except that you will be warned if you attempt to push too many items on the stack, or if you try to pop an item from an empty stack. Here's the listing for STAKEN:

```
// staken.cpp
// overloading functions in base and derived classes
#include <iostream>
using namespace std;
#include <process.h>              //for exit()
/////////////////////////////////////////////////////////////
class Stack
    {
    protected:                    //NOTE: can't be private
        enum { MAX = 3 };         //size of stack array
        int st[MAX];              //stack: array of integers
        int top;                  //index to top of stack
    public:
        Stack()                   //constructor
            { top = -1; }
        void push(int var)        //put number on stack
            { st[++top] = var; }
        int pop()                 //take number off stack
            { return st[top--]; }
    };
/////////////////////////////////////////////////////////////
class Stack2 : public Stack
    {
```

```
    public:
      void push(int var)            //put number on stack
         {
         if(top >= MAX-1)           //error if stack full
            { cout << "\nError: stack is full"; exit(1); }
         Stack::push(var);          //call push() in Stack class
         }
      int pop()                     //take number off stack
         {
         if(top < 0)                //error if stack empty
            { cout << "\nError: stack is empty\n"; exit(1); }
         return Stack::pop();       //call pop() in Stack class
         }
   };
/////////////////////////////////////////////////////////////////
int main()
   {
   Stack2 s1;

   s1.push(11);                     //push some values onto stack
   s1.push(22);
   s1.push(33);

   cout << endl << s1.pop();        //pop some values from stack
   cout << endl << s1.pop();
   cout << endl << s1.pop();
   cout << endl << s1.pop();        //oops, popped one too many...
   cout << endl;
   return 0;
   }
```

In this program the `Stack` class is just the same as it was in the STAKARAY program, except that the data members have been made `protected`.

Which Function Is Used?

The `Stack2` class contains two functions, `push()` and `pop()`. These functions have the same names, and the same argument and return types, as the functions in `Stack`. When we call these functions from `main()`, in statements like

`s1.push(11);`

how does the compiler know which of the two `push()` functions to use? Here's the rule: When the same function exists in both the base class and the derived class, the function in the derived class will be executed. (This is true of objects of the derived class. Objects of the base class don't know anything about the derived class and will always use the base class functions.) We say that the derived class function *overrides* the base class function. So in the statement above, since `s1` is an object of class `Stack2`, the `push()` function in `Stack2` will be executed, not the one in `Stack`.

The push() function in Stack2 checks to see if the stack is full. If it is, it displays an error message and causes the program to exit. If it isn't, it calls the push() function in Stack. Similarly, the pop() function in Stack2 checks to see if the stack is empty. If it is, it prints an error message and exits; otherwise, it calls the pop() function in Stack.

In main() we push three items onto the stack, but we pop four. The last pop elicits an error message:

```
33
22
11
Error: stack is empty
```

and terminates the program.

Scope Resolution with Overridden Functions

How do push() and pop() in Stack2 access push() and pop() in Stack? They use the scope resolution operator, ::, in the statements.

```
Stack::push(var);
```

and

```
return Stack::pop();
```

These statements specify that the push() and pop() functions in Stack are to be called. Without the scope resolution operator, the compiler would think the push() and pop() functions in Stack2 were calling themselves, which—in this case—would lead to program failure. Using the scope resolution operator allows you to specify exactly what class the function is a member of.

Inheritance in the English Distance Class

Here's a somewhat more complex example of inheritance. So far in this book the various programs that used the English Distance class assumed that the distances to be represented would always be positive. This is usually the case in architectural drawings. However, if we were measuring, say, the water level of the Pacific Ocean as the tides varied, we might want to be able to represent negative feet-and-inches quantities. (Tide levels below mean-lower-low-water are called *minus tides*; they prompt clam diggers to take advantage of the larger area of exposed beach.)

Let's derive a new class from Distance. This class will add a single data item to our feet-and-inches measurements: a sign, which can be positive or negative. When we add the sign, we'll also need to modify the member functions so they can work with signed distances. Here's the listing for ENGLEN:

```
// englen.cpp
// inheritance using English Distances
#include <iostream>
using namespace std;
enum posneg { pos, neg };          //for sign in DistSign
/////////////////////////////////////////////////////////////
class Distance                     //English Distance class
   {
   protected:                      //NOTE: can't be private
      int feet;
      float inches;
   public:                         //no-arg constructor
      Distance() : feet(0), inches(0.0)
         {  }                      //2-arg constructor)
      Distance(int ft, float in) : feet(ft), inches(in)
         {  }
      void getdist()               //get length from user
         {
         cout << "\nEnter feet: ";  cin >> feet;
         cout << "Enter inches: ";  cin >> inches;
         }
      void showdist() const        //display distance
         { cout << feet << "\'-" << inches << '\"'; }
   };
/////////////////////////////////////////////////////////////
class DistSign : public Distance  //adds sign to Distance
   {
   private:
      posneg sign;                 //sign is pos or neg
   public:
                                   //no-arg constructor
      DistSign() : Distance()      //call base constructor
         { sign = pos; }           //set the sign to +

                                   //2- or 3-arg constructor
      DistSign(int ft, float in, posneg sg=pos) :
            Distance(ft, in)       //call base constructor
         { sign = sg; }            //set the sign

      void getdist()               //get length from user
         {
         Distance::getdist();      //call base getdist()
         char ch;                  //get sign from user
         cout << "Enter sign (+ or -): ";  cin >> ch;
         sign = (ch=='+') ? pos : neg;
         }
      void showdist() const        //display distance
         {
         cout << ( (sign==pos) ? "(+)" : "(-)" );  //show sign
         Distance::showdist();                     //ft and in
         }
   };
/////////////////////////////////////////////////////////////
```

```
int main()
   {
   DistSign alpha;                    //no-arg constructor
   alpha.getdist();                   //get alpha from user

   DistSign beta(11, 6.25);           //2-arg constructor

   DistSign gamma(100, 5.5, neg);     //3-arg constructor

                                      //display all distances
   cout << "\nalpha = ";  alpha.showdist();
   cout << "\nbeta = ";   beta.showdist();
   cout << "\ngamma = ";  gamma.showdist();
   cout << endl;
   return 0;
   }
```

Here the `DistSign` class adds the functionality to deal with signed numbers. The `Distance` class in this program is just the same as in previous programs, except that the data is protected. Actually in this case it could be private, because none of the derived-class functions accesses it. However, it's safer to make it protected so that a derived-class function could access it if necessary.

Operation of ENGLEN

The `main()` program declares three different signed distances. It gets a value for `alpha` from the user and initializes `beta` to (+)11'-6.25" and `gamma` to (–)100'-5.5". In the output we use parentheses around the sign to avoid confusion with the hyphen separating feet and inches. Here's some sample output:

```
Enter feet: 6
Enter inches: 2.5
Enter sign (+ or -): -

alpha = (-)6'-2.5"
beta = (+)11'-6.25"
gamma = (-)100'-5.5"
```

The `DistSign` class is derived from `Distance`. It adds a single variable, `sign`, which is of type `posneg`. The `sign` variable will hold the sign of the distance. The `posneg` type is defined in an `enum` statement to have two possible values: `pos` and `neg`.

Constructors in DistSign

`DistSign` has two constructors, mirroring those in `Distance`. The first takes no arguments, the second takes either two or three arguments. The third, optional, argument in the second constructor is a sign, either `pos` or `neg`. Its default value is `pos`. These constructors allow us to define variables (objects) of type `DistSign` in several ways.

Both constructors in `DistSign` call the corresponding constructors in `Distance` to set the feet-and-inches values. They then set the `sign` variable. The no-argument constructor always sets it to `pos`. The second constructor sets it to `pos` if no third-argument value has been provided, or to a value (`pos` or `neg`) if the argument is specified.

The arguments `ft` and `in`, passed from `main()` to the second constructor in `DistSign`, are simply forwarded to the constructor in `Distance`.

Member Functions in `DistSign`

Adding a sign to `Distance` has consequences for both its member functions. The `getdist()` function in the `DistSign` class must ask the user for the sign as well as for feet-and-inches values, and the `showdist()` function must display the sign along with the feet and inches. These functions call the corresponding functions in `Distance`, in the lines

```
Distance::getdist();
```

and

```
Distance::showdist();
```

These calls get and display the feet and inches values. The body of `getdist()` and `showdist()` in `DistSign` then go on to deal with the sign.

Abetting Inheritance

C++ is designed to make it efficient to create a derived class. Where we want to use parts of the base class, it's easy to do so, whether these parts are data, constructors, or member functions. Then we add the functionality we need to create the new improved class. Notice that in ENGLEN we didn't need to duplicate any code; instead we made use of the appropriate functions in the base class.

Class Hierarchies

In the examples so far in this chapter, inheritance has been used to add functionality to an existing class. Now let's look at an example where inheritance is used for a different purpose: as part of the original design of a program.

Our example models a database of employees of a widget company. We've simplified the situation so that only three kinds of employees are represented. Managers manage, scientists perform research to develop better widgets, and laborers operate the dangerous widget-stamping presses.

The database stores a name and an employee identification number for all employees, no matter what category they are. However, for managers, it also stores their titles and golf club dues. For scientists it stores the number of scholarly articles they have published. Laborers need no additional data beyond their names and numbers.

Our example program starts with a base class `employee`. This class handles the employee's last name and employee number. From this class three other classes are derived: `manager`, scientist, and laborer. The manager and scientist classes contain additional information about these categories of employee, and member functions to handle this information, as shown in Figure 9.5.

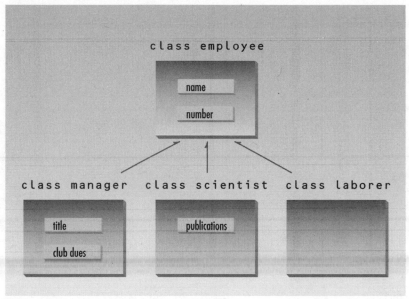

Figure 9.5 Class Hierarchy in EMPLOY.

Here's the listing for EMPLOY:

```cpp
// employ.cpp
// models employee database using inheritance
#include <iostream>
using namespace std;
const int LEN = 80;                 //maximum length of names
//////////////////////////////////////////////////////////////
class employee                      //employee class
   {
   private:
      char name[LEN];               //employee name
      unsigned long number;         //employee number
   public:
      void getdata()
         {
         cout << "\n   Enter last name: "; cin >> name;
         cout << "   Enter number: ";      cin >> number;
         }
      void putdata() const
         {
         cout << "\n   Name: " << name;
```

```
               cout << "\n   Number: " << number;
               }
         };
/////////////////////////////////////////////////////////////////
class manager : public employee     //management class
   {
   private:
      char title[LEN];                //"vice-president" etc.
      double dues;                    //golf club dues
   public:
      void getdata()
         {
         employee::getdata();
         cout << "   Enter title: ";           cin >> title;
         cout << "   Enter golf club dues: "; cin >> dues;
         }
      void putdata() const
         {
         employee::putdata();
         cout << "\n   Title: " << title;
         cout << "\n   Golf club dues: " << dues;
         }
   };
/////////////////////////////////////////////////////////////////
class scientist : public employee  //scientist class
   {
   private:
      int pubs;                       //number of publications
   public:
      void getdata()
         {
         employee::getdata();
         cout << "   Enter number of pubs: "; cin >> pubs;
         }
      void putdata() const
         {
         employee::putdata();
         cout << "\n   Number of publications: " << pubs;
         }
   };
/////////////////////////////////////////////////////////////////
class laborer : public employee     //laborer class
   {
   };
/////////////////////////////////////////////////////////////////
int main()
   {
   manager m1, m2;
   scientist s1;
   laborer l1;
```

```
      cout << endl;              //get data for several employees
      cout << "\nEnter data for manager 1";
      m1.getdata();

      cout << "\nEnter data for manager 2";
      m2.getdata();

      cout << "\nEnter data for scientist 1";
      s1.getdata();

      cout << "\nEnter data for laborer 1";
      l1.getdata();
                                //display data for several employees
      cout << "\nData on manager 1";
      m1.putdata();

      cout << "\nData on manager 2";
      m2.putdata();

      cout << "\nData on scientist 1";
      s1.putdata();

      cout << "\nData on laborer 1";
      l1.putdata();
      cout << endl;
      return 0;
      }
```

The `main()` part of the program declares four objects of different classes: two managers, a scientist, and a laborer. (Of course many more employees of each type could be defined, but the output would become rather large.) It then calls the `getdata()` member functions to obtain information about each employee, and the `putdata()` function to display this information. Here's a sample interaction with EMPLOY. First the user supplies the data.

```
Enter data for manager 1
   Enter last name: Wainsworth
   Enter number: 10
   Enter title: President
   Enter golf club dues: 1000000
Enter data on manager 2
   Enter last name: Bradley
   Enter number: 124
   Enter title: Vice-President
   Enter golf club dues: 500000
Enter data for scientist 1
   Enter last name: Hauptman-Frenglish
   Enter number: 234234
   Enter number of pubs: 999
Enter data for laborer 1
   Enter last name: Jones
   Enter number: 6546544
```

The program then plays it back.

```
Data on manager 1
  Name: Wainsworth
  Number: 10
  Title: President
  Golf club dues: 1000000
Data on manager 2
  Name: Bradley
  Number: 124
  Title: Vice-President
  Golf club dues: 500000
Data on scientist 1
   Name: Hauptman-Frenglish
  Number: 234234
  Number of publications: 999
Data on laborer 1
  Name: Jones
  Number: 6546544
```

A more sophisticated program would use an array or some other container to arrange the data so that a large number of employee objects could be accommodated.

"Abstract" Base Class

Notice that we don't define any objects of the base class `employee`. We use this as a general class whose sole purpose is to act as a base from which other classes are derived.

The `laborer` class operates identically to the `employee` class, since it contains no additional data or functions. It may seem that the `laborer` class is unnecessary, but by making it a separate class we emphasize that all classes are descended from the same source, `employee`. Also, if in the future we decided to modify the `laborer` class, we would not need to change the declaration for `employee`.

Classes used only for deriving other classes, as `employee` is in EMPLOY, are sometimes loosely called *abstract classes*, meaning that no actual instances (objects) of this class are created. However, the term *abstract* has a more precise definition that we'll look at in Chapter 11, "Virtual Functions."

Constructors and Member Functions

There are no constructors in either the base or derived classes, so the compiler creates objects of the various classes automatically when it encounters definitions like

```
manager m1, m2;
```

using the default constructor for `manager` calling the default constructor for `employee`.

The `getdata()` and `putdata()` functions in `employee` accept a name and number from the user and display a name and number. Functions also called `getdata()` and `putdata()` in the `manager` and `scientist` classes use the functions in `employee`, and also do their own work. In `manager` the `getdata()` function asks the user for a title and the amount of golf club dues, and **putdata()** displays these values. In **scientist** these functions handle the number of publications.

Inheritance and Graphics Shapes

In the CIRCLES program in Chapter 6, "Objects and Classes," we saw a program in which a class represented graphics circles that could be displayed on the screen. Of course, there are other kinds of shapes besides circles, such as squares, triangles, and so on. The very phrase "kinds of shapes" implies an inheritance relationship between something called a "shape" and specific kinds of shapes like circles and squares. We can use this relationship to make a program that is more robust and easier to understand than a program that treats different shapes as being unrelated.

In particular, we'll make a **shape** class that's a base class (parent) of three derived classes: a **circle** class, a **rect** (for rectangle) class, and a **tria** (for triangle) class. As with other programs that use the Console Graphics Lite functions, you may need to read Appendix E, "Console Graphics Lite," and either Appendix C, "Microsoft Visual C++," or Appendix D, "Borland C++" for your specific compiler to learn how to build the graphics files into your program. Here's the listing for MULTSHAP:

```
// multshap.cpp
// balls, rects, and polygons
#include "msoftcon.h"          //for graphics functions
////////////////////////////////////////////////////////////////
class shape                    //base class
   {
   protected:
      int xCo, yCo;            //coordinates of shape
      color fillcolor;         //color
      fstyle fillstyle;        //fill pattern
   public:                     //no-arg constructor
      shape() : xCo(0), yCo(0), fillcolor(cWHITE),
                                    fillstyle(SOLID_FILL)
         { }                   //4-arg constructor
      shape(int x, int y, color fc, fstyle fs) :
                 xCo(x), yCo(y), fillcolor(fc), fillstyle(fs)
         { }
      void draw() const        //set color and fill style
         {
         set_color(fillcolor);
         set_fill_style(fillstyle);
         }
   };
////////////////////////////////////////////////////////////////
class circle : public shape
   {
   private:
      int radius;              //(xCo, yCo) is center
   public:
      circle() : shape()       //no-arg constr
```

```
                    { }
                                        //5-arg constructor
            circle(int x, int y, int r, color fc, fstyle fs)
                        : shape(x, y, fc, fs), radius(r)
                    { }
            void draw() const        //draw the circle
                {
                shape::draw();
                draw_circle(xCo, yCo, radius);
                }
        };
////////////////////////////////////////////////////////////////
class rect : public shape
    {
    private:
        int width, height;        //(xCo, yCo) is upper-left corner
    public:
        rect() : shape(), height(0), width(0)     //no-arg ctor
            { }                                   //6-arg ctor
        rect(int x, int y, int h, int w, color fc, fstyle fs) :
                        shape(x, y, fc, fs), height(h), width(w)
            { }
        void draw() const        //draw the rectangle
            {
            shape::draw();
            draw_rectangle(xCo, yCo, xCo+width, yCo+height);
            set_color(cWHITE);    //draw diagonal
            draw_line(xCo, yCo, xCo+width, yCo+height);
            }
        };
////////////////////////////////////////////////////////////////
class tria : public shape
    {
    private:
        int height;                //(xCo, yCo) is tip of pyramid
    public:
        tria() : shape(), height(0) //no-arg constructor
            { }                     //5-arg constructor
        tria(int x, int y, int h, color fc, fstyle fs) :
                                shape(x, y, fc, fs), height(h)
            { }
        void draw() const        //draw the triangle
            {
            shape::draw();
            draw_pyramid(xCo, yCo, height);
            }
        };
////////////////////////////////////////////////////////////////
int main()
    {
    init_graphics();             //initialize graphics system

    circle cir(40, 12, 5, cBLUE, X_FILL);       //create circle
```

```
rect rec(12, 7, 10, 15, cRED, SOLID_FILL); //create rectangle
tria tri(60, 7,  11, cGREEN, MEDIUM_FILL); //create triangle

cir.draw();                 //draw all shapes
rec.draw();
tri.draw();
set_cursor_pos(1, 25);      //lower-left corner
return 0;
}
```

When executed, this program produces three different shapes: a blue circle, a red rectangle, and a green triangle. Figure 9.6 shows the output of MULTSHAP.

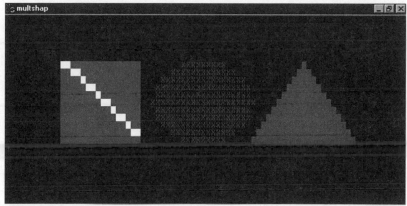

Figure 9.6   Output of the MULTSHAP program.

The characteristics that are common to all shapes, such as their location, color, and fill pattern, are placed in the **shape** class. Individual shapes have more specific attributes. A circle has a radius, for example, while a rectangle has a height and width. A **draw()** routine in **shape** handles the tasks specific to all shapes: setting their color and fill pattern. Overloaded **draw()** functions in the **circle**, **rect**, and **tria** classes take care of drawing their specific shapes once the color and pattern are determined.

As in the last example, the base class **shape** is an example of an "abstract" class, in that there is no meaning to instantiating an object of this class. What shape does a **shape** object display? The question doesn't make sense. Only a specific shape can display itself. The **shape** class exists only as a repository of attributes and actions that are common to all shapes.

Public and Private Inheritance

C++ provides a wealth of ways to fine-tune access to class members. One such access-control mechanism is the way derived classes are declared. Our examples so far have used publicly derived classes, with declarations like

```
class manager : public employee
```

which appeared in the EMPLOY example.

What is the effect of the **public** keyword in this statement, and what are the alternatives? Listen up: The keyword **public** specifies that objects of the derived class are able to access public member functions of the base class. The alternative is the keyword **private**. When this keyword is used, objects of the derived class cannot access public member functions of the base class. Since objects can never access **private** or **protected** members of a class, the result is that no member of the base class is accessible to objects of the derived class.

Access Combinations

There are so many possibilities for access that it's instructive to look at an example program that shows what works and what doesn't. Here's the listing for PUBPRIV:

```
// pubpriv.cpp
// tests publicly- and privately-derived classes
#include <iostream>
using namespace std;
/////////////////////////////////////////////////////////////////
class A                    //base class
   {
   private:
      int privdataA;        //(functions have the same access
   protected:                //rules as the data shown here)
      int protdataA;
   public:
      int pubdataA;
   };
/////////////////////////////////////////////////////////////////
class B : public A         //publicly-derived class
   {
   public:
      void funct()
         {
         int a;
         a = privdataA;  //error: not accessible
         a = protdataA;  //OK
         a = pubdataA;    //OK
         }
   };
/////////////////////////////////////////////////////////////////
class C : private A        //privately-derived class
   {
   public:
      void funct()
         {
         int a;
         a = privdataA;  //error: not accessible
         a = protdataA;  //OK
         a = pubdataA;    //OK
         }
   };
```

```
//////////////////////////////////////////////////////////
int main()
  {
  int a;

  B objB;
  a = objB.privdataA;    //error: not accessible
  a = objB.protdataA;    //error: not accessible
  a = objB.pubdataA;     //OK (A public to B)

  C objC;
  a = objC.privdataA;    //error: not accessible
  a = objC.protdataA;    //error: not accessible
  a = objC.pubdataA;     //error: not accessible (A private to C)
  return 0;
  }
```

The program specifies a base class, A, with private, protected, and public data items. Two classes, B and C, are derived from A. B is publicly derived and C is privately derived.

As we've seen before, functions in the derived classes can access protected and public data in the base class. Objects of the derived classes cannot access private or protected members of the base class.

What's new is the difference between publicly derived and privately derived classes. Objects of the publicly derived class B can access public members of the base class A, while objects of the privately derived class C cannot; they can only access the public members of their own derived class. This is shown in Figure 9.7.

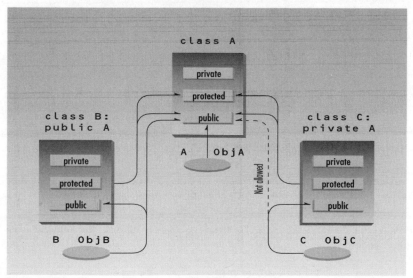

Figure 9.7 Public and private derivation.

If you don't supply any access specifier when creating a class, **private** is assumed.

Access Specifiers: When to Use What

How do you decide when to use private as opposed to public inheritance? In most cases a derived class exists to offer an improved?md?or a more specialized?md]version of the base class. We've seen examples of such derived classes; for instance the `CountDn` class that adds the decrement operator to the `Counter` class and the `manager` class that is a more specialized version of the `employee` class. In such cases it makes sense for objects of the derived class to access the public functions of the base class if they want to perform a basic operation, and to access functions in the derived class to perform the more specialized operations that the derived class provides. In such cases public derivation is appropriate.

In some situations, however, the derived class is created as a way of completely modifying the operation of the base class, hiding or disguising its original interface. For example, imagine that you have already created a really nice `Array` class that acts like an array but provides protection against out-of-bounds array indexes. Then suppose you want to use this `Array` class as the basis for a `Stack` class, instead of using a basic array. You might derive `Stack` from `Array`, but you wouldn't want the users of `Stack` objects to treat them as if they were arrays, using the `[ ]` operator to access data items, for example. Objects of `Stack` should always be treated as if they were stacks, using `push()` and `pop()`. That is, you want to disguise the `Array` class as a `Stack` class. In this situation, private derivation would allow you to conceal all the `Array` class functions from objects of the derived `Stack` class.

Levels of Inheritance

Classes can be derived from classes that are themselves derived. Here's a miniprogram that shows the idea:

```
class A
   { };
class B : public A
   { };
class C : public B
   { };
```

Here `B` is derived from `A`, and `C` is derived from `B`. The process can be extended to an arbitrary number of levels—`D` could be derived from `C`, and so on.

As a more concrete example, suppose that we decided to add a special kind of laborer called a *foreman* to the EMPLOY program. We'll create a new program, EMPLOY2, that incorporates objects of class `foreman`.

Since foremen are a kind of laborer, the `foreman` class is derived from the `laborer` class, as shown in Figure 9.8.

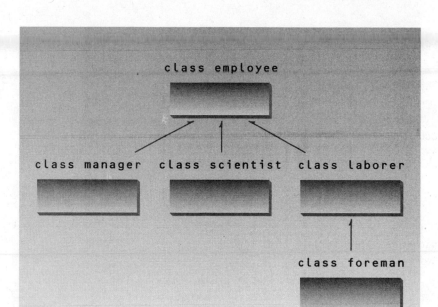

Figure 9.8 Class hierarchy in EMPLOY2.

Foremen oversee the widget-stamping operation, supervising groups of laborers. They are responsible for the widget production quota for their group. A foreman's ability is measured by the percentage of production quotas successfully met. The **quotas** data item in the foreman class represents this percentage. Here's the listing for EMPLOY2:

```
// employ2.cpp
// multiple levels of inheritance
#include <iostream>
using namespace std;
const int LEN = 80;                //maximum length of names
////////////////////////////////////////////////////////////////
class employee
   {
   private:
      char name[LEN];              //employee name
      unsigned long number;        //employee number
   public:
      void getdata()
         {
         cout << "\n   Enter last name: "; cin >> name;
         cout << "   Enter number: ";      cin >> number;
         }
      void putdata() const
         {
         cout << "\n   Name: " << name;
```

```
                    cout << "\n   Number: " << number;
                    }
                };
   /////////////////////////////////////////////////////////////////
   class manager : public employee      //manager class
      {
      private:
         char title[LEN];                //"vice-president" etc.
         double dues;                    //golf club dues
      public:
         void getdata()
            {
            employee::getdata();
            cout << "   Enter title: ";            cin >> title;
            cout << "   Enter golf club dues: "; cin >> dues;
            }
         void putdata() const
            {
            employee::putdata();
            cout << "\n   Title: " << title;
            cout << "\n   Golf club dues: " << dues;
            }
      };
   /////////////////////////////////////////////////////////////////
   class scientist : public employee  //scientist class
      {
      private:
         int pubs;                      //number of publications
      public:
         void getdata()
            {
            employee::getdata();
            cout << "   Enter number of pubs: "; cin >> pubs;
            }
         void putdata() const
            {
            employee::putdata();
            cout << "\n   Number of publications: " << pubs;
            }
      };
   /////////////////////////////////////////////////////////////////
   class laborer : public employee      //laborer class
      {
      };
   /////////////////////////////////////////////////////////////////
   class foreman : public laborer       //foreman class
      {
      private:
         float quotas;  //percent of quotas met successfully
      public:
```

```
            void getdata()
                {
                laborer::getdata();
                cout << "   Enter quotas: "; cin >> quotas;
                }
            void putdata() const
                {
                laborer::putdata();
                cout << "\n   Quotas: " << quotas;
                }
        };
//////////////////////////////////////////////////////////////////
int main()
    {
    laborer l1;
    foreman f1;

    cout << endl;
    cout << "\nEnter data for laborer 1";
    l1.getdata();
    cout << "\nEnter data for foreman 1";
    f1.getdata();

    cout << endl;
    cout << "\nData on laborer 1";
    l1.putdata();
    cout << "\nData on foreman 1";
    f1.putdata();
    cout << endl;
    return 0;
    }
```

Notice that a class hierarchy is not the same as an organization chart. An organization chart shows lines of command. A class hierarchy results from generalizing common characteristics. The more general the class, the higher it is on the chart. Thus a laborer is more general than a foreman, who is a specialized kind of laborer, so **laborer** is shown above **foreman** in the class hierarchy, although a foreman is probably paid more than a laborer.

Multiple Inheritance

A class can be derived from more than one base class. This is called *multiple inheritance*. Figure 9.9 shows how this looks when a class C is derived from base classes A and B.

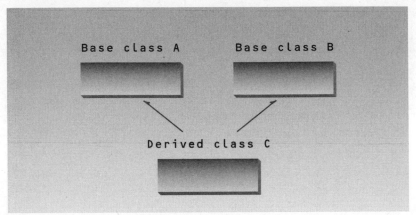

Figure 9.9 Multiple inheritance.

The syntax for multiple inheritance is similar to that for single inheritance. In the situation shown in Figure 9.9, the relationship is expressed like this:

```
class A                          // base class A
   {
   };
class B                          // base class B
   {
   };
class C : public A, public B     // C is derived from A and B
   {
   };
```

The base classes from which C is derived are listed following the colon in C's specification; they are separated by commas.

Member Functions in Multiple Inheritance

As an example of multiple inheritance, suppose that we needed to record the educational experience of some of the employees in the EMPLOY program. Let's also suppose that, perhaps in a different project, we had already developed a class called **student** that models students with different educational backgrounds. We decide that instead of modifying the **employee** class to incorporate educational data, we will add this data by multiple inheritance from the **student** class.

The **student** class stores the name of the school or university last attended and the highest degree received. Both these data items are stored as strings. Two member functions, **getedu()** and **putedu()**, ask the user for this information and display it.

Educational information is not relevant to every class of employee. Let's suppose, somewhat undemocratically, that we don't need to record the educational experience of laborers; it's only relevant for managers and scientists. We therefore modify `manager` and `scientist` so that they inherit from both the `employee` and `student` classes, as shown in Figure 9.10.

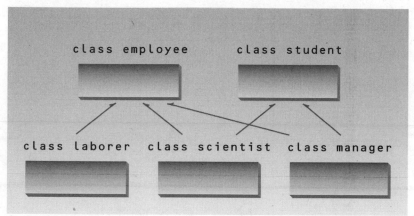

Figure 9.10 Class hierarchy in EMPMULT.

Here's a miniprogram that shows these relationships (but leaves out everything else):

```
class student
   { };
class employee
   { };
class manager : private employee, private student
   { };
class scientist : private employee, private student
   { };
class laborer : public employee
   { };
```

And here, featuring considerably more detail, is the listing for EMPMULT:

```
//empmult.cpp
//multiple inheritance with employees and degrees
#include <iostream>
using namespace std;
const int LEN = 80;           //maximum length of names
//////////////////////////////////////////////////////////////////
class student                 //educational background
   {
   private:
      char school[LEN];       //name of school or university
      char degree[LEN];       //highest degree earned
   public:
```

```cpp
         void getedu()
            {
            cout << "   Enter name of school or university: ";
            cin >> school;
            cout << "   Enter highest degree earned \n";
            cout << "   (Highschool, Bachelor's, Master's, PhD): ";
            cin >> degree;
            }
         void putedu() const
            {
            cout << "\n   School or university: " << school;
            cout << "\n   Highest degree earned: " << degree;
            }
      };
//////////////////////////////////////////////////////////////////
class employee
   {
   private:
      char name[LEN];         //employee name
      unsigned long number;    //employee number
   public:
      void getdata()
         {
         cout << "\n   Enter last name: "; cin >> name;
         cout << "   Enter number: ";      cin >> number;
         }
      void putdata() const
         {
         cout << "\n   Name: " << name;
         cout << "\n   Number: " << number;
         }
   };
//////////////////////////////////////////////////////////////////
class manager : private employee, private student  //management
   {
   private:
      char title[LEN];        //"vice-president" etc.
      double dues;            //golf club dues
   public:
      void getdata()
         {
         employee::getdata();
         cout << "   Enter title: ";           cin >> title;
         cout << "   Enter golf club dues: "; cin >> dues;
         student::getedu();
         }
      void putdata() const
         {
         employee::putdata();
         cout << "\n   Title: " << title;
         cout << "\n   Golf club dues: " << dues;
         student::putedu();
         }
   };
```

```
/////////////////////////////////////////////////////////////////
class scientist : private employee, private student  //scientist
   {
   private:
      int pubs;       //number of publications
   public:
      void getdata()
         {
         employee::getdata();
         cout << "    Enter number of pubs: "; cin >> pubs;
         student::getedu();
         }
      void putdata() const
         {
         employee::putdata();
         cout << "\n   Number of publications: " << pubs;
         student::putedu();
         }
   };
/////////////////////////////////////////////////////////////////
class laborer : public employee              //laborer
   {
   };
/////////////////////////////////////////////////////////////////
int main()
   {
   manager m1;
   scientist s1, s2;
   laborer l1;

   cout << endl;
   cout << "\nEnter data for manager 1";     //get data for
   m1.getdata();                             //several employees

   cout << "\nEnter data for scientist 1";
   s1.getdata();

   cout << "\nEnter data for scientist 2";
   s2.getdata();

   cout << "\nEnter data for laborer 1";
   l1.getdata();

   cout << "\nData on manager 1";            //display data for
   m1.putdata();                             //several employees

   cout << "\nData on scientist 1";
   s1.putdata();

   cout << "\nData on scientist 2";
   s2.putdata();

   cout << "\nData on laborer 1";
```

```
l1.putdata();
cout << endl;
return 0;
}
```

The `getdata()` and `putdata()` functions in the `manager` and `scientist` classes incorporate calls to functions in the `student` class, such as

```
student::getedu();
```

and

```
student::putedu();
```

These routines are accessible in `manager` and `scientist` because these classes are descended from `student`.

Here's some sample interaction with EMPMULT:

```
Enter data for manager 1
   Enter last name: Bradley
   Enter number: 12
   Enter title: Vice-President
   Enter golf club dues: 100000
   Enter name of school or university: Yale
   Enter highest degree earned
   (Highschool, Bachelor's, Master's, PhD): Bachelor's

Enter data for scientist 1
   Enter last name: Twilling
   Enter number: 764
   Enter number of pubs: 99
   Enter name of school or university: MIT
   Enter highest degree earned
   (Highschool, Bachelor's, Master's, PhD): PhD

Enter data for scientist 2
   Enter last name: Yang
   Enter number: 845
   Enter number of pubs: 101
   Enter name of school or university: Stanford
   Enter highest degree earned
   (Highschool, Bachelor's, Master's, PhD): Master's

Enter data for laborer 1
   Enter last name: Jones
   Enter number: 48323
```

As we saw in the EMPLOY and EMPLOY2 examples, the program then displays this information in roughly the same form.

private Derivation in EMPMULT

The manager and scientist classes in EMPMULT are privately derived from the employee and student classes. There is no need to use public derivation because objects of manager and scientist never call routines in the employee and student base classes. However, the laborer class must be publicly derived from employer, since it has no member functions of its own and relies on those in employee.

Constructors in Multiple Inheritance

EMPMULT has no constructors. Let's look at an example that does use constructors, and see how they're handled in multiple inheritance.

Imagine that we're writing a program for building contractors, and that this program models lumber-supply items. It uses a class that represents a quantity of lumber of a certain type: 100 8-foot-long construction grade 2×4s, for example.

The class should store various kinds of data about each such lumber item. We need to know the length (3'-6" or whatever) and we need to store the number of such pieces of lumber and their unit cost.

We also need to store a description of the lumber we're talking about. This has two parts. The first is the nominal dimensions of the cross-section of the lumber. This is given in inches. For instance, lumber 2 inches by 4 inches (for you metric folks, about 5 cm by 10 cm) is called a *two-by-four*. This is usually written 2×4. We also need to know the grade of lumber—rough-cut, construction grade, surfaced-four-sides, and so on. We find it convenient to create a Type class to hold this data. This class incorporates member data for the nominal dimensions and the grade of the lumber, both expressed as strings, such as 2×6 and *construction*. Member functions get this information from the user and display it.

We'll use the Distance class from previous examples to store the length. Finally we create a Lumber class that inherits both the Type and Distance classes. Here's the listing for ENGLMULT:

```
// englmult.cpp
// multiple inheritance with English Distances
#include <iostream>
#include <string>
using namespace std;
/////////////////////////////////////////////////////////////////
class Type                        //type of lumber
   {
   private:
      string dimensions;
      string grade;
   public:                        //no-arg constructor
      Type() : dimensions("N/A"), grade("N/A")
         {  }

                                  //2-arg constructor
```

```cpp
      Type(string di, string gr) : dimensions(di), grade(gr)
         {  }
      void gettype()                  //get type from user
         {
         cout << "   Enter nominal dimensions (2x4 etc.): ";
         cin >> dimensions;
         cout << "   Enter grade (rough, const, etc.): ";
         cin >> grade;
         }
      void showtype() const       //display type
         {
         cout << "\n   Dimensions: " << dimensions;
         cout << "\n   Grade: " << grade;
         }
   };
////////////////////////////////////////////////////////////////
class Distance                        //English Distance class
   {
   private:
      int feet;
      float inches;
   public:                            //no-arg constructor
      Distance() : feet(0), inches(0.0)
         {  }                          //constructor (two args)
      Distance(int ft, float in) : feet(ft), inches(in)
         {  }
      void getdist()                  //get length from user
         {
         cout << "   Enter feet: ";  cin >> feet;
         cout << "   Enter inches: ";  cin >> inches;
         }
      void showdist() const       //display distance
         { cout  << feet << "\'-" << inches << '\"'; }
   };
////////////////////////////////////////////////////////////////
olaee Lumber : public Type, public Distance
   {
   private:
      int quantity;                        //number of pieces
      double price;                        //price of each piece
   public:                                 //constructor (no args)
      Lumber() : Type(), Distance(), quantity(0), price(0.0)
         {  }
                      //constructor (6 args)
      Lumber( string di, string gr,        //args for Type
              int ft, float in,            //args for Distance
              int qu, float prc ) :        //args for our data
              Type(di, gr),                //call Type ctor
              Distance(ft, in),            //call Distance ctor
              quantity(qu), price(prc)     //initialize our data
         {  }
      void getlumber()
         {
```

```
         Type::gettype();
         Distance::getdist();
         cout << "   Enter quantity: "; cin >> quantity;
         cout << "   Enter price per piece: "; cin >> price;
         }
      void showlumber() const
         {
         Type::showtype();
         cout << "\n   Length: ";
         Distance::showdist();
         cout << "\n   Price for " << quantity
              << " pieces: $" << price * quantity;
         }
   };
/////////////////////////////////////////////////////////////////
int main()
   {
   Lumber siding;                       //constructor (no args)

   cout << "\nSiding data:\n";
   siding.getlumber();                  //get siding from user

                                        //constructor (6 args)
   Lumber studs( "2x4", "const", 8, 0.0, 200, 4.45F );

                                        //display lumber data
   cout << "\nSiding";   siding.showlumber();
   cout << "\nStuds";       studs.showlumber();
   cout << endl;
   return 0;
   }
```

The major new feature in this program is the use of constructors in the derived class **Lumber**. These constructors call the appropriate constructors in **Type** and **Distance**.

No-Argument Constructor

The no-argument constructor in **Type** looks like this:

```
Type()
   { strcpy(dimensions, "N/A"); strcpy(grade, "N/A"); }
```

This constructor fills in "N/A" (not available) for the **dimensions** and **grade** variables so the user will be made aware if an attempt is made to display data for an uninitialized lumber object.

You're already familiar with the no-argument constructor in the **Distance** class:

```
Distance() : feet(0), inches(0.0)
   { }
```

The no-argument constructor in **Lumber** calls both these constructors.

```
Lumber() : Type(), Distance(), quantity(0), price(0.0)
      { }
```

The names of the base-class constructors follow the colon and are separated by commas. When the `Lumber()` constructor is invoked, these base-class constructors—`Type()` and `Distance()`—will be executed. The `quantity` and `price` attributes are also initialized.

Multi-Argument Constructors

Here is the two-argument constructor for `Type`:

```
Type(string di, string gr) : dimensions(di), grade(gr)
      { }
```

This constructor copies string arguments to the dimensions and grade member data items. Here's the constructor for `Distance`, which is again familiar from previous programs:

```
Distance(int ft, float in) : feet(ft), inches(in)
   { }
```

The constructor for `Lumber` calls both these constructors, so it must supply values for their arguments. In addition it has two arguments of its own: the quantity of lumber and the unit price. Thus this constructor has six arguments. It makes two calls to the two constructors, each of which takes two arguments, and then initializes its own two data items. Here's what it looks like:

```
Lumber( string di, string gr,      //args for Type
        int ft, float in,          //args for Distance
        int qu, float prc ) :      //args for our data
        Type(di, gr),              //call Type ctor
        Distance(ft, in),          //call Distance ctor
        quantity(qu), price(prc)   //initialize our data
   { }
```

Ambiguity in Multiple Inheritance

Odd sorts of problems may surface in certain situations involving multiple inheritance. Here's a common one. Two base classes have functions with the same name, while a class derived from both base classes has no function with this name. How do objects of the derived class access the correct base class function? The name of the function alone is insufficient, since the compiler can't figure out which of the two functions is meant.

Here's an example, AMBIGU, that demonstrates the situation:

```
// ambigu.cpp
// demonstrates ambiguity in multiple inheritance
#include <iostream>
using namespace std;
//////////////////////////////////////////////////////////////
class A
   {
```

```
   public:
      void show()  { cout << "Class A\n"; }
   };
class B
   {
   public:
      void show()  { cout << "Class B\n"; }
   };
class C : public A, public B
   {
   };
//////////////////////////////////////////////////////////////
int main()
   {
   C objC;                //object of class C
// objC.show();           //ambiguous--will not compile
   objC.A::show();        //OK
   objC.B::show();        //OK
   return 0;
   }
```

The problem is resolved using the scope-resolution operator to specify the class in which the function lies. Thus

```
objC.A::show();
```

refers to the version of show() that's in the A class, while

```
objC.B::show();
```

refers to the function in the B class. Stroustrup (See Appendix H, "Bibliography,") calls this *disambiguation*.

Another kind of ambiguity arises if you derive a class from two classes that are each derived from the same class. This creates a diamond-shaped inheritance tree. The DIAMOND program shows how this looks.

```
//diamond.cpp
//investigates diamond-shaped multiple inheritance
#include <iostream>
using namespace std;
//////////////////////////////////////////////////////////////
class A
   {
   public:
      void func();
   };
class B : public A
   { };
class C : public A
   { };
class D : public B, public C
   { };
//////////////////////////////////////////////////////////////
```

```
int main()
   {
   D objD;
   objD.func();  //ambiguous: won't compile
   return 0;
   }
```

Classes **B** and **C** are both derived from class **A**, and class **D** is derived by multiple inheritance from both **B** and **C**. Trouble starts if you try to access a member function in class **A** from an object of class **D**. In this example **objD** tries to access **func()**. However, both **B** and **C** contain a copy of **func()**, inherited from **A**. The compiler can't decide which copy to use, and signals an error.

There are various advanced ways of coping with this problem, but the fact that such ambiguities can arise causes many experts to recommend avoiding multiple inheritance altogether. You should certainly not use it in serious programs unless you have considerable experience.

Containership: Classes Within Classes

In inheritance, if a class **B** is derived from a class **A**, we can say that "**B** is a kind of **A**." This is because **B** has all the characteristics of **A**, and in addition some of its own. It's like saying that a starling is a kind of bird: A starling has the characteristics shared by all birds (wings, feathers, and so on) but has some distinctive characteristics of its own (such as dark iridescent plumage). For this reason inheritance is often called a "kind of" relationship.

There's another type of relationship, called a "has a" relationship, or *containership*. We say that a starling *has a* tail, meaning that each starling includes an instance of a tail. In object-oriented programming the "has a" relationship occurs when one object is contained in another. Here's a case where an object of class **A** is contained in a class **B**:

```
class A
   {
   };
class B
   {
   A objA;  // define objA as an object of class A
   };
```

In some situations inheritance and containership relationships can serve similar purposes. For example, we can rewrite the EMPMULT program to use containership instead of inheritance. In EMPMULT the **manager** and **scientist** classes are derived from the **employee** and **student** classes using the inheritance relationship. In our new program, EMPCONT, the **manager** and **scientist** classes contain instances of the **employee** and **student** classes, as shown in Figure 9.11.

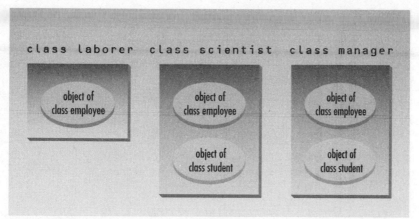

Figure 9.11   Class hierarchy in EMPCONT.

The following miniprogram shows these relationships in a different way:

```cpp
class student
   {};
class employee
   {};
class manager
   {
   student stu;      // stu is an object of class student
   employee emp;     // emp is an object of class employee
   };
class scientist
   {
   student stu;      // stu is an object of class student
   employee emp;     // emp is an object of class employee
   };
class laborer
   {
   employee emp;     // emp is an object of class employee
   };
```

Here's the full-scale listing for EMPCONT:

```cpp
// empcont.cpp
// containership with employees and degrees
#include <iostream>
#include <string>
using namespace std;
/////////////////////////////////////////////////////////////
class student                    //educational background
   {
   private:
      string school;             //name of school or university
      string degree;             //highest degree earned
```

```cpp
   public:
      void getedu()
         {
         cout << "   Enter name of school or university: ";
         cin >> school;
         cout << "   Enter highest degree earned \n";
         cout << "   (Highschool, Bachelor's, Master's, PhD): ";
         cin >> degree;
         }
      void putedu() const
         {
         cout << "\n   School or university: " << school;
         cout << "\n   Highest degree earned: " << degree;
         }
   };
/////////////////////////////////////////////////////////////////
class employee
   {
   private:
      string name;              //employee name
      unsigned long number;     //employee number
   public:
      void getdata()
         {
         cout << "\n   Enter last name: "; cin >> name;
         cout << "   Enter number: ";      cin >> number;
         }
      void putdata() const
         {
         cout << "\n   Name: " << name;
         cout << "\n   Number: " << number;
         }
   };
/////////////////////////////////////////////////////////////////
class manager                 //management
   {
   private:
      string title;           //"vice-president" etc.
      double dues;            //golf club dues
      employee emp;          //object of class employee
      student stu;           //object of class student
   public:
      void getdata()
         {
         emp.getdata();
         cout << "   Enter title: ";           cin >> title;
         cout << "   Enter golf club dues: "; cin >> dues;
         stu.getedu();
         }
      void putdata() const
         {
```

```
            emp.putdata();
            cout << "\n    Title: " << title;
            cout << "\n    Golf club dues: " << dues;
            stu.putedu();
            }
        };
//////////////////////////////////////////////////////////////
class scientist                 //scientist
    {
    private:
        int pubs;                   //number of publications
        employee emp;               //object of class employee
        student stu;                //object of class student
    public:
        void getdata()
            {
            emp.getdata();
            cout << "    Enter number of pubs: "; cin >> pubs;
            stu.getedu();
            }
        void putdata() const
            {
            emp.putdata();
            cout << "\n    Number of publications: " << pubs;
            stu.putedu();
            }
        };
//////////////////////////////////////////////////////////////
class laborer                   //laborer
    {
    private:
        employee emp;               //object of class employee
    public:
        void getdata()
            { emp.getdata(); }
        void putdata() const
            { emp.putdata(); }
        };
//////////////////////////////////////////////////////////////
int main()
    {
    manager m1;
    scientist s1, s2;
    laborer l1;

    cout << endl;
    cout << "\nEnter data for manager 1";      //get data for
    m1.getdata();                              //several employees

    cout << "\nEnter data for scientist 1";
    s1.getdata();
```

```
        cout << "\nEnter data for scientist 2";
        s2.getdata();

        cout << "\nEnter data for laborer 1";
        l1.getdata();

        cout << "\nData on manager 1";            //display data for
        m1.putdata();                             //several employees

        cout << "\nData on scientist 1";
        s1.putdata();

        cout << "\nData on scientist 2";
        s2.putdata();

        cout << "\nData on laborer 1";
        l1.putdata();
        cout << endl;
        return 0;
        }
```

The **student** and **employee** classes are the same in EMPCONT as they were in EMPMULT, but they are used in a different way by the **manager** and **scientist** classes.

Containership is clearly useful with classes that act like a data type, as does the **Distance** class, for example. Then an object of that type can be used in a class in almost the same way a basic type like **int** would be. In other situations you will need to examine the problem carefully and perhaps try different approaches to see what makes sense. Often the inheritance relationship is simpler to implement and offers a clearer conceptual framework.

Inheritance and Program Development

The program-development process, as practiced for decades by programmers everywhere, is being fundamentally altered by object-oriented programming. This is due not only to the use of classes in OOP but to inheritance as well. Let's see how this comes about.

Programmer A creates a class. Perhaps it's something like the **Distance** class, with a complete set of member functions for arithmetic operations on a user-defined data type.

Programmer B likes the **Distance** class but thinks it could be improved by using signed distances. The solution is to create a new class, like **DistSign** in the ENGLEN example, that is derived from **Distance** but incorporates the extensions necessary to implement signed distances.

Programmers C and D then write applications that use the **DistSign** class.

Programmer B may not have access to the source code for the **Distance** member functions, and programmers C and D may not have access to the source code for **DistSign**.

Yet, because of the software reusability feature of C++, B can modify and extend the work of A, and C and D can make use of the work of B (and A).

Notice that the distinction between software tool developers and application writers is becoming blurred. Programmer A creates a general-purpose programming tool, the `Distance` class. Programmer B creates a specialized version of this class, the `DistSign` class. Programmers C and D create applications. A is a tool developer, and C and D are applications developers. B is somewhere in between. In any case OOP is making the programming scene more flexible and at the same time more complex.

In Chapter 13 we'll see how a class can be divided into a client-accessible part and a part that is distributed only in object form, so it can be used by other programmers without the distribution of source code.

Summary

A class, called the *derived class*, can inherit the features of another class, called the *base class*. The derived class can add other features of its own, so it becomes a specialized version of the base class. Inheritance provides a powerful way to extend the capabilities of existing classes, and to design programs using hierarchical relationships.

Accessibility of base class members from derived classes and from objects of derived classes is an important issue. Data or functions in the base class that are prefaced by the keyword *protected* can be accessed from derived classes but not by any other objects, including objects of derived classes. Classes may be publicly or privately derived from base classes. Objects of a publicly derived class can access public members of the base class, while objects of a privately derived class cannot.

A class can be derived from more than one base class. This is called *multiple inheritance*. A class can also be contained within another class.

Inheritance permits the reusability of software: Derived classes can extend the capabilities of base classes with no need to modify—or even access the source code of—the base class. This leads to new flexibility in the software development process, and to a wider range of roles for software developers.

Questions

Answers to questions can be found in Appendix G, "Answers to Questions and Exercises."

1. Inheritance is a way to

    a. make general classes into more specific classes.

    b. pass arguments to objects of classes.

    c. add features to existing classes without rewriting them.

    d. improve data hiding and encapsulation.

2. A "child" class is said to be _____ from a base class.

3. Advantages of inheritance include

    a. providing class growth through natural selection.

    b. facilitating class libraries.

    c. avoiding the rewriting of code.

    d. providing a useful conceptual framework.

4. Write the first line of the specifier for a class `Bosworth` that is publicly derived from a class `Alphonso`.

5. True or false: Adding a derived class to a base class requires fundamental changes to the base class.

6. To be accessed from a member function of the derived class, data or functions in the base class must be `public` or _____.

7. If a base class contains a member function `basefunc()`, and a derived class does not contain a function with this name, can an object of the derived class access `basefunc()`?

8. Assume that the classes mentioned in Question 4 and the class `Alphonso` contain a member function called `alfunc()`. Write a statement that allows object `BosworthObj` of class `Bosworth` to access `alfunc()`.

9. True or false: If no constructors are specified for a derived class, objects of the derived class will use the constructors in the base class.

10. If a base class and a derived class each include a member function with the same name, which member function will be called by an object of the derived class, assuming the scope-resolution operator is not used?

11. Write a declarator for a no-argument constructor of the derived class `Bosworth` of Question 4 that calls a no-argument constructor in the base class `Alphonso`.

12. The scope-resolution operator usually

    a. limits the visibility of variables to a certain function.

    b. tells what base class a class is derived from.

    c. specifies a particular class.

    d. resolves ambiguities.

13. True or false: It is sometimes useful to specify a class from which no objects will ever be created.

14. Assume there is a class `Derv` that is derived from a base class `Base`. Write the declarator for a derived-class constructor that takes one argument and passes this argument along to the constructor in the base class.

15. Assume a class **Derv** that is privately derived from class **Base**. An object of class **Derv** located in **main()** can access

    a. public members of **Derv**.

    b. protected members of **Derv**.

    c. private members of **Derv**.

    d. public members of **Base**.

    e. protected members of **Base**.

    f. private members of **Base**.

16. True or false: A class **D** can be derived from a class **C**, which is derived from a class **B**, which is derived from a class **A**.

17. A class hierarchy

    a. shows the same relationships as an organization chart.

    b. describes "has a" relationships.

    c. describes "is a kind of" relationships.

    d. shows the same relationships as a family tree.

18. Write the first line of a specifier for a class **Tire** that is derived from class **Wheel** and from class **Rubber**.

19. Assume a class **Derv** derived from a base class **Base**. Both classes contain a member function **funo()** that takes no arguments. Write a statement to go in a member function of **Derv** that calls **func()** in the base class.

20. True or false: It is illegal to make objects of one class members of another class.

Exercises

Answers to starred exercises can be found in Appendix G.

*1. Imagine a publishing company that markets both book and audiocassette versions of its works. Create a class **publication** that stores the title (a string) and price (type **float**) of a publication. From this class derive two classes: **book**, which adds a page count (type **int**); and **tape**, which adds a playing time in minutes (type **float**). Each of these three classes should have a **getdata()** function to get its data from the user at the keyboard, and a **putdata()** function to display its data.

Write a `main()` program to test the **book** and **tape** classes by creating instances of them, asking the user to fill in data with `getdata()`, and then displaying the data with `putdata()`.

*2. Recall the STRCONV example from Chapter 8. The **String** class in this example has a flaw: It does not protect itself if its objects are initialized to have too many characters. (The **SZ** constant has the value 80.) For example, the definition

```
String s = "This string will surely exceed the width of the "
           "screen, which is what the SZ constant represents.";
```

will cause the **str** array in **s** to overflow, with unpredictable consequences, such as crashing the system.

With **String** as a base class, derive a class **Pstring** (for "protected string") that prevents buffer overflow when too long a string constant is used in a definition. A new constructor in the derived class should copy only SZ-1 characters into **str** if the string constant is longer, but copy the entire constant if it's shorter. Write a `main()` program to test different lengths of strings.

*3. Start with the **publication**, **book**, and **tape** classes of Exercise 1. Add a base class **sales** that holds an array of three **float**s so that it can record the dollar sales of a particular publication for the last three months. Include a `getdata()` function to get three sales amounts from the user, and a `putdata()` function to display the sales figures. Alter the **book** and **tape** classes so they are derived from both **publication** and **sales**. An object of class **book** or **tape** should input and output sales data along with its other data. Write a `main()` function to create a **book** object and a **tape** object and exercise their input/output capabilities.

4. Assume that the publisher in Exercises 1 and 3 decides to add a third way to distribute books: on computer disk, for those who like to do their reading on their laptop. Add a **disk** class that, like **book** and **tape**, is derived from **publication**. The **disk** class should incorporate the same member functions as the other classes. The data item unique to this class is the disk size: either 3-1/2 inches or 5-1/4 inches. ~~You can use an enum Boolean type to store this item, but the complete size should be displayed.~~ The user could select the appropriate size by typing 3 or 5.

5. Derive a class called **employee2** from the **employee** class in the EMPLOY program in this chapter. This new class should add a type **double** data item called **compensation**, and also an enum type called **period** to indicate whether the employee is paid hourly, weekly, or monthly. For simplicity you can change the **manager**, **scientist**, and **laborer** classes so they are derived from **employee2** instead of **employee**. However, note

that in many circumstances it might be more in the spirit of OOP to create a separate base class called compensation and three new classes manager2, scientist2, and laborer2, and use multiple inheritance to derive these three classes from the original manager, scientist, and laborer classes and from compensation. This way none of the original classes needs to be modified.

6. Start with the ARROVER3 program in Chapter 8. Keep the safearay class the same as in that program, and, using inheritance, derive the capability for the user to specify both the upper and lower bounds of the array in a constructor. This is similar to Exercise 9 in Chapter 8, except that inheritance is used to derive a new class (you can call it safehilo) instead of modifying the original class.

7. Start with the COUNTEN2 program in this chapter. It can increment or decrement a counter, but only using prefix notation. Using inheritance, add the ability to use postfix notation for both incrementing and decrementing. (See Chapter 8 for a description of postfix notation.)

8. Operators in some computer languages, such as BASIC, allow you to select parts of an existing string and assign them to other strings. (The Standard C++ string class offers a different approach.) Using inheritance, add this capability to the Pstring class of Exercise 2. In the derived class, Pstring2, incorporate three new functions: left(), mid(), and right().

```
s2.left(s1, n)      // s2 is assigned the leftmost n characters
                    //    from s1
s2.mid(s1, s, n)    // s2 is assigned the middle n characters
                    //    from s1, starting at character number s
                    //    (leftmost character is 0)
s2.right(s1, n)     // s2 is assigned the rightmost n characters
                    //    from s1
```

You can use for loops to copy the appropriate parts of s1, character by character, to a temporary Pstring2 object, which is then returned. For extra credit, have these functions return by reference, so they can be used on the left side of the equal sign to change parts of an existing string.

9. Start with the publication, book, and tape classes of Exercise 1. Suppose you want to add the date of publication for both books and tapes. From the publication class, derive a new class called publication2 that includes this member data. Then change book and tape so they are derived from publication2 instead of publication. Make all the necessary changes in member functions so the user can input and output dates along with the other data. For the dates, you can use the date class from Exercise 5 in Chapter 6, which stores a date as three ints, for month, day, and year.

10. There is only one kind of manager in the EMPMULT program in this chapter. Any serious company has executives as well as managers. From the `manager` class derive a class called `executive`. (We'll assume an executive is a high-end kind of manager.) The additional data in the `executive` class will be the size of the employee's yearly bonus and the number of shares of company stock held in his or her stock-option plan. Add the appropriate member functions so these data items can be input and displayed along with the other `manager` data.

11. Various situations require that pairs of numbers be treated as a unit. For example, each screen coordinate has an x (horizontal) component and a y (vertical) component. Represent such a pair of numbers as a structure called `pair` that comprises two `int` member variables.

    Now, assume you want to be able to store `pair` variables on a stack. That is, you want to be able to place a pair (which contains two integers) onto a stack using a single call to a `push()` function, with a structure of type `pair` as an argument; and retrieve a pair using a single call to a `pop()` function, which will return a structure of type `pair`. Start with the `Stack2` class in the STAKEN program in this chapter, and from it derive a new class called `pairStack`. This new class need contain only two members: the overloaded `push()` and `pop()` functions. The `pairStack::push()` function will need to make two calls to `Stack2::push()` to store the two integers in its pair, and the `pairStack::pop()` function will need to make two calls to `Stack2::pop()` (although not necessarily in the same order).

12. Amazing as it may seem, the old British pounds-shillings-pence money notation (£9.19.11, see Exercise 10 in Chapter 4, "Structures") isn't the whole story. A penny was further divided into halfpennies and farthings, with a farthing being worth 1/4 of a penny. There was a halfpenny coin, a farthing coin, and a halffarthing coin. Fortunately all this can be expressed numerically in eighths of a penny:

1/8 penny is a halffarthing
1/4 penny is a farthing
3/8 penny is a farthing and a half
1/2 penny is a halfpenny (pronounced ha'penny)
5/8 penny is a halfpenny plus a halffarthing
3/4 penny is a halfpenny plus a farthing
7/8 penny is a halfpenny plus a farthing and a half

Let's assume we want to add to the `sterling` class the ability to handle such fractional pennies. The I/O format can be something like £1.1.1-1/4 or £9.19.11-7/8, where the hyphen separates the fraction from the pennies.

Derive a new class called `sterfrac` from `sterling`. It should be able to perform the four arithmetic operations on sterling quantities that include eighths of a penny. Its only member data is an `int` indicating the number of eighths; you can call it `eighths`. You'll need to overload many of the functions in `sterling` to handle the eighths. The user should be able to type any fraction in lowest terms, and the display should also show fractions in lowest terms. It's not necessary to use the full-scale `fraction` class (see Exercise 11 in Chapter 6) but you could try that for extra credit.

CHAPTER 10

POINTERS

You will learn about the following in this chapter:

- Address constants and variables
- Pointers and arrays
- Pointers and function arguments
- Pointers and strings

- Memory management with NEW and DELETE
- Pointers and objects
- Linked list

Pointers are the hobgoblin of C++ (and C) programming; seldom has such a simple idea inspired so much perplexity for so many. But fear not. In this chapter we will try to demystify pointers and show practical uses for them in C++ programming.

What are pointers for? Here are some common uses:

- Accessing array elements

- Passing arguments to a function when the function needs to modify the original argument

- Passing arrays and strings to functions

- Obtaining memory from the system

- Creating data structures such as linked lists

Pointers are much more commonly used in C++ (and C) than in many other languages (such as BASIC, Pascal, and certainly Java, which has no pointers). Is this emphasis on pointers really necessary? You can do a lot without them, as their absence from the preceding chapters demonstrates. Some operations that use pointers in C++ can be carried out in other ways. For example, array elements can be accessed with array notation rather than pointer notation (we'll see the difference soon), and a function can modify arguments passed by reference, as well as those passed by pointers.

However, in some situations pointers provide an essential tool for increasing the power of C++. A notable example is the creation of data structures such as linked lists and binary trees. In fact, several key features of C++, such as virtual functions, the **new** operator, and the `this` pointer (discussed in Chapter 11, "Virtual Functions"), require the use of pointers. So, although you can do a lot of programming in C++ without using pointers, you will find them essential to obtaining the most from the language.

In this chapter we'll introduce pointers gradually, starting with fundamental concepts and working up to complex pointer applications.

If you already know C, you can probably skim over the first half of the chapter. However, you should read the sections in the second half on the `new` and `delete` operators, accessing member functions using pointers, arrays of pointers to objects, and linked-list objects.

Addresses and Pointers

The ideas behind pointers are not complicated. Here's the first key concept: Every byte in the computer's memory has an *address*. Addresses are numbers, just as they are for houses on a street. The numbers start at 0 and go up from there—1, 2, 3, and so on. If you have 1MB of memory, the highest address is 1,048,575. (Of course you probably have much more.)

Your program, when it is loaded into memory, occupies a certain range of these addresses. That means that every variable and every function in your program starts at a particular address. Figure 10.1 shows how this looks.

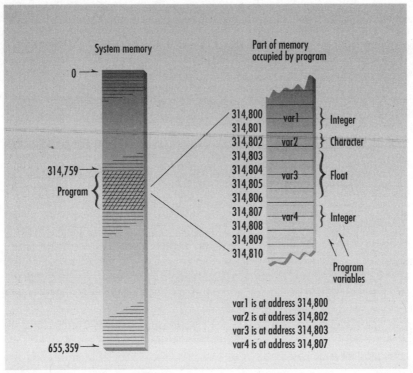

Figure 10.1 Memory addresses.

The Address-of Operator &

You can find the address occupied by a variable by using the *address-of* operator &. Here's a short program, VARADDR, that demonstrates how to do this:

```
// varaddr.cpp
// addresses of variables
#include <iostream>
using namespace std;

int main()
   {
   int var1 = 11;           //define and initialize
   int var2 = 22;           //three variables
   int var3 = 33;

   cout << &var1 << endl    //print the addresses
        << &var2 << endl    //of these variables
        << &var3 << endl;
   return 0;
   }
```

This simple program defines three integer variables and initializes them to the values 11, 22, and 33. It then prints out the addresses of these variables.

The actual addresses occupied by the variables in a program depend on many factors, such as the computer the program is running on, the size of the operating system, and whether any other programs are currently in memory. For these reasons you probably won't get the same addresses we did when you run this program. Here's the output on our machine:

```
0x8f4ffff4      ←——————— address of var1
0x8f4ffff2      ←——————— address of var2
0x8f4ffff0      ←——————— address of var3
```

Remember that the *address* of a variable is not at all the same as its *contents*. The contents of the three variables are 11, 22, and 33. Figure 10.2 shows the three variables in memory.

The << insertion operator interprets the addresses in hexadecimal arithmetic, as indicated by the prefix 0x before each number. This is the usual way to show memory addresses. If you aren't familiar with the hexadecimal number system, don't worry. All you really need to know is that each variable starts at a unique address. However, you might note in the output above that each address differs from the next by exactly 2 bytes. That's because integers occupy 2 bytes of memory (assuming it's a 16-bit system). If we had used variables of type char, they would have adjacent addresses, since a char occupies 1 byte; and if we had used type double, the addresses would have differed by 8 bytes.

The addresses appear in descending order because automatic variables are stored on the stack, which grows downward in memory. If we had used external variables, they would have ascending addresses, since external variables are stored on the heap, which grows upward. Again, you don't need to worry too much about these considerations, since the compiler keeps track of the details for you.

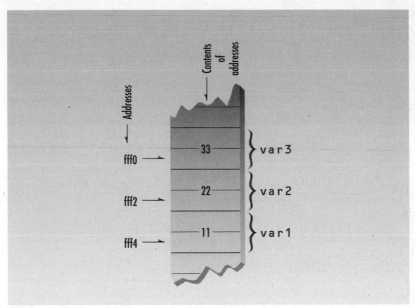

Figure 10.2 Addresses and contents of variables.

Don't confuse the address-of operator **&**, which precedes a variable name in a variable declaration, with the reference operator **&**, which follows the type name in a function prototype or definition. (References were discussed in Chapter 5, "Functions.")

Pointer Variables

Addresses by themselves are rather limited. It's nice to know that we can find out where things are in memory, as we did in VARADDR, but printing out address values is not all that useful. The potential for increasing our programming power requires an additional idea: *variables that hold address values.* We've seen variable types that store characters, integers, floating-point numbers, and so on. Addresses are stored similarly. A variable that holds an address value is called a *pointer variable*, or simply a *pointer*.

What is the data type of pointer variables? It's not the same as the variable whose address is being stored; a pointer to **int** is not type **int**. You might think a pointer data type would be called something like **pointer** or **ptr**. However, things are slightly more complicated. The next program, PTRVAR, shows the syntax for pointer variables.

```
// ptrvar.cpp
// pointers (address variables)
```

```
#include <iostream>
using namespace std;

int main()
    {
    int var1 = 11;              //two integer variables
    int var2 = 22;

    cout << &var1 << endl       //print addresses of variables
        << &var2 << endl << endl;

    int* ptr;                   //pointer to integers

    ptr = &var1;                //pointer points to var1
    cout << ptr << endl;        //print pointer value

    ptr = &var2;                //pointer points to var2
    cout << ptr << endl;        //print pointer value
    return 0;
    }
```

This program defines two integer variables, var1 and var2, and initializes them to the values 11 and 22. It then prints out their addresses.

The program next defines a *pointer variable* in the line

```
int* ptr;
```

To the uninitiated this is a rather bizarre syntax. The asterisk means *pointer to*. Thus the statement defines the variable ptr as a *pointer to* int. This is another way of saying that this variable can hold the addresses of integer variables.

What's wrong with the idea of a general-purpose pointer type that holds pointers to any data type? If we called it type pointer we could write declarations like

```
pointer ptr;
```

The problem is that the compiler needs to know *what kind of variable the pointer points to*. (We'll see why when we talk about pointers and arrays.) The syntax used in C++ allows pointers to any type to be declared.

```
char* cptr;          // pointer to char
int* iptr;           // pointer to int
float* fptr;         // pointer to float
Distance* distptr;   // pointer to user-defined Distance class
```

and so on.

Syntax Quibbles

We should note that it is common to write pointer definitions with the asterisk closer to the variable name than to the type.

```
char *charptr;
```

It doesn't matter to the compiler, but placing the asterisk next to the type helps emphasize that the asterisk is part of the variable type (pointer to `char`), not part of the name itself.

If you define more than one pointer of the same type on one line, you need only insert the type-pointed-to once, but you need to place an asterisk before each variable name.

```
char* ptr1, * ptr2, * ptr3;  // three variables of type char*
```

Or you can use the asterisk-next-to-the-name approach.

```
char *ptr1, *ptr2, *ptr3;  // three variables of type char*
```

Pointers Must Have a Value

An address like 0x8f4ffff4 can be thought of as a *pointer constant*. A pointer like `ptr` can be thought of as a *pointer variable*. Just as the integer variable `var1` can be assigned the constant value 11, so can the pointer variable `ptr` be assigned the constant value 0x8f4ffff4.

When we first define a variable, it holds no value (unless we initialize it at the same time). It may hold a garbage value, but this has no meaning. In the case of pointers, a garbage value is the address of something in memory, but probably not of something that we want. So before a pointer is used, a specific address must be placed in it. In the PTRVAR program, `ptr` is first assigned the address of `var1` in the line

```
ptr = &var1;      ←──────put address of var1 in ptr
```

Following this the program prints out the value contained in `ptr`, which should be the same address printed for `&var1`. The same pointer variable `ptr` is then assigned the address of `var2`, and this value is printed out. Figure 10.3 shows the operation of the PTRVAR program. Here's the output of PTRVAR:

```
0x8f51fff4    ←─────── address of var1
0x8f51fff2    ←─────── address of var2

0x8f51fff4    ←─────── ptr set to address of var1
0x8f51fff2    ←─────── ptr set to address of var2
```

To summarize: A pointer can hold the address of any variable of the correct type; it's a receptacle awaiting an address. However, it must be given some value, otherwise it will point to an address we don't want it to point to, such as into our program code or the operating system. Rogue pointer values can result in system crashes and are difficult to debug, since the compiler gives no warning. The moral: Make sure you give every pointer variable a valid address value before using it.

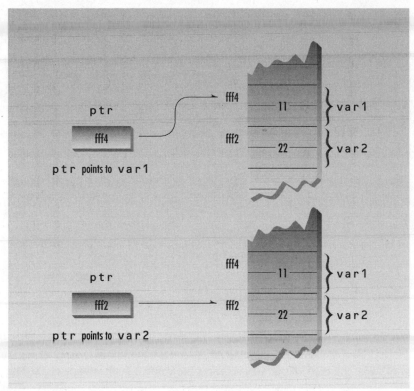

Figure 10.3 Changing values in `ptr`.

Accessing the Variable Pointed To

Suppose that we don't know the name of a variable but we do know its address. Can we access the contents of the variable? (It may seem like mismanagement to lose track of variable names, but we'll soon see that there are many variables whose names we don't know.)

There is a special syntax to access the value of a variable using its address instead of its name. Here's an example program, PTRACC, that shows how it's done:

```
// ptracc.cpp
// accessing the variable pointed to
#include <iostream>
using namespace std;

int main()
   {
```

```
int var1 = 11;                  //two integer variables
int var2 = 22;

int* ptr;                       //pointer to integers

ptr = &var1;                    //pointer points to var1
cout << *ptr << endl;           //print contents of pointer (11)

ptr = &var2;                    //pointer points to var2
cout << *ptr << endl;           //print contents of pointer (22)
return 0;
}
```

This program is very similar to PTRVAR, except that instead of printing the address values in **ptr**, we print the integer value stored at the address that's stored in **ptr**. Here's the output:

```
11
22
```

The expression that accesses the variables **var1** and **var2** is ***ptr**, which occurs in each of the two **cout** statements.

When an asterisk is used in front of a variable name, as it is in the ***ptr** expression, it is called the *indirection operator*. It means *the value of the variable pointed to by*. Thus the expression ***ptr** represents the value of the variable pointed to by **ptr**. When **ptr** is set to the address of **var1**, the expression ***ptr** has the value 11, since **var1** is 11. When **ptr** is changed to the address of **var2**, the expression ***ptr** acquires the value 22, since **var2** is 22. The indirection operator is sometimes called the *contents of* operator, which is another way to say the same thing. Figure 10.4 shows how this looks.

You can use a pointer not only to display a variable's value, but also to perform any operation you would perform on the variable directly. Here's a program, PTRTO, that uses a pointer to assign a value to a variable, and then to assign that value to another variable:

```
// ptrto.cpp
// other access using pointers
#include <iostream>
using namespace std;

int main()
   {
   int var1, var2;           //two integer variables
   int* ptr;                 //pointer to integers

   ptr = &var1;              //set pointer to address of var1
   *ptr = 37;                //same as var1=37
   var2 = *ptr;              //same as var2=var1

   cout << var2 << endl;     //verify var2 is 37
   return 0;
   }
```

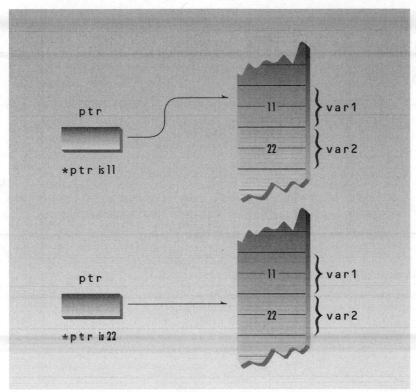

Figure 10.4 Access via pointer.

Remember that the asterisk used as the indirection operator has a different meaning than the asterisk used to declare pointer variables. The indirection operator *precedes* the variable and means *value of the variable pointed to by*. The asterisk used in a declaration means *pointer to*.

```
int* ptr;     //declaration: pointer to int
*ptr = 37;    //indirection: value of variable pointed to by ptr
```

Using the indirection operator to access the value stored in an address is called *indirect addressing*, or sometimes *dereferencing*, the pointer.

Here's a capsule summary of what we've learned so far:

```
int v;        //defines variable v of type int
int* p;       //defines p as a pointer to int
p = &v;       //assigns address of variable v to pointer p
v = 3;        //assigns 3 to v
*p = 3;       //also assigns 3 to v
```

The last two statements show the difference between normal or direct addressing, where we refer to a variable by name, and pointer or indirect addressing, where we refer to the same variable using its address.

In the example programs we've shown so far in this chapter, there's really no advantage to using the pointer expression to access variables, since we can access them directly. Pointers come into their own when you can't access a variable directly, as we'll see later.

Pointer to `void`

Before we go on to see pointers at work, we should note one peculiarity of pointer data types. Ordinarily, the address that you put in a pointer must be the same type as the pointer. You can't assign the address of a `float` variable to a pointer to `int`, for example:

```
float flovar = 98.6;
int* ptrint = &flovar;  //ERROR: can't assign float* to int*
```

However, there is an exception to this. There is a sort of general-purpose pointer that can point to any data type. This is called a pointer to `void`, and is defined like this:

```
void* ptr;   //ptr can point to any data type
```

Such pointers have certain specialized uses, such as passing pointers to functions that operate independently of the data type pointed to.

The next example uses a pointer to `void` and also shows that, if you don't use `void`, you must be careful to assign pointers an address of the same type as the pointer. Here's the listing for PTRVOID:

```
// ptrvoid.cpp
// pointers to type void
#include <iostream>
using namespace std;

int main()
   {
   int intvar;                //integer variable
   float flovar;              //float variable

   int* ptrint;               //define pointer to int
   float* ptrflo;             //define pointer to float
   void* ptrvoid;             //define pointer to void

   ptrint = &intvar;          //ok, int* to int*
// ptrint = &flovar;          //error, float* to int*
// ptrflo = &intvar;          //error, int* to float*
   ptrflo = &flovar;          //ok, float* to float*

   ptrvoid = &intvar;         //ok, int* to void*
   ptrvoid = &flovar;         //ok, float* to void*
   return 0;
   }
```

You can assign the address of `intvar` to `ptrint` because they are both type `int*`, but you can't assign the address of `flovar` to `ptrint` because the first is type `float*` and the second is type `int*`. However, `ptrvoid` can be given any pointer value, such as `int*`, because it is a pointer to `void`.

If for some unusual reason you really need to assign one kind of pointer type to another, you can use the reinterpret_cast. For the lines commented out in PTRVOID, that would look like this:

```
ptrint = reinterpret_cast<int*>(flovar);
ptrflo = reinterpret_cast<float*>(intvar);
```

The use of reinterpret_cast in this way is not recommended, but occasionally it's the only way out of a difficult situation. Static casts won't work with pointers. Old-style C casts can be used, but are always a bad idea in C++. We'll see examples of reinterpret_cast in Chapter 12, "Streams and Files," where it's used to alter the way a data buffer is interpreted.

Pointers and Arrays

There is a close association between pointers and arrays. We saw in Chapter 7, "Arrays and Strings," how array elements are accessed. The following program, ARRNOTE, provides a review.

```
// arrnote.cpp
// array accessed with array notation
#include <iostream>
using namespace std;

int main()
   {                                        //array
   int intarray[5] = { 31, 54, 77, 52, 93 };

   for(int j=0; j<5; j++)                   //for each element,
      cout << intarray[j] << endl;          //print value
   return 0;
   }
```

The cout statement prints each array element in turn. For instance, when j is 3, the expression intarray[j] takes on the value intarray[3] and accesses the fourth array element, the integer 52. Here's the output of ARRNOTE:

```
31
54
77
52
93
```

Surprisingly, array elements can be accessed using pointer notation as well as array notation. The next example, PTRNOTE, is similar to ARRNOTE except that it uses pointer notation.

```
// ptrnote.cpp
// array accessed with pointer notation
#include <iostream>
using namespace std;

int main()
```

```
{                                           //array
int intarray[5] = { 31, 54, 77, 52, 93 };

for(int j=0; j<5; j++)                      //for each element,
   cout << *(intarray+j) << endl;           //print value
return 0;
}
```

The expression *(intarray+j) in PTRNOTE has exactly the same effect as intarray[j] in ARRNOTE, and the output of the programs is identical. But how do we interpret the expression *(intarray+j)? Suppose j is 3, so the expression is equivalent to *(intarray+3). We want this to represent the contents of the fourth element of the array (52). Remember that the name of an array is its address. The expression intarray+j is thus an address with something added to it. You might expect that intarray+3 would cause 3 bytes to be added to intarray. But that doesn't produce the result we want: intarray is an array of integers, and 3 bytes into this array is the middle of the second element, which is not very useful. We want to obtain the fourth *integer* in the array, not the fourth byte, as shown in Figure 10.5. (This figure assumes 2-byte integers.)

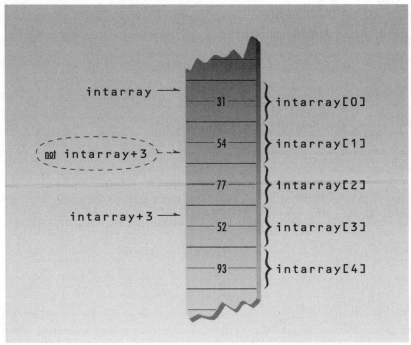

Figure 10.5   Counting by integers.

The C++ compiler is smart enough to take the size of the data into account when it performs arithmetic on data addresses. It knows that `intarray` is an array of type `int` because it was declared that way. So when it sees the expression `intarray+3`, it interprets it as the address of the fourth *integer* in `intarray`, not the fourth byte.

But we want the *value* of this fourth array element, not the *address*. To take the value, we use the indirection operator `*`. The resulting expression, when j is 3, is `*(intarray+3)`, which is the content of the fourth array element, or 52.

Now we see why a pointer declaration must include the type of the variable pointed to. The compiler needs to know whether a pointer is a pointer to `int` or a pointer to `double` so that it can perform the correct arithmetic to access elements of the array. It multiplies the index value by 2 in the case of type `int`, but by 8 in the case of `double`.

Pointer Constants and Pointer Variables

Suppose that, instead of adding j to `intarray` to step through the array addresses, you wanted to use the increment operator. Could you write `*(intarray++)`?

The answer is no, and the reason is that you can't increment a constant (or indeed change it in any way). The expression `intarray` is the address where the system has chosen to place your array, and it will stay at this address until the program terminates. `intarray` is a pointer constant. You can't say `intarray++` any more than you can say `7++`. (In a multitasking system, variable addresses may change during program execution. An active program may be swapped out to disk and then reloaded at a different memory location. However, this process is invisible to your program.)

But while you can't increment an address, you can increment a pointer that holds an address. The next example, PTRINC, shows how:

```
// ptrinc.cpp
// array accessed with pointer
#include <iostream>
using namespace std;

int main()
   {
   int intarray[] = { 31, 54, 77, 52, 93 }; //array
   int* ptrint;                             //pointer to int
   ptrint = intarray;                       //points to intarray

   for(int j=0; j<5; j++)                   //for each element,
      cout << *(ptrint++) << endl;          //print value
   return 0;
   }
```

Here we define a pointer to `int`—ptrint—and give it the value `intarray`, the address of the array. Now we can access the contents of the array elements with the expression

`*(ptrint++)`

The variable `ptrint` starts off with the same address value as `intarray`, thus allowing the first array element, `intarray[0]`, which has the value 31, to be accessed as before. But, because `ptrint` is a variable and not a constant, it can be incremented. After it is incremented, it points to the second array element, `intarray[1]`. The expression `*(ptrint++)` then represents the contents of the second array element, or 54. The loop causes the expression to access each array element in turn. The output of PTRINC is the same as that for PTRNOTE.

Pointers and Functions

In Chapter 5 we noted that there are three ways to pass arguments to a function: by value, by reference, and by pointer. If the function is intended to modify variables in the calling program, then these variables cannot be passed by value, since the function obtains only a copy of the variable. However, either a reference argument or a pointer can be used in this situation.

Passing Simple Variables

We'll first review how arguments are passed by reference, and then compare this to passing pointer arguments. The PASSREF program shows passing by reference.

```
// passref.cpp
// arguments passed by reference
#include <iostream>
using namespace std;

int main()
   {
   void centimize(double&);     //prototype

   double var = 10.0;           //var has value of 10 inches
   cout << "var = " << var << " inches" << endl;

   centimize(var);              //change var to centimeters
   cout << "var = " << var << " centimeters" << endl;
   return 0;
   }
//----------------------------------------------------------------
void centimize(double& v)
   {
   v *= 2.54;                   //v is the same as var
   }
```

Here we want to convert a variable `var` in `main()` from inches to centimeters. We pass the variable by reference to the function `centimize()`. (Remember that the `&` following the data type `double` in the prototype for this function indicates that the argument is passed by reference.) The `centimize()` function multiplies the original variable by 2.54. Notice how the function refers to the variable. It simply uses the argument name `v`; `v` and `var` are different names for the same thing.

Once it has converted var to centimeters, main() displays the result. Here's the output of PASSREF:

```
var = 10 inches
var = 25.4 centimeters
```

The next example, PASSPTR, shows an equivalent situation when pointers are used:

```
// passptr.cpp
// arguments passed by pointer
#include <iostream>
using namespace std;

int main()
   {
   void centimize(double*);     //prototype

   double var = 10.0;           //var has value of 10 inches
   cout << "var = " << var << " inches" << endl;

   centimize(&var);             //change var to centimeters
   cout << "var = " << var << " centimeters" << endl;
   return 0;
   }
//-------------------------------------------------------------
void centimize(double* ptrd)
   {
   *ptrd *= 2.54;               //*ptrd is the same as var
   }
```

The output of PASSPTR is the same as that of PASSREF.

The function **centimize()** is declared as taking an argument that is a pointer to **double**:

```
void centimize(double*)   // argument is pointer to double
```

When **main()** calls the function it supplies the address of the variable as the argument:

```
centimize(&var);
```

Remember that this is not the variable itself, as it is in passing by reference, but the variable's address.

Because the **centimize()** function is passed an address, it must use the indirection operator, *ptrd, to access the value stored at this address:

```
*ptrd *= 2.54;  // multiply the contents of ptrd by 2.54
```

Of course this is the same as

```
*ptrd = *ptrd * 2.54;  // multiply the contents of ptrd by 2.54
```

where the standalone asterisk means multiplication. (This operator really gets around.)

Since **ptrd** contains the address of **var**, anything done to ***ptrd** is actually done to **var**. Figure 10.6 shows how changing ***ptrd** in the function changes **var** in the calling program.

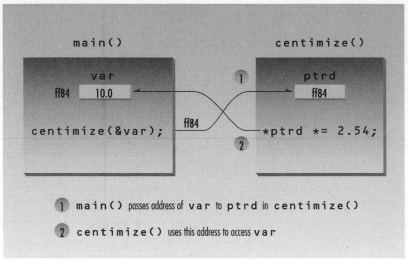

Figure 10.6 Pointer passed to function.

Passing a pointer as an argument to a function is in some ways similar to passing a reference. They both permit the variable in the calling program to be modified by the function. However, the mechanism is different. A reference is an alias for the original variable, while a pointer is the address of the variable.

Passing Arrays

We've seen numerous examples, starting in Chapter 7, of arrays passed as arguments to functions, and their elements being accessed by the function. Until this chapter, since we had not yet learned about pointers, this was done using array notation. However, it's more common to use pointer notation instead of array notation when arrays are passed to functions. The PASSARR program shows how this looks:

```
// passarr.cpp
// array passed by pointer
#include <iostream>
using namespace std;
const int MAX = 5;              //number of array elements

int main()
   {
   void centimize(double*);  //prototype

   double varray[MAX] = { 10.0, 43.1, 95.9, 59.7, 87.3 };

   centimize(varray);          //change elements of varray to cm

   for(int j=0; j<MAX; j++)  //display new array values
      cout << "varray[" << j << "]="
           << varray[j] << " centimeters" << endl;
   return 0;
```

```
    }
//------------------------------------------------------------
void centimize(double* ptrd)
    {
    for(int j=0; j<MAX; j++)
       *ptrd++ *= 2.54;          //ptrd points to elements of varray
    }
```

The prototype for the function is the same as in PASSPTR; the function's single argument is a pointer to **double**. In array notation this is written as

```
void centimize(double[]);
```

That is, **double*** is equivalent here to **double[]**, although the pointer syntax is more commonly used.

Since the name of an array is the array's address, there is no need for the address operator & when the function is called:

```
centimize(varray);  // pass array address
```

In **centimize()** this array address is placed in the variable **ptrd**. To point to each element of the array in turn, we need only increment **ptrd**:

```
*ptrd++ *= 2.54;
```

Figure 10.7 shows how the array is accessed. Here's the output of PASSARR:

```
varray[0]=25.4 centimeters
varray[1]=109.474 centimeters
varray[2]=243.586 centimeters
varray[3]=151.638 centimeters
varray[4]=221.742 centimeters
```

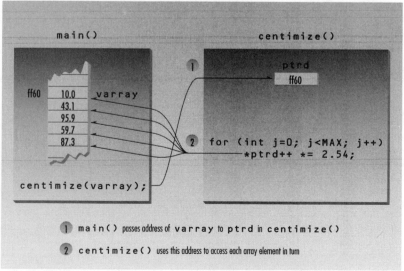

Figure 10.7 Accessing an array from function.

Here's a syntax question: How do we know that the expression `*ptrd++` increments the pointer and not the pointer contents? In other words, does the compiler interpret it as `*(ptrd++)`, which is what we want, or as `(*ptrd)++`? It turns out that `*` (when used as the indirection operator) and `++` have the same precedence. However, operators of the same precedence are distinguished in a second way: by *associativity*. Associativity is concerned with whether the compiler performs operations starting with an operator on the right or an operator on the left. If a group of operators has right associativity, the compiler performs the operation on the right side of the expression first, then works its way to the left. The unary operators like `*` and `++` have right associativity, so the expression is interpreted as `*(ptrd++)`, which increments the pointer, not what it points to. That is, the pointer is incremented first and the indirection operator is applied to the resulting address.

Sorting Array Elements

As a further example of using pointers to access array elements, let's see how to sort the contents of an array. We'll use two program examples—the first to lay the groundwork, and the second, an expansion of the first, to demonstrate the sorting process.

Ordering with Pointers

The first program is similar to the REFORDER program in Chapter 6, "Objects and Classes," except that it uses pointers instead of references. It orders two numbers passed to it as arguments, exchanging them if the second is smaller than the first. Here's the listing for PTRORDER:

```
// ptrorder.cpp
// orders two arguments using pointers
#include <iostream>
using namespace std;

int main()
   {
   void order(int*, int*);          //prototype

   int n1=99, n2=11;                //one pair ordered, one not
   int n3=22, n4=88;

   order(&n1, &n2);                 //order each pair of numbers
   order(&n3, &n4);

   cout << "n1=" << n1 << endl;     //print out all numbers
   cout << "n2=" << n2 << endl;
   cout << "n3=" << n3 << endl;
   cout << "n4=" << n4 << endl;
   return 0;
   }
//--------------------------------------------------------------
void order(int* numb1, int* numb2) //orders two numbers
   {
```

```
if(*numb1 > *numb2)              //if 1st larger than 2nd,
   {
   int temp = *numb1;            //swap them
   *numb1 = *numb2;
   *numb2 = temp;
   }
}
```

The function order() works the same as it did in REFORDER, except that it is passed the addresses of the numbers to be ordered, and it accesses the numbers using pointers. That is, *numb1 accesses the number in main() passed as the first argument, and *numb2 accesses the second.

Here's the output from PTRORDER:

```
n1=11   ←——— t h i s  a n d
n2=99   ←——— this are swapped, since they weren't in order
n3=22   ←——— t h i s
n4=88   ←——— and this are not swapped, since they were in order
```

We'll use the order() function from PTRORDER in our next example program, PTRSORT, which sorts an array of integers.

```
// ptrsort.cpp
// sorts an array using pointers
#include <iostream>
using namespace std;

int main()
   {
   void bsort(int*, int);        //prototype
   const int N = 10;             //array size
                                 //test array
   int arr[N] = { 37, 84, 62, 91, 11, 65, 57, 28, 19, 49 };

   bsort(arr, N);                //sort the array

   for(int j=0; j<N; j++)        //print out sorted array
      cout << arr[j] << " ";
   cout << endl;
   return 0;
   }
//--------------------------------------------------------------
void bsort(int* ptr, int n)
   {
   void order(int*, int*);       //prototype
   int j, k;                     //indexes to array

   for(j=0; j<n-1; j++)          //outer loop
      for(k=j+1; k<n; k++)       //inner loop starts at outer
         order(ptr+j, ptr+k);    //order the pointer contents
   }
//--------------------------------------------------------------
void order(int* numb1, int* numb2)  //orders two numbers
   {
```

```
    if(*numb1 > *numb2)         //if 1st larger than 2nd,
        {
        int temp = *numb1;      //swap them
        *numb1 = *numb2;
        *numb2 = temp;
        }
    }
```

The array `arr` of integers in `main()` is initialized to unsorted values. The address of the array, and the number of elements, are passed to the `bsort()` function. This sorts the array, and the sorted values are then printed. Here's the output of the PTRSORT:

```
11 19 28 37 49 57 62 65 84 91
```

The Bubble Sort

The `bsort()` function sorts the array using a variation of the bubble sort. This is a simple (although notoriously slow) approach to sorting. Here's how it works, assuming we want to arrange the numbers in the array in ascending order. First the first element of the array (`arr[0]`) is compared in turn with each of the other elements (starting with the second). If it's greater than any of them, the two are swapped. When this is done we know that at least the first element is in order; it's now the smallest element. Next the second element is compared in turn with all the other elements, starting with the third, and again swapped if it's bigger. When we're done we know that the second element has the second-smallest value. This process is continued for all the elements until the next-to-the-last, at which time the array is assumed to be ordered. Figure 10.8 shows the bubble sort in action (with fewer items than in PTRSORT).

In PTRSORT, the number in the first position, 37, is compared with each element in turn, and swapped with 11. The number in the second position, which starts off as 84, is compared with each element. It's swapped with 62; then 62 (which is now in the second position) is swapped with 37, 37 is swapped with 28, and 28 is swapped with 19. The number in the third position, which is 84 again, is swapped with 62, 62 is swapped with 57, 57 with 37, and 37 with 28. The process continues until the array is sorted.

The `bsort()` function in PTRSORT consists of two nested loops, each of which controls a pointer. The outer loop uses the loop variable `j`, and the inner one uses `k`. The expressions `ptr+j` and `ptr+k` point to various elements of the array, as determined by the loop variables. The expression `ptr+j` moves down the array, starting at the first element (the top) and stepping down integer by integer until one short of the last element (the bottom). For each position taken by `ptr+j` in the outer loop, the expression `ptr+k` in the inner loop starts pointing one below `ptr+j` and moves down to the bottom of the array. Each time through the inner loop, the elements pointed to by `ptr+j` and `ptr+k` are compared, using the `order()` function, and if the first is greater than the second, they're swapped. Figure 10.9 shows this process.

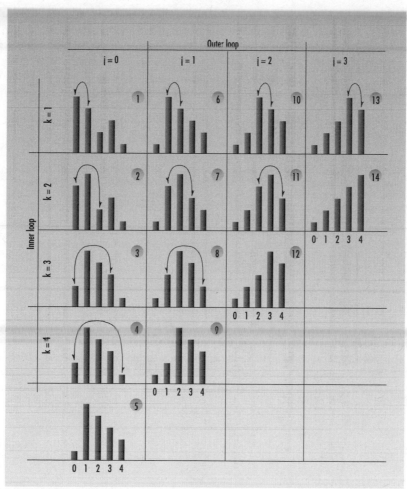

Figure 10.8 Operation of the bubble sort.

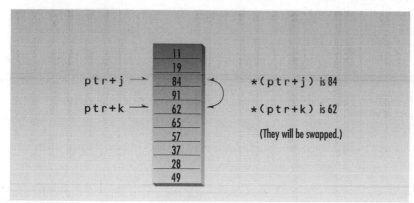

Figure 10.9 Operation of PTRSORT.

The PTRSORT example begins to reveal the power of pointers. They provide a consistent and efficient way to operate on array elements and other variables whose names aren't known to a particular function.

Pointers and C-type Strings

As we noted in Chapter 7, C-type strings are simply arrays of type **char**. Thus pointer notation can be applied to the characters in strings, just as it can to the elements of any array.

Pointers to String Constants

Here's an example, TWOSTR, in which two strings are defined, one using array notation as we've seen in previous examples, and one using pointer notation:

```
// twostr.cpp
// strings defined using array and pointer notation
#include <iostream>
using namespace std;

int main()
    {
    char str1[] = "Defined as an array";
    char* str2 = "Defined as a pointer";

    cout << str1 << endl;      // display both strings
    cout << str2 << endl;

// str1++;                     // can't do this; str1 is a constant
    str2++;                     // this is OK, str2 is a pointer

    cout << str2 << endl;      // now str2 starts "Defined..."
    return 0;
    }
```

In many ways these two types of definition are equivalent. You can print out both strings as the example shows, use them as function arguments, and so on. But there is a subtle difference: **str1** is an address—that is, a pointer constant—while **str2** is a pointer variable. So **str2** can be changed, while **str1** cannot, as shown in the program. Figure 10.10 shows how these two kinds of strings look in memory.

We can increment **str2**, since it is a pointer, but once we do, it no longer points to the first character in the string. Here's the output of TWOSTR:

```
Defined as an array
Defined as a pointer
Defined as a pointer      ←——— following str2++
```

A string defined as a pointer is considerably more flexible than one defined as an array. The following examples will make use of this flexibility.

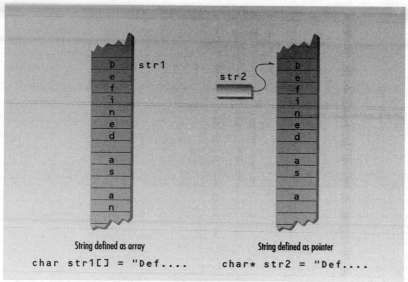

Figure 10.10   Strings as arrays and pointers.

Strings As Function Arguments

Here's an example that shows a string used as a function argument. The function simply prints the string, by accessing each character in turn. Here's the listing for PTRSTR:

```cpp
// ptrstr.cpp
// displays a string with pointer notation
#include <iostream>
using namespace std;

int main()
   {
   void dispstr(char*);       //prototype
   char str[] = "Idle people have the least leisure.";

   dispstr(str);              //display the string
   return 0;
   }
//------------------------------------------------------------
void dispstr(char* ps)
   {
   while( *ps )               //until null character,
      cout << *ps++;          //print characters
   cout << endl;
   }
```

The array address `str` is used as the argument in the call to function `dispstr()`. This address is a constant, but since it is passed by value, a copy of it is created in `dispstr()`.

This copy is a pointer, **ps**. A pointer can be changed, so the function increments **ps** to display the string. The expression ***ps++** returns the successive characters of the string. The loop cycles until it finds the null character (**'\0'**) at the end of the string. Since this has the value 0, which represents *false*, the **while** loop terminates at this point.

Copying a String Using Pointers

We've seen examples of pointers used to obtain values from an array. Pointers can also be used to insert values into an array. The next example, COPYSTR, demonstrates a function that copies one string to another:

```
// copystr.cpp
// copies one string to another with pointers
#include <iostream>
using namespace std;

int main()
   {
   void copystr(char*, const char*);  //prototype
   char* str1 = "Self-conquest is the greatest victory.";
   char str2[80];                     //empty string

   copystr(str2, str1);               //copy str1 to str2
   cout << str2 << endl;              //display str2
   return 0;
   }
//--------------------------------------------------------------
void copystr(char* dest, const char* src)
   {
   while( *src )                      //until null character,
      *dest++ = *src++;               //copy chars from src to dest
   *dest = '\0';                      //terminate dest
   }
```

Here the **main()** part of the program calls the function **copystr()** to copy **str1** to **str2**. In this function the expression

```
*dest++ = *src++;
```

takes the value at the address pointed to by **src** and places it in the address pointed to by **dest**. Both pointers are then incremented, so the next time through the loop the next character will be transferred. The loop terminates when a null character is found in **src**; at this point a null is inserted in **dest** and the function returns. Figure 10.11 shows how the pointers move through the strings.

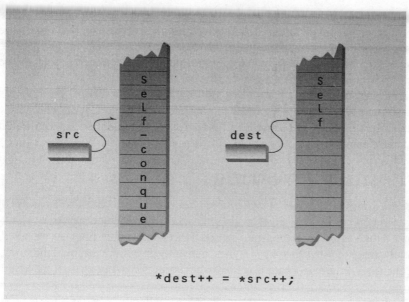

Figure 10.11 Operation of COPYSTR.

Library String Functions

Many of the library functions we have already used for strings have string arguments that are specified using pointer notation. As an example you can look at the description of strcpy() in your compiler's documentation (or in the STRING.H header file). This function copies one string to another; we can compare it with our homemade copystr() function in the COPYSTR example. Here's the syntax for the strcpy() library function:

```
char* strcpy(char* dest, const char* src);
```

This function takes two arguments of type char*. (The next section, "The const Modifier and Pointers," explains the meaning of const in this context.) The strcpy() function also returns a pointer to char; this is the address of the dest string. In other respects this function works very much like our homemade copystr() function.

The const Modifier and Pointers

The use of the const modifier with pointer declarations can be confusing, because it can mean one of two things, depending on where it's placed. The following statements show the two possibilities:

```
const int* cptrInt;   //cptrInt is a pointer to constant int
int* const ptrcInt;   //ptrcInt is a constant pointer to int
```

Following the first declaration, you cannot change the value of whatever `cptrInt` points to, although you can change `cptrInt` itself. Following the second declaration, you can change what `ptrcInt` points to, but you cannot change the value of `ptrcInt` itself. You can remember the difference by reading from right to left, as indicated in the comments. You can use `const` in both positions to make the pointer and what it points to constant.

In the declaration of `strcpy()` just shown, the argument `const char* src` specifies that the characters pointed to by `src` cannot be changed by `strcpy()`. It does not imply that the `src` pointer itself cannot be modified. To do that the argument declaration would need to be `char* const src`.

Arrays of Pointers to Strings

Just as there are arrays of variables of type `int` or type `float`, there can also be arrays of pointers. A common use for this construction is an array of pointers to strings.

In Chapter 7 the STRARAY program demonstrated an array of `char*` strings. As we noted, there is a disadvantage to using an array of strings, in that the subarrays that hold the strings must all be the same length, so space is wasted when strings are shorter than the length of the subarrays (see Figure 7.10 in Chapter 7).

Let's see how to use pointers to solve this problem. We will modify STRARAY to create an array of pointers to strings, rather than an array of strings. Here's the listing for PTRTOSTR:

```
// ptrtostr.cpp
// an array of pointers to strings
#include <iostream>
using namespace std;
const int DAYS = 7;              //number of pointers in array

int main()
    {                            //array of pointers to char
    char* arrptrs[DAYS] = { "Sunday", "Monday", "Tuesday",
            "Wednesday", "Thursday",
            "Friday", "Saturday"  };

    for(int j=0; j<DAYS; j++)    //display every string
       cout << arrptrs[j] << endl;
    return 0;
    }
```

The output of this program is the same as that for STRARAY:

```
Sunday
Monday
Tuesday
Wednesday
Thursday
Friday
Saturday
```

When strings are not part of an array, C++ places them contiguously in memory, so there is no wasted space. However, to find the strings, there must be an array that holds pointers to them. A string is itself an array of type char, so an array of pointers to strings is an array of pointers to char. That is the meaning of the definition of **arrptrs** in PTRTOSTR. Now recall that a string is always represented by a single address: the address of the first character in the string. It is these addresses that are stored in the array. Figure 10.12 shows how this looks.

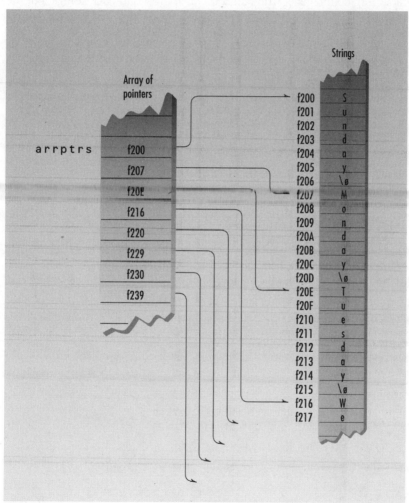

Figure 10.12 Array of pointers and strings.

Memory Management: new and delete

We've seen many examples where arrays are used to set aside memory. The statement

```
int arr1[100];
```

reserves memory for 100 integers. Arrays are a useful approach to data storage, but they have a serious drawback: We must know at the time we write the program how big the array will be. We can't wait until the program is running to specify the array size. The following approach won't work:

```
cin >> size;        // get size from user
int arr[size];      // error; array size must be a constant
```

The compiler requires the array size to be a constant.

But in many situations we don't know how much memory we need until runtime. We might want to store a string that was typed in by the user, for example. In this situation we can define an array sized to hold the largest string we expect, but this wastes memory. (As we'll learn in Chapter 15, "The Standard Template Library," you can also use a vector, which is a sort of expandable array.)

The new Operator

C++ provides a different approach to obtaining blocks of memory: the new operator. This versatile operator obtains memory from the operating system and returns a pointer to its starting point. The NEWINTRO example shows how new is used:

```cpp
// newintro.cpp
// introduces operator new
#include <iostream>
#include <cstring>              //for strlen
using namespace std;

int main()
   {
   char* str = "Idle hands are the devil's workshop.";
   int len = strlen(str);       //get length of str

   char* ptr;                   //make a pointer to char
   ptr = new char[len+1];       //set aside memory: string + '\0'

   strcpy(ptr, str);            //copy str to new memory area ptr

   cout << "ptr=" << ptr << endl;  //show that ptr is now in str

   delete[] ptr;                //release ptr's memory
   return 0;
   }
```

The expression

```
ptr = new char[len+1];
```

returns a pointer to a section of memory just large enough to hold the string **str**, whose length **len** we found with the **strlen()** library function, plus an extra byte for the null character '**\0**' at the end of the string. Figure 10.13 shows the syntax of a statement using the **new** operator. Remember to use brackets around the size; the compiler won't object if you mistakenly use parentheses, but the results will be incorrect.

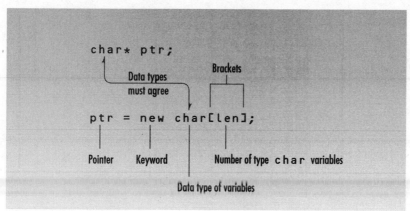

Figure 10.13   Syntax of new operator.

Figure 10.14 shows the memory obtained by **new** and the pointer to it.

In NEWINTRO we use **strcpy()** to copy string **str** to the newly created memory area pointed to by **ptr**. Since we made this area equal in size to the length of **str**, the string fits exactly. The output of NEWINTRO is:

```
ptr=Idle hands are the devil's workshop.
```

C programmers will recognize that **new** plays a role similar to the **malloc()** family of library functions. The **new** approach is superior in that it returns a pointer to the appropriate data type, while **malloc()**'s pointer must be cast to the appropriate type. There are other advantages as well.

C programmers may wonder if there is a C++ equivalent to **realloc()** for changing the size of memory that has already been reallocated. Sorry, there's no **renew** in C++. You'll need to fall back on the ploy of creating a larger (or smaller) space with **new**, and copying your data from the old area to the new one.

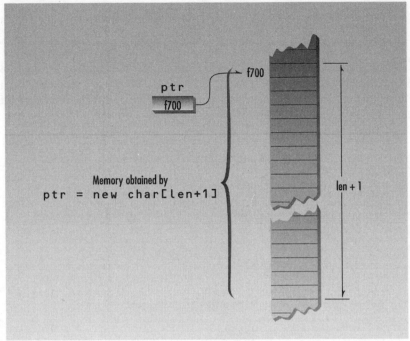

Figure 10.14 Memory obtained by new operator

The delete Operator

If your program reserves many chunks of memory using **new**, eventually all the available memory will be reserved and the system will crash. To ensure safe and efficient use of memory, the **new** operator is matched by a corresponding **delete** operator that returns memory to the operating system. In NEWINTRO the statement

```
delete[] ptr;
```

returns to the system whatever memory was pointed to by **ptr**.

Actually, there is no need for this operator in NEWINTRO, since memory is automatically returned when the program terminates. However, suppose you use **new** in a function. If the function uses a local variable as a pointer to this memory, then when the function terminates, the pointer will be destroyed but the memory will be left as an orphan, taking up space that is inaccessible to the rest of the program. Thus it is always good practice, and often essential, to **delete** memory when you're through with it.

Deleting the memory doesn't delete the pointer that points to it (**str** in NEWINTRO), and doesn't change the address value in the pointer. However, this address is no longer valid; the memory it points to may be changed to something entirely different. Be careful that you don't use pointers to memory that has been **delete**d.

The brackets following **delete** indicate that we're deleting an array. If you create a single object with **new**, you don't need the brackets when you delete it.

```
ptr = new SomeClass;   // allocate a single object
. . .
delete ptr;                  // no brackets following delete
```

However, don't forget the brackets when deleting arrays of objects. Using them ensures that all the members of the array are deleted, and that the destructor is called for each one.

A String Class Using new

The new operator often appears in constructors. As an example, we'll modify the String class, last seen in examples such as STRPLUS in Chapter 8, "Operator Overloading." You may recall that a potential defect of that class was that all String objects occupied the same fixed amount of memory. A string shorter than this fixed length wasted memory, and a longer string—if one were mistakenly generated—could crash the system by extending beyond the end of the array. Our next example uses new to obtain exactly the right amount of memory. Here's the listing for NEWSTR:

```cpp
// newstr.cpp
// using new to get memory for strings
#include <iostream>
#include <cstring>          //for strcpy(), etc
using namespace std;
//////////////////////////////////////////////////////////////////
class String                 //user-defined string type
   {
   private:
      char* str;                       //pointer to string
   public:
      String(char* s)                  //constructor, one arg
         {
         int length = strlen(s);    //length of string argument
         str = new char[length+1];  //get memory
         strcpy(str, s);            //copy argument to it
         }
      ~String()                        //destructor
         {
         delete[] str;                 //release memory
         }
      void display()                   //display the String
         {
         cout << str << endl;
         }
   };
//////////////////////////////////////////////////////////////////
int main()
   {                                   //uses 1-arg constructor
   String s1 = "Who knows nothing doubts nothing.";

   cout << "s1=";                      //display string
   s1.display();
   return 0;
   }
```

The `String` class has only one data item: a pointer to `char`, called `str`. This pointer will point to the string held by the `String` object. There is no array within the object to hold the string. The string is stored elsewhere; only the pointer to it is a member of `String`.

Constructor in NEWSTR

The constructor in this example takes a normal `char*` string as its argument. It obtains space in memory for this string with `new`; `str` points to the newly obtained memory. The constructor then uses `strcpy()` to copy the string into this new space.

Destructor in NEWSTR

We haven't seen many destructors in our examples so far, but now that we're allocating memory with `new`, destructors become important. If we allocate memory when we create an object, it's reasonable to deallocate the memory when the object is no longer needed. As you may recall from Chapter 7, a destructor is a routine that is called automatically when an object is destroyed. The destructor in NEWSTR looks like this:

```
~String()
   {
   delete[] str;
   }
```

This destructor gives back to the system the memory obtained when the object was created. Objects (like other variables) are typically destroyed when the function in which they were defined terminates. This destructor ensures that memory obtained by the `String` object will be returned to the system, and not left in limbo, when the object is destroyed.

We should note a potential glitch in using destructors as shown in NEWSTR. If you copy one `String` object to another, say with a statement like `s2 = s1`, you're really only copying the pointer to the actual (`char*`) string. Both objects now point to the same string in memory. But if you now delete one string, the destructor will delete the `char*` string, leaving the other object with an invalid pointer. This can be subtle, because objects can be deleted in non-obvious ways, such as when a function, in which a local object has been created, returns. In Chapter 11 we'll see how to make a smarter destructor that counts how many `String` objects are pointing to a string.

Pointers to Objects

Pointers can point to objects as well as to simple data types and arrays. We've seen many examples of objects defined and given a name, in statements like

```
Distance dist;
```

where an object called `dist` is defined to be of the `Distance` class.

Sometimes, however, we don't know, at the time that we write the program, how many objects we want to create. When this is the case we can use `new` to create objects while the program is running. As we've seen, `new` returns a pointer to an unnamed object. Let's look at a short example program, ENGLPTR, that compares the two approaches to creating objects.

```
// englptr.cpp
// accessing member functions by pointer
#include <iostream>
using namespace std;
//////////////////////////////////////////////////////////////
class Distance                  //English Distance class
   {
   private:
      int feet;
      float inches;
   public:
      void getdist()            //get length from user
         {
         cout << "\nEnter feet: ";  cin >> feet;
         cout << "Enter inches: ";  cin >> inches;
         }
      void showdist()           //display distance
         { cout << feet << "\'-" << inches << '\"'; }
   };
//////////////////////////////////////////////////////////////
int main()
   {
   Distance dist;               //define a named Distance object
   dist.getdist();              //access object members
   dist.showdist();             //   with dot operator

   Distance* distptr;           //pointer to Distance
   distptr = new Distance;      //points to new Distance object
   distptr->getdist();          //access object members
   distptr->showdist();         //   with -> operator
   cout << endl;
   return 0;
   }
```

This program uses a variation of the English **Distance** class seen in previous chapters. The **main()** function defines **dist**, uses the **Distance** member function **getdist()** to get a distance from the user, and then uses **showdist()** to display it.

Referring to Members

ENGLPTR then creates another object of type **Distance** using the **new** operator, and returns a pointer to it called **distptr**.

The question is, how do we refer to the member functions in the object pointed to by **distptr**? You might guess that we would use the dot (.) membership-access operator, as in

```
distptr.getdist();   // won't work; distptr is not a variable
```

but this won't work. The dot operator requires the identifier on its left to be a variable. Since **distptr** is a pointer to a variable, we need another syntax. One approach is to *dereference* (get the contents of the variable pointed to by) the pointer:

```
(*distptr).getdist();   // ok but inelegant
```

However, this is slightly cumbersome because of the parentheses. (The parentheses are necessary because the dot operator (.) has higher precedence than the indirection operator (*). An equivalent but more concise approach is furnished by the membership-access operator ->, which consists of a hyphen and a greater-than sign:

```
distptr->getdist();    // better approach
```

As you can see in ENGLPTR, the -> operator works with pointers to objects in just the same way that the . operator works with objects. Here's the output of the program:

```
Enter feet: 10 ←——— this object uses the dot operator

Enter inches: 6.25
10'-6.25"

Enter feet: 6    ←——— this object uses the -> operator
Enter inches: 4.75
6'-4.75"
```

Another Approach to new

You may come across another—less common—approach to using **new** to obtain memory for objects.

Since **new** can return a pointer to an area of memory that holds an object, we should be able to refer to the original object by dereferencing the pointer. The ENGLREF example shows how this is done.

```
// englref.cpp
// dereferencing the pointer returned by new
#include <iostream>
using namespace std;
/////////////////////////////////////////////////////////////////
class Distance                       // English Distance class
   {
   private:
      int feet;
      float inches;
   public:
      void getdist()                 // get length from user
         {
         cout << "\nEnter feet: ";  cin >> feet;
         cout << "Enter inches: ";  cin >> inches;
         }
      void showdist()                // display distance
         { cout << feet << "\'-" << inches << '\"'; }
   };
/////////////////////////////////////////////////////////////////
int main()
   {
   Distance& dist = *(new Distance);  // create Distance object
                                      // alias is "dist"
   dist.getdist();                    // access object members
```

```
dist.showdist();                    //   with dot operator
cout << endl;
return 0;
}
```

The expression

```
new Distance
```

returns a pointer to a memory area large enough for a **Distance** object, so we can refer to the original object as

```
*(new Distance)
```

This is the object pointed to by the pointer. Using a reference, we define **dist** to be an object of type **Distance**, and we set it equal to *(new Distance). Now we can refer to members of **dist** using the dot membership operator, rather than ->.

This approach is less common than using pointers to objects obtained with **new**, or simply declaring an object, but it works in a similar way.

An Array of Pointers to Objects

A common programming construction is an array of pointers to objects. This arrangement allows easy access to a group of objects, and is more flexible than placing the objects themselves in an array. (For instance, in the PERSORT example in this chapter we'll see how a group of objects can be sorted by sorting an array of pointers to them, rather than sorting the objects themselves.)

Our next example, PTROBJS, creates an array of pointers to the **person** class. Here's the listing:

```
// ptrobjs.cpp
// array of pointers to objects
#include <iostream>
using namespace std;
/////////////////////////////////////////////////////////////
class person                        //class of persons
   {
   protected:
      char name[40];                //person's name
   public:
      void setName()                //set the name
         {
         cout << "Enter name: ";
         cin >> name;
         }
      void printName()              //get the name
         {
         cout << "\n   Name is: " << name;
         }
   };
/////////////////////////////////////////////////////////////
int main()
   {
```

```
        person* persPtr[100];      //array of pointers to persons
        int n = 0;                 //number of persons in array
        char choice;

        do                                    //put persons in array
          {
          persPtr[n] = new person;            //make new object
          persPtr[n]->setName();              //set person's name
          n++;                                //count new person
          cout << "Enter another (y/n)? "; //enter another
          cin >> choice;                      //person?
          }
        while( choice=='y' );                 //quit on 'n'

        for(int j=0; j<n; j++)                //print names of
          {                                   //all persons
          cout << "\nPerson number " << j+1;
          persPtr[j]->printName();
          }
        cout << endl;
        return 0;
        }  //end main()
```

The class person has a single data item, `name`, which holds a string representing a person's name. Two member functions, `setName()` and `printName()`, allow the name to be set and displayed.

Program Operation

The `main()` function defines an array, `persPtr`, of 100 pointers to type `person`. In a **do** loop it then asks the user to enter a name. With this name it creates a `person` object using `new`, and stores a pointer to this object in the array `persPtr`. To demonstrate how easy it is to access the objects using the pointers, it then prints out the `name` data for each `person` object.

Here's a sample interaction with the program:

```
Enter name: Stroustrup       ←——— user enters names
Enter another (y/n)? y
Enter name: Ritchie
Enter another (y/n)? y
Enter name: Kernighan
Enter another (y/n)? n
Person number 1     ←——— program displays all names stored
   Name is: Stroustrup
Person number 2
   Name is: Ritchie
Person number 3
   Name is: Kernighan
```

Accessing Member Functions

We need to access the member functions `setName()` and `printName()` in the `person` objects pointed to by the pointers in the array `persPtr`. Each of the elements of the array `persPtr` is specified in array notation to be `persPtr[j]` (or equivalently by pointer notation to be `*(persPtr+j)`). The elements are pointers to objects of type `person`. To access a member of an object using a pointer, we use the `->` operator. Putting this all together, we have the following syntax for `getname()`:

```
persPtr[j]->getName()
```

This executes the `getname()` function in the `person` object pointed to by element `j` of the `persPtr` array. (It's a good thing we don't have to program using English syntax.)

A Linked List Example

Our next example shows a simple linked list. What is a linked list? It's another way to store data. You've seen numerous examples of data stored in arrays. Another data structure is an array of pointers to data members, as in the PTRTOSTRS and PTROBJS examples. Both the array and the array of pointers suffer from the necessity to declare a fixed-size array before running the program.

A Chain of Pointers

The linked list provides a more flexible storage system in that it doesn't use arrays at all. Instead, space for each data item is obtained as needed with `new`, and each item is connected, or *linked*, to the next data item using a pointer. The individual items don't need to be located contiguously in memory the way array elements are; they can be scattered anywhere.

In our example the entire linked list is an object of class `linklist`. The individual data items, or links, are represented by structures of type `link`. Each such structure contains an integer—representing the object's single data item—and a pointer to the next link. The list itself stores a pointer to the link at the head of the list. This arrangement is shown in Figure 10.15.

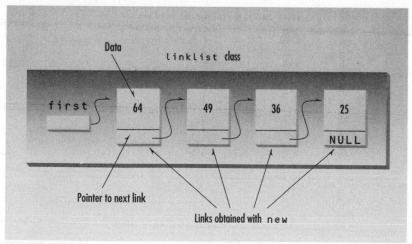

Figure 10.15 A linked list.

Here's the listing for LINKLIST:

```cpp
// linklist.cpp
// linked list
#include <iostream>
using namespace std;
/////////////////////////////////////////////////////////////////
struct link                             //one element of list
   {
   int data;                            //data item
   link* next;                          //pointer to next link
   };
/////////////////////////////////////////////////////////////////
class linklist                          //a list of links
   {
   private:
      link* first;                      //pointer to first link
   public:
      linklist()                        //no-argument constructor
         { first = NULL; }              //no first link
      void additem(int d);              //add data item (one link)
      void display();                   //display all links
   };
//---------------------------------------------------------------
void linklist::additem(int d)           //add data item
   {
   link* newlink = new link;            //make a new link
   newlink->data = d;                   //give it data
   newlink->next = first;               //it points to next link
   first = newlink;                     //now first points to this
   }
//---------------------------------------------------------------
void linklist::display()                //display all links
   {
   link* current = first;               //set ptr to first link
   while( current != NULL )             //quit on last link
      {
      cout << current->data << endl;    //print data
      current = current->next;          //move to next link
      }
   }
/////////////////////////////////////////////////////////////////
int main()
   {
   linklist li;            //make linked list
```

```
li.additem(25);      //add four items to list
li.additem(36);
li.additem(49);
li.additem(64);

li.display();        //display entire list
return 0;
}
```

The `linklist` class has only one member data item: the pointer to the start of the list. When the list is first created, the constructor initializes this pointer, which is called `first`, to NULL. The NULL constant is defined to be 0. This value serves as a signal that a pointer does not hold a valid address. In our program a link whose next member has a value of NULL is assumed to be at the end of the list.

Adding an Item to the List

The `additem()` member function adds an item to the linked list. A new link is inserted at the beginning of the list. (We could write the `additem()` function to insert items at the end of the list, but that is a little more complex to program.) Let's look at the steps involved in inserting a new link.

First, a new structure of type `link` is created by the line

```
link* newlink = new link;
```

This creates memory for the new `link` structure with `new` and saves the pointer to it in the `newlink` variable.

Next we want to set the members of the newly created structure to appropriate values. A structure is similar to a class in that, when it is referred to by pointer rather than by name, its members are accessed using the `->` member-access operator. The following two lines set the `data` variable to the value passed as an argument to `additem()`, and the `next` pointer to point to whatever address was in `first`, which holds the pointer to the start of the list.

```
newlink->data = d;
newlink->next = first;
```

Finally, we want the `first` variable to point to the new link:

```
first = newlink;
```

The effect is to uncouple the connection between `first` and the old first link, insert the new link, and move the old first link into the second position. Figure 10.16 shows this process.

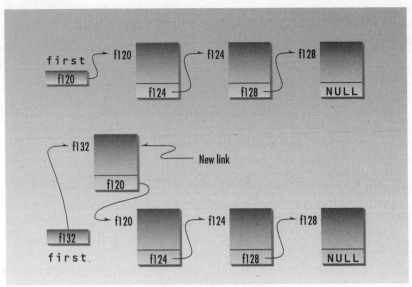

Figure 10.16 Adding to a linked list.

Displaying the List Contents

Once the list is created it's easy to step through all the members, displaying them (or performing other operations). All we need to do is follow from one **next** pointer to another until we find a **next** that is **NULL**, signaling the end of the list. In the function **display()**, the line

```
cout << endl << current->data;
```

prints the value of the data, and

```
current = current->next;
```

moves us along from one link to another, until

```
current != NULL
```

in the **while** expression becomes false. Here's the output of LINKLIST:

```
64
49
36
25
```

Linked lists are perhaps the most commonly used data storage arrangements after arrays. As we noted, they avoid the wasting of memory space engendered by arrays. The disadvantage is that finding a particular item on a linked list requires following the chain of links from the head of the list until the desired link is reached. This can be time consuming. An array element, on the other hand, can be accessed quickly, provided its index is known in advance. We'll have more to say about linked lists and other data-storage techniques in Chapter 15, "The Standard Template Library."

Self-Containing Classes

We should note a possible pitfall in the use of self-referential classes and structures. The **link** structure in LINKLIST contained a pointer to the same kind of structure. You can do the same with classes:

```
class sampleclass
   {
   sampleclass* ptr;  // this is fine
   };
```

However, while a class can contain a pointer to an object of its own type, it cannot contain an *object* of its own type:

```
class sampleclass
   {
   sampleclass obj;  // can't do this
   };
```

This is true of structures as well as classes.

Augmenting LINKLIST

The general organization of LINKLIST can serve for a more complex situation than that shown. There could be more data in each link. Instead of an integer, a link could hold a number of data items or it could hold a pointer to a structure or object.

Additional member functions could perform such activities as adding and removing links from an arbitrary part of the chain. Another important member function is a destructor. As we mentioned, it's important to delete blocks of memory that are no longer in use. A destructor that performs this task would be a highly desirable addition to the **linklist** class. It could go through the list using **delete** to free the memory occupied by each link.

Pointers to Pointers

Our next example demonstrates an array of pointers to objects, and shows how to sort these pointers based on data in the object. This involves the idea of pointers to pointers, and may help demonstrate why people lose sleep over pointers.

The idea in the next program is to create an array of pointers to objects of the **person** class. This is similar to the PTROBJS example, but we go further and add variations of the **order()** and **bsort()** functions from the PTRSORT example so that we can sort a group of **person** objects based on the alphabetical order of their names. Here's the listing for PERSORT:

```cpp
// persort.cpp
// sorts person objects using array of pointers
#include <iostream>
#include <string>               //for string class
using namespace std;
///////////////////////////////////////////////////////////////
class person                    //class of persons
   {
   protected:
      string name;              //person's name
   public:
      void setName()            //set the name
         { cout << "Enter name: "; cin >> name; }
      void printName()          //display the name
         { cout << endl << name; }
      string getName()          //return the name
         { return name; }
   };
///////////////////////////////////////////////////////////////
int main()
   {
   void bsort(person**, int);   //prototype
   person* persPtr[100];        //array of pointers to persons
   int n = 0;                   //number of persons in array
   char choice;                 //input char

   do {                         //put persons in array
      persPtr[n] = new person;  //make new object
      persPtr[n]->setName();    //set person's name
      n++;                      //count new person
      cout << "Enter another (y/n)? "; //enter another
      cin >> choice;            //    person?
      }
   while( choice=='y' );        //quit on 'n'

   cout << "\nUnsorted list:";
   for(int j=0; j<n; j++)       //print unsorted list
      { persPtr[j]->printName(); }

   bsort(persPtr, n);           //sort pointers

   cout << "\nSorted list:";
   for(j=0; j<n; j++)           //print sorted list
      { persPtr[j]->printName(); }
   cout << endl;
   return 0;
   }  //end main()
//-------------------------------------------------------------
void bsort(person** pp, int n)   //sort pointers to persons
   {
   void order(person**, person**);  //prototype
   int j, k;                     //indexes to array
```

```
for(j=0; j<n-1; j++)            //outer loop
    for(k=j+1; k<n; k++)        //inner loop starts at outer
        order(pp+j, pp+k);          //order the pointer contents
}
//-------------------------------------------------------------
void order(person** pp1, person** pp2)  //orders two pointers
    {                                //if 1st larger than 2nd,
    if( (*pp1)->getName() > (*pp2)->getName() )
        {
        person* tempptr = *pp1;      //swap the pointers
        *pp1 = *pp2;
        *pp2 = tempptr;
        }
    }
```

When the program is first executed it asks for a name. When the user gives it one, it creates an object of type **person** and sets the **name** data in this object to the name entered by the user. The program also stores a pointer to the object in the **persPtr** array.

When the user types **n** to indicate that no more names will be entered, the program calls the **bsort()** function to sort the **person** objects based on their **name** member variables. Here's some sample interaction with the program:

```
Enter name: Washington
Enter another (y/n)? y
Enter name: Adams
Enter another (y/n)? y
Enter name: Jefferson
Enter another (y/n)? y
Enter name: Madison
Enter another (y/n)? n
(continued on next page)
(continued from previous page)
Unsorted list:
Washington
Adams
Jefferson
Madison

Sorted list:
Adams
Jefferson
Madison
Washington
```

Sorting Pointers

Actually, when we sort **person** objects, we don't move the objects themselves; we move the pointers to the objects. This eliminates the need to shuffle the objects around in memory, which can be very time consuming if the objects are large. The process is shown in Figure 10.17.

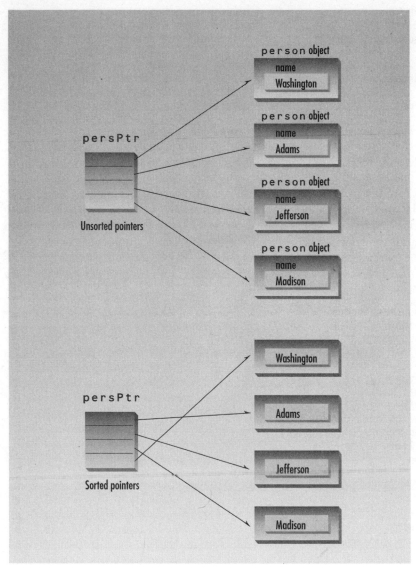

Figure 10.17   Sorting an array of pointers.

To facilitate the sorting activity we've added a `getName()` member function to the `person` class, so we can access the names from `order()` to decide when to swap pointers.

The `person**` Data Type

You will notice that the first argument to the `bsort()` function, and both arguments to `order()`, have the type `person**`. What do the two asterisks mean? These arguments are used to pass the address of the array persPtr, or—in the case of order()—the addresses of elements of the array. If this were an array of type person, then the address of the array would be type person*. However, the array is of type *pointers* to person, or person*, so its address is type person**. The address of a pointer is a pointer to a pointer. Figure 10.18 shows how this looks.

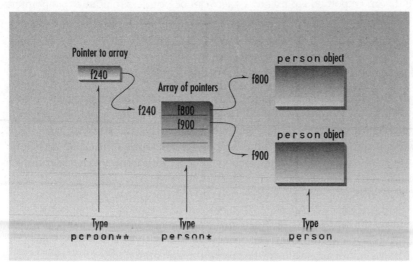

Figure 10.18   Pointer to an array of pointers.

Compare this program with PTRSORT, which sorted an array of type int. You'll find that the data types passed to functions in PERSORT all have one more asterisk than they did in PTRSORT, because the array is an array of pointers.

Since the persPtr array contains pointers, the construction

```
persPtr[j]->printName()
```

executes the printName() function in the object pointed to by element j of persPtr.

Comparing Strings

The order() function in PERSORT has been modified to order two strings lexigraphically— that is, by putting them in alphabetical order. To do this it compares the strings using the C++ library function strcmp(). This function takes the two strings s1 and s2 as arguments, as in strcmp(s1, s2), and returns one of the following values.

Value	Condition
<0	s1 comes before s2
0	s1 is the same as s2
>0	s1 comes after s2

The strings are accessed using the syntax

```
(*pp1)->getname()
```

The argument **pp1** is a pointer to a pointer, and we want the name pointed to by the pointer it points to. The member-access operator **->** dereferences one level, but we need to dereference another level, hence the asterisk preceding **pp1**.

Just as there can be pointers to pointers, there can be pointers to pointers to pointers, and so on. Fortunately such complexities are seldom encountered.

A Parsing Example

Programmers are frequently faced with the problem of unravelling or *parsing* a string of symbols. Examples are commands typed by a user at the keyboard, sentences in natural languages (like English), statements in a programming language, and algebraic expressions. Now that we've learned about pointers and strings, we can handle this sort of problem.

Our next (somewhat longer) example in this chapter will show how to parse arithmetic expressions like

```
6/3+2*3-1
```

The user enters the expression, the program works its way through it, character by character, figures out what it means in arithmetic terms, and displays the resulting value (7 in the example). Our expressions will use the four arithmetic operators: +, -, *, and /. We'll simplify the numbers we use to make the programming easier by restricting them to a single digit. Also, we won't allow parentheses.

This program makes use of our old friend the **Stack** class (see the STAKARAY program in Chapter 7). We've modified this class so it stores data of type **char**. We use the stack to store both numbers and operators (both as characters). The stack is a useful storage mechanism because, when parsing expressions, we frequently need to access the last item stored, and a stack is a last-in-first-out (LIFO) container.

Besides the **Stack** class, we'll use a class called **express** (short for *expression*), representing an entire arithmetic expression. Member functions for this class allow us to initialize an object with an expression in the form of a string (entered by the user), parse the expression, and return the resulting arithmetic value.

Parsing Arithmetic Expressions

Here's how we parse an arithmetic expression. We start at the left, and look at each character in turn. It can be either a *number* (always a single digit; a character between '**0**' and '**9**'), or an *operator* (the characters '**+**', '**-**', '*****', and '**/**').

If the character is a number, we always push it onto the stack. We also push the first operator we encounter. The trick is how we handle subsequent operators. Note that we can't execute the current operator, because we haven't yet read the number that follows it. Finding an operator is merely the signal that we can execute the previous operator, which is stored on the stack. That is, if the sequence 2+3 is on the stack, then we wait until we find another operator before carrying out the addition.

Thus whenever we find that the current character is an operator (except the first), we pop the previous number (3 in the preceding example) and the previous operator (+) off the stack, placing them in the variables lastval and lastop. Finally we pop the first number (2) and carry out the arithmetic operation on the two numbers (obtaining 5). Can we always execute the previous operator? No. Remember that * and / have a higher precedence than + and -. In the expression 3+4/2, we can't execute the + until we've done the division. So when we get to the / in this expression, we must put the 2 and the + back on the stack until we've carried out the division.

On the other hand, if the current operator is a + or -, we know we can always execute the previous operator. That is, when we see the + in the expression 4-5+6, we know it's all right to execute the -, and when we see the - in 6/2-3 , we know it's OK to do the division. Table 10.1 shows the four possibilities.

Table 10.1.   Operators and Parsing Actions

Previous Operator	Current Operator	Example	Action
+ or -	* or /	2+4/	Push previous operator and previous number (+, 4)
* or /	* or /	9/3*	Execute previous operator, push result (3)
+ or -	+ or -	6+3+	Execute previous operator, push result (9)
* or /	+ or -	8/2-	Execute previous operator, push result (4)

The parse() member function carries out this process of going through the input expression and performing those operations it can. However, there is more work to do. The stack still contains either a single number or several sequences of number-operator-number. Working down through the stack, we can execute these sequences. Finally, a single number is left on the stack; this is the value of the original expression. The solve() member function carries out this task, working its way down through the stack until only a single number is left. In general, parse() puts things on the stack, and solve() takes them off.

The PARSE Program

Some typical interaction with PARSE might look like this:

```
Enter an arithmetic expression
of the form 2+3*4/3-2.
No number may have more than one digit.
Don't use any spaces or parentheses.
Expression: 9+6/3

The numerical value is: 11
Do another (Enter y or n)?
```

Note that it's all right if the *results* of arithmetic operations contain more than one digit. They are limited only by the numerical size of type char, from ñ128 to +127. Only the input string is limited to numbers from 0 to 9.

Here's the listing for the program:

```cpp
// parse.cpp
// evaluates arithmetic expressions composed of 1-digit numbers
#include <iostream>
#include <cstring>                     //for strlen(), etc
using namespace std;
const int LEN = 80;     //length of expressions, in characters
const int MAX = 40;     //size of stack
//////////////////////////////////////////////////////////////
class Stack
    {
    private:
        char st[MAX];                   //stack: array of chars
        int top;                        //number of top of stack
    public:
        Stack()                         //constructor
            { top = 0; }
        void push(char var)             //put char on stack
            { st[++top] = var; }
        char pop()                      //take char off stack
            { return st[top--]; }
        int gettop()                    //get top of stack
            { return top; }
    };
//////////////////////////////////////////////////////////////
class express                          //expression class
    {
    private:
        Stack s;                        //stack for analysis
        char* pStr;                     //pointer to input string
        int len;                        //length of input string
    public:
        express(char* ptr)              //constructor
            {
            pStr = ptr;                 //set pointer to string
            len = strlen(pStr);         //set length
            }
        void parse();                   //parse the input string
        int solve();                    //evaluate the stack
    };
//------------------------------------------------------------
void express::parse()                  //add items to stack
    {
    char ch;                           //char from input string
```

```
      char lastval;                       //last value
      char lastop;                        //last operator

      for(int j=0; j<len; j++)            //for each input character
         {
         ch = pStr[j];                    //get next character

         if(ch>='0' && ch<='9')           //if it's a digit,
            s.push(ch-'0');               //save numerical value
                                          //if it's operator
         else if(ch=='+' || ch=='-' || ch=='*' || ch=='/')
            {
            if(s.gettop()==1)             //if it's first operator
               s.push(ch);                //put on stack
            else                          //not first operator
               {
               lastval = s.pop();         //get previous digit
               lastop = s.pop();          //get previous operator
               //if this is * or / AND last operator was + or -
               if( (ch=='*' || ch=='/') &&
                   (lastop=='+' || lastop=='-') )
                  {
                  s.push(lastop);         //restore last two pops
                  s.push(lastval);
                  }
               else                       //in all other cases
                  {
                  switch(lastop)          //do last operation
                     {                    //push result on stack
                     case '+': s.push(s.pop() + lastval); break;
                     case '-': s.push(s.pop() - lastval); break;
                     case '*': s.push(s.pop() * lastval); break;
                     case '/': s.push(s.pop() / lastval); break;
                     default:  cout << "\nUnknown oper"; exit(1);
                     } //end switch
                  } //end else, in all other cases
               s.push(ch);                //put current op on stack
               } //end else, not first operator
            } //end else if, it's an operator
         else                             //not a known character
            { cout << "\nUnknown input character"; exit(1); }
         } //end for
      } //end parse()
//------------------------------------------------------------
int express::solve()                      //remove items from stack
   {
   char lastval;                          //previous value

   while(s.gettop() > 1)
      {
```

```
        lastval = s.pop();                //get previous value
        switch( s.pop() )                 //get previous operator
            {                             //do operation, push answer
          case '+': s.push(s.pop() + lastval); break;
          case '-': s.push(s.pop() - lastval); break;
          case '*': s.push(s.pop() * lastval); break;
          case '/': s.push(s.pop() / lastval); break;
          default:  cout << "\nUnknown operator"; exit(1);
            } //end switch
        } //end while
    return int( s.pop() );                //last item on stack is ans
    } //end solve()
////////////////////////////////////////////////////////////////
int main()
    {
    char ans;                             //'y' or 'n'
    char string[LEN];                     //input string from user

    cout << "\nEnter an arithmetic expression"
            "\nof the form 2+3*4/3-2."
            "\nNo number may have more than one digit."
            "\nDon't use any spaces or parentheses.";
    do {
        cout << "\nEnter expresssion: ";
        cin >> string;                    //input from user
        express* eptr = new express(string);  //make expression
        eptr->parse();                    //parse it
        cout << "\nThe numerical value is: "
                << eptr->solve();         //solve it
        delete eptr;                      //delete expression
        cout << "\nDo another (Enter y or n)? ";
        cin >> ans;
        } while(ans == 'y');
    return 0;
    }
```

This is a longish program, but it shows how a previously designed class, `Stack`, can come in handy in a new situation; it demonstrates the use of pointers in a variety of ways; and it shows how useful it can be to treat a string as an array of characters.

Simulation: A Horse Race

As our final example in this chapter we'll show a horse-racing game. In this game a number of horses appear on the screen, and, starting from the left, race to a finish line on the right. This program will demonstrate pointers in a new situation, and also a little bit about object-oriented design.

Each horse's speed is determined randomly, so there is no way to figure out in advance which one will win. The program uses console graphics, so the horses are easily, although somewhat crudely, displayed. You'll need to compile the program with the MSOFTCON.H or

BORLACON.H header file (depending on your compiler), and the MSOFTCON.CPP or BORLACON.CPP source file. (See Appendix E, "Console Graphics Lite," for more information.)

When our program, HORSE, is started, it asks the user to supply the race's distance and the number of horses that will run in it. The classic unit of distance for horse racing (at least in English-speaking countries) is the *furlong*, which is 1/8 of a mile. Typical races are 6, 8, 10, or 12 furlongs. You can enter from 1 to 7 horses. The program draws vertical lines corresponding to each furlong, along with start and finish lines. Each horse is represented by a rectangle with a number in the middle. Figure 10.19 shows the screen with a race in progress.

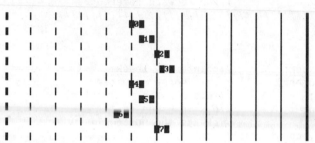

Figure 10.19   Output of the HORSE program.

Designing the Horse Race

How do we approach an OOP design for our horse race? Our first question might be, is there a group of similar entities that we're trying to model? The answer is yes, the horses. So it seems reasonable to make each horse an object. There will be a class called **horse**, which will contain data specific to each horse, such as its number and the distance it has run so far (which is used to display the horse in the correct screen position).

However, there is also data that applies to the entire race track, rather than to individual horses. This includes the track length, the elapsed time in minutes and seconds (0:00 at the start of the race), and the total number of horses. It makes sense then to have a track object, which will be a single member of the **track** class. You can think of other real-world objects associated with horse racing, such as riders and saddles, but they aren't relevant to the program.

Are there other ways to design the program? For example, what about using inheritance to make the horses descendants of the track? This doesn't make much sense, because the horses aren't a "kind of" race track; they're a completely different thing. Another option is to make the track data into static data of the horse class. However, it's generally better to make each different kind of thing in the problem domain (the real world) a separate object in the program.

How will the horse objects and the track object communicate? An array of pointers to `horse` objects can be a member of the `track` class, so the track can access the horses through these pointers. The track will create the horses when it's created. As it does so, it will pass a pointer to itself to each horse, so the horse can access the track.

Here's the listing for HORSE:

```
// horse.cpp
// models a horse race
#include "msoftcon.h"              //for console graphics
#include <iostream>                //for I/O
#include <cstdlib>                 //for random()
#include <ctime>                   //for time()
using namespace std;
const int CPF = 5;                 //columns per furlong
const int maxHorses = 7;           //maximum number of horses
class track;                       //for forward references
/////////////////////////////////////////////////////////////////
class horse
   {
   private:
      const track* ptrTrack;       //pointer to track
      const int horse_number;      //this horse's number
      float finish_time;           //this horse's finish time
      float distance_run;          //distance run so far
   public:                         //create the horse
      horse(const int n, const track* ptrT) :
             horse_number(n), ptrTrack(ptrT),
             distance_run(0.0)     //haven't moved yet
         { }
      ~horse()                     //destroy the horse
         { /*empty*/ }             //display the horse
      void display_horse(const float elapsed_time);
   }; //end class horse
/////////////////////////////////////////////////////////////////
class track
   {
   private:
      horse* hArray[maxHorses];    //array of ptrs-to-horses
      int total_horses;            //total number of horses
      int horse_count;             //horses created so far
      const float track_length;    //track length in furlongs
      float elapsed_time;          //time since start of race

   public:
      track(float lenT, int nH);   //2-arg constructor
      ~track();                    //destructor
      void display_track();        //display track
      void run();                  //run the race
      float get_track_len() const; //return total track length
   }; //end class track
//-----------------------------------------------------------------
void horse::display_horse(float elapsed_time) //for each horse
   {                               //display horse & number
```

```
set_cursor_pos( 1 | int(distance_run * CPF),
        2 + horse_number*2 );
                                    //horse 0 is blue
    set_color(static_cast<color>(cBLUE+horse_number));
    cout << " \xDB" << horse_number << "\xDB";
                                    //until finish,
    if( distance_run < ptrTrack->get_track_len() + 1.0 / CPF )
        {
        if( rand() % 3 )             //skip about 1 of 3 ticks
            distance_run += 0.2F;    //advance 0.2 furlongs
        finish_time = elapsed_time;  //update finish time
        }
    else
        {                            //display finish time
        int mins = int(finish_time)/60;
        int secs = int(finish_time) - mins*60;
        cout << " Time=" << mins << ":" << secs;
        }
    } //end display_horse()
//--------------------------------------------------------------
track::track(float lenT, int nH) :  //track constructor
                    track_length(lenT), total_horses(nH),
                    horse_count(0), elapsed_time(0.0)
        {
        init_graphics();             //start graphics
        total_horses =               //not more than 7 horses
         (total_horses > maxHorses) ? maxHorses : total_horses;
        for(int j=0; j<total_horses; j++)   //make each horse
          hArray[j] = new horse(horse_count++, this);

        time_t aTime;                //initialize random numbers
        srand( static_cast<unsigned>(time(&aTime)) );
        display_track();
        } //end track constructor
//--------------------------------------------------------------
track::~track()                      //track destructor
    {
    for(int j=0; j<total_horses; j++) //delete each horse
        delete hArray[j];
    }
//--------------------------------------------------------------
void track::display_track()
    {
    clear_screen();                  //clear screen
                                     //display track
    for(int f=0; f<=track_length; f++)    //for each furlong
        for(int r=1; r<=total_horses*2 + 1; r++) //and screen row
            {
            set_cursor_pos(f*CPF + 5, r);
            if(f==0 || f==track_length)
                cout << '\xDE';      //draw start or finish line
            else
                cout << '\xB3';      //draw furlong marker
            }
```

```
      } //end display_track()
//---------------------------------------------------------------→
void track::run()
   {
   while( !kbhit() )
      {
      elapsed_time += 1.75;          //update time
                                     //update each horse
      for(int j=0; j<total_horses; j++)
         hArray[j]->display_horse(elapsed_time);
      wait(500);
      }
   getch();                          //eat the keystroke
   cout << endl;
   }
//---------------------------------------------------------------
float track::get_track_len() const
   { return track_length; }
/////////////////////////////////////////////////////////////////
int main()
   {
   float length;
   int total;
                                     //get data from user
   cout << "\nEnter track length (furlongs): ";
   cin >> length;
   cout << "\nEnter number of horses (1 to 7): ";
   cin >> total;
   track theTrack(length, total);    //create the track
   theTrack.run();                   //run the race
   return 0;
   } //end main()
```

Keeping Time

Simulation programs usually involve an activity taking place over a period of time. To model the passage of time, such programs typically energize themselves at fixed intervals. In the HORSE program, the main() program calls the track's run() function. This function makes a series of calls within a while loop, one for each horse, to a function display_horse(). This function redraws each horse in its new position. The while loop then pauses 500 milliseconds, using the console graphics wait() function. Then it does the same thing again, until the race is over or the user presses a key.

Deleting an Array of Pointers to Objects

At the end of the program the destructor for the track must delete the horse objects, which it obtained with new in its constructor. Notice that we can't just say

```
delete[] hArray;   //deletes pointers, but not horses
```

This deletes the array of pointers, but not what the pointers point to. Instead we must go through the array element by element, and delete each horse individually:

```
for(int j=0; j<total_horses; j++)  //deletes horses
   delete hArray[j];
```

Debugging Pointers

Pointers can be the source of mysterious and catastrophic program bugs. The most common problem is that the programmer has failed to place a valid address in a pointer variable. When this happens the pointer can end up pointing anywhere in memory. It could be pointing to the program code, or to the operating system. If the programmer then inserts a value into memory using the pointer, the value will write over the program or operating instructions, and the computer will crash or evince other uncharming behavior.

A particular version of this scenario takes place when the pointer points to address 0, which is called NULL. This happens, for example, if the pointer variable is defined as an *external variable*, since external variables are automatically initialized to 0. Instance variables in classes are also initialized to 0. Here's a miniprogram that demonstrates the situation:

```
int* intptr;         //external variable, initialized to 0
void main()
   {                 //failure to put valid address in intptr
   *intptr = 37;     //attempts to put 37 in address at 0
   }                 //result iserror
```

When intptr is defined, it is given the value 0, since it is external. The single program statement will attempt to insert the value 37 into the address at 0.

Fortunately, however, the runtime error-checking unit built into the program by the compiler is waiting for attempts to access address 0, and will display an error message (perhaps an *access violation*, *null pointer assignment*, or *page fault*) and terminate the program. If you see such a message, one possibility is that you have failed to properly initialize a pointer.

Summary

This has been a whirlwind tour through the land of pointers. There is far more to learn, but the topics we've covered here will provide a basis for the examples in the balance of the book and for further study of pointers.

We've learned that everything in the computer's memory has an address, and that addresses are *pointer constants*. We can find the addresses of variables using the address-of operator &.

Pointers are variables that hold address values. Pointers are defined using an asterisk (*) to mean *pointer to*. A data type is always included in pointer definitions (except void*), since the compiler must know what is being pointed to, so that it can perform arithmetic correctly on the pointer. We access the thing pointed to using the asterisk in a different way, as the *indirection operator*, meaning *contents of the variable pointed to by*.

The special type `void*` means a pointer to *any* type. It's used in certain difficult situations where the same pointer must hold addresses of different types.

Array elements can be accessed using array notation with brackets or pointer notation with an asterisk. Like other addresses, the address of an array is a constant, but it can be assigned to a variable, which can be incremented and changed in other ways.

When the address of a variable is passed to a function, the function can work with the original variable. (This is not true when arguments are passed by value.) In this respect passing by pointer offers the same benefits as passing by reference, although pointer arguments must be *dereferenced* or accessed using the indirection operator. However, pointers offer more flexibility in some cases.

A string constant can be defined as an array or as a pointer. The pointer approach may be more flexible, but there is a danger that the pointer value will be corrupted. Strings, being arrays of type `char`, are commonly passed to functions and accessed using pointers.

The `new` operator obtains a specified amount of memory from the system and returns a pointer to the memory. This operator is used to create variables and data structures during program execution. The `delete` operator releases memory obtained with `new`.

When a pointer points to an object, members of the object's class can be accessed using the access operator `->`. The same syntax is used to access structure members.

Classes and structures may contain data members that are pointers to their own type. This permits the creation of complex data structures like linked lists.

There can be pointers to pointers. These variables are defined using the double asterisk; for example, `int** pptr`.

Questions

Answers to questions can be found in Appendix G, "Answers to Questions and Exercises."

1. Write a statement that displays the address of the variable `testvar`.

2. The contents of two pointers that point to adjacent variables of type `float` differ by _____.

3. A pointer is

   a. the address of a variable.

   b. an indication of the variable to be accessed next.

   c. a variable for storing addresses.

   d. the data type of an address variable.

4. Write expressions for the following:

   a. The address of `var`

   b. The contents of the variable pointed to by `var`

   c. The variable `var` used as a reference argument

   d. The data type pointer-to-`char`

5. An address is a _____, while a pointer is a _____.

6. Write a definition for a variable of type pointer to float.

7. One way pointers are useful is to refer to a memory address that has no _____.

8. If a pointer testptr points to a variable testvar, write a statement that represents the contents of testvar but does not use its name.

9. An asterisk placed after a data type means _____. An asterisk placed in front of a variable name means _____.

10. The expression *test can be said to

   a. be a pointer to test.

   b. refer to the contents of test.

   c. dereference test.

   d. refer to the value of the variable pointed to by test.

11. Is the following code correct?

```
int intvar = 333;
int* intptr;
cout << *intptr;
```

12. A pointer to void can hold pointers to _____.

13. What is the difference between intarr[3] and *(intarr+3)?

14. Write some code that uses pointer notation to display every value in the array intarr, which has 77 elements.

15. If intarr is an array of integers, why is the expression intarr++ not legal?

16. Of the three ways to pass arguments to functions, only passing by _____ and passing by _____ allow the function to modify the argument in the calling program.

17. The type of variable a pointer points to must be part of the pointer's definition so that

   a. data types don't get mixed up when arithmetic is performed on them.

   b. pointers can be added to one another to access structure members.

   c. no one's religious conviction will be offended.

   d. the compiler can perform arithmetic correctly to access array elements.

18. Using pointer notation, write a prototype (declaration) for a function called `func()` that returns type `void` and takes a single argument that is an array of type `char`.

19. Using pointer notation, write some code that will transfer 80 characters from the string `s1` to the string `s2`.

20. The first element in a string is

    a. the name of the string.

    b. the first character in the string.

    c. the length of the string.

    d. the name of the array holding the string.

21. Using pointer notation, write the prototype for a function called `revstr()` that returns a string value and takes one argument that represents a string.

22. Write a definition for an array `numptrs` of pointers to the strings `One`, `Two`, and `Three`.

23. The `new` operator

    a. returns a pointer to a variable.

    b. creates a variable called `new`.

    c. obtains memory for a new variable.

    d. tells how much memory is available.

24. Using `new` may result in less _____ memory than using an array.

25. The `delete` operator returns _____ to the operating system.

26. Given a pointer `p` that points to an object of type `upperclass`, write an expression that executes the `exclu()` member function in this object.

27. Given an object with index number 7 in array `objarr`, write an expression that executes the `exclu()` member function in this object.

28. In a linked list

    a. each link contains a pointer to the next link.

    b. an array of pointers point to the links.

    c. each link contains data or a pointer to data.

    d. the links are stored in an array.

29. Write a definition for an array `arr` of 8 pointers that point to variables of type `float`.

30. If you wanted to sort many large objects or structures, it would be most efficient to

    a. place them in an array and sort the array.

    b. place pointers to them in an array and sort the array.

    c. place them in a linked list and sort the linked list.

    d. place references to them in an array and sort the array.

Exercises

Answers to starred exercises can be found in Appendix G.

*1. Write a program that reads a group of numbers from the user and places them in an array of type `float`. Once the numbers are stored in the array, the program should average them and print the result. Use pointer notation wherever possible.

*2. Start with the `string` class from the NEWSTR example in this chapter. Add a member function called `upit()` that converts the string to all uppercase. You can use the `toupper()` library function, which takes a single character as an argument and returns a character that has been converted (if necessary) to uppercase. This function uses the CCTYPE header file. Write some code in `main()` to test `upit()`.

*3. Start with an array of pointers to strings representing the days of the week, as found in the PTRTOSTR program in this chapter. Provide functions to sort the strings into alphabetical order, using variations of the `bsort()` and `order()` functions from the PTRSORT program in this chapter. Sort the pointers to the strings, not the actual strings.

*4. Add a destructor to the LINKLIST program. It should delete all the links when a `linklist` object is destroyed. It can do this by following along the chain, deleting each link as it goes. You can test the destructor by having it display a message each time it deletes a link; it should delete the same number of links that were added to the list. (A destructor is called automatically by the system for any existing objects when the program exits.)

5. Suppose you have a `main()` with three local arrays, all the same size and type (say `float`). The first two are already initialized to values. Write a function called `addarrays()` that accepts the addresses of the three arrays as arguments; adds the contents of the first two arrays together, element by element; and places the results in the third array before returning. A fourth argument to this function can carry the size of the arrays. Use pointer notation throughout; the only place you need brackets is in defining the arrays.

6. Make your own version of the library function `strcmp(s1, s2)`, which compares two strings and returns ñ1 if `s1` comes first alphabetically, 0 if `s1` and `s2` are the same, and 1 if `s2` comes first alphabetically. Call your function `compstr()`. It should take two `char*` strings as arguments, compare them character by character, and return an `int`. Write a `main()` program to test the function with different combinations of strings. Use pointer notation throughout.

7. Modify the **person** class in the PERSORT program in this chapter so that it includes not only a name, but also a `salary` item of type `float` representing the person's salary. You'll need to change the `setName()` and `printName()` member functions to `setData()` and `printData()`, and include in them the ability to set and display the salary as well as the name. You'll also need a `getSalary()` function. Using pointer notation, write a `salsort()` function that sorts the pointers in the `persPtr` array by salary rather than by name. Try doing all the sorting in `salsort()`, rather than calling another function as PERSORT does. If you do this, don't forget that `->` takes precedence over `*`, so you'll need to say

```
if( (*(pp+j))->getSalary() > (*(pp+k))->getSalary() )
    { // swap the pointers }
```

8. Revise the `additem()` member function from the LINKLIST program so that it adds the item at the end of the list, rather than the beginning. This will cause the first item inserted to be the first item displayed, so the output of the program will be

```
25
36
49
64
```

To add the item you'll need to follow the chain of pointers to the end of the list, then change the last link to point to the new link.

9. Let's say that you need to store 100 integers so that they're easily accessible. However, let's further assume that there's a problem: The memory in your computer is so fragmented that the largest array that you can use holds only 10 integers. (Such problems actually arise, although usually with larger memory objects.) You can solve this problem by defining 10 separate int arrays of 10 integers each, and an array of 10 pointers to these arrays. The int arrays can have names like a0, a1, a2, and so on. The address of each of these arrays can be stored in the pointer array of type int*, which can have a name like ap (for array of pointers). You can then access individual integers using expressions like ap[j][k], where j steps through the pointers in ap and k steps through individual integers in each array. This looks like you're accessing a two-dimensional array, but it's really a group of one-dimensional arrays.

   Fill such a group of arrays with test data (say the numbers 0, 10, 20, and so on up to 990). Then display the data to make sure it's correct.

10. As presented, Exercise 9 is rather inelegant because each of the 10 int arrays is declared in a different program statement, using a different name. Each of their addresses must also be obtained using a separate statement. You can simplify things by using new, which allows you to allocate the arrays in a loop and assign pointers to them at the same time:

    ```
    for(j=0; j<NUMARRAYS; j++)        // allocate NUMARRAYS arrays
        *(ap+j) = new int[MAXSIZE];    // each MAXSIZE ints long
    ```

    Rewrite the program in Exercise 9 to use this approach. You can access the elements of the individual arrays using the same expression mentioned in Exercise 9, or you can use pointer notation: *(*(ap+j)+k). The two notations are equivalent.

11. Create a class that allows you to treat the 10 separate arrays in Exercise 10 as a single one-dimensional array, using array notation with a single index. That is, statements in main() can access their elements using expressions like a[j], even though the class member functions must access the data using the two-step approach. Overload the subscript operator [] (see Chapter 9, "Inheritance") to achieve this result. Fill the arrays with test data and then display it. Although array notation is used in the class interface in main() to access "array" elements, you should use only pointer notation for all the operations in the implementation (within the class member functions).

12. Pointers are complicated, so let's see if we can make their operation more understandable (or possibly more impenetrable) by simulating their operation with a class.

To clarify the operation of our homemade pointers, we'll model the computer's memory using arrays. This way, since array access is well understood, you can see what's really going on when we access memory with pointers.

We'd like to use a single array of type `char` to store all types of variables. This is what a computer memory really is: an array of bytes (which are the same size as type `char`), each of which has an address (or, in array-talk, an index). However, C++ won't ordinarily let us store a `float` or an `int` in an array of type `char`. (We could use unions, but that's another story.) So we'll simulate memory by using a separate array for each data type we want to store. In this exercise we'll confine ourselves to one numerical type, `float`, so we'll need an array of this type; call it `fmemory`. However, pointer values (addresses) are also stored in memory, so we'll need another array to store them. Since we're using array indexes to model addresses, and indexes for all but the largest arrays can be stored in type `int`, we'll create an array of this type, call it `pmemory`, to hold these "pointers."

An index to `fmemory`, call it `fmem_top`, points to the next available place where a `float` value can be stored. There's a similar index to `pmemory`, call it `pmem_top`. Don't worry about running out of "memory." We'll assume these arrays are big enough so that each time we store something we can simply insert it at the next index number in the array. Other than this, we won't worry about memory management.

Create a class called `Float`. We'll use it to model numbers of type `float` that are stored in `fmemory` instead of real memory. The only instance data in `Float` is its own "address"; that is, the index where its `float` value is stored in `fmemory`. Call this instance variable `addr`. Class `Float` also needs two member functions. The first is a one-argument constructor to initialize the `Float` with a `float` value. This constructor stores the `float` value in the element of `fmemory` pointed to by `fmem_top`, and stores the value of `fmem_top` in `addr`. This is similar to how the compiler and linker arrange to store an ordinary variable in real memory. The second member function is the overloaded `&` operator. It simply returns the pointer (really the index, type `int`) value in `addr`.

Create a second class called `ptrFloat`. The instance data in this class holds the address (index) in `pmemory` where some other address (index) is stored. A member function initializes this "pointer" with an `int` index value. The second member function is the overloaded `*` (indirection, or "contents of") operator. Its operation is a tad more complicated. It obtains the address from `pmemory`, where its data, which is also an address, is stored. It then uses this new address as an index into `fmemory` to obtain the float value pointed to by its address data.

```
float& ptrFloat::operator*()
   {
   return fmemory[ pmemory[addr] ];
   }
```

In this way it models the operation of the indirection operator (*). Notice that you need to return by reference from this function so that you can use * on the left side of the equal sign.

The two classes `Float` and `ptrFloat` are similar, but `Float` stores `float`s in an array representing memory, and `ptrFloat` stores `int`s (representing memory pointers, but really array index values) in a different array that also represents memory.

Here's a typical use of these classes, from a sample `main()`:

```
Float var1 = 1.234;          // define and initialize two Floats
Float var2 = 5.678;

ptrFloat ptr1 = &var1;       // define two pointers-to-Floats,
ptrFloat ptr2 = &var2;       // initialize to addresses of Floats

cout << " *ptr1=" << *ptr1;  // get values of Floats indirectly
cout << " *ptr2=" << *ptr2;  // and display them

*ptr1 = 7.123;               // assign new values to variables
*ptr2 = 8.456;               // pointed to by ptr1 and ptr2

cout << " *ptr1=" << *ptr1;  // get new values indirectly
cout << " *ptr2=" << *ptr2;  // and display them
```

Notice that, aside from the different names for the variable types, this looks just the same as operations on real variables. Here's the output from the program:

```
*ptr1=1.234
*ptr2=2.678

*ptr1=7.123
*ptr2=8.456
```

This may seem like a roundabout way to implement pointers, but by revealing the inner workings of the pointer and address operator, we have provided a different perspective on their true nature.

CHAPTER 11

VIRTUAL FUNCTIONS

> **You will learn about the following in this chapter:**
>
> - Virtual functions
> - Friend functions
> - Static functions
>
> - Overloaded assignment operator
> - Overloaded copy constructor
> - The THIS pointer

Finding An object's class with TYPEID()11

Now that we understand something about pointers, we can delve into more advanced C++ topics. This chapter covers a rather loosely related collection of such subjects: virtual functions, friend functions, static functions, the overloaded = operator, the overloaded copy constructor, and the **this** pointer. These are advanced features; they are not necessary for every C++ program, especially very short ones. However, they are widely used, and are essential for most full-size programs. Virtual functions in particular are essential for polymorphism, one of the cornerstones of object-oriented programming.

Virtual Functions

Virtual means *existing in appearance but not in reality*. When virtual functions are used, a program that appears to be calling a function of one class may in reality be calling a function of a different class. Why are virtual functions needed? Suppose you have a number of objects of different classes but you want to put them all in an array and perform a particular operation on them using the same function call. For example, suppose a graphics program includes several different shapes: a triangle, a ball, a square, and so on, as in the MULTSHAP program in Chapter 9, "Inheritance." Each of these classes has a member function `draw()` that causes the object to be drawn on the screen.

Now suppose you plan to make a picture by grouping a number of these elements together, and you want to draw the picture in a convenient way. One approach is to create an array that holds pointers to all the different objects in the picture. The array might be defined like this:

```
shape* ptrarr[100];   // array of 100 pointers to shapes
```

If you insert pointers to all the shapes into this array, you can then draw an entire picture using a simple loop:

```
for(int j=0; j<N; j++)
   ptrarr[j]->draw();
```

This is an amazing capability: Completely different functions are executed by the same function call. If the pointer in `ptrarr` points to a ball, the function that draws a ball is called; if it points to a triangle, the triangle-drawing function is called. This is called *polymorphism*, which means *different forms*. The functions have the same appearance, the `draw()` expression, but different actual functions are called, depending on the contents of `ptrarr[j]`. Polymorphism is one of the key features of object-oriented programming, after classes and inheritance.

For the polymorphic approach to work, several conditions must be met. First, all the different classes of shapes, such as balls and triangles, must be derived from a single base class (called `shape` in MULTSHAP). Second, the `draw()` function must be declared to be `virtual` in the base class.

This is all rather abstract, so let's start with some short programs that show parts of the situation, and put everything together later.

Normal Member Functions Accessed with Pointers

Our first example shows what happens when a base class and derived classes all have functions with the same name, and you access these functions using pointers but without using virtual functions. Here's the listing for NOTVIRT:

```
// notvirt.cpp
// normal functions accessed from pointer
#include <iostream>
using namespace std;
/////////////////////////////////////////////////////////////
class Base                         //base class
   {
   public:
      void show()                  //normal function
         { cout << "Base\n"; }
   };
/////////////////////////////////////////////////////////////
```

```
class Derv1 : public Base          //derived class 1
   {
   public:
      void show()
         { cout << "Derv1\n"; }
   };
/////////////////////////////////////////////////////////////////
class Derv2 : public Base          //derived class 2
   {
   public:
      void show()
         { cout << "Derv2\n"; }
   };
/////////////////////////////////////////////////////////////////
int main()
   {
   Derv1 dv1;          //object of derived class 1
   Derv2 dv2;          //object of derived class 2
   Base* ptr;          //pointer to base class

   ptr = &dv1;         //put address of dv1 in pointer
   ptr->show();        //execute show()

   ptr = &dv2;         //put address of dv2 in pointer
   ptr->show();        //execute show()
   return 0;
   }
```

The **Derv1** and **Derv2** classes are derived from class **Base**. Each of these three classes has a member function **show()**. In **main()** we create objects of class **Derv1** and **Derv2**, and a pointer to class **Base**. Then we put the address of a derived class object in the base class pointer in the line

```
ptr = &dv1;  // derived class address in base class pointer
```

But wait—how can we get away with this? Doesn't the compiler complain that we're assigning an address of one type (**Derv1**) to a pointer of another (**Base**)? On the contrary, the compiler is perfectly happy, because type checking has been relaxed in this situation, for reasons that will become apparent soon. The rule is that pointers to objects of a derived class are type-compatible with pointers to objects of the base class.

Now the question is, when you execute the line

```
ptr->show();
```

what function is called? Is it **Base::show()** or **Derv1::show()**? Again, in the last two lines of NOTVIRT we put the address of an object of class **Derv2** in the pointer, and again execute

```
ptr->show();
```

Which of the **show()** functions is called here? The output from the program answers these questions:

```
Base
Base
```

As you can see, the function in the base class is always executed. The compiler ignores the *contents* of the pointer **ptr** and chooses the member function that matches the *type* of the pointer, as shown in Figure 11.1.

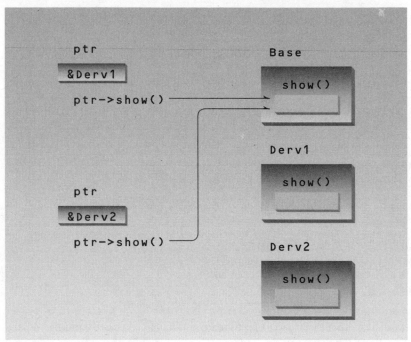

Figure 11.1 Nonvirtual pointer access.

Sometimes this is what we want, but it doesn't solve the problem posed at the beginning of this section: accessing objects of different classes using the same statement.

Virtual Member Functions Accessed with Pointers

Let's make a single change in our program: We'll place the keyword *virtual* in front of the declarator for the **show()** function in the base class. Here's the listing for the resulting program, VIRT:

```
// virt.cpp
// virtual functions accessed from pointer
#include <iostream>
using namespace std;
/////////////////////////////////////////////////////////////
```

```
class Base                              //base class
    {
    public:
       virtual void show()          //virtual function
          { cout << "Base\n"; }
    };
//////////////////////////////////////////////////////////////////
class Derv1 : public Base               //derived class 1
    {
    public:
       void show()
          { cout << "Derv1\n"; }
    };
//////////////////////////////////////////////////////////////////
class Derv2 : public Base               //derived class 2
    {
    public:
       void show()
          { cout << "Derv2\n"; }
    };
//////////////////////////////////////////////////////////////////
int main()
    {
    Derv1 dv1;              //object of derived class 1
    Derv2 dv2;              //object of derived class 2
    Base* ptr;             //pointer to base class

    ptr = &dv1;             //put address of dv1 in pointer
    ptr->show();            //execute show()

    ptr = &dv2;             //put address of dv2 in pointer
    ptr->show();            //execute show()
    return 0;
    }
```

The output of this program is:

```
Derv1
Derv2
```

Now, as you can see, the member functions of the derived classes, not the base class, are executed. We change the contents of ptr from the address of Derv1 to that of Derv2, and the particular instance of show() that is executed also changes. So the same function call,

```
ptr->show();
```

executes different functions, depending on the contents of ptr. The rule is that the compiler selects the function according to the *contents* of the pointer ptr, not on the *type* of the pointer, as in NOTVIRT. This is shown in Figure 11.2.

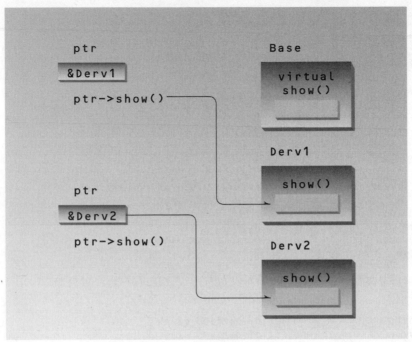

Figure 11.2 Virtual pointer access.

Late Binding

The astute reader may wonder how the compiler knows what function to compile. In NOTVIRT the compiler has no problem with the expression

```
ptr->show();
```

It always compiles a call to the **show()** function in the base class. But in VIRT the compiler doesn't know what class the contents of **ptr** may contain. It could be the address of an object of the **Derv1** class or of the **Derv2** class. Which version of **draw()** does the compiler call? In fact the compiler doesn't know what to do, so it arranges for the decision to be deferred until the program is running. At runtime, when it is known what class is pointed to by **ptr**, the appropriate version of **draw** will be called. This is called *late binding* or *dynamic binding*. (Choosing functions in the normal way, during compilation, is called *early binding*, or *static binding*.) Late binding requires some overhead but provides increased power and flexibility.

We'll put these ideas to use in a moment, but first let's consider a refinement to the idea of virtual functions.

Abstract Classes and Pure Virtual Functions

Think of the shape class in the multshap program in Chapter 9. We'll never make an object of the shape class; we'll only make specific shapes such as circles and triangles. When we will never want to instantiate objects of a base class, we call it an *abstract class*. Such a class exists only to act as a parent of derived classes that will be used to instantiate objects. It may also provide an interface for the class hierarchy.

How can we make it clear to someone using our family of classes that we don't want anyone to instantiate objects of the base class? We could just say this in the documentation, and count on the users of the class to remember it, but of course it's much better to write our classes so that such instantiation is impossible. How can we can do that? By placing at least one *pure virtual function* in the base class. A pure virtual function is one with the expression =0 added to the declaration. This is shown in the VIRTPURE example.

```cpp
// virtpure.cpp
// pure virtual function
#include <iostream>
using namespace std;
/////////////////////////////////////////////////////////////////
class Base                         //base class
   {
   public:
      virtual void show() = 0;     //pure virtual function
   };
/////////////////////////////////////////////////////////////////
class Derv1 : public Base          //derived class 1
   {
   public:
      void show()
         { cout << "Derv1\n"; }
   };
/////////////////////////////////////////////////////////////////
class Derv2 : public Base          //derived class 2
   {
   public:
      void show()
         { cout << "Derv2\n"; }
   };
/////////////////////////////////////////////////////////////////
int main()
   {
// Base bad;           //can't make object from abstract class
   Base* arr[2];       //array of pointers to base class
   Derv1 dv1;          //object of derived class 1
   Derv2 dv2;          //object of derived class 2

   arr[0] = &dv1;      //put address of dv1 in array
   arr[1] = &dv2;      //put address of dv2 in array

   arr[0]->show();     //execute show() in both objects
   arr[1]->show();
   return 0;
   }
```

```
        if( persPtr[j]->isOutstanding() )
            cout << "   This person is outstanding\n";
        }
    return 0;
    }  //end main()
```

The Classes

The **person** class is an abstract class because it contains the pure virtual functions **getData()** and **isOutstanding()**. No **person** objects can ever be created. This class exists only to be the base class for the **student** and **professor** classes. The **student** and **professor** classes add new data items to the base class. The **student** class contains a variable **gpa** of type **float**, which represents the student's grade point average (GPA). The **professor** class contains a variable **numPubs,** of type **int**, which represents the number of scholarly publications the professor has published. A student with a GPA of over 3.5, and a professor who has published more than 100 publications, are considered outstanding. (We'll refrain from comment on the desirability of these criteria for judging educational excellence.)

The isOutstanding() Function

The **isOutstanding()** function is declared as a pure virtual function in **person**. In the **student** class this function returns a **bool true** if the student's GPA is greater than 3.5, and **false** otherwise. In **professor** it returns **true** if the professor's **numPubs** variable is greater than 100. The **getData()** function asks the user for the GPA for a **student**, but for the number of publications for a **professor**.

The main() Program

In **main()** we first let the user enter a number of student and teacher names. For students, the program also asks for the GPA, and for professors it asks for the number of publications. When the user is finished, the program prints out the names of all the students and professors, noting those that are outstanding. Here's some sample interaction:

```
Enter student or professor (s/p): s
    Enter name: Timmy
    Enter student's GPA: 1.2
    Enter another (y/n)? y
Enter student or professor (s/p): s
    Enter name: Brenda
    Enter student's GPA: 3.9
    Enter another (y/n)? y
Enter student or professor (s/p): s
    Enter name: Sandy
    Enter student's GPA: 2.4
    Enter another (y/n)? y
Enter student or professor (s/p): p
    Enter name: Shipley
    Enter number of professor's publications: 714
    Enter another (y/n)? y
```

```
Enter student or professor (s/p): p
   Enter name: Wainright
   Enter number of professor's publications: 13
   Enter another (y/n)? n

Name is: Timmy
Name is: Brenda
   This person is outstanding
Name is: Sandy
Name is: Shipley
   This person is outstanding
Name is: Wainright
```

Virtual Functions in a Graphics Example

Let's try another example of virtual functions, this one is a graphics example derived from the MULTSHAP program in Chapter 11, "Inheritance." As we noted at the beginning of this section, you may want to draw a number of shapes using the same statement. The VIRTSHAP program does this. Remember that you must build this program with the appropriate console graphics file, as described in Appendix E, "Console Graphics Lite."

```cpp
// virtshap.cpp
// virtual functions with shapes
#include <iostream>
using namespace std;
#include "msoftcon.h"           //for graphics functions
////////////////////////////////////////////////////////////
class shape                     //base class
   {
   protected:
      int xCo, yCo;             //coordinates of center
      color fillcolor;         //color
      fstyle fillstyle;        //fill pattern
   public:                      //no-arg constructor
      shape() : xCo(0), yCo(0), fillcolor(cWHITE),
                                   fillstyle(SOLID_FILL)
         {  }                   //4-arg constructor
      shape(int x, int y, color fc, fstyle fs) :
                  xCo(x), yCo(y), fillcolor(fc), fillstyle(fs)
         {  }
      virtual void draw()       //virtual draw function
         {
         set_color(fillcolor);
         set_fill_style(fillstyle);
         }
   };
////////////////////////////////////////////////////////////
class ball : public shape
   {
   private:
      int radius;               //(xCo, yCo) is center
   public:
```

```cpp
      ball() : shape()          //no-arg constr
         { }
                                  //5-arg constructor
      ball(int x, int y, int r, color fc, fstyle fs)
                   : shape(x, y, fc, fs), radius(r)
         { }
      void draw()               //draw the ball
         {
         shape::draw();
         draw_circle(xCo, yCo, radius);
         }
   };
//////////////////////////////////////////////////////////////////
class rect : public shape
   {
   private:
      int width, height;        //(xCo, yCo) is upper left corner
   public:
      rect() : shape(), height(0), width(0)      //no-arg ctor
         { }                                      //6-arg ctor
      rect(int x, int y, int h, int w, color fc, fstyle fs) :
                   shape(x, y, fc, fs), height(h), width(w)
         { }
      void draw()               //draw the rectangle
         {
         shape::draw();
         draw_rectangle(xCo, yCo, xCo+width, yCo+height);
         set_color(cWHITE);   //draw diagonal
         draw_line(xCo, yCo, xCo+width, yCo+height);
         }
   };
//////////////////////////////////////////////////////////////////
class tria : public shape
   {
   private:
      int height;               //(xCo, yCo) is tip of pyramid
   public:
      tria() : shape(), height(0) //no-arg constructor
         { }                      //5-arg constructor
      tria(int x, int y, int h, color fc, fstyle fs) :
                             shape(x, y, fc, fs), height(h)
         { }
      void draw()               //draw the triangle
         {
         shape::draw();
         draw_pyramid(xCo, yCo, height);
         }
   };
//////////////////////////////////////////////////////////////////
int main()
   {
```

```
    int j;
    init_graphics();                 //initialize graphics system

    shape* pShapes[3];               //array of pointers to shapes
                                     //define three shapes
    pShapes[0] = new ball(40, 12, 5, cBLUE, X_FILL);
    pShapes[1] = new rect(12, 7, 10, 15, cRED, SOLID_FILL);
    pShapes[2] = new tria(60, 7,  11, cGREEN, MEDIUM_FILL);

    for(j=0; j<3; j++)               //draw all shapes
        pShapes[j]->draw();

    for(j=0; j<3; j++)               //delete all shapes
        delete pShapes[j];
    set_cursor_pos(1, 25);
    return 0;
    }
```

The class specifiers in VIRTSHAP are similar to those in MULTSHAP, except that the `draw()` function in the **shape** class has been made into a pure virtual function.

In main(), we set up an array, **ptrarr**, of pointers to shapes. Next we create three objects, one of each class, and place their addresses in an array. Now it's easy to draw all three shapes. The statement

```
ptrarr[j]->draw();
```

does this as the loop variable j changes.

This is a powerful approach to combining graphics elements, especially when a large number of objects need to be grouped together and drawn as a unit.

Virtual Destructors

Base class destructors should always be virtual. Suppose you use **delete** with a base class pointer to a derived class object to destroy the derived-class object. If the base-class destructor is not virtual, then **delete**, like a normal member function, calls the destructor for the base class, not the destructor for the derived class. This will cause only the base part of the object to be destroyed. The VIRTDEST program shows how this looks.

```
//vertdest.cpp
//tests non-virtual and virtual destructors
#include <iostream>
using namespace std;
/////////////////////////////////////////////////////////////
class Base
    {
    public:
        ~Base()                          //non-virtual destructor
//      virtual ~Base()                  //virtual destructor
            { cout << "Base destroyed\n"; }
    };
/////////////////////////////////////////////////////////////
```

```
class Derv : public Base
  {
  public:
    ~Derv()
       { cout << "Derv destroyed\n"; }
  };
////////////////////////////////////////////////////////////////
int main()
  {
  Base* pBase = new Derv;
  delete pBase;
  return 0;
  }
```

The output for this program as written is

```
Base destroyed
```

This shows that the destructor for the **Derv** part of the object isn't called. In the listing the base class destructor is not virtual, but you can make it so by commenting out the first definition for the destructor and substituting the second. Now the output is

```
Derv destroyed
Base destroyed
```

Now both parts of the derived class object are destroyed properly. Of course, if none of the destructors has anything important to do (like deleting memory obtained with **new**) then virtual destructors aren't important. But in general, to ensure that derived-class objects are destroyed properly, you should make destructors in all base classes virtual.

Virtual Base Classes

Before leaving the subject of virtual programming elements, we should mention *virtual base classes as they relate to multiple inheritance*.

Consider the situation shown in Figure 11.3, with a base class, **Parent**; two derived classes, **Child1** and **Child2**; and a fourth class, **Grandchild**, derived from both **Child1** and **Child2**.

In this arrangement, a problem can arise if a member function in the **Grandchild** class wants to access data or functions in the **Parent** class. The NORMBASE program shows what happens.

```
// normbase.cpp
// ambiguous reference to base class

class Parent
  {
  protected:
    int basedata;
  };
class Child1 : public Parent
  { };
class Child2 : public Parent
  { };
```

```
class Grandchild : public Child1, public Child2
    {
    public:
        int getdata()
            { return basedata; }    // ERROR: ambiguous
    };
```

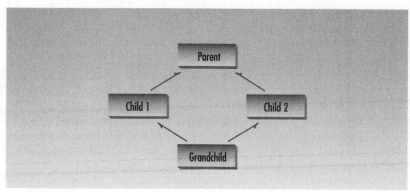

Figure 11.3 Virtual base classes.

A compiler error occurs when the `getdata()` member function in `Grandchild` attempts to access `basedata` in `Parent`. Why? When the `Child1` and `Child2` classes are derived from `Parent`, each inherits a copy of `Parent`; this copy is called a *subobject*. Each of the two subobjects contains its own copy of `Parent`'s data, including `basedata`. Now, when `Grandchild` refers to `basedata`, which of the two copies will it access? The situation is ambiguous, and that's what the compiler reports.

To eliminate the ambiguity, we make `Child1` and `Child2` into virtual base classes, as shown by the example VIRTBASE.

```
// virtbase.cpp
// virtual base classes

class Parent
    {
    protected:
        int basedata;
    };
class Child1 : virtual public Parent    // shares copy of Parent
    { };
class Child2 : virtual public Parent    // shares copy of Parent
    { };
class Grandchild : public Child1, public Child2
    {
    public:
        int getdata()
            { return basedata; }     // OK: only one copy of Parent
    };
```

The use of the keyword `virtual` in these two classes causes them to share a single common subobject of their base class `Parent`. Since there is only one copy of `basedata`, there is no ambiguity when it is referred to in `Grandchild`.

Friend Functions

The concepts of encapsulation and data hiding dictate that nonmember functions should not be able to access an object's private or protected data. The policy is, if you're not a member, you can't get in. However, there are situations where such rigid discrimination leads to considerable inconvenience.

Friends As Bridges

Imagine that you want a function to operate on objects of two different classes. Perhaps the function will take objects of the two classes as arguments, and operate on their private data. In this situation there's nothing like a `friend` function. Here's a simple example, FRIEND, that shows how `friend` functions can act as a bridge between two classes:

```
// friend.cpp
// friend functions
#include <iostream>
using namespace std;
/////////////////////////////////////////////////////////////
class beta;                    //needed for frifunc declaration

class alpha
   {
   private:
      int data;
   public:
      alpha() : data(0) {  }            //no-arg constructor
      friend int frifunc(alpha, beta);  //friend function
   };
/////////////////////////////////////////////////////////////
class beta
   {
   private:
      int data;
   public:
      beta() : data(7) {  }             //no-arg constructor
      friend int frifunc(alpha, beta);  //friend function
   };
/////////////////////////////////////////////////////////////
int frifunc(alpha a, beta b)            //function definition
   {
   return( a.data + b.data );
   }
//-----------------------------------------------------------
int main()
   {
```

```
alpha aa;
beta bb;

cout << frifunc(aa, bb) << endl;      //call the function
return 0;
}
```

In this program, the two classes are `alpha` and `beta`. The constructors in these classes initialize their single data items to fixed values (3 in `alpha` and 7 in `beta`).

We want the function `frifunc()` to have access to both these private data members, so we make it a `friend` function. It's declared with the `friend` keyword in both classes:

```
friend int frifunc(alpha, beta);
```

This declaration can be placed anywhere in the class; it doesn't matter if it goes in the `public` or the `private` section.

An object of each class is passed as an argument to the function `frifunc()`, and it accesses the private `data` member of both classes through these arguments. The function doesn't do much: It adds the data items and returns the sum. The `main()` program calls this function and prints the result.

A minor point: Remember that a class can't be referred to until it has been declared. Class `beta` is referred to in the declaration of the function `frifunc()` in class `alpha`, so `beta` must be declared before `alpha`. Hence the declaration

```
class beta;
```

at the beginning of the program.

Breaching the Walls

We should note that `friend` functions are controversial. During the development of C++, arguments raged over the desirability of including this feature. On the one hand, it adds flexibility to the language; on the other, it is not in keeping with *data hiding*, the philosophy that only member functions can access a class's private data.

How serious is the breach of data integrity when `friend` functions are used? A `friend` function must be declared as such within the class whose data it will access. Thus a programmer who does not have access to the source code for the class cannot make a function into a `friend`. In this respect the integrity of the class is still protected. Even so, `friend` functions are conceptually messy, and potentially lead to a spaghetti-code situation if numerous `friend`s muddy the clear boundaries between classes. For this reason `friend` functions should be used sparingly. If you find yourself using many `friend`s, you may need to rethink the design of the program.

English Distance Example

However, sometimes `friend` functions are too convenient to avoid. Perhaps the most common example is when `friend`s are used to increase the versatility of overloaded operators. The following program shows a limitation in the use of such operators when friends are not used. This example is a variation on the ENGLPLUS and ENGLCONV programs in Chapter 8, "Operator Overloading." It's called NOFRI.

```cpp
// nofri.cpp
// limitation to overloaded + operator
#include <iostream>
using namespace std;
//////////////////////////////////////////////////////////////
class Distance                      //English Distance class
   {
   private:
      int feet;
      float inches;
   public:
      Distance() : feet(0), inches(0.0)  //constructor (no args)
         { }                             //constructor (one arg)
      Distance(float fltfeet)     //convert float to Distance
         {                        //feet is integer part
         feet = static_cast<int>(fltfeet);
          inches = 12*(fltfeet-feet); //inches is what's left
         }
      Distance(int ft, float in)  //constructor (two args)
         { feet = ft; inches = in; }
      void showdist()                 //display distance
         { cout << feet << "\'-" << inches << '\"'; }
      Distance operator + (Distance);
   };
//-------------------------------------------------------------
                                   //add this distance to d2
Distance Distance::operator + (Distance d2)    //return the sum
   {
   int f = feet + d2.feet;         //add the feet
   float i = inches + d2.inches;   //add the inches
   if(i >= 12.0)                   //if total exceeds 12.0,
      { i -= 12.0; f++;  }         //less 12 inches, plus 1 foot
   return Distance(f,i);           //return new Distance with sum
   }
//////////////////////////////////////////////////////////////
int main()
   {
   Distance d1 = 2.5;              //constructor converts
   Distance d2 = 1.25;             //float feet to Distance
   Distance d3;
   cout << "\nd1 = "; d1.showdist();
   cout << "\nd2 = "; d2.showdist();

   d3 = d1 + 10.0;                 //distance + float: OK
   cout << "\nd3 = "; d3.showdist();
// d3 = 10.0 + d1;                 //float + Distance: ERROR
// cout << "\nd3 = "; d3.showdist();
   cout << endl;
   return 0;
   }
```

In this program, the + operator is overloaded to add two objects of type `Distance`. Also, there is a one-argument constructor that converts a value of type `float`, representing feet and decimal fractions of feet, into a `Distance` value. (That is, it converts 10.25′ into 10′-3″.)

When such a constructor exists, you can make statements like this in `main()`:

```
d3 = d1 + 10.0;
```

The overloaded + is looking for objects of type `Distance` both on its left and on its right, but if the argument on the right is type `float`, the compiler will use the one-argument constructor to convert this `float` to a `Distance` value, and then carry out the addition.

Here is what appears to be a subtle variation on this statement:

```
d3 = 10.0 + d1;
```

Does this work? No, because the object of which the overloaded + operator is a member must be the variable to the left of the operator. When we place a variable of a different type there, or a constant, then the compiler uses the + operator that adds that type (`float` in this case), not the one that adds `Distance` objects. Unfortunately, this operator does not know how to convert `float` to `Distance`, so it can't handle this situation. Here's the output from NOFRI:

```
d1 = 2'-6"
d2 = 1'-3"
d3 = 12'-6"
```

The second addition won't compile, so these statements are commented out. We could get around this problem by creating a new object of type `Distance`:

```
d3 = Distance(10, 0) + d1;
```

but this is non-intuitive and inelegant. How can we write natural-looking statements that have nonmember data types to the left of the operator? As you may have guessed, a `friend` can help you out of this dilemma. The FRENGL program shows how.

```cpp
// frengl.cpp
// friend overloaded + operator
#include <iostream>
using namespace std;
//////////////////////////////////////////////////////////////////
class Distance                       //English Distance class
   {
   private:
      int feet;
      float inches;
   public:
      Distance()                     //constructor (no args)
         { feet = 0; inches = 0.0; }
      Distance( float fltfeet )      //constructor (one arg)
         {                           //convert float to Distance
         feet = int(fltfeet);           //feet is integer part
         inches = 12*(fltfeet-feet);    //inches is what's left
         }
```

```
        Distance(int ft, float in)  //constructor (two args)
           { feet = ft; inches = in; }
        void showdist()             //display distance
           { cout << feet << "\'-" << inches << '\"'; }
        friend Distance operator + (Distance, Distance); //friend
   };
//
Distance operator + (Distance d1, Distance d2) //add D1 to d2
   {
   int f = d1.feet + d2.feet;       //add the feet
   float i = d1.inches + d2.inches; //add the inches
   if(i >= 12.0)                    //if inches exceeds 12.0,
      { i -= 12.0; f++;  }          //less 12 inches, plus 1 foot
   return Distance(f,i);            //return new Distance with sum
   }
//-------------------------------------------------------------
int main()
   {
   Distance d1 = 2.5;               //constructor converts
   Distance d2 = 1.25;              //float-feet to Distance
   Distance d3;
   cout << "\nd1 = "; d1.showdist();
   cout << "\nd2 = "; d2.showdist();

   d3 = d1 + 10.0;                  //distance + float: OK
   cout << "\nd3 = "; d3.showdist();
   d3 = 10.0 + d1;                  //float + Distance: OK
   cout << "\nd3 = "; d3.showdist();
   cout << endl;
   return 0;
   }
```

The overloaded + operator is made into a `friend`:

```
friend Distance operator + (Distance, Distance);
```

Notice that, while the overloaded + operator took one argument as a member function, it takes two as a `friend` function. In a member function, one of the objects on which the + operates is the object of which it was a member, and the second is an argument. In a `friend`, both objects must be arguments.

The only change to the body of the overloaded + function is that the variables **feet** and **inches**, used in NOFRI for direct access to the object's data, have been replaced in FRENGL by **d1.feet** and **d1.inches**, since this object is supplied as an argument.

Remember that, to make a function a friend, only the function declaration within the class is preceded by the keyword `friend`. The class definition is written normally, as are calls to the function.

friends for Functional Notation

Sometimes a `friend` allows a more obvious syntax for calling a function than does a member function. For example, suppose we want a function that will square (multiply by itself) an object of the English `Distance` class and return the result in square feet, as a type `float`. The MISQ example shows how this might be done with a member function.

```
// misq.cpp
// member square() function for Distance
#include <iostream>
using namespace std;
//////////////////////////////////////////////////////////////
class Distance                         //English Distance class
   {
   private:
      int feet;
      float inches;
   public:                             //constructor (no args)
      Distance() : feet(0), inches(0.0)
         { }                           //constructor (two args)
      Distance(int ft, float in) : feet(ft), inches(in)
         { }
      void showdist()                  //display distance
         { cout << feet << "\'-" << inches << '\"'; }
      float square();                  //member function
   };
//-------------------------------------------------------------
float Distance::square()              //return square of
   {                                   //this Distance
   float fltfeet = feet + inches/12;   //convert to float
   float feetsqrd = fltfeet * fltfeet; //find the square
   return feetsqrd;                    //return square feet
   }
//////////////////////////////////////////////////////////////
int main()
   {
   Distance dist(3, 6.0);              //two-arg constructor (3'-6")
   float sqft;

   sqft = dist.square();              //return square of dist
                                       //display distance and square
   cout << "\nDistance = "; dist.showdist();
   cout << "\nSquare = " << sqft << " square feet\n";
   return 0;

   }
```

The `main()` part of the program creates a `Distance` value, squares it, and prints out the result. The output shows the original distance and the square:

```
Distance = 3'-6"
Square = 12.25 square feet
```

In `main()` we use the statement

```
sqft = dist.square();
```

to find the square of **dist** and assign it to **sqft**. This works all right, but if we want to work with **Distance** objects using the same syntax that we use with ordinary numbers, we would probably prefer a functional notation:

```
sqft = square(dist);
```

We can achieve this effect by making **square()** a **friend** of the **Distance** class, as shown in FRISQ:

```
// frisq.cpp
// friend square() function for Distance
#include <iostream>
using namespace std;
////////////////////////////////////////////////////////////////
class Distance                      //English Distance class
    {
    private:
        int feet;
        float inches;
    public:
        Distance() : feet(0), inches(0.0) //constructor (no args)
            { }
                                           //constructor (two args)
        Distance(int ft, float in) : feet(ft), inches(in)
            { }
        void showdist()                    //display distance
            { cout << feet << "\'-" << inches << '\"'; }
        friend float square(Distance);     //friend function
    };
//--------------------------------------------------------------
float square(Distance d)            //return square of
    {                               //this Distance
    float fltfeet = d.feet + d.inches/12;  //convert to float
    float feetsqrd = fltfeet * fltfeet;    //find the square
    return feetsqrd;                //return square feet
    }
////////////////////////////////////////////////////////////////
int main()
    {
    Distance dist(3, 6.0);          //two-arg constructor (3'-6")
    float sqft;

    sqft = square(dist);            //return square of dist
                                    //display distance and square
    cout << "\nDistance = "; dist.showdist();
    cout << "\nSquare = " << sqft << " square feet\n";
    return 0;
    }
```

Where **square()**, as a member function in MISQ, takes no arguments, it takes one as a **friend** in FRISQ. In general, the **friend** version of a function requires one more argument than when the function is a member. The **square()** function in FRISQ is similar to that in MISQ, but it refers to the data in the source **Distance** object as **d.feet** and **d.inches**, instead of as **feet** and **inches**.

friend Classes

The member functions of a class can all be made friends at the same time when you make the entire class a friend. The program FRICLASS shows how this looks.

```cpp
// friclass.cpp
// friend classes
#include <iostream>
using namespace std;
///////////////////////////////////////////////////////////
class alpha
    {
    private:
        int data1;
    public:
        alpha() : data1(99) {  }     //constructor
        friend class beta;           //beta is a friend class
    };
///////////////////////////////////////////////////////////
class beta
    {                                //all member functions can
    public:                          //access private alpha data
        void func1(alpha a)  { cout << "\ndata1=" << a.data1; }
        void func2(alpha a)  { cout << "\ndata1=" << a.data1; }
    };
///////////////////////////////////////////////////////////
int main()
    {
    alpha a;
    beta b;

    b.func1(a);
    b.func2(a);
    cout << endl;
    return 0;

    }
```

In class **alpha** the entire class **beta** is proclaimed a friend. Now all the member functions of **beta** can access the private data of **alpha** (in this program the single data item **data1**).

Note that in the **friend** declaration we specify that **beta** is a class using the **class** keyword:

```cpp
friend class beta;
```

We could also have declared **beta** to be a class before the **alpha** class specifier, as in previous examples.

```cpp
class beta;
```

and then, within **alpha**, referred to **beta** without the **class** keyword:

```cpp
friend beta;
```

Static Functions

In the STATIC example in Chapter 6, "Objects and Classes," we introduced **static** data members. As you may recall, a static data member is not duplicated for each object; rather a single data item is shared by all objects of a class. The STATIC example showed a class that kept track of how many objects of itself there were. Let's extend this concept by showing how functions as well as data may be **static**. Besides showing static functions, our example will model a class that provides an ID number for each of its objects. This allows you to query an object to find out which object it is—a capability that is sometimes useful in debugging a program, among other situations. The program also casts some light on the operation of destructors. Here's the listing for STATFUNC:

```cpp
// statfunc.cpp
// static functions and ID numbers for objects
#include <iostream>
using namespace std;
///////////////////////////////////////////////////////////////
class gamma
    {
    private:
       static int total;        //total objects of this class
                                 //   (declaration only)
       int id;                   //ID number of this object
    public:
       gamma()                   //no-argument constructor
          {
          total++;               //add another object
          id = total;            //id equals current total
          }
       ~gamma()                  //destructor
          {
          total ;
          cout << "Destroying ID number " << id  << endl;
          }
       static void showtotal()  //static function
          {
          cout << "Total is " << total << endl;
          }
       void showid()            //non-static function
          {
          cout << "ID number is " << id << endl;
          }
    };
//-------------------------------------------------------------
int gamma::total = 0;            //definition of total
///////////////////////////////////////////////////////////////
int main()
    {
```

```
gamma g1;
gamma::showtotal();

gamma g2, g3;
gamma::showtotal();

g1.showid();
g2.showid();
g3.showid();
cout << "----------end of program----------\n";
return 0;
}
```

Accessing `static` Functions

In this program there is a static data member, `total`, in the class `gamma`. This data keeps track of how many objects of the class there are. It is incremented by the constructor and decremented by the destructor.

Suppose we want to access `total` from outside the class. We construct a function, `showtotal()`, that prints the `total`'s value. But how do we access this function?

When a data member is declared `static`, there is only one such data value for the entire class, no matter how many objects of the class are created. In fact, there may be no such objects at all, but we still want to be able to learn this fact. We could create a dummy object to use in calling a member function, as in

```
gamma dummyObj;           // make an object so we can call function
dummyObj.showtotal();  // call function
```

But this is rather inelegant. We shouldn't need to refer to a specific object when we're doing something that relates to the entire class. It's more reasonable to use the name of the class itself with the scope-resolution operator.

```
gamma::showtotal();   // more reasonable
```

However, this won't work if `showtotal()` is a normal member function; an object and the dot member-access operator are required in such cases. To access `showtotal()` using only the class name, we must declare it to be a `static` member function. This is what we do in STATFUNC. Now the function can be accessed using only the class name. Here's the output:

```
Total is 1
Total is 3
ID number is 1
ID number is 2
ID number is 3
----------end of program--------
Destroying ID number 3
Destroying ID number 2
Destroying ID number 1
```

We define one object, g1, and then print out the value of `total`, which is 1. Then we define two more objects, g2 and g3, and again print out the total, which is now 3.

Numbering the Objects

We've placed another function in `gamma()` to print out the ID number of individual members. This ID number is set equal to `total` when an object is created, so each object has a unique number. The `showid()` function prints out the ID of its object. We call it three times in `main()`, in the statements

```
g1.showid();
g2.showid();
g3.showid();
```

As the output shows, each object has a unique number. The g1 object is numbered 1, g2 is 2, and g3 is 3.

Investigating Destructors

Now that we know how to number objects, we can investigate an interesting fact about destructors. STATFUNC prints an *end of program* message in its last statement, but it's not done yet, as the output shows. The three objects created in the program must be destroyed before the program terminates, so that memory is not left in an inaccessible state. The compiler takes care of this by invoking the destructor.

We can see that this happens by inserting a statement in the destructor that prints a message. Since we've numbered the objects, we can also find out the order in which the objects are destroyed. As the output shows, the last object created, g3, is destroyed first. One can infer from this last-in-first-out approach that local objects are stored on the stack.

Assignment and Copy Initialization

The C++ compiler is always busy on your behalf, doing things you can't be bothered to do. If you take charge, it will defer to your judgment; otherwise it will do things its own way. Two important examples of this process are the assignment operator and the copy constructor.

You've used the assignment operator many times, probably without thinking too much about it. Suppose a1 and a2 are objects. Unless you tell the compiler otherwise, the statement

```
a2 = a1;        // set a2 to the value of a1
```

will cause the compiler to copy the data from a1, member by member, into a2. This is the default action of the assignment operator, =.

You're also familiar with initializing variables. Initializing an object with another object, as in

```
alpha a2(a1);   // initialize a2 to the value of a1
```

causes a similar action. The compiler creates a new object, a2, and copies the data from a1, member by member, into a2. This is the default action of the copy constructor.

Both these default activities are provided, free of charge, by the compiler. If member-by-member copying is what you want, you need take no further action. However, if you want assignment or initialization to do something more complex, then you can override the default functions. We'll discuss the techniques for overloading the assignment operator and the copy constructor separately, and then put them together in an example that gives a String class a more efficient way to manage memory.

Overloading the Assignment Operator

Let's look at a short example that demonstrates the technique of overloading the assignment operator. Here's the listing for ASSIGN:

```cpp
// assign.cpp
// overloads assignment operator (=)
#include <iostream>
using namespace std;
/////////////////////////////////////////////////////////////////
class alpha
   {
   private:
      int data;
   public:
      alpha()                    //no-arg constructor
         { }
      alpha(int d)               //one-arg constructor
         { data = d; }
      void display()             //display data
         { cout << data; }
      alpha operator = (alpha& a)  //overloaded = operator
         {
         data = a.data;          //not done automatically
         cout << "\nAssignment operator invoked";
         return alpha(data);     //return copy of this alpha
         }
   };
/////////////////////////////////////////////////////////////////
int main()
   {
   alpha a1(37);
   alpha a2;

   a2 = a1;                      //invoke overloaded =
   cout << "\na2="; a2.display(); //display a2

   alpha a3 = a2;                //does NOT invoke =
   cout << "\na3="; a3.display(); //display a3
   cout << endl;
   return 0;
   }
```

The `alpha` class is very simple; it contains only one data member. Constructors initialize the data, and a member function can print out its value. The new aspect of ASSIGN is the function `operator=()`, which overloads the = operator.

In `main()`, we define `a1` and give it the value 37, and define `a2` but give it no value. Then we use the assignment operator to set `a2` to the value of `a1`:

```
a2 = a1;    // assignment statement
```

This causes our overloaded `operator=()` function to be invoked. Here's the output from ASSIGN:

```
Assignment operator invoked
a2=37
a3=37
```

Initialization Is Not Assignment

In the last two lines of ASSIGN we initialize the object `a3` to the value `a2`, and display it. Don't be confused by the syntax here. The equal sign in

```
alpha a3 = a2;    // copy initialization, not an assignment
```

is not an assignment but an initialization, with the same effect as

```
alpha a3(a2);    // alternative form of copy initialization
```

This is why the assignment operator is executed only once, as shown by the single invocation of the line

```
Assignment operator invoked
```

in the output of ASSIGN.

Taking Responsibility

When you overload the = operator you assume responsibility for doing whatever the default assignment operator did. Often this involves copying data members from one object to another. The `alpha` class in ASSIGN has only one data item, `data`, so the `operator=()` function copies its value with the statement

```
data = a.data;
```

The function also prints the `Assignment operator invoked` message so that we can tell when it executes.

Passing by Reference

Notice that the argument to `operator=()` is passed by reference. It is not absolutely necessary to do this, but it's usually a good idea. Why? As you know, an argument passed by value generates a copy of itself in the function to which it is passed. The argument passed to the `operator=()` function is no exception. If such objects are large, the copies can waste a lot of memory. Values passed by reference don't generate copies, and thus help to conserve memory.

Also, there are certain situations in which you want to keep track of the number of objects (as in the STATFUNC example, where we assigned numbers to the objects). If the compiler is generating extra objects every time you use the assignment operator, you may wind up with more objects than you expected. Passing by reference helps avoid such spurious object creation.

Returning a Value

As we've seen, a function can return information to the calling program by value or by reference. When an object is returned by value, a new object is created and returned to the calling program. In the calling program the value of this object can be assigned to a new object, or it can be used in other ways. When an object is returned by reference, no new object is created. A reference to the original object in the function is all that's returned to the calling program.

The `operator=()` function in ASSIGN returns a value by creating a temporary **alpha** object and initializing it using the one-argument constructor in the statement

```
return alpha(data);
```

The value returned is a copy of, but not the same object as, the object of which the overloaded = operator is a member. Returning a value makes it possible to chain = operators:

```
a3 = a2 = a1;
```

However, returning by value has the same disadvantages as passing an argument by value: It creates an extra copy that wastes memory and can cause confusion. Can we return this value with a reference, using the declarator shown here for the overloaded = operator?

```
alpha& operator = (alpha& a)  // bad idea in this case
```

Unfortunately, we can't use reference returns on variables that are local to a function. Remember that local (**automatic**) variables—that is, those created within a function (and not designated **static**)—are destroyed when the function returns. A return by reference returns only the address of the data being returned, and, for local data, this address points to data within the function. When the function is terminated and this data is destroyed, the pointer is left with a meaningless value. Your compiler may flag this usage with a warning. (We'll see one way to solve this problem in the section "The **this** Pointer" later in this chapter.)

Not Inherited

The assignment operator is unique among operators in that it is not inherited. If you overload the assignment operator in a base class, you can't use this same function in any derived classes.

The Copy Constructor

As we discussed, you can define and at the same time initialize an object to the value of another object with two kinds of statements:

```
alpha a3(a2);    // copy initialization
alpha a3 = a2;   // copy initialization, alternate syntax
```

Both styles of definition invoke a copy constructor: a constructor that creates a new object and copies its argument into it. The default copy constructor, which is provided automatically by the compiler for every object, performs a member-by-member copy. This is similar to what the assignment operator does; the difference is that the copy constructor also creates a new object.

Like the assignment operator, the copy constructor can be overloaded by the user. The XOFXREF example shows how it's done.

```cpp
// xofxref.cpp
// copy constructor: X(X&)
#include <iostream>
using namespace std;
/////////////////////////////////////////////////////////////
class alpha
   {
   private:
      int data;
   public:
      alpha()                    //no-arg constructor
         { }
      alpha(int d)               //one-arg constructor
         { data = d; }
      alpha(alpha& a)            //copy constructor
         {
         data = a.data;
         cout << "\nCopy constructor invoked";
         }
      void display()             //display
         { cout << data; }
      void operator = (alpha& a) //overloaded = operator
         {
         data = a.data;
         cout << "\nAssignment operator invoked";
         }
   };
/////////////////////////////////////////////////////////////
int main()
   {
   alpha a1(37);
   alpha a2;

   a2 = a1;                            //invoke overloaded =
   cout << "\na2="; a2.display();  //display a2
```

```
    alpha a3(a1);             //invoke copy constructor
//  alpha a3 = a1;            //equivalent definition of a3
    cout << "\na3="; a3.display();  //display a3
    cout << endl;
    return 0;
    }
```

This program overloads both the assignment operator and the copy constructor. The overloaded assignment operator is similar to that in the ASSIGN example. The copy constructor takes one argument: an object of type **alpha**, passed by reference. Here's its declarator:

alpha(alpha&)

This declarator has the form **X(X&)** (pronounced "X of X ref"). Here's the output of XOFXREF:

```
Assignment operator invoked
a2=37
Copy constructor invoked
a3=37
```

The statement

a2 = a1;

invokes the assignment operator, while

alpha a3(a1);

invokes the copy constructor. The equivalent statement

alpha a3 = a1;

could also be used to invoke the copy constructor.

We've seen that the copy constructor may be invoked when an object is defined. It is also invoked when arguments are passed by value to functions and when values are returned from functions. Let's mention these situations briefly.

Function Arguments

The copy constructor is invoked when an object is passed by value to a function. It creates the copy that the function operates on. Thus if the function

void func(alpha);

were declared in XOFXREF, and this function were called by the statement

func(a1);

then the copy constructor would be invoked to create a copy of the **a1** object for use by **func()**. (Of course, the copy constructor is not invoked if the argument is passed by reference or if a pointer to it is passed. In these cases no copy is created; the function operates on the original variable.)

Function Return Values

The copy constructor also creates a temporary object when a value is returned from a function. Suppose there were a function like this in XOFXREF:

```
alpha func();
```

and this function was called by the statement

```
a2 = func();
```

then the copy constructor would be invoked to create a copy of the value returned by `func()`, and this value would be assigned (invoking the assignment operator) to `a2`.

Why Not an X(X) Constructor?

Do we need to use a reference in the argument to the copy constructor? Could we pass by value instead? No, the compiler complains that it is **out of memory** if we try to compile

```
alpha(alpha a)
```

Why? Because when an argument is passed by value, a copy of it is constructed. What makes the copy? The copy constructor. But this *is* the copy constructor, so it calls itself. In fact it calls itself over and over until the compiler runs out of memory. So, in the copy constructor, the argument must be passed by reference, which creates no copies.

Watch Out for Destructors

In the sections "Passing by Reference" and "Returning a Value," we discussed passing arguments to a function by value and returning by value. These situations cause the destructor to be called as well, when the temporary objects created by the function are destroyed when the function returns. This can cause considerable consternation if you're not expecting it. The moral is, when working with objects that require more than member-by-member copying, pass and return by reference—not by value—whenever possible.

Define Both Copy Constructor and Assignment Operator

When you overload the assignment operator, you almost always want to overload the copy constructor as well (and vice versa). You don't want your custom copying routine used in some situations, and the default member-by-member scheme used in others. Even if you don't think you'll use one or the other, you may find the compiler using them in non-obvious situations, such as passing an argument to a function by value, and returning from a function by value.

In fact, if the constructor to a class involves the use of system resources such as memory or disk files, you should almost always overload both the assignment operator and the copy constructor, and make sure they do what you want.

How to Prohibit Copying

We've discussed how to customize the copying of objects using the assignment operator and the copy constructor. Sometimes, however, you may want to prohibit the copying of an object using these operations. For example, it might be essential that each member of a class be created with a unique value for some member, which is provided as an argument to the constructor. If an object is copied, the copy would be given the same value. To avoid copying, overload the assignment operator and the copy constructor as private members.

```
class alpha
   {
   private:
      alpha& operator = (alpha&);  // private assignment operator
      alpha(alpha&);               // private copy constructor
   };
```

As soon as you attempt a copying operation, such as

```
alpha a1, a2;
a1 = a2;          // assignment
alpha a3(a1);     // copy constructor
```

the compiler will tell you that the function is not accessible. You don't need to define the functions, since they will never be called.

A Memory-Efficient String Class

The ASSIGN and XOFXREF examples don't really need to have overloaded assignment operators and copy constructors. They use straightforward classes with only one data item, so the default assignment operator and copy constructor would work just as well. Let's look at an example where it is essential for the user to overload these operators.

Defects with the `String` Class

We've seen various versions of our homemade `String` class in previous chapters. However, these versions are not very sophisticated. It would be nice to overload the = operator so that we could assign the value of one `String` object to another with the statement

```
s2 = s1;
```

If we overload the = operator, the question arises of how we will handle the actual string (the array of type `char`), which is the principal data item in the `String` class.

One possibility is for each `String` object to have a place to store a string. If we assign one `String` object to another (from `s1` into `s2` in the previous statement), we simply copy the string from the source into the destination object. If you're concerned with conserving memory, the problem with this is that the same string now exists in two (or more) places in memory. This is not very efficient, especially if the strings are long. Figure 11.4 shows how this looks.

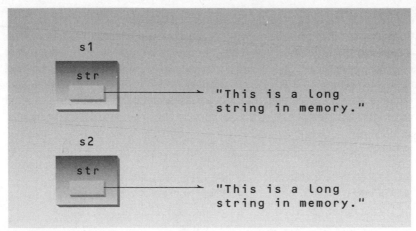

Figure 11.4   Replicating strings.

Instead of having each **String** object contain its own **char*** string, we could arrange for it to contain only a *pointer* to a string. Now, if we assign one **String** object to another, we need only copy the pointer from one object to another; both pointers will point to the same string. This is efficient, since only a single copy of the string itself needs to be stored in memory. Figure 11.5 shows how this looks.

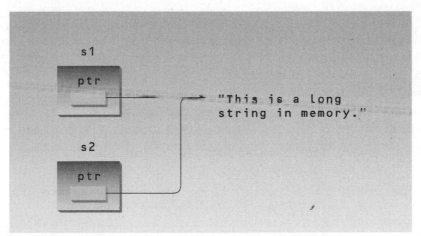

Figure 11.5   Replicating pointers to strings.

However, if we use this system we need to be careful when we destroy a **String** object. If a **String**'s destructor uses **delete** to free the memory occupied by the string, and if there are several objects with pointers pointing to the string, then these other objects will be left with pointers pointing to memory that may no longer hold the string they think it does; they become dangling pointers.

To use pointers to strings in **String** objects, we need a way to keep track of how many **String** objects point to a particular string, so that we can avoid using **delete** on the string until the last **String** that points to it is itself deleted. Our next example, STRIMEM, does just this.

A String-Counter Class

Suppose we have several **String** objects pointing to the same string and we want to keep a count of how many **Strings** point to the string. Where will we store this count?

It would be cumbersome for every **String** object to maintain a count of how many of its fellow **Strings** were pointing to a particular string, so we don't want to use a member variable in **String** for the count. Could we use a static variable? This is a possibility; we could create a static array and use it to store a list of string addresses and counts. However, this requires considerable overhead. It's more efficient to create a new class to store the count. Each object of this class, which we call **strCount**, contains a count and also a pointer to the string itself. Each **String** object contains a pointer to the appropriate **strCount** object. Figure 11.6 shows how this looks.

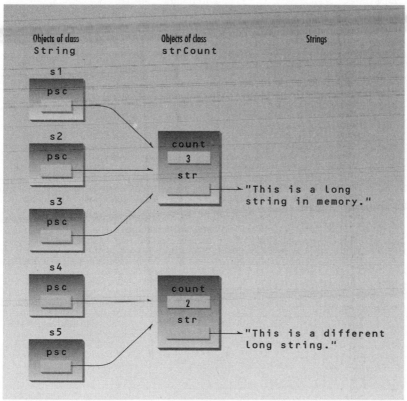

Figure 11.6   String and strCount classes.

To ensure that `String` objects have access to `strCount` objects, we make `String` a `friend` of `strCount`. Also, we want to ensure that the `strCount` class is used only by the `String` class. To prevent access to any of its functions, we make all member functions of `strCount` private. Because `String` is a friend, it can nevertheless access any part of `strCount`. Here's the listing for STRIMEM:

```
// strimem.cpp
// memory-saving String class
// overloaded assignment and copy constructor
#include <iostream>
#include <cstring>                    //for strcpy(), etc.
using namespace std;
/////////////////////////////////////////////////////////////
class strCount                        //keep track of number
   {                                  //of unique strings
   private:
      int count;                      //number of instances
      char* str;                      //pointer to string
      friend class String;            //make ourselves available
      //member functions are private
//-----------------------------------------------------------
      strCount(char* s)               //one-arg constructor
         {
         int length = strlen(s);   //length of string argument
         str = new char[length+1];  //get memory for string
         strcpy(str, s);             //copy argument to it
         count=1;                    //start count at 1
         }
//-----------------------------------------------------------
      ~strCount()                     //destructor
         { delete[] str; }           //delete the string
   };
/////////////////////////////////////////////////////////////
class String                          //String class
   {
   private:
      strCount* psc;                  //pointer to strCount
   public:
      String()                        //no-arg constructor
         { psc = new strCount("NULL"); }
//-----------------------------------------------------------
      String(char* s)                 //1-arg constructor
         { psc = new strCount(s); }
//-----------------------------------------------------------
      String(String& S)               //copy constructor
         {
```

```
                psc = S.psc;
                (psc->count)++;
                }
    //------------------------------------------------------------
        ~String()                      //destructor
            {
            if(psc->count==1)          //if we are its last user,
                delete psc;            //    delete our strCount
            else                       //    otherwise,
                (psc->count)--;        //    decrement its count
            }
    //------------------------------------------------------------
        void display()                 //display the String
            {
            cout << psc->str;                  //print string
            cout << " (addr=" << psc << ")";   //print address
            }
    //------------------------------------------------------------
        void operator = (String& S) //assign the string
            {
            if(psc->count==1)          //if we are its last user,
                delete psc;            //    delete our strCount
            else                       //    otherwise,
                (psc->count)--;        //    decrement its count
            psc = S.psc;               //use argument's strCount
            (psc->count)++;            //increment its count
            }
        };
    ///////////////////////////////////////////////////////////////
    int main()
        {
        String s3 = "When the fox preaches, look to your geese.";
        cout << "\ns3="; s3.display();    //display s3

        String s1;                        //define String
        s1 = s3;                          //assign it another String
        cout << "\ns1="; s1.display();    //display it

        String s2(s3);                    //initialize with String
        cout << "\ns2="; s2.display();    //display it
        cout << endl;
        return 0;
        }
```

In the main() part of STRIMEM we define a **String** object, **s3**, to contain the proverb "When
the fox preaches, look to your geese." We define another **String s1** and set it equal to **s3**;

then we define **s2** and initialize it to **s3**. Setting **s1** equal to **s3** invokes the overloaded assignment operator; initializing **s2** to **s3** invokes the overloaded copy constructor. We print out all three strings, and also the address of the **strCount** object pointed to by each object's **psc** pointer, to show that these objects are all the same. Here's the output from STRIMEM:

```
s3=When the fox preaches, look to your geese. (addr=0x8f510e00)
s1=When the fox preaches, look to your geese. (addr=0x8f510e00)
s2=When the fox preaches, look to your geese. (addr=0x8f510e00)
```

The other duties of the **String** class are divided between the **String** and **strCount** classes. Let's see what they do.

The **strCount** Class

The **strCount** class contains the pointer to the actual string and the count of how many **String** class objects point to this string. Its single constructor takes a pointer to a string as an argument and creates a new memory area for the string. It copies the string into this area and sets the count to 1, since just one **String** points to it when it is created. The destructor in **strCount** frees the memory used by the string. (We use **delete[]** with brackets because a string is an array.)

The **String** Class

The **String** class uses three constructors. If a new string is being created, as in the zero- and one-argument constructors, a new **strCount** object is created to hold the string, and the **psc** pointer is set to point to this object. If an existing **String** object is being copied, as in the copy constructor and the overloaded assignment operator, then the pointer **psc** is set to point to the old **strCount** object, and the count in this object is incremented.

The overloaded assignment operator, as well as the destructor, must also delete the old **strCount** object pointed to by **psc** if the count is 1. (We don't need brackets on **delete** because we're deleting only a single **strCount**object.) Why must the assignment operator worry about deletion? Remember that the **String** object on the left of the equal sign (call it **s1**) was pointing at some **strCount** object (call it **oldStrCnt**) before the assignment. After the assignment **s1** will be pointing to the object on the right of the equal sign. If there are now no **String** objects pointing to **oldStrCnt**, it should be deleted. If there are other objects pointing to it, its count must be decremented. Figure 11.7 shows the action of the overloaded assignment operator, and Figure 11.8 shows the copy constructor.

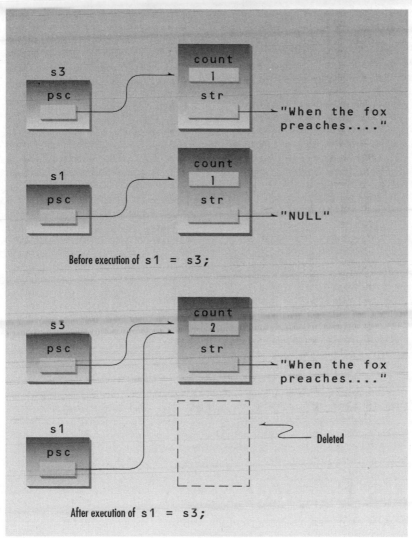

Figure 11.7 Assignment operator in STRIMEM.

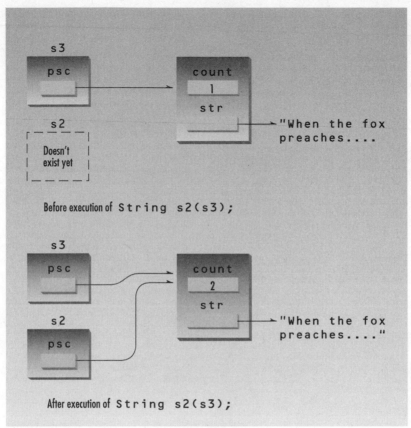

Figure 11.8 Copy Constructor in STRIMEM.

The `this` Pointer

The member functions of every object have access to a sort of magic pointer named **this**, which points to the object itself. Thus any member function can find out the address of the object of which it is a member. Here's a short example, WHERE, that shows the mechanism:

```cpp
// where.cpp
// the this pointer
#include <iostream>
using namespace std;
////////////////////////////////////////////////////////////////
class where
    {
    private:
        char charray[10];    //occupies 10 bytes
    public:
```

```
        void reveal()
            { cout << "\nMy object's address is " << this; }
        };
//////////////////////////////////////////////////////////////////
int main()
    {
    where w1, w2, w3;          //make three objects
    w1.reveal();               //see where they are
    w2.reveal();
    w3.reveal();
    cout << endl;
    return 0;
    }
```

The `main()` program in this example creates three objects of type `where`. It then asks each object to print its address, using the `reveal()` member function. This function prints out the value of the `this` pointer. Here's the output:

```
My object's address is 0x8f4effec
My object's address is 0x8f4effe2
My object's address is 0x8f4effd8
```

Since the data in each object consists of an array of 10 bytes, the objects are spaced 10 bytes apart in memory. (EC minus E2 is 10 decimal, as is E2 minus D8.) Some compilers may place extra bytes in objects, making them slightly larger than 10 bytes.

Accessing Member Data with `this`

When you call a member function, it comes into existence with the value of `this` set to the address of the object for which it was called. The `this` pointer can be treated like any other pointer to an object, and can thus be used to access the data in the object it points to, as shown in the DOTHIS program:

```
// dothis.cpp
// the this pointer referring to data
#include <iostream>
using namespace std;
//////////////////////////////////////////////////////////////////
class what
    {
    private:
        int alpha;
    public:
        void tester()
            {
            this->alpha = 11;      //same as alpha = 11;
            cout << this->alpha;   //same as cout << alpha;
            }
    };
//////////////////////////////////////////////////////////////////
int main()
    {
    what w;
```

```
    w.tester();
    cout << endl;
    return 0;
    }
```

This program simply prints out the value 11. Notice that the `tester()` member function accesses the variable `alpha` as

```
this->alpha
```

This is exactly the same as referring to `alpha` directly. This syntax works, but there is no reason for it except to show that `this` does indeed point to the object.

Using `this` for Returning Values

A more practical use for `this` is in returning values from member functions and overloaded operators.

Recall that in the ASSIGN program we could not return an object by reference, because the object was local to the function returning it and thus was destroyed when the function returned. We need a more permanent object if we're going to return it by reference. The object of which a function is a member is more permanent than its individual member functions. An object's member functions are created and destroyed every time they're called, but the object itself endures until it is destroyed by some outside agency (for example, when it is `delete`d). Thus returning by reference the object of which a function is a member is a better bet than returning a temporary object created in a member function. The `this` pointer makes this easy.

Here's the listing for ASSIGN2, in which the `operator=()` function returns by reference the object that invoked it:

```
//assign2.cpp
// returns contents of the this pointer
#include <iostream>
using namespace std;
/////////////////////////////////////////////////////////////////
class alpha
    {
    private:
        int data;
    public:
        alpha()                     //no-arg constructor
            { }
        alpha(int d)                //one-arg constructor
            { data = d; }
        void display()              //display data
            { cout << data; }
        alpha& operator = (alpha& a) //overloaded = operator
            {
            data = a.data;          //not done automatically
            cout << "\nAssignment operator invoked";
            return *this;           //return copy of this alpha
            }
```

```
   };
///////////////////////////////////////////////////////////////////
int main()
   {
   alpha a1(37);
   alpha a2, a3;

   a3 = a2 = a1;                       //invoke overloaded =, twice
   cout << "\na2="; a2.display();      //display a2
   cout << "\na3="; a3.display();      //display a3
   cout << endl;
   return 0;
   }
```

In this program we can use the declaration

```
alpha& operator = (alpha& a)
```

which returns by reference, instead of

```
alpha operator = (alpha& a)
```

which returns by value. The last statement in this function is

```
return *this;
```

Since this is a pointer to the object of which the function is a member, *this is that object itself, and the statement returns it by reference. Here's the output of ASSIGN2:

```
Assignment operator invoked
Assignment operator invoked
a2=37
a3=37
```

Each time the equal sign is encountered in

```
a3 = a2 = a1;
```

the overloaded operator=() function is called, which prints the messages. The three objects all end up with the same value.

You usually want to return by reference from overloaded assignment operators, using *this, to avoid the creation of extra objects.

Revised STRIMEM Program

Using the this pointer we can revise the operator=() function in STRIMEM to return a value by reference, thus making possible multiple assignment operators for String objects, such as

```
s1 = s2 = s3;
```

At the same time, we can avoid the creation of spurious objects, such as those that are created when objects are returned by value. Here's the listing for STRIMEM2:

```cpp
// strimem2.cpp
// memory-saving String class
// the this pointer in overloaded assignment
#include <iostream>
#include <cstring>                 //for strcpy(), etc
using namespace std;
//////////////////////////////////////////////////////////////////
class strCount                     //keep track of number
   {                               //of unique strings
   private:
      int count;                   //number of instances
      char* str;                   //pointer to string
      friend class String;         //make ourselves available
   //member functions are private
      strCount(char* s)            //one-arg constructor
         {
         int length = strlen(s);   //length of string argument
         str = new char[length+1]; //get memory for string
         strcpy(str, s);           //copy argument to it
         count=1;                  //start count at 1
         }
//-------------------------------------------------------------
      ~strCount()                  //destructor
         { delete[] str; }         //delete the string
   };
//////////////////////////////////////////////////////////////////
class String                       //String class
   {
   private:
      strCount* psc;               //pointer to strCount
   public:
      String()                     //no-arg constructor
         { psc = new strCount("NULL"); }
//-------------------------------------------------------------
      String(char* s)              //1-arg constructor
         { psc = new strCount(s); }
//-------------------------------------------------------------
      String(String& S)            //copy constructor
         {
         cout << "\nCOPY CONSTRUCTOR";
         psc = S.psc;
            (psc->count)++;
         }
//-------------------------------------------------------------
      ~String()                    //destructor
         {
         if(psc->count==1)         //if we are its last user,
            delete psc;            //   delete our strCount
         else                      //   otherwise,
            (psc->count)--;        //   decrement its count
         }
//-------------------------------------------------------------
      void display()                  //display the String
```

```
      {
      cout << psc->str;                    //print string
      cout << " (addr=" << psc << ")";    //print address
      }
//-----------------------------------------------------------------
   String& operator = (String& S)          //assign the string
      {
      cout << "\nASSIGNMENT";
      if(psc->count==1)        //if we are its last user,
         delete psc;           //delete our strCount
      else                     // otherwise,
         (psc->count)--;       // decrement its count
      psc = S.psc;             //use argument's strCount
      (psc->count)++;          //increment count
      return *this;            //return this object
      }
   };

int main()
   {
   String s3 = "When the fox preaches, look to your geese.";
   cout << "\ns3="; s3.display();  //display s3

   String s1, s2;                  //define strings
   s1 = s2 = s3;                   //assign them
   cout << "\ns1="; s1.display();  //display it
   cout << "\ns2="; s2.display();  //display it
   cout << endl;                   //wait for keypress
   return 0;
   }
```

Now the declarator for the = operator is

```
String& operator = (String& S)   // return by reference
```

And, as in ASSIGN2, this function returns a pointer to **this**. Here's the output:

```
s3=When the fox preaches, look to your geese. (addr=0x8f640d3a)
ASSIGNMENT
ASSIGNMENT
s1=When the fox preaches, look to your geese. (addr=0x8f640d3a)
s2=When the fox preaches, look to your geese. (addr=0x8f640d3a)
```

The output shows that, following the assignment statement, all three **String** objects point to the same **strCount** object.

We should note that the **this** pointer is not available in static member functions, since they are not associated with a particular object.

Beware of Self-Assignment

A corollary of Murphy's Law states that whatever is possible, someone will eventually do. This is certainly true in programming, so you can expect that if you have overloaded the = operator, someone will use it to set an object equal to itself:

```
alpha = alpha;
```

Your overloaded assignment operator should be prepared to handle such self-assignment. Otherwise, bad things may happen. For example, in the `main()` part of the STRIMEM2 program, if you set a `String` object equal to itself, the program will crash (unless there are other `String` objects using the same `strCount` object). The problem is that the code for the assignment operator deletes the `strCount` object if it thinks the object that called it is the only object using the `strCount`. Self assignment will cause it to believe this, even though nothing should be deleted.

To fix this, you should check for self-assignment at the start of any overloaded assignment operator. You can do this in most cases by comparing the address of the object for which the operator was called with the address of its argument. If the addresses are the same, the objects are identical and you should return immediately. (You don't need to assign one to the other; they're already the same.) For example, in STRIMEM2, you can insert the lines

```
if(this == &S)
   return *this;
```

at the start of `operator=()`. That should solve the problem.

Dynamic Type Information

It's possible to find out information about an object's class and even change the class of an object at runtime. We'll look briefly at two mechanisms: the `dynamic_cast` operator, and the `typeid` operator. These are advanced capabilities, but you may find them useful someday.

These capabilities are usually used in situations where a variety of classes are descended (sometimes in complicated ways) from a base class. For dynamic casts to work, the base class must be polymorphic; that is, it must have at least one virtual function.

For both `dynamic_cast` and `typeid` to work, your compiler must enable Run-Time Type Information (RTTI). Borland C++ Builder has this capability enabled by default, but in Microsoft Visual C++ you'll need to turn it on overtly. See Appendix C, "Microsoft Visual C++," for details on how this is done. You'll also need to include the header file TYPEINFO.

Checking the Type of a Class with `dynamic_cast`

Suppose some other program sends your program an object (as the operating system might do with a call-back function). It's supposed to be a certain type of object, but you want to check it to be sure. How can you tell if an object is a certain type? The `dynamic_cast` operator provides a way, assuming that the classes whose objects you want to check are all descended from a common ancestor. The DYNCAST1 program shows how this looks.

```
//dyncast1.cpp
//dynamic cast used to test type of object
//RTTI must be enabled in compiler
#include <iostream>
#include <typeinfo>                //for dynamic_cast
```

```
using namespace std;
//////////////////////////////////////////////////////////////
class Base
    {
    virtual void vertFunc()      //needed for dynamic cast
        { }
    };
class Derv1 : public Base
    { };
class Derv2 : public Base
    { };
//////////////////////////////////////////////////////////////
//checks if pUnknown points to a Derv1
bool isDerv1(Base* pUnknown)  //unknown subclass of Base
    {
    Derv1* pDerv1;
    if( pDerv1 = dynamic_cast<Derv1*>(pUnknown) )
        return true;
    else
        return false;
    }
//-------------------------------------------------------------
int main()
    {
    Derv1* d1 = new Derv1;
    Derv2* d2 = new Derv2;

    if( isDerv1(d1) )
        cout << "d1 is a member of the Derv1 class\n";
    else
        cout << "d1 is not a member of the Derv1 class\n";

    if( isDerv1(d2) )
        cout << "d2 is a member of the Derv1 class\n";
    else
        cout << "d2 is not a member of the Derv1 class\n";
    return 0;
    }
```

Here we have a base class **Base** and two derived classes **Derv1** and **Derv2**. There's also a function, **isDerv1()**, which returns true if the pointer it received as an argument points to an object of class **Derv1**. This argument is of class **Base**, so the object passed can be either **Derv1** or **Derv2**. The **dynamic_cast** operator attempts to convert this unknown pointer **pUnknown** to type **Derv1**. If the result is not zero, then **pUnknown** did point to a **Derv1** object. If the result is zero, it pointed to something else.

Changing Pointer Types with `dynamic_cast`

The dynamic cast operator allows you to cast upward and downward in the inheritance tree. However, it allows such casting only in a limited ways. The DYNCAST2 program shows examples of such casts.

```cpp
//dyncast2.cpp
//tests dynamic casts
//RTTI must be enabled in compiler
#include <iostream>
#include <typeinfo>                //for dynamic_cast
using namespace std;
//////////////////////////////////////////////////////////////
class Base
   {
   protected:
      int ba;
   public:
      Base() : ba(0)
         {  }
      Base(int b) : ba(b)
         {  }
      virtual void vertFunc()   //needed for dynamic_cast
         {  }
      void show()
         { cout << "Base: ba=" << ba << endl; }
   };
//////////////////////////////////////////////////////////////
class Derv : public Base
   {
   private:
      int da;
   public:
      Derv(int b, int d) : da(d)
         { ba = b; }
      void show()
         { cout << "Derv: ba=" << ba << ", da=" << da << endl; }
   };
//////////////////////////////////////////////////////////////
int main()
   {
   Base* pBase = new Base(10);          //pointer to Base
   Derv* pDerv = new Derv(21, 22);      //pointer to Derv

   //derived-to-base: upcast -- points to Base subobject of Derv
   pBase = dynamic_cast<Base*>(pDerv);
   pBase->show();                       //"Base: ba=21"

   pBase = new Derv(31, 32);            //normal
   //base-to-derived: downcast -- (pBase must point to a Derv)
   pDerv = dynamic_cast<Derv*>(pBase);
   pDerv->show();                       //"Derv: ba=31, da=32"
   return 0;
   }
```

Here we have a base and a derived class. We've given each of these classes a data item to better demonstrate the effects of dynamic casts.

In an upcast, you attempt to change a derived-class object into a base-class object. What you get is the base part of the derived class object. In the example we make an object of class Derv. The base class part of this object holds member data ba, which has a value of 21, and the derived part holds data member da, which has the value 22. After the cast, pBase points to the base-class part of this Derv class object, so when called upon to display itself, it prints Base: ba=21. Upcasts are fine if all you want is the base part of the object.

In a downcast, we put a derived class object, which is pointed to by a base-class pointer, into a derived-class pointer.

The typeid Operator

Sometimes you want more information about an object than simply verifying that it's of a certain class. You can obtain information about the types of unknown objects, such as its class name, using the typeid operator. The TYPEID program demonstrates how it works.

```
// typeid.cpp
// demonstrates typeid() function
// RTTI must be enabled in compiler
#include <iostream>
#include <typeinfo>              //for typeid()
using namespace std;
/////////////////////////////////////////////////////////////////
class Base
    {
    virtual void virtFunc()     //needed for typeid
        { }
    };
class Derv1 : public Base
    { };
class Derv2 : public Base
    { };
/////////////////////////////////////////////////////////////////
void displayName(Base* pB)
    {
    cout << "pointer to an object of ";   //display name of class
    cout << typeid(*pB).name() << endl;   //pointed to by pB
    }
//-----------------------------------------------------------------
int main()
    {
    Base* pBase = new Derv1;
    displayName(pBase);    //"pointer to an object of class Derv1"

    pBase = new Derv2;
    displayName(pBase);    //"pointer to an object of class Derv2"
    return 0;
    }
```

In this example the `displayName()` function displays the name of the class of the object passed to it. To do this, it uses the `name` member of the `type_info` class, along with the `typeid` operator. In `main()` we pass this function two objects of class `Derv1` and `Derv2` respectively, and the program's output is:

```
pointer to an object of class Derv1
pointer to an object of class Derv2
```

Besides its name, other information about a class is available using `typeid`. For example, you can check for equality of classes using an overloaded == operator. We'll show an example of this in the EMPL_IO program in Chapter 12, "Streams and Files." Although the examples in this section have used pointers, `dynamic_cast` and `typeid` work equally well with references.

Summary

Virtual functions provide a way for a program to decide, when it is running, what function to call. Ordinarily such decisions are made at compile time. Virtual functions make possible greater flexibility in performing the same kind of action on different kinds of objects. In particular, they allow the use of functions called from an array of type pointer-to-base that actually holds pointers (or references) to a variety of derived types. This is an example of *polymorphism*. Typically a function is declared virtual in the base class, and other functions with the same name are declared in derived classes.

The use of one or more pure virtual functions in a class makes the class *abstract*, which means that no objects can be instantiated from it.

A `friend` function can access a class's private data, even though it is not a member function of the class. This is useful when one function must have access to two or more unrelated classes and when an overloaded operator must use, on its left side, a value of a class other than the one of which it is a member. `friend`s are also used to facilitate functional notation.

A `static` function is one that operates on the class in general, rather than on objects of the class. In particular it can operate on static variables. It can be called with the class name and scope-resolution operator.

The assignment operator = can be overloaded. This is necessary when it must do more than merely copy one object's contents into another. The copy constructor, which creates copies during initialization, and also when arguments are passed and returned by value, can also be overloaded. This is necessary when the copy constructor must do more than simply copy an object.

The `this` pointer is predefined in member functions to point to the object of which the function is a member. The `this` pointer is useful in returning the object of which the function is a member.

The `dynamic_cast` operator plays several roles. It can be used to determine what type of object a pointer points to, and, in certain situations, it can change the type of a pointer. The `typeid` operator can discover certain information about an object's class, such as its name.

Questions

Answers to questions can be found in Appendix G, "Answers to Questions and Exercises."

1. Virtual functions allow you to

    a. create an array of type pointer-to-base class that can hold pointers to derived classes.

    b. create functions that can never be accessed.

    c. group objects of different classes so they can all be accessed by the same function code.

    d. use the same function call to execute member functions of objects from different classes.

2. True or false: A pointer to a base class can point to objects of a derived class.

3. If there is a pointer p to objects of a base class, and it contains the address of an object of a derived class, and both classes contain a nonvirtual member function, `ding()`, then the statement `p->ding();` will cause the version of `ding()` in the _____ class to be executed.

4. Write a declarator for a virtual function called `dang()` that returns type `void` and takes one argument of type `int`.

5. Deciding—after a program starts to execute—what function will be executed by a particular function call statement is called _____.

6. If there is a pointer, `p`, to objects of a base class, and it contains the address of an object of a derived class, and both classes contain a virtual member function, `ding()`, then the statement `p->ding();` will cause the version of `ding()` in the _____ class to be executed.

7. Write the declaration for a pure virtual function called `aragorn` that returns no value and takes no arguments.

8. A pure virtual function is a virtual function that

    a. causes its class to be abstract.

    b. returns nothing.

    c. is used in a base class.

    d. takes no arguments.

9. Write the definition of an array called `parr` of 10 pointers to objects of class `dong`.

10. An abstract class is useful when

    a. no classes should be derived from it.

    b. there are multiple paths from one derived class to another.

    c. no objects should be instantiated from its.

    d. you want to defer the declaration of the class.

11. True or false: A `friend` function can access a class's private data without being a member of the class.

12. A `friend` function can be used to

    a. mediate arguments between classes.

    b. allow access to classes whose source code is unavailable.

    c. allow access to an unrelated class.

    d. increase the versatility of an overloaded operator.

13. Write the declaration for a friend function called `harry()` that returns type `void` and takes one argument of class `george`.

14. The keyword `friend` appears in

    a. the class allowing access to another class.

    b. the class desiring access to another class.

    c. the private section of a class.

    d. the public section of a class.

15. Write a declaration that, in the class in which it appears, will make every member of the class `harry` a `friend` function.

16. A static function

    a. should be called when an object is destroyed.

    b. is closely connected to an individual object of a class.

    c. can be called using the class name and function name.

    d. is used when a dummy object must be created.

17. Explain what the default assignment operator = does when applied to objects.

18. Write a declaration for an overloaded assignment operator in class `zeta`.

19. An assignment operator might be overloaded to

    a. help keep track of the number of identical objects.

    b. assign a separate ID number to each object.

    c. ensure that all member data is copied exactly.

    d. signal when assignment takes place.

20. True or false: The user must always define the operation of the copy constructor.

21. The operation of the assignment operator and that of the copy constructor are

    a. similar, except that the copy constructor creates a new object.

    b. similar, except that the assignment operator copies member data.

    c. different, except that they both create a new object.

    d. different, except that they both copy member data.

22. Write the declaration of a copy constructor for a class called Bertha.

23. True or false: A copy constructor could be defined to copy only part of an object's data.

24. The lifetime of a variable that is defined as

    a. automatic if a member function coincides with the lifetime of the function.

    b. external coincides with the lifetime of a class.

    c. nonstatic member data of an object coincides with the lifetime of the object.

    d. static in a member function coincides with the lifetime of the function.

25. True or false: There is no problem with returning the value of a variable defined as automatic within a member function so long as it is returned by value.

26. Explain the difference in operation between these two statements.
```
person p1(p0);
person p1 = p0;
```

27. A copy constructor is invoked when

   a. a function returns by value.

   b. an argument is passed by value.

   c. a function returns by reference.

   d. an argument is passed by reference.

28. What does the **this** pointer point to?

29. If, within a class, **da** is a member variable, will the statement **this.da=37;** assign 37 to **da**?

30. Write a statement that a member function can use to return the entire object of which it is a member, without creating any temporary objects.

Exercises

Answers to starred exercises can be found in Appendix G.

*1. Imagine the same publishing company described in Exercise 1 in Chapter 9 that markets both book and audiocassette versions of its works. As in that exercise, create a class called **publication** that stores the title (a string) and price (type **float**) of a publication. From this class derive two classes: **book**, which adds a page count (type **int**); and **tape**, which adds a playing time in minutes (type **float**). Each of the three classes should have a **getdata()** function to get its data from the user at the keyboard, and a **putdata()** function to display the data.

   Write a **main()** program that creates an array of pointers to **publication**. This is similar to the VIRTPERS example in this chapter. In a loop, ask the user for data about a particular book or tape, and use **new** to create an object of type **book** or **tape** to hold the data. Put the pointer to the object in the array. When the user has finished entering the data for all books and tapes, display the resulting data for all the books and tapes entered, using a **for** loop and a single statement such as

   ```
   pubarr[j]->putdata();
   ```

   to display the data from each object in the array.

*2. In the **Distance** class, as shown in the FRENGL and FRISQ examples in this chapter, create an overloaded ***** operator so that two distances can be multiplied together. Make it a **friend** function so that you can use such expressions as

   ```
   Wdist1 = 7.5 * dist2;
   ```

You'll need a one-argument constructor to convert floating-point values into `Distance` values. Write a `main()` program to test this operator in several ways.

*3. As we saw earlier, it's possible to make a class that acts like an array. The CLARRAY example shown here is a complete program that shows one way to create your own array class:

```cpp
// clarray.cpp
// creates array class
#include <iostream>
using namespace std;
///////////////////////////////////////////////////////////////
class Array                           //models a normal C++ array
   {
   private:
      int* ptr;                       //pointer to Array contents
      int size;                       //size of Array
   public:
      Array(int s)                    //one-argument constructor
         {
         size = s;                    //argument is size of Array
         ptr = new int[s];            //make space for Array
         }
      ~Array()                        //destructor
         { delete[] ptr; }
      int& operator [] (int j)   //overloaded subscript operator
         { return *(ptr+j); }
   };
///////////////////////////////////////////////////////////////
int main()
   {
   const int ASIZE = 10;              //size of array
   Array arr(ASIZE);                  //make an array

   for(int j=0; j<ASIZE; j++)         //fill it with squares
      arr[j] = j*j;

   for(j=0; j<ASIZE; j++)             //display its contents
      cout << arr[j] << ' ';
   cout << endl;
   return 0;
   }
```

The output of this program is

```
0  1  4  9  16  25  36  49  64  81
```

Starting with CLARRAY, add an overloaded assignment operator and an overloaded copy constructor to the **Array** class. Then add statements such as

```
Array arr2(arr1);
```

and

```
arr3 = arr1;
```

to the **main()** program to test whether these overloaded operators work. The copy constructor should create an entirely new **Array** object with its own memory for storing array elements. Both the copy constructor and the assignment operator should copy the contents of the old **Array** object to the new one. What happens if you assign an **Array** of one size to an **Array** of a different size?

4. Start with the program of Exercise 1 in this chapter, and add a member function of type **bool** called **isOversize()** to the **book** and **tape** classes. Let's say that a book with more than 800 pages, or a tape with a playing time longer than 90 minutes (which would require two cassettes), is considered oversize. You can access these function from **main()** and display the string "Oversize" for oversize books and tapes when you display their other data. If **book** and **tape** objects are to be accessed using pointers to them that are stored in an array of type **publication**, what do you need to add to the **publication** base class? Can you instantiate members of this base class?

5. Start with the program of Exercise 8 in Chapter 8, which overloaded five arithmetic operators for money strings. Add the two operators that couldn't be overloaded in that exercise. These operations,

```
long double * bMoney   // number times money
long double / bMoney   // number divided by money
```

require **friend** functions, since an object appears on the right side of the operator while a numerical constant appears on the left. Make sure that the **main()** program allows the user to enter two money strings and a floating-point value, and then carries out all seven arithmetic operations on appropriate pairs of these values.

6. As in the previous exercise, start with the program of Exercise 8 in Chapter 9. This time, add a function that rounds a **bMoney** value to the nearest dollar. It should be used like this:

```
mo2 = round(mo1);
```

As you know, amounts of $0.49 and less are rounded down, while those $0.50 and above are rounded up. A library function called `modfl()` is useful here. It separates a type `long double` variable into a fractional part and an integer part. If the fractional part is less than 0.50, return the integer part as is; otherwise add 1.0. In `main()`, test the function by sending it a sequence of `bMoney` amounts that go from less than 49 cents to more than 50 cents.

7. Remember the PARSE program from Chapter 12? It would be nice to improve this program so it could evaluate expressions with real numbers, say type `float`, instead of single-digit numbers. For example,

```
3.14159 / 2.0 + 75.25 * 3.333 + 6.02
```

As a first step toward this goal, you need to develop a stack that can hold both operators (type `char`) and numbers (type `float`). But how can you store two different types on a stack, which is basically an array? After all, type `char` and type `float` aren't even the same size. Could you store pointers to different types? They're the same size, but the compiler still won't allow you to store type `char*` and type `float*` in the same array. The only way two different types of pointers can be stored in the same array is if they are derived from the same base class. So we can encapsulate a `char` in one class and a `float` in another, and arrange for both classes to be derived from a base class. Then we can store both kinds of pointers in an array of pointers to the base class. The base class doesn't need to have any data of its own; it can be an abstract class from which no objects will be instantiated.

Constructors can store the values into the derived classes in the usual way, but you'll need to use pure virtual functions to get the values back out again. Here's a possible scenario:

```
class Token                        // abstract base class
   {
   public:
      virtual float getNumber()=0;    // pure virtual functions
      virtual char getOperator()=0;
   };
class Operator : public Token
   {
   private:
      char oper;                   // operators +, -, *, /
   public:
      Operator(char);             // constructor sets value
      char getOperator();         // gets value
      float getNumber();          // dummy function
   };
class Number : public Token
   {
```

```
    private:
        float fnum;              // the number
    public:
        Number(float);           // constructor sets value
        float getNumber();       // gets value
        char getOperator();      // dummy function
    };

Token* atoken[100];              // holds types Operator* and Number*
```

Base-class virtual functions need to be instantiated in all derived classes, or the classes themselves become abstract. Thus the `Operand` class needs a `getNumber()` function, even though it doesn't store a number, and the `Number` class needs `getOperand()`, even though it doesn't store an operand.

Expand this framework into a working program by adding a `Stack` class that holds `Token` objects, and a `main()` that pushes and pops various operators (such as + and *) and floating-point numbers (1.123) on and off the stack.

8. Let's put a little twist into the HORSE example of Chapter 10 by making a class of extra-competitive horses. We'll assume that any horse that's ahead by the halfway point in the race starts to feel its oats and becomes almost unbeatable. From the horse class, derive a class called `comhorse` (for competitive horse). Overload the `horse_tick()` function in this class so that each horse can check if it's the front-runner and if there's another horse close behind it (say 0.1 furlong). If there is, it should speed up a bit. Perhaps not enough to win every time, but enough to give it a decided advantage.

How does each horse know where the other horses are? It must access the memory that holds them, which in the HORSE program is `hArray`. Be careful, however. You want to create comhorses, not horses. So the `comhorse` class will need to overload `hArray`. You may need to derive a new track class, `comtrack`, to create the comhorses.

You can continuously check if your horse is ahead of the (otherwise) leading horse, and if it's by a small margin, accelerate your horse a bit.

9. Exercise 4 in Chapter 10 involved adding an overloaded destructor to the `linklist` class. Suppose we fill an object of such a destructor-enhanced class with data, and then assign the entire class with a statement such as

```
list2 = list1;
```

using the default assignment operator. Now, suppose we later delete the list1 object. Can we still use list2 to access the same data? No, because when list1 was deleted, its destructor deleted all its links. The only data actually contained in a linklist object is a pointer to the first link. Once the links are gone, the pointer in list2 becomes invalid, and attempts to access the list lead to meaningless values or a program crash.

One way to fix this is to overload the assignment operator so that it copies all the data links, as well as the linklist object itself. You'll need to follow along the chain, copying each link in turn. As we noted earlier, you should overload the copy constructor as well. To make it possible to delete linklist objects in main(), you may want to create them using pointers and new. That makes it easier to test the new routines. Don't worry if the copy process reverses the order of the data.

Notice that copying all the data is not very efficient in terms of memory usage. Contrast this approach with that used in the STRIMEM example in Chapter 10, which used only one set of data for all objects, and kept track of how many objects pointed to this data.

10. Carry out the modification, discussed in Exercise 7, to the PARSE program of Chapter 10. That is, make it possible to parse expressions containing floating-point numbers. Combine the classes from Exercise 7 with the algorithms from PARSE. You'll need to operate on pointers to tokens instead of characters. This involves statements of the kind

```
Number* ptrN = new Number(ans);
s.push(ptrN);
```

and

```
Operator* ptrO = new Operator(ch);
s.push(ptrO);
```

CHAPTER 12

STREAMS AND FILES

You will learn about the following in this chapter:

- The stream class hierarchy
- IOS and error-handling
- Objects and disk files
- Overloading << and >>
- Command-line arguments
- Printer output

This chapter focuses on the C++ stream classes. We'll start off with a look at the hierarchy in which these classes are arranged, and we'll summarize their important features. The largest part of this chapter is devoted to showing how to perform file-related activities using C++ streams. We'll show how to read and write data to files in a variety of ways, how to handle errors, and how files and OOP are related. Later in the chapter we'll examine several other features of C++ that are related to files, including in-memory text formatting, command-line arguments, overloading the insertion and extraction operators, and sending data to the printer.

Stream Classes

A *stream* is a general name given to a flow of data. In C++ a stream is represented by an object of a particular class. So far we've used the `cin` and `cout` stream objects. Different streams are used to represent different kinds of data flow. For example, the `ifstream` class represents data flow from input disk files.

Advantages of Streams

C programmers may wonder what advantages there are to using the stream classes for I/O, instead of traditional C functions such as `printf()` and `scanf()`, and—for files—`fprintf()`, `fscanf()`, and so on.

One reason is simplicity. If you've ever used a `%d` formatting character when you should have used a `%f` in `printf()`, you'll appreciate this. There are no such formatting characters in streams, since each object already knows how to display itself. This removes a major source of errors.

Another reason is that you can overload existing operators and functions, such as the insertion (<<) and extraction (>>) operators, to work with classes that you create. This makes your own classes work in the same way as the built-in types, which again makes programming easier and more error free (not to mention more aesthetically satisfying).

You may wonder if stream I/O is important if you plan to program in an environment with a Graphics User Interface such as Windows, where direct text output to the screen is not used. Do you still need to know about C++ streams? Yes, because they are the best way to write data to files, and also to format data in memory for later use in text input/output windows and other GUI elements.

The Stream Class Hierarchy

The stream classes are arranged in a rather complex hierarchy. Figure 12.1 shows the arrangement of the most important of these classes.

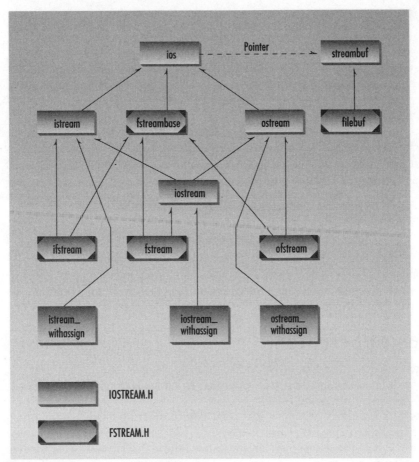

Figure 12.1   Stream class hierarchy.

We've already made extensive use of some stream classes. The extraction operator >> is a member of the `istream` class, and the insertion operator << is a member of the `ostream` class. Both of these classes are derived from the `ios` class. The `cout` object, representing the standard output stream, which is usually directed to the video display, is a predefined object of the `ostream_withassign` class, which is derived from the `ostream` class. Similarly `cin` is an object of the `istream_withassign` class, which is derived from `istream`.

The classes used for input and output to the video display and keyboard are declared in the header file IOSTREAM, which we routinely included in our examples in previous chapters. The classes used specifically for disk file I/O are declared in the file FSTREAM. Figure 12.1 shows which classes are in which two header files. (Also, some manipulators are declared in IOMANIP, and in-memory classes are declared in STRSTREAM.) You may find it educational to print out these header files and trace the relationships among the various classes. They're in your compiler's INCLUDE subdirectory. Many questions about streams can be answered by studying their class and constant declarations.

As you can see from Figure 12.1, the `ios` class is the base class for the hierarchy. It contains many constants and member functions common to input and output operations of all kinds. Some of these, such as the `showpoint` and `fixed` formatting flags, we've seen already. The `ios` class also contains a pointer to the `streambuf` class, which contains the actual memory buffer into which data is read or written, and the low-level routines for handling this data. Ordinarily you don't need to worry about the `streambuf` class, which is referenced automatically by other classes.

The `istream` and `ostream` classes are derived from `ios` and are dedicated to input and output, respectively. The `istream` class contains such functions as `get()`, `getline()`, `read()`, and the overloaded extraction (>>) operators, while `ostream` contains `put()` and `write()`, and the overloaded insertion (<<)operators.

The `iostream` class is derived from both `istream` and `ostream` by multiple inheritance. Classes derived from it can be used with devices, such as disk files, that may be opened for both input and output at the same time. Three classes—`istream_withassign`, `ostream_withassign`, and `iostream_withassign`—are inherited from `istream`, `ostream`, and `iostream`, respectively. They add assignment operators to these classes.

The following summary of stream classes may seem rather abstract. You may want to skim it now, and return to it later when you need to know how to perform a particular stream-related activity.

The `ios` Class

The `ios` class is the granddaddy of all the stream classes, and contains the majority of the features you need to operate C++ streams. The three most important features are the formatting flags, the error-status flags, and the file operation mode. We'll look at formatting flags and error-status flags next. We'll save the file operations mode for later, when we talk about disk files.

Formatting Flags

Formatting flags are a set of **enum** definitions in **ios**. They act as on/off switches that specify choices for various aspects of input and output format and operation. We won't provide a detailed discussion of each flag, since we've already seen some of them in use, and others are more or less self-explanatory. Some we'll discuss later in this chapter. Table 12.1 is a complete list of the formatting flags.

Table 12.1 **ios** Formatting Flags

Flag	Meaning
skipws	Skip (ignore) whitespace on input
left	Left adjust output [12.34]
right	Right adjust output [12.34]
internal	Use padding between sign or base indicator and number [+ 12.34]
dec	Convert to decimal
oct	Convert to octal
hex	Convert to hexadecimal
boolalpha	Convert bool to "true" or "false" strings
showbase	Use base indicator on output (0 for octal, 0x for hex)
showpoint	Show decimal point on output
uppercase	Use uppercase X, E, and hex output letters (**ABCDEF**)—the default is lowercase
showpos	Display + before positive integers
scientific	Use exponential format on floating-point output [9.1234E2]
fixed	Use fixed format on floating-point output [912.34]
unitbuf	Flush all streams after insertion
stdio	Flush **stdout**, **stderror** after insertion

There are several ways to set the formatting flags, and different ones can be set in different ways. Since they are members of the **ios** class, you must usually precede them with the name **ios** and the scope-resolution operator (for example, **ios::skipws**). All the flags can be set using the **setf()** and **unsetf() ios** member functions. Look at the following example:

```
cout.setf(ios::left);   // left justify output text
cout >> "This text is left-justified";
cout.unsetf(ios::left); // return to default (right justified)
```

Many formatting flags can be set using manipulators, so let's look at them now.

Manipulators

Manipulators are formatting instructions inserted directly into a stream. We've seen examples before, such as the manipulator `endl`, which sends a newline to the stream and flushes it:

```
cout << "To each his own." << endl;
```

We've also used the `setiosflags()` manipulator (see the SALEMON program in Chapter 7, "Arrays and Strings"):

```
cout << setiosflags(ios::fixed)      // use fixed decimal point
     << setiosflags(ios::showpoint)  // always show decimal point
     << var;
```

As these examples demonstrate, manipulators come in two flavors: those that take an argument and those that don't. Table 12.2 summarizes the important no-argument manipulators.

Table 12.2 No-Argument `ios` Manipulators

Manipulator	Purpose
ws	Turn on whitespace skipping on input
dec	Convert to decimal
oct	Convert to octal
hex	Convert to hexadecimal
endl	Insert newline and flush the output stream
ends	Insert null character to terminate an output string
flush	Flush the output stream
lock	Lock file handle
unlock	Unlock file handle

You insert these manipulators directly into the stream. For example, to output `var` in hexadecimal format, you can say

```
cout << hex << var;
```

Note that manipulators affect only the data that follows them in the stream, not the data that precedes them. Table 12.3 summarizes the important manipulators that take arguments. You need the IOMANIP header file for these functions.

Table 12.3 ios Manipulators with Arguments

Manipulator	Argument	Purpose
setw()	field width (int)	Set field width for output
setfill()	fill character (int)	Set fill character for output (default is a space)
setprecision()	precision (int)	Set precision (number of digits displayed)
setiosflags()	formatting flags (long)	Set specified flags
resetiosflags()	formatting flags (long)	Clear specified flags

Functions

The **ios** class contains a number of functions that you can use to set the formatting flags and perform other tasks. Table 12.4 shows most of these functions, except those that deal with errors, which we'll examine separately.

Table 12.4 ios Functions

Function	Purpose
ch = fill();	Return the fill character (fills unused part of field; default is space)
fill(ch);	Set the fill character
p = precision();	Get the precision (number of digits displayed for floating-point)
precision(p);	Set the precision
w = width();	Get the current field width (in characters)
width(w);	Set the current field width
setf(flags);	Set specified formatting flags (for example, ios::left)
unsetf(flags);	Unset specified formatting flags
setf(flags, field);	First clear field, then set flags

These functions are called for specific stream objects using the normal dot operator. For example, to set the field width to 12, you can say

```
cout.width(14);
```

The following statement sets the fill character to an asterisk (as for check printing):

```
cout.fill('*');
```

You can use several functions to manipulate the **ios** formatting flags directly. For example, to set left justification, use

```
cout.setf(ios::left);
```

To restore right justification, use

```
cout.unsetf(ios::left);
```

A two-argument version of **setf()** uses the second argument to reset all the flags of a particular type or *field*. Then the flag specified in the first argument is set. This makes it easier to reset the relevant flags before setting a new one. Table 12.5 shows the arrangement.
For example,

```
cout.setf(ios::left, ios::adjustfield);
```

clears all the flags dealing with text justification and then sets the **left** flag for left-justified output.

Table 12.5   Two-Argument Version of **setf()**

First Argument: Flags to Set	Second Argument: Field to Clear
dec, oct, hex	basefield
left, right, internal	adjustfield
scientific, fixed	floatfield

By using the techniques shown here with the formatting flags, you can usually figure out a way to format I/O not only for the keyboard and display, but, as we'll see later in this chapter, for files as well.

The **istream** Class

The **istream** class, which is derived from **ios**, performs input-specific activities, or extraction. It's easy to confuse extraction and the related output activity, insertion. Figure 12.2 emphasizes the difference.
Table 12.6 lists the functions you'll most commonly use from the **istream** class.

Table 12.6   **istream** Functions

Function	Purpose
>>	Formatted > member function>>>>>extraction for all basic (and overloaded) types.
get(ch);	Extract one character into ch.
get(str)	Extract characters into array str, until '0'.

continued on next page

continued from previous page

Function	Purpose
get(str, MAX)	Extract up to MAX characters into array.
get(str, DELIM)	Extract characters into array str until specified delimiter (typically '\n'). Leave delimiting char in stream.
get(str, MAX, DELIM)	Extract characters into array str until MAX characters or the DELIM character. Leave delimiting char in stream.
getline(str, MAX, DELIM)	Extract characters into array str, until MAX characters or the DELIM character. Extract delimiting character.
putback(ch)	Insert last character read back into input stream.
ignore(MAX, DELIM)	Extract and discard up to MAX characters until (and including) the specified delimiter (typically '\n').
peek(ch)	Read one character, leave it in stream.
count = gcount()	Return number of characters read by a (immediately preceding) call to get(), getline(), or read().
read(str, MAX)	For files—extract up to MAX characters into str, until EOF.
seekg()	Set distance (in bytes) of file pointer from start of file.
seekg(pos, seek_dir)	Set distance (in bytes) of file pointer from specified place in file. seek_dir can be ios::beg, ios::cur, ios::end.
pos = tellg(pos)	Return position (in bytes) of file pointer from start of file.

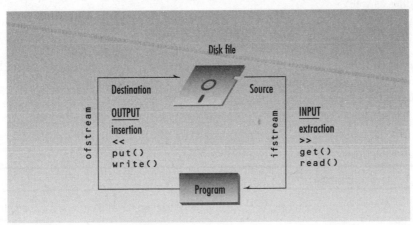

Figure 12.2   File input and output.

You've seen some of these functions, such as get(), before. Most of them operate on the cin object, which usually represents the data flow from the keyboard. However, the last four deal specifically with disk files.

The ostream Class

The ostream class handles output or insertion activities. Table 12.7 shows the most commonly used member functions of this class. The last four functions in this table deal specifically with disk files.

Table 12.7   ostream Functions

Function	Purpose
<<	Formatted insertion for all basic (and overloaded) types.
put(ch)	Insert character ch into stream.
flush()	Flush buffer contents and insert newline.
write(str, SIZE)	Insert SIZE characters from array str into file
seekp(position)	Set distance in bytes of file pointer from start of file.
seekp(position, seek_dir)	Set distance in bytes of file pointer from specified place in file. seek_dir can be ios::beg, ios::cur, or ios::end.
poo = tellp()	Return position of file pointer, in bytes.

The iostream and the _withassign Classes

The iostream class, which is derived from both istream and ostream, acts only as a base class from which other classes, specifically iostream_withassign, can be derived. It has no functions of its own (except constructors and destructors). Classes derived from iostream can perform both input and output.

There are three _withassign classes:

- istream_withassign, derived from istream
- ostream_withassign, derived from ostream
- iostream_withassign, derived from iostream

These _withassign classes are much like those they're derived from except that they include overloaded assignment operators so their objects can be copied.

Why do we need separate copyable and uncopyable stream classes? In general, it's not a good idea to copy stream class objects. The reason is that each such object is associated with a particular `streambuf` object, which includes an area in memory to hold the object's actual data. If you copy the stream object, it causes confusion if you also copy the `streambuf` object. However, in a few cases it's important to be able to copy a stream.

Accordingly, the `istream`, `ostream`, and `iostream` classes are made uncopyable (by making their overloaded copy constructors and assignment operators private), while the `_withassign` classes derived from them can be copied.

Predefined Stream Objects

We've already made extensive use of two predefined stream objects that are derived from the `_withassign` classes: `cin` and `cout`. These are normally connected to the keyboard and display, respectively. The two other predefined objects are `cerr` and `clog`.

- `cin`, an object of `istream_withassign`, normally used for keyboard input
- `cout`, an object of `ostream_withassign`, normally used for screen display
- `cerr`, an object of `ostream_withassign`, for error messages
- `clog`, an object of `ostream_withassign`, for log messages

The `cerr` object is often used for error messages and program diagnostics. Output sent to `cerr` is displayed immediately, rather than being buffered, as `cout` is. Also, it cannot be redirected (more on this later). For these reasons you have a better chance of seeing a final output message from `cerr` if your program dies prematurely. Another object, `clog`, is similar to `cerr` in that it is not redirected, but its output is buffered, while `cerr`'s output is not.

Stream Errors

So far in this book we've mostly used a rather straightforward approach to input and output, using statements of the form

```
cout << "Good morning";
```

and

```
cin >> var;
```

However, as you may have discovered, this approach assumes that nothing will go wrong during the I/O process. This isn't always the case, especially on input. What happens if a user enters the string "nine" instead of the integer 9, or pushes the [Enter] key without entering anything? Or what happens if there's a hardware failure? In this section we'll explore such problems. Many of the techniques we'll see here are applicable to file I/O as well.

Error-Status Bits

The stream error-status flags are an `ios` enum member that reports errors that occurred in an input or output operation. They're summarized in Table 12.8. Figure 12.3 shows how these flags look. Various `ios` functions can be used to read (and even set) these error flags, as shown in Table 12.9.

Table 12.8 Error-Status Flags

Name	Meaning
goodbit	No errors (no flags set, value = 0)
eofbit	Reached end of file
failbit	Operation failed (user error, premature EOF)
badbit	Invalid operation (no associated streambuf)
hardfail	Unrecoverable error

Table 12.9 Functions for Error Flags

Function	Purpose
int = eof();	Returns true if EOF flag set
int = fail();	Returns true if failbit or badbit or hardfail flag set
int = bad();	Returns true if badbit or hardfail flag set
int = good();	Returns true if everything OK; no flags set
clear(int=0);	With no argument, clears all error bits; otherwise sets specified flags, as in clear(ios::failbit)

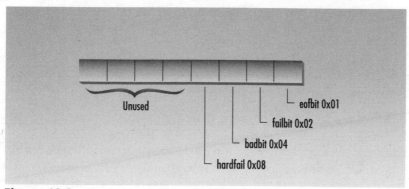

Figure 12.3 Stream status flags.

Inputting Numbers

Let's see how to handle errors when inputting numbers. This approach applies to both numbers read from the keyboard and from disk, as we'll see later. The idea is to check the value of **goodbit**, signal an error if it's not true, and give the user another chance to enter the correct input.

```
    while(true)                              // cycle until input OK
       {
       cout << "\nEnter an integer: ";
       cin >> i;
       if( cin.good() )                      // if no errors
          {
          cin.ignore(10, '\n');              // remove newline
          break;                             // exit loop
          }
       cin.clear();                          // clear the error bits
       cout << "Incorrect input";
       cin.ignore(10, '\n');                 // remove newline
       }
    cout << "integer is " << i;              // error-free integer
```

The most common error this scheme detects when reading keyboard input is the user typing nondigits (like "nine" instead of 9). This causes the **failbit** to be set. However, it also detects system-related failures that are more common with disk files.

Floating-point numbers (**float**, **double**, and **long double**) can be analyzed for errors in the same way as integers.

Too Many Characters

Too many characters sounds like a difficulty experienced by movie directors, but extra characters can also present a problem when reading from input streams. This is especially true when there are errors. Typically, extra characters are left in the input stream after the input is supposedly completed. They are then passed along to the next input operation, even though they are not intended for it. Often it's a new line that remains behind, but sometimes other characters are left over as well. To get rid of these extraneous characters the **ignore(MAX, DELIM)** member function of **istream** is used. It reads and throws away up to **MAX** characters, including the specified delimiter character. In our example, the line

```
cin.ignore(10, '\n');
```

causes **cin** to read up to 10 characters, including the '\n', and remove them from the input.

No-Input Input

Whitespace characters, such as tab space and '\n', are normally ignored (skipped) when inputting numbers. This can have some undesirable side effects. For example, users, prompted to enter a number, may simply press the (Enter) key without typing any digits. (Perhaps they think that this will enter 0, or perhaps they are simply confused.) In the code shown above, as well as the simple statement

```
cin >> i;
```

pressing (Enter) causes the cursor to drop down to the next line, while the stream continues to wait for the number. What's wrong with the cursor dropping to the next line? First, inexperienced users, seeing no acknowledgment when they press (Enter), may assume the computer is broken. Second, pressing (Enter) repeatedly normally causes the cursor to drop lower and lower until the entire screen begins to scroll upward. This is all right in teletype-style interaction, where the program and the user simply type at each other. However, in text-based graphics programs (such as the ELEV program in Chapter 13, "Multifile Programs"), scrolling the screen disarranges and eventually obliterates the display.

Thus it's important to be able to tell the input stream *not* to ignore whitespace. This is handled by clearing the **skipws** flag:

```
cout << "\nEnter an integer: ";
cin.unsetf(ios::skipws);          // don't ignore whitespace
cin >> i;
if( cin.good() )
   {
   // no error
   }
// error
```

Now if the user types ⌷Enter⌷ without any digits, the **failbit** will be set and an error generated. The program can then tell the user what to do, or reposition the cursor so the screen does not scroll.

Inputting Strings and Characters

The user can't really make any serious errors inputting strings and characters, since all input, even numbers, can be interpreted as a string. However, if coming from a disk file, characters and strings should still be checked for errors, in case an EOF or something worse is encountered. Unlike the situation with numbers, you often do want to ignore whitespace when inputting strings and characters.

Error-Free Distances

Let's look at a program in which user input to the English **Distance** class is checked for errors. This program simply accepts **Distance** values in feet and inches from the user and displays them. However, if the user commits an entry error, the program rejects the input with an appropriate explanation to the user, and prompts for new input.

The program is very simple except that the member function **getdist()** has been expanded to handle errors. Parts of this new code follow the approach of the fragment shown above. However, we've also added some statements to ensure that the user does not enter a floating-point number for feet. This is important because, while the feet value is an integer, the inches value is floating-point, and the user could easily become confused.

Ordinarily, if it's expecting an integer, the extraction operator simply terminates when it sees a decimal point, without signaling an error. We want to know about such an error, so we read the feet value as a string instead of an **int**. We then examine the string with a homemade function **isFeet()**, which returns true if the string proves to be a correct value for feet. To pass the feet test, it must contain only digits, and they must evaluate to a number between –999 and 999. (We assume the Distance class will never be used for measuring larger feet values.) If the string passes the feet test, we convert it to an actual **int** with the library function **atoi()**.

The inches value is a floating-point number. We want to check its range, which should be 0 or greater but less than 12.0. We also check it for **ios** error flags. Most commonly, the **failbit** will be set because the user typed non digits instead of a number. Here's the listing for ENGLERR:

```cpp
// englerr.cpp
// input checking with English Distance class
#include <iostream>
#include <string>
#include <cstdlib>                     //for atoi(), atof()
using namespace std;
int isFeet(string);                    //declaration
//////////////////////////////////////////////////////////////////
class Distance                         //English Distance class
   {
   private:
      int feet;
      float inches;
   public:
      Distance()                       //constructor (no args)
         { feet = 0; inches = 0.0; }
      Distance(int ft, float in)  //constructor (two args)
         { feet = ft; inches = in; }
      void showdist()                  //display distance
         { cout << feet << "\'-" << inches << '\"'; }
      void getdist();                  //get length from user
   };
//----------------------------------------------------------------
void Distance::getdist()               //get length from user
   {
   string instr;                       //for input string

   while(true)                         //cycle until feet are right
      {
      cout << "\n\nEnter feet: ";
      cin.unsetf(ios::skipws);         //do not skip white space
      cin >> instr;                    //get feet as a string
      if( isFeet(instr) )              //is it a correct feet value?
         {                             //yes
         cin.ignore(10, '\n');         //eat chars, including newline
         feet = atoi( instr.c_str() ); //convert to integer
         break;                        //break out of 'while'
         }                             //no, not an integer
      cin.ignore(10, '\n');            //eat chars, including newline
      cout << "Feet must be an integer less than 1000\n";
      }  //end while feet

   while(true)                         //cycle until inches are right
      {
      cout << "Enter inches: ";
      cin.unsetf(ios::skipws);         //do not skip white space
      cin >> inches;                   //get inches (type float)
      if(inches>=12.0 || inches<0.0)
```

```
            {
            cout << "Inches must be between 0.0 and 11.99\n";
            cin.clear(ios::failbit); //"artificially" set fail bit
            }
        if( cin.good() )              //check for cin failure
            {                         //(most commonly a non-digit)
            cin.ignore(10, '\n');     //eat the newline
            break;                    //input is OK, exit 'while'
            }
        cin.clear();                  //error; clear the error state
        cin.ignore(10, '\n');         //eat chars, including newline
        cout << "Incorrect inches input\n";  //start again
        }  //end while inches
    }
//-------------------------------------------------------------
int isFeet(string str)               //return true if the string
    {                                //   is a correct feet value
    int slen = str.size();           //get length
    if(slen==0 || slen > 5)          //if no input, or too long
        return 0;                    //not an int
    for(int j=0; j<slen; j++)        //check each character
                                     //if not digit or minus
        if( (str[j] < '0' || str[j] > '9') && str[j] != '-' )
            return 0;                //string is not correct feet
    double n = atof( str.c_str() );  //convert to double
    if( n<-999.0 || n>999.0 )        //is it out of range?
        return 0;                    //if so, not correct feet
    return 1;                        //it is correct feet
    }
////////////////////////////////////////////////////////////////
int main()
    {
    Distance d;                      //make a Distance object
    char ans;
    do
        {
        d.getdist();                 //get its value from user
        cout << "\nDistance = ";
        d.showdist();                //display it
        cout << "\nDo another (y/n)? ";
        cin >> ans;
        cin.ignore(10, '\n');        //eat chars, including newline
        } while(ans != 'n');         //cycle until 'n'
    return 0;
    }
```

We've used another dodge here: setting an error-state flag manually. We do this because we want to ensure that the inches value is greater than 0 but less than 12.0. If it isn't, we turn on the **failbit** with the statement

```
cin.clear(ios::failbit);  // set failbit
```

When the program checks for errors with **cin.good()**, it will find the **failbit** set and signal that the input is incorrect.

Disk File I/O with Streams

Most programs need to save data to disk files and read it back in. Working with disk files requires another set of classes: `ifstream` for input, `fstream` for both input and output, and `ofstream` for output. Objects of these classes can be associated with disk files, and we can use their member functions to read and write to the files.

Referring back to Figure 12.1, you can see that `ifstream` is derived from `istream`, `fstream` is derived from `iostream`, and `ofstream` is derived from `ostream`. These ancestor classes are in turn derived from `ios`. Thus the file-oriented classes derive many of their member functions from more general classes. The file-oriented classes are also derived, by multiple inheritance, from the `fstreambase` class. This class contains an object of class `filebuf`, which is a file-oriented buffer; and its associated member functions, derived from the more general `streambuf` class. You don't usually need to worry about these buffer classes.

The `ifstream`, `ofstream`, and `fstream` classes are declared in the FSTREAM file.

C programmers will note that the approach to disk I/O used in C++ is quite different from that in C. The old C functions, such as `fread()` and `fwrite()`, will still work in C++, but they are not so well suited to the object-oriented environment. The new C++ approach is considerably cleaner and easier to implement. (Incidentally, be careful about mixing the old C functions with C++ streams. They don't always work together gracefully, although there are ways to make them cooperate.)

Formatted File I/O

In formatted I/O, numbers are stored on disk as a series of characters. Thus 6.02, rather than being stored as a 4-byte type `float` or an 8-byte type `double`, is stored as the characters `'6'`, `'.'`, `'0'`, and `'2'`. This can be inefficient for numbers with many digits, but it's appropriate in many situations and easy to implement. Characters and strings are stored more or less normally.

Writing Data

The following program writes a character, an integer, a type `double`, and two `string` objects to a disk file. There is no output to the screen. Here's the listing for FORMATO:

```
// formato.cpp
// writes formatted output to a file, using <<
#include <fstream>                   //for file I/O
#include <iostream>
#include <string>
using namespace std;

int main()
   {
   char ch = 'x';
   int j = 77;
   double d = 6.02;
```

```
string str1 = "Kafka";          //strings without
string str2 = "Proust";         //  embedded spaces

ofstream outfile("fdata.txt"); //create ofstream object

outfile << ch                   //insert (write) data
        << j
        << ' '                  //needs space between numbers
        << d
        << str1
        << ' '                  //needs spaces between strings
        << str2;
cout << "File written\n";
return 0;
}
```

Here we define an object called **outfile** to be a member of the **ofstream** class. At the same time, we initialize it to the file FDATA.TXT. This initialization sets aside various resources for the file, and accesses or *opens* the file of that name on the disk. If the file doesn't exist, it is created. If it does exist, it is truncated and the new data replaces the old. The **outfile** object acts much as **cout** did in previous programs, so we can use the insertion operator (<<) to output variables of any basic type to the file. This works because the insertion operator is appropriately overloaded in **ostream**, from which **ofstream** is derived.

When the program terminates, the **outfile** object goes out of scope. This calls its destructor, which closes the file, so we don't need to close the file explicitly.

There are several potential formatting glitches. First, you must separate numbers (such as 77 and 6.02) with nonnumeric characters. Since numbers are stored as a sequence of characters, rather than as a fixed-length field, this is the only way the extraction operator will know, when the data is read back from the file, where one number stops and the next one begins. Second, strings must be separated with whitespace for the same reason. This implies that strings cannot contain imbedded blanks. In this example we use the space character (' ') for both kinds of delimiters. Characters need no delimiters, since they have a fixed length.

You can verify that FORMATO has indeed written the data by examining the FDATA.TXT file with the Windows WORDPAD accessory or the DOS command TYPE.

Reading Data

We can read the file generated by FERMATO by using an **ifstream** object, initialized to the name of the file. The file is automatically opened when the object is created. We can then read from it using the extraction (>>) operator.

Here's the listing for the FORMATI program, which reads the data back in from the FDATA.TXT file:

```
// formati.cpp
// reads formatted output from a file, using >>
#include <fstream>                  //for file I/O
#include <iostream>
```

```
#include <string>
using namespace std;

int main()
   {
   char ch;
   int j;
   double d;
   string str1;
   string str2;
```
>) operator>>) operator>> (extraction) operator>
```
   ifstream infile("fdata.txt");   //create ifstream object
                                   //extract (read) data from it
   infile >> ch >> j >> d >> str1 >> str2;

   cout << ch << endl           //display the data
        << j << endl
        << d << endl
        << str1 << endl
        << str2 << endl;
   return 0;
   }
```

Here the `ifstream` object, which we name `infile`, acts much the way `cin` did in previous programs. Provided that we have formatted the data correctly when inserting it into the file, there's no trouble extracting it, storing it in the appropriate variables, and displaying its contents. The program's output looks like this:

```
x
77
6.02
Kafka
Proust
```

Of course the numbers are converted back to their binary representations for storage in the program. That is, the 77 is stored in the variable j as a type *int*, not as two characters; and the 6.02 is stored as a **double**.

Strings with Embedded Blanks

The technique of our last examples won't work with **char*** strings containing embedded blanks. To handle such strings, you need to write a specific delimiter character after each string, and use the **getline()** function, rather than the extraction operator, to read them in. Our next program, OLINE, outputs some strings with blanks embedded in them.

```
// oline.cpp
// file output with strings
#include <fstream>                      //for file I/O
using namespace std;

int main()
```

```
    {
    ofstream outfile("TEST.TXT");        //create file for output
                                         //send text to file
    outfile << "I fear thee, ancient Mariner!\n";
    outfile << "I fear thy skinny hand\n";
    outfile << "And thou art long, and lank, and brown,\n";
    outfile << "As is the ribbed sea sand.\n";
    return 0;
    }
```

When you run the program, the lines of text (from Samuel Taylor Coleridge's *The Rime of the Ancient Mariner*) are written to a file. Each one is specifically terminated with a new-line ('\n') character. Note that these are **char*** strings, not objects of the **string** class. Many stream operations work more easily with **char*** strings.

To extract the strings from the file, we create an **ifstream** and read from it one line at a time using the **getline()** function, which is a member of **istream**. This function reads characters, including whitespace, until it encounters the '\n' character, and places the resulting string in the buffer supplied as an argument. The maximum size of the buffer is given as the second argument. The contents of the buffer is displayed after each line.

```
// iline.cpp
// file input with strings
#include <fstream>                     //for file functions
#include <iostream>
using namespace std;

int main()
    {
    const int MAX = 80;                 //size of buffer
    char buffer[MAX];                   //character buffer
    ifstream infile("TEST.TXT");        //create file for input
    while( !infile.eof() )              //until end-of-file
        {
        infile.getline(buffer, MAX);    //read a line of text
        cout << buffer << endl;         //display it
        }
    return 0;
    }
```

The output of ILINE to the screen is the same as the data written to the TEST.TXT file by OLINE: the four-line Coleridge stanza. The program has no way of knowing in advance how many strings are in the file, so it continues to read one string at a time until it encounters an end-of-file. Incidentally, don't use this program to read random text files. It requires all the text lines to terminate with the '\n' character, and if you encounter a file in which this is not the case, the program will hang.

Detecting End-of-File

As we have seen, objects derived from **ios** contain error-status flags that can be checked to determine the results of operations. When we read a file little by little, as we do here, we will eventually encounter an end-of-file (EOF) condition. The EOF is a signal sent to the program from the operating system when there is no more data to read. In ILINE we could have checked for this in the line

```
while( !infile.eof() )    // until eof encountered
```

However, checking specifically for an **eofbit** means that we won't detect the other error flags, such as the **failbit** and **badbit**, which may also occur, although more rarely. To do this, we can change our loop condition:

```
while( infile.good() )    // until any error encountered
```

You can also test the stream directly. Any stream object, such as **infile**, has a value that can be tested for the usual error conditions, including EOF. If any such condition is true, the object returns a zero value. If everything is going well, the object returns a nonzero value. This value is actually a pointer, but the "address" returned has no significance except to be tested for a zero or nonzero value. Thus we can rewrite our **while** loop again:

```
while( infile )           // until any error encountered
```

This is certainly simple, but it may not be quite so clear to the uninitiated what it does.

Character I/O

The **put()** and **get()** functions, which are members of **ostream** and **istream**, respectively, can be used to output and input single characters. Here's a program, OCHAR, that outputs a string, one character at a time:

```
// ochar.cpp
// file output with characters
#include <fstream>                //for file functions
#include <iostream>
#include <string>
using namespace std;

int main()
   {
   string str = "Time is a great teacher, but unfortunately "
                "it kills all its pupils.  Berlioz";

   ofstream outfile("TEST.TXT");    //create file for output
   for(int j=0; j<str.size(); j++)  //for each character,
      outfile.put( str[j] );        //write it to file
   cout << "File written\n";
   return 0;
   }
```

In this program an **ofstream** object is created as it was in OLINE. The length of the **string** object **str** is found using the **size()** member function, and the characters are output using **put()** in a **for** loop. The aphorism by Hector Berlioz (a 19th-century composer of operas and program music) is written to the file TEST.TXT. We can read this file back in and display it using the ICHAR program.

```
// ichar.cpp
```

```
// file input with characters
#include <fstream>                  //for file functions
#include <iostream>
using namespace std;

int main()
    {
    char ch;                        //character to read
    ifstream infile("TEST.TXT");    //create file for input
    while( infile )                 //read until EOF or error
        {
        infile.get(ch);            //read character
        cout << ch;                 //display it
        }
    cout << endl;
    return 0;
    }
```

This program uses the `get()` function and continues reading until the EOF is reached (or an error occurs). Each character read from the file is displayed using `cout`, so the entire aphorism appears on the screen.

Another approach to reading characters from a file is the `rdbuf()` function, a member of the `ios` class. This function returns a pointer to the `streambuf` (or `filebuf`) object associated with the stream object. This object contains a buffer that holds the characters read from the stream, so you can use the pointer to it as a data object in its own right. Here's the listing for ICHAR2:

```
// ichar2.cpp
// file input with characters
#include <fstream>                  //for file functions
#include <iostream>
using namespace std;

int main()
    {
    ifstream infile("TEST.TXT");    //create file for input

    cout << infile.rdbuf();         //send its buffer to cout
    cout << endl;
    return 0;
    }
```

This program has the same effect as ICHAR. It also takes the prize for the shortest file-oriented program. Note that `rdbuf()` knows that it should return when it encounters an EOF.

Binary I/O

You can write a few numbers to disk using formatted I/O, but if you're storing a large amount of numerical data it's more efficient to use binary I/O, in which numbers are stored as they are in the computer's RAM memory, rather than as strings of characters. In binary I/O an `int` is always stored in 2 bytes, whereas its text version might be "12345", requiring 5 bytes. Similarly, a `float` is always stored in 4 bytes, while its formatted version might be "6.02314e13", requiring 10 bytes.

Our next example shows how an array of integers is written to disk and then read back into memory, using binary format. We use two new functions: `write()`, a member of `ofstream`; and `read()`, a member of `ifstream`. These functions think about data in terms of bytes (type `char`). They don't care how the data is formatted, they simply transfer a buffer full of bytes from and to a disk file. The parameters to `write()` and `read()` are the address of the data buffer and its length. The address must be cast, using `reinterpret_cast`, to type `char*`, and the length is the length in bytes (characters), *not* the number of data items in the buffer. Here's the listing for BINIO:

```
// binio.cpp
// binary input and output with integers
#include <fstream>                          //for file streams
#include <iostream>
using namespace std;
const int MAX = 100;                        //size of buffer
int buff[MAX];                              //buffer for integers

int main()
   {
   for(int j=0; j<MAX; j++)                 //fill buffer with data
      buff[j] = j;                          //(0, 1, 2, ...)
                                            //create output stream
   ofstream os("edata.dat", ios::binary);
                                            //write to it
   os.write( reinterpret_cast<char*>(buff), MAX*sizeof(int) );
   os.close();                             //must close it

   for(j=0; j<MAX; j++)                     //erase buffer
      buff[j] = 0;
                                            //create input stream
   ifstream is("edata.dat", ios::binary);
                                            //read from it
   is.read( reinterpret_cast<char*>(buff), MAX*sizeof(int) );

   for(j=0; j<MAX; j++)                     //check data
      if( buff[j] != j )
         { cerr << "Data is incorrect\n"; return 1; }
   cout << "Data is correct\n";
   return 0;
   }
```

You must use the `ios::binary` argument in the second parameter to `write()` and `read()` when working with binary data. This is because the default, text mode, takes some liberties with the data. For example, in text mode the `'\n'` character is expanded into two bytes— a carriage-return and a linefeed—before being stored to disk. This makes a formatted text file more readable by DOS-based utilities like TYPE, but it causes confusion when it is applied to binary data, since every byte that happens to have the ASCII value 10 is translated into

2 bytes. The `ios::binary` argument is an example of a *mode bit*. We'll say more about this when we discuss the `open()` function later in this chapter.

The `reinterpret_cast` Operator

In the BINIO program (and many others to follow) we use the `reinterpret_cast` operator to make it possible for a buffer of type `int` to look to the `read()` and `write()` functions like a buffer of type `char`.

```
is.read( reinterpret_cast<char*>(buff), MAX*sizeof(int) );
```

The `reinterpret_cast` operator is how you tell the compiler, "I know you won't like this, but I want to do it anyway." It changes the type of a section of memory without caring if it makes sense, so it's up to you to use it judiciously.

You can also use `reinterpret_cast` to change pointer values into integers and vice versa. This is a dangerous practice, but one which is sometimes necessary.

Closing Files

So far in our example programs there has been no need to close streams explicitly because they are closed automatically when they go out of scope; this invokes their destructors and closes the associated file. However, in BINIO, since both the output stream `os` and the input stream `is` are associated with the same file, EDATA.DAT, the first stream must be closed before the second is opened. We use the `close()` member function for this.

You may want to use an explicit `close()` every time you close a file, without relying on the stream's destructor. This is potentially more reliable, and certainly makes the listing more readable.

Object I/O

Since C++ is an object-oriented language, it's reasonable to wonder how objects can be written to and read from disk. The next examples show the process. The `person` class, used in several previous examples (for example, the VIRTPERS program in Chapter 11, "Virtual Functions"), supplies the objects.

Writing an Object to Disk

When writing an object we generally want to use binary mode. This writes the same bit configuration to disk that was stored in memory, and ensures that numerical data contained in objects is handled properly. Here's the listing for OPERS, which asks the user for information about an object of class `person`, and then writes this object to the disk file PERSON.DAT:

```
// opers.cpp
// saves person object to disk
#include <fstream>                 //for file streams
#include <iostream>
using namespace std;
```

```
/////////////////////////////////////////////////////////////
class person                        //class of persons
   {
   protected:
      char name[80];                 //person's name
      short age;                     //person's age
   public:
      void getData()                 //get person's data
         {
         cout << "Enter name: "; cin >> name;
         cout << "Enter age: "; cin >> age;
         }
   };
/////////////////////////////////////////////////////////////
int main()
   {
   person pers;                      //create a person
   pers.getData();                   //get data for person
                                     //create ofstream object
   ofstream outfile("PERSON.DAT", ios::binary);
                                     //write to it
   outfile.write(reinterpret_cast<char*>(&pers), sizeof(pers));
   return 0;
   }
```

The `getData()` member function of `person` is called to prompt the user for information, which it places in the `pers` object. Here's some sample interaction:

```
Enter name: Coleridge
Enter age: 62
```

The contents of the `pers` object are then written to disk, using the `write()` function. We use the `sizeof` operator to find the length of the `pers` object.

Reading an Object from Disk

Reading an object back from the PERSON.DAT file requires the `read()` member function. Here's the listing for IPERS:

```
// ipers.cpp
// reads person object from disk
#include <fstream>                   //for file streams
#include <iostream>
using namespace std;
/////////////////////////////////////////////////////////////
class person                        //class of persons
   {
   protected:
      char name[80];                 //person's name
      short age;                     //person's age
```

```
   public:
      void showData()                //display person's data
         {
         cout << "Name: " << name << endl;
         cout << "Age: " << age << endl;
         }
   };
////////////////////////////////////////////////////////////////////
int main()
   {
   person pers;                        //create person variable
   ifstream infile("PERSON.DAT", ios::binary); //create stream
                                       //read stream
   infile.read( reinterpret_cast<char*>(&pers), sizeof(pers) );
   pers.showData();                    //display person
   return 0;
   }
```

The output from IPERS reflects whatever data the OPERS program placed in the PERSON.DAT file:

```
Name: Coleridge
Age: 62
```

Compatible Data Structures

To work correctly, programs that read and write objects to files, as do OPERS and IPERS, must be talking about the same class of objects. Objects of class **person** in these programs are exactly 42 bytes long, with the first 40 being occupied with a string representing the person's name, and the last 2 containing an integer of type **short**, representing the person's age. If two programs thought the name field was a different length, for example, neither could accurately read a file generated by the other.

Notice, however, that while the **person** classes in OPERS and IPERS have the same data, they may have different member functions. The first includes the single function **getData()**, while the second has only **showData()**. It doesn't matter what member functions you use, since they are not written to disk along with the object's data. The data must have the same format, but inconsistencies in the member functions have no effect. However, this is true only in simple classes that don't use virtual functions.

If you read and write objects of derived classes to a file, you must be even more careful. Objects of derived classes include a mysterious number placed just before the object's data in memory. This number helps identify the object's class when virtual functions are used. When you write an object to disk, this number is written along with the object's other data. If you change a class's member functions, this number changes as well. If you write an object of one class to a file, and then read it back into an object of a class that has identical data but a different member function, you'll encounter big trouble if you try to use virtual functions on the object. The moral: Make sure a class that reads an object is *identical* to the class that wrote it.

I/O with Multiple Objects

The OPERS and IPERS programs wrote and read only one object at a time. Our next example opens a file and writes as many objects as the user wants. Then it reads and displays the entire contents of the file. Here's the listing for DISKFUN:

```
// diskfun.cpp
// reads and writes several objects to disk
#include <fstream>                  //for file streams
#include <iostream>
using namespace std;
/////////////////////////////////////////////////////////////
class person                        //class of persons
   {
   protected:
      char name[80];                //person's name
      int age;                      //person's age
   public:
      void getData()                //get person's data
         {
         cout << "\n   Enter name: "; cin >> name;
         cout << "   Enter age: "; cin >> age;
         }
      void showData()               //display person's data
         {
         cout << "\n   Name: " << name;
         cout << "\n   Age: " << age;
         }
   };
/////////////////////////////////////////////////////////////
int main()
   {
   char ch;
   person pers;                     //create person object
   fstream file;                    //create input/output file
                                    //open for append
   file.open("GROUP.DAT", ios::app | ios::out |
                                     ios::in | ios::binary );
   do                               //data from user to file
      {
      cout << "\nEnter person's data:";
      pers.getData();               //get one person's data
                                    //write to file
      file.write( reinterpret_cast<char*>(&pers), sizeof(pers) );
      cout << "Enter another person (y/n)? ";
      cin >> ch;
      }
   while(ch=='y');                  //quit on 'n'
   file.seekg(0);                   //reset to start of file
                                    //read first person
   file.read( reinterpret_cast<char*>(&pers), sizeof(pers) );
```

```
   while( !file.eof() )              //quit on EOF
      {
      cout << "\nPerson:";           //display person
      pers.showData();               //read another person
      file.read( reinterpret_cast<char*>(&pers), sizeof(pers) );
      }
   cout << endl;
   return 0;
   }
```

Here's some sample interaction with DISKFUN. The output shown assumes that the program has been run before and that two **person** objects have already been written to the file.

```
Enter person's data:
   Enter name: McKinley
   Enter age: 22
Enter another person (y/n)? n

Person:
   Name: Whitney
   Age: 20
Person:
   Name: Rainier
   Age: 21
Person:
   Name: McKinley
   Age: 22
```

Here one additional object is added to the file, and the entire contents, consisting of three objects, is then displayed.

The `fstream` Class

So far in this chapter the file objects we created were for either input or output. In DISK-FUN we want to create a file that can be used for both input and output. This requires an object of the **fstream** class, which is derived from **iostream**, which is derived from both **istream** and **ostream** so it can handle both input and output.

The `open()` Function

In previous examples we created a file object and initialized it in the same statement:

```
ofstream outfile("TEST.TXT");
```

In DISKFUN we use a different approach: We create the file in one statement and open it in another, using the **open()** function, which is a member of the **fstream** class. This is a useful approach in situations where the open may fail. You can create a stream object once, and then try repeatedly to open it, without the overhead of creating a new stream object each time.

The Mode Bits

We've seen the mode bit **ios::binary** before. In the **open()** function we include several new mode bits. The mode bits, defined in **ios**, specify various aspects of how a stream object will be opened. Table 12.10 shows the possibilities.

Table 12.10 Mode Bits for **open()** Function

Mode Bit	Result
in	Open for reading (default for **ifstream**)
out	Open for writing (default for **ofstream**)
ate	Start reading or writing at end of file (**AT End**)
app	Start writing at end of file (**APPend**)
trunc	Truncate file to zero length if it exists (**TRUNCate**)
nocreate	Error when opening if file does not already exist
noreplace	Error when opening for output if file already exists, unless **ate** or **app** is set
binary	Open file in binary (not text) mode

In DISKFUN we use **ios::app** because we want to preserve whatever was in the file before. That is, we can write to the file, terminate the program, and start up the program again, and whatever we write to the file will be added following the existing contents. We use in and out because we want to perform both input and output on the file, and we use binary because we're writing binary objects. The vertical bars between the flags cause the bits representing these flags to be logically combined into a single integer, so that several flags can apply simultaneously.

We write one **person** object at a time to the file, using the **write()** function. When we've finished writing, we want to read the entire file. Before doing this we must reset the file's current position. We do this with the **seekg()** function, which we'll examine in the next section. It ensures we'll start reading at the beginning of the file. Then, in a **while** loop, we repeatedly read a **person** object from the file and display it on the screen.

This continues until we've read all the **person** objects—a state that we discover using the **eof()** function, which returns the state of the **ios::eofbit**.

File Pointers

Each file object has associated with it two integer values called the *get pointer* and the *put pointer*. These are also called the *current get position* and the *current put position*, or—if it's clear which one is meant—simply the *current position*. These values specify the byte number in the file where writing or reading will take place. (The term *pointer* in this context should not be confused with normal C++ pointers used as address variables.)

Often you want to start reading an existing file at the beginning and continue until the end. When writing, you may want to start at the beginning, deleting any existing contents, or at the end, in which case you can open the file with the `ios::app` mode specifier. These are the default actions, so no manipulation of the file pointers is necessary. However, there are times when you must take control of the file pointers yourself so that you can read from and write to an arbitrary location in the file. The `seekg()` and `tellg()` functions allow you to set and examine the get pointer, and the `seekp()` and `tellp()` functions perform these same actions on the put pointer.

Specifying the Position

We saw an example of positioning the get pointer in the DISKFUN program, where the `seekg()` function set it to the beginning of the file so that reading would start there. This form of `seekg()` takes one argument, which represents the absolute position in the file. The start of the file is byte 0, so that's what we used in DISKFUN. Figure 12.4 shows how this looks.

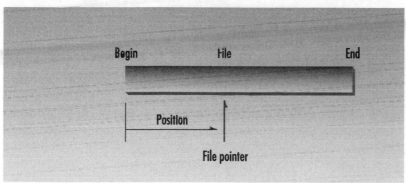

Figure 12.4   The `seekg()` function with one argument.

Specifying the Offset

The `seekg()` function can be used in two ways. We've seen the first, where the single argument represents the position from the start of the file. You can also use it with two arguments, where the first argument represents an offset from a particular location in the file, and the second specifies the location from which the offset is measured. There are three possibilities for the second argument: **beg** is the beginning of the file, **cur** is the current pointer position, and **end** is the end of the file. The statement

```
seekp(-10, ios::end);
```

for example, will set the put pointer to 10 bytes before the end of the file. Figure 12.5 shows how this looks.

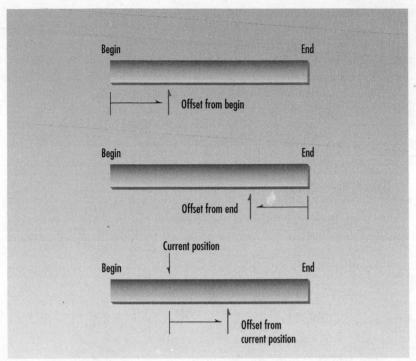

Figure 12.5 The *seekg( )* function with two arguments.

Here's an example that uses the two-argument version of **seekg()** to find a particular **person** object in the GROUP.DAT file, and to display the data for that particular person. Here's the listing for SEEKG:

```cpp
// seekg.cpp
// seeks particular person in file
#include <fstream>                    //for file streams
#include <iostream>
using namespace std;
///////////////////////////////////////////////////////////////
class person                          //class of persons
   {
   protected:
      char name[80];                  //person's name
      int age;                        //person's age
   public:
      void getData()                  //get person's data
         {
         cout << "\n   Enter name: "; cin >> name;
         cout << "   Enter age: "; cin >> age;
         }
```

```
         void showData(void)              //display person's data
            {
            cout << "\n   Name: " << name;
            cout << "\n   Age: " << age;
            }
         };
/////////////////////////////////////////////////////////////////////
int main()
   {
   person pers;                      //create person object
   ifstream infile;                  //create input file
   infile.open("GROUP.DAT", ios::in | ios::binary);  //open file

   infile.seekg(0, ios::end);        //go to 0 bytes from end
   int endposition = infile.tellg();         //find where we are
   int n = endposition / sizeof(person);     //number of persons
   cout << "\nThere are " << n << " persons in file";

   cout << "\nEnter person number: ";
   cin >> n;
   int position = (n-1) * sizeof(person);  //number times size
   infile.seekg(position);           //bytes from start
                                     //read one person
   infile.read( reinterpret_cast<char*>(&pers), sizeof(pers) );
   pers.showData();                  //display the person
   cout << endl;
   return 0;
   }
```

Here's the output from the program, assuming that the GROUP.DAT file is the same as that just accessed in the DISKFUN example:

```
There are 3 persons in file
Enter person number: 2

   Name: Rainier
   Age: 21
```

For the user, we number the items starting at 1, although the program starts numbering at 0; so person 2 is the second person of the three in the file.

The `tellg()` Function

The first thing the program does is figure out how many persons are in the file. It does this by positioning the get pointer at the end of the file with the statement

```
infile.seekg(0, ios::end);
```

The `tellg()` function returns the current position of the get pointer. The program uses this function to return the pointer position at the end of the file; this is the length of the file in bytes. Next, the program calculates how many **person** objects there are in the file by dividing by the size of a person; it then displays the result.

In the output shown, the user specifies the second object in the file, and the program calculates how many bytes into the file this is, using `seekg()`. It then uses `read()` to read one person's worth of data starting from that point. Finally, it displays the data with `showData()`.

Error Handling in File I/O

In the file-related examples so far we have not concerned ourselves with error situations. In particular, we have assumed that the files we opened for reading already existed, and that those opened for writing could be created or appended to. We've also assumed that there were no failures during reading or writing. In a real program it is important to verify such assumptions and take appropriate action if they turn out to be incorrect. A file that you think exists may not, or a filename that you assume you can use for a new file may already apply to an existing file. Or, there may be no more room on the disk, or no disk in the drive, and so on.

Reacting to Errors

Our next program shows how such errors are most conveniently handled. All disk operations are checked after they are performed. If an error has occurred, a message is printed and the program terminates. We've used the technique, discussed earlier, of checking the return value from the object itself to determine its error status. The program opens an output stream object, writes an entire array of integers to it with a single call to `write()`, and closes the object. Then it opens an input stream object and reads the array of integers with a call to `read()`.

```
// rewerr.cpp
// handles errors during input and output
#include <fstream>      //for file streams
#include <iostream>
using namespace std;
#include <process.h>    //for exit()

const int MAX = 1000;
int buff[MAX];

int main()
    {
    for(int j=0; j<MAX; j++)            //fill buffer with data
        buff[j] = j;
    ofstream os;                        //create output stream
                                        //open it
    os.open("a:edata.dat", ios::trunc | ios::binary);
    if(!os)
        { cerr << "Could not open output file\n"; exit(1); }

    cout << "Writing...\n";             //write buffer to it
    os.write( reinterpret_cast<char*>(buff), MAX*sizeof(int) );
    if(!os)
```

```
      { cerr << "Could not write to file\n"; exit(1); }
   os.close();                         //must close it

   for(j=0; j<MAX; j++)                //clear buffer
      buff[j] = 0;

   ifstream is;                        //create input stream
   is.open("a:edata.dat", ios::binary);
   if(!is)
      { cerr << "Could not open input file\n"; exit(1); }

   cout << "Reading...\n";             //read file
   is.read( reinterpret_cast<char*>(buff), MAX*sizeof(int) );
   if(!is)
      { cerr << "Could not read from file\n"; exit(1); }

   for(j=0; j<MAX; j++)                //check data
      if( buff[j] != j )
         { cerr << "\nData is incorrect\n"; exit(1); }
   cout << "Data is correct\n";
   return 0;
   }
```

Analyzing Errors

In the REWERR example we determined whether an error occurred in an I/O operation by examining the return value of the entire stream object.

```
if(!is)
   // error occurred
```

Here **is** returns a pointer value if everything went well, but 0 if it didn't. This is the shotgun approach to errors: No matter what the error is, it's detected in the same way and the same action is taken. However, it's also possible, using the **ios** error-status flags, to find out more specific information about a file I/O error. We've already seen some of these status flags at work in screen and keyboard I/O. Our next example, FERRORS, shows how they can be used in file I/O.

```
// ferrors.cpp
// checks for errors opening file
#include <fstream>              // for file functions
#include <iostream>
using namespace std;

int main()
   {
   ifstream file;
   file.open("a:test.dat");

   if( !file )
      cout << "\nCan't open GROUP.DAT";
   else
```

```
    cout << "\nFile opened successfully.";
cout << "\nfile = " << file;
cout << "\nError state = " << file.rdstate();
cout << "\ngood() = " << file.good();
cout << "\neof() = " << file.eof();
cout << "\nfail() = " << file.fail();
cout << "\nbad() = " << file.bad() << endl;
file.close();
return 0;
}
```

This program first checks the value of the object file. If its value is zero, then probably the file could not be opened because it didn't exist. Here's the output from FERRORS when that's the case:

```
Can't open GROUP.DAT
file = 0x1c730000
Error state = 4
good() = 0
eof() = 0
fail() = 4
bad() = 4
```

The error state returned by `rdstate()` is 4. This is the bit that indicates that the file doesn't exist; it's set to 1. The other bits are all set to 0. The `good()` function returns 1 (true) only when no bits are set, so it returns 0 (false). We're not at EOF, so `eof()` returns 0. The `fail()` and `bad()` functions return nonzero, since an error occurred.

In a serious program some or all of these functions should be used after every I/O operation to ensure that things went as expected.

File I/O with Member Functions

So far we've let the `main()` function handle the details of file I/O. When you use more sophisticated classes it's natural to include file I/O operations as member functions of the class. In this section we'll show two programs that do this. The first uses ordinary member functions in which each object is responsible for reading and writing itself to a file. The second shows how static member functions can read and write all the objects of a class at once.

Objects That Read and Write Themselves

Sometimes it makes sense to let each member of a class read and write itself to a file. This is a simple approach, and works well if there aren't many objects to be read or written at once. In this example we add member functions—`diskOut()` and `diskIn()`—to the `person` class. These functions allow a `person` object to write itself to disk and read itself back in.

We've made some simplifying assumptions. First, all objects of the class will be stored in the same file, called PERSFILE.DAT. Second, new objects are always appended to the end of the file. An argument to the `diskIn()` function allows us to read the data for any person in the file. To prevent an attempt to read data beyond the end of the file, we include a static member function, diskCount(), that returns the number of persons stored in the file. Here's the listing for REWOBJ:

```cpp
// rewobj.cpp
// person objects do disk I/O
#include <fstream>              //for file streams
#include <iostream>
using namespace std;
/////////////////////////////////////////////////////////////////
class person                    //class of persons
   {
   protected:
      char name[40];            //person's name
      int age;                  //person's age
   public:
      void getData(void)        //get person's data
         {
         cout << "\n   Enter name: "; cin >> name;
         cout << "   Enter age: "; cin >> age;
         }
      void showData(void)       //display person's data
         {
         cout << "\n   Name: " << name;
         oout << "\n   Age: " << age;
         }
      void diskIn(int);         //read from file
      void diskOut();           //write to file
      static int diskCount();   //return number of
                                //   persons in file
   };
//-------------------------------------------------------------
void person::diskIn(int pn)     //read person number pn
   {                            //from file
   ifstream infile;                             //make stream
   infile.open("PERSFILE.DAT", ios::binary);   //open it
   infile.seekg( pn*sizeof(person) );          //move file ptr
   infile.read( (char*)this, sizeof(*this) );  //read one person
   }
//-------------------------------------------------------------
void person::diskOut()          //write person to end of file
   {
   ofstream outfile;            //make stream
                                //open it
   outfile.open("PERSFILE.DAT", ios::app | ios::binary);
   outfile.write( (char*)this, sizeof(*this) );  //write to it
   }
//-------------------------------------------------------------
int person::diskCount()         //return number of persons
   {                            //in file
   ifstream infile;
   infile.open("PERSFILE.DAT", ios::binary);
   infile.seekg(0, ios::end);   //go to 0 bytes from end
```

```
                                      //calculate number of persons
        return (int)infile.tellg() / sizeof(person);
        }
/////////////////////////////////////////////////////////////////
int main()
    {
    person p;                         //make an empty person
    char ch;

    do {                              //save persons to disk
       cout << "Enter data for person:";
       p.getData();                   //get data
       p.diskOut();                   //write to disk
       cout << "Do another (y/n)? ";
       cin >> ch;
       } while(ch=='y');              //until user enters 'n'

    int n = person::diskCount();   //how many persons in file?
    cout << "There are " << n << " persons in file\n";
    for(int j=0; j<n; j++)            //for each one,
       {
       cout << "\nPerson " << j;
       p.diskIn(j);                   //read person from disk
       p.showData();                  //display person
       }
    cout << endl;
    return 0;
    }
```

There shouldn't be too many surprises here; you've seen most of the elements of this program before. It operates in the same way as the DISKFUN program. Notice, however, that all the details of disk operation are invisible to `main()`, having been hidden away in the `person` class.

We don't know in advance where the data is that we're going to read and write, since each object is in a different place in memory. However, the this pointer always tells us where we are when we're in a member function. In the `read()` and `write()` stream functions, the address of the object to be read or written is this and its size is `sizeof(*this)`.

Here's some output, assuming there were already two persons in the file when the program was started:

```
Enter data for person:
   Enter name: Acheson
   Enter age: 63
Enter another (y/n)? y

Enter data for person:
   Enter name: Dulles
   Enter age: 72
Enter another (y/n)? n

Person #1
   Name: Stimson
```

```
      Age: 45
Person #2
   Name: Hull
   Age: 58
Person #3
   Name: Acheson
   Age: 63
Person #4
   Name: Dulles
   Age: 72
```

If you want the user to be able to specify the filename used by the class, instead of hard-wiring it into the member functions as we do here, you could create a static member variable (say `char fileName[]`) and a static function to set it. Or, you might want to give each object the name of the file it was associated with, using a nonstatic function.

Classes That Read and Write Themselves

Let's assume you have many objects in memory, and you want to write them all to a file. It's not efficient to have a member function for each object open the file, write one object to it, and then close it, as in the REWOBJ example. It's much faster—and the more objects there are the truer this is—to open the file once, write all the objects to it, and then close it.

Static Functions

One way to write many objects at once is to use a static member function, which applies to the class as a whole rather than to each object. This function can write all the objects at once. How will such a function know where all the objects are? It can access an array of pointers to the objects, which can be stored as static data. As each object is created, a pointer to it is stored in this array. A static data member also keeps track of how many objects have been created. The static write function can open the file; then in a loop go through the array, writing each object in turn; and finally close the file.

Size of Derived Objects

To make things really interesting, let's make a further assumption: that the objects stored in memory are different sizes. Why would this be true? This situation typically arises when several classes are derived from a base class. For example, consider the EMPLOY program in Chapter 9, "Inheritance." Here we have an `employee` class that acts as a base class for the `manager`, `scientist`, and `laborer` classes. Objects of these three derived classes are different sizes, since they contain different amounts of data. Specifically, in addition to the name and employee number, which apply to all employees, there are a title and golf-club dues for the manager and the number of publications for the scientist.

We would like to write the data from a list containing all three types of derived objects (`manager`, `scientist`, and `laborer`) using a simple loop and the `write()` member function of `ofstream`. But to use this function we need to know how large the object is, since that's its second argument.

Suppose we have an array of pointers (call it `arrap[]`) to objects of type `employee`. These pointers can point to objects of the three derived classes. (See the VIRTPERS program in Chapter 11 for an example of an array of pointers to objects of derived classes.) We know that if we're using virtual functions we can make statements like

```
arrap[j]->putdata();
```

The version of the `putdata()` function that matches the object pointed to by the pointer will be used, rather than the function in the base class. But can we also use the `sizeof()` function to return the size of a pointer argument? That is, can we say

```
ouf.write( (char*)arrap[j], sizeof(*arrap[j]) );  // no good
```

No, because `sizeof()` isn't a virtual function. It doesn't know that it needs to consider the type of object pointed to, rather than the type of the pointer. It will always return the size of the base class object.

Using the `typeid()` Function

How can we find the size of an object, if all we have is a pointer to it? One answer to this is the `typeid()` function, introduced in Chapter 11. We can use this function to find the class of an object, and use this class name in `sizeof()`. To use `typeid()` you may need to enable a compiler option called *Run-Time Type Information* (RTTI). At least this is true in the current Microsoft compiler, as described in Appendix C, "Microsoft Visual C++."

Our next example shows how this works. Once we know the size of the object, we can use it in the `write()` function to write the object to disk.

We've added a simple user interface to the EMPLOY program, and made the member-specific functions virtual so we can use an array of pointers to objects. We've also incorporated some of the error-detection techniques discussed in the last section.

This is a rather ambitious program, but it demonstrates many of the techniques that could be used in a full-scale database application. It also shows the real power of OOP. How else could you use a single statement to write objects of different sizes to a file? Here's the listing for EMPL_IO:

```cpp
// empl_io.cpp
// performs file I/O on employee objects
// handles different sized objects
#include <fstream>              //for file-stream functions
#include <iostream>
#include <typeinfo>             //for typeid()
using namespace std;
#include <process.h>           //for exit()

const int LEN = 32;            //maximum length of last names
const int MAXEM = 100;         //maximum number of employees

enum employee_type {tmanager, tscientist, tlaborer};
//////////////////////////////////////////////////////////////
class employee                 //employee class
   {
   private:
```

```
        char name[LEN];           //employee name
        unsigned long number;     //employee number
        static int n;             //current number of employees
        static employee* arrap[]; //array of ptrs to emps
    public:
        virtual void getdata()
           {
           cin.ignore(10, '\n');
           cout << "   Enter last name: "; cin >> name;
           cout << "   Enter number: ";      cin >> number;
           }
        virtual void putdata()
           {
           cout << "\n   Name: " << name;
           cout << "\n   Number: " << number;
           }
        virtual employee_type get_type();  //get type
        static void add();        //add an employee
        static void display();    //display all employees
        static void read();       //read from disk file
        static void write();      //write to disk file
    };
//------------------------------------------------------------
//static variables
int employee::n;                  //current number of employees
employee* employee::arrap[MAXEM]; //array of ptrs to emps
/////////////////////////////////////////////////////////////
//manager class
class manager : public employee
    {
    private:
        char title[LEN];          //"vice-president" etc.
        double dues;              //golf club dues
    public:
        void getdata()
           {
           employee::getdata();
           cout << "   Enter title: ";          cin >> title;
           cout << "   Enter golf club dues: "; cin >> dues;
           }
        void putdata()
           {
           employee::putdata();
           cout << "\n   Title: " << title;
           cout << "\n   Golf club dues: " << dues;
           }
    };
/////////////////////////////////////////////////////////////
//scientist class
class scientist : public employee
    {
    private:
        int pubs;                 //number of publications
```

```
     public:
        void getdata()
           {
           employee::getdata();
           cout << "   Enter number of pubs: "; cin >> pubs;
           }
        void putdata()
           {
           employee::putdata();
           cout << "\n   Number of publications: " << pubs;
           }
     };
/////////////////////////////////////////////////////////////////
//laborer class
class laborer : public employee
   {
   };
/////////////////////////////////////////////////////////////////
//add employee to list in memory
void employee::add()
   {
   char ch;
   cout << "'m' to add a manager"
           "\n's' to add a scientist"
           "\n'l' to add a laborer"
           "\nEnter selection: ";
   cin >> ch;
   switch(ch)
      {                           //create specified employee type
      case 'm': arrap[n] = new manager;   break;
      case 's': arrap[n] = new scientist; break;
      case 'l': arrap[n] = new laborer;   break;
      default: cout << "\nUnknown employee type\n"; return;
      }
   arrap[n++]->getdata();      //get employee data from user
   }
//-------------------------------------------------------------
//display all employees
void employee::display()
   {
   for(int j=0; j<n; j++)
      {
      cout  << (j+1);            //display number
      switch( arrap[j]->get_type() )   //display type
         {
         case tmanager:    cout << ". Type: Manager";   break;
         case tscientist:  cout << ". Type: Scientist"; break;
         case tlaborer:    cout << ". Type: Laborer";   break;
         default: cout << ". Unknown type";
         }
      arrap[j]->putdata();     //display employee data
      cout << endl;
      }
```

```
      }
//--------------------------------------------------------------
//return the type of this object
employee_type employee::get_type()
   {
   if( typeid(*this) == typeid(manager) )
      return tmanager;
   else if( typeid(*this)==typeid(scientist) )
      return tscientist;
   else if( typeid(*this)==typeid(laborer) )
      return tlaborer;
   else
      { cerr << "\nBad employee type"; exit(1); }
   return tmanager;
   }
//--------------------------------------------------------------
//write all current memory objects to file
void employee::write()
   {
   int size;
   cout << "Writing " << n << " employees.\n";
   ofstream ouf;                //open ofstream in binary
   employee_type etype;         //type of each employee object

   ouf.open("EMPLOY.DAT", ios::trunc ¦ ios::binary);
   if(!ouf)
      { cout << "\nCan't open file\n"; return; }
   for(int j=0; j<n; j++)       //for every employee object
      {                         //get it's type
      etype = arrap[j]->get_type();
                                //write type to file
      ouf.write( (char*)&etype, sizeof(etype) );
      switch(etype)             //find its size
         {
         case tmanager:   size=sizeof(manager); break;
         case tscientist: size=sizeof(scientist); break;
         case tlaborer:   size=sizeof(laborer); break;
         }                      //write employee object to file
      ouf.write( (char*)(arrap[j]), size );
      if(!ouf)
         { cout << "\nCan't write to file\n"; return; }
      }
   }
//--------------------------------------------------------------
//read data for all employees from file into memory
void employee::read()
   {
   int size;                    //size of employee object
   employee_type etype;         //type of employee
   ifstream inf;                //open ifstream in binary
   inf.open("EMPLOY.DAT", ios::binary);
   if(!inf)
      { cout << "\nCan't open file\n"; return; }
```

```
      n = 0;                        //no employees in memory yet
   while(true)
      {                             //read type of next employee
      inf.read( (char*)&etype, sizeof(etype) );
      if( inf.eof() )         //quit loop on eof
         break;
      if(!inf)                //error reading type
         { cout << "\nCan't read type from file\n"; return; }
      switch(etype)
         {                          //make new employee
         case tmanager:        //of correct type
            arrap[n] = new manager;
            size=sizeof(manager);
            break;
         case tscientist:
            arrap[n] = new scientist;
            size=sizeof(scientist);
            break;
         case tlaborer:
            arrap[n] = new laborer;
            size=sizeof(laborer);
            break;
         default: cout << "\nUnknown type in file\n"; return;
         }                          //read data from file into it
      inf.read( (char*)arrap[n], size  );
      if(!inf)                //error but not eof
         { cout << "\nCan't read data from file\n"; return; }
      n++;                    //count employee
      }  //end while
   cout << "Reading " << n << " employees\n";
   }
////////////////////////////////////////////////////////////////
int main()
   {
   char ch;
   while(true)
      {
      cout << "'a' -- add data for an employee"
              "\n'd' -- display data for all employees"
              "\n'w' -- write all employee data to file"
              "\n'r' -- read all employee data from file"
              "\n'x' -- exit"
              "\nEnter selection: ";
      cin >> ch;
      switch(ch)
         {
         case 'a':              //add an employee to list
            employee::add(); break;
         case 'd':              //display all employees
            employee::display(); break;
         case 'w':              //write employees to file
            employee::write(); break;
         case 'r':              //read all employees from file
```

```
                    employee::read(); break;
            case 'x': exit(0);    //exit program
            default: cout << "\nUnknown command";
            }  //end switch
      }  //end while
   return 0;
   }  //end main()
```

Code Number for Object Type

We know how to find the class of an object that's in memory, but how do we know the class of the object whose data we're about to read from the disk? There's no magic function to help us with this one. When we write an object's data to disk, we need to write a code number (the enum variable **employee_type**) directly to the disk just before the object's data. Then when we are about to read an object back from the file to memory, we read this value and create a new object of the type indicated. Finally we copy the data from the file into this new object.

No Homemade Objects, Please

Incidentally, you might be tempted to read an object's data into just anyplace, say into an array of type **char**, and then set a pointer-to-object to point to this area, perhaps with a cast to make it kosher.

```
char someArray[MAX];
aClass* aPtr_to_Obj;
aPtr_to_Obj = reinterpret_cast<aClass*>(someArray);  // don't do this
```

However, this does not create an object, and attempts to use the pointer as if it pointed to an object will lead to trouble. There are only two legitimate ways to create an object. You can define it explicitly at compile time:

```
aClass anObj;
```

or you can create it with **new** at runtime, and assign its location to a pointer:

```
aPtr_to_Obj = new aClass;
```

When you create an object properly its constructor is invoked. This is necessary even if you have not defined a constructor and are using the default constructor. An object is more than an area of memory with data in it; it is also a set of member functions, some of which you don't even see.

Interaction with EMPL_IO

Here's some sample interaction with the program, in which we create a **manager**, a **scientist**, and a **laborer** in memory, write them to disk, read them back in, and display them. (For simplicity, multi-word names and titles are not allowed; say VicePresident, not Vice President.)

```
'a' -- add data for an employee
'd' -- display data for all employees
```

```
'w' -- write all employee data to file
'r' -- read all employee data from file
'x' -- exit
Type selection: a
'm' to add a manager
's' to add a scientist
'l' to add a laborer
Type selection: m
   Enter last name: Johnson
   Enter number: 1111
   Enter title: President
   Enter golf club dues: 20000

'a' -- add data for an employee
'd' -- display data for all employees
'w' -- write all employee data to file
'r' -- read all employee data from file
'x' -- exit
Type selection: a
'm' to add a manager
's' to add a scientist
'l' to add a laborer
Type selection: s
   Enter last name: Faraday
   Enter number: 2222
   Enter number of pubs: 99

'a' -- add data for an employee
'd' -- display data for all employees
'w' -- write all employee data to file
'r' -- read all employee data from file
'x' -- exit
Type selection: a
'm' to add a manager
's' to add a scientist
'l' to add a laborer
Type selection: l
   Enter last name: Smith
   Enter number: 3333

'a' -- add data for an employee
'd' -- display data for all employees
'w' -- write all employee data to file
'r' -- read all employee data from file
'x' -- exit
Type selection: w
Writing 3 employees

'a' -- add data for an employee
'd' -- display data for all employees
'w' -- write all employee data to file
'r' -- read all employee data from file
'x' -- exit
```

```
Type selection: r
Reading 3 employees

'a' -- add data for an employee
'd' -- display data for all employees
'w' -- write all employee data to file
'r' -- read all employee data from file
(continued on next page)
(continued from previous page)
'x' -- exit
Type selection: d
1. Type: Manager
   Name: Johnson
   Title: President
   Golf club dues: 20000
2. Type: Scientist
   Name: Faraday
   Number: 2222
   Number of publications: 99
3. Type: Laborer
   Name: Smith
   Number: 3333
```

Of course you can also exit the program after writing the data to disk. When you start it up again, you can read the file back in and all the data will reappear.

It would be easy to add functions to this program to delete an employee, retrieve data for a single employee from the file, search the file for employees with particular characteristics, and so forth.

Overloading the Extraction and Insertion Operators

Let's move on to another stream-related topic: overloading the extraction and insertion operators. This is a powerful feature of C++. It lets you treat I/O for user-defined data types in the same way as basic types like **int** and **double**. For example, if you have an object of class **crawdad** called **cd1**, you can display it with the statement

```
cout << "\ncd1=" << cd1;
```

just as if it were a basic data type.

We can overload the extraction and insertion operators so they work with the display and keyboard (**cout** and **cin**) alone. With a little more care, we can also overload them so they work with disk files as well. We'll look at examples of both these situations.

Overloading for `cout` and `cin`

Here's an example, ENGLIO, that overloads the insertion and extraction operators for the **Distance** class so they work with **cout** and **cin**.

```
// englio.cpp
// overloaded << and >> operators
#include <iostream>
using namespace std;
/////////////////////////////////////////////////////////////////
class Distance                             //English Distance class
   {
   private:
      int feet;
      float inches;
   public:
      Distance() : feet(0), inches(0.0)  //constructor (no args)
         {  }
                                          //constructor (two args)
      Distance(int ft, float in) : feet(ft), inches(in)
         {  }
      friend istream& operator >> (istream& s, Distance& d);
      friend ostream& operator << (ostream& s, Distance& d);
   };
//---------------------------------------------------------------
istream& operator >> (istream& s, Distance& d)  //get Distance
   {                                            //from user
   cout << "\nEnter feet: ";  s >> d.feet;      //using
   cout << "Enter inches: ";  s >> d.inches;    //overloaded
   return s;                                    //>> operator
   }
//---------------------------------------------------------------
ostream& operator << (ostream& s, Distance& d)  //display
   {                                            //Distance
   s << d.feet << "\'-" << d.inches << '\"';    //using
   return s;                                    //overloaded
   }                                            //<< operator
/////////////////////////////////////////////////////////////////
int main()
   {
   Distance dist1, dist2;        //define Distances
   Distance dist3(11, 6.25);     //define, initialize dist3

   cout << "\nEnter two Distance values:";
   cin >> dist1 >> dist2;        //get values from user
                                 //display distances
   cout << "\ndist1 = " << dist1 << "\ndist2 = " << dist2;
   cout << "\ndist3 = " << dist3 << endl;
   return 0;
   }
```

This program asks for two **Distance** values from the user, and then prints out these values and another value that was initialized in the program. Here's a sample interaction:

```
Enter feet: 10
Enter inches: 3.5

Enter feet: 12
```

```
Enter inches: 0
```

```
dist1 = 10'-3.5"
dist2 = 12'-6"
dist3 = 11'-6.25"
```

Notice how convenient and natural it is to treat `Distance` objects like any other data type, using statements like

```
cin >> dist1 >> dist2;
```

and

```
cout << "\ndist1=" << dist1 << "\ndist2=" << dist2;
```

The `<<` and `>>` operators are overloaded in similar ways. They return, by reference, an object of `istream` (for `>>`) or `ostream` (for `<<`). These return values permit chaining. The operators take two arguments, both passed by reference. The first argument for `>>` is an object of `istream` (such as `cin`). For `<<` it's an object of `ostream` (such as `cout`). The second argument is an object of the class to be displayed, `Distance` in this example. The `>>` operator takes input from the stream specified in the first argument and puts it in the member data of the object specified by the second argument. The `<<` operator removes the data from the object specified by the second argument and sends it into the stream specified by the first argument.

The `operator<<()` and `operator>>()` functions must be friends of the `Distance` class, since the `istream` and `ostream` objects appear on the left side of the operator. (See the discussion of friend functions in Chapter 11.)

You can overload the insertion and extraction operators for other classes by following these same steps.

Overloading for Files

Our next example shows how we might overload the `<<` and `>>` operators in the `Distance` class so they work with file I/O as well as with `cout` and `cin`.

```
// englio2.cpp
// overloaded << and >> operators can work with files
#include <fstream>
#include <iostream>
using namespace std;
/////////////////////////////////////////////////////////////////
class Distance                          //English Distance class
   {
   private:
      int feet;
      float inches;
   public:
      Distance() : feet(0), inches(0.0) //constructor (no args)
         { }                            //constructor (two args)
      Distance(int ft, float in) : feet(ft), inches(in)
         { }
      friend istream& operator >> (istream& s, Distance& d);
```

```
                friend ostream& operator << (ostream& s, Distance& d);
        };
//----------------------------------------------------------------
istream& operator >> (istream& s, Distance& d)   //get Distance
        {                                        //from file or
        char dummy;   //for ('), (-), and (")    //keyboard
                                                 //with
        s >> d.feet >> dummy >> dummy >> d.inches >> dummy;
        return s;                                //overloaded
        }                                        //>> operator
//----------------------------------------------------------------
ostream& operator << (ostream& s, Distance& d)   //send Distance
        {                                        //to file or
        s << d.feet << "\'-" << d.inches << '\"';  //screen with
        return s;                                //overloaded
        }                                        //<< operator
////////////////////////////////////////////////////////////////
int main()
        {
        char ch;
        Distance dist1;
        ofstream ofile;                          //create and open
        ofile.open("DIST.DAT");                  //output stream

        do {
           cout << "\nEnter Distance: ";
           cin >> dist1;                         //get distance from user
           ofile << dist1;                       //write it to output str
           cout << "Do another (y/n)? ";
           cin >> ch;
           } while(ch != 'n');
        ofile.close();                           //close output stream

        ifstream ifile;                          //create and open
        ifile.open("DIST.DAT");                  //input stream

        cout << "\nContents of disk file is:\n";
        while(true)
           {
           ifile >> dist1;                       //read dist from stream
           if( ifile.eof() )                     //quit on EOF
              break;
           cout << "Distance = " << dist1 <<endl;  //display distance
           }
        return 0;
        }
```

We've made minimal changes to the overloaded operators themselves. The >> operator no longer prompts for input, since it doesn't make sense to prompt a file. We assume the user knows exactly how to enter a feet-and-inches value, including the various punctuation marks. The << operator is unchanged. The program asks for input from the user, writing each Distance value to the file as it's obtained. When the user is finished with input, the program then reads and displays all the values from the file. Here's some sample inter-action:

```
Enter Distance: 3'-4.5"
Do another (y/n)? yes

Enter Distance: 7'-11.25"
Do another (y/n)? yes

Enter Distance: 11'-6"
Do another (y/n)? no

Contents of disk file is:
Distance = 3'-4.5"
Distance = 7'-11.25"
Distance = 11'-6"
```

The distances are stored character by character to the file. In this example the contents of the file would be as follows:

```
3'-4.5"7'-11.25"11'-6
```

If the user fails to enter the distances with the correct punctuation, they won't be written to the file correctly and the file won't be readable for the << operator. In a real program error checking the input is essential.

Memory As a Stream Object

You can treat a section of memory as a stream object, inserting data into it just as you would a file. This is useful when you need to format your output in a particular way (such as displaying exactly two digits to the right of the decimal point), but you also need to use a text-output function that requires a string as input. This is common when calling output functions in a GUI environment such as Windows, since these functions often require a string as an argument. (C programmers will remember using the sprintf() function for this purpose.)

A family of stream classes implements such in-memory formatting. For output to memory there is ostrstream, which is derived from (among other classes) ostream. For input from memory there is istrstream, derived from istream; and for memory objects that do both input and output there is strstream, derived from iostream.

Most commonly you will want to use ostrstream. Our next example shows how this works. You start with a data buffer in memory. Then you create an ostrstream object, using the memory buffer and its size as arguments to the stream's constructor. Now you can output formatted text to the memory buffer as if it were a stream object. Here's the listing for OSTRSTR:

```
// ostrstr.cpp
// writes formatted data into memory
#include <strstream>
#include <iostream>
#include <iomanip>                       //for setiosflags()
using namespace std;
```

```
const int SIZE = 80;                  //size of memory buffer

int main()
    {
    char ch = 'x';                    //test data
    int j = 77;
    double d = 67890.12345;
    char str1[] = "Kafka";
    char str2[] = "Freud";

    char membuff[SIZE];               //buffer in memory
    ostrstream omem(membuff, SIZE);   //create stream object

    omem << "ch=" << ch << endl       //insert formatted data
         << "j=" << j << endl         //into object
         << setiosflags(ios::fixed)   //format with decimal point
         << setprecision(2)           //two digits to right of dec
         << "d=" << d << endl
         << "str1=" << str1 << endl
         << "str2=" << str2 << endl
         << ends;                     //end the buffer with '\0'
    cout << membuff;                  //display the memory buffer
    return 0;
    }
```

When you run the program, `membuff` will be filled with the formatted text:

```
ch=x\nj=77\nd=67890.12\nstr1=Kafka\nstr2=Freud\n\0
```

We can format floating-point numbers using the usual methods. Here we specify a fixed decimal format (rather than exponential) with `ios::fixed`, and two digits to the right of the decimal point. The manipulator `ends` inserts a `'\0'` character at the end of the string to provide an EOF. Displaying this buffer in the usual way with **cout** produces the program's output:

```
ch=x
j=77
d=67890.12
str1=Kafka
str2=Freud
```

In this example the program displays the contents of the buffer only to show what it looks like. Ordinarily you would have a more sophisticated use for this formatted data.

Command-Line Arguments

If you've ever used MS-DOS, you are probably familiar with command-line arguments, used when invoking a program. They are typically used to pass the name of a data file to an application. For example, you can invoke a word processor application and the document it will work on at the same time:

```
C>wordproc afile.doc
```

Here `afile.doc` is a command-line argument. How can we get a C++ program to read the command-line arguments? Here's an example, COMLINE, that reads and displays as many command-line arguments as you care to type (they're separated by spaces):

```
// comline.cpp
// demonstrates command-line arguments
#include <iostream>
using namespace std;

int main(int argc, char* argv[] )
   {
   cout << "\nargc = " << argc << endl;  //number of arguments

   for(int j=0; j<argc; j++)              //display arguments
      cout << "Argument " << j << " = " << argv[j] << endl;
   return 0;
   }
```

And here's a sample interaction with the program:

```
C:\C++BOOK\Chap12>comline uno dos tres

argc = 4
Argument 0 = C:\CPP\CHAP12\COMLINE.EXE
Argument 1 = uno
Argument 2 = dos
Argument 3 = tres
```

To read command-line arguments, the `main()` function (don't forget it's a function!) must itself be given two arguments. The first, `argc` (for *argument count*), represents the total number of command-line arguments. The first command-line argument is always the pathname of the current program. The remaining command-line arguments are those typed by the user; they are delimited by the space character. In the preceding example they are *uno, dos,* and *tres*.

The system stores the command-line arguments as strings in memory, and creates an array of pointers to these strings. In the example the array is called `argv` (for *argument values*). Individual strings are accessed through the appropriate pointer, so the first string (the pathname) is `argv[0]`, the second (`uno` in this example) is `argv[1]`, and so on. COMLINE accesses the arguments in turn and prints them out in a `for` loop that uses `argc`, the number of command-line arguments, as its upper limit.

You don't need to use the particular names `argc` and `argv` as arguments to `main()`, but they are so common that any other names would cause consternation to everyone but the compiler.

Here's a program that uses a command-line argument for something useful. It displays the contents of a text file whose name is supplied by the user on the command line. Thus it imitates the DOS command TYPE. Here's the listing for OTYPE:

```
// otype.cpp
// imitates TYPE command
#include <fstream>                    //for file functions
#include <iostream>
```

```
using namespace std;
#include <process.h>            //for exit()

int main(int argc, char* argv[] )
   {
   if( argc != 2 )
      {
      cerr << "\nFormat: otype filename";
      exit(-1);
      }
   char ch;                     //character to read
   ifstream infile;             //create file for input
   infile.open( argv[1] );      //open file
   if( !infile )                //check for errors
      {
      cerr << "\nCan't open " << argv[1];
      exit(-1);
      }
   while( infile.get(ch) != 0 ) //read a character
      cout << ch;               //display the character
   return 0;
   }
```

This program first checks to see if the user has entered the correct number of command-line arguments. Remember that the pathname of OTYPE.E XE itself is always the first command-line argument. The second argument is the name of the file to be displayed, which the user should have entered when invoking the program:

```
C>otype ichar.cpp
```

Thus the total number of command-line arguments should equal 2. If it doesn't, the user probably doesn't understand how to use the program, and the program sends an error message via **cerr** to clarify matters.

If the number of arguments is correct, the program tries to open the file whose name is the second command-line argument (**argv[1]**). Again, if the file can't be opened, the program signals an error. Finally, in a **while** loop, the program reads the file character by character and writes it to the screen.

A value of 0 for the character signals an EOF. This is another way to check for EOF. You can also use the value of the file object itself, as we've done before:

```
while( infile )
   {
   infile.get(ch);
   cout << ch;
   }
```

You could also replace this entire **while** loop with the statement

```
cout << infile.rdbuf();
```

as we saw earlier in the ICHAR2 program.

Printer Output

It's fairly easy to use console-mode programs to send data to the printer. A number of special filenames for hardware devices are defined by the operating system. These make it possible to treat the devices as if they were files. Table 12.11 shows these predefined names.

Table 12.11 Hardware Device Names

Name	Device
con	Console (keyboard and screen)
aux or com1	First serial port
com2	Second serial port
prn or lpt1	First parallel printer
lpt2	Second parallel printer
lpt3	Third parallel printer
nul	Dummy (nonexistent) device

In most systems the printer is connected to the first parallel port, so the filename for the printer should be prn or lpt1. (You can substitute the appropriate name if your system is configured differently.)

The following program, EZPRINT, sends a string and a number to the printer, using formatted output with the insertion operator.

```
// ezprint.cpp
// demonstrates simple output to printer
#include <fstream>                 //for file streams
using namespace std;

int main()
   {
   char* s1 = "\nToday's winning number is ";
   int   n1 = 17982;

   ofstream outfile;              //make a file
   outfile.open("PRN");           //open it for printer
   outfile << s1 << n1 << endl;   //send data to printer
   outfile << '\x0C';             //formfeed to eject page
   return 0;
   }
```

You can send any amount of formatted output to the printer this way. The '\x0C' character causes the page to eject from the printer.

The next example, OPRINT, prints the contents of a disk file, specified on the command line, to the printer. It uses the character-by-character approach to this data transfer.

```
// oprint.cpp
// imitates print command
#include <fstream>                    //for file functions
#include <iostream>
using namespace std;
#include <process.h>                  //for exit()

int main(int argc, char* argv[] )
   {
   if(argc != 2)
      {
      cerr << "\nFormat: oprint filename";
      exit(-1);
      }
   char ch;                           //character to read
   ifstream infile;                   //create file for input
   infile.open( argv[1] );            //open file
   if( !infile )                      //check for errors
      {
      cerr << "\nCan't open " << argv[1];
      exit(-1);
      }
   ofstream outfile;                  //make file
   outfile.open("PRN");               //open it for printer
   while( infile.get(ch) != 0 )       //read a character
      outfile.put(ch);                //write character to printer
   outfile.put('\x0C');               //formfeed to eject page
   return 0;
   }
```

You can use this program to print any text file, such as any of your .CPP source files. It acts much the same as the DOS PRINT command. Like the OTYPE example, this program checks for the correct number of command-line arguments, and for a successful opening of the specified file.

Summary

In this chapter we briefly examined the hierarchy of stream classes and showed how to handle various kinds of I/O errors. Then we saw how to perform file I/O in a variety of ways. Files in C++ are associated with objects of various classes, typically **ofstream** for output, **ifstream** for input, and **fstream** for both input and output. Member functions of these or base classes are used to perform I/O operations. Such operators and functions as <<, **put()**, and **write()** are used for output, while >>, **get()**, and **read()** are used for input.

The **read()** and **write()** functions work in binary mode, so that entire objects can be saved to disk no matter what sort of data they contain. Single objects can be stored, as can arrays or other data structures of many objects. File I/O can be handled by member functions. This can be the responsibility of individual objects, or the class itself can handle I/O using static member functions.

A check for error conditions should be made after each file operation. The file object itself takes on a value of 0 if an error occurred. Also, several member functions can be used to determine specific kinds of errors. The extraction operator >> and the insertion operator << can be overloaded so that they work with programmer-defined data types. Memory can be considered a stream, and data sent to it as if it were a file.

Questions

Answers to questions can be found in Appendix G, "Answers to Questions and Exercises."

1. A C++ stream is

    a. the flow of control through a function.

    b. a flow of data from one place to another.

    c. associated with a particular class.

    d. a file.

2. The base class for most stream classes is the _____ class.

3. Name three stream classes commonly used for disk I/O.

4. Write a statement that will create an object called **salefile** of the ofstream class and associate it with a file called SALES.JUN.

5. True or false: Some streams work with input, and some with output.

6. Write an **if** statement that checks if an **ifstream** object called **foobar** has reached the end of file or has encountered an error.

7. We can output text to an object of class ofstream using the insertion operator << because

    a. the ofstream class is a stream.

    b. the insertion operator works with all classes.

    c. we are actually outputting to **cout**.

    d. the insertion operator is overloaded in ofstream.

8. Write a statement that writes a single character to an object called **fileOut**, which is of class ofstream.

9. To write data that contains variables of type `float` to an object of type `ofstream`, you should use

   a. the insertion operator.

   b. `seekg()`.

   c. `write()`.

   d. `put()`.

10. Write a statement that will read the contents of an `ifstream` object called `ifile` into an array called `buff`.

11. Mode bits such as `app` and `ate`

    a. are defined in the ios class.

    b. can specify if a file is open for reading or writing.

    c. work with the `put()` and `get()` functions.

    d. specify ways of opening a file.

12. Define what *current position* means when applied to files.

13. True or false: A file pointer always contains the address of the file.

14. Write a statement that moves the current position 13 bytes backward in a stream object called `f1`.

15. The statement

    `f1.write( (char*)&obj1, sizeof(obj1) );`

    a. writes the member functions of `obj1` to `f1`.

    b. writes the data in `obj1` to `f1`.

    c. writes the member functions and the data of `obj1` to `f1`.

    d. writes the address of `obj1` to `f1`.

16. Command-line arguments are

    a. disagreements in the military.

    b. typed following a program name at the command prompt.

    c. accessed through arguments to `main()`.

    d. accessible only from disk files.

17. Used with `cin`, what does the `skipws` flag accomplish?

18. Write a declarator for `main()` that will enable command-line arguments.

19. In console mode programs, the printer can be accessed using the predefined filename _____.

20. Write the declarator for the overloaded >> operator that takes output from an object of class `istream` and displays it as the contents of an object of class `Sample`.

Exercises

Answers to starred exercises can be found in Appendix G.

*1. Start with the `Distance` class from the ENGLCON example in Chapter 6, "Objects and Classes." Using a loop similar to that in the DISKFUN example in this chapter, get a number of `Distance` values from the user, and write them to a disk file. Append them to existing values in the file, if any. When the user signals that no more values will be input, read the file and display all the values.

*2. Write a program that emulates the DOS COPY command. That is, it should copy the contents of a text file (such as any .CPP file) to another file. Invoke the program with two command-line arguments—the source file and the destination file—like this:

```
C>ocopy srcfile.cpp destfile.cpp
```

In the program, check that the user has typed the correct number of command-line arguments, and that the files specified can be opened.

*3. Write a program that returns the size in bytes of a program entered on the command line:

```
C>filesize program.ext
```

4. In a loop, prompt the user to enter *name data* consisting of a first name, middle initial, last name, and employee number (type `unsigned long`). Then, using formatted I/O with the insertion (<<) operator, write these four data items to an `ofstream` object. Don't forget that strings must be terminated with a space or other whitespace character. When the user indicates that no more name data will be entered, close the `ofstream` object, open an `ifstream` object, read and display all the data in the file, and terminate the program.

5. Create a `time` class that includes integer member values for `hours`, `minutes`, and `seconds`. Make a member function `get_time()` that gets a time value from the user, and a function `put_time()` that displays a time in 12:59:59 format. Add error checking to the `get_time()` function to minimize user mistakes. This function should request hours, minutes,

and seconds separately, and check each one for **ios** error status flags and the correct range. Hours should be between 0 and 23, and minutes and seconds between 0 and 59. Don't input these values as strings and then convert them; read them directly as integers. This implies that you won't be able to screen out entries with superfluous decimal points, as does the ENGL_IO program in this chapter, but we'll assume that's not important.

In **main()**, use a loop to repeatedly get a **time** value from the user with **get_time()** and then display it with **put_time()**, like this:

```
Enter hours: 11
Enter minutes: 59
Enter seconds: 59
time = 11:59:59

Do another (y/n)? y
Enter hours: 25
Hours must be between 0 and 23
Enter hours: 1
Enter minutes: 10
Enter seconds: five
Incorrect seconds input
Enter seconds: 5
time = 1:10:05
```

6. Make a class called **name** from the data in Exercise 4 (first name, middle initial, last name, employee number). Create member functions for this class that read and write an object's data to a disk file, using **ofstream**, and read it back using **ifstream**. Use formatted data with the **<<** and **>>** operators. The read and write member functions should be self-contained: they should include statements to open the appropriate stream and read or write a record.

   The write function can simply append its data to the end of the file. The read function will need a way to select which record it's going to read. One way to do this is to call it with a parameter representing the record number. Once it knows which record it should read, how does the read function find the record? You might think you could use the **seekg()** function, but that isn't much help because in formatted I/O the records are all different lengths (depending on the number of characters in the strings and the number of digits in the integer). So you'll need to actually read records until you've skipped forward to the one you want.

   In **main()**, call these member functions to allow the user to enter data for a number of objects that are written to a file as they are entered. The program then displays all this data by reading it from the file.

7. Another approach to adding file stream I/O to an object is to make the file stream itself a static member of the object. Why do that? Well, it's

often conceptually easier to think of the stream as being related to the class as a whole than to the individual objects of the class. Also, it's more efficient to open a stream only once, then read and write objects to it as needed. For example, once the file is opened, each time the read function is called it can return the data for the next object in the file. The file pointer will progress automatically through the file because the file is not closed between reads.

Rewrite the program in Exercises 4 and 6 to use an **fstream** object as a static data item of the name class. Keep the same functionality that is in those exercises. Write a static function to open this stream, and another static function to reset the file pointer to the beginning of the file. You can use this reset function when you're done writing and want to read all the records back from the file.

8. Starting with the LINKLIST program in Chapter 10, "Pointers," create a program that gives the user four options, which can be selected by pressing a key.

   - Add a link to the list in memory (the user supplies the data, which is one integer)

   - Display the data from all the links in memory

   - Write the data for all the links to a disk file (creating or truncating the file as necessary)

   - Read all the data back from the file, and construct a new linked list in which to store it

   The first two options can use the member functions already implemented in LINKLIST. You'll need to write functions to read to, and write from, the disk file. You can use the same file for all reads and writes. The file should store only the data; there's no sense in its storing the contents of pointers, which will probably not be relevant when the list is read back in.

9. Start with Exercise 7 in Chapter 8,"Operator Overloading," and overload the insertion (<<) and extraction (>>) operators for the **frac** class in the four-function calculator. Note that you can chain the operators, so asking for a fraction, an operator, and a fraction should require only one statement:

```
cin >> frac1 >> op >> frac2;
```

10. Add error checking to the extraction (>>) operator of the **frac** class in Exercise 9 in this chapter. With error checking it's probably better to prompt for the first fraction, then for the operator, and then for the second fraction, rather than using a single statement as shown in Exercise 9.

This makes the format more comprehensible when it is interspersed with error messages.

```
Enter first fraction: 5/0
Denominator cannot be 0
   Enter fraction again: 5/1
Enter operator (+, -, *, /): +
Enter second fraction: one third
Input error
   Enter fraction again: 1/3
Answer is ------------------- 16/3
Do another (y/n)?
```

As implied in this sample interaction, you should check for **ios** error flags and also for a denominator of 0. If there's an error, prompt the user to enter the fraction again.

11. Start with the **bMoney** class, last seen in Exercise 5 in Chapter 11. Overload the insertion (<<) and extraction (>>) operators to perform I/O on **bMoney** quantities. Perform some sample I/O in **main()**.

12. To the EMPL_IO program in this chapter add the ability to search through all the employee objects in a disk file, looking for one with a specified employee number. If it finds a match, it should display the data for the employee. The user can invoke this **find()** function by typing the f character. The function should then prompt for the employee number. Ask yourself if the function should be static, virtual, or something else. This search and display operation should not interfere with the data in memory.

Note

Note: Don't try to read a file generated with the EMPL_IO program. The classes are not the same because of the **find()** member function in the new program, and disaster will result if their data is mixed, as discussed in this chapter. You may need to turn on an "Enable RTTI" option in your compiler. Consult Appendix C, "Microsoft Visual C++," or Appendix D, "Borland C++," as appropriate.

CHAPTER 13

MULTIFILE PROGRAMS

You will learn about the following in this chapter:

- Reasons for multifile programs

- Public and private components

- Creating multifile programs

- Program: a class of very large numbers

- Program: simulating high-rise elevators

- Program: modeling a water system

*I*n previous chapters we've seen how the various parts of a C++ program—such as class declarations, member functions, and a `main()` function—are combined. However, the programs in those chapters all consisted of a single file. Now let's look at program organization from a more global perspective, involving multiple files.

Besides demonstrating multifile programs, this chapter will introduce some longer and more ambitious applications. Our aim in these programs is not that you necessarily understand every detail of their operation, but that you acquire a general understanding of how the elements of larger programs relate to one another. These programs also show how classes can be used in more realistic applications than the short examples we've seen so far. On the other hand, they are not so long that it takes all spring to wade through them.

Reasons for Multifile Programs

There are several reasons for using multifile programs. These include the use of class libraries, the organization of programmers working on a project, and the conceptual design of a program. Let's reflect briefly on these issues.

Class Libraries

In traditional procedure-oriented languages it has long been customary for software vendors to furnish libraries of functions. Other programmers then combine these libraries with their own custom-written routines to create an application for the end-user.

Libraries provide ready-made functions for a wide variety of fields. For instance, a vendor might supply a library of functions for handling statistics calculations, or one for advanced memory management.

Since C++ is organized around classes rather than functions, it's not surprising that libraries for C++ programs consist of classes. What may be surprising is how superior a class library is to an old-fashioned function library. Because classes encapsulate both data and functions, and because they more closely model objects in real life, the interface between a class library and the application that makes use of it can be much cleaner than that provided by a function library.

For these reasons class libraries assume a more important role in C++ programming than function libraries do in traditional programming. A class library can take over a greater portion of the programming burden. An applications programmer, if the right class library is available, may find that only a minimal amount of programming is necessary to create a final product. Also, as more and more class libraries are created, the chances of finding one that solves your particular programming problem continues to increase.

We'll see an important example of a class library in Chapter 15, "The Standard Template Library."

A class library usually includes two components: the *interface* and the *implementation*. Let's see what the difference is.

Interface

Let's say that the person who wrote a class library is called the *class developer*, and the person who uses the library is called the *programmer*.

To use a class library, the programmer needs to access various declarations, including class declarations. These declarations can be thought of as the public part of the library and are usually furnished in source-code form as a header file, with the .H extension. This file is typically combined with the client's source code using an `#include` statement.

The declarations in such a header file need to be public for several reasons. First, it's a convenience to the client to see the actual class definitions rather than to have to read a description of them. More importantly, the programmer will need to declare objects based on these classes and call on member functions from these objects. Only by declaring the classes in the source file is this possible.

These declarations are called the *interface* because that's what a user of the class (the programmer) sees and interacts with. The programmer need not be concerned with the other part of the library, the *implementation*.

Implementation

On the other hand, the inner workings of the member functions of the various classes don't need to be known by the programmer. The class developers, like any other software developers, don't want to release source code if they can help it, since it might be illegally modified or pirated. Member functions—except for short inline functions—are therefore often distributed in object form, as .OBJ files or as library (.LIB) files. (Various other extensions may be used for Windows-specific classes such as ActiveX and COM and for various other specialized situations.)

Figure 13.1 shows how the various files are related in a multifile system.

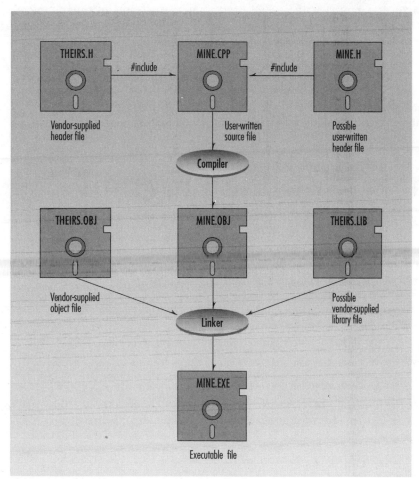

Figure 13.1   Files in a multifile application.

In this chapter we'll show several larger programs organized according to these principles. The first program introduces a class of very large numbers. By "very large," we mean numbers with an almost unlimited number of digits. Such numbers are important in various kinds of mathematics, such as calculating pi to thousands of digits. The second example simulates an elevator system in a high-rise building, using classes for the elevators and the building. The final program provides classes that allow you to create your own water-distribution system. You can connect valves, tanks, pipes, and similar components to model water systems such as the cooling system in a nuclear reactor.

Organization and Conceptualization

Programs may be broken down into multiple files for reasons other than the accommodation of class libraries. As in other programming languages, such as C, a common situation involves a project with several programmers (or teams of programmers). Confining each programmer's responsibility to a separate file helps organize the project and define more cleanly the interface among different parts of the program.

It is also often the case that a program is divided into separate files according to functionality: One file can handle the code involved in a graphics display, for example, while another file handles mathematical analysis, and a third handles disk I/O. In large programs, a single file may simply become too large to handle conveniently.

The techniques used for working with multifile programs are similar, whatever the reasons for dividing the program.

Creating a Multifile Program

Suppose that you have purchased a prewritten class file called THEIRS.OBJ. (A library file with the .LIB extension is dealt with in much the same way.) It probably comes with a header file, say THEIRS.H. You have also written your own program to use the classes in the library; your source file is called MINE.CPP. Now you want to combine these component files—THEIRS.OBJ, THEIRS.H, and MINE.CPP—into a single executable program.

Header Files

The header file THEIRS.H is easily incorporated into your own source file, MINE.CPP, with an `#include` statement:

```
#include "THEIRS.H"
```

Quotes rather than angle brackets around the filename tell the compiler to look first for the file in the current directory, rather than in the default include directory.

Directory

Make sure all the component files, THEIRS.OBJ, THEIRS.H, and MINE.CPP, are in the same directory. In fact, you will probably want to create a separate directory for the project, to avoid confusion. (This isn't strictly necessary, but it's the simplest approach.)

Projects

Most compilers manage multiple files using a project metaphor. A project contains all the files necessary for the application. It also contains instructions for combining these files, often in a special file called a *project file*. The extension for this file varies with the compiler vendor. It's .BPR for Borland, and .DSP for Microsoft. Modern compilers construct and maintain this file automatically, so you don't need to worry about it. In general you must tell the compiler about all the source (.CPP) files you plan to use so they can be added to the project. You can add .OBJ and .LIB files in a similar way. Header files are dealt with differently by different compilers. Some compilers require them to be added to the project, while others will go out and look for them automatically when they see the #include directive in a source file.

Appendices C and D provide details on creating multifile programs for specific compilers.

Only a single command needs to be given to the compiler for it to compile all the source (.CPP and .H) files and link the resulting .OBJ files (and any other .OBJ or .LIB files) into a final .EXE file. This is called the *build* process. Often the .EXE file can be executed as well. (In Windows and other advanced programming there are many more types of files.)

One of the nice things about a project is that it keeps track of the dates when you compiled each source file. Only those source files that have been modified since the last build are recompiled; this can save considerable time, especially on large projects. Some compilers distinguish between a Make command and a Build command. Make compiles only those source files that have changed since the last build, whereas Build compiles all files regardless of date.

A Very Long Number Class

Sometimes even the basic data type unsigned long does not provide enough precision for certain integer arithmetic operations. unsigned long is the largest integer type in Standard C++, holding integers up to 4,294,967,295, or about ten digits. This is about the same number of digits a pocket calculator can handle. But if you need to work with integers containing more significant digits than this, you have a problem.

Our next example offers a solution. It provides a class that holds integers up to 1,000 digits long. If you want to make even longer numbers (or shorter ones), you can change a single constant in the program.

Numbers As Strings

The verylong class stores numbers as strings of digits. These are old-fashioned char* C-strings, which are easier to work with in this context than the string class. The use of C-strings explains the large digit capacity: C++ can handle long C-strings, since they are simply arrays. By representing numbers as C-strings we can make them as long as we want. There are two data members in verylong: a char array to hold the string of digits, and an int to tell how long the string is. (This length of data isn't strictly necessary, but it saves using strlen() repeatedly to find the string length.) The digits in the string are stored in reverse order, with the least significant digit stored first, at vlstr[0]. This simplifies various operations on the string. Figure 13.2 shows a number stored as a string.

We've provided user-accessible routines for addition and multiplication of verylong numbers. (We leave it as an exercise for the reader to write subtraction and division routines.)

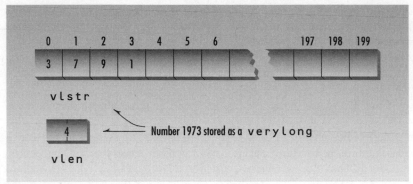

Figure 13.2 A VERYLONG number.

The Class Specifier

Here's the header file for VERYLONG. It shows the specifiers for the **verylong** class.

```
// verylong.h
// class specifier for very long integer type
#include <iostream>
#include <string.h>          //for strlen(), etc.
#include <stdlib.h>          //for ltoa()
using namespace std;

const int SZ = 1000;
        //maximum digits in verylongs

class verylong
    {
    private:
        char vlstr[SZ];         //verylong number, as a string
        int vlen;               //length of verylong string
        verylong multdigit(const int) const;   //prototypes for
        verylong mult10(const verylong) const; //private functions
    public:
        verylong() : vlen(0)            //no-arg constructor
            { vlstr[0]='\0'; }
        verylong(const char s[SZ])      //one-arg constructor
            { strcpy(vlstr, s); vlen=strlen(s); }   //for string
        verylong(const unsigned long n)  //one-arg constructor
            {                                   //for long int
            ltoa(n, vlstr, 10);             //convert to string
            strrev(vlstr);                  //reverse it
            vlen=strlen(vlstr);             //find length
            }
        void putvl() const;             //display verylong
        void getvl();                   //get verylong from user
        verylong operator + (const verylong); //add verylongs
        verylong operator * (const verylong); //multiply verylongs
    };
```

In addition to the data members, there are two private-member functions in class verylong. One multiplies a verylong number by a single digit, and the other multiplies a verylong number by 10. These routines are used internally by the multiplication routine.

There are three constructors. One sets the verylong to 0 by inserting a terminating null at the beginning of the array and setting the length to 0. The second initializes it to a string (which is in reverse order), and the third initializes it to a long int value.

The putvl() member function displays a verylong, and getvl() gets a verylong value from the user. You can type as many digits as you like, up to 1000. Note that there is no error checking in this routine; if you type a non-digit the results will be inaccurate.

Two overloaded operators, + and *, perform addition and multiplication. You can use expressions like

```
alpha = beta * gamma + delta;
```

to do verylong arithmetic.

The Member Functions

Here's VERYLONG.CPP, the file that holds the member function definitions:

```
// verylong.cpp
// implements very long integer type
#include "verylong.h"           //header file for verylong
//--------------------------------------------------------------
void verylong::putvl() const              //display verylong
   {
   char temp[SZ];
   strcpy(temp,vlstr);                    //make copy
   cout << strrev(temp);                  //reverse the copy
   }                                      //and display it
//--------------------------------------------------------------
void verylong::getvl()                    //get verylong from user
   {
   cin >> vlstr;                          //get string from user
   vlen = strlen(vlstr);                  //find its length
   strrev(vlstr);                         //reverse it
   }
//--------------------------------------------------------------
verylong verylong::operator + (const verylong v) //add verylongs
   {
   char temp[SZ];
   int j;
                   //find longest number
   int maxlen = (vlen > v.vlen) ? vlen : v.vlen;
   int carry = 0;                         //set to 1 if sum >= 10
   for(j = 0; j<maxlen; j++)              //for each position
      {
      int d1 = (j > vlen-1)   ? 0 : vlstr[j]-'0';   //get digit
      int d2 = (j > v.vlen-1) ? 0 : v.vlstr[j]-'0'; //get digit
      int digitsum = d1 + d2 + carry;              //add digits
      if( digitsum >= 10 )               //if there's a carry,
         { digitsum -= 10; carry=1; }    //decrease sum by 10,
```

```
       else                                 //set carry to 1
          carry = 0;                         //otherwise carry is 0
       temp[j] = digitsum+'0';              //insert char in string
       }
    if(carry==1)                            //if carry at end,
       temp[j++] = '1';                      //last digit is 1
    temp[j] = '\0';                         //terminate string
    return verylong(temp);                  //return temp verylong
    }
//--------------------------------------------------------------
verylong verylong::operator * (const verylong v)   //multiply
    {                                              //verylongs
    verylong pprod;                         //product of one digit
    verylong tempsum;                       //running total
    for(int j=0; j<v.vlen; j++)             //for each digit in arg
       {
       int digit = v.vlstr[j]-'0';          //get the digit
       pprod = multdigit(digit);            //multiply this by digit
       for(int k=0; k<j; k++)               //multiply result by
          pprod = mult10(pprod);            //    power of 10
       tempsum = tempsum + pprod;           //add product to total
       }
    return tempsum;                         //return total of prods
    }
//--------------------------------------------------------------
verylong verylong::mult10(const verylong v) const //multiply
    {                                              //arg by 10
    char temp[SZ];
    for(int j=v.vlen-1; j>=0; j--)          //move digits one
       temp[j+1] = v.vlstr[j];              //    position higher
    temp[0] = '0';                          //put zero on low end
    temp[v.vlen+1] = '\0';                  //terminate string
    return verylong(temp);                  //return result
    }
//--------------------------------------------------------------
verylong verylong::multdigit(const int d2) const
    {                                       //multiply this verylong
    char temp[SZ];                          //by digit in argument
    int j, carry = 0;
    for(j = 0; j<vlen; j++)                 //for each position
       {                                    //    in this verylong
       int d1 = vlstr[j]-'0';               //get digit from this
       int digitprod = d1 * d2;             //multiply by that digit
       digitprod += carry;                  //add old carry
       if( digitprod >= 10 )                //if there's a new carry,
          {
          carry = digitprod/10;             //carry is high digit
          digitprod -= carry*10;            //result is low digit
          }
       else
          carry = 0;                        //otherwise carry is 0
       temp[j] = digitprod+'0';             //insert char in string
       }
```

```
if(carry != 0)                    //if carry at end,
    temp[j++] = carry+'0';        //it's last digit
temp[j] = '\0';                   //terminate string
return verylong(temp);            //return verylong
}
```

The `putvl()` and `getvl()` functions are fairly straightforward. They use the `strrev()` C library function to reverse the C-string, so it is stored in reverse order but input is displayed normally.

The `operator+()` function adds two `verylong`s and leaves the result in a third `verylong`. It does this by considering their digits one at a time. It adds digit 0 from both numbers, storing a carry if necessary. Then it adds the digits in position 1, adding the carry if necessary. It continues until it has added all the digits in the larger of the two numbers. If the numbers are different lengths, the nonexistent digits in the shorter number are set to 0 before being added. Figure 13.3 shows the process.

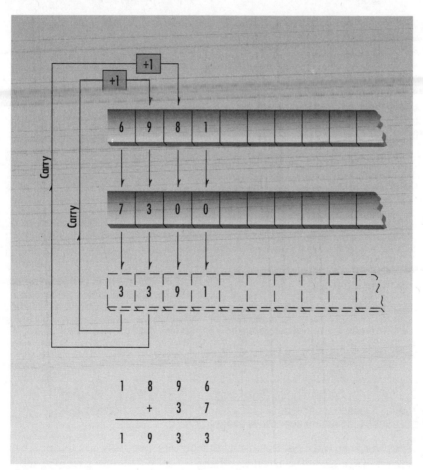

Figure 13.3   Adding `verylong` numbers.

Multiplication uses the `operator*()` function. This function performs multiplication by multiplying the multiplicand (the top number when you write it by hand) by each separate digit in the multiplier (the bottom number). It calls the `multdigit()` routine to this. The results are then multiplied by 10 an appropriate number of times to shift the result to match the position of the digit, using the `mult10()` function. The results of these separate calculations are then added together using the `operator+()` function.

The Application Program

To test the `verylong` class we use a variation of the FACTOR program from Chapter 3, "Loops and Decisions," to calculate the factorial of a number entered by the user. Here's the listing for VL_APP.CPP:

```
// vl_app.cpp
// calculates factorials of larger numbers using verylong class
#include "verylong.h"                    //verylong header file

int main()
   {
   unsigned long numb, j;
   verylong fact=1;                      //initialize verylong

   cout << "\n\nEnter number: ";
   cin >> numb;                          //input a long int

   for(j=numb; j>0; j--)                 //factorial is numb *
      fact = fact * j;                   //   numb-1 * numb-2 *
   cout << "Factorial is ";              //   numb-3 and so on
   fact.putvl();                         //display factorial
   cout << endl;
   return 0;
   }
```

In this program `fact` is a `verylong` variable. The other variables, numb and `j`, don't need to be `verylong`s because they don't get so big. To calculate the factorial of 100, for example, `numb` and `j` require only three digits, while `fact` requires 158.

Notice how, in the expression

```
fact = fact * j;
```

the long variable `j` is automatically converted to `verylong`, using the one-argument constructor, before the multiplication is carried out.

Here's the output when we ask the program to find the factorial of 100:

```
Enter number: 100
Factorial is 93326215443944152681699238856266700490711596826438162
146859296389521759999322991560894146397615651828625369792082722 3
758251185210916864000000000000000000000000
```

Try *that* using type `long` variables! Surprisingly, the routines are fairly fast; this program executes in a fraction of a second. You can calculate the factorial of numbers up to about 400 before you exceed the 1000 digit capacity of the program.

A High-Rise Elevator Simulation

The next time you're waiting for an elevator in a high-rise office building, ask yourself how the elevators figure out where to go. In the old days, of course, there was a human elevator operator on each car. ("Good morning, Mr. Burberry," "Good morning, Carl.") Riders needed to tell the operator their destination floor when getting on ("Seventeen, please."). A panel of signal lights lit up inside the car to show which floors were requesting service up or down. Operators decided which way to go and where to stop on the basis of these verbal requests and their observation of the signal lights.

Nowadays enough intelligence is built into elevator systems to permit the cars to operate on their own. In our next example we use C++ classes to model an elevator system.

What are the components of such a system? In a typical building there are a number of similar elevators. On each floor there are up and down buttons. Note that there is usually only one such pair of buttons per floor; when you push a button you don't know which elevator will stop for you. Within the elevator there is a larger number of buttons: one for each floor. After entering the elevator, riders push a button to indicate their destination. Our simulation program will model all these components.

Running the ELEV Program

When you start up the ELEV program you'll see four elevators sitting at the bottom of the screen, and a list of numbers on the left, starting at 1 on the bottom of the screen and continuing up to 20 at the top. The elevators are initially on the ground (first) floor. This is shown in Figure 13.4.

Figure 13.4 The ELEV program initial screen.

Making a Floor Request

If you press (Enter), text at the bottom of the screen prompts

```
Enter the floor you're on:
```

You can enter any floor number from 1 to 20. If you've just arrived for work on the ground floor, you'll enter 1. If you're leaving a higher floor to go out to lunch, you'll enter your floor's number. The next prompt is

```
Enter direction you want to go (u or d):
```

If you're on the first floor you must go up, and if you're on the 20th floor you must go down. For intermediate floors you can go either way. When you've completed your floor request, a triangle will appear next to the appropriate floor number on the left. It will point either up or down, depending on the direction you requested. As more requests are made, triangles will appear beside additional floor numbers.

If there is an elevator car already at a floor where a request has been made, the door will open immediately. You'll see a happy-face character materialize outside the car, then move into the open door. If there is no car on the floor making the request, one will move up or down toward the floor and open its door once it reaches the floor.

Entering Destinations

Once a car arrives at a floor and the happy-face passenger is inside, a prompt appears on the bottom of the screen:

```
Car 1 has stopped at floor 1
Enter destination floors (0 when finished)
Destination 1: 13
```

Here the passenger has entered 13. However, the happy face can represent more than one passenger getting on at once. Each passenger may request a different destination, so the program allows multiple destinations to be entered. Enter as many numbers as you want (at least 1, but no more than 20) and enter 0 when you're done.

The destinations requested by passengers within a particular car are indicated by small rectangles displayed outside the car, just to its left, opposite the floor number requested. Each car has its own set of destinations (unlike floor requests, which are shared by all the cars).

You can make as many floor requests as you like. The system will remember the requests, along with the destinations selected from within each car, and attempt to service them all. All four cars may be in motion at the same time. Figure 13.5 shows a situation with multiple floor requests and multiple destinations.

Designing the System

The elevator cars are all roughly the same, so it seems reasonable to make them objects of a single class, called `elevator`. This class will contain data specific to each car: its present location, the direction it's going, the destination floor numbers requested by its occupants, and so on.

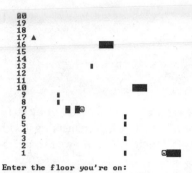

Figure 13.5 Elevators in action.

However, there is also data that applies to the building as a whole. This data will be part of the **building** class. First there is an array of *floor requests*. This is a list of floors where people, waiting for the elevator, have pushed the up or down button to request that an elevator stop at their floor. Any elevator may respond to such a floor request, so each one needs to know about them. We use an N-by-2 array of type **bool**, where N is the number of floors and the 2 allows separate array elements for up and down for each floor. All the elevators can look at this array when they're trying to figure out where to go next.

Besides knowing about the floor requests, each elevator car must also be aware of where the other elevators are. If we're on the first floor, there's no point in rushing up to the 15th floor to answer a request if there's already another car available on the 10th floor. The closest car should head toward the request. To make it easy for each car to find out about the others, the second data item in **building** is an array of pointers to elevators. Each elevator car stores its memory address on this list when it's first created, so the other cars can find it.

The third data item in the **building** class is the number of cars created so far. This allows each car to number itself sequentially when it's created.

Managing Time

The **main()** program calls a member function of building at fixed intervals to put things into motion. This function is called **master_tick()**. It in turn calls a function for each elevator car, called **car_tick1()**. This function, among other things, displays each car on the screen and calls another function to decide what the car should do next. The choices are to go up, to go down, to stop, to load a passenger, or to unload a passenger.

Each car must then be moved to its new position. However, things get slightly complicated here. Because each car must figure out where the other ones are before it can decide what to do, all the cars must go through the decision process before any of them moves. To make sure this happens, we use two time ticks for each car. Thus after **car_tick1()** has been called to decide where each car will go, another function, **car_tick2()**, is called to actually move each car. It causes the cars to move by changing the variable **current_floor**.

The process of loading passengers follows a fixed sequence of steps, during which the car is stopped at the desired floor. The program draws, in order

1. Car with closed door, no happy face.

2. Car with open door, happy face on left.

3. Car with happy face in open door, get destinations from user.

4. Car with closed door, no happy face.

The reverse sequence applies to unloading. These sequences are carried out by starting a timer (an integer variable) and letting it count down from 3 to 0, decrementing it with each time tick. A **case** statement in the **car_display()** function then draws the appropriate version of the car for each stage of the process.

Because the ELEV program uses various console graphics functions, it requires a header file; either MSOFTCON.H for Microsoft compilers or BORLACON.H for Borland compilers. (See Appendix E, "Console Graphics Lite.")

Listings for ELEV

We've divided the program into four files. Two of these files, ELEV.H and ELEV.CPP, might be created by a vendor supplying elevator-design software. This software would then be purchased by an engineering company interested in designing an elevator system for a particular building. (This program is not certified by the National Elevator Board, so don't try it with real elevators.) The engineering company would then write another pair of files, ELEV_APP.H and ELEV_APP.CPP. The ELEV_APP.H file specifies the characteristics of the high-rise building. It needs to be a separate file because these characteristics must be known by the elevator class member functions, and the easiest way to do this is to include ELEV_APP.H in the ELEV.H file. The ELEV_APP.CPP file initializes the elevators and then calls elevator functions at fixed intervals to simulate the passage of time.

Class Specifier

The ELEV.H file contains the specification for the elevator class. The array of pointers to elevators, **car_list[]**, allows each elevator to query all the others about their location and direction. Here's the listing:

```
// elev.h
// header file for elevators -- contains class declarations

#include "elev_app.h"              //provided by client
#include <msoftcon.h>             //for console graphics
#include <iostream>
#include <iomanip>                //for setw()
#include <conio.h>                //for screen output
#include <stdlib.h>               //for itoa()
#include <process.h>              //for exit()
using namespace std;

enum direction { UP, DN, STOP };
const int LOAD_TIME =    3;   //loading/unloading time (ticks)
```

```
const int SPACING =       7;    //visual spacing between cars
const int BUF_LENGTH =   80;    //length of utility string buffer

class building;
/////////////////////////////////////////////////////////////
class elevator
   {
   private:
   building* ptrBuilding;            //ptr to parent building
   const int car_number;            //our number (0 to nc-1)
   int current_floor;               //where are we? (0 to nf-1)
   int old_floor;                   //where were we? (0 to nf-1)
   direction current_dir;           //which way are we going?
   bool destination[NUM_FLOORS];    //selected by occupants
   int loading_timer;               //non-zero if loading
   int unloading_timer;             //non-zero if unloading

   public:
   elevator(building*, int);        //constructor
   void car_tick1();                //time tick 1 for each car
   void car_tick2();                //time tick 2 for each car
   void car_display();              //display elevator
   void dests_display() const;      //display elevator requests
   void decide();                   //decide what to do
   void move();                     //move the car
   void get_destinations();         //get destinations
   int get_floor() const;           //get current floor
   direction get_direction() const; //get current direction
   };
/////////////////////////////////////////////////////////////
class building
   {
   private:
   elevator* car_list[NUM_CARS];    //ptrs to cars
   int num_cars;                    //cars created so far
                                    //array of up/down buttons
   bool floor_request[2][NUM_FLOORS]; //false=UP, true=DN

   public:
   building();                      //constructor
   ~building();                     //destructor
   void master_tick();              //send ticks to all cars
   int get_cars_floor(const int) const; //find where a car is
                                    //find which way car is going
   direction get_cars_dir(const int) const;
                                    //check specific floor req
   bool get_floor_req(const int, const int) const;
                                    //set specific floor req
   void set_floor_req(const int, const int, const bool);
   void record_floor_reqs();        //get floor requests
   void show_floor_reqs() const;    //show floor requests
   };
```

Member Functions

The ELEV.CPP file contains the definitions of the **elevator** class and **building** class member functions and data. Functions in **building** initialize the system, provide a master time tick, display the floor requests, and get floor requests from the user. Functions in **elevator** initialize individual cars (with the constructor), provide two time ticks for each car, display it, display its destinations, decide what to do, move the car to a new floor, and get destinations from the user. Here's the listing:

```cpp
// elev.cpp
// contains class data and member function definitions

#include "elev.h"      //include class declarations
/////////////////////////////////////////////////////////////////
//            function definitions for class building
/////////////////////////////////////////////////////////////////
building::building()                      //constructor
   {
   char ustring[BUF_LENGTH];              //string for floor numbers

   init_graphics();                       //initialize graphics
   clear_screen();                        //clear screen
   num_cars = 0;
   for(int k=0; k<NUM_CARS; k++)          //make elevators
      {
      car_list[k] = new elevator(this, num_cars);
      num_cars++;
      }
   for(int j=0; j<NUM_FLOORS; j++)        //for each floor
      {
      set_cursor_pos(3, NUM_FLOORS-j);   //put floor number
      itoa(j+1, ustring, 10);            //on screen
      cout << setw(3) << ustring;
      floor_request[UP][j] = false;      //no floor requests yet
      floor_request[DN][j] = false;
      }
   } //end constructor
//------------------------------------------------------------
building::~building()                     //destructor
   {
   for(int k=0 k<NUM_CARS; k++)
      delete car_list[k];
   }
//------------------------------------------------------------
void building::master_tick()              //master time tick
   {
   int j;
   show_floor_reqs();                     //display floor requests
   for(j=0; j<NUM_CARS; j++)              //for each elevator
      car_list[j]->car_tick1();           //send it time tick 1
   for(j=0; j<NUM_CARS; j++)              //for each elevator
      car_list[j]->car_tick2();           //send it time tick 2
   } //end master_tick()
```

```
//••••••••••••••••••••••••••••••••••••••••••••••••••••••••••••••••••
void building::show_floor_reqs() const  //display floor requests
   {
   for(int j=0; j<NUM_FLOORS; j++)
      {
      set_cursor_pos(SPACING, NUM_FLOORS-j);
      if(floor_request[UP][j]==true)
         cout << '\x1E';                //up arrow
      else
         cout << ' ';
      set_cursor_pos(SPACING+3, NUM_FLOORS-j);
      if(floor_request[DN][j]==true)
         cout << '\x1F';                //down arrow
      else
         cout << ' ';
      }
   } //end show_floor_reqs()
//------------------------------------------------------------------
//record_floor_reqs() -- get requests from riders outside car
void building::record_floor_reqs()
   {
   char ch = 'x';             //utility char for input
   char ustring[BUF_LENGTH];  //utility string for input
   int iFloor;                //floor from which request made
   char chDirection;          //'u' or 'd' for up or down

   set_cursor_pos(1,22);      //bottom of screen
   cout << "Press [Enter] to call an elevator: ";
   if( !kbhit() )             //wait for keypress (must be CR)
      return;
   cin.ignore(10, '\n');
   if(ch=='\x1B')             //if escape key, end program
      exit(0);
   set_cursor_pos(1,22); clear_line();  //clear old text
   set_cursor_pos(1,22);      //bottom of screen
   cout << "Enter the floor you're on: ";
   cin.get(ustring, BUF_LENGTH);        //get floor
   cin.ignore(10, '\n');      //eat chars, including newline
   iFloor = atoi(ustring);    //convert to integer

   cout << "Enter direction you want to go (u or d): ";
   cin.get(chDirection);      //(avoid multiple linefeeds)
   cin.ignore(10, '\n');      //eat chars, including newline

   if(chDirection=='u' || chDirection=='U')
      floor_request[UP][iFloor-1] = true;  //up floor request
   if(chDirection=='d' || chDirection=='D')
      floor_request[DN][iFloor-1] = true;  //down floor request
   set_cursor_pos(1,22); clear_line();     //clear old text
   set_cursor_pos(1,23); clear_line();
   set_cursor_pos(1,24); clear_line();
   } //end record_floor_reqs()
//------------------------------------------------------------------
```

```
//get_floor_req() -- see if there's a specific request
bool building::get_floor_req(const int dir,
                                const int floor) const
   {
   return floor_request[dir][floor];
   }
//--------------------------------------------------------------
//set_floor_req() -- set specific floor request
void building::set_floor_req(const int dir, const int floor,
                             const bool updown)
   {
   floor_request[dir][floor] = updown;
   }
//--------------------------------------------------------------
//get_cars_floor() -- find where a car is
int building::get_cars_floor(const int carNo) const
   {
   return car_list[carNo]->get_floor();
   }
//--------------------------------------------------------------
//get_cars_dir() -- find which way car is going
direction building::get_cars_dir(const int carNo) const
   {
   return car_list[carNo]->get_direction();
   }
//--------------------------------------------------------------


/////////////////////////////////////////////////////////////////
//            function definitions for class elevator
/////////////////////////////////////////////////////////////////
                                      //constructor
elevator::elevator(building* ptrB, int nc) :
                            ptrBuilding(ptrB), car_number(nc)
   {
   current_floor = 0;                 //start at 0 (user's 1)
   old_floor = 0;                     //remember previous floor
   current_dir = STOP;                //stationary at start
   for(int j=0; j<NUM_FLOORS; j++)    //occupants have not pushed
      destination[j] = false;         //    any buttons yet
   loading_timer = 0;                 //not loading yet
   unloading_timer = 0;               //not unloading yet
                                   } //end constructor
//--------------------------------------------------------------
int elevator::get_floor() const      //get current floor
   {
   return current_floor;
   }
//--------------------------------------------------------------
direction elevator::get_direction() const  //get current
   {                                        //  direction
   return current_dir;
   }
//--------------------------------------------------------------
```

```cpp
Void elevator::car_tick1()              //tick 1 for each car
   {
   car_display();                       //display elevator box
   dests_display();                     //display destinations
   if(loading_timer)                    //count down load time
      --loading_timer;
   if(unloading_timer)                  //count down unload time
      --unloading_timer;
   decide();                            //decide what to do
   } //end car_tick()
//------------------------------------------------------------
//all cars must decide before any of them move
void elevator::car_tick2()              //tick 2 for each car
   {
   move();                              //move car if appropriate
   }
//------------------------------------------------------------
void elevator::car_display()            //display elevator image
   {
   set_cursor_pos(SPACING+(car_number+1)*SPACING, NUM_FLOORS-old_floor);
   cout << "   ";                       //erase old position
   set_cursor_pos(SPACING-1+(car_number+1)*SPACING,
                               NUM_FLOORS-current_floor);
   switch(loading_timer)
      {
      case 3:
         cout << "\x01\xDB \xDB ";      //draw car with open door
         break;                         //happy face on left
      case 2:
         cout << " \xDB\x01\xDB ";      //happy face in open door
         get_destinations();            //get destinations
         break;
      case 1:
         cout << " \xDB\xDB\xDB ";      //draw with closed door
         break;                         //no happy face
      case 0:
         cout << " \xDB\xDB\xDB ";      //closed door, no
         break;                         //happy face (default)
      }
   set_cursor_pos(SPACING+(car_number+1)*SPACING,
                               NUM_FLOORS-current_floor);
   switch(unloading_timer)
      {
      case 3:
         cout << "\xDB\x01\xDB ";       //draw car with open door
         break;                         //happy face in car
      case 2:
         cout << "\xDB \xDB\x01";       //draw car with open door
         break;                         //happy face on right
      case 1:
         cout << "\xDB\xDB\xDB ";       //draw with closed door
         break;                         //no happy face
      case 0:
```

```cpp
        cout << "\xDB\xDB\xDB ";      //closed door, no
        break;                        //happy face (default)
      }
   old_floor = current_floor;         //remember old floor
   }  //end car_display()
//-------------------------------------------------------------
void elevator::dests_display() const //display destinations
   {                                  //    selected by buttons
   for(int j=0; j<NUM_FLOORS; j++)    //    inside the car
      {
      set_cursor_pos(SPACING-2+(car_number+1)*SPACING, NUM_FLOORS-j);
      if( destination[j] == true )
         cout << '\xFE';              //small box
      else
         cout << ' ';                 //blank
      }
   }  //end dests_display()
//-------------------------------------------------------------
void elevator::decide()                    //decide what to do
   {
   int j;
   //flags indicate if destinations or requests above/below us
   bool destins_above, destins_below;    //destinations
   bool requests_above, requests_below;  //requests
   //floor number of closest request above us and below us
   int nearest_higher_req = 0;
   int nearest_lower_req = 0;
   //flags indicate if there is another car, going in the same
   //direction, between us and the nearest floor request (FR)
   bool car_between_up, car_between_dn;
   //flags indicate if there is another car, going in the
   //opposite direction, on the opposite side of the nearest FR
   bool car_opposite_up, car_opposite_dn;
   //floor and direction of other car (not us)
   int ofloor;                              //floor
   direction odir;                          //direction

   //ensure we don't go too high or too low
   if( (current_floor==NUM_FLOORS-1 && current_dir==UP)
      || (current_floor==0 && current_dir==DN) )
      current_dir = STOP;

   //if there's a destination on this floor, unload passengers
   if( destination[current_floor]==true )
      {
      destination[current_floor] = false;  //erase destination
      if( !unloading_timer)                //unload
         unloading_timer = LOAD_TIME;
      return;
      }
   //if there's an UP floor request on this floor,
   //and if we're going up or stopped, load passengers
   if( (ptrBuilding->get_floor_req(UP, current_floor) &&
```

```
                ourrent_dir != DN) )
      {
    current_dir = UP;  //(in case it was STOP)
    //remove floor request for direction we're going
    ptrBuilding->set_floor_req(current_dir,
                               current_floor, false);
    if( !loading_timer)                   //load
       loading_timer = LOAD_TIME;
    return;
    }
//if there's a down floor request on this floor,
//and if we're going down or stopped, load passengers
if( (ptrBuilding->get_floor_req(DN, current_floor) &&
     current_dir != UP) )
      {
    current_dir = DN;  //(in case it was STOP)
    //remove floor request for direction we're going
    ptrBuilding->set_floor_req(current_dir,
                              current_floor, false);
    if( !loading_timer)                   //load passengers
       loading_timer = LOAD_TIME;
    return;
    }
//check if there are other destinations or requests
//record distance to nearest request
destins_above = destins_below = false;
requests_above = requests_below = false;
for(j=current_floor+1; j<NUM_FLOORS; j++)
    {                                     //check floors above
    if( destination[j] )                  //if destinations
       destins_above = true;              //set flag
    if( ptrBuilding->get_floor_req(UP, j) ||
       ptrBuilding->get_floor_req(DN, j) )
         {                                //if requests
       requests_above = true;             //set flag
       if( !nearest_higher_req )          //if not set before
          nearest_higher_req = j;         //   set nearest req
       }
    }
for(j=current_floor-1; j>=0; j--)         //check floors below
   {
   if(destination[j] )                    //if destinations
      destins_below = true;               //set flag
   if( ptrBuilding->get_floor_req(UP, j) ||
      ptrBuilding->get_floor_req(DN, j) )
        {                                 //if requests
      requests_below = true;              //set flag
      if( !nearest_lower_req )            //if not set before
         nearest_lower_req = j;           //   set nearest req
      }
   }
//if no requests or destinations above or below, stop
if( !destins_above && !requests_above &&
```

```
         !destins_below && !requests_below)
         {
      current_dir = STOP;
      return;
         }
//if destinations and we're stopped, or already going the
//right way, go toward destinations
if( destins_above && (current_dir==STOP ¦¦ current_dir==UP) )
      {
   current_dir = UP;
   return;
      }
if( destins_below && (current_dir==STOP ¦¦ current_dir==DN) )
      {
   current_dir = DN;
   return;
      }
//find out if there are other cars, (a) going in the same
//direction, between us and the nearest floor request;
//or (b) going in the opposite direction, on the other
//side of the floor request
car_between_up = car_between_dn = false;
car_opposite_up = car_opposite_dn = false;

for(j=0; j<NUM_CARS; j++)                //check each car
      {
   if(j != car_number)                   //if it's not us
         {                               //get its floor
      ofloor = ptrBuilding->get_cars_floor(j);   //and
      odir = ptrBuilding->get_cars_dir(j); //direction

         //if it's going up and there are requests above us
         if( (odir==UP ¦¦ odir==STOP) && requests_above )
            //if it's above us and below the nearest request
            if( (ofloor > current_floor
               && ofloor <= nearest_higher_req)
            //or on same floor as us but is lower car number
              ¦¦ (ofloor==current_floor && j < car_number) )
               car_between_up = true;
         //if it's going down and there are requests below us
         if( (odir==DN ¦¦ odir==STOP) && requests_below )
            //if it's below us and above the nearest request
            if( (ofloor < current_floor
               && ofloor >= nearest_lower_req)
               //or on same floor as us but is lower car number
               ¦¦ (ofloor==current_floor && j < car_number) )
               car_between_dn = true;
         //if it's going up and there are requests below us
         if( (odir==UP ¦¦ odir==STOP) && requests_below )
            //it's below request and closer to it than we are
            if(nearest_lower_req >= ofloor
               && nearest_lower_req - ofloor
                  < current_floor - nearest_lower_req)
```

```
                       car_opposite_up = true;
            //if it's going down and there are requests above us
            if( (odir==DN || odir==STOP) && requests_above )
               //it's above request and closer to it than we are
               if(ofloor >= nearest_higher_req
                   && ofloor - nearest_higher_req
                       < nearest_higher_req - current_floor)
                   car_opposite_dn = true;
            }  //end if(not us)
      }  //end for(each car)

   //if we're going up or stopped, and there is an FR above us,
   //and there are no other cars going up between us and the FR,
   //or above the FR going down and closer than we are,
   //then go up
   if( (current_dir==UP || current_dir==STOP)
      && requests_above && !car_between_up && !car_opposite_dn )
      {
      current_dir = UP;
      return;
      }

   //if we're going down or stopped, and there is an FR below
   //us, and there are no other cars going down between us and
   //the FR, or below the FR going up and closer than we are,
   //then go down
   if( (current_dir==DN || current_dir==STOP)
      && requests_below && !car_between_dn && !car_opposite_up )
      {
      current_dir = DN;
      return;
      }
   //if nothing else happening, stop
   current_dir = STOP;
   }  //end decide(), finally
//----------------------------------------------------------------
void elevator::move()
   {                              //if loading or unloading,
   if(loading_timer || unloading_timer)  //don't move
      return;
   if(current_dir==UP)         //if going up, go up
      current_floor++;
   else if(current_dir==DN)    //if going down, go down
      current_floor--;
   }  //end move()
//----------------------------------------------------------------
void elevator::get_destinations()     //stop, get destinations
   {
   char ustring[BUF_LENGTH];           //utility buffer for input
   int dest_floor;                     //destination floor

   set_cursor_pos(1,22); clear_line();  //clear top line
   set_cursor_pos(1, 22);
```

```
        cout << "Car " << (car_number+1)
            << " has stopped at floor " << (current_floor+1)
            << "\nEnter destination floors (0 when finished)";
    for(int j=1; j<NUM_FLOORS; j++)     //get floor requests
        {                               //maximum; usually fewer
        set_cursor_pos(1, 24);
        cout << "Destination " << j << ": ";

        cin.get(ustring, BUF_LENGTH);   //(avoid multiple LFs)
        cin.ignore(10, '\n');           //eat chars, including newline
        dest_floor = atoi(ustring);
        set_cursor_pos(1,24); clear_line(); //clear old input line
        if(dest_floor==0)               //if no more requests,
            {                           //clear bottom three lines
            set_cursor_pos(1,22); clear_line();
            set_cursor_pos(1,23); clear_line();
            set_cursor_pos(1,24); clear_line();
            return;
            }
        --dest_floor;                   //start at 0, not 1
        if(dest_floor==current_floor)   //chose this very floor
            { --j; continue; }          //   so forget it
        //if we're stopped, first choice made sets direction
        if(j==1 && current_dir==STOP)
            current_dir = (dest_floor < current_floor) ? DN : UP;
        destination[dest_floor] = true; //record selection
        dests_display();                //display destinations
        }
    } //end get_destinations()
```

Application

The next two files, ELEV_APP.H and ELEV_APP.CPP, are created by someone with a particular building in mind. They want to customize the software for their building. ELEV_APP.H does this by defining two constants that specify the number of floors and the number of elevators the building will have. Here's its listing:

```
// elev_app.h
// provides constants to specify building characteristics

const int NUM_FLOORS = 20;   //number of floors
const int NUM_CARS = 4;      //number of elevator cars
```

ELEV_APP.CPP initializes the data in the **building** class and creates a number of **elevator** objects, using **new**. (An array could also be used.) Then, in a loop, it calls the **building** functions **master_tick()** and **get_floor_requests()** over and over. The **wait()** function (declared in MSOFTCON.H or BORLACON.H) slows things down to a human-oriented speed. When the user is answering a prompt, time (the program's time, as opposed to the user's time) stops. Here's the listing for ELEV_APP.CPP:

```
// elev_app.cpp
// client-supplied file
```

```
#include "elev.h"              //for class declarations

void main(void)
   {
   building theBuilding;
   while(true)
      {
      theBuilding.master_tick(); //send time tick to all cars
      wait(1000);                //pause
                                 //get floor requests from user
      theBuilding.record_floor_reqs();
      }
   }
```

Elevator Strategy

Building the necessary intelligence into the elevator cars is not trivial. It's handled in the decide() function, which consists of a series of rules. These rules are arranged in order of priority. If any one applies, then the appropriate action is carried out; the following rules are not queried. Here is a slightly simplified version:

1. If the elevator is about to crash into the bottom of the shaft, or through the roof, then stop.

2. If this is a destination floor, then unload the passengers.

3. If there is an up floor request on this floor, and we are going up, then load the passengers.

4. Is there is a down floor request on this floor, and we are going down, then load the passengers.

5. If there are no destinations or requests above or below, then stop.

6. If there are destinations above us, then go up.

7. If there are destinations below us, then go down.

8. If we're stopped or going up, and there is a floor request above us, and there are no other cars going up between us and the request, or above it and going down and closer than we are, then go up.

9. If we're stopped or going down, and there is a floor request below us, and there are no other cars going down between us and the request, or below it and going up and closer than we are, then go down.

10. If no other rules apply, stop.

Rules 8 and 9 are rather complicated. They attempt to keep two or more cars from rushing to answer the same floor request. However, the results are not perfect. In some situations cars are slow to answer requests because they are afraid another car is on its way, when in fact the other car is answering a different floor request. The program's strategy could be improved by allowing the `decide()` function to distinguish between up and down requests when it checks whether there are requests above or below the current car. However, this would further complicate `decide()`, which is already long enough. We'll leave such refinements to the reader.

A Water-Distribution System

Have you ever wondered how your house is supplied with water? Or how the cooling system in a nuclear reactor operates? The next application can help you answer these questions. It models a liquid-distribution system consisting of pipes, valves, tanks, and other components. This example shows how easy it is to create a set of classes for a specialized situation. A similar approach could be used in other process-control applications, such as the hydraulic systems used to operate aircraft. The general approach is even applicable to electrical distribution systems, or economic systems that track the flow of money.

Figure 13.6 shows a water-distribution system for a small community built on a hillside. This water system is modeled in the PIPES program.

As in the previous program, we break this program into three files. PIPES.H contains the class declarations, and PIPES.CPP contains the definitions of the member functions. These files can be assumed to be provided by a vendor of class libraries. The PIPE_APP.CPP file is the one we write ourselves to specify a water system with a particular arrangement of tanks, valves, and pipes.

Components of a Water System

In this application we find that physical objects in the real world—objects we can see and touch—correspond closely with objects in the program. Let's see what these objects are.

- A *source* supplies water to the system. In the real world it might correspond to a spring, well, or reservoir. The water from the source is assumed to be always available but cannot be supplied faster than a certain fixed rate.

- A *sink* is a user of water. It represents a house, factory, or farm, or a group of such water consumers. A sink absorbs water from the system at a fixed rate.

- A *pipe* carries water over a distance. A pipe has a characteristic resistance that limits the amount of water that can flow through it. The water flowing into a pipe equals the water flowing out.

- A *tank* stores water. It also decouples the input/output flows: The rate at which water flows into the tank can be different from the rate at which it flows out. For example, if the input flow is greater than the output, the contents of the tank increase. A tank has a characteristic maximum output flow rate, determined (in this model, at least) by the size of the outlet in the tank.

- To keep a tank from overflowing, and to make sure it doesn't run out of water, we can associate switches with the tank. A *switch* turns on when the amount of water in the tank reaches a certain quantity. Switches are usually used to actuate a valve, which in turn controls the level of water in the tank.

- A *valve* regulates the flow of water. It can be on, causing no resistance to the flow, or off, which stops the flow entirely. A valve is assumed to be operated by some sort of servo-mechanism, and is typically controlled by switches associated with a tank.

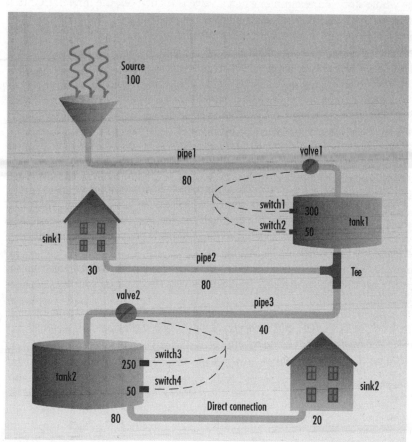

Figure 13.6 A typical water system.

Flow, Pressure, and Back Pressure

Every component in the system has three important aspects: flow, pressure, and back pressure. When we connect one component to another, we're connecting these three aspects.

Flow

The bottom-line characteristic of components in the water system is *flow*. This is the amount of water passing through the component per unit time. It's usually what we're interested in measuring when we model a system.

Often the flow into a component is the same as the flow out. This is true of pipes and of valves. However, as noted above, it is not true of tanks.

Pressure

Flow isn't the whole story. For example, when a valve is turned off, the flow both into it and out of it stops, but water may still be trying to flow through the valve. This potential for flow is *pressure*. A source or a tank provides water at a certain pressure. If the rest of the system permits, this pressure will cause a proportional flow: The greater the pressure, the greater the flow. But if a valve is turned off, the flow will stop, regardless of what the pressure is. Pressure, like flow, is transmitted downstream from one component to another.

A tank decouples pressure as well as flow. The pressure downstream from a tank is determined by the tank, not by the upstream pressure.

Back Pressure

In opposition to pressure is *back pressure*. This is caused by the resistance to flow of some components. A small-diameter pipe, for instance, will slow the flow of water, so that no matter how much pressure is supplied, the flow will still be small. This back pressure will slow the flow not only into the component causing the back pressure, but into all components upstream.

Back pressure goes the opposite way from flow and pressure. It's transmitted from the downstream component to the upstream component. Tanks decouple back pressure as they do pressure and flow.

Component Input and Output

Sometimes the flow, pressure, or back pressure are the same on both ends of a component. The flow into one end of a pipe, for example, is the same as the flow out the other end (we assume no leaks). However, these characteristics can also be different on the upstream and downstream sides. When a valve is turned off, the pressure on its downstream side becomes zero, no matter what the pressure on the upstream side is. The flow into a tank may be different from the flow out; the difference between input and output flow is reflected in changes to the contents of the tank. The output pressure of a pipe may be less than the input pressure because of the pipe's resistance.

Thus each component, at any given instant, can be characterized by six values. There are three inputs: pressure (from the upstream component), back pressure (from downstream), and flow (from upstream). There are also three outputs: pressure (on the downstream component), back pressure (on the upstream component), and flow (to the downstream component). This situation is shown in Figure 13.7.

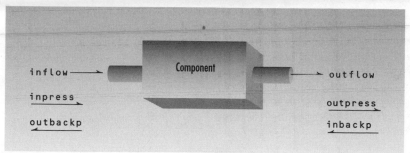

Figure 13.7 A component's characteristics.

The outputs of a component are calculated from its inputs, and also from the internal characteristics and state of the component, such as the resistance of a pipe or whether a valve is open or closed. A member function of each component, called `Tick()` because it occurs at fixed time intervals, is used to calculate the components' output based on their input and internal characteristics. If the input pressure to a pipe is increased, for example, the flow will increase correspondingly (unless the back pressure caused by the pipe's resistance and other components beyond it in the line is too high).

Making Connections

To create a water system we need to connect the various components together. It should be possible to connect any component to any other component so that water flows from one to another. (Switches are not connected in this way, since they don't carry water.) Besides flow, both pressure and back pressure must be connected, since they are also transmitted from component to component.

Thus, making a connection means setting the output pressure and output flow from the upstream object to the input pressure and input flow of the downstream object, and setting the output back pressure from the downstream object to the input back pressure of the upstream object. This is shown in Figure 13.8.

Simplifying Assumptions

To avoid complex mathematics we've made some simplifying assumptions.

What we call back pressure in the program should probably be called something like *ease of flow*. The values we use for this characteristic are *proportional* to the resulting flow, being small if only a small amount can flow, and large when the flow can be large. Real back pressure would be the reciprocal of the resulting flow, but this would unduly complicate the program.

Both pressure and back pressure are assumed to be measured in the same units as flow. To calculate the flow, we examine the pressure pushing water into the system, and the back pressure resisting its flow. The resulting flow is the smallest of these two numbers. Thus if a source provides 100 gallons/minute, and a pipe has a resistance of 60 gallons/minute, which causes a back pressure of 60 gallons/minute, the flow will be 60 gallons/minute.

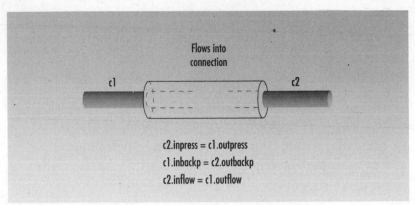

Figure 13.8   Connections between components.

These assumptions don't model exactly the real world of hydraulic flow, in which flow is determined by complex formulas relating pressure and back pressure, but they do provide a good first approximation.

We assume the output pressure of a tank is a constant. In reality it would depend on the contents of the tank. However, for tanks considerably higher in elevation than the sink, this is a reasonable approximation.

There is also an unavoidable built-in kind of imperfection in our approach to this problem. The physical system we are modeling is an analog system that changes continuously with time. But our model is "digital": It samples the state of the components at discrete "ticks," or time intervals. Thus when something changes, like a valve opening, it may take several loop cycles for the resulting pressure and flow changes to propagate throughout the system. These transients can be ignored in analyzing the system's behavior.

Program Design

Our goal in this program is to create a family of classes that make it easy to model different water-distribution systems. In this application it's easy to see what the classes should represent. We create a class for each kind of component—a valve class, a tank class, a pipe class, and so on. Once these classes are established, the programmer can then connect components as necessary to model a specific system.

Here is the listing for the PIPES.H file. We assume this file is supplied by a class software vendor.

```
// pipes.h
// header file for pipes
#include <iostream>        //for cout, etc.
#include <iomanip>         //for setw
#include <conio.h>         //for getch()
using namespace std;

const int infinity = 32767;    //infinite back pressure
enum offon { off, on };        //status of valves and switches
```

```
class Tank;                      //for using Tank in Switch
//////////////////////////////////////////////////////////////
class Component                  //components (Pipe, Valve, etc.)
   {
   protected:
      int inpress, outpress;    //pressures in and out
      int inbackp, outbackp;    //back pressures in and out
      int inflow, outflow;      //flow in and out
   public:
      Component() : inpress(0), outpress(0), inbackp(0),
                    outbackp(0), inflow(0), outflow(0)
         { }
      virtual ~Component()       //virtual destructor
         { }
      int Flow() const
         { return inflow; }
      friend void operator >= (Component&, Component&);
      friend void Tee(Component&, Component&, Component&);
   };
//////////////////////////////////////////////////////////////
class Source : public Component    //flow begins here
   {
   public:
      Source(int outp)
         { outpress = inpress = outp; }
      void Tick();               //update
   };
//////////////////////////////////////////////////////////////
class Sink : public Component      //flow ends here
   {
   public:
      Sink(const int obp)         //initialize backpressure
         { outbackp = inbackp = obp; }
      void Tick();               //update
   };
//////////////////////////////////////////////////////////////
class Pipe : public Component      //connects other components,
   {                              //has resistance to flow
   private:
      int resist;
   public:
      Pipe(const int r)           //initialize
         { inbackp = resist = r; }
      void Tick();               //update
   };
//////////////////////////////////////////////////////////////
class Valve : public Component    //turns flow on or off
   {
   private:
      offon status;              //on (open) or off (closed)
   public:
      Valve(const offon s)        //initialize status
         { status = s; }
```

```cpp
      offon& Status()                  //get and set status
         { return status; }
      void Tick();                     //update
   };
/////////////////////////////////////////////////////////////////
class Tank : public Component         //stores water
   {
   private:
      int contents;                    //water in tank (gals)
      int maxoutpress;                 //max output pressure
   public:
      Tank(const int mop)              //initialize to empty tank
         { maxoutpress = mop; contents = 0; }
      int Contents() const             //get contents
         { return(contents); }
      void Tick();
   };
/////////////////////////////////////////////////////////////////
class Switch                          //activated by tank level
   {                                  //can operate valves
   private:
      offon status;                    //'on' if contents > triggercap
      int cap;                         //capacity where switch turns on
      Tank* tankptr;                   //pointer to owner tank
   public:
      Switch(Tank *tptr, const int tcap)  //initialize
         { tankptr = tptr; cap = tcap; status = off; }
      int Status() const               //get status
         { return(status); }
      void Tick()                      //update status
         { status = (tankptr->Contents() > cap) ? on : off; }
   };
```

Here's the listing for the PIPES.CPP file, which contains the definitions of the class member functions. Like PIPES.H, it's supplied by the class vendor.

```cpp
// pipes.cpp
// function definitions for pipes

#include "pipes.h"               //class declarations
//------------------------------------------------------------
                               //"flows into" operator: c1 >= c2
void operator >= (Component& c1, Component& c2)
   {
   c2.inpress = c1.outpress;
   c1.inbackp = c2.outbackp;
   c2.inflow =  c1.outflow;
   }
//------------------------------------------------------------
                               //"tee" divides flow into two
void Tee(Component& src, Component& c1, Component& c2)
   {
                               //avoid division by 0
   if( (c1.outbackp==0 && c2.outbackp==0) ||
```

```
            (c1.outbackp==0 && c2.outbackp==0) )
         {
         c1.inpress = c2.inpress = 0;
         src.inbackp = 0;
         c1.inflow = c2.inflow = 0;
         return;
         }                         //proportion for each output
      float f1 = (float)c1.outbackp / (c1.outbackp + c2.outbackp);
      float f2 = (float)c2.outbackp / (c1.outbackp + c2.outbackp);
                                   //pressures for two outputs
      c1.inpress = src.outpress * f1;
      c2.inpress = src.outpress * f2;
                                   //back pressure for single input
      src.inbackp = c1.outbackp + c2.outbackp;
                                   //flow for two outputs
      c1.inflow = src.outflow * f1;
      c2.inflow = src.outflow * f2;
      }
//-----------------------------------------------------------
void Source::Tick()            //update source
   {                                 //output pressure fixed
   outbackp = inbackp;
   outflow = (outpress < outbackp) ? outpress : outbackp;
   inflow = outflow;
   }
//-----------------------------------------------------------
void Sink::Tick()              //update sink
   {                                 //output back pressure fixed
   outpress = inpress;
   outflow = (outbackp < outpress) ? outbackp : outpress;
   inflow = outflow;
   }
//-----------------------------------------------------------
void Pipe::Tick(void)          //update pipes
   {
   outpress = (inpress < resist) ? inpress : resist;
   outbackp = (inbackp < resist) ? inbackp : resist;

   //outflow is the lesser of outpress, outbackp, and resist
   if(outpress < outbackp && outpress < resist)
      outflow = outpress;
   else if(outbackp < outpress && outbackp < resist)
      outflow = outbackp;
   else
      outflow = resist;
   }
//-----------------------------------------------------------
void Valve::Tick(void)         //update valves
   {
   if(status==on)              //if valve open
      {
      outpress = inpress;
      outbackp = inbackp;
```

```
        outflow = (outpress < outbackp) ? outpress : outbackp;
        }
    else                            //if valve closed
        {
        outpress = 0;
        outbackp = 0;
        outflow = 0;
        }
    }
//--------------------------------------------------------------
void Tank::Tick(void)              //update tanks
    {
    outbackp = infinity;           //will take all the flow
                                   //    you can give it
    if( contents > 0 )             //if not empty
        {
        outpress = (maxoutpress<inbackp) ? maxoutpress : inbackp;
        outflow = outpress;
        }
    else                           //if empty
        {
        outpress = 0;              //no out pressure,
        outflow = 0;               //no flow
        }
    contents += inflow - outflow;   //always true
    }
```

Programming the Connections

A key part of program usability is a simple, intuitive way of describing connections in the program. We could use a function, such as

```
Connect(valve1, tank1);
```

However, this can be confusing: Is the upstream component the right argument or the left?

A better approach is to overload an operator to represent connections between components. We'll choose the greater-than-or-equal-to operator, >=, which provides a visual indication of flow direction from left to right. We can call it the *flows-into* operator. A program statement establishing a connection would look like this:

```
valve1 >= tank1;
```

meaning that water from valve1 flows into tank1.

Base and Derived Classes

When designing our program we look first for similarities among the various objects. The common attributes can be placed in a base class, while the individual features that distinguish the components can be placed in derived classes.

The Component Base Class

In this application we note that all the objects (except switches) have water flowing through them and can be connected to each other. We will therefore create a base class that permits connections. We'll call it `Component`.

```
class Component                     // components (Pipe, Valve, etc.)
   {
   protected:
      int inpress, outpress;     // pressures in and out
      int inbackp, outbackp;     // back pressures in and out
      int inflow, outflow;       // flow in and out
   public:
      Component(void) : inpress(0), outpress(0), inbackp(0),
                        outbackp(0), inflow(0), outflow(0)
         { }
      int Flow(void)
           { return inflow; }
      friend void operator >= (Component&, Component&);
      friend void Tee(Component&, Component&, Component&);
   };
```

A component has pressure, back pressure, and flow. These all have two values: input to the component, and output from it. For input we have the flow into the object from upstream, the pressure exerted by objects on its upstream side, and the back pressure exerted by objects on the downstream side. For output there is the flow out of the object, the pressure it transmits to the downstream object, and the back pressure it transmits to the upstream object. These values are all stored in objects of the `Component` class. A constructor for this class initializes all the data items to 0, and another member function returns the flow, which is, for most components, what we want to measure to see how the system is working.

The Flows-Into Operator

The flows-into operator, >=, connects an upstream component with a downstream component. Three inputs (the downstream object's pressure and flow and the upstream object's back pressure) are set equal to three outputs (the upstream object's pressure and flow and the downstream object's back pressure).

```
// "flows into" operator: c1 >= c2
void operator >= (Component& c1, Component& c2)
   {
   c2.inpress = c1.outpress;
   c1.inbackp = c2.outbackp;
   c2.inflow  = c1.outflow;
   }
```

The >= operator is defined as a `friend` of the `Component` class. It could also be defined as a member function, but another kind of connection, the `Tee()` function, must be a `friend`, so we'll make >= a `friend` for consistency. Both arguments to >= are passed by reference, since the original arguments must both be modified.

Since the >= operator applies to objects of the base class `Component`, it works on objects of the derived classes, such as tanks, valves, and pipes. This saves you from having to write a separate function to handle each kind of connection, such as

```
friend void operator >= (Pipe&, Valve&);
friend void operator >= (Valve&, Tank&);
friend void operator >= (Tank&, Sink&);
```

and so on ad infinitum.

Derived Classes

The classes that model the physical objects in the system are derived from the base class `Component`. These are `Source`, `Sink`, `Pipe`, `Valve`, and `Tank`. Each has specific characteristics. A `Source` has a fixed input pressure. A `Sink` has a fixed back pressure. A `Pipe` has a fixed internal resistance; its output back pressure can never be greater than a fixed value. A `Valve` has a status of type `offon`, `off`, or `on` (defined in an `enum` statement). A `Tank` has contents—how full it is. A valve's status and a tank's contents change as the program runs.

Variables that will be constant throughout the program, such as the resistance of a pipe or the output pressure of a tank, are initialized when the object is first created.

As we noted, all these derived classes, and the `Switch` class as well, include member functions called `Tick()`. This function is called for each object in the system—once each time period—to update the internal state of the object and to calculate the three outputs (pressure, back pressure, and flow) from the three inputs.

The Tee() Function

The `Tee()` function divides a single input flow into two output flows. The proportion of flow going into each downstream component is proportional to the back pressure of each component. A pipe with a lot of resistance will get a smaller proportion of the flow than one with low resistance. (See the listing for this function.)

`Tee()` is called with three arguments: the source component and the two downstream components, in order:

```
Tee(input, output1, output2);
```

It would be nice to use a more intuitive operator than a function with three parameters to connect three components. For instance,

```
input >= output1 + output2;
```

Unfortunately there is no ternary operator (one that takes three arguments) that can be overloaded in C++.

The Switch Class

The `Switch` class has a special relationship to the `Tank` class. Each tank is typically associated with two switches. One switch is set to turn on when the tank level is a certain minimum value (when the tank is almost empty). The other turns on when the level is above a certain maximum value (when the tank is full). This maximum determines the capacity of the tank.

Let's define the relationship between switches and tanks by saying that a switch is "owned" by a tank. When a switch is defined, it's given two values. One is the address of the tank that owns it. The other is the contents level at which it will turn on. The `Tick()` member function in `switch` uses the address of its owner tank to access the tank contents directly. This is how it figures out whether to turn itself on or off.

Switches are typically used to control a valve that regulates the flow of water into a tank. When the tank is full, the valve turns off; when it's nearing empty, the valve turns on again.

The PIPE_APP.CPP File

The `main()` part of the program would be written by an application programmer to model a specific water system. Here's the listing for PIPE_APP.CPP. This file contains only one function: `main()`.

```cpp
// pipe_app.cpp
// models a water supply system

#include "pipes.h"              //pipes header file

int main()
   {
   char ch = 'a';
   Source src(100);            //source(maximum capacity)
   Pipe pipe1(80);             //pipe(resistance)
   Valve valve1(on);           //valve(initially on)

   Tank tank1(60);             //tank1(maximum outflow)
   Switch switch1(&tank1, 300); //tank1 high switch
   Switch switch2(&tank1, 50);  //tank1 low switch

   Pipe pipe2(80);             //pipe
   Sink sink1(30);             //sink(maximum capacity)
   Pipe pipe3(40);             //pipe
   Valve valve2(on);           //valve

   Tank tank2(80);             //tank2
   Switch switch3(&tank2, 250); //tank2 high switch
   Switch switch4(&tank2, 50);  //tank2 low switch

   Sink sink2(20);             //sink

   cout << "Press Enter for new time tick, 'x' to exit\n";
   while(ch != 'x')            //quit on 'x' key
      {                        //make connections
      src >= pipe1;            //    source flows into pipe1
      pipe1 >= valve1;         //    pipe1 flows into valve1
      valve1 >= tank1;         //    valve1 flows into tank1
      Tee(tank1, pipe2, pipe3); //    output of tank1 splits
      pipe2 >= sink1;          //    pipe2 flows into sink1
```

```
            pipe3 >= valve2;            //   pipe3 flows into valve2
            valve2 >= tank2;            //   valve2 flows into tank2
            tank2 >= sink2;             //   tank2 flows into sink2

            src.Tick();                 //update all components
            pipe1.Tick();               //   and switches
            valve1.Tick();
            tank1.Tick();
            switch1.Tick();
            switch2.Tick();
            pipe2.Tick();
            sink1.Tick();
            pipe3.Tick();
            valve2.Tick();
            tank2.Tick();
            switch3.Tick();
            switch4.Tick();
            sink2.Tick();
                                        //if tank1 gets too high
            if( valve1.Status()==on && switch1.Status()==on )
               valve1.Status() = off;
                                        //if tank1 gets too low
            if( valve1.Status()==off && switch2.Status()==off )
               valve1.Status() = on;
                                        //if tank2 gets too high
            if( valve2.Status()==on && switch3.Status()==on )
               valve2.Status() = off;
                                        //if tank2 gets too low
            if( valve2.Status()==off && switch4.Status()==off )
               valve2.Status() = on;
                                        //output
            cout << "Src=" << setw(2) << src.Flow();
            cout << "  P1=" << setw(2) << pipe1.Flow();
            if( valve1.Status()==off )
               cout << "  V1=off";
            else
               cout << "  V1=on ";
            cout << "  T1=" << setw(3) << tank1.Contents();
            cout << "  P2=" << setw(2) << pipe2.Flow();
            cout << "  Snk1=" << setw(2) << sink1.Flow();
            cout << "  P3=" << setw(2) << pipe3.Flow();
            if( valve2.Status()==off )
               cout << "  V2=off";
            else
               cout << "  V2=on ";
            cout << "  T2=" << setw(3) << tank2.Contents();
            cout << "  Snk2=" << setw(2) << sink2.Flow();
            ch = getch();
            cout << '\n';
            } //end while
      return 0;
      } //end main()
```

Declaring the Components

In `main()` the various components—pipes, valves, tanks, and so on—are first declared. At this time their fixed characteristics are initialized: A pipe is given a fixed resistance, and a tank's contents are initialized to empty.

Connecting and Updating

The bulk of the work in `main()` is carried out in a loop. Each time through the loop represents one time period, or tick of the clock. Pressing the Enter key causes a new tick; thus the program's user acts as the system's clock. To exit from the loop and terminate the program, press the X key.

The first business in the loop is to connect the various components. The source `src` is connected to `pipe1`, `pipe1` is connected to `valve1`, and so on. The resulting system was shown earlier in Figure 13.6.

Once the connections are made, the internal states of all the components are updated by calling their `Tick()` functions.

Valves are opened and closed in `if` statements, based on the previous state of the valves and on switches. The goal is to keep the contents of the tank between the upper switch and the lower switch by opening and closing the valve as appropriate. When the tank contents reach the high switch, this switch is turned on, and the if statement causes the valve to close. When the contents drop below the bottom switch, turning it off, the valve is opened.

Output

To see what's happening in the system, we use `cout` statements to print out the flow of various components, the capacity of the tanks, and the status of the valves as they change with time. Figure 13.9 shows some sample output.

Notice in this figure that some values occasionally fall below zero. This is due to the digital nature of the simulation, mentioned earlier. Such transients can be ignored.

The goal of most water systems is to supply a continuous flow of water to the various sources. The output of PIPES shows that there are some problems in the system modeled. The flow to `sink1` alternates between 25 and 30 gallons/minute, depending on whether `tank2` is filling or not. The water-system client would probably prefer that the supply was constant. Even worse, `sink2` experiences periods of no flow at all. It would seem that some components of the system need to be resized to eliminate these defects.

Of course, `cout` provides a very unsophisticated output system. It would be easy to provide a graphic output, where pictures of the components appear on the screen. A `Display()` function built into each component would draw a picture of that component. Pictures would be connected as they are in the program—valve to tank, tank to pipe, and so on. The user could watch tanks fill and empty and valves open and close. Numbers beside pipes could display the flow within. This would make it easier to interpret the system's operation. It would also make the program larger and more complicated, which is why it is not implemented here.

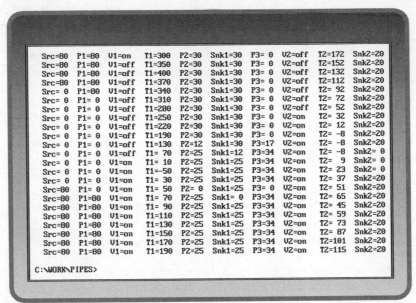

```
Src=80  P1=80  V1=on   T1=300  P2=30  Snk1=30  P3= 0  V2=off  T2=172  Snk2=20
Src=80  P1=80  V1=off  T1=350  P2=30  Snk1=30  P3= 0  V2=off  T2=152  Snk2=20
Src=80  P1=80  V1=off  T1=400  P2=30  Snk1=30  P3= 0  V2=off  T2=132  Snk2=20
Src=80  P1=80  V1=off  T1=370  P2=30  Snk1=30  P3= 0  V2=off  T2=112  Snk2=20
Src= 0  P1=80  V1=off  T1=340  P2=30  Snk1=30  P3= 0  V2=off  T2= 92  Snk2=20
Src= 0  P1= 0  V1=off  T1=310  P2=30  Snk1=30  P3= 0  V2=off  T2= 72  Snk2=20
Src= 0  P1= 0  V1=off  T1=280  P2=30  Snk1=30  P3= 0  V2=off  T2= 52  Snk2=20
Src= 0  P1= 0  V1=off  T1=250  P2=30  Snk1=30  P3= 0  V2=on   T2= 32  Snk2=20
Src= 0  P1= 0  V1=off  T1=220  P2=30  Snk1=30  P3= 0  V2=on   T2= 12  Snk2=20
Src= 0  P1= 0  V1=off  T1=190  P2=30  Snk1=30  P3= 0  V2=on   T2= -8  Snk2=20
Src= 0  P1= 0  V1=off  T1=130  P2=12  Snk1=30  P3=17  V2=on   T2= -8  Snk2=20
Src= 0  P1= 0  V1=off  T1= 70  P2=25  Snk1=12  P3=34  V2=on   T2= -8  Snk2= 0
Src= 0  P1= 0  V1=on   T1= 10  P2=25  Snk1=25  P3=34  V2=on   T2=  9  Snk2= 0
Src= 0  P1= 0  V1=on   T1=-50  P2=25  Snk1=25  P3=34  V2=on   T2= 23  Snk2= 0
Src= 0  P1= 0  V1=on   T1= 30  P2=25  Snk1=25  P3=34  V2=on   T2= 37  Snk2=20
Src=80  P1= 0  V1=on   T1= 50  P2= 0  Snk1=25  P3= 0  V2=on   T2= 51  Snk2=20
Src=80  P1=80  V1=on   T1= 70  P2=25  Snk1= 0  P3=34  V2=on   T2= 65  Snk2=20
Src=80  P1=80  V1=on   T1= 90  P2=25  Snk1=25  P3=34  V2=on   T2= 45  Snk2=20
Src=80  P1=80  V1=on   T1=110  P2=25  Snk1=25  P3=34  V2=on   T2= 59  Snk2=20
Src=80  P1=80  V1=on   T1=130  P2=25  Snk1=25  P3=34  V2=on   T2= 73  Snk2=20
Src=80  P1=80  V1=on   T1=150  P2=25  Snk1=25  P3=34  V2=on   T2= 87  Snk2=20
Src=80  P1=80  V1=on   T1=170  P2=25  Snk1=25  P3=34  V2=on   T2=101  Snk2=20
Src=80  P1=80  V1=on   T1=190  P2=25  Snk1=25  P3=34  V2=on   T2=115  Snk2=20

C:\WORK\PIPES>
```

Figure 13.9   Output of the PIPES program.

Summary

Vendor-provided object libraries are often distributed as a public component (the interface) containing class declarations in an .H header file, and a private component (the implementation) containing member function definitions in an .OBJ object file or .LIB library file.

C++ compilers allow you to combine several source or object files into a single executable file. This permits files provided by one vendor to be combined with files from another, to create a final application. The project feature simplifies keeping track of what files need to be compiled. It compiles any source file that has been modified since the last linking, and links the resulting object files.

Questions

Answers to questions can be found in Appendix G, "Answers to Questions and Exercises."

1. Breaking a program into several files is desirable because

   a. some files don't need to be recompiled each time.

   b. a program can be divided functionally.

   c. files can be marketed in object form.

   d. different programmers can work on a different files.

2. An .H file is associated with a .CPP file using the _____.

3. An .OBJ file is attached to a .CPP file using _____.

4. A *project* file contains

    a. the contents of the files in the project.

    b. the dates of the files in the project.

    c. instructions for compiling and linking.

    d. definitions for C++ variables.

5. A group of related classes, supplied as a separate product, is often called a _____.

6. True or false: A header file may need to be accessed by more than one source file in a project.

7. The so-called private files of a class library

    a. require a password.

    b. can be accessed by `friend` functions.

    c. help prevent code from being pirated.

    d. may consist only of object code.

8. True or false: Class libraries can be more powerful than function libraries.

9. True or false: the interface is private and the implementation is public.

10. The public part of a class library usually contains

    a. member function declarations.

    b. member function definitions.

    c. class declarations.

    d. definitions of inline functions.

Projects

Unfortunately, we don't have room in this book for exercises that involve the kind of larger programs discussed in this chapter. However, here are some suggestions for projects you may wish to pursue on your own.

1. Create member functions to perform subtraction and division for the **verylong** class in the VERYLONG example. These should overload the - and / operators. Warning: There's some work involved here. When you include subtraction, you must assume that any **verylong** can be negative

as well as positive. This complicates the addition and multiplication routines, which must do different things depending on the signs of the numbers.

To see one way to perform division, do a long-division example by hand and write down every step. Then incorporate these steps into a division member function. You'll find that you need some comparisons, so you'll need to write a comparison routine, among other things.

2. Modify the ELEV program to be more efficient in the way it handles requests. As an example of its current non-optimal behavior, start the program and make a down request on floor 20. Then make a down request on floor 10. Car 1 will immediately head up to 20, but car 2, which should head up to 10, waits until car 1 has passed 10 before starting. Modify `decide()` so this doesn't happen.

3. Add a `Pump` class to the PIPES example, so you can model water systems that don't rely on gravity. Create a water system that incorporates such a class. (Hint: A pump should derive its input from a tank.)

4. Create a class library that models something you're interested in. Create a `main()` or "client" program to test it. Market your class library and become rich and famous.

CHAPTER 14

TEMPLATES AND EXCEPTIONS

You will learn about the following in this chapter:

- Function templates
- Class templates
- Exceptions

- Multiple exceptions
- Exceptions with arguments
- Built-in exceptions

This chapter introduces two advanced C++ features: templates and exceptions. Templates make it possible to use one function or class to handle many different data types. Exceptions provide a convenient, uniform way to handle errors that occur within classes. These features are combined in a single chapter largely for historical reasons, becoming part of C++ at the same time. They were not part of the original specification for C++, but were introduced as "Experimental" topics in Ellis and Stroustrup (1990, see Appendix H, "Bibliography"). Subsequently they were incorporated into Standard C++.

The template concept can be used in two different ways: with functions and with classes. We'll look at function templates first, then go on to class templates, and finally to exceptions.

Function Templates

Suppose you want to write a function that returns the absolute value of two numbers. As you no doubt remember from high school algebra, the absolute value of a number is its value without regard to its sign: The absolute value of 3 is 3, and the absolute value of −3 is also 3. Ordinarily this function would be written for a particular data type:

```
int abs(int n)              //absolute value of ints
   {
   return (n<0) ? -n : n;   //if n is negative, return -n
   }
```

Here the function is defined to take an argument of type int and to return a value of this same type. But now suppose you want to find the absolute value of a type long. You will need to write a completely new function:

```
long abs(long n)              //absolute value of longs
   {
   return (n<0) ? -n : n;
   }
```

And again, for type `float`:

```
float abs(float n)            //absolute value of floats
   {
   return (n<0) ? -n : n;
   }
```

The body of the function is written the same way in each case, but they are completely different functions because they handle arguments and return values of different types. It's true that in C++ these functions can all be overloaded to have the same name, but you must nevertheless write a separate definition for each one. (In the C language, which does not support overloading, functions for different types can't even have the same name. In the C function library this leads to families of similarly named functions, such as `abs()`, `fabs()`, `fabsl()`, `labs()`, `cabs()`, and so on.)

Rewriting the same function body over and over for different types is time consuming and wastes space in the listing. Also, if you find you've made an error in one such function, you'll need to remember to correct it in each function body. Failing to do this correctly is a good way to introduce inconsistencies into your program.

It would be nice if there were a way to write such a function just once, and have it work for many different data types. This is exactly what function templates do for you. The idea is shown schematically in Figure 14.1.

A Simple Function Template

Our first example shows how to write our absolute-value function as a template, so that it will work with any basic numerical type. This program defines a template version of `abs()` and then, in `main()`, invokes this function with different data types to prove that it works. Here's the listing for TEMPABS:

```
// tempabs.cpp
// template used for absolute value function
#include <iostream>
using namespace std;
//-----------------------------------------------------------
template <class T>                 //function template
T abs(T n)
   {
   return (n < 0) ? -n : n;
   }
//-----------------------------------------------------------
int main()
   {
   int int1 = 5;
   int int2 = -6;
   long lon1 = 70000L;
```

```
long lon2 = -80000L;
double dub1 = 9.95;
double dub2 = -10.15;
                            //calls instantiate functions
cout << "\nabs(" << int1 << ")=" << abs(int1);  //abs(int)
cout << "\nabs(" << int2 << ")=" << abs(int2);  //abs(int)
cout << "\nabs(" << lon1 << ")=" << abs(lon1);  //abs(long)
cout << "\nabs(" << lon2 << ")=" << abs(lon2);  //abs(long)
cout << "\nabs(" << dub1 << ")=" << abs(dub1);  //abs(double)
   cout << "\nabs(" << dub2 << ")=" << abs(dub2);  //abs(double)
   cout << endl;
   return 0;
}
```

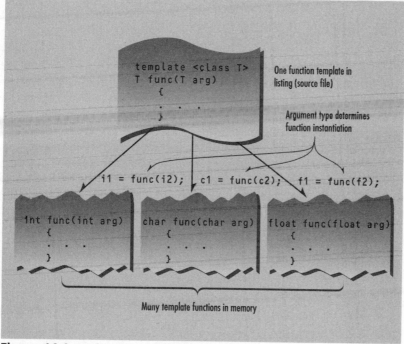

Figure 14.1 A function template.

Here's the output of the program:

```
abs(5)=5
abs(-6)=6
abs(70000)=70000
abs(-80000)=80000
abs(9.95)=9.95
abs(-10.15)=10.15
```

As you can see, the `abs()` function now works with all three of the data types (`int`, `long`, and `double`) that we use as arguments. It will work on other basic numerical types as well, and it will even work on user-defined data types, provided that the less-than operator (`<`) and the unary minus operator (`-`) are appropriately overloaded.

Here's how we specify the `abs()` function to work with multiple data types:

```
template <class T>          //function template
T abs(T n)
  {
  return (n<0) ? -n : n;
  }
```

This entire syntax, with a first line starting with the keyword `template` and the function definition following, is called a *function template*. How does this new way of writing `abs()` give it such amazing flexibility?

Function Template Syntax

The key innovation in function templates is to represent the data type used by the function not as a specific type such as `int`, but by a name that can stand for *any* type. In the preceding function template, this name is `T`. (There's nothing magic about this name; it can be anything you want, like `Type`, or `anyType`, or `FooBar`.) The `template` keyword signals the compiler that we're about to define a function template. The keyword `class`, within the angle brackets, might just as well be called `type`. As we've seen, you can define your own data types using classes, so there's really no distinction between types and classes. The variable following the keyword class (`T` in this example) is called the *template argument*.

Throughout the definition of the function, whenever a specific data type like `int` would ordinarily be written, we substitute the template argument, `T`. In the `abs()` function this name appears only twice, both in the first line (the function declarator), as the argument type and return type. In more complex functions it may appear numerous times throughout the function body as well (in variable definitions, for example).

What the Compiler Does

What does the compiler do when it sees the `template` keyword and the function definition that follows it? Well, nothing right away. The function template itself doesn't cause the compiler to generate any code. It can't generate code because it doesn't know yet what data type the function will be working with. It simply remembers the template for possible future use.

Code generation doesn't take place until the function is actually called (invoked) by a statement within the program. In TEMPABS this happens in expressions like `abs(int1)` in the statement

```
cout << "\nabs(" << int << ")=" << abs(int1);
```

When the compiler sees such a function call, it knows that the type to use is `int`, because that's the type of the argument `int1`. So it generates a specific version of the `abs()` function for type `int`, substituting `int` wherever it sees the name `T` in the function template.

This is called *instantiating* the function template, and each instantiated version of the function is called a *template function*. (That is, a *template function* is a specific instance of a *function template*. Isn't English fun?)

The compiler also generates a call to the newly instantiated function, and inserts it into the code where abs(int1) is. Similarly, the expression abs(lon1) causes the compiler to generate a version of abs() that operates on type long and a call to this function; while the abs(dub1) call generates a function that works on type double. Of course, the compiler is smart enough to generate only one version of abs() for each data type. Thus, even though there are two calls to the int version of the function, the code for this version appears only once in the executable code.

Simplifies the Listing

Notice that the amount of RAM used by the program is the same whether we use the template approach or actually write three separate functions. What we've saved is having to type three separate functions into the source file. This makes the listing shorter and easier to understand. Also, if we want to change the way the function works, we need to make the change in only one place in the listing instead of three places.

The Deciding Argument

The compiler decides how to compile the function based entirely on the data type used in the function call's argument (or arguments). The function's return type doesn't enter into this decision. This is similar to the way the compiler decides which of several overloaded functions to call.

Another Kind of Blueprint

We've seen that a function template isn't really a function, since it does not actually cause program code to be placed in memory. Instead it is a pattern, or blueprint, for making many functions. This fits right into the philosophy of OOP. It's similar to the way a class isn't anything concrete (such as program code in memory), but a blueprint for making many similar objects.

Function Templates with Multiple Arguments

Let's look at another example of a function template. This one takes three arguments: two that are template arguments and one of a basic type. The purpose of this function is to search an array for a specific value. The function returns the array index for that value if it finds it, or ñl if it can't find it. The arguments are a pointer to the array, the value to search for, and the size of the array. In main() we define four different arrays of different types, and four values to search for. We treat type char as a number. Then we call the template function once for each array. Here's the listing for TEMPFIND:

```
// tempfind.cpp
// template used for function that finds number in array
#include <iostream>
```

```
using namespace std;
//---------------------------------------------------------------
//function returns index number of item, or -1 if not found
template <class atype>
int find(atype* array, atype value, int size)
    {
    for(int j=0; j<size; j++)
       if(array[j]==value)
           return j;
    return -1;
    }
//---------------------------------------------------------------
char chrArr[] =   {1, 3, 5, 9, 11, 13};  //array
char ch = 5;                             //value to find
int intArr[] =   {1, 3, 5, 9, 11, 13};
int in = 6;
long lonArr[] =   {1L, 3L, 5L, 9L, 11L, 13L};
long lo = 11L;
double dubArr[] = {1.0, 3.0, 5.0, 9.0, 11.0, 13.0};
double db = 4.0;

int main()
    {
    cout << "\n 5 in chrArray: index=" << find(chrArr, ch, 6);
    cout << "\n 6 in intArray: index=" << find(intArr, in, 6);
    cout << "\n11 in lonArray: index=" << find(lonArr, lo, 6);
    cout << "\n 4 in dubArray: index=" << find(dubArr, db, 6);
      cout << endl;
      return 0;
    }
```

Here we name the template argument **atype**. It appears in two of the function's arguments: as the type of a pointer to the array, and as the type of the item to be matched. The third function argument, the array size, is always type **int**; it's not a template argument. Here's the output of the program:

```
 5 in chrArray: index=2
 6 in intArray: index=-1
11 in lonArray: index=4
 4 in dubArray: index=-1
```

The compiler generates four different versions of the function, one for each type used to call it. It finds a 3 at index 2 in the character array, does not find a 4 in the integer array, and so on.

Template Arguments Must Match

When a template function is invoked, all instances of the same template argument must be of the same type. For example, in **find()**, if the array name is of type **int**, the value to search for must also be of type **int**. You can't say

```
int intarray[] = {1, 3, 5, 7};         //int array
float f1 = 5.0;                        //float value
int value = find(intarray, f1, 4);     //uh, oh
```

because the compiler expects all instances of `atype` to be the same type. It can generate a function

```
find(int*, int, int);
```

but it can't generate

```
find(int*, float, int);
```

because the first and second arguments must be the same type.

Syntax Variation

Some programmers put the `template` keyword and the function declarator on the same line:

```
template<class atype> int find(atype* array, atype value, int size)
   {
   //function body
   }
```

Of course the compiler is happy enough with this format, but we find it more forbidding and less clear than the multiline approach.

More Than One Template Argument

You can use more than one template argument in a function template. For example, suppose you like the idea of the `find()` function template, but you aren't sure how large an array it might be applied to. If the array is too large, then type `long` would be necessary for the array size, instead of type `int`. On the other hand, you don't want to use type `long` if you don't need to. You want to select the type of the array size, as well as the type of data stored, when you call the function. To make this possible, you could make the array size into a template argument as well. We'll call it `btype`:

```
template <class atype, class btype>
btype find(atype* array, atype value, btype size)
   {
   for(btype j=0; j<size; j++)    //note use of btype
      if(array[j]==value)
         return j;
   return static_cast<btype>(-1);
   }
```

Now you can use either type `int` or type `long` (or even a user-defined type) for the size, whichever is appropriate. The compiler will generate different functions based not only on the type of the array and the value to be searched for, but also on the type of the array size.

Note that multiple template arguments can lead to many functions being instantiated from a single template. Two such arguments, if there were six basic types that could reasonably be used for each one, would allow the creation of 36 functions. This can take up a lot of memory if the functions are large. On the other hand, you don't instantiate a version of the function unless you actually call it.

Why Not Macros?

Old-time C programmers may wonder why we don't use macros to create different versions of a function for different data types. For example, the `abs()` function could be defined as

```
#define abs(n) ( (n<0) ? (-n) : (n) )
```

This has a similar effect to the class template in TEMPABS, because it performs a simple text substitution and can thus work with any type. However, as we've noted before, macros aren't much used in C++. There are several problems with them. One is that macros don't perform any type checking. There may be several arguments to the macro that should be of the same type, but the compiler won't check whether or not they are. Also, the type of the value returned isn't specified, so the compiler can't tell if you're assigning it to an incompatible variable. In any case, macros are confined to functions that can be expressed in a single statement. There are also other, more subtle, problems with macros. On the whole it's best to avoid them.

What Works?

How do you know whether you can instantiate a template function for a particular data type? For example, could you use the `find()` function from TEMPFIND to find a C-string (type `char*`) in an array of C-strings? To see if this is possible, check the operators used in the function. If they all work on the data type, then you can probably use it. In `find()`, however, we compare two variables using the equal-to (`==`) operator. You can't use this operator with C-strings; you must use the `strcmp()` library function. Thus `find()` won't work on C-strings. However, it would work on the `string` class because that class overloads the `==` operator.

Start with a Normal Function

When you write a template function you're probably better off starting with a normal function that works on a fixed type; `int` or whatever. You can design and debug it without having to worry about template syntax and multiple types. Then, when everything works properly, you can turn the function definition into a template and check that it works for additional types.

Class Templates

The template concept can be extended to classes. Class templates are generally used for data storage (container) classes. (We'll see a major example of this in the next chapter, "The Standard Template Library.") Stacks and linked lists, which we encountered in previous chapters, are examples of data storage classes. However, the examples of these classes that we presented could store data of only a single basic type. The `Stack` class in the STAKARAY program in Chapter 7, "Arrays and Strings," for example, could store data only of type `int`. Here's a condensed version of that class.

```
class Stack
    {
    private:
        int st[MAX];           //array of ints
        int top;               //index number of top of stack
    public:
        Stack();               //constructor
        void push(int var);    //takes int as argument
        int pop();             //returns int value
    };
```

If we wanted to store data of type long in a stack we would need to define a completely new class:

```
class LongStack
    {
    private:
        long st[MAX];          //array of longs
        int top;               //index number of top of stack
    public:
        LongStack();           //constructor
        void push(long var);   //takes long as argument
        long pop();            //returns long value
    };
```

Similarly, we would need to create a new stack class for every data type we wanted to store. It would be nice to be able to write a single class specification that would work for variables of all types, instead of a single basic type. As you may have guessed, class templates allow us to do this. We'll create a variation of STAKARAY that uses a class template. Here's the listing for TEMPSTAK:

```
// tempstak.cpp
// implements stack class as a template
#include <iostream.h>
using namespace std;
const int MAX = 100;           //size of array
//////////////////////////////////////////////////////////////////
template <class Type>
class Stack
    {
    private:
        Type st[MAX];              //stack: array of any type
        int top;                   //number of top of stack
    public:
        Stack()                    //constructor
            { top = -1; }
        void push(Type var)        //put number on stack
            { st[++top] = var; }
        Type pop()                 //take number off stack
            { return st[top--]; }
    };
//////////////////////////////////////////////////////////////////
int main()
    {
```

```
Stack<float> s1;        //s1 is object of class Stack<float>

s1.push(1111.1F);       //push 3 floats, pop 3 floats
s1.push(2222.2F);
s1.push(3333.3F);
cout << "1: " << s1.pop() << endl;
cout << "2: " << s1.pop() << endl;
cout << "3: " << s1.pop() << endl;

Stack<long> s2;         //s2 is object of class Stack<long>

s2.push(123123123L);    //push 3 longs, pop 3 longs
s2.push(234234234L);
s2.push(345345345L);
cout << "1: " << s2.pop() << endl;
cout << "2: " << s2.pop() << endl;
cout << "3: " << s2.pop() << endl;
return 0;
}
```

Here the class **Stack** is presented as a template class. The approach is similar to that used in function templates. The **template** keyword and **class Stack** signal that the entire class will be a template.

```
template <class Type>
class Stack
   {
   //data and member functions using template argument Type
   };
```

A template argument, named **Type** in this example, is then used (instead of a fixed data type like **int**) every place in the class specification where there is a reference to the type of the array **st**. There are three such places: the definition of **st**, the argument type of the **push()** function, and the return type of the **pop()** function.

Class templates differ from function templates in the way they are instantiated. To create an actual function from a function template, you call it using arguments of a specific type. Classes, however, are instantiated by defining an object using the template argument.

```
Stack<float> s1;
```

This creates an object, **s1**, a stack that stores numbers of type **float**. The compiler provides space in memory for this object's data, using type **float** wherever the template argument **Type** appears in the class specification. It also provides space for the member functions (if these have not already been placed in memory by another object of type **Stack<float>**). These member functions also operate exclusively on type **float**. Figure 14.2 shows how a class template and definitions of specific objects cause these objects to be placed in memory.

Creating a **Stack** object that stores objects of a different type, as in

```
Stack<long> s2;
```

creates not only a different space for data, but also a new set of member functions that operate on type **long**.

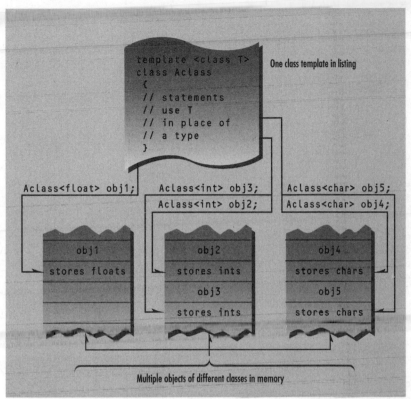

```
template <class T>
class Aclass              One class template in listing
{
// statements
// use T
// in place of
// a type
}
```

```
Aclass<float> obj1;    Aclass<int> obj3;      Aclass<char> obj5;
                       Aclass<int> obj2;      Aclass<char> obj4;
```

```
        obj1                  obj2                  obj4

   stores floats         stores ints            stores chars

                            obj3                  obj5

                         stores ints            stores chars
```

Multiple objects of different classes in memory

Figure 14.2 A class template.

Note that the name of the type of **s1** consists of the class name **Stack** *plus the template argument*: **Stack<float>**. This distinguishes it from other classes that might be created from the same template, such as **Stack<int>** or **Stack<long>**.

In TEMPSTAK we exercise the **s1** and **s2** stacks by pushing and popping three values on each one and displaying each popped value. Here's the output:

```
1: 3333.3        //float stack
2: 2222.2
3: 1111.1
1: 345345345     //long stack
2: 234234234
3: 123123123
```

In this example, the template approach gives us two classes for the price of one, and we could instantiate class objects for other numerical types with just a single line of code.

Class Name Depends on Context

In the TEMPSTAK example, the member functions of the class template were all defined within the class. If the member functions are defined externally (outside of the class specification), we need a new syntax. The next program shows how this works. Here's the listing for TEMPSTAK2:

```cpp
// temstak2.cpp
// implements stack class as a template
// member functions are defined outside the class
#include <iostream>
using namespace std;
const int MAX = 100;
//////////////////////////////////////////////////////////////
template <class Type>
class Stack
   {
   private:
      Type st[MAX];           //stack: array of any type
      int top;                //number of top of stack
   public:
      Stack();                //constructor
      void push(Type var);    //put number on stack
      Type pop();             //take number off stack
   };
//////////////////////////////////////////////////////////////
template<class Type>
Stack<Type>::Stack()          //constructor
   {
   top = -1;
   }
//------------------------------------------------------------
template<class Type>
void Stack<Type>::push(Type var) //put number on stack
   {
   st[++top] = var;
   }
//------------------------------------------------------------
template<class Type>
Type Stack<Type>::pop()          //take number off stack
   {
   return st[top--];
   }
//------------------------------------------------------------
int main()
   {
   Stack<float> s1;       //s1 is object of class Stack<float>

   s1.push(1111.1F);      //push 3 floats, pop 3 floats
   s1.push(2222.2F);
   s1.push(3333.3F);
   cout << "1: " << s1.pop() << endl;
   cout << "2: " << s1.pop() << endl;
   cout << "3: " << s1.pop() << endl;

   Stack<long> s2;        //s2 is object of class Stack<long>

   s2.push(123123123L);   //push 3 longs, pop 3 longs
```

```
s2.push(264234234L);
s2.push(345345345L);
cout << "1: " << s2.pop() << endl;
cout << "2: " << s2.pop() << endl;
cout << "3: " << s2.pop() << endl;
return 0;
}
```

The expression **template<class Type>** must precede not only the class definition, but each externally defined member function as well. Here's how the **push()** function looks:

```
template<class Type>
void Stack<Type>::push(Type var)
   {
   st[++top] = var;
   }
```

The name **Stack<Type>** is used to identify the class of which **push()** is a member. In a normal non-template member function the name **Stack** alone would suffice:

```
void Stack::push(int var)  //Stack() as a non-template function
   {
   st[++top] = var;
   }
```

but for a function template we need the template argument as well: **Stack<Type>**.

Thus we see that the name of the template class is expressed differently in different contexts. Within the class specification, it's simply the name itself: **Stack**. For externally defined member functions, it's the class name plus the template argument name: **Stack<Type>**. When you define actual objects for storing a specific data type, it's the class name plus this specific type: **Stack<float>** (or whatever).

```
class Stack                        //Stack class specifier
   {  };

void Stack<Type>::push(Type var)   //push() definition
   {  }

Stack<float> s1;                   //object of type Stack<float>
```

You must exercise considerable care to use the correct name in the correct context. It's easy to forget to add the **<Type>** or **<float>** to the **Stack**. The compiler hates it when you get it wrong.

Although it's not demonstrated in this example, you must also be careful of the syntax when a member function returns a value of its own class. Suppose we define a class **Int** that provided safety features for integers, as discussed in Exercise 4 in Chapter 8, "Operator Overloading." If you used an external definition for a member function **xfunc()** of this class that returned type **Int**, you would need to use **Int<Type>** for the return type as well as preceding the scope resolution operator:

```
Int<Type> Int<Type>::xfunc(Int arg)
   {  }
```

The class name used as a type of a function argument, on the other hand, doesn't need to include the <Type> designation.

A Linked List Class Using Templates

Let's look at another example where templates are used for a data storage class. This is a modification of our LINKLIST program from Chapter 10, "Pointers," which you are encouraged to reexamine. It requires not only that the `linklist` class itself be made into a template, but that the `link` structure, which actually stores each data item, be made into a template as well. Here's the listing for TEMPLIST:

```cpp
// templist.cpp
// implements linked list as a template
#include <iostream>
using namespace std;
/////////////////////////////////////////////////////////////
template<class TYPE>                //struct link<TYPE>
struct link                         //one element of list
//within this struct definition 'link' means link<TYPE>
   {
   TYPE data;                       //data item
   link* next;                      //pointer to next link
   };
/////////////////////////////////////////////////////////////
template<class TYPE>                //class linklist<TYPE>
class linklist                      //a list of links
//within this class definition 'linklist' means linklist<TYPE>
   {
   private:
      link<TYPE>* first;            //pointer to first link
   public:
      linklist()                    //no-argument constructor
         { first = NULL; }          //no first link
      //note: destructor would be nice; not shown for simplicity
      void additem(TYPE d);         //add data item (one link)
      void display();               //display all links
   };
/////////////////////////////////////////////////////////////
template<class TYPE>
void linklist<TYPE>::additem(TYPE d)   //add data item
(continued on next page)
(continued from previous page)
   {
   link<TYPE>* newlink = new link<TYPE>;   //make a new link
   newlink->data = d;               //give it data
   newlink->next = first;           //it points to next link
   first = newlink;                 //now first points to this
   }
//-----------------------------------------------------------
template<class TYPE>
void linklist<TYPE>::display()      //display all links
   {
```

```
    link<TYPE>* current = first;      //set ptr to first link
    while( current != NULL )          //quit on last link
        {
        cout << endl << current->data;  //print data
        current = current->next;        //move to next link
        }
    }
//--------------------------------------------------------------
int main()
    {
    linklist<double> ld; //ld is object of class linklist<double>

    ld.additem(151.5);     //add three doubles to list ld
    ld.additem(262.6);
    ld.additem(373.7);
    ld.display();          //display entire list ld

    linklist<char> lch;    //lch is object of class linklist<char>

    lch.additem('a');      //add three chars to list lch
    lch.additem('b');
    lch.additem('c');
    lch.display();         //display entire list lch
    cout << endl;
    return 0;
    }
```

In `main()` we define two linked lists: one to hold numbers of type `double`, and one to hold characters of type `char`. We then exercise the lists by placing three items on each one with the `additem()` member function, and displaying all the items with the `display()` member function. Here's the output of TEMPLIST:

```
373.7
262.6
151.5
c
b
a
```

Both the `linklist` class and the `link` structure make use of the template argument `TYPE` to stand for any type. (Well, not really any type; we'll discuss later what types can actually be stored.) Thus not only `linklist` but also `link` must be templates, preceded by the line

```
template<class TYPE>
```

Notice that it's not just a class that's turned into a template. Any other programming constructs that use a variable data type must also be turned into templates, as the `link` structure is here.

As before, we must pay attention to how the class (and in this program, a structure as well) are named in different parts of the program. Within its own specification we can use the name of the class or structure alone: `linklist` and `link`. In external member functions, we must use the class or structure name and the template argument: `linklist<TYPE>`. When we actually define objects of type `linklist`, we must use the specific data type that the list is to store:

```
linklist<double> ld;  //defines object ld of class linklist<double>
```

Storing User-Defined Data Types

In our programs so far, we've used template classes to store basic data types. For example, in the TEMPLIST program we stored numbers of type `double` and type `char` in a linked list. Is it possible to store objects of user-defined types (classes) in these same template classes? The answer is yes, but with a caveat.

Employees in a Linked List

Examine the `employee` class in the EMPLOY program in Chapter 9, "Inheritance." (Don't worry about the derived classes.) Could we store objects of type `employee` on the linked list of the TEMPLIST example? As with template functions, we can find out if a template class can operate on objects of a particular class by checking the operations the template class performs on those objects. The `linklist` class uses the overloaded insertion (<<) operator to display the objects it stores:

```
void linklist<TYPE>::display()
   {
   ...
   cout << endl << current->data;  //uses insertion operator (<<)
   ...
   };
```

This is not a problem with basic types, for which the insertion operator is already defined. Unfortunately, however, the `employee` class in the EMPLOY program does not overload this operator. Thus we'll need to modify the `employee` class to include it. Also, to simplify getting employee data from the user, we overload the extraction (>>) operator as well. Data from this operator is placed in a temporary object `emptemp` before being added to the linked list. Here's the listing for TEMLIST2:

```
// temlist2.cpp
// implements linked list as a template
// demonstrates list used with employee class

#include <iostream>
using namespace std;
const int LEN = 80;            //maximum length of
names/////////////////////////////////////////////////////////
////class employee                          //employee class
   {
   private:
      char name[LEN];                //employee name
      unsigned long number;          //employee number
   public:
```

```
            friend istream& operator >> (istream& s, employee& e);
            friend ostream& operator << (ostream& s, employee& e);
        };
//---------------------------------------------------------------
istream& operator >> (istream& s, employee& e)
    {
    cout << "\n   Enter last name: "; cin >> e.name;
    cout << "   Enter number: ";      cin >> e.number;
    return s;
    }
//---------------------------------------------------------------
ostream& operator << (ostream& s, employee& e)
    {
    cout << "\n   Name: " << e.name;
    cout << "\n   Number: " << e.number;
    return s;
    }
////////////////////////////////////////////////////////////////
template<class TYPE>                   //struct "link<TYPE>"
struct link                            //one element of list
    {
    TYPE data;                         //data item
    link* next;                        //pointer to next link
    };
////////////////////////////////////////////////////////////////
template<class TYPE>                   //class "linklist<TYPE>"
class linklist                         //a list of links
    {
    private:
        link<TYPE>* first;             //pointer to first link
    public:
        linklist()                     //no-argument constructor
            { first = NULL; }          //no first link
        void additem(TYPE d);          //add data item (one link)
        void display();                //display all links
    };
//---------------------------------------------------------------
template<class TYPE>
void linklist<TYPE>::additem(TYPE d)  //add data item
    {
    link<TYPE>* newlink = new link<TYPE>;  //make a new link
    newlink->data = d;                 //give it data
    newlink->next = first;             //it points to next link
    first = newlink;                   //now first points to this
    }
//---------------------------------------------------------------
template<class TYPE>
void linklist<TYPE>::display()         //display all links
    {
    link<TYPE>* current = first;       //set ptr to first link
    while( current != NULL )           //quit on last link
        {
        cout << endl << current->data; //display data
```

```
         current = current->next;          //move to next link
         }
      }
/////////////////////////////////////////////////////////////////
int main()
   {                         //lemp is object of
   linklist<employee> lemp;  //class "linklist<employee>"
   employee emptemp;         //temporary employee storage
   char ans;                 //user's response ('y' or 'n')

   do
      {
      cin >> emptemp;          //get employee data from user
      lemp.additem(emptemp);   //add it to linked list 'lemp'
      cout << "\nAdd another (y/n)? ";
      cin >> ans;
      } while(ans != 'n');     //when user is done,
   lemp.display();             //display entire linked list
   cout << endl;
   return 0;
   }
```

In `main()` we instantiate a linked list called `lemp`. Then, in a loop, we ask the user to input data for an employee, and we add that employee object to the list. When the user terminates the loop, we display all the employee data. Here's some sample interaction:

```
   Enter last name: Mendez
   Enter number: 1233
Add another(y/n)? y

   Enter last name: Smith
   Enter number: 2344
Add another(y/n)? y

   Enter last name: Chang
   Enter number: 3455
Add another(y/n)? n

   Name: Chang
   Number: 3455

   Name: Smith
   Number: 2344

   Name: Mendez
   Number: 1233
```

Notice that the `linklist` class does not need to be modified in any way to store objects of type `employee`. This is the beauty of template classes: They will work not only with basic types, but with user-defined types as well.

What Can You Store?

We noted that you can tell whether you can store variables of a particular type in a data-storage template class by checking the operators in the member functions of that class. Is it possible to store a string (class **string**) in the **linklist** class in the TEMLIST2 program? Member functions in this class use the insertion (<<) and extraction (>>) operators. These operators work perfectly well with strings, so there's no reason we can't use this class to store strings, as you can verify yourself. But if any operators exist in a storage class member function that don't operate on a particular data type, then you can't use the class to store that type.

Exceptions

Exceptions, the second major topic in this chapter, provide a systematic, object-oriented approach to handling run-time errors generated by C++ classes. Exceptions are errors that occur at run time. They are caused by a wide variety exceptional circumstance, such as running out of memory, not being able to open a file, trying to initialize an object to an impossible value, or using an out-of-bounds index to a vector.

Why Do We Need Exceptions?

Why do we need a new mechanism to handle errors? Let's look at how the process was handled in the past. In C-language programs, an error is often signaled by returning a particular value from the function in which it occurred. For example, disk-file functions often return NULL or 0 to signal an error. Each time you call one of these functions you check the return value:

```
if( somefunc() == ERROR_RETURN_VALUE )
    //handle the error or call error-handler function
else
    //proceed normally
if( anotherfunc() == NULL )
    //handle the error or call error-handler function
else
    //proceed normally
if( thirdfunc() == 0 )
    //handle the error or call error-handler function
else
    //proceed normally
```

One problem with this approach is that every single call to such a function must be examined by the program. Surrounding each function call with an **if...else** statement, and adding statements to handle the error (or call an error-handler routine), requires a lot of code and makes the listing convoluted and hard to read.

The problem becomes more complex when classes are used, since errors may take place without a function being explicitly called. For example, suppose an application defines objects of a class:

```
SomeClass obj1, obj2, obj3;
```

How will the application find out if an error occurred in the class constructor? The constructor is called implicitly, so there's no return value to be checked.

Things are complicated even further when an application uses class libraries. A class library and the application that makes use of it are often created by separate people: the class library by a vendor and the application by a programmer who buys the class library. This makes it even harder to arrange for error values to be communicated from a class member function to the program that's calling the function. The problem of communicating errors from deep within class libraries is probably the most important problem solved by exceptions. We'll return to this topic at the end of this section.

Old-time C programmers may remember another approach to catching errors: the `setjmp()` and `longjmp()` combination of functions. However, this approach is not appropriate for an object-oriented environment because it does not properly handle the destruction of objects.

Exception Syntax

Imagine an application that creates and interacts with objects of a certain class. Ordinarily the application's calls to the class member functions cause no problems. Sometimes, however, the application makes a mistake, causing an error to be detected in a member function. This member function then informs the application that an error has occurred. When exceptions are used, this is called *throwing* an exception. In the application we install a separate section of code to handle the error. This code is called an *exception handler* or *catch block*; it *catches* the exceptions thrown by the member function. Any code in the application that uses objects of the class is enclosed in a *try block*. Errors generated in the try block will be caught in the catch block. Code that doesn't interact with the class need not be in a try block. Figure 14.3 shows the arrangement.

The exception mechanism uses three new C++ keywords: `throw`, `catch`, and `try`. Also, we need to create a new kind of entity called an **exception class**. XSYNTAX is not a working program, but a skeleton program to show the syntax.

```
// xsyntax.cpp
// not a working program
///////////////////////////////////////////////////////////
class AClass                    //a class
   {
   public:
   class AnError                //exception class
      {
      };
   void Func()                  //a member function
      {
      if( /* error condition */ )
         throw AnError();       //throw exception
      }
   };
///////////////////////////////////////////////////////////
int main()                      //application
   {
   try                          //try block
      {
```

```
    AClass obj1;               //interact with AClass objects
    obj1.Func();               //may cause error
    }
catch(AClass::AnError)         //exception handler
    {                          //(catch block)
    //tell user about error, etc.
    }
return 0;
}
```

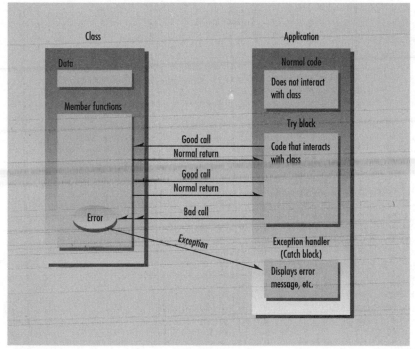

Figure 14.3   The exception mechanism.

We start with a class called **AClass**, which represents any class in which errors might occur. An exception class, **AnError**, is specified in the public part of **AClass**. In **AClass**'s member functions we check for errors. If we find one, we throw an exception, using the keyword throw followed by the constructor for the error class:

```
throw AnError();   //'throw' followed by constructor for AnError class
```

In the **main()** part of the program we enclose any statements that interact with **AClass** in a try block. If any of these statements causes an error to be detected in an **AClass** member function, an exception will be thrown and control will go to the catch block that immediately follows the try block.

A Simple Exception Example

Let's look at a working program example that uses exceptions. This example is derived from the STAKARAY program in Chapter 7, which created a stack data structure in which integer data values could be stored. Unfortunately, this earlier example could not detect two common errors. The application program might attempt to push too many objects onto the stack, thus exceeding the capacity of the array, or it might try to pop too many objects off the stack, thus obtaining invalid data. In the XSTAK program we use an exception to handle these two errors.

```cpp
// xstak.cpp
// demonstrates exceptions
#include <iostream>
using namespace std;
const int MAX = 3;              //stack holds 3 integerss
/////////////////////////////////////////////////////////////////
class Stack
    {
    private:
        int st[MAX];                //array of integers
        int top;                    //index of top of stack
    public:
        class Range                 //exception class for Stack
            {                       //note: empty class body
            };

        Stack()                     //constructor
            { top = -1; }

        void push(int var)
            {
            if(top >= MAX-1)        //if stack full,
                throw Range();      //throw exception
            st[++top] = var;        //put number on stack
            }
        int pop()
            {
            if(top < 0)             //if stack empty,
                throw Range();      //throw exception
            return st[top--];       //take number off stack
            }
    };
/////////////////////////////////////////////////////////////////
int main()
    {
    Stack s1;
        {
    try
        s1.push(11);
        s1.push(22);
```

```
        s1.push(33);
//      s1.push(44);                        //oops: stack full
        cout << "1: " << s1.pop() << endl;
        cout << "2: " << s1.pop() << endl;
        cout << "3: " << s1.pop() << endl;
        cout << "4: " << s1.pop() << endl;  //oops: stack empty
        }
    catch(Stack::Range)                     //exception handler
        {
        cout << "Exception: Stack Full or Empty" << endl;
        }

    cout << "Arrive here after catch (or normal exit)" << endl;
    return 0;
    }
```

Note that we've made the stack small so that it's easier to trigger an exception by pushing too many items.

Let's examine the features of this program that deal with exceptions. There are four of them. In the class specification there is an exception class. There are also statements that throw exceptions. In the **main()** part of the program there is a block of code that may cause exceptions (the try block), and a block of code that handles the exception (the catch block).

Specifying the Exception Class

The program first specifies an exception class within the **Stack** class:

```
class Range
    {   //note: empty class body
    };
```

Here the body of the class is empty, so objects of this class have no data and no member functions. All we really need in this simple example is the class name, **Range**. This name is used to connect a throw statement with a catch block. (The class body need not always be empty, as we'll see later.)

Throwing an Exception

In the **Stack** class an exception occurs if the application tries to pop a value when the stack is empty or tries to push a value when the stack is full. To let the application know that it has made such a mistake when manipulating a **Stack** object, the member functions of the **Stack** class check for these conditions using **if** statements, and throw an exception if they occur. In XSTAK the exception is thrown in two places, both using the statement

```
throw Range();
```

The Range() part of this statement invokes the (implicit) constructor for the **Range** class, which creates an object of this class. The **throw** part of the statement transfers program control to the exception handler (which we'll examine in a moment).

The `try` Block

All the statements in `main()` that might cause this exception—that is, statements that manipulate `Stack` objects—are enclosed in braces and preceded by the `try` keyword:

```
try
   {
   //code that operates on objects that might cause an exception
   }
```

This is simply part of the application's normal code; it's what you would need to write even if you weren't using exceptions. Not all the code in the program needs to be in a try block; just the code that interacts with the `Stack` class. Also, there can be many try blocks in your program, so you can access `Stack` objects from different places.

The Exception Handler (Catch Block)

The code that handles the exception is enclosed in braces, preceded by the `catch` keyword, with the exception class name in parentheses. The exception class name must include the class in which it is located. Here it's `Stack::Range.`

```
catch(Stack::Range)
   {
   //code that handles the exception
   }
```

This construction is called the *exception handler*. It must immediately follow the try block. In XSTAK the exception handler simply prints an error message to let the user know why the program failed.

Control "falls through" the bottom of the exception handler, so you can continue processing at that point. Or the exception handler may transfer control elsewhere, or (often) terminate the program.

Sequence of Events

Let's summarize the sequence of events when an exception occurs.

1. Code is executing normally outside a try block.

2. Control enters the try block.

3. A statement in the try block causes an error in a member function.

4. The member function throws an exception.

5. Control transfers to the exception handler (catch block) following the try block.

That's all there is to it. Notice how clean the resulting code is. Any of the statements in the try block could cause an exception, but we don't need to worry about checking a return value for each one, because the try-throw-catch arrangement handles them all automatically. In this particular example we've deliberately created two statements that cause exceptions. The first,

```
s1.push(44);  //pushes too many items
```

causes an exception if you remove the comment symbol preceding it, and the second,

```
cout << "4: " << s1.pop() << endl;  //pops item from empty stack
```

causes an exception if the first statement is commented out. Try it each way. In both cases the same error message will be displayed:

```
Stack Full or Empty
```

Multiple Exceptions

You can design a class to throw as many exceptions as you want. To show how this works, we'll modify the XSTAK program to throw separate exceptions for attempting to push data on a full stack and attempting to pop data from an empty stack. Here's the listing for XSTAK2:

```
// xstak2.cpp
// demonstrates two exception handlers
#include <iostream>
using namespace std;
const int MAX = 3;               //stack holds 3 integerss
////////////////////////////////////////////////////////////
class Stack
    {
    private:
        int st[MAX];             //stack: array of integers
        int top;                 //index of top of stack
    public:
        class Full { };          //exception class
        class Empty { };         //exception class
//-----------------------------------------------------------
        Stack()                  //constructor
            { top = -1; }
//-----------------------------------------------------------
        void push(int var)       //put number on stack
            {
            if(top >= MAX-1)     //if stack full,
                throw Full();    //throw Full exception
            st[++top] = var;
            }
//-----------------------------------------------------------
        int pop()                //take number off stack
            {
            if(top < 0)          //if stack empty,
                throw Empty();   //throw Empty exception
            return st[top-];
            }
    };
////////////////////////////////////////////////////////////
int main()
    {
    Stack s1;
```

```
       try
          {
          s1.push(11);
          s1.push(22);
          s1.push(33);
//        s1.push(44);                              //oops: stack full
          cout << "1: " << s1.pop() << endl;
          cout << "2: " << s1.pop() << endl;
          cout << "3: " << s1.pop() << endl;
          cout << "4: " << s1.pop() << endl;  //oops: stack empty
          }
       catch(Stack::Full)
          {
          cout << "Exception: Stack Full" << endl;
          }
       catch(Stack::Empty)
          {
          cout << "Exception: Stack Empty" << endl;
          }
       return 0;
       }
```

In XSTAK2 we specify two exception classes:

```
class Full  {  };
class Empty  {  };
```

The statement

```
throw Full();
```

is executed if the application calls **push()** when the stack is already full, and

```
throw Empty();
```

is executed if **pop()** is called when the stack is empty.

A separate catch block is used for each exception:

```
try
   {
   //code that operates on Stack objects
   }
catch(Stack::Full)
   {
   //code to handle Full exception
   }
catch(Stack::Empty)
   {
   //code to handle Empty exception
   }
```

All the catch blocks used with a particular try block must immediately follow the try block. In this case each catch block simply prints a message: "Stack Full" or "Stack Empty". Only one catch block is activated for a given exception. A group of catch blocks, or a *catch ladder*, operates a little like a **switch** statement, with only the appropriate section of code being executed. When an exception has been handled, control passes to the statement following all the catch blocks. (Unlike a switch statement, you don't need to end each catch block with a break. In this way catch blocks act more like functions.)

Exceptions with the `Distance` Class

Let's look at another example of exceptions, this one applied to the infamous `Distance` class from previous chapters. A `Distance` object has an integer value of feet and a floating-point value for inches. The inches value should always be less than 12.0. A problem with this class in previous examples has been that it couldn't protect itself if the user initialized an object with an inches value of 12.0 or greater. This could lead to trouble when the class tried to perform arithmetic, since the arithmetic routines (such as `operator +()`) assumed inches would be less than 12.0. Such impossible values could also be displayed, thus confounding the user with dimensions like 7'-15".

Let's rewrite the `Distance` class to use an exception to handle this error, as shown in XDIST:

```cpp
// xdist.cpp
// exceptions with Distance class
#include <iostream>
using namespace std;
////////////////////////////////////////////////////////////////
class Distance                     //English Distance class
   {
   private:
      int feet;
      float inches;
   public:
      class InchesEx { };          //exception class
//-------------------------------------------------------------
      Distance()                   //constructor (no args)
         { feet = 0; inches = 0.0; }
//-------------------------------------------------------------
      Distance(int ft, float in)  //constructor (two args)
         {
         if(in >= 12.0)            //if inches too big,
            throw InchesEx();      //throw exception
         feet = ft;
         inches = in;
         }
//-------------------------------------------------------------
      void getdist()               //get length from user
         {
         cout << "\nEnter feet: ";  cin >> feet;
         cout << "Enter inches: ";  cin >> inches;
         if(inches >= 12.0)        //if inches too big,
            throw InchesEx();      //throw exception
         }
//-------------------------------------------------------------
      void showdist()              //display distance
         { cout << feet << "\'-" << inches << '\"'; }
```

```
    };
////////////////////////////////////////////////////////////////
int main()
    {
    try
        {
        Distance dist1(17, 3.5);    //2-arg constructor
        Distance dist2;             //no-arg constructor
        dist2.getdist();            //get distance from user
                                    //display distances
        cout << "\ndist1 = ";  dist1.showdist();
        cout << "\ndist2 = ";  dist2.showdist();
        }
    catch(Distance::InchesEx)       //catch exceptions
        {
        cout << "\nInitialization error: "
                "inches value is too large.";
        }
    cout << endl;
    return 0;
    }
```

We install an exception class called **InchesEx** in the **Distance** class. Then, whenever the user attempts to initialize the inches data to a value greater than or equal to 12.0, we throw the exception. This happens in two places: in the two-argument constructor, where the programmer may make an error supplying initial values, and in the **getdist()** function, where the user may enter an incorrect value at the *Enter inches* prompt. We could also check for negative values and other input mistakes.

In **main()** all interaction with **Distance** objects is enclosed in a try block, and the catch block displays an error message.

In a more sophisticated program, of course, you might want to handle a user error (as opposed to a programmer error) differently. It would be more user friendly to go back to the beginning of the try block and give the user a chance to enter a another distance value.

Exceptions with Arguments

What happens if the application needs more information about what caused an exception? For instance, in the XDIST example, it might help the programmer to know what the bad inches value actually was. Also, if the same exception is thrown by different member functions, as it is in XDIST, it would be nice to know which of the functions was the culprit. Is there a way to pass such information from the member function, where the exception is thrown, to the application that catches it?

This question can be answered by remembering that throwing an exception involves not only transferring control to the handler, but also creating an object of the exception class by calling its constructor. In XDIST, for example, we create an object of type **InchesEx** when we throw the exception with the statement

```
throw InchesEx();
```

If we add data members to the exception class, we can initialize them when we create the object. The exception handler can then retrieve the data from the object when it catches the exception. It's like writing a message on a baseball and throwing it over the fence to your neighbor. We'll modify the XDIST program to do this. Here's the listing for XDIST2:

```cpp
// xdist2.cpp
// exceptions with arguments
#include <iostream>
#include <string>
using namespace std;
/////////////////////////////////////////////////////////////////
class Distance                      //English Distance class
   {
   private:
      int feet;
      float inches;
   public:
//-----------------------------------------------------------------
      class InchesEx                //exception class
         {
         public:
            string origin;          //for name of routine
            float iValue;           //for faulty inches value

            InchesEx(string or, float in)  //2-arg constructor
               {
               origin = or;         //store string
               iValue = in;         //store inches
               }
         };                         //end of exception class
//-----------------------------------------------------------------
      Distance()                    //constructor (no args)
         { feet = 0; inches = 0.0; }
//-----------------------------------------------------------------
      Distance(int ft, float in)    //constructor (two args)
         {
         if(in >= 12.0)
            throw InchesEx("2-arg constructor", in);
         feet = ft;
         inches = in;
         }
//-----------------------------------------------------------------
      void getdist()                //get length from user
         {
         cout << "\nEnter feet: ";  cin >> feet;
         cout << "Enter inches: ";  cin >> inches;
         if(inches >= 12.0)
            throw InchesEx("getdist() function", inches);
         }
//-----------------------------------------------------------------
      void showdist()               //display distance
         { cout << feet << "\'-" << inches << '\"'; }
   };
```

```cpp
//////////////////////////////////////////////////////////////
int main()
   {
   try
      {
      Distance dist1(17, 3.5);    //2-arg constructor
      Distance dist2;             //no-arg constructor
      dist2.getdist();            //get value
                                  //display distances
      cout << "\ndist1 = ";  dist1.showdist();
      cout << "\ndist2 = ";  dist2.showdist();
      }
   catch(Distance::InchesEx ix)   //exception handler
      {
      cout << "\nInitialization error in " << ix.origin
           << ".\n   Inches value of " << ix.iValue
           << " is too large.";
      }
   cout << endl;
   return 0;
   }
```

There are three parts to the operation of passing data when throwing an exception: specifying the data members and a constructor for the exception class, initializing this constructor when we throw an exception, and accessing the object's data when we catch the exception. Let's look at these in turn.

Specifying Data in an Exception Class

It's convenient to make the data in an exception class public so it can be accessed directly by the exception handler. Here's the specification for the new **InchesEx** exception class in XDIST2:

```cpp
class InchesEx                         //exception class
   {
   public:
      string origin;               //for name of routine
      float iValue;                //for faulty inches value

      InchesEx(string or, float in)  //2-arg constructor
         {
         origin = or;          //put string in object
         iValue = in;                //put inches value in object
         }
   };
```

There are public variables for a **string** object, which will hold the name of the member function being called, and a type **float**, for the faulty inches value.

Initializing an Exception Object

How do we initialize the data when we throw an exception? In the two-argument constructor for the **Stack** class we say

```
throw InchesEx("2-arg constructor", in);
```

and in the `getdist()` nmember function for Stack it's

```
throw InchesEx("getdist() function", inches);
```

When the exception is thrown, the handler will display the string and inches values. The string will tell us which member function is throwing the exception, and the value of **inches** will report the faulty inches value detected by the member function. This additional data will make it easier for the programmer or user to figure out what caused the error.

Extracting Data from the Exception Object

How do we extract this data when we catch the exception? The simplest way is to make the data a public part of the exception class, as we've done here. Then in the catch block we can declare **ix** as the name of the exception object we're catching. Using this name we can refer to its data in the usual way, using the dot operator:

```
catch(Distance::InchesEx ix)
    {
    //access 'ix.origin' and 'ix.iValue' directly
    }
```

We can then display the value of **ix.origin** and **ix.iValue**. Here's some interaction with XDIST2, when the user enters too large a value for inches:

```
Enter feet: 7
Enter inches: 13.5

Initialization error in getdist() function.
   Inches value of 13.5 is too large.
```

Similarly, if the programmer changes the definition of **dist1** in **main()** to

```
Distance dist1(17, 22.25);
```

the resulting exception will cause this error message:

```
Initialization error in 2-arg constructor.
   Inches value of 22.25 is too large.
```

Of course we can make whatever use of the exception arguments we want, but they generally carry information that helps us diagnose the error that triggered the exception.

The `bad_alloc` Class

Standard C++ contains several built-in exception classes. The most commonly used is probably `bad_alloc`, which is thrown if an error occurs when attempting to allocate memory with `new`. (This exception was called `xalloc` in earlier versions of C++. At this writing this older approach is still used in Microsoft Visual C++.) If you set up the appropriate `try` and `catch` blocks, you can make use of `bad_alloc` with very little effort. Here's a short example, BADALLOC, that shows how it's used:

```
// badalloc.cpp
// demonstrates bad_alloc exception
#include <iostream>
using namespace std;

int main()
   {
   const unsigned long SIZE = 10000;      //memory size
   char* ptr;                             //pointer to memory

   try
      {
      ptr = new char[SIZE];               //allocate SIZE bytes
      }
   catch(bad_alloc)                       //exception handler
      {
      cout << "\nbad_alloc exception: can't allocate memory.\n";
      return(1);
      }
   delete[] ptr;                          //deallocate memory
   cout << "\nMemory use is successful.\n";
   return 0;
   }
```

Put all the statements that use `new` in a try block. The catch block that follows handles the exception; often by displaying an error message and terminating the program.

Exception Notes

We've shown only the simplest and most common approach to using exceptions. We won't go into further detail, but we'll conclude with a few thoughts about exception usage.

Function Nesting

The statement that causes an exception need not be located directly in the try block; it can also be in a function that is called by a statement in the try block. (Or in a function called by a function that is called by a statement in the try block, and so on.) So you only need to install a try block on the program's upper level. Lower-level functions need not be so encumbered, provided they are called directly or indirectly by functions in the try block.

Exceptions and Class Libraries

An important problem solved by exceptions is that of errors in class libraries. A library routine may discover an error, but typically it doesn't know what to do about it. After all, the library routine was written by a different person at a different time than was the program that called it. What the library routine needs to do is pass the error along to whatever program called it, saying in effect "There's been an error, I don't know what you want to do about it, but here it is." The calling program can thus handle the error as it sees fit.

The exception mechanism provides this capability because exceptions are transmitted up through nested functions until a catch block is encountered. The throw statement may be in a library routine, but the catch block can be in the program that knows how to deal with the error.

If you're writing a class library, you should cause it to throw exceptions for anything that could cause problems to the program using it. If you're writing a program that uses a class library, you should provide try and catch blocks for any exceptions that it throws.

Not for Every Situation

Exceptions should not be used for every kind of error. They impose a certain overhead in terms of program size and (when an exception occurs) in time. For example, exceptions should probably not be used for user input errors (such as inserting letters into numerical input) that are easily detectable by the program. Instead the program should use normal decisions and loops to check the user's input and request the user to try again if necessary.

Destructors Called Automatically

The exception mechanism is surprisingly sophisticated. When an exception is thrown, a destructor is called automatically for any object that was created by the code up to that point in the try block. This is necessary because the application won't know which statement caused the exception, and if it wants to recover from the error, it will (at the very least) need to start over at the top of the try block. The exception mechanism guarantees that the code in the try block will have been "reset," at least as far as the existence of objects is concerned.

Handling Exceptions

After you catch an exception, you will sometimes want to terminate your application. The exception mechanism gives you a chance to indicate the source of the error to the user, and to perform any necessary clean-up chores before terminating. It also makes clean-up easier by executing the destructors for objects created in the try block. This allows you to release system resources, such as memory, that such objects may be using.

In other cases you will not want to terminate your program. Perhaps your program can figure out what caused the error and correct it, or the user can be asked to input different data. When this is the case, the try and catch blocks are typically embedded in a loop, so control can be returned to the beginning of the try block (which the exception mechanism has attempted to restore to its initial state).

If there is no exception handler that matches the exception thrown, the program is unceremoniously terminated by the operating system.

Summary

Templates allow you to generate a family of functions, or a family of classes, to handle different data types. Whenever you find yourself writing several identical functions that perform the same operation on different data types, you should consider using a function template instead. Similarly, whenever you find yourself writing several different class specifications that differ only in the type of data acted on, you should consider using a class template. You'll save yourself time and the result will be a more robust and more easily maintained program that is also (once you understand templates) easier to understand.

Exceptions are a mechanism for handling C++ errors in a systematic, OOP-oriented way. An exception is typically caused by a faulty statement in a try block that operates on objects of a class. The class member function discovers the error and throws an exception, which is caught by the program using the class, in exception-handler code following the try block.

Questions

Answers to questions can be found in Appendix G, "Answers to Questions and Exercises."

1. A template provides a convenient way to make a family of

   a. variables.

   b. functions.

   c. classes.

   d. programs.

2. A template argument is preceded by the keyword _____.

3. True or false: Templates automatically create different versions of a function, depending on user input.

4. Write a template for a function that always returns its argument times 2.

5. A template class

   a. is designed to be stored in different containers.

   b. works with different data types.

   c. generates objects which must all be identical.

   d. generates classes with different numbers of member functions.

6. True or false: There can be more than one template argument.

7. Creating an actual function from a template is called _____ the function.

8. Actual code for a template function is generated when

    a. the function declaration appears in the source code.

    b. the function definition appears in the source code.

    c. a call to the function appears in the source code.

    d. the function is executed at run time.

9. The key concept in the template concept is replacing a _____ with a name that stands for _____.

10. Templates are often used for classes that _____ _____.

11. An exception is typically caused by

    a. the programmer who writes an application's code.

    b. the creator of a class who writes the class member functions.

    c. a run-time error.

    d. an operating system malfunction that terminates the program.

12. The C++ keywords used with exceptions are _____, _____, and _____.

13. Write a statement that throws an exception using the class `BoundsError`, which has an empty body.

14. True or false: Statements that might cause an exception must be part of a catch block.

15. Exceptions are thrown

    a. from the catch block to the try block.

    b. from a throw statement to the try block.

    c. from the point of the error to a catch block.

    d. from a throw statement to a catch block.

16. Write the specification for an exception class that stores an error number and an error name. Include a constructor.

17. True or false: A statement that throws an exception does not need to be located in a try block.

18. The following are errors for which an exception would typically be thrown.

    a. An excessive amount of data threatens to overflow an array

    b. The user presses the (Control)-(C) key combination to terminate the program

    c. A power failure shuts down the system.

    d. `new` cannot obtain the requested memory

19. Additional information sent when an exception is thrown may be placed in

    a. the `throw` keyword.

    b. the function that caused the error.

    c. the catch block.

    d. an object of the exception class.

20. True or false: A program can continue to operate after an exception has occurred.

Exercises

Answers to starred exercises can be found in Appendix G.

*1. Write a template function that returns the average of all the elements of an array. The arguments to the function should be the array name and the size of the array (type `int`). In `main()`, exercise the function with arrays of type `int`, `long`, `double`, and `char`.

*2. A queue is a data-storage device. It's like a stack, except that, instead of being last-in-first-out, it's first-in-first-out, like the line at a bank teller's window. If you put in 1, 2, 3, you get back 1, 2, 3 in that order.

A stack needs only one index to an array (top in the STAKARAY program in Chapter 7). A queue, on the other hand, must keep track of two indexes to an array: one to the tail, where new items are added, and one to the head, where old items are removed. The tail follows the head through the array as items are added and removed. If either the tail or the head reaches the end of the array, it is reset back to the beginning.

Write a class template for a queue class. Assume the programmer using the queue won't make any mistakes, like exceeding the capacity of the queue, or trying to remove an item when the queue is empty. Define several queues of different data types and insert and remove data from them.

*3. Add exceptions to the queue template in Exercise 2. Throw two exceptions: one if the capacity of the queue is exceeded, the other if the program tries to remove an item from an empty queue. One way to handle this is to add a new data member to the queue: a count of the number of items currently in the queue. Increment the count when you insert an item, and decrement it when you remove an item. Throw an exception if this count exceeds the capacity of the queue, or if it becomes less than 0.

You might try making the `main()` part of this exercise interactive, so the user can put values on a queue and take them off. This makes it easier to exercise the queue. Following an exception, the program should allow the user to recover from a mistake without corrupting the contents of the queue.

4. Create a function called `swaps()` that interchanges the values of the two arguments sent to it. (You will probably want to pass these arguments by reference.) Make the function into a template, so it can be used with all numerical data types (`char`, `int`, `float`, and so on). Write a `main()` program to exercise the function with several types.

5. Create a function called `amax()` that returns the value of the largest element in an array. The arguments to the function should be the address of the array and its size. Make this function into a template so it will work with an array of any numerical type. Write a `main()` program that applies this function to arrays of various types.

6. Start with the `safearay` class from the ARROVER3 program in Chapter 8. Make this class into a template, so the safe array can store any kind of data. In `main()`, create safe arrays of at least two different types, and store some data in them.

7. Start with the `frac` class and the four-function fraction calculator of Exercise 7 in Chapter 8. Make the `frac` class into a template so it can be instantiated using different data types for the numerator and denominator. These must be integer types, which pretty much restricts you to `char`, `short`, `int`, and `long` (unless you develop an integer type of your own). In `main()`, instantiate a class `frac<char>` and use it for the four-function calculator. Class `frac<char>` will take less memory than `frac<int>`, but won't be able to handle large fractions.

8. Add an exception class to the ARROVER3 program in Chapter 8 so that an out-of-bounds index will trigger the exception. The catch block can print an error message for the user.

9. Modify the exception class in Exercise 8 (adapted from ARROVER3) so that the error message in the catch block reports the value of the index that caused the exception.

10. There are various philosophies about when to use exceptions. Refer to the ENGLERR program from Chapter 12, "Streams and Files." Should user-input errors be exceptions? For this exercise, let's assume so. Add an exception class to the **Distance** class in that program. (See also the XDIST and XDIST2 examples in this chapter.) Throw an exception in all the places where ENGLERR displayed an error message. Use an argument to the exception constructor to report where the error occurred and the specific cause of the error (inches not a number, inches out of range, and so on). Also, throw an exception when an error is found within the **isint()** function (nothing entered, too many digits, nondigit character, integer out of range). Question: If it throws exceptions, can **isint()** remain an independent function?

    You can insert both the try block and the catch block within the **do** loop so that after an exception you go back to the top of the loop, ready to ask the user for more input.

    You might also want to throw an exception in the two-argument constructor, in case the programmer initializes a **Distance** value with its inches member out of range.

11. Start with the STRPLUS program in Chapter 8. Add an exception class, and throw an exception in the one-argument constructor if the initialization string is too long. Throw another in the overloaded + operator if the result will be too long when two strings are concatenated. Report which of these errors has occurred.

12. Sometimes the easiest way to use exceptions is to create a new class of which an exception class is a member. Try this with a class that uses exceptions to handle file errors. Make a class **dofile** that includes an exception class and member functions to read and write files. A constructor to this class can take the filename as an argument and open a file with that name. You may also want a member function to reset the file pointer to the beginning of the file. Use the REWERR program in Chapter 12 as a model, and write a **main()** program that provides the same functionality, but does so by calling on members of the **dofile** class.

CHAPTER 15

THE STANDARD TEMPLATE LIBRARY

Most computer programs exist to process data. The data may represent a wide variety of real-world information: personnel records, inventories, text documents, the results of scientific experiments, and so on. Whatever it represents, data is stored in memory and manipulated in similar ways. University computer science programs typically include a course called "Data structures and Algorithms." Data structures refers to the ways data is stored in memory, and algorithms refers to how it is manipulated.

C++ classes provide an excellent mechanism for creating a library of data structures. In the past, compiler vendors and many third-party developers offered libraries of *container classes* to handle the storage and processing of data. Now, however, Standard C++ includes its own built-in container class library. It's called the Standard Template Library (STL), and was developed by Alexander Stepanov and Meng Lee of Hewlett Packard. The STL is part of the Standard C++ class library, and can be used as a standard approach to storing and processing data.

This chapter describes the STL and how to use it. The STL is large and complex, so we won't by any means describe everything about it; that would require a large book. (Many books are available on the STL; see Appendix H, "Bibliography.") We will introduce the STL and give examples of the more common algorithms and containers.

Introduction to the STL

The STL contains several kinds of entities. The three most important are containers, algorithms, and iterators.

A *container* is a way that stored data is organized in memory. In earlier chapters we've explored two kinds of containers: stacks and linked lists. Another container, the array, is so common that it's built into C++ (and most other computer languages). However, there are many other kinds of containers, and the STL includes the most useful. The STL containers are implemented by template classes, so they can be easily customized to hold different kinds of data.

Algorithms in the STL are procedures that are applied to containers to process their data in various ways. For example, there are algorithms to sort, copy, search, and merge data. Algorithms are represented by template functions. These functions are not member functions of the container classes. Rather they are standalone functions. Indeed, one of the striking characteristics of the STL is that its algorithms are so general. You can use them not only on STL containers, but on ordinary C++ arrays and on containers you create yourself. (Containers also include member functions for more specific tasks.)

Iterators are a generalization of the concept of pointers: they point to elements in a container. You can increment an iterator, as you can a pointer, so it points in turn to each element in a container. Iterators are a key part of the STL because they connect algorithms with containers. Think of them as a software version of cables, like the cables that connect stereo components together or a computer to its peripherals.

Figure 15.1 shows these three main components of the STL. In this section we'll discuss containers, algorithms, and iterators in slightly more detail. In subsequent sections we'll explore these concepts further with program examples.

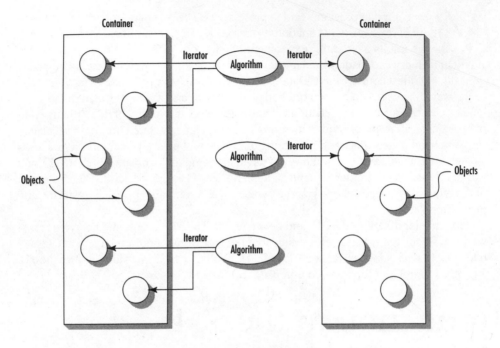

Algorithms use iterators to act on objects in containers

Figure 15.1   Containers, algorithms, and iterators.

Containers

A container is a way to store data, whether the data consists of built-in types like `int` and `float`, or of class objects. The STL makes seven basic kinds of containers available, as well as three more that are derived from the basic kinds. In addition, you can create your own containers based on the basic kinds. You may wonder why we need so many kinds of containers. Why not use C++ arrays in all data storage situations? The answer is efficiency. An array is awkward or slow in many situations.

Containers in the STL fall into two main categories: *sequence* and *associative*. The sequence containers are *vector*, *list*, and *deque*. The associative containers are *set*, *multiset*, *map*, and *multimap*. In addition, several specialized containers are derived from the sequence containers. These are *stack*, *queue*, and *priority_queue*. We'll look at these categories in turn.

Sequence Containers

A sequence container stores a set of elements in what you can visualize as a line, like houses on a street. Each element is related to the other elements by its position along the line. Each element (except at the ends) is preceded by one specific element and followed by another. An ordinary C++ array is an example of a sequence container.

One problem with a C++ array is that you must specify its size at compile time; that is, in the source code. Unfortunately, you usually don't know, when you write the program, how much data will be stored in the array. So you must specify an array large enough to hold what you guess is the maximum amount of data. When the program runs, you will either waste space in memory by not filling the array, or elicit an error message (or even blow up the program) by running out of space. The STL provides the *vector* container to avoid these difficulties.

Here's another problem with arrays. Say you're storing employee records, and you've arranged them in alphabetical order by the employee's last name. If you now want to insert a new employee whose name starts with L, you must move all the employees from M to Z to make room. This can be very time consuming. The STL provides the *list* container, which is based on the idea of a linked list, to solve this problem. Recall from the LINKLIST example in Chapter 10, "Pointers," that it's easy to insert a new item in a linked list by rearranging several pointers.

The third sequence container is the *deque*, which can be thought of as a combination of a stack and a queue. A stack, as you may recall from previous examples, works on a last-in-first-out principle. Both input and output take place on the top of the stack. A queue, on the other hand, uses a first-in-first-out arrangement: data goes in at the front and comes out at the back, like a line of customers in a bank. A deque combines these approaches so you can insert or delete data from either end. The word deque is derived from Double-Ended QUEue. It's a versatile mechanism that's not only useful in its own right, but can be used as the basis for stacks and queues, as you'll see later.

Table 15.1 summarizes the characteristics of the STL sequence containers. It includes the ordinary C++ array for comparison.

Table 15.1   Basic Sequence Containers

	Characteristic	Advantages and Disadvantages
ordinary C++ array	Fixed size	Quick random access (by index number)
		Slow to insert or erase in the middle
		Size cannot be changed at run time

continued on next page

continued from previous page

	Characteristic	Advantages and Disadvantages
vector	Relocating, expandable array	Quick random access (by index number)
		Slow to insert or erase in the middle
		Quick to insert or erase at end
list	Doubly linked list	Quick to insert or delete at any location
		Quick access to both ends
		Slow random access
deque	Like vector, but can be accessed at either end	Quick random access (using index number)
		Slow to insert or erase in the middle
		Quick insert or erase (push and pop) at either the beginning or the end

Instantiating an STL container object is easy. First you must include an appropriate header file. Then you use the template format with the kind of objects to be stored as the parameter. Examples might be

```
vector<int> aVect;  //create a vector of ints
```

or

```
list<airtime> departure_list;  //create a list of airtimes
```

Notice that there's no need to specify the size of STL containers. The containers themselves take care of all memory allocation.

Associative Containers

An associative container is not sequential; instead it uses *keys* to access data. The keys, typically numbers or stings, are used automatically by the container to arrange the stored elements in a specific order. It's like an ordinary English dictionary, in which you access data by looking up words arranged in alphabetical order. You start with a key value (say the word "aardvark," to use the dictionary example), and the container converts this key to the element's location in memory. If you know the key, you can access the associated value swiftly.

There are two kinds of associative containers in the STL: *sets* and *maps*. These both store data in a structure called a *tree*, which offers fast searching, insertion, and deletion. Sets and maps are thus very versatile general data structures suitable for a wide variety of applications. However, it is inefficient to sort them and perform other operations that require random access.

Sets are simpler and more commonly used than maps. A set stores a number of items which contain *keys*. The keys are the attributes used to order the items. For example, a set might store objects of the **person** class, which are ordered alphabetically using their **name** attributes as keys. In this situation, you can quickly locate a desired **person** object by searching for the object with a specified `name`. If a set stores values of a basic type like `int`, then the key is the entire item stored. Some writers refer to an entire object stored in a set as a *key*, but we'll call it the *key object* to emphasize that the the attribute used to order it (the key) isn't the entire item.

A map stores pairs of objects: a key object and a value object. A map is often used as a container that's somewhat like an array, except instead of accessing its elements with index numbers, you access them with indices that can be of an arbitrary type. That is, the key object serves as the index, and the value object is the value at that index.

The *map* and *set* containers allow only one key of a given value to be stored. This makes sense in, say, a list of employees arranged by unique employee numbers. On the other hand, the *multimap* and *multiset* containers allow multiple keys. In an English dictionary there might be several entries for the word "set," for example.

Table 15.2 summarizes the associative containers available in the STL.

Table 15.2   Basic Associative Containers

	Characteristics
set	Stores only the key objects Only one key of each value allowed
multiset	Stores only the key objects Multiple key values allowed
map	Associates key object with value object Only one key of each value allowed
multimap	Associates key object with value object Multiple key values allowed

Creating associative containers is just like creating sequential ones:

```
set<int> intSet;  //create a set of ints
```

or

```
multiset<employee> machinists;  //create a multiset of employees
```

Member Functions

Algorithms are the heavy hitters of the STL, carrying out complex operations like sorting and searching. However, containers also need member functions to perform simpler tasks that are specific to a particular type of container.

Table 15.3 shows some frequently-used member functions whose name and purpose (not the actual implementation) are common to most container classes.

Table 15.3 Some Member Functions Common to All Containers

Name	Purpose
`size()`	Returns the number of items in the container
`empty()`	Returns true if container is empty
`max_size()`	Returns size of the largest possible container
`begin()`	Returns an iterator to the start of the container, for iterating forwards through the container
`end()`	Returns an iterator to the past-the-end location in the container, used to end forward iteration
`rbegin()`	Returns a reverse iterator to the end of the container, for iterating backward through the container
`rend()`	Returns a reverse iterator to the beginning of the container; used to end backward iteration

Many other member functions appear only in certain containers, or certain categories of containers. You'll learn more about these as we go along. Appendix F, "Debugging," includes a table showing the STL member functions and which ones exist for which containers.

Container Adapters

It's possible to create special-purpose containers from the normal containers mentioned above using a construct called *container adapters*. These special-purpose containers have simpler interfaces than the more general containers. The specialized containers implemented with container adapters in the STL are stacks, queues, and priority queues. As we noted, a stack restricts access to pushing and popping a data item on and off the top of the stack. In a queue you push items at one end and pop them off the other. In a priority queue you push data in the front in random order, but when you pop the data off the other end, you always pop the *largest item* stored: the priority queue automatically sorts the data for you.

Stacks, queues, and priority queues can be created from different sequence containers, although the deque is often used. Table 15.4 shows the abstract data types and the sequence containers that can be used in their implementation.

Table 15.4 Adapter-Based Containers

Container	Implementation	Characteristics
`stack`	Can be implemented as vector, list, or deque	Insert (push) and remove (pop) at one end only
`queue`	Can be implemented as list or deque	Insert (push) at one end, remove (pop) at other
`priority_queue`	Can be implemented as vector or deque	Insert(push) in random order at one end, remove (pop) in sorted order from other end

You use a template within a template to instantiate these classes. For example, here's a stack object that holds type `int`, instantiated from the deque class:

```
stack< deque<int> > aStak;
```

A detail to note about this format is that you must insert a space between the two closing angle brackets. You can't write

```
stack<deque<int>> astak;   //syntax error
```

because the compiler will interpret the `>>` as an operator.

Algorithms

An algorithm is a function that does something to the items in a container (or containers). As we noted, algorithms in the STL are not member functions or even friends of container classes, as they are in earlier container libraries, but are standalone template functions. You can use them with built-in C++ arrays, or with container classes you create yourself (provided the class includes certain basic functions).

Table 15.5 shows a few representative algorithms. We'll examine others as we go along. Appendix F contains a table listing most of the STL algorithms.

Table 15.5   Some Typical STL Algorithms

Algorithm	Purpose
find	Returns first element equivalent to a specified value
count	Counts the number of elements that have a specified value
equal	Compares the contents of two containers and returns true if all corresponding elements are equal
search	Looks for a sequence of values in one container that correspond with the same sequence in another container
copy	Copies a sequence of values from one container to another (or to a different location in the same container)
swap	Exchanges a value in one location with a value in another
iter_swap	Exchanges a sequence of values in one location with a sequence of values in another location
fill	Copies a value into a sequence of locations
ort	Sorts the values in a container according to a specified ordering
merge	Combines two sorted ranges of elements to make a larger sorted range
accumulate	Returns the sum of the elements in a given range
for_each	Executes a specified function for each element in the container

Suppose you create an array of type `int`, with data in it:

```
int arr[8] = {42, 31, 7, 80, 2, 26, 19, 75};
```

You can then use the STL `sort()` algorithm to sort this array by saying

```
sort(arr, arr+8);
```

where `arr` is the address of the beginning of the array, and `arr+8` is the past-the-end address (one item past the end of the array).

Iterators

Iterators are pointer-like entities that are used to access individual data items (which are usually called *elements*), in a container. Often they are used to move sequentially from element to element, a process called *iterating* through the container. You can increment iterators with the ++ operator so they point to the next element, and dereference them with the * operator to obtain the value of the element they point to. In the STL an iterator is represented by an object of an `iterator` class.

Different classes of iterators must be used with different types of container. There are three major classes of iterators: forward, bi-directional, and random access. A *forward iterator* can only move forward through the container, one item at a time. Its ++ operator accomplishes this. It can't move backward and it can't be set to an arbitrary location in the middle of the container. A *bidirectional iterator* can move backward as well as forward, so both its ++ and -- operators are defined. A *random access iterator*, in addition to moving backward and forward, can jump to an arbitrary location. You can tell it to access location 27, for example.

There are also two specialized kinds of iterators. An *input iterator* can "point to" an input device (`cin` or a file) to read sequential data items into a container, and an *output iterator* can "point to" an output device (`cout` or a file) and write elements from a container to the device.

While the values of forward, bi-directional, and random access iterators can be stored (so they can be used later), the values of input and output iterators cannot be. This makes sense: the first three iterators point to memory locations, while input and output iterators point to I/O devices for which stored "pointer" values have no meaning. Table 15.6 shows the characteristics of these different kinds of iterators.

Table 15.6   Iterator Characteristics

Iterator Type	Read/Write	Iterator Can Be Saved	Direction	Access
Random access	Read and write	Yes	Forward and back	Random
Bidirectional	Read and write	Yes	Forward and back	Linear
Forward	Read and write	Yes	Forward only	Linear
Output	Write only	No	Forward only	Linear
Input	Read only	No	Forward only	Linear

Potential Problems with the STL

The sophistication of the STL's template classes places a strain on compilers, and not all of them respond well. Let's look at some potential problems.

First, it's sometimes hard to find errors because the compiler reports them as being deep in a header file when they're really in the class user's code. You may need to resort to brute force methods such as commenting out one line of your code at a time to find the culprit.

Precompilation of header files, which speeds up compilation dramatically on compilers that offer it, may cause problems with the STL. If things don't seem to be working, try turning off precompiled headers.

The STL may generate spurious compiler warnings. "Conversion may lose significant digits" is a favorite. These appear to be harmless, and can be ignored or turned off.

These minor complaints aside, the STL is a surprisingly robust and versatile system. Errors tend to be caught at compile time rather than at run time. The different algorithms and containers present a very consistent interface; what works with one container or algorithm will usually work with another (assuming it's used appropriately).

This quick overview probably leaves you with more questions than answers. The balance of this chapter should provide enough specific details of STL operation to make things clearer.

Algorithms

The STL algorithms perform operations on collections of data. These algorithms were designed to work with STL containers, but one of the nice things about them is that you can apply them to ordinary C++ arrays. This may save you considerable work when programming arrays. It also offers an easy way to learn about the algorithms, unencumbered with containers. In this section we'll examine how some representative algorithms are used. (Remember that the algorithms are listed in Appendix F.)

The `find()` Algorithm

The `find()` algorithm looks for the first element in a container that has a specified value. The FIND example program shows how this looks when we're trying to find a value in an array of `int`s.

```
// find.cpp
// finds the first object with a specified value
#include <iostream>
#include <algorithm>                      //for find()
using namespace std;

int arr[] = { 11, 22, 33, 44, 55, 66, 77, 88 };

int main()
   {
   int* ptr;
   ptr = find(arr, arr+8, 33);            //find first 33
```

```
cout << "First object with value 33 found at offset "
    << (ptr-arr) << endl;
return 0;
}
```

The output from this program is

```
First object with value 33 found at offset 2.
```

As usual, the first element in the array is number 0, so the 33 is at offset 2, not 3.

Header Files

In this program we've included the header file ALGORITHM. Notice that, as with other header files in the Standard C++ library, there is no file extension (like .H or .CPP). This file contains the declarations of the STL algorithms. Other header files are used for containers and for other purposes. If you're using an older version of the STL you may need to include a header file with a somewhat different name, like ALGO.H.

Ranges

The first two parameters to `find()` specify the range of elements to be examined. These values are specified by iterators. In this example we use normal C++ pointer values, which are a special case of iterators.

The first parameter is the iterator of (or in this case the pointer to) the first value to be examined. The second parameter is the iterator of the location one past the last element to be examined. Since there are 8 elements, this value is the first value plus 8. This is called a *past-the-end* value; it points to the element just past the end of the range to be examined.

This syntax is reminiscent of the normal C++ idiom in a **for** loop:

```
for(int j=0; j<8; j++)    //from 0 to 7
  {
  if(arr[j] == 33)
    {
    cout << "First object with value 33 found at offset "
        << j << endl;
    break;
    }
  }
```

In the FIND example the `find()` algorithm saves you the trouble of writing this **for** loop. In more complicated situations, algorithms may save you from writing far more complicated code.

The `count()` Algorithm

Let's look at another algorithm, `count()`, which counts how many elements in a container have a specified value and returns this number. The COUNT example shows how this looks:

```
// count.cpp
// counts the number of objects with a specified value
#include <iostream>
```

```
#include <algorithm>                  //for count()
using namespace std;

int arr[] = { 33, 22, 33, 44, 33, 55, 66, 77 };

int main()
   {
   int n = count(arr, arr+8, 33);   //count number of 33's
   cout << "There are " << n << " 33's in arr." << endl;
   return 0;
   }
```

The output is

```
There are 3 33's in arr.
```

The `sort()` Algorithm

You can guess what the `sort()` algorithm does. Here's an example, called SORT, of this algorithm applied to an array:

```
// sort.cpp
// sorts an array of integers
#include <iostream>
#include <algorithm>
using namespace std;
                              //array of numbers
int arr[] = {45, 2, 22, -17, 0, -30, 25, 55};

int main()
   {
   sort(arr, arr+8);             //sort the numbers

   for(int j=0; j<8; j++)        //display sorted array
      cout << arr[j] << ' ';
   return 0;
   }
```

The output from the program is

```
-30, -17, 0, 2, 22, 25, 45, 55
```

We'll look at some variations of this algorithm later.

The `search()` Algorithm

Some algorithms operate on two containers at once. For instance, while the `find()` algorithm looks for a specified value in a single container, the `search()` algorithm looks for a sequence of values, specified by one container, within another container. The SEARCH example shows how this looks.

```
// search.cpp
// searches one container for a sequence in another container
#include <iostream>
```

```
#include <algorithm>
using namespace std;

int source[] =  { 11, 44, 33, 11, 22, 33, 11, 22, 44 };
int pattern[] = { 11, 22, 33 };

int main()
   {
   int* ptr;
   ptr = search(source, source+9, pattern, pattern+3);
   if(ptr == source+9)                  //if past-the-end
      cout << "No match found\n";
   else
      cout << "Match at " << (ptr - source) << endl;
   return 0;
}
```

The algorithm looks for the sequence 11, 22, 33, specified by the array **pattern**, within the array **source**. As you can see by inspection, this sequence is found in **source** starting at the fourth element (element 3). The output is

```
Match at 3
```

If the iterator value **ptr** ends up one past the end of the source, then no match has been found.

The arguments to algorithms such as **search()** don't need to be the same type of container. The source could be in an STL vector, and the pattern in an array, for example. This kind of generality is a very powerful feature of the STL.

The `merge()` Algorithm

Here's an algorithm that works with three containers, merging the elements from two source containers into a destination container. The MERGE example shows how it works.

```
// merge.cpp
// merges two containers into a third
#include <iostream>
#include <algorithm>            //for merge()
using namespace std;

int src1[] = { 2, 3, 4, 6, 8 };
int src2[] = { 1, 3, 5 };
int dest[8];

int main()
   {                            //merge src1 and src2 into dest
   merge(src1, src1+5, src2, src2+3, dest);
   for(int j=0; j<8; j++)       //display dest
      cout << dest[j] << ' ';
   cout << endl;
   return 0;
   }
}
```

The output, which displays the contents of the destination container, looks like this:

```
1 2 3 3 4 5 6 8
```

As you can see, merging preserves the ordering, interweaving the two sequences of source elements into the destination container.

Function Objects

Some algorithms can take something called a *function object* as an argument. A function object looks, to the user, much like a template function. However, it's actually an object of a template class that has a single member function: the overloaded () operator. This sounds mysterious, but it's easy to use.

Suppose you want to sort an array of numbers into descending instead of ascending order. The SORTEMP program shows how to do it:

```
// sortemp.cpp
// sorts array of doubles in backward order,
// uses greater<>() function object
#include <iostream>
#include <algorithm>                  //for sort()
#include <functional>                 //for greater<>
using namespace std;
                                      //array of doubles
double fdata[] = { 19.2, 87.4, 33.6, 55.0, 11.5, 42.2 };

int main()
   {                                  //sort the doubles
   sort( fdata, fdata+6, greater<double>() );

   for(int j=0; j<6; j++)             //display sorted doubles
      cout << fdata[j] << ' ';
   cout << endl;
   return 0;
   }
```

The sort() algorithm usually sorts in ascending order, but the use of the greater<>() function object, the third argument of sort(), reverses the sorting order. Here's the output:

```
87.4 55 42.2 33.6 19.2 11.5
```

Besides comparisons, there are function objects for arithmetical and logical operations. We'll look at function objects more closely in the last section in this chapter.

User-written Functions in Place of Function Objects

Function objects operate only on basic C++ types and on classes for which the appropriate operators (+, <, ==, and so on) are defined. If you're working with values for which this is not the case, you can substitute a user-written function for a function object. For example, the operator < is not defined for ordinary char* strings, but we can write a function to perform the comparison, and use this function's address (its name) in place of the function object. The SORTCOM example shows how to sort an array of char* strings:

```
// sortcom.cpp
// sorts array of strings with user-written comparison function
#include <iostream>
#include <string>                            //for strcmp()
#include <algorithm>
using namespace std;
                                            //array of strings
char* names[] = { "George", "Penny", "Estelle",
               "Don", "Mike", "Bob" };

bool alpha_comp(char*, char*);              //prototype

int main()
   {
   sort(names, names+6, alpha_comp);        //sort the strings

   for(int j=0; j<6; j++)                    //display sorted strings
      cout << names[j] << endl;
   return 0;
   }

bool alpha_comp(char* s1, char* s2)         //returns true if s1<s2
   {
   return ( strcmp(s1, s2)<0 ) ? true : false;
   }
```

The third argument to the `sort()` algorithm is the address of the `alpha_comp()` function, which compares two `char*` strings and returns `true` or `false`, depending on whether the first is lexicographically (that is, alphabetically) less than the second. It uses the C library function `strcmp()`, which returns a value less than 0 if its first argument is less than its second. The output from this program is what you would expect:

```
Bob
Don
Estelle
George
Mike
Penny
```

Actually, you don't need to write your own function objects to handle text. If you use the `string` class from the standard library, you can use built-in function objects like `less<>()` and `greater<>()`.

Adding _if to Algorithms

Some algorithms have versions that end in `_if`. These algorithms take an extra parameter called a *predicate*, which is a function object or a function. For example, the `find()` algorithm finds all elements equal to a specified value. We can also create a function that works with the `find_if()` algorithm to find elements with any arbitrary characteristic.

Our example uses `string` objects. The `find_if()` algorithm is supplied with a user-written `isDon()` function to find the first `string` in an array of `string` objects that has the value "Don". Here's the listing for FIND_IF:

```
// find_if.cpp
// searches array of strings for first name that matches "Don"
#include <iostream>
#include <string>
#include <algorithm>
using namespace std;
//------------------------------------------------------------
bool isDon(string name)        //returns true if name=="Don"
   {
   return name == "Don";
   }
//------------------------------------------------------------
string names[] = { "George", "Estelle", "Don", "Mike", "Bob" };

int main()
   {
   string* ptr;
   ptr = find_if( names, names+5, isDon );

   if(ptr==names+5)
      cout << "Don is not on the list.\n";
   else
      cout << "Don is element "
           << (ptr-names)
           << " on the list.\n";
   return 0;
   }
```

Since "Don" is indeed one of the names in the array, the output from the program is

```
Don is element 2 on the list.
```

The address of the function isDon() is the third argument to find_if(), while the first and second arguments are, as usual, the first and the past-the-end addresses of the array.

The find_if() algorithm applies the isDon() function to every element in the range. If isDon() returns true for any element, then find_if() returns the value of that element's pointer (iterator). Otherwise, it returns a pointer to the past-the-the end address of the array.

Various other algorithms, such as count(), replace(), and remove(), have _if versions.

The for_each() Algorithm

The for_each() algorithm allows you to do something to every item in a container. You write your own function to determine what that "something" is. Your function can't change the elements in the container, but it can use or display their values.

Here's an example in which for_each() is used to convert all the values of an array from inches to centimeters and display them. We write a function called in_to_cm() that multiplies a value by 2.54, and use this function's address as the third argument to for_each(). Here's the listing for FOR_EACH:

```
// for_each.cpp
// uses for_each() to output inches array elements as centimeters
#include <iostream>
```

```
#include <algorithm>
using namespace std;

void in_to_cm(double);        //prototype

int main()
   {                              //array of inches values
   double inches[] = { 3.5, 6.2, 1.0, 12.75, 4.33 };
                                //output as centimeters
   for_each(inches, inches+5, in_to_cm);
   cout << endl;
   return 0;
   }

void in_to_cm(double in)    //convert and display as centimeters
   {
   cout << (in * 2.54) << ' ';
   }
```

The output looks like this:

```
8.89 15.748 2.54 32.385 10.9982
```

The `transform()` Algorithm

The `transform()` algorithm does something to every item in a container, and places the resulting values in a different container (or the same one). Again, a user-written function determines what will be done to each item. The return type of this function must be the same as that of the destination container. Our example is similar to FOR_EACH, except that instead of displaying the converted values, our `in_to_cm()` function puts the centimeter values into a different array, `centi[]`. The main program then displays the contents of `centi[]`. Here's the listing for TRANSFO:

```
// transfo.cpp
// uses transform() to change array of inches values to cm
#include <iostream>
#include <algorithm>
using namespace std;

int main()
   {                              //array of inches values
   double inches[] = { 3.5, 6.2, 1.0, 12.75, 4.33 };
   double centi[5];
   double in_to_cm(double);    //prototype
                                //transform into array centi[]
   transform(inches, inches+5, centi, in_to_cm);

   for(int j=0; j<5; j++)      //display array centi[]
      cout << centi[j] << ' ';
   cout << endl;
   return 0;
   }
```

```
double in_to_om(double in)      //convert inches to centimeters
   {
   return (in * 2.54);          //return result
   }
```

The output is the same as that from the FOR_EACH program.

We've looked at just a few of the algorithms in the STL. There are many others, but what we've shown here should give you an idea of the kinds of algorithms that are available, and how to use them.

Sequential Containers

As we noted earlier, there are two major categories of containers in the STL: sequence containers and associative containers. In this section we'll introduce the three sequence containers: vectors, lists, and deques, focusing on how these containers work and on their member functions. We haven't learned about iterators yet, so there will be some operations that we can't perform on these containers. We'll examine iterators in the next section.

Each program example in the following sections will introduce several member functions for the container being described. Remember, however, that different kinds of containers use member functions with the same names and characteristics, so what you learn about, say, push_back() for vectors will also be relevant to lists and queues.

Vectors

You can think of vectors as smart arrays. They manage storage allocation for you, expanding and contracting the size of the vector as you insert or erase data. You can use vectors much like arrays, accessing elements with the [ ] operator. Such random access is very fast with vectors. It's also fast to add (or *push*) a new data item onto the end (the *back*) of the vector. When this happens the vector's size is automatically increased to hold the new item.

Member Functions push_back(), size(), and operator[]

Our first example, VECTOR, shows the most common vector operations.

```
// vector.cpp
// demonstrates push_back(), operator[], size()
#include <iostream>
#include <vector>
using namespace std;

int main()
   {
   vector<int> v;                    //create a vector of ints

   v.push_back(10);                  //put values at end of array
   v.push_back(11);
   v.push_back(12);
   v.push_back(13);
```

```
    v[0] = 20;                      //replace with new values
    v[3] = 23;

    for(int j=0; j<v.size(); j++)   //display vector contents
       cout << v[j] << ' ';         //20 11 12 23
    cout << endl;
    return 0;
    }
```

We use the vector's default (no-argument) constructor to create a vector v. As with all STL containers, the template format is used to specify the type of variable the container will hold; in this case type int. We don't specify the container's size, so it starts off at 0.

The push_back() member function inserts the value of its argument at the back of the vector. (The back is where the element with the highest index number is.) The front of a vector (the element with index 0), unlike that of a list or queue, cannot be used for inserting new elements. Here we push the values 10, 11, 12 and 13, so that v[0] contains 10, v[1] contains 11, v[2] contains 12, and v[3] contains 13.

Once a vector has some data in it, this data can be accessed—both read and written to—using the overloaded [ ] operator, just as if it were in an array. We use this operator to change the first element from 10 to 20, and the last element from 13 to 23. Here's the output from VECTOR:

20 11 12 23

The size() member function returns the number of elements currently in the container, which in VECTOR is 4. We use this value in the **for** loop to print out the values of the elements in the container.

Another member function, max_size() (which we don't demonstrate here), returns the maximum size to which a container can be expanded. This number depends on the type of data being stored in the container (the bigger the elements, the fewer of them you can store), the type of container, and the operating system. For example, on our system max_size() returns 1,073,741,823 for a vector type int.

Member Functions swap(), empty(), back() and pop_back()

The next example, VECTCON, shows some additional vector constructors and member functions.

```
// vectcon.cpp
// demonstrates constructors, swap(), empty(), back(), pop_back()
#include <iostream>
#include <vector>
using namespace std;

int main()
   {                                   //an array of doubles
   double arr[] = { 1.1, 2.2, 3.3, 4.4 };

   vector<double> v1(arr, arr+4);   //initialize vector to array
   vector<double> v2(4);            //empty vector of size 4
```

```
   v1.swap(v2);                       //swap contents of v1 and v2

   while( !v2.empty() )               //until vector is empty,
      {
      cout << v2.back() << ' ';       //display the last element
      v2.pop_back();                  //remove the last element
      }                               //output: 4.4 3.3 2.2 1.1
   cout << endl;
   return 0;
   }
```

We've used two new vector constructors in this program. The first initializes the vector **v1** with the values of a normal C++ array passed to it as an argument. The arguments to this constructor are pointers to the start of the array and to the element one past the end. The second constructor sets **v2** to an initial size of 4, but does not supply any initial values. Both vectors hold type **double**.

The **swap()** member function exchanges all the data in one vector with all the data in another, keeping the elements in the same order. In this program there is only garbage data in **v2**, so it's swapped with the data in **v1**. We display **v2** to show it now contains the data that was in **v1**. The output is

4.4, 3.3, 2.2, 1.1

The **back()** member function returns the value of the last element in the vector. We display this value with **cout**. The **pop_back()** member function removes the last element in the vector. Thus each time through the loop there is a different last element. (It's a little surprising that **pop_back()** does not simultaneously return the value of the last element and remove it from the vector, as we've seen **pop()** do in previous examples with stacks, but it doesn't, so **back()** must be used as well.)

Some member functions, such as **swap()**, also exist as algorithms. When this is the case, the member function version is usually provided because it's more efficient for that particular container than the algorithm version. Sometimes you can use the algorithm as well. For example, you can use it to swap elements in two different kinds of containers.

Member Functions `insert()` and `erase()`

The **insert()** and **erase()** member functions insert or remove an element from an arbitrary location in a container. These functions aren't very efficient with vectors, since all the elements above the insertion or erasure must be moved to make space for the new element or close up the space where the erased item was. However, insertion and erasure may nevertheless be useful if speed is not a factor. The next example, VECTINS, shows how these member functions are used:

```
// vectins.cpp
// demonstrates insert(), erase()
#include <iostream>
#include <vector>
using namespace std;

int main()
   {
```

```
       int arr[] = { 100, 110, 120, 130 };   //an array of ints

       vector<int> v(arr, arr+4);            //initialize vector to array

     cout << "\nBefore insertion: ";
     for(int j=0; j<v.size(); j++)           //display all elements
        cout << v[j] << ' ';

     v.insert( v.begin()+2, 115);            //insert 115 at element 2

     cout << "\nAfter insertion:  ";
     for(j=0; j<v.size(); j++)               //display all elements
         cout << v[j] << ' ';

     v.erase( v.begin()+2 );                 //erase element 2

     cout << "\nAfter erasure:    ";
     for(j=0; j<v.size(); j++)               //display all elements
         cout << v[j] << ' ';
     cout << endl;
     return 0;
     }
```

The `insert()` member function (at least this version of it) takes two arguments: the place where an element will be inserted in a container, and the value of the element. We add 2 to the `begin()` member function to specify element 2 (the third element) in the vector. The elements from the insertion point to the end of the container are moved upward to make room, and the size of the container is increased by 1.

The `erase()` member function removes the element at the specified location. The elements above the deletion point are moved downward, and the size of the container is decreased by 1. Here's the output from VECTINS:

```
Before insertion: 100 110 120 130
After insertion:  100 110 115 120 130
After erasure:    100 110 120 130
```

Lists

An STL list container is a doubly linked list, in which each element contains a pointer not only to the next element but also to the preceding one. The container stores the address of both the front (first) and the back (last) elements, which makes for fast access to both ends of the list.

Member Functions `push_front()`, `front()`, and `pop_front`

Our first example, LIST, shows how data can be pushed, read, and popped from both the front and the back.

```
//list.cpp
//demonstrates push_front(), front(), pop_front()
#include <iostream>
```

```
#include <list>
using namespace std;

int main()
   {
   list<int> ilist;

   ilist.push_back(30);              //push items on back
   ilist.push_back(40);
   ilist.push_front(20);             //push items on front
   ilist.push_front(10);

   int size = ilist.size();          //number of items

   for(int j=0; j<size; j++)
      {
      cout << ilist.front() << ' ';  //read item from front
      ilist.pop_front();             //pop item off front
      }
   cout << endl;
   return 0;
   }
```

We push data on the back (the end) and front of the list in such a way that when we display and remove the data from the front it's in normal order:

10 20 30 40

The push_front(),pop_front(), and front()member functions are similar to push_back(), pop_back(), and back(), which we've already seen at work with vectors.

Note that you can't use random access for list elements, because such access is too slow. For this reason the [ ] operator is not defined for lists. If it were, this operator would need to traverse along the list, counting elements as it went, until it reached the correct one, a time-consuming operation. If you need random access, you should use a vector or a deque.

Lists are appropriate when you will make frequent insertions and deletions in the middle of the list. This is not efficient for vectors and deques, because all the elements above the insertion or deletion point must be moved. However, it's quick for lists because only a few pointers need to be changed to insert or delete a new item. (However, it may still be time-consuming to find the correct insertion point.)

The insert()and erase() member functions are used for list insertion and deletion, but they require the use of iterators, so we'll postpone a discussion of these functions.

Member Functions reverse(), merge(), and unique()

Some member functions exist only for lists; no such member functions are defined for other containers, although there are algorithms that do the same things. Our next example, LISTPLUS, shows some of these functions. It begins by filling two list-of-**int** objects with the contents of two arrays.

```
listplus.cpp
// demonstrates reverse(), merge(), and unique()
#include <iostream>
```

```
#include <list>
using namespace std;

int main()
   {
   int j;
   list<int> list1, list2;

   int arr1[] = { 40, 30, 20, 10 };
   int arr2[] = { 15, 20, 25, 30, 35 };

   for(j=0; j<4; j++)
      list1.push_back( arr1[j] );     //list1: 40, 30, 20, 10
   for(j=0; j<5; j++)
      list2.push_back( arr2[j] );     //list2: 15, 20, 25, 30, 35

   list1.reverse();                   //reverse list1: 10 20 30 40
   list1.merge(list2);                //merge list2 into list1
   list1.unique();                    //remove duplicate 20 and 30

   int size = list1.size();
   while( !list1.empty() )
      {
      cout << list1.front() << ' ';   //read item from front
      list1.pop_front();              //pop item off front
      }
   cout << endl;
   return 0;
   }
```

The first list is in backward order, so we return it to normal sorted order using the **reverse()** member function. (It's quick to reverse a list container because both ends are accessible.) This is necessary because the second member function, **merge()**, operates on two lists and requires both of them to be in sorted order. Following the reversal, the two lists are

```
10, 20, 30, 40
15, 20, 25, 30, 35
```

Now the **merge()** function merges **list2** into **list1**, keeping everything sorted and expanding **list1** to hold the new items. The resulting content of **list1** is

```
10, 15, 20, 20, 25, 30, 30, 35, 40
```

Finally we apply the **unique()** member function to **list1**. This function finds adjacent elements with the same value, and removes all but the first. The contents of **list1** are then displayed. The output of LISTPLUS is

```
10, 15, 20, 25, 30, 35, 40
```

To display the contents of the list we use the `front()` and `pop_front()` member functions in a `for` loop. Each element, from front to back, is displayed and then popped off the list. The result is that the process of displaying the list destroys it. This may not always be what you want, but for the moment it's the only way we have learned to access successive list elements. Iterators, described in the next section, will solve this problem.

Deques

A deque is like a vector in some ways and like a linked list in others. Like a vector, it supports random access using the `[]` operator. However, like a list a deque can be accessed at the front as well as the back. It's a sort of double-ended vector, supporting `push_front()`, `pop_front()`, and `front()`.

Memory is allocated differently for vectors and queues. A vector always occupies a contiguous region of memory. If a vector grows too large, it may need to be moved to a new location where it will fit. A deque, on the other hand, can be stored in several non-contiguous areas; it is segmented. A member function, `capacity()`, returns the largest number of elements a vector can store without being moved, but `capacity()` isn't defined for deques because they don't need to be moved.

```cpp
// deque.cpp
// demonstrates push_back(), push_front(), front()
#include <iostream>
#include <deque>
using namespace std;

int main()
   {
   deque<int> deq;

   deq.push_back(30);              //push items on back
   deq.push_back(40);
   deq.push_back(50);
   deq.push_front(20);             //push items on front
   deq.push_front(10);

   deq[2] = 33;                    //change middle item

   for(int j=0; j<deq.size(); j++)
      cout << deq[j] << ' ';       //display items
   cout << endl;
   return 0;
   }
```

We've already seen examples of `push_back()`, `push_front()`, and `operator []`. They work the same for deques as for other containers. The output of this program is

```
10 20 33 40 50
```

Figure 15.2 shows some important member functions for the three sequential containers.

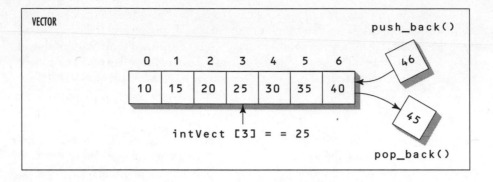

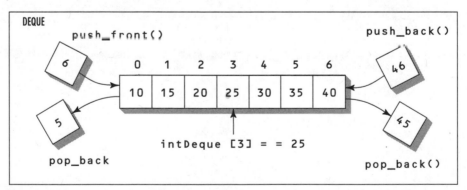

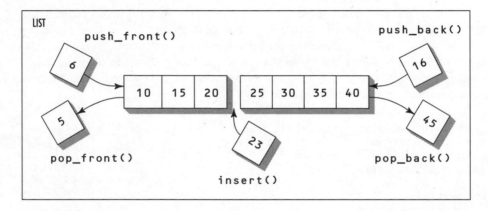

Figure 15.2 Sequential containers.

Iterators

Iterators may seem a bit mysterious, yet they are central to the operation of the STL. In this section we'll first discuss the twin roles played by iterators: as smart pointers and as a connection between algorithms and containers. Then we'll show some examples of their use.

Iterators as Smart Pointers

It's often necessary to perform an operation on all the elements in the container (or perhaps a range of elements). Displaying the value of each element in the container, or adding its value to a total, are examples. In an ordinary C++ array, such operations are carried out using a pointer (or the [] operator, which is the same underlying mechanism). For example, the following code iterates through a float array, displaying the value of each element:

```
float* ptr = start_address;
for(int j=0; j<SIZE; j++)
   cout << *ptr++;
```

We dereference the pointer ptr with the * operator to obtain the value of the item it points to, and increment it with the ++ operator so it points to the next item.

Ordinary Pointers Underpowered

However, with more sophisticated containers, plain C++ pointers have disadvantages. For one thing, if the items stored in the container are not placed contiguously in memory, handling the pointer becomes much more complicated; we can't simply increment it to point to the next value. For example, in moving to the next item in a linked list we can't assume the item is adjacent to the previous one; we must follow the chain of pointers.

We may also want to store the address of some container element in a pointer variable so we can access the element at some future time. What happens to this stored pointer value if we insert or erase something from the middle of the container? It may not continue to be valid if the container's contents are rearranged. It would be nice if we didn't need to worry about revising all our stored pointer values when insertions and deletions take place.

One solution to these kinds of problems is to create a class of "smart pointers." An object of such a class basically wraps its member functions around an ordinary pointer. The ++ and * operators are overloaded so they know how to operate on the elements in their container, even if the elements are not contiguous in memory or change their locations. Here's how that might look, in skeleton form:

```
class SmartPointer
   {
   private:
      float* p;    //an ordinary pointer
   public:
      float operator*()
         {  }
      float operator++()
         {  }
   };

void main()
   {
   ...
   SmartPointer sptr = start_address;
   for(int j=0; j<SIZE; j++)
      cout << *sptr++;
   }
```

Whose Responsibility?

Should the smart pointer class be embedded in a container, or should it be a separate class? The approach chosen by the STL is to make smart pointers, called *iterators*, into a completely separate class (actually a family of templetized classes). The class user creates iterators by defining them to be objects of such classes.

Iterators as an Interface

Besides acting as smart pointers to items in containers, iterators serve another important purpose in the STL. They determine which algorithms can be used with which containers. Why is this necessary?

In some theoretical sense you should be able to apply every algorithm to every container. And, in fact, many algorithms will work with all the STL containers. However, it turns out that some algorithms are very inefficient (that is, slow) when used with some containers. The `sort()` algorithm, for example, needs random access to the container it's trying to sort; otherwise it would need to iterate through the container to find each element before moving it, a time-consuming approach. Similarly, to be efficient, the `reverse()` algorithm needs to iterate backward as well as forward through a container.

Iterators provide a surprisingly elegant way to match appropriate algorithms with containers. As we noted, you can think of an iterator as a cable, like the cable used to connect a computer and printer. One end of the cable plugs into a container, and the other plugs into an algorithm. However, not all cables plug into all containers, and not all cables plug into all algorithms. If you try to use an algorithm that's too powerful for a given container type, then you won't be able to find a cable (an iterator) to connect them. If you try it, you will receive a compiler error, alerting you to the problem.

How many kinds of iterators (cables) do you need to make this scheme work? As it turns out, only five types are necessary. Figure 15.3 shows these five categories, arranged from bottom to top in order of increasing sophistication, except that input and output are equally unsophisticated. (This is *not* an inheritance diagram.)

If an algorithm needs only to step through a container in a forward direction, reading (but not writing to) one item after another, it can use an *input* iterator to connect itself to the container. Actually, input iterators are typically used, not with containers, but when reading from files or `cin`.

If an algorithm steps through the container in a forward direction but writes to the container instead of reading from it, it can use an *output* iterator. Output iterators are typically used when writing to files or `cout`.

If an algorithm steps along in the forward direction and may either read or write to a container, it must use a *forward* iterator.

If an algorithm must be able to step both forward and back through a container, it must use a *bidirectional* iterator.

Finally, if an algorithm must access any item in the container instantly, without stepping along to it, it must use a *random access* iterator. Random access iterators are like arrays, in that you can access any element. They are the only iterators that can be manipulated with arithmetic operations, as in

```
iter2 = iter1 + 7;
```

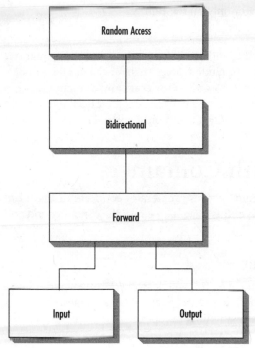

Figure 15.3   Iterator categories.

Table 15.7 shows which operations each iterator supports.

Table 15.7   Capabilities of Different Iterator Categories

Iterator Type	Step Forward ++	Read value=*i	Write *i=value	Step Back --	Random Access [n]
Random access iterator	x	x	x	x	x
Bidirectional iterator	x	x	x	x	
Forward iterator	x	x	x		
Output iterator	x		x		
Input iterator	x	x			

As you can see, all the iterators support the ++ operator for stepping forward through the container. The input iterator can use the * operator on the right side of the equal sign (but not on the left):

```
value = *iter;
```

The output iterator can use the * operator only on the right:

```
*iter = value;
```

The forward iterator handles both reading and writing, and the bidirectional iterator can be decremented as well as incremented. The random access iterator can use the [ ] operator (as well as simple arithmetic operators like + and -) to access any element quickly.

An algorithm can always use an iterator with *more* capability than it needs. If it needs a forward iterator, for example, it's all right to plug it into a bidirectional iterator or a random access iterator.

Matching Algorithms with Containers

We've used a cable as an analogy to an iterator, because an iterator connects an algorithm and a container. Let's focus on the two ends of this imaginary cable: the container end and the algorithm end.

Plugging the Cable into a Container

If you confine yourself to the basic STL containers, you will be using only two kinds of iterators. As shown in Table 15.8, the vector and deque accept any kind of iterator, while the list, set, multiset, map, and multimap accept anything except the random iterator.

Table 15.8 Iterator Types Accepted by Containers

	Vector	List	Deque	Set	Multiset	Map	Multimap
Random Access	X		X				
Bidirectional	X	X	X	X	X	X	X
Forward	X	X	X	X	X	X	X
Input	X	X	X	X	X	X	X
Output	X	X	X	X	X	X	X

How does the STL enforce the use of the correct iterator for a given container? When you define an iterator you must specify what kind of container it will be used for. For example, if you've defined a list holding elements of type `int`,

```
list<int> iList;              //list of ints
```

then to define an iterator to this list you say

```
list<int>::iterator iter;  //iterator to list-of-ints
```

When you do this, the STL automatically makes this iterator a bidirectional iterator, because that's what a list requires. An iterator to a vector or a deque is automatically created as a random-access iterator.

This automatic selection process is implemented by having an iterator class for a specific container be derived (inherited) from a more general iterator class that's appropriate to a specific container. Thus the iterators to vectors and deques are derived from the `random_access_iterator` class, while iterators to lists are derived from the `bidirectional_iterator` class.

We now see how containers are matched to their end of our fanciful iterator—cables. A cable doesn't actually plug into a container; it is (figuratively speaking) hardwired to it, like the cord on a toaster. Vectors and deques are always wired to random-access cables, while lists (and all the associative containers, which we'll encounter later in this chapter) are always wired to bidirectional cables.

Plugging the Cables into the Algorithm

Now that we've seen how one end of an iterator cable is "wired" to the container, we're ready to look at the other end of the cable. How do iterators plug into algorithms? Every algorithm, depending on what it will do to the elements in a container, requires a certain kind of iterator. If the algorithm must access elements at arbitrary locations in the container, it requires a random-access iterator. If it will merely step forward through the iterator, it can use the less powerful forward iterator. Table 15.9 shows a sampling of algorithms and the iterators they require. (A complete version of this table is shown in Appendix F.)

Table 15.9   Type of Iterator Required by Representative Algorithms

	Input	Output	Forward	Bidirec-tional	Random Access
for_each	X				
find	X				
count	X				
copy	X	X			
replace			X		
unique			X		
reverse				X	
sort					X
nth_element					X
merge	X	X			
accumulate	X				

Again, although each algorithm requires an iterator with a certain level of capability, a more powerful iterator will also work. The `replace()` algorithm requires a forward iterator, but it will work with a bidrectional or a random access iterator as well.

Now, imagine that algorithms have connectors with pins sticking out, like the cable connectors on your computer. This is shown in Figure 15.4. Those requiring random access iterators have 5 pins, those requiring bidirectional iterators have 4 pins, those requiring forward iterators have 3 pins, and so on.

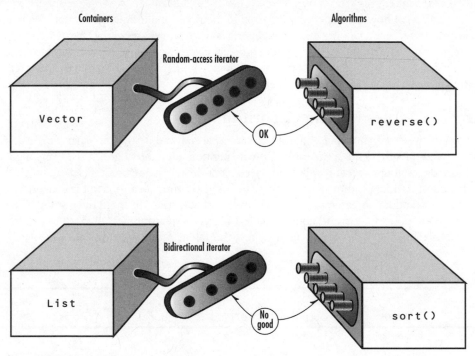

Figure 15.4   Iterators connecting containers and algorithms.

The algorithm end of an iterator (a cable) has a connector with a certain number of holes. You can plug a 5-hole iterator into a 5-pin algorithm, and you can also plug it into an algorithm with 4 or fewer pins. However, you can't plug a 4-hole (bidirectional) iterator into a 5-pin (random-access) algorithm. So vectors and deques, with random access iterators, can be plugged into any algorithm, while lists and associative containers, with only a 4-hole bidirectional iterator, can only be plugged into less powerful algorithms.

The Tables Tell the Story

From Table 15.8 and 15.9 you can figure out whether an algorithm will work with a given container. Table 15.9 shows that the **sort()** algorithm, for example, requires a random-access iterator. Table 15.8 indicates that the only containers that can handle random-access iterators are vectors and deques. There's no use trying to apply the **sort()** algorithm to lists, sets, maps, and so on.

Any algorithm that does *not* require a random-access iterator will work with any kind of STL container, because all these containers use bidirectional iterators, which is only one grade below random access. (If there were a singly-linked list in the STL it would use only a forward iterator, so it could not be used with the `reverse()` algorithm.

As you can see, comparatively few algorithms require random-access iterators. Therefore most algorithms work with most containers.

Overlapping Member Functions and Algorithms

Sometimes you must choose between using a member function or an algorithm with the same name. The `find()` algorithm, for example, requires only an input iterator, so it can be used with any container. However, sets and maps have their own `find()` member function (unlike sequential containers). Which version of `find()` should you use? Generally, if a member-function version exists, it's because, for that container, the algorithm version is not as efficient as it could be; so in these cases you should probably use the member-function version.

Iterators at Work

Using iterators is considerably simpler than talking about them. We've already seen several examples of one of the more common uses, where iterator values are returned by a container's `begin()` and `end()` member functions. We've disguised the fact that these functions return iterator values by treating them as if they were pointers. Now let's see how actual iterators are used with these and other functions.

Data Access

In containers that provides random access iterators (vector and queue) it's easy to iterate through the container using the `[]` operator. Containers such as lists, which don't support random access, require a different approach. In previous examples we've used a "destructive readout" to display the contents of a list by popping off the items one by one, as in the LIST and LISTPLUS examples. A more practical approach is to define an iterator for the container. The LISTOUT program shows how that might look:

```
// listout.cpp
// iterator and for loop for output
#include <iostream>
#include <list>
#include <algorithm>
using namespace std;

int main()
   {
   int arr[] = { 2, 4, 6, 8 };
   list<int> theList;

   for(int k=0; k<4; k++)       //fill list with array elements
      theList.push_back( arr[k] );

   list<int>::iterator iter;   //iterator to list-of-ints
```

```
for(iter = theList.begin(); iter != theList.end(); iter++)
   cout << *iter << ' ';      //display the list
cout << endl;
return 0;
}
```

The program simply displays the contents of the `theList` container. The output is

`2 4 6 8`

We define an iterator of type `list<int>` to match the container type. As with a pointer variable, we must give an iterator a value before using it. In the `for` loop we initialize it to `iList.begin()`, the start of the container. We can increment it with the `++` operator so that it steps through the elements in a container, and we can dereference it with the `*` operator to obtain the value of each element it points to. We can also compare it for equality using the `!=` operator, so we can exit the loop when it reaches the end of the container at `iList.end()`.

An equivalent approach, using a `while` loop instead of a `for` loop, might be

```
iter = iList.begin();
while( iter != iList.end() )
   cout << *iter++ << ' ';
```

The `*iter++` syntax is the same as it would be for a pointer.

Data Insertion

We can use similar code to place data into existing elements in a container, as shown in LISTFILL:

```
// listfill.cpp
// uses iterator to fill list with data
#include <iostream>
#include <list>
using namespace std;

int main()
   {
   list<int> iList(5);      //empty list holds 5 ints
   list<int>::iterator it;  //iterator
   int data = 0;
                            //fill list with data
   for(it = iList.begin(); it != iList.end(); it++)
      *it = data += 2;
                            //display list
   for(it = iList.begin(); it != iList.end(); it++)
      cout << *it << ' ';
   cout << endl;
   return 0;
   }
```

The first loop fills the container with the `int` values 2, 4, 6, 8, 10, showing that the overloaded `*` operator works on the left side of the equal sign as well as the right. The second loop displays these values.

Algorithms and Iterators

Algorithms, as we've discussed, use iterators as arguments (and sometimes as return values). The ITERFIND example shows the `find()` algorithm applied to a list. (We know we can use the `find()` algorithm with lists, because it requires only an input iterator.)

```
// iterfind.cpp
// find() returns a list iterator
#include <iostream>
#include <algorithm>
#include <list>
using namespace std;

int main()
   {
   list<int> theList(5);        //empty list holds 10 ints
   list<int>::iterator iter;    //iterator
   int data = 0;
                                //fill list with data
   for(iter = theList.begin(); iter != theList.end(); iter++)
      *iter = data += 2;        //2, 4, 6, 8, 10
                                //look for number 8
   iter = find(theList.begin(), theList.end(), 8);
   if( iter != theList.end() )
      cout << "\nFound 8.\n";
   else
      cout << "\nDid not find 8.\n";
   return 0;
   }
```

As an algorithm, `find()` takes three arguments. The first two are iterator values specifying the range to be searched, and the third is the value to be found. Here we fill the container with the same 2, 4, 6, 8, 10 values as in the last example. Then we use the `find()` algorithm to look for the number 8. If `find()` returns `iList.end()`, we know it's reached the end of the container without finding a match. Otherwise, it must have located an item with the value 8. Here the output is

```
Found 8.
```

Can we use the value of the iterator to tell where in the container the 8 is located? You might think the offset of the matching item from the beginning of the container could be calculated from `(iter - iList.begin())`. However, this is not a legal operation on the iterators used for lists. A list iterator is only a bidirectional iterator, so you can't perform arithmetic with it. You can do arithmetic with random access iterators, such as those used with vectors and queues. Thus if you were searching a vector `v` rather than a list `iList`, you could rewrite the last part of ITERFIND like this:

```
iter = find(v.begin(), v.end(), 8);
if( iter != v.end() )
   cout << "\nFound 8 at location " << (iter-v.begin() );
else
   cout << "\nDid not find 8.";
```

The output would be

```
Found 8 at location 3
```

Here's another example in which an algorithm uses iterators as arguments. This one uses the **copy()** algorithm with a vector. The user specifies a range of locations to be copied from one vector to another, and the program copies them. Iterators specify this range.

```
// itercopy.cpp
// uses iterators for copy() algorithm
#include <iostream>
#include <vector>
#include <algorithm>
using namespace std;

int main()
   {
   int beginRange, endRange;
   int arr[] = { 11, 13, 15, 17, 19, 21, 23, 25, 27, 29 };
   vector<int> v1(arr, arr+10);   //initialized vector
   vector<int> v2(10);            //uninitialized vector

   cout << "Enter range to be copied (example: 2 5): ";
   cin >> beginRange >> endRange;

   vector<int>::iterator iter1 = v1.begin() + beginRange;
   vector<int>::iterator iter2 = v1.begin() + endRange;
   vector<int>::iterator iter3;
                              //copy range from v1 to v2
   iter3 = copy( iter1, iter2, v2.begin() );
                              //(it3 -> last item copied)
   iter1 = v2.begin();        //iterate through range
   while(iter1 != iter3)      //in v2, displaying values
      cout << *iter1++ << ' ';
   cout << endl;
   return 0;
   }
```

Some interaction with this program is

```
Enter range to be copied (example: 2 5): 3 6
17 19 21
```

We don't display the entire contents of **v2**, only the range of items copied. Fortunately, **copy()** returns an iterator that points to the last item (actually one past the last item) that was copied to the destination container, **v2** in this case. The program uses this value in the **while** loop to display only the items copied.

Specialized Iterators

In this section we'll examine two specialized forms of iterators: iterator adapters, which can change the behavior of iterators in interesting ways, and stream iterators, which allow input and output streams to behave like iterators.

Iterator Adapters

The STL provides three variations on the normal iterator. These are the *reverse iterator*, the *insert iterator*, and the *raw storage iterator*. The reverse iterator allows want you to iterate backward through a container. The insert iterator want changes the behavior of various algorithms, such as `copy()` and `merge()`, so they insert data into a container rather than overwriting existing data. The raw storage iterator allowswant output iterators to store data in uninitialized memory, but it's used in specialized situations and we'll ignore it here.

Reverse Iterators

Suppose you want to iterate backward through a container, from the end to the beginning. You might think you could say something like

```
list<int>::iterator iter;        //normal iterator
iter = iList.end();              //start at end
while( iter != iList.begin() )   //go to beginning
   cout << *iter-- << ' ';       //decrement iterator
```

but unfortunately this doesn't work. For one thing, the range will be wrong (from n to 1, instead of from n-1 to 0).

To iterate backward you can use a *reverse iterator*. The ITEREV program shows an example where a reverse iterator is used to display the contents of a list in reverse order.

```
// iterev.cpp
// demonstrates reverse iterator
#include <iostream>
#include <list>
using namespace std;

int main()
   {
   int arr[] = { 2, 4, 6, 8, 10 };       //array of ints
   list<int> theList;

   for(int j=0; j<5; j++)                //transfer array
      theList.push_back( arr[j] );       //to list

   list<int>::reverse_iterator revit;    //reverse iterator

   revit = theList.rbegin();             //iterate backward
   while( revit != theList.rend() )      //through list,
      cout << *revit++ << ' ';           //displaying output
   cout << endl;
   return 0;
   }
```

The output of this program is

```
10 8 6 4 2
```

You must use the member functions `rbegin()` and `rend()` when you use a reverse iterator. (Don't try to use them with a normal forward iterator.) Confusingly, you're starting at the end of the container, but the member function is called `rbegin()`. Also, you must increment the iterator. Don't try to decrement a reverse iterator; `revit--` doesn't do what you want. With a `reverse_iterator`, always go from `rbegin()` to `rend()` using the increment operator.

Insert Iterators

Some algorithms, such as `copy()`, overwrite the existing contents (if any) of the destination container. The COPYDEQ program, which copies from one deque to another, provides an example:

```
// copydeq.cpp
//demonstrates normal copy with queues
#include <iostream>
#include <deque>
#include <algorithm>
using namespace std;

int main()
   {
   int arr1[] = { 1, 3, 5, 7, 9 };
   int arr2[] = { 2, 4, 6, 8, 10 };
   deque<int> d1;
   deque<int> d2;

   for(int j=0; j<5; j++)            //transfer arrays to deques
      {
      d1.push_back( arr1[j] );
      d2.push_back( arr2[j] );
      }                             //copy d1 to d2
   copy( d1.begin(), d1.end(), d2.begin() );

   for(int k=0; k<d2.size(); k++)  //display d2
      cout << d2[k] << ' ';
   cout << endl;
   return 0;
   }
```

The output of this program is

```
1 3 5 7 9
```

The contents of **d2** have been written over the contents of **d1**, so when we display **d2** there's no trace of its former (even-numbered) contents. Usually this behavior is what you want. Sometimes, however, you'd rather that `copy()` inserted new elements into a container along with the old ones, instead of overwriting the old ones. You can cause this behavior by using an *insert iterator*. There are three flavors of this iterator:

- `back_inserter` inserts new items at the end
- `front_inserter` inserts new items at the beginning
- `inserter` inserts new items at a specified location

The DINSITER program shows how to use a back inserter.

```
//dinsiter.cpp
//demonstrates insert iterators with queues
#include <iostream>
#include <deque>
#include <algorithm>
using namespace std;

int main()
    {
    int arr1[] = { 1, 3, 5, 7, 9 };   //initialize d1
    int arr2[] = {2, 4, 6};           //initialize d2
    deque<int> d1;
    deque<int> d2;

    for(int i=0; i<5; i++)            //transfer arrays to deques
        d1.push_back( arr1[i] );
    for(int j=0; j<3; j++)
        d2.push_back( arr2[j] );
                                      //copy d1 to back of d2
    copy( d1.begin(), d1.end(), back_inserter(d2) );

    cout << "\nd2: ";                 //display d2
    for(int k=0; k<d2.size(); k++)
        cout << d2[k] << ' ';
    cout << endl;
    return 0;
    }
```

The back inserter uses the container's **push_back()** member function to insert the new items at the end of the target container **d2**, following the existing items. The source container **d1** is unchanged. The output of the program, which displays the new contents of **d2**, is

2 4 6 1 3 5 7 9

If we specified a front inserter instead,

```
copy( d1.begin(), d1.end(), front_inserter(d2) );
```

then the new items would be inserted into the front of the container. The underlying mechanism of the front inserter is the container's **push_front()** member function, which pushes the items into the front of the container, effectively reversing their order. The output would be

9 7 5 3 1 2 4 6

You can also insert the new items starting at any arbitrary element by using the *inserter* version of the insert iterator. For example, to insert the new items at the beginning of **d2**, we would say

```
copy( d1.begin(), d1.end(), inserter(d2, d2.begin()) );
```

The first argument to `inserter` is the container to be copied into, and the second is an iterator pointing to the location where copying should begin. Because `inserter` uses the container's `insert()` member function, the order of the elements is not reversed. The output resulting from this statement would be

```
1 3 5 7 9 2 4 6
```

By changing the second argument to `inserter` we could cause the new data to be inserted anywhere in `d2`.

Note that a `front_inserter` can't be used with a vector, because vectors don't have a `push_front()` member function; they can only be accessed at the end.

Stream Iterators

Stream iterators allow you to treat files and I/O devices (such as `cin` and `cout`) as if they were iterators. This makes it easy to use files and I/O devices as arguments to algorithms. (This is another demonstration of the versatility of using iterators to link algorithms and containers.)

The major purpose of the input and output iterator categories is to support these stream iterator classes. Input and output iterators make it possible for appropriate algorithms to be used directly on input and output streams.

Stream iterators are actually objects of classes that are templetized for different types of input or output. There are two stream iterators: `ostream_iterator` and `istream_iterator`. Let's look at them in turn.

The `ostream_iterator` Class

An `ostream_iterator` object can be used as an argument to any algorithm that specifies an output iterator. In the OUTITER example we'll use it as an argument to `copy()`:

```cpp
//outiter.cpp
//demonstrates ostream_iterator
#include <iostream>
#include <algorithm>
#include <list>
using namespace std;

int main()
   {
   int arr[] = { 10, 20, 30, 40, 50 };
   list<int> theList;

   for(int j=0; j<5; j++)                  //transfer array to list
      theList.push_back( arr[j] );

   ostream_iterator<int> ositer(cout, ", ");  //ostream iterator

   cout << "\nContents of list: ";
```

```
    copy(theList.begin(), theList.end(), ositer);  //display list
    cout << endl;
    return 0;
    }
```

We define an ostream iterator for reading type **int** values. The two arguments to this constructor are the stream to which the **int** values will be written, and a string value that will be displayed following each value. The stream value is typically a filename or **cout**; here it's **cout**. When writing to **cout** the delimiting string can consist of any characters you want; here we use a comma and a space.

The **copy()** algorithm copies the contents of the list to **cout**. The ostream iterator is used as the third argument to **copy()**; it's the destination.

The output of OUTITER is

```
Contents of list: 10, 20, 30, 40, 50,
```

Our next example, FOUTITER, shows how to use an ostream iterator to write to a file:

```
//foutiter.cpp
//demonstrates ostream_iterator with files
#include <fstream>
#include <algorithm>
#include <list>
using namespace std;

int main()
    {
    int arr[] = { 11, 21, 31, 41, 51 };
    list<int> theList;

    for(int j=0; j<5; j++)              //transfer array
        theList.push_back( arr[j] );    //   to list
    ofstream outfile("ITER.DAT");       //create file object

    ostream_iterator<int> ositer(outfile, " ");  //iterator
                                        //write list to file
    copy(theList.begin(), theList.end(), ositer);
    return 0;
    }
```

You must define an **ofstream** file object and associate it with a file, here called ITER.DAT. This object is the first argument to the **ostream_itertor**. When writing to a file, use a white-space character in the string argument, not characters like "--". This makes it easier to read the data back from the file. Here we use a space (" ") character.

There's no displayable output from FOUTITER, but you can use a text editor (like the Notepad utility in Windows) to examine the file ITER.DAT, which was created by the ITER program. It should contain the data

```
11 21 31 41 51
```

The `istream_iterator` Class

An `istream_iterator` object can be used as an argument to any algorithm that specifies an input iterator. Our example, INITER, shows such objects used as the first two arguments to `copy()`. This program reads floating-point numbers entered into `cin` (the keyboard) by the user, and stores them in a list.

```cpp
// initer.cpp
// demonstrates istream_iterator
#include <iostream>
#include <list>
#include <algorithm>
using namespace std;

int main()
   {
   list<float> fList(5);              //uninitialized list

   cout << "\nEnter 5 floating-point numbers: ";
                                      //istream iterators
   istream_iterator<float> cin_iter(cin);   //cin
   istream_iterator<float> end_of_stream;   //eos
                                      //copy from cin to fList
   copy( cin_iter, end_of_stream, fList.begin() );

   cout << endl;                      //display fList
   ostream_iterator<float> ositer(cout, "--");
   copy(fList.begin(), fList.end(), ositer);
   cout << endl;
   return 0;
   }
```

Some interaction with INITER is

```
Enter 5 floating-point numbers: 1.1  2.2  3.3  4.4  5.5
1.1--2.2--3.3--4.4--5.5--
```

Notice that for `copy()`, because the data coming from `cin` is the source and not the destination, we must specify both the beginning and the end of the range of data to be copied. The beginning is an `istream_iterator` connected to `cin`, which we define as `cin_iter` using the one-argument constructor. But what about the end of the range? The no-argument (default) constructor to `istream_iterator` plays a special role here. It always creates an `istream_iterator` object that represents the end of the stream.

How does the user generate this end-of-stream value when inputting data? By typing the Ctrl-z key combination, which transmits the end-of-file character normally used for streams. Sometimes several presses of Ctrl-z are necessary. Pressing Enter won't end the file, although it will delimit the numbers.

We use an `ostream_iterator` to display the contents of the list, although of course there are many other ways to do this.

You must perform any display output, such as the "Enter 5 floating-point numbers" prompt, not only before using the istream iterator, but even before defining it. As soon as this iterator is defined, it locks up the display, waiting for input.

Our next example, FINITER, uses a file instead of `cin` as input to the `copy()` algorithm.

```cpp
// finiter.cpp
// demonstrates istream_iterator with files
#include <iostream>
#include <list>
#include <fstream>
#include <algorithm>
using namespace std;

int main()
    {
    list<int> iList;                //empty list
    ifstream infile("ITER.DAT");  //create input file object
                                  //(ITER.DAT must already exist)
                                  //istream iterators
    istream_iterator<int> file_iter(infile);  //file
    istream_iterator<int> end_of_stream;       //eos
                                  //copy from infile to iList
    copy( file_iter, end_of_stream, back_inserter(iList) );

    cout << endl;                 //display iList
    ostream_iterator<int> ositer(cout, "--");
    copy(iList.begin(), iList.end(), ositer);
    cout << endl;
    return 0;
    }
```

The output from FINITER is

```
11--21--31--31--41--51--
```

We define an `ifstream` object to represent the ITER.DAT file, which must already exist and contain data. (The FOUTITER program, if you ran it, will have generated this file.)

Instead of using `cout`, as in the `istream` iterator in the INITER example, we use the `ifstream` object named `infile`. The end-of-stream object is the same.

We've made another change in this program: it uses a `back_inserter` to insert data into `iList`. This makes it possible to define `iList` as an empty container instead of one with a specified size. This often makes sense when reading input, since you may not know how many items will be entered.

Associative Containers

We've seen that the sequence containers (vector, list and deque) store data items in a fixed linear sequence. Finding an item (unless its index number is known or it's located at an end of the container) will involve the slow process of stepping through the items in the container one by one.

In an associative container the items are not arranged in sequence. Instead they are arranged in a more complex way that makes it much faster to find a given item. This arrangement is typically a tree structure, although different approaches (such as hash tables) are possible. The speed of searching is the main advantage of associative containers.

Searching is done using a *key*, which is usually a single value like a number or string. This value is an attribute of the objects in the container, or it may be the entire object.

The two main categories of associative containers in the STL are sets and maps.

A set stores objects containing keys. A map stores pairs, where the first part of the pair is an object containing a key and the second part is an object containing a value.

In both a set and a map, only one example of each key can be stored. It's like a dictionary that forbids more than one entry for each word. However, the STL has alternative versions of set and map that relax this restriction. A *multiset* and a *multimap* are similar to a set and a map, but can include multiple instances of the same key.

Associative containers share many member functions with other containers. However, some algorithms, such as `lower_bound()` and `equal_range()`, exist only for associative containers. Also, some member functions that do exist for other containers, such as the push and pop family (`push_back()` and so on) have no versions for associative containers. It wouldn't make sense to use push and pop with associative containers, because elements must always be inserted in their ordered locations, not at the beginning or end of the container.

Sets and Multisets

Sets are often used to hold objects of user-defined classes such as employees in a database. (You'll see examples of this later in this chapter.) However, sets can also hold simpler elements such as strings. Figure 15.5 shows how this looks. The objects are arranged in order, and the entire object is the key.

Our first example, SET, shows a set that stores objects of class **string**.

```
// set.cpp
// set stores string objects
#include <iostream>
#include <set>
#pragma warning (disable:4786)  //for set (microsoft compilers only)
#include <string>
using namespace std;

int main()
   {                              //array of string objects
   string names[] = {"Juanita", "Robert",
                     "Mary", "Amanda", "Marie"};
                              //initialize set to array
   set<string, less<string> > nameSet(names, names+5);
                              //iterator to set
   set<string, less<string> >::iterator iter;

   nameSet.insert("Yvette");  //insert more names
   nameSet.insert("Larry");
   nameSet.insert("Robert");  //no effect; already in set
```

```
nameSet.insert("Barry");
nameSet.erase("Mary");        //erase a name
                              //display size of set
cout << "\nSize=" << nameSet.size() << endl;
iter = nameSet.begin();       //display members of set
while( iter != nameSet.end() )
   cout << *iter++ << '\n';

string searchName;            //get name from user
cout << "\nEnter name to search for: ";
cin >> searchName;
                              //find matching name in set
iter = nameSet.find(searchName);
if( iter == nameSet.end() )
   cout << "The name " << searchName << " is NOT in the set.";
else
   cout << "The name " << *iter << " IS in the set.";
cout << endl;
return 0;
}
```

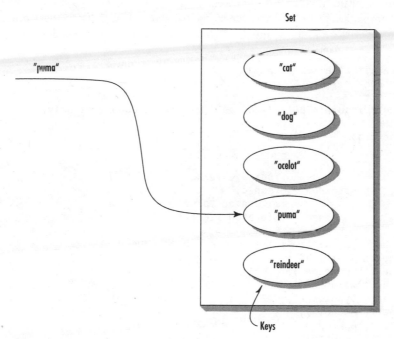

Figure 15.5 A set of string objects.

To define a set we specify the type of objects to be stored (in this case class **string**) and also the function object that will be used to order the members of the set. Here we use **less<>()** applied to string objects.

As you can see, a set has an interface similar to other STL containers. We can initialize a set to an array, and insert new members into a set with the `insert()` member function. To display the set we can iterate through it.

To find a particular entry in the set we use the `find()` member function. (Sequential containers use `find()` in its algorithm version.) Here's some sample interaction with SET, where the user enters "George" as the name to be searched for:

```
Size = 7
Amanda
Barry
Juanita
Larry
Marie
Robert
Yvette

Enter name to search for: George
The name George is NOT in the set.
```

Of course the speed advantage of searching an associative container isn't apparent until you have many more entries than in this example.

Let's look at an important pair of member functions available only with associative containers. Our example, SETRANGE, shows the use of `lower_bound()` and `upper_bound()`:

```cpp
// setrange.cpp
// tests ranges within a set
#include <iostream>
#include <set>
#pragma warning (disable:4786)  //for set (microsoft compilers only)
#include <string>
using namespace std;

int main()
   {                                //set of string objects
   set<string, less<string> > organic;
                                    //iterator to set
   set<string, less<string> >::iterator iter;

   organic.insert("Curine");  //insert organic compounds
   organic.insert("Xanthine");
   organic.insert("Curarine");
   organic.insert("Melamine");
   organic.insert("Cyanimide");
   organic.insert("Phenol");
   organic.insert("Aphrodine");
   organic.insert("Imidazole");
   organic.insert("Cinchonine");
   organic.insert("Palmitamide");
   organic.insert("Cyanimide");

   iter = organic.begin();     //display set
   while( iter != organic.end() )
      cout << *iter++ << '\n';
```

```
string lower, upper;        //display entries in range
cout << "\nEnter range (example C Czz): ";
cin >> lower >> upper;
iter = organic.lower_bound(lower);
while( iter != organic.upper_bound(upper) )
    cout << *iter++ << '\n';
return 0;
}
```

The program first displays an entire set of organic compounds. The user is then prompted to type in a pair of key values, and the program displays those keys that lie within this range. Here's some sample interaction:

```
Aphrodine
Cinchonine
Curarine
Curine
Cyanimide
Imidazole
Melamine
Palmitamide
Phenol
Xanthine

Enter range (example C Czz): Aaa Ourb
Aphrodine
Cinchonine
Curarine
```

The `lower_bound()` member function takes an argument that is a value of the same type as the key. It returns an iterator to the first entry that is not less than this argument (where the meaning of "less" is determined by the function object used in the set's definition). The `upper_bound()` function returns an iterator to the first entry that is greater than its argument. Together, these functions allow you to access a specified range of values.

Maps and Multimaps

A *map* stores pairs. A pair consists of a *key object* and a *value object*. The key object contains a key that will be searched for. The value object contains additional data. As in a set, the key objects can be strings, numbers, or objects of more complex classes. The values are often strings or numbers, but they can also be objects or even containers.

For example, the key could be a word, and the value could be a number representing how many times that word appears in a document. Such a map constitutes a *frequency table*. Or the key could be a word and the value could be a list of page numbers. This arrangement could represent an index, like the one at the back of this book. Figure 15.6 shows a situation in which the keys are words and the values are definitions, as in an ordinary dictionary.

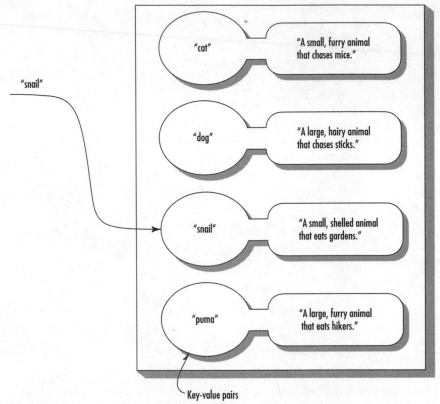

Figure 15.6   A map of word-phrase pairs.

One common way to use maps is as associative arrays. In an ordinary C++ array the array index, which is used to access a particular element, is an integer. Thus in the expression anArray[3], the 3 is the array index. An associative array works in a similar way except that you can choose the data type of the array index. If you've defined the index to be a string, for example, you can say anArray["jane"].

An Associative Array

Let's look at a simple example of a map used as an associative array. The keys will be the names of states, and the values will be the populations of the states. Here's the listing for ASSO_ARR:

```
// asso_arr.cpp
// demonstrates map used as associative array
#include <iostream>
#include <string>
#include <map>
#pragma warning (disable:4786)  //for map (Microsoft only)
using namespace std;
```

```
int main()
   {
   string name;
   int pop;

   string states[] = { "Wyoming", "Colorado", "Nevada",
                        "Montana", "Arizona", "Idaho"};
   int pops[] = { 470, 2890, 800, 787, 2718, 944 };

   map<string, int, less<string> > mapStates;        //map
   map<string, int, less<string> >::iterator iter;  //iterator

   for(int j=0; j<6; j++)
      {
      name = states[j];                    //get data from arrays
      pop = pops[j];
      mapStates[name] = pop;               //put it in map
      }
   cout << "Enter state: ";                //get state from user
   cin >> name;
   pop = mapStates[name];                  //find population
   cout << "Population: " << pop << ",000\n";

   cout << endl;                           //display entire map
   for(iter = mapStates.begin(); iter != mapStates.end(); iter++)
      cout << (*iter).first << ' ' << (*iter).second << ",000\n";
   return 0;
   }
```

When the program runs, the user is prompted to type the name of a state. The program then looks in the map, using the state name as an index, and returns the population of the state. Finally it displays all the name-population pairs in the map. Here's some sample output:

```
Enter state: Wyoming
Population: 470,000

Arizona 2718,000
Colorado 2890,000
Idaho 944,000
Montana 787,000
Nevada 800,000
Wyoming 470,000
```

Search speed is where sets and maps excel. Here the program quickly finds the appropriate population when the user enters a state's name. (This would be more meaningful if there were millions of data items.) Iterating through the container, as is shown by the list of states and populations, isn't as fast as in a sequential container, but it's still fairly efficient. Notice that the states are ordered alphabetically, although the original data was not.

The definition of a map takes three template arguments:

```
map<string, int, less<string> > maStates;
```

The first is the type of the key. In this case it's `string`, representing the state name. The second is the type of the value; in this case it's `int`, which represents the population, in 1,000s. The third argument specifies the ordering that will be used for the keys. We choose to have it ordered alphabetically by the names of the states; that's what `less<string>` does. We also define an iterator to this map.

Our input data is in two separate arrays. (In a real program it would probably come from a file.) To put this data into the map we read it into the variables `name` and `pop`, and execute the statement

```
mapStates[name] = pop;
```

This is a particularly elegant construction, looking just like an insertion into an ordinary array. However, the array index `name` is a string, not an integer.

When the user types in a state name, the program finds the appropriate population with the statement

```
pop = mapStates[name];
```

Besides using the array-index syntax, we can also access the two parts of an entry in the map, the key, and the value, using an iterator. The key is obtained from `(*iter).first`, and the value from `(*iter).second`. Otherwise the iterator works as it does in other containers.

Storing User-Defined Objects

Until now our example programs have stored objects of basic types. However, the big payoff with the STL is that you can use it to store and manipulate objects of classes that you write yourself (or that someone else has written). In this section we'll show how this is done.

A Set of `person` Objects

We'll start with a `person` class that includes a person's last name, first name, and telephone number. We'll create some members of this class and insert them in a set, thus creating a phone book database. The user interacts with the program by entering a person's name. The program then searches the list and displays the data for that person, if it finds a match. We'll use a multiset so two or more `person` objects can have the same name. Here's the listing for SETPERS:

```
// setpers.cpp
// uses a multiset to hold person objects
#include <iostream>
#include <set>
#pragma warning (disable:4786)   //for set (Microsoft only)
#include <string>
using namespace std;

class person
   {
   private:
      string lastName;
```

```
        string firstName;
        long phoneNumber;
    public:                         //default constructor
        person() : lastName("blank"),
                   firstName("blank"), phoneNumber(0)
           {  }
                                //3-arg constructor
        person(string lana, string fina, long pho) :
               lastName(lana), firstName(fina), phoneNumber(pho)
           {  }
        friend bool operator<(const person&, const person&);
        friend bool operator==(const person&, const person&);

        void display() const    //display person's data
           {
           cout << endl << lastName << ",\t" << firstName
                << "\t\tPhone: " << phoneNumber;
           }
    };
                                //operator < for person class
bool operator<(const person& p1, const person& p2)
    {
    if(p1.lastName == p2.lastName)
        return (p1.firstName < p2.firstName) ? true : false;
    return (p1.lastName < p2.lastName) ? true : false;
    }
                                //operator == for person class
bool operator==(const person& p1, const person& p2)
    {
    return (p1.lastName == p2.lastName &&
            p1.firstName == p2.firstName ) ? true : false;
    }
////////////////////////////////////////////////////////////////
int main()
    {                               //create person objects
    person pers1("Deauville", "William", 8435150);
    person pers2("McDonald", "Stacey", 3327563);
    person pers3("Bartoski", "Peter", 6946473);
    person pers4("KuangThu", "Bruce", 4157300);
    person pers5("Wellington", "John", 9207404);
    person pers6("McDonald", "Amanda", 8435150);
    person pers7("Fredericks", "Roger", 7049982);
    person pers8("McDonald", "Stacey", 7764987);
                                //multiset of persons
    multiset< person, less<person> > persSet;
                                //iterator to a multiset of persons
    multiset<person, less<person> >::iterator iter;

    persSet.insert(pers1);      //put persons in multiset
    persSet.insert(pers2);
    persSet.insert(pers3);
    persSet.insert(pers4);
    persSet.insert(pers5);
    persSet.insert(pers6);
```

```
            persSet.insert(pers7);
            persSet.insert(pers8);

            cout << "\nNumber of entries = " << persSet.size();

            iter = persSet.begin();    //display contents of multiset
            while( iter != persSet.end() )
               (*iter++).display();
                                      //get last and first name
            string searchLastName, searchFirstName;
            cout << "\n\nEnter last name of person to search for: ";
            cin >> searchLastName;
            cout << "Enter first name: ";
            cin >> searchFirstName;
                                      //create person with this name
            person searchPerson(searchLastName, searchFirstName, 0);

                                      //get count of such persons
            int cntPersons = persSet.count(searchPerson);
            cout << "Number of persons with this name = " << cntPersons;

                                      //display all matches
            iter = persSet.lower_bound(searchPerson);
            while( iter != persSet.upper_bound(searchPerson) )
               (*iter++).display();
            cout << endl;
            return 0;
            }  //end main()
```

Necessary Member Functions

To work with STL containers, the **person** class needs a few common member functions. These are a default (no-argument) constructor (which is actually not necessary in this example but is usually essential), the overloaded < operator, and the overloaded -- operator. These member functions are used by the list class and by various algorithms. You may need other member functions in other specific situations. (As in most classes, you should probably also provide overloaded assignment and copy constructors and a destructor, but we'll ignore these here to avoid complicating the listing.)

The overloaded < and == operators should use **const** arguments. Generally it's best to make them friends, but you can use member functions as well.

Ordering

The overloaded < operator specifies the way the elements in the set will be ordered. In SETPERS we define this operator to order the last name of the person, and, if the last names are the same, to order the first names.

Here's some interaction with SETPERS. The program first displays the entire list. (Of course this would not be practical on a real database with a large number of elements.) Because they are stored in a multiset, the elements are ordered automatically. Then, at the prompt, the user enters the name "McDonald" followed by "Stacey" (last name first). There are two persons on the list with this particular name, so they are both displayed.

```
Number of entries = 8
Bartoski,       Peter         phone: 6946473
Deauville,      William       phone: 8435150
Fredericks,     Roger         phone: 7049982
KuangThu,       Bruce         phone: 4157300
McDonald,       Amanda        phone: 8435150
McDonald,       Stacey        phone: 3327563
McDonald,       Stacey        phone: 7764987
Wellington,     John          phone: 9207404

Enter last name of person to search for: McDonald
Enter first name: Stacey
Number of persons with this name = 2
McDonald,       Stacey        phone: 3327563
McDonald,       Stacey        phone: 7764987
```

Just Like Basic Types

As you can see, once a class has been defined, objects of that class are handled by the container in the same way as variables of basic types.

We first use the `size()` member function to display the total number of entries. Then we iterate through the list, displaying all the entries.

Because we're using a multiset, the `lower_bound()` and `upper_bound()` member functions are available to display all elements that fall within a range. In the example output the lower and upper bound are the same, so all persons with the same name are displayed. Notice that we must create a "fictitious" person with the same name as the person (or persons) we want to find. The `lower_bound()` and `upper_bound()` functions then match this person against those on the list.

A List of `person` Objects

It's very fast to search a set or multiset for a person with a given name, as in the SETPERS example. If, however, we're more concerned with being able to quickly insert or delete a **person** object, we might decide to use a list instead. The LISTPERS example shows how this looks.

```cpp
// listpers.cpp
// uses a list to hold person objects
#include <iostream>
#include <list>
#include <algorithm>
#include <string>
using namespace std;

class person
    {
    private:
        string lastName;
        string firstName;
        long phoneNumber;
```

```cpp
   public:
      person() :                    //no-arg constructor
         lastName("blank"), firstName("blank"), phoneNumber(0L)
         {  }
                                    //3-arg constructor
      person(string lana, string fina, long pho) :
            lastName(lana), firstName(fina), phoneNumber(pho)
         {  }
      friend bool operator<(const person&, const person&);
      friend bool operator==(const person&, const person&);
      friend bool operator!=(const person&, const person&);
      friend bool operator>(const person&, const person&);

      void display() const   //display all data
         {
         cout << endl << lastName << ",\t" << firstName
              << "\t\tPhone: " << phoneNumber;
         }

      long get_phone() const //return phone number
         { return phoneNumber; }
   };
                                    //overloaded < for person class

                                    //overloaded == for person class
bool operator==(const person& p1, const person& p2)
   {
   return (p1.lastName == p2.lastName &&
           p1.firstName == p2.firstName ) ? true : false;
   }
bool operator<(const person& p1, const person& p2)
   {
   if(p1.lastName == p2.lastName)
      return (p1.firstName < p2.firstName) ? true : false;
   return (p1.lastName < p2.lastName) ? true : false;
   }
bool operator!=(const person& p1, const person& p2)
   { return !(p1==p2); }
bool operator>(const person& p1, const person& p2)
   { return !(p1<p2) && !(p1==p2); }
//////////////////////////////////////////////////////////////
int main()
   {
   list<person> persList;       //list of persons
                                //iterator to a list of persons
   list<person>::iterator iter1;
                                //put persons in list
   persList.push_back( person("Deauville", "William", 8435150) );
   persList.push_back( person("McDonald", "Stacey", 3327563) );
   persList.push_back( person("Bartoski", "Peter", 6946473) );
   persList.push_back( person("KuangThu", "Bruce", 4157300) );
   persList.push_back( person("Wellington", "John", 9207404) );
   persList.push_back( person("McDonald", "Amanda", 8435150) );
   persList.push_back( person("Fredericks", "Roger", 7049982) );
```

```
       persList.push_back( person("McDonald", "Stacey", 7764987) );

       cout << "\nNumber of entries = " << persList.size();

     iter1 = persList.begin();  //display contents of list
     while( iter1 != persList.end() )
        (*iter1++).display();

//find person or persons with specified name (last and first)
     string searchLastName, searchFirstName;
     cout << "\n\nEnter last name of person to search for: ";
     cin >> searchLastName;
     cout << "Enter first name: ";
     cin >> searchFirstName;
                               //make a person with that name
     person searchPerson(searchLastName, searchFirstName, 0L);
                               //search for first match of names
     iter1 = find(persList.begin(), persList.end(), searchPerson);
     if( iter1 != persList.end() )  //find additional matches
        {
        cout << "Person(s) with that name is(are)";
        do
           {
           (*iter1).display();  //display match
           ++iter1;                 //search again, one past match
           iter1 = find(iter1, persList.end(), searchPerson);
           } while( iter1 != persList.end() );
        }
     else
        cout << "There is no person with that name.";

//find person or persons with specified phone number
     cout << "\n\nEnter phone number (format 1234567): ";
     long sNumber;                  //get search number
     cin >> sNumber;
                               //iterate through list
     bool found_one = false;
     for(iter1=persList.begin(); iter1 != persList.end(); ++iter1)
        {
        if( sNumber == (*iter1).get_phone() )  //compare numbers
           {
           if( !found_one )
              {
              cout << "Person(s) with that phone number is(are)";
              found_one = true;
              }
           (*iter1).display();  //display the match
           }
        } //end for
     if( !found_one )
        cout << "There is no person with that phone number";
     cout << endl;
     return 0;
     } //end main()
```

Finding All Persons with a Specified Name

We can't use the `lower_bound()`/`upper_bound()` member functions because we're dealing with a list, not a set or map. Instead we use the `find()` member function to find all the persons with a given name. If this function reports a hit, we must apply it again, starting one person past the original hit, to see if there are other persons with the same name. This complicates the programming; we must use a loop and two calls to `find()`.

Finding All Persons with a Specified Phone Number

It's harder to search for a person with a specified phone number than one with a specified name, because the class member functions like `find()` are intended to be used to find the primary search characteristic. In this example we use the brute force approach to finding the phone number, iterating through the list and making a "manual" comparison of the number we're looking for and each member of the list:

```
if( sNumber == (*iter1).getphone() )
   ...
```

The program first displays all the entries, then asks the user for a name and finds the matching person or persons. It then asks for a phone number and again finds any matching persons. Here's some interaction with LISTPERS:

```
Number of entries = 8
Deauville,      William          phone: 8435150
McDonald,       Stacey           phone: 3327563
Bartoski,       Peter            phone: 6946473
KuangThu,       Bruce            phone: 4157300
Wellington,     John             phone: 9207404
McDonald,       Amanda           phone: 8435150
Fredericks,     Roger            phone: 7049982
McDonald,       Stacey           phone: 7764987

Enter last name of person to search for: Wellington
Enter first name: John
Person(s) with that name is(are)
Wellington,     John             phone: 9207404

Enter phone number (format 1234567): 8435150
Person(s) with that number is(are)
Deauville,      William          phone: 8435150
McDonald,       Amanda           phone: 8435150
```

Here the program has found one person with the specified name and two people with the specified phone number.

When using lists to store class objects we must declare four comparison operators for that class: `==`, `!=`, `<`, and `>`. Depending on what algorithms you actually use, you may not need to define (provide function bodies for) all these operators. In this example we only need to define the `==` operator, although for completeness we define all four. If we used the `sort()` algorithm on the list, we would need to define the `<` operator as well.

Function Objects

Function objects are used extensively in the STL. One important use for them is as arguments to certain algorithms. They allow you to customize the operation of these algorithms. We mentioned function objects earlier in this chapter, and used one in the SORTEMP program. There we showed an example of the predefined function object `greater<>()` used to sort data in reverse order. In this section we'll examine other predefined function objects, and also see how to write your own so that you have even greater control over what the STL algorithms do.

Recall that a function object is a function that has been wrapped in a class so that it looks like an object. The class, however, has no data and only one member function, which is the overloaded `()` operator. The class is often templetized so it can work with different types.

Predefined Function Objects

The predefined STL function objects, located in the FUNCTIONAL header file, are shown in Table 15.10. There are function objects corresponding to all the major C++ operators. In the table, the letter T indicates any class, either user-written or a basic type. The variables x and y represent objects of class T passed to the function object as arguments.

Table 15.10   Predefined Function Objects

Function object	Return value
T = plus(T, T)	x+y
T = minus(T, T)	x-y
T = times(T, T)	x*y
T = divide(T, T)	x/y
T = modulus(T, T)	x%y
T = negate(T)	-x
bool = equal_to(T, T)	x == y
bool = not_equal_to(T, T)	x != y
bool = greater(T, T)	x > y
bool = less(T, T)	x < y
bool = greater_equal(T, T)	x >= y
bool = less_equal(T, T)	x <= y
bool = logical_and(T, T)	x && y

continued on next page

continued from previous page

Function object	Return value
bool = `logical_or`(T, T)	x ‖ y
bool = `logical_not`(T)	!x

There are function objects for arithmetic operations, comparisons, and logical operations. Let's look at an example where an arithmetic function object might come in handy. Our example uses a class called **airtime**, which represents time values consisting of hours and minutes, but no seconds. This data type is appropriate for flight arrival and departure times in airports. The example shows how the **plus<>()** function object can be used to add all the **airtime** values in a container. Here's the listing for PLUSAIR:

```cpp
//plusair.cpp
//uses accumulate() algorithm and plus() function object
#include <iostream>
#include <list>
#include <numeric>               //for accumulate()
using namespace std;
/////////////////////////////////////////////////////////////
class airtime
   {
   private:
      int hours;                 //0 to 23
      int minutes;               //0 to 59
   public:
                                 //default constructor
      airtime() : hours(0), minutes(0)
         {  }
                                 //2-arg constructor
      airtime(int h, int m) : hours(h), minutes(m)
         {  }
      void display() const  //output to screen
         { cout << hours << ':' << minutes; }

      void get()             //input from user
         {
         char dummy;
         cout << "\nEnter airtime (format 12:59): ";
         cin >> hours >> dummy >> minutes;
         }
                                 //overloaded + operator
      airtime operator + (const airtime right) const
         {                       //add members
         int temph = hours + right.hours;
         int tempm = minutes + right.minutes;
         if(tempm >= 60)    //check for carry
            { temph++; tempm -= 60; }
         return airtime(temph, tempm); //return sum
         }
                                 //overloaded == operator
      bool operator == (const airtime& at2) const
```

```
                   { return (hours == at2.hours) &&
                          (minutes == at2.minutes); }
                                  //overloaded < operator
        bool operator < (const airtime& at2) const
            { return (hours < at2.hours) ||
                     (hours == at2.hours && minutes < at2.minutes); }
                                  //overloaded != operator
        bool operator != (const airtime& at2) const
           { return !(*this==at2); }
                             //overloaded > operator
        bool operator > (const airtime& at2) const
           { return !(*this<at2) && !(*this==at2); }
    };  //end class airtime
//////////////////////////////////////////////////////////////
int main()
    {
    char answer;
    airtime temp, sum;
    list<airtime> airlist;    //list of airtimes

    do {                      //get airtimes from user
        temp.get();
        airlist.push_back(temp);
        cout << "Enter another (y/n)? ";
        cin >> answer;
        } while (answer != 'n');
                             //sum all the airtimes
    sum = accumulate( airlist.begin(), airlist.end(),
                      airtime(0, 0), plus<airtime>() );
    cout << "\nsum = ";
    sum.display();            //display sum
    cout << endl;
    return 0;
    }
```

This program features the **accumulate()** algorithm. There are two versions of this function. The three-argument version always sums (using the + operator) a range of values. In the four-argument version shown here, any of the arithmetic function objects shown in Table 15.10 can be used.

The four arguments to this version of **accumulate()** are the iterators of the first and last elements in the range, the initial value of the sum (often 0), and the operation to be applied to the elements. In this example we add them using **plus<>()**, but we could subtract them, multiply them, or perform other operations using different function objects. Here's some interaction with PLUSAIR:

```
Enter airtime (format 12:59) : 3:45
Enter another (y/n)? y

Enter airtime (format 12:59) : 5:10
Enter another (y/n)? y

Enter airtime (format 12:59) : 2:25
Enter another (y/n)? y
```

```
Enter airtime (format 12:59) : 0:55
Enter another (y/n)? n

sum = 12:15
```

The `accumulate()` algorithm is not only easier and clearer than iterating through the container yourself to add the elements, it's also (unless you put a lot of work into your code) more efficient.

The `plus<>()` function object requires that the + operator be overloaded for the `airtime` class. This operator should be a `const` function, since that's what the `plus<>()` function object expects.

The other arithmetic function objects work in a similar way. The logical function objects such as `logical_and<>()` can be used on objects of classes for which these operations make sense (for example, type `bool` variables).

Writing Your Own Function Objects

If one of the standard function objects doesn't do what you want, you can write your own. Our next example shows two situations where this might be desirable, one involving the `sort()` algorithm and one involving `for_each()`.

It's easy to sort a group of elements based on the relationship specified in the class < operator. However, what happens if you want to sort a container that contains pointers to objects, rather than the objects themselves? Storing pointers is a good way to improve efficiency, especially for large objects, because it avoids the copying process that takes place whenever an object is placed in a container. However, if you try to sort the pointers, you'll find that the objects are arranged by pointer address, rather than by some attribute of the object.

To make the `sort()` algorithm work the way we want in a container of pointers, we must supply it with a function object that defines how we want the data ordered.

Our example program starts with a vector of pointers to `person` objects. These objects are placed in the vector, then sorted in the usual way, which leads to the pointers, not the persons, being sorted. This isn't what we want, and in this case causes no change in the ordering at all, because the items were inserted in order of increasing addresses. Next the vector is sorted correctly, using the function object `comparePersons()`. This orders items using the *contents* of pointers, rather than the pointers themselves. The result is that the `person` objects are sorted alphabetically by name. Here's the listing for SORTPTRS.

```
// sortptrs.cpp
// sorts person objects stored by pointer
#include <iostream>
#include <vector>
#include <algorithm>
#include <string>
using namespace std;

class person
   {
   private:
      string lastName;
      string firstName;
```

```
        long phoneNumber;
    public:
        person() :                  //default constructor
            lastName("blank"), firstName("blank"), phoneNumber(0L)
          {  }
                                    //3-arg constructor
        person(string lana, string fina, long pho) :
                lastName(lana), firstName(fina), phoneNumber(pho)
            {  }
        friend bool operator<(const person&, const person&);
        friend bool operator==(const person&, const person&);

        void display() const   //display person's data
           {
           cout << endl << lastName << ",\t" << firstName
                << "\t\tPhone: " << phoneNumber;
           }
        long get_phone() const //return phone number
           { return phoneNumber; }
      }; //end class person
//-------------------------------------------------------------
//overloaded < for person class
bool operator<(const person& p1, const person& p2)
   {
   if(p1.lastName == p2.lastName)
      return (p1.firstName < p2.firstName) ? true : false;
   return (p1.lastName < p2.lastName) ? true : false;
   }
//-------------------------------------------------------------
//overloaded == for person class
bool operator==(const person& p1, const person& p2)
   {
   return (p1.lastName == p2.lastName &&
           p1.firstName == p2.firstName ) ? true : false;
   }
//-------------------------------------------------------------
//function object to compare persons using pointers
class comparePersons
   {
   public:
   bool operator() (const person* ptrP1,
                    const person* ptrP2) const
     { return *ptrP1 < *ptrP2; }
   };
//-------------------------------------------------------------
//function object to display a person, using a pointer
class displayPerson
   {
   public:
   void operator() (const person* ptrP) const
     { ptrP->display(); }
   };
```

```
//////////////////////////////////////////////////////////////
int main()
   {                               //a vector of ptrs to persons
   vector<person*> vectPtrsPers;
                                //make persons
   person* ptrP1 = new person("KuangThu", "Bruce", 4157300);
   person* ptrP2 = new person("Deauville", "William", 8435150);
   person* ptrP3 = new person("Wellington", "John", 9207404);
   person* ptrP4 = new person("Bartoski", "Peter", 6946473);
   person* ptrP5 = new person("Fredericks", "Roger", 7049982);
   person* ptrP6 = new person("McDonald", "Stacey", 7764987);

   vectPtrsPers.push_back(ptrP1);  //put persons in set
   vectPtrsPers.push_back(ptrP2);
   vectPtrsPers.push_back(ptrP3);
   vectPtrsPers.push_back(ptrP4);
   vectPtrsPers.push_back(ptrP5);
   vectPtrsPers.push_back(ptrP6);

   for_each(vectPtrsPers.begin(),                  //display vector
            vectPtrsPers.end(), displayPerson() );
                                                //sort pointers
   sort( vectPtrsPers.begin(), vectPtrsPers.end() );
   cout << "\n\nSorted pointers";
   for_each(vectPtrsPers.begin(),                  //display vector
            vectPtrsPers.end(), displayPerson() );

   sort( vectPtrsPers.begin(),                     //sort persons
         vectPtrsPers.end(), comparePersons() );
   cout << "\n\nSorted persons";
   for_each(vectPtrsPers.begin(),                  //display vector
            vectPtrsPers.end(), displayPerson() );
   while( !vectPtrsPers.empty() )
      {
      delete vectPtrsPers.back();                //delete person
      vectPtrsPers.pop_back();                   //pop pointer
      }
   cout << endl;
   return 0;
   }  //end main()
```

Here's the output of SORTPTRS:

```
KuangThu,        Bruce           phone: 4157300
Deauville,       William         phone: 8435150
Wellington,      John            phone: 9207404
Bartoski,        Peter           phone: 6946473
Fredericks,      Roger           phone: 7049982
McDonald,        Stacey          phone: 7764987

Sorted pointers
KuangThu,        Bruce           phone: 4157300
Deauville,       William         phone: 8435150
```

```
Wellington,     John            phone: 9207404
Bartoski,       Peter           phone: 6946473
Fredericks,     Roger           phone: 7049982
McDonald,       Stacey          phone: 7764987

Sorted persons
Bartoski,       Peter           phone: 6946473
Deauville,      William         phone: 8435150
Fredericks,     Roger           phone: 7049982
KuangThu,       Bruce           phone: 4157300
McDonald,       Stacey          phone: 7764987
Wellington,     John            phone: 9207404
```

First the original order is shown, then the ordering sorted incorrectly by pointer, and finally the order sorted correctly by name.

The comparePersons() Function Object

If we use the two-argument version of the sort() algorithm,

```
sort( vectPtrsPers.begin(), vectPtrsPers.end() );
```

then only the pointers are sorted, by their addresses in memory. This is not usually what we want. To sort the person objects by name, we use the three-argument version of sort(), with the comparePersons() function object as the third argument:

```
sort( vectPtrsPers.begin(),
     bectPtrsPers.end(), comparePersons() );
```

The function object comparePersons() is defined like this in the SORTPTRS program:

```
//function object to compare persons using pointers
class comparePersons
  {
  public:
  bool operator() (const person* ptrP1,
                   const person* ptrP2) const
    { return *ptrP1 < *ptrP2; }
  };
```

The operator() takes two arguments that are pointers to persons and compares their contents, rather than the pointers themselves.

The displayPerson() Function Object

We use a different approach to display the contents of a container than we have before. Instead of interacting through the container, we use the for_each() function, with a function object as its third argument.

```
for_each(vectPtrsPers.begin(),
        bectPtrsPers.end(), displayPeson() );
```

This causes the `displayPerson()` function object to be called once for each person in the vector. Here's how `displayPerson()` looks:

```
//function object to display a person, using a pointer
class displayPerson
  {
  public:
  void operator() (const person* ptrP) const
    { ptrP->display(); }
  };
```

With this arrangement a single function call displays all the `person` objects in the vector.

Function objects Used to Modify Container Behavior

In SORTPTRS we showed function objects used to modify the behavior of algorithms. Function objects can also modify the behavior of containers. For example, if you want a set of pointers to objects to sort itself automatically based on the objects instead of the pointers, you can use an appropriate function object when you define the container. No `sort()` algorithm need be used. We'll examine this approach in an exercise.

Summary

This chapter has presented a quick and dirty introduction to the STL. However, we've touched on the major topics, and you should have acquired enough information to begin using the STL in a useful way. For a fuller understanding of the STL we recommend that readers avail themselves of a complete text on the topic.

You've learned that the STL consists of three main components: containers, algorithms, and iterators. Containers are divided into two groups: sequential and associative. Sequential containers are the vector, list, and deque. Associative containers are the set and map, and the closely-related multiset and multimap. Algorithms carry out operations on containers, such as sorting, copying, and searching. Iterators act like pointers to container elements and provide connections between algorithms and containers.

Not all algorithms are appropriate for all containers. Iterators are used to ensure that algorithms and containers are appropriately matched. Iterators are defined for specific kinds of containers, and used as arguments to algorithms. If the container's iterators don't match the algorithm, a compiler error results.

Input and output iterators connect directly to I/O streams, thus allowing data to be piped directly between I/O devices and containers. Specialized iterators allow backward iteration and can also change the behavior of some algorithms so that they insert data rather than overwriting existing data.

Algorithms are standalone functions that can work on many different containers. In addition, each container has its own specific member functions. In some cases the same function is available as both an algorithm and a member function.

STL containers and algorithms will work with objects of any class, provided certain member functions, such as the < operator, are overloaded for that class.

The behavior of certain algorithms such as `find_if()` can be customized using function objects. A function object is instantiated from a class containing only an `()` operator.

Questions

Answers to questions can be found in Appendix G, "Answers to Questions and Exercises."

1. An STL container can be used to

    a. hold objects of class employee.

    b. store elements in a way that makes them quickly accessible.

    c. compile C++ programs.

    d. organize the way objects are stored in memory.

2. The STL sequence containers are v_____, l_____, and d_____.

3. Two important STL associative containers are s_____ and ma_____.

4. An STL algorithm is

    a. a standalone function that operates on containers.

    b. a link between member functions and containers.

    c. a friend function of appropriate container classes.

    d. a member function of appropriate container classes.

5. True or false: one purpose of an iterator in the STL is to connect algorithms and containers.

6. The `find()` algorithm

    a. finds matching sequences of elements in two containers.

    b. finds a container that matches a specified container.

    c. takes iterators as its first two arguments.

    d. takes container elements as its first two arguments.

7. True or false: algorithms can be used only on STL containers.

8. A range is often supplied to an algorithm by two i_____ values.

9. What entity is often used to customize the behavior of an algorithm?

10. A vector is an appropriate container if you

    a. want to insert lots of new elements at arbitrary locations in the vector.

    b. want to insert new elements, but always at the front of the container.

    c. are given an index number and you want to quickly access the corresponding element.

    d. are given an element's key value and you want to quickly access the corresponding element.

11. True or false: the `back()` member function removes the element at the back of the container.

12. If you define a vector v with the default constructor, and define another vector w with a one-argument constructor to a size of 11, and insert 3 elements into each of these vectors with `push_back()`, then the `size()` member function will return _____ for v and _____ for w.

13. The `unique()` algorithm removes all _____ element values from a container.

14. In a deque,

    a. data can be quickly inserted or deleted at any arbitrary location.

    b. data can be inserted or deleted at any arbitrary location, but the process is relatively slow.

    c. data can be quickly inserted or deleted at either end.

    d. data can be inserted or deleted at either end, but the process is relatively slow.

15. In iterator _____ a specific element in a container.

16. True or false: an iterator can always move forward or backward through a container.

17. You must use at least a _____ iterator for a list.

18. If `iter` is an iterator to a container, write an expression that will have the value of the object pointed to by `iter`, and will then cause `iter` to point to the next element.

19. The `copy()` algorithm returns an iterator to

    a. the last element copied from.

    b. the last element copied to.

    c. the element one past the last element copied from.

    d. the element one past the last element copied to.

20. To use a `reverse_iterator`, you should

    a. begin by initializing it to `end()`.

    b. begin by initializing it to `rend()`.

    c. increment it to move backward through the container.

    d. decrement it to move backward through the container.

21. True or false: the `back_inserter` iterator always causes the new elements to be inserted following the existing ones

22. Stream iterators allow you to treat the display and keyboard devices, and files, as if they were _____.

23. What does the second argument to an `ostream_iterator` specify?

24. In an associative container,

    a. values are stored in sorted order.

    b. keys are stored in sorted order.

    c. sorting is always in alphabetical or numerical order.

    d. you must use the `sort()` algorithm to keep the contents sorted.

25. When defining a set, you must specify how _____.

26. True or false: in a set, the `insert()` member function inserts a key in sorted order.

27. A map stores _____ of objects (or values).

28. True or false: a map can have two or more elements with the same key value.

29. If you store pointers to objects, instead of objects, in a container, then

    a. the objects won't need to be copied to implement storage in the container.

    b. only associative containers can be used.

    c. you can't sort the objects using object attributes as keys.

    d. the containers will often require less memory.

30. If you want an associative container like `set` to order itself automatically, you can define the ordering in a function object and specify that function object in the container's _____.

Exercises

Answers to exercises can be found in Appendix G.

*1. Write a program that applies the **sort()** algorithm to an array of floating point values entered by the user, and displays the result.

*2. Apply the **sort()** algorithm to an array of words entered by the user, and display the result. Use **push_back()** to insert the words, and the **[ ]** operator and **size()** to display them.

*3. Start with a list of **int** values. Use two normal (not reverse) iterators, one moving forward through the list and one moving backward, in a **while** loop, to reverse the contents of the list. You can use the **swap()** algorithm to save a few statements. (Make sure your solution works for both even and odd numbers of items.) To see how the experts do it, look at the **reverse()** function in your compiler's ALGORITHM header file.

*4. Start with the **person** class, and create a multiset to hold pointers to **person** objects. Define the multiset with the **comparePersons** function object, so it will be sorted automatically by names of persons. Define a half-dozen persons, put them in the multiset, and display its contents. Several of the persons should have the same name, to verify that the multiset stores multiple objects with the same key.

5. Fill an array with even numbers and a set with odd numbers. Use the **merge()** algorithm to merge these containers into a vector. Display the vector contents to show that all went well. [merge.cpp]

6. In Exercise 15.3 two ordinary (non-reverse) iterators were used to reverse the contents of a container. Now use one forward and one reverse iterator to carry out the same task, this time on a vector. [reverse2.cpp]

7. We showed the four-argument version of the **accumulate()** algorithm in the PLUSAIR example. Rewrite this example using the three-argument version. [accumulate.cpp]

8. You can use the **copy()** algorithm to copy sequences within a container. However, you must be careful when the destination sequence overlaps the source sequence. Write a program that lets you copy any sequence to a different location within an array, using **copy()**. Have the user enter values for **first1**, **last1**, and **first2**. Use the program to verify that you can shift a sequence that overlaps its destination to the left, but not to the right. (For example, you can shift several items from 10 to 9, but not from 10 to 11.) This is because **copy()** starts with the leftmost element. [copy1.cpp]

9. We listed the function objects corresponding to the C++ operators in Table 15.10, and, in the PLUSAIR program earlier in this chapter, we showed the function object plus<>() used with the accumulate() algorithm. It wasn't necessary to provide arguments to the function objects in that example, but sometimes it is. However, you can't put the argument within the parentheses of the function object, as you might expect. Instead, you use a function adapter called bind1st or bind2nd to bind the argument to the function. For example, suppose you were looking for a particular string (call it searchName) in a container of strings (called names). You can say

    ```
    ptr = find_if(names.begin(), names.end(),
                bind2nd(equal_to<string>(), searchName) );
    ```

    Here equal_to<>() and searchName are arguments to bind2nd(). This statement returns an iterator to the first string in the container equal to searchName. Write a program that incorporates this statement or a similar one to find a string in a container of strings. It should display the position of searchName in the container. [bind2nd.cpp]

10. You can use the copy_backword() algorithm to overcome the problem described in Exercise 7. That is, you can't shift a sequence to the left if any of the source overlaps any of the destination. Write a program that uses both copy() and copy_backward() to enable shifting any sequence anywhere within a container, regardless of overlap. [copy2.cpp]

11. Write a program that copies a source file of integers to a destination file, using stream iterators. The user should supply both source and destination filenames to the program. You can use a while loop approach. Within the loop, read each integer value from the input iterator and write it immediately to the output iterator, then increment both iterators. The ITER.DAT file created by the FOUTITER program in this chapter makes a suitable source file. [copyfile.cpp]

12. A frequency table lists words and the number of times each word appears in a text file. Write a program that creates a frequency table for a file whose name is entered by the user. You can use a map of string-int pairs. You may want to use the C library function ispunct() (in header file CTYPE.H) to check for punctuation so you can strip it off the end of a word, using the string member function substr(). Also, the tolower() function may prove handy for uncapitalizing words. [wordfreq.cpp]

CHAPTER 16

OBJECT-ORIENTED DESIGN

You will learn about the following in this chapter:

- CRC Cards
- USE Cases
- Class relationships

- Class diagrams
- Translating design into code

An object-oriented programmer faces a major question at the start of every programming project: "What classes should I use?" Understanding how to break a programming problem into classes is not a trivial undertaking. The process is called *object-oriented design* (OOD). Many books have been written, and many more will be written, on this subject, which is still in a state of rapid evolution.

In a single chapter we can't cover everything there is to know about OOD, but we can give you an idea of the issues involved and some of the major techniques.

Much writing about OOD is abstract and theoretical. To make our discussion as concrete as possible, we'll use a case study, focusing on a specific situation and describing the actual steps you might take to design a program.

Our Approach to OOD

In this chapter we're going to focus on three major phases in the process of translating a programming problem into classes. These are:

- CRC cards
- Use cases
- Class diagrams

Briefly, creating CRC cards gives us a first approximation of the classes we will need and what they do. Use cases then allow us to add detail to what we learned with CRC cards. Finally, class diagrams specify how our classes are related, and provide a bridge to the actual program code.

CRC Cards

CRC cards are a non-technical, non-threatening way to analyze a problem. They allow the people who understand the problem, or who are going to use the finished program, to guide the design process. These people are sometimes referred to with a highfalutin' name like *business domain experts* (BDEs). The BDEs may not know anything about programming, but they know (or can figure out) what they want the program to do. CRC cards are effective because the BDEs can generate them with no knowledge of programming.

Each CRC card corresponds to an object in the business domain, such as a person or report. Because of the correspondence between real-world and program objects, each CRC card also corresponds to an object in the program code. Thus the CRC-card approach allows non-programmers to play a major role in program design.

Use Cases

A *use case* is a description of a specific operation carried out by the program. Such an operation is usually initiated by a human user of the program. This user may ask a class to do something. Then this class may ask other classes for help carrying out the user's request. A detailed description of this process constitutes the use case.

As use cases are generated, it may become clearer that new classes are needed, or that existing classes need to be modified. Such perceptions can be reflected in new or modified CRC cards.

Class Diagrams

Once CRC cards and use cases have been generated, *class diagrams* provide a way to express the relationships among the classes, and to record the information on the CRC cards. The Universal Modeling Language (UML) specifies how class relationships are depicted on class diagrams. Exploring class relationships with the class diagrams may again reveal that additions or changes need to be made to the original classes, resulting in further revisions to the CRC cards.

When the CRC cards, use cases, and class diagrams have been completed, the final program design is ready to be coded.

In the balance of this chapter we'll describe how CRC cards, use cases, and class diagrams are used to design a specific program. We'll then discuss how the design is translated into actual code, and show the program listings for the completed program.

The Programming Problem

The program we'll design in this chapter is called *Landlord*. Using a specific program will keep the discussion grounded in something specific. You may or may not like your landlord, but you can understand the sorts of data (such as rents and expenses) that the landlord must deal with. This gets us started with an easily-understood *business domain* (what we're writing the program about).

Let's suppose that you're an independent programmer, and you're approached by a potential customer whose name is Beverly Smith. Beverly is a small-time landlord; she owns an apartment building with 12 units. She wants you to write a program that will make it easier for her to record data and print reports regarding the finances of the apartment building.

Hand-Written Forms

Currently Beverly is recording all the information about her apartment building by hand, in old-fashioned ledger books. She shows you the forms she's currently using. There are three of them:

- The Rental Income Record
- The Expense Record
- The Annual Summary

The *Rental Income Record* is used to record and display the incoming rent payments. It contains 12 columns, one for each month; and one row for each apartment number. Each time Beverly receives a rent payment from a tenant, she records it in the appropriate row and column of the Rental Income Record, which is shown in Figure 16.1.

Monthly Rental Income Record

Apartment No	Jan	Feb	Mar	Apr	May	June	July	Aug
101	695	695	695	695	695			
102	595	595	595	595	595			
103	810	810	825	825	825			
104	720	720	720	720	720			
201	680	680	680	680	680			
202	510	510	510	530	530			
203	790	790	790	790	790			
204	495	495	495	495	495			
301	585	585	585	585	585			
302	530	530	530	530	550			
303	810	810	810	810	810			
304	745	745	745	745	745			

Figure 16.1 The Rental Income record.

The layout of the Rental Income Record makes it easy to see which rents have been paid.

The *Expense Record* records outgoing payments. It's similar to your personal check register. It has columns for the date, the payee (the company or person to whom Beverly writes the check), and the amount being paid. In addition, there's a column where Beverly can specify the budget category to which the payment should be charged. Budget categories include Mortgage, Repairs, Utilities, Taxes, Insurance, and so on. The Expense Record is shown in Figure 16.2.

Expense Record

Date	Payee	Amount	Budget Category
1/3	First Megabank	5187.30	Mortgage
1/5	City Water	963.10	Utilities
1/9	Steady State	4840.00	Insurance
1/15	P.G. & E.	727.23	Utilities
1/22	Sam's Hardware	54.81	Supplies
1/25	Ernie Glotz	150.00	Repairs
2/3	First Megabank	5187.30	Mortgage
2/7	City Water	845.93	Utilities
2/15	P.G. & E.	754.20	Utilities
2/18	Ploty & Sheems	1200.00	Legal Fees
3/2	First Megabank	5187.30	Mortgage
3/7	City Water	890.27	Utilities
3/10	County of Springfield	9427.00	Property Taxes
3/14	P.G. & E.	772.35	Utilities
3/20	Gotham Courier	26.40	Advertising
3/25	Ernie Glotz	450.00	Repairs
3/27	Acme Painting	600.00	Maintenance
4/3	First Megabank	5187.30	Mortgage

Figure 16.2   The Expense record.

The *Annual Report* uses data from the Rental Income Record and the Expense Record to summarize how much money came in and how much went out during the year. All the rents are summed and the result is displayed. The expenses are summed and displayed by budget category, which makes it easy to see, for example, how much was spent on repairs during the year. Figure 16.3 shows the Annual Report. Finally expenses are subtracted from income to show how much money Beverly made (or lost) during the year.

In Beverly's existing system, the annual report isn't created until the end of the year, and all the rents and expenses for December have been recorded.

Beverly tells you she wants the program to pretty much duplicate what she's currently doing on the paper forms. She wants to be able to enter data about rents and expenses, and print out the Rental and Expense records and the Annual Report.

Assumptions

Of course we've already made some simplifying assumptions. There are other kinds of data associated with running an apartment building, such as damage deposits, depreciation, mortgage interest, and income from late fees and the rental of laundry machines. We won't consider these details.

	Annual Summary of Business and Statement of Income	
1		
2	INCOME	
3	Rent	102.264.00
4	TOTAL INCOME	102.264.00
5		
6	EXPENSES	
7	Mortgage	62.247.60
8	Property taxes	9.487.00
9	Insurance	4.840.00
10	Utilities	18.326.76
11	Supplies	1.129.23
12	Repairs	4.274.50
13	Maintenance	2.609.42
14	Legal fees	1.200.00
15	Landscaping	900.00
16	Advertising	79.64
17		
18	TOTAL EXPENSES	105.034.15
19		
20	NET PROFIT OR (LOSS)	(2.770.15)
21		

Figure 16.3   The Annual report.

There are also other kinds of reports Beverly might want, such as a Net Worth statement. It might even be nice to have the program interface with an income tax program and online banking. And from a big-picture perspective, there are commercial landlord programs available, so it might not be smart for Beverly to contract to have one custom-written. We'll ignore all of these distractions to make the problem more tractable.

The CRC Modeling Team

In the early days of software development, a programming team would ask the client to write a specification describing exactly what they wanted the program to do. Once they had completed the specification, the client's part of the job was over. The programmers would go back to their office and write the program based on the specification. After some period of time (usually lengthy) they would deliver the final result to the client.

This might seem like a reasonable approach, but the results were often disappointing for the client. The programmers' interpretation of the specification was often not what the client had expected. The problem was that there wasn't enough interaction between the client and the programmers. Experience has shown that the more closely the client is involved in the design of the actual program, the more satisfactory the outcome.

Object-oriented programming makes a close association with the client much easier because objects in the program correspond so closely with objects in the real world. First the client defines the objects that are important in the real world situation, which as we noted is called the *problem domain* or *business domain*. Then the programmer translates these objects into objects in the program.

The approach we'll describe for an initial approach to finding user requirements is called *CRC modeling*. CRC stands for Class-Requirements-Collaborators.

Members of the Team

CRC modeling is carried out by a team of people. The first step in beginning the CRC modeling process is to get your team together. There are three kinds of people on the team:

- Business Domain Experts
- A facilitator
- Scribes

The majority of the people on a CRC team are business domain experts (BDEs), people who understand the business and how the program will be used. For a large application there might be a half-dozen or more BDEs, but for our simple landlord program the only BDEs are Beverly and her accountant, a CPA named Bryan.

The *facilitator* guides the process of developing the CRC cards. Ideally the facilitator has considerable experience in object-oriented design, the use of CRC modeling, and object-oriented programming. In addition, the facilitator should be someone who communicates well with people and can encourage them to express their ideas.

The *scribe* writes down business details that aren't recorded on the CRC cards. A large project may have several scribes. Our landlord project is small, so you yourself, in your role as independent software developer, can play the role of both the facilitator and the scribe.

You'll need to a meeting room with a nice big table for the CRC team. You'll use this table to spread out and arrange the CRC cards once they've been created.

The Problem Summary Statement

The goal of the CRC modeling process is to discover the classes that are appropriate for modeling the problem. One way to begin this process is to create a formal written statement of the problem. This statement is called the *Problem Summary Statement*.

As facilitator, you suggest that Beverly take a crack at writing this statement. Beverly comes up with the following:

> The Landlord program handles the financial data necessary for operating a small apartment building. The program's user should be able to input rents paid by individual tenants, and expenses incurred in operating the building. On demand, the program should display a Rent Record, which shows the rents paid by each tenant for each month; and an Expense Record, which, for each expense, records the date, payee, amount, and budget category.

"How does that look to you?" you ask Bryan.

Bryan examines the statement. "You left out the Annual Report," he tells Beverly. "Good point," she responds. She adds another sentence to the statement:

> The program should also be able to display an Annual Summary, which shows total rents paid for the year and total expenses paid in each budget category.

This amended Problem Summary Statement looks good to you, so you declare it finished. In a more complicated situation many people would collaborate on the creation of the Problem Summary Statement, but in this case Beverly knows the business well enough to get it right the first time, with a little help from Bryan.

"So far so good," you tell Beverly. "Now let's see what classes we can extract from this statement. Every noun is a potential candidate for becoming a class." You make a list of all the nouns in the Program Summary Statement. However, you cross a few of them out, such as "Landlord program" and "financial data" because they're too general or too vague. You're left with the following list:

- Program user
- Rent
- Tenant
- Expense
- Apartment
- Building
- Rent Record
- Expense Record
- Date
- Payee
- Amount
- Budget Category
- Annual Summary
- Total Expenses

During the development process, we'll find that some of these candidate classes will be deleted, some will remain, and some new ones will be added. For the time being they're a starting point.

Constructing the CRC Cards

A CRC card starts as a blank 4-by-6 or 3-by-5 filing card. This may seem like a mundane basis for such a high tech activity as object-oriented design, but filing cards have many advantages. They're cheap, readily available, and not threatening to non-programmers. No one cares if you make a mistake and need to throw one away. They can also be moved around on the table to make the relationships among classes easier to visualize. Perhaps most importantly, their size is limited, so you can't write too much on them. This forces you to keep things reasonably simple.

The name CRC comes from the three areas into which we divide the front of the card. These are:

- Class

- Responsibilities

- Collaborators

Figure 16.4 shows a CRC card. The top of the card holds the class name, the left side lists responsibilities, and the right side lists collaborators.

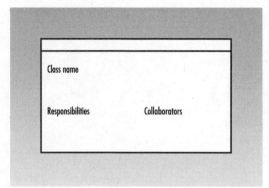

Class name

Responsibilities   Collaborators

Figure 16.4   CRC card.

We've learned about classes in previous chapters. *Responsibilities* are the things a class needs to know and the actions it must take. *Collaborators* are other classes that a class may need to help it carry out its responsibilities. We'll return to Responsibilities and Collaborators in a moment.

Classes

You tell everyone in your little CRC modeling group that the next step is to write the name of each of the candidate classes at the top of a CRC card. The three of you divide up the work and soon there are CRC cards spread all over the table.

Have you missed any classes that should be in the program? It's quite likely. Experience has shown that there are some categories that are often candidates for classhood. These are

- Any human beings associated with the program

- Any objects associated with the program

- Money used for specific purposes

- Input screens (often called *forms*)

- Output screens (often called *reports*)

"These categories provide a different way of coming up with classes," you explain. "Is there anything in any of these categories that we haven't already put on a card?"

"Well, tenants and payees are the only human beings I need to deal with, and we've got both of them," says Beverly. "Of course there are all sorts of other objects in the building, like bathtubs and fire extinguishers. Do we need to include them?"

"I don't think so," you tell her. "Things like that are really just things you buy, so they're recorded as expenses. The actual items you buy aren't important to this program. You just care about recording who sold you the item and how much you paid for it."

"As for possible money items," Bryan says, "the only money involved is for rents and expenses, and we've covered those already."

"I think we've covered all the reports, too," you say. "We've got the Rent Record, the Expense Record, and the Annual Report."

"But we don't have any input screens!" Beverly says. "Don't we need some?"

"We certainly do," you say. "You'll need some sort of screen to enter rents, and another to enter expenses."

"Won't I also need some kind of main screen?" Beverly asks. "You know, like a main menu or something, where I tell the program what I want to do next."

"Good point," you tell her. "Let's call it the User Interface Screen. So we'll add three more classes." You create three more CRC cards:

- Rent Input Screen

- Expense Input Screen

- User Interface Screen

The resulting cards are shown in Figure 16.5.

Responsibilities

"The next step," you tell everyone, "is to add responsibilities to each card."

"What are responsibilities again?" Bryan asks.

"Anything a class needs to know or do. For example, let's look at class Tenant. Objects of this class represent real tenants that live in Beverly's apartments. Tenants will know things, like their names, addresses, and phone numbers. They may also do things. For example, we may need an object of the Tenant class to display its name. Any of these are potential responsibilities."

You don't explain that "things that a class knows" corresponds to class member data (attributes) in the program, and that "things that a class does" corresponds to member functions (methods). Bryan and Beverly aren't programmers, and don't know or care about the technical terms.

We should note that some experts don't consider attributes to be responsibilities, and put them in a separate place on the card, such as on the back. To keep things simple we'll consider attributes to be responsibilities, along with methods.

"Wait a minute," says Beverly. "Isn't a tenant's main responsibility to pay the rent?"

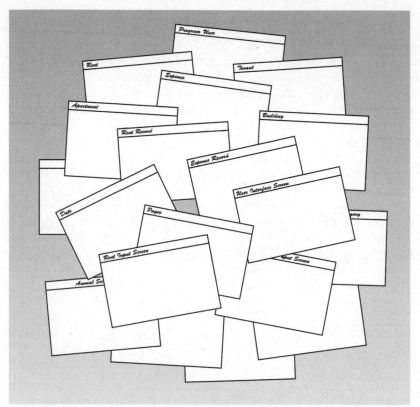

Figure 16.5   The initial CRC cards.

"That's true in a legal sense," you say. "But we're only talking about responsibilities within the program. As the user of the program you're going to enter the rent amounts yourself, when you receive a check from a real tenant. So the Tenant object in the program doesn't have the responsibility of paying the rent."

"I thought objects in the program corresponded to objects in real life," Bryan says.

"It's not an exact correspondence," you explain. "Objects in the program are usually less complex than the equivalent object in the real world. Remember that we're really only interested in responsibilities that will be used by other parts of the program. If no other class cares about some responsibility, we don't need it."

"Then what about the phone number you mentioned?" asks Bryan. "No other part of the program is going to call anyone, so we don't need that."

"That's a good point," you tell Bryan. "We need the names of the tenants to identify them, and we'll need their apartment numbers, so each rent amount can be placed in the correct row of the Rent Record. But that's probably all the data we need for each tenant. We can forget about phone numbers and other details."

"But if it doesn't pay the rent, what does a Tenant object do?" asks Beverly.

"Besides displaying its name, I'm not actually sure at this point," you say. "We'll learn more as we go along."

"You don't know yet?" asks Beverly incredulously. "But you're supposed to be the expert."

"No, you're the experts in what you want the program to do," you tell her. It's a group effort. And no one gets everything right the first time. That's why it's important to go through this process. We help each other discover things."

"I have a another question," Bryan says. "How do we get data into a Tenant object in the first place? Isn't one of its responsibilities to find out what its name is and where it lives?"

"Yes, but we can do that in the constructor. Oh, sorry!" You realize you've used too technical a term. "I mean, Tenant objects can be born knowing their name and apartment number. We don't need to specify separate responsibilities for that."

Collaborators

You move on to collaborators, explaining that a *collaborator* is any other class that our class needs to help do something. That is, one or more collaborators may be necessary to implement each "what it does" responsibility. A collaborator may simply provide information, or it may carry out a more extensive task.

"All the Tenant class does is display itself," says Bryan. "I don't see that it needs any collaborators for that."

You agree, but take time to explain that collaborators are usually shown only on the CRC card for the class that initiates the collaboration, not on the card that carries out the request. Thus if class A asks for some information from class B, then B is listed as a collaborator on class A's CRC card, but A isn't listed on B's card. "Maybe a *collaborator* should be called an *assistant*," you conclude, "to make it clearer the relationship only goes one way."

The Tenant CRC Card

You write down the responsibilities you've discussed so far on the Tenant class CRC card, which is shown in Figure 16.6. You leave the collaborator field blank.

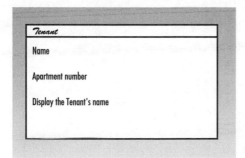

Figure 16.6   The initial CRC card for the Tenant class.

The Expense CRC Card

Next you pick up the card for the Expense class. "Responsibilities?" you ask.

"OK, says Bryan, I'm getting the hang of this. It's all in the Problem Summary Statement. Each Expense object needs to know the payee, the amount, and the budget category.".

"And the date," interjects Beverly.

"Oh, right," says Bryan.

"Wait a minute," Beverly points to the cards on the table. "We already have CRC cards for the payee, date, amount, and budget category. They can't be classes and also responsibilities of the Expense class at the same time, can they?"

"Very perceptive," you tell her. "And if you think about it, those four things are pretty simple. The amount is just a single number, and the payee and budget are just strings."

"You mean they're not complex enough to be classes?" Bryan asks.

"It could be," you say. "There's usually no point creating a class for something that's basically a simple variable. It was probably a mistake to make CRC cards for them. The date could be a class, but let's say we're going to treat it as two separate numbers, for the day and the month. So those four things should be responsibilities, not classes."

You throw the CRC cards for the Amount, Payee, Budget Category, and Date into the waste basket. Then you write these names down in the Responsibilities column of the Expense CRC card, changing Date to Month and Day. You don't need a year column because the program handles data for only one year at a time.

"Now, what about things an Expense object does?"

"We'll want to see every expense displayed in the Expense Record," says Beverly. "So an Expense object should be able to display itself." You add the Display responsibility to the card. Again there doesn't seem to be a need for any collaborators. The initial CRC card for the Expense class is shown in Figure 16.7.

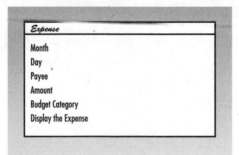

Figure 16.7   The initial CRC card for the Expense class.

The Rent Input Screen CRC card

"OK, let's try the Rent Input Screen," you say. "What are its responsibilities?"

"It's the screen I'll use when I receive a rent check," says Beverly. "I'll input the date of the check, the name of tenant who wrote it, and the amount. So those three things are what the class knows."

"And what this class does," Bryan says, "is to get this information from the user, and pass it along to the Rent Record."

"So that makes the Rent Record a collaborator," Beverly says.

That's good, you think. They're catching on fast. You fill out the CRC card as they suggest, as shown in Figure 16.8.

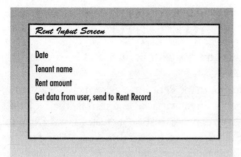

Figure 16.8   The initial CRC card for the Rent Input Screen class.

The Rent Record CRC Card

"That leads to the Rent Record CRC card," Beverly says.

"I have a feeling it's going to be a little more complicated," you say. "What are its responsibilities?"

"It's got to hold all the rent amounts, so it will need a list of rents," Beverly says.

"And a way to insert a new rent, and a way to display itself," adds Bryan. You decide no collaborators are necessary, and come up with the CRC card shown in Figure 16.9.

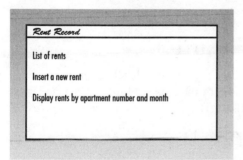

Figure 16.9   The initial CRC card for the Rent Record class.

"Hang on a minute," says Bryan. "Shouldn't we have made a Rent class CRC card before we did the Rent Input Screen and the Rent Record? Rent is one of the nouns from our Problem Summary Statement, and the Rent Record will need to collaborate with it."

"Well, we could do it that way," you tell Bryan. "The rent amount, and maybe also the month it was for and the apartment number, could be attributes of a Rent class. But my sense is that the Rent Record can take care of remembering which month and apartment number applies to which rent. Then the rent is just a single number, and that's probably not worth making into a class." You hold the Rent CRC card over the wastebasket. "Any objections?" No one says anything, so you drop it in.

The Expense Input Screen CRC Card

You work through the remaining cards in a similar way, with Beverly and Bryan making initial suggestions, which you sometimes modify.

The Expense Input Screen is somewhat analogous to the Rent Input Screen class. However, because an Expense is a class object rather than a single variable as a rent is, the Expense Input Screen doesn't need to "know" the details of an expense. Instead it creates a new Expense object, based on the information typed in by the user, and passes this object along to the Expense Report for storage. Figure 16.10 shows the Expense Input Screen CRC card.

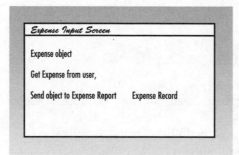

Figure 16.10   The initial CRC card for the Expense Input Screen class.

The Expense Record CRC Card

The Expense Record CRC card contains a list of expenses. It will be responsible for inserting a new object into the list when requested by the Expense Input Screen, and it will also need to display all the expenses when asked. The result is shown in Figure 16.11.

The Annual Report CRC Card

The Annual Report displays a summary of the data in the Rent Record and the Expense Record. It doesn't need to "know" anything because all the data it needs is in these two records, which therefore act as collaborators. The card is shown in Figure 16.12.

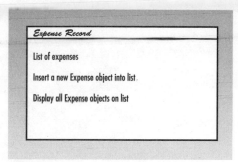

Figure 16.11   The CRC card for the Expense Record class.

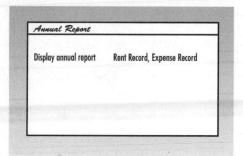

Figure 16.12   The initial CRC card for the Annual Report class.

The User Interface CRC Card

The User Interface class takes care of interacting with the user. In fact, that's its single responsibility. It doesn't need to know anything, but what it does, depending on the instructions from the user, is insert data or display reports. More specifically, it tells the Rent Input Screen to insert a rent amount, and the Expense Input Screen to insert an expense. It also displays the Rent Record, Expense Record, or Annual Report. It must therefore collaborate with all these classes. Figure 16.13 shows the User Interface CRC card.

"What about doing the Apartment class next?" Beverly asks.

"Hmm." You think for a moment. "I'm not sure what responsibilities this class would have. None of the classes we've done so far need to collaborate with the Apartment class. It's true a real tenant lives in a real apartment, but in this program all we really care about is the apartment number associated with a tenant, and that's just a single number. Maybe we could use an Apartment class instead of a Tenant class, but we've already figured out the Tenant class."

"I see what you mean," Beverly says. "All right, let's keep the Tenant class and forget about the Apartment class. Now what about the Building class?"

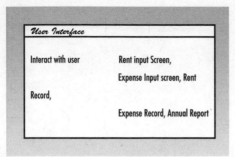

Figure 16.13 The initial CRC card for the User Interface class.

"We don't need that either," you tell her. "The assumption in this program is that Beverly only owns one building. So we never need to specify the building, or know anything about it. I'd suggest scrapping it. Also, I don't think we need a class called Program User. We already have one called User Interface."

After a some more discussion you toss away the CRC cards for Apartment, Building, and Program User. You now have CRC cards for the following classes:

- User Interface
- Tenant
- Rent Input Screen
- Rent Record
- Expense
- Expense Input Screen
- Expense Record
- Annual Report

You spread these cards out on the table where everyone can see them.

The Scribe

During the whole process of constructing the CRC cards, the scribe (you yourself, in this case) has been taking notes on details not captured on the CRC cards. These notes will be made available to programmers and others later on, in case details of the operation aren't clear.

Use Cases

Having created a set of CRC cards, the members of your group probably feel that they have correctly identified all the relevant classes, responsibilities, and collaborators. However, they may be overly optimistic. A different approach, called *use cases*, may help to uncover additional classes and responsibilities.

A use case is a detailed description of a specific task carried out by the program.

An *actor* is a human (or organizational) entity that interacts with the program. Actors often initiate tasks. In this program there's only one actor, which we call the user.

Rereading the Problem Summary Statement (including the addition of the Annual Summary), we can see that it mentions five activities. Each of these is a candidate for a use case. All these activities are initiated by an actor: the user. Here they are:

1. User inputs an expense

2. User inputs a rent

3. User asks to see the Expense Record

4. User asks to see the Rent Record

5. User asks to see the Annual Summary

Use Case 1: User Inputs an Expense

"OK," you tell the CRC group. "Let's take a new filing card and write down the detailed steps for the user inputting an expense. This isn't a CRC card, it's just a handy place to make a list."

"How do we begin?" asks Beverly.

"Ask yourself what's the first thing that happens when the user inputs an expense. Who does what to whom?"

"Well, I guess the first thing is that the user tells the User Interface object that she wants to input an expense," Beverly says, thinking out loud.

"Right, and then the User Interface calls up the Expense Input Screen," adds Bryan.

"Good. Then what?" You prompt.

"The Expense Input Screen calls the Expense Record?" asks Bryan.

"There's another detail we should interject here," you say. "The Expense Input Screen needs to create a new Expense object. Then it passes that object to the Expense Record."

"OK," says Bryan, "and then the Expense Record stores the new Expense object in its list."

"Sounds good," you say. You finish adding these steps to a card. The result is shown in Figure 16.14.

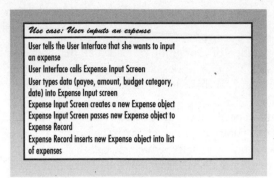

Use case: User inputs an expense

User tells the User Interface that she wants to input
an expense
User Interface calls Expense Input Screen
User types data (payee, amount, budget category,
date) into Expense Input screen
Expense Input Screen creates a new Expense object
Expense Input Screen passes new Expense object to
Expense Record
Expense Record inserts new Expense object into list
of expenses

Figure 16.14   Use-case card for inputting an expense.

Use Case 2: The User Inputs a Rent

"The use case for the user inputting a rent starts the same way," Bryan says. "In fact, all the use cases start with the user asking the user interface to do something."

"True," you say. "That's because this is a relatively simple program. In a more complicated situation we might have Manager actors and Salesmen actors and Client actors, as well as other parts of the program initiating an action."

"OK," says Beverly, ignoring this complexity, "then the User Interface calls up the Rent Input Screen, and the user types in the date, the tenant's name, and the rent amount."

"Then the Rent Input Screen passes that information to the Rent Record," Bryan says, "and the Rent Record stores it in its list of rents." The resulting use case is shown in Figure 16.15.

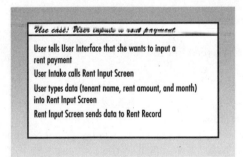

Use case: User inputs a rent payment

User tells User Interface that she wants to input a
rent payment
User Intake calls Rent Input Screen
User types data (tenant name, rent amount, and month)
into Rent Input Screen
Rent Input Screen sends data to Rent Record

Figure 16.15   Preliminary use case: user inputs a rent.

Trouble with the "User Inputs a Rent" Use Case

"I see a problem with that last step," you say. "The Rent Record stores the rent according to apartment number and month (see Figure 16.2). But the Rent Input Screen is passing the tenant's name to the Rent Record, not the apartment number."

"Maybe the Rent Input Screen should get the apartment number from the user instead of the name," Bryan suggests.

"That's no good," Beverly says. "When I get a check from someone, it has their name on it, not the apartment number. I want to be able to type in the name."

"If you type the tenant's name, can't the program figure out the apartment number?" asks Bryan.

"Where would it look that up?" you ask. "We don't have a list of tenants anywhere."

"Uh oh," says Bryan gloomily. "Trouble."

A New Tenant List Class

"Well, maybe we should have a tenant list," says Beverly.

"I think you're right," you say. "We haven't thought about it, but we need a place to put all the Tenant objects after they're created. They can't just float around randomly in the program." You make a new CRC card with the title Tenant List. "What should this class know?" you ask.

"I can't think of anything," Beverly says. "It just stores the tenants."

"But one of its responsibilities should be finding a tenant's apartment number if you tell it the tenant's name," says Bryan. "That's what we need in the *User inputs a rent* use case.

"And it needs a way for the user to add a new tenant to it," you say. "That's how we'll get new tenants into the program."

"And it should be able to display itself," Beverly says. "It would be handy to see who's living where."

You make a new CRC card for the Tenant List, as shown in Figure 16.16.

"All right," you say. "Now we've added another class to the program, and we can finish up the use case for the user entering a rent."

A New Tenant Input Screen Class

"Not so fast," Beverly says. "The user needs to insert tenants into the Tenant List object, but we don't have a tenant input screen."

"My fault," you say. "You're absolutely right, we should add a class to represent that screen." Beverly, you think, is turning out to be very good at this. You make up a new CRC card, as shown in Figure 16.17.

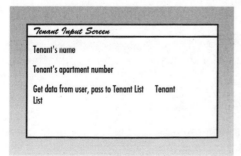

Figure 16.17   A new CRC Card for the Tenant Input Screen class.

"Now," you ask, "can we can get back to the use case for *User inputting a rent payment*?" This time there are no objections, and you modify the card as shown in Figure 16.18.

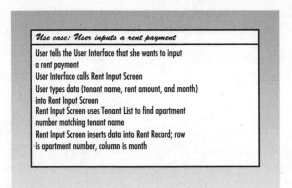

Figure 16.18   Final use case: user inputs a rent.

Use Case: The User Inputs a Tenant

"I hate to say this," you tell the group, "but I think we need another use case."

"I know what you're thinking," Beverly says. "Inputting the data for a new tenant."

"Exactly." You make up a new card for this use case, as shown in Figure 16.19

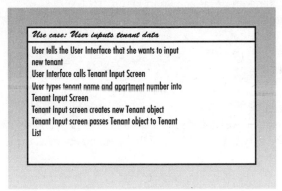

Figure 16.19   Use case: user inputs a tenant.

"Well at least this use case didn't reveal the need for any new classes," Beverly says, breathing a sigh of relief.

Revised CRC card for Rent Input Screen

"But there's something else," Bryan says. "If the Rent Input Screen has to look up each tenant on this new Tenant List object to find the tenant's apartment number, doesn't that make Tenant List a collaborator of the Rent Input Screen?"

You think about that for a moment. "That's a good point," you tell Bryan. You revise the Rent Input Screen CRC card, as shown in Figure 16.20.

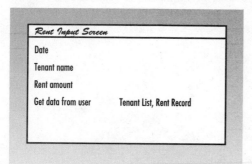

Figure 16.20 The revised CRC Card for the Rent Input Screen.

Revised CRC Card for User Interface Class

"Adding the Tenant List class is certainly having a ripple effect," says Beverly. "We're adding new classes and use cases all over the place."

"It's chaotic!" Bryan says. "It's making me uneasy. I thought we had everything all figured out, and now we've added all kinds of new stuff." He's looking a little panic-stricken.

"That's how this process is supposed to work," you explain to him. "You can't get all the classes right just with the CRC cards, so you try the use-case approach to see if more classes show up. In this case, they did."

"It's not a science at all," complains Bryan. "More like a town meeting."

"What's worse," you tell Bryan, "Is that we're not done. If the user is going to be able to add a new tenant, then what happens to the Interface object?"

"We need to add the Tenant Input Screen as a collaborator of the User Interface class," Beverly says.

You make the change, as shown in Figure 16.21.

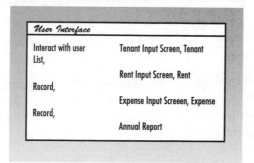

Figure 16.21 The revised CRC card for the User Interface class.

The Remaining Use Cases

Creating the remaining use cases doesn't lead to any complications. Figures 16.22, 16.23, and 16.24 show how they look.

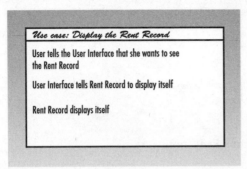

Figure 16.22   Use case: user displays the Rent Record.

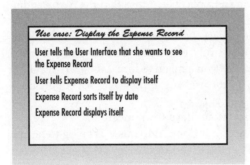

Figure 16.23   Use case: user displays the Expense Record.

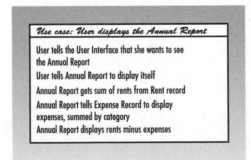

Figure 16.24   Use case: user displays the Annual Report.

You rewrite the original list of use cases:

- User inputs a tenant

- User inputs a rent payment

- User inputs an expense

- User displays the Rent Record

- User displays the Expense Record

- User displays the Annual Report

At this point our CRC modeling group has done its job, creating a group of CRC cards representing classes, along with their responsibilities and collaborators. We'll let Beverly and Bryan get back to their normal lives. You, in your role as software developer, still have considerable work ahead of you.

Simplifications

In the preceding discussion, we simplified the creation of the use cases by leaving out various alternative scenarios that might occur if the user does something unusual. For example, what happens if the user enters a rent payment and the program can't find a name on the tenant list that matches the name the user types in? Or what happens if the user asks to see the Expense Report, but no expense amounts have been entered? Typically, the alternative scenarios are numbered and included in the same use case description. Figure 16.25 shows a use case that includes two alternative scenarios.

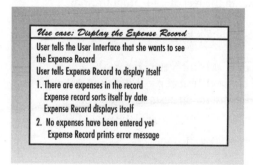

Figure 16.25   Revised use case: user displays the Expense Record.

During the creation of the use cases, it's quite possible that the BDEs will come up with additions they would like to make to the program's capabilities. Beverly might realize, for example, that being able to delete a tenant from the Tenant List might be useful, in case a real tenant moved out. It might also be useful to be able to modify entries in all the reports. Including new program capabilities would involve adding new responsibilities to some CRC cards and possibly adding new classes. For simplicity, we haven't included these possibilities in our example.

Another issue we've ignored is that of persistence. A *persistent* object is one whose data can be saved to disk. In the Landlord program, you would probably want to make the Tenant List, the Rent Record, and the Expense Record into persistent classes, so the information contained in them would not be lost when the program terminates. Again, for simplicity, we ignore this feature.

Class Relationships

Class relationships describe how classes within a program interact with each other. They're important in object-oriented design because they help us understand how a program is organized, and this understanding helps us write the actual code for the program. In the development of the Landlord program we'll apply what we learn about class relationships to creating a class diagram for the program. The class diagram will then help with the actual coding.

When we use natural languages like English to describe object-oriented programs, we generally use verbs to describe relationships between classes, while nouns are used to describe the classes themselves. For example, one of the statements in the use cases described earlier is "Rent Input Screen uses Tenant List to find apartment number." Here the relationship between the Rent Input Screen class and the Tenant List class is described by the verb "uses."

This is another way in which the object-oriented paradigm is analogous to the real world. In natural-language descriptions we use verbs to describe relationships between nouns: "Chris *buys* groceries," "Sandy *asks* Bob."

In this section we'll discuss three important class relationships: association, aggregation, and generalization. Be aware that the names of some class relationships are different in the realm of object-oriented design than they are in the rest of C++ programming. For example, we use the term "inheritance" in C++, but "generalization" in OOD. OOD was originally developed in association with the Smalltalk language, which has its own vocabulary.

If you do further reading in OOD, you should also know that, before the advent of UML, writers used a variety of terms to describe class relationships. What the UML calls association, for example, was called a *uses relationship*, an *instance relationship*, and other terms in older books. Even today, different writers use relationship terms in different ways.

Attribute

Let's start with a class relationship we already know about: attributes, which is another name for member data. Basic variable types like `int` are typically used as attributes. However, it's also possible for attributes to consist of objects of other classes. For example, we've seen examples where a string object called name is an attributes of the employee class.

An attribute is said to model the *has a* relationship. We say that an employee has a name, for example.

Because the attribute is entirely enclosed within the class, we don't usually consider it when working with class diagrams, which depict relationships between classes. However, we're mentioning it here to clarify the difference between attributes and other class relationships.

Some writers say that an attribute class has a *weak association* with the class that contains it. This differentiates attributes from normal associations, which we'll look at next.

Association

An association is the most commonly-used relationship between objects. In an association, one object uses another object to help it carry out a task. For this reason, association is often called a *uses* relationship.

Use cases (or sometimes the Problem Summary Statement) may contain clues to associations. Terms like "uses," "sends to," "gets from," "depends on," "requests," or "tells" probably indicate associations.

In our Landlord program, in the "User displays the Annual Report" use case described earlier, there are the sentences "Annual Report gets sum of rents from Rent Record" and "Annual Report tells Expense Record to display expenses." From these statements we can infer that there are associations between Annual Report and Rent Record, and between Annual Report and Expense Record.

In UML class diagrams, associations are indicated by lines, as shown in Figure 16.26.

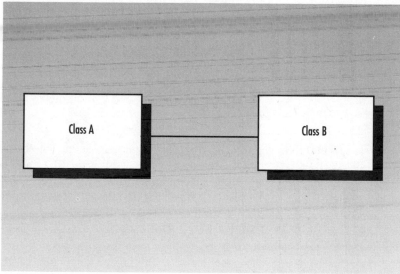

Figure 16.26   Association.

Classes that collaborate are usually related through associations. Thus we can use the collaboration part of the CRC cards to indicate when an association exists on the class diagram.

Navigability

Associations can go both ways at once, with both classes being able to make requests of the other. More often they go only one way, with class A asking class B to help it out, but class B not asking class A for anything.

The direction of an association is called *navigability*, and is represented on UML class diagrams by a small open arrowhead pointing toward the collaborator (B). If each class asks the other to do something, then no arrows are used; just an unadorned line. Figure 16.27 shows association with navigability from A to B.

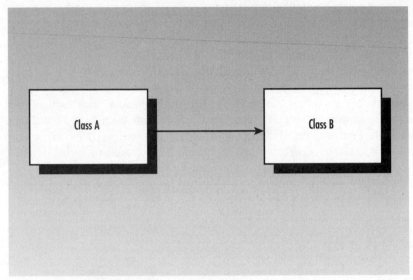

Figure 16.27 Association with navigability.

Aggregation

The second major class relationship is *aggregation*. Aggregation means that one object (call it A) *contains* other objects (say B, C, and D). Another way to say this is that B, C, and D are *part of* A. Examples are an Address Book object containing many People objects, and a Seminar containing many Students. Aggregation is sometimes called the *part-of* relationship.

In UML terminology the object that contains the *parts* is called the *whole*. In the paragraph above, A is the whole, while B, C, and D are the parts.

In UML class diagrams, aggregation is depicted by lines from the parts meeting at an empty diamond-shaped arrowhead pointing to the whole. This is shown in Figure 16.28.

Composition

Composition is a stronger kind of aggregation, in which the parts are necessary to the whole and are more permanently bound to it. For example, a calculator object might be composed of a screen object, some button objects, and an Integrated Circuit object.

Formally, a composition relationship must satisfy three criteria. First, as in aggregation, Classes B, C, and D are part of A. Second, B, C, and D cannot be part of any other class. Third, B, C, and D have lifetimes contemporaneous with A. That is, they are created when A is created, and destroyed when A is destroyed.

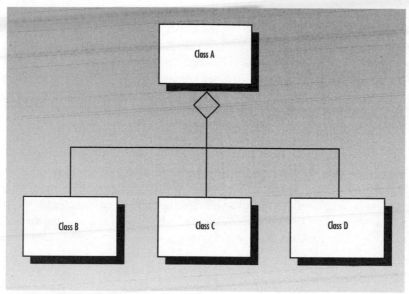

Figure 16.28 Aggregation.

In UML class diagrams, composition is depicted with lines from the parts that meet at a filled-in diamond-shaped arrowhead pointing to the whole. This is shown in Figure 16.29. (Composition may also be shown by placing the icon for the contained class within the icon for the class that contains it.)

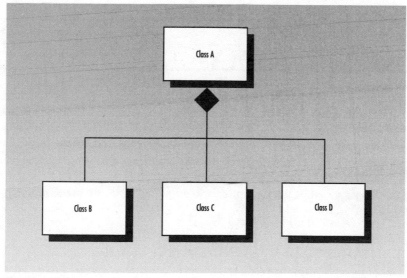

Figure 16.29 Composition.

Objects and Classes

Association, aggregation, and composition are actually relationships between objects, not classes. This is confusing, because the rectangular symbols on a class diagram seem to represent classes, not objects. How then can lines between these rectangles represent relationships between objects? The best way to think about this is to consider the rectangles as representing both a class and at the same time objects of that class.

Multiplicity

Sometimes exactly one object of class A relates to exactly one object of class B. In other situations, many objects of class A will relate to one object of class B. The number of objects involved on both sides of a relationship is called the *multiplicity* of the relationship. In class diagrams, symbols are used at both ends of the relationship line to indicate multiplicity. Table 16.1 shows the UML multiplicity symbols.

Table 16.1 The UML Multiplicity Symbols

Symbol	Meaning
0	None
1	One
*	Some (0 to infinity)
0..1	None or one
1..*	One or more
2..4	Two, three, or four
7,11	Seven or eleven

Figure 16.30 shows some relationships between classes, with their associated multiplicities. Each object of class A is an aggregate of exactly four objects of class B. Each object of class A may be associated with zero or more objects of class C, and each object of class C is associated with exactly one object of class A. Each object of class A is also associated with two, three, or four objects of class D. Each object of class B may or may not be associated with one object of class E.

This information provided by the multiplicity notation will be useful to the programmer in writing actual code.

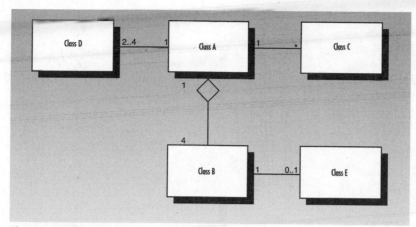

Figure 16.30 Multiplicity.

Generalization

Generalization is another name for inheritance (actually public inheritance). In OOD the terms *superclass* and *subclass* are often used instead of base class and derived class. The superclass is a generalization of the subclass, in the same way the Mammal class is a generalization of the Tiger class. Generalization is often called the *is a kind of* or simply the *is a* (or even *is a*) relationship.

Generalization (unlike association and composition) is a relationship defined at the class level, not the object level. Being defined on the class level means that all the objects of the class must obey the relationship.

Generalizations can often be identified from use cases or the Problem Summary Statement by looking for phrases like "is a kind of."

In UML class diagrams, generalization is indicated by a line from the subclass (child) terminating in an open triangle-shaped arrowhead pointing to the superclass (parent). Figure 16.31 shows how this looks where B is a subclass of A.

There aren't any generalization relationships in the Landlord program. However, you might imagine a situation in which the three data input screen classes, "Tenant Input Screen," "Rent Input Screen," and "Expense Input Screen," are descended from a superclass called "Input Screen." In this case each of the three specific input screen classes could be described (perhaps in the Problem Summary Statement) as a "*kind of* Input Screen class."

In the Landlord program this generalization isn't implemented because no responsibilities are shared by these classes, despite their similar names. (If a GUI were used in the program, and the input screens were windows, generalization would probably be more appropriate because there would be more common responsibilities.)

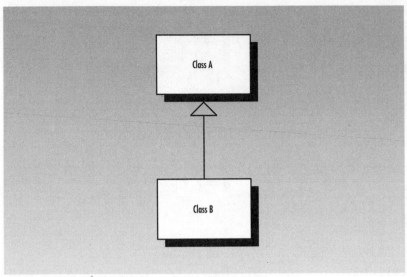

Figure 16.31 Generalization.

Coupling and Cohesion

Coupling describes the strength of the connections between classes. In a good program design, classes are coupled as loosely as possible. This makes it easier to understand the class relationships and implement robust, maintainable code.

If you find two classes that are highly coupled (send many kinds of messages to each other, for example), maybe you should consider merging them into a single class.

Attribution is considered to be the weakest coupling, followed by association. Aggregation and generalization constitute stronger coupling.

Cohesion refers to the conceptual unity of a class. A class should represent a single, easily-understood concept, and its responsibilities should all relate directly to this concept. Such a concept is often called the *key abstraction* of the class. In a good design, all classes have tight cohesion.

If you find yourself with a class with loose cohesion (its purpose is vague, or involves two or more major abstractions), you might consider breaking it into several classes.

Class Diagrams

Now that we've learned something about class relationships, let's try to put together a class diagram that depicts the class relationships for the Landlord program. This is our last step before we start writing code.

Why do we need a class diagram? The CRC cards and the collection of use cases is not a very convenient way to transmit information. The class diagram provides a clear and compact way to show class relationships. Also, developing the class diagram gives us another chance to rethink class relationships, and see if we've forgotten any classes or responsibilities.

Arranging the CRC Cards

Start off by arranging the CRC cards so each card is near its collaborators. Cards with more collaborators should be placed in the center, cards with fewer collaborators near the periphery.

The way the cards are arranged on the table will be duplicated on the class diagram. It's a lot easier to move the cards around than to draw and redraw a bunch of rectangles on a sheet of paper or even on a whiteboard.

Figure 16.32 shows a possible arrangement for the CRC cards for the Landlord program.

Figure 16.32   Landlord CRC cards arrangement.

Once you've arranged the CRC cards to your satisfaction, you can copy the contents of each CRC card into a rectangle drawn on the class diagram. If you're using a big piece of paper or a whiteboard, you can include responsibilities within each class rectangle. Leave out collaborators, which will be represented on the class diagram by relationships. Figure 16.33 shows a class rectangle that includes this information.

If you want to keep everything on letter-size paper, then you'll probably need to leave out the responsibilities and include only a class name inside each class rectangle. You can show responsibilities on separate sheets of paper.

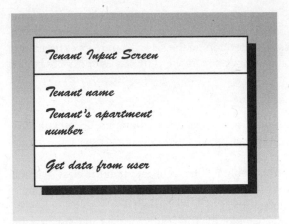

Figure 16.33   Class rectangle with responsibilities.

Associations in Landlord

Generally speaking, collaborations in the CRC cards translate into associations in the class diagram. Table 16.2 shows a list of collaborations, taken from the CRC cards.

Table 16.2   List of Collaborations

Class	Collaborator
Tenant	none
Expense	none
Rent Input Screen	Tenant List, Rent Record
Rent Record	none
Expense Input Screen	Expense Record
Expense Record	none
Tenant Input Screen	Tenant List
Annual Report	Rent Record, Expense Record
User Interface	Tenant Input Screen, Tenant List, Rent Input Screen, Rent Record, Expense Input Screen, Expense Record Annual Report

Wherever there was a collaboration in the CRC cards, draw a line representing an association from the initiating class to the servant class. As we've seen, associations are drawn as lines from one class to another, with a small arrowhead pointing to the server.

Aggregations in Landlord

We have two instances of aggregation in the Landlord program. Class Tenant List holds a number of Tenant objects, and class Expense Record holds a number of Expense objects. (There's no aggregation in the Rent Record class because rents are basic variables, not class objects.)

There are no generalization relationships (inheritance) in the Landlord program, nor are there any examples of composition.

Figure 16.34 shows the class diagram for the Landlord program. Because of space limitations it shows only the class names, not their responsibilities.

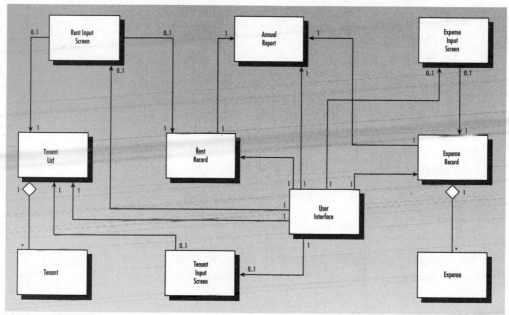

Figure 16.34   Class diagram for the Landlord program.

Writing the Program

Finally, armed with the CRC cards, use cases, the class diagram, and the detailed notes recorded by the scribe, you can crank up your compiler and start writing the actual code.

The Header file

The best place to start coding is the .H file, where you define class interfaces, rather than the details of their implementations. As we've discussed before, the declarations in the .H file are the public part of the classes, the part that users of these classes see. The function bodies in the .CPP file are the implementations, which should be invisible to class users.

The creation of the .H file is an intermediate step between design and the nitty-gritty of writing method bodies. Here's the LANDLORD.H file:

```
//landlord.h
//header file for landlord.cpp -- contains class declarations, etc.
#include <iostream>
#include <vector>
#pragma warning (disable:4786)  //for set (microsoft compilers only)
#include <set>
#include <string>
#include <algorithm>            //for sort()
#include <numeric>              //for accumulate()

using namespace std;
/////////////////////////////external methods//////////////////////////
void getaLine(string& inStr);   // get line of text
char getaChar();                // get a character

/////////////////////////////class tenant//////////////////////////////
class tenant
    {
    private:
    string name;      // tenant's name
    int aptNumber;    // tenant's apartment number
    // other tenant information (phone, etc.) could go here

    public:
    tenant(string n, int aNo);
    ~tenant();
    int getAptNumber();
    // needed for use in 'set'
    friend bool operator < (const tenant&, const tenant&);
    friend bool operator == (const tenant&, const tenant&);
    // for I/O
    friend ostream& operator << (ostream&, const tenant&);
};  // end class tenant
/////////////////////////class compareTenants//////////////////////////
class compareTenants  //function object --  compares tenants
    {
    public:
    bool operator () (tenant*, tenant*) const;
    };

/////////////////////////class tenantList//////////////////////////////
class tenantList
    {
    private:
    // set of pointers to tenants
    set<tenant*, compareTenants> setPtrsTens;
    set<tenant*, compareTenants>::iterator iter;

    public:
    ~tenantList();                // destructor (deletes tenants)
    void insertTenant(tenant*);   // put tenant on list
```

```cpp
   int getAptNo(string);          // return apartment number
   void display();                // display tenant list
   };  // end class tenantList


/////////////////////////class tenantInputScreen////////////////////
class tenantInputScreen
   {
   private:
   tenantList* ptrTenantList;
   string tName;
   int aptNo;

   public:
   tenantInputScreen(tenantList* ptrTL) : ptrTenantList(ptrTL)
      { /* empty */ }
   void getTenant();
   };  //end class tenantInputScreen

/////////////////////////////class rentRow/////////////////////////////
// one row of the rent record: an address and 12 rent amounts
class rentRow
   {
   private:
   int aptNo;
   float rent[12];

   public:
   rentRow(int);                  // 1-arg ctor
   void setRent(int, float);      // record rent for one month
   float getSumOfRow();           // return sum of rents in row
   // needed to store in 'set'
   friend bool operator < (const rentRow&, const rentRow&);
   friend bool operator == (const rentRow&, const rentRow&);
   // for output
   friend ostream& operator << (ostream&, const rentRow&);
   };  // end class rentRow

////////////////////////////////////////////////////////////////////////
class compareRows  //function object --  compares rentRows
   {
   public:
      bool operator () (rentRow*, rentRow*) const;
   };

/////////////////////////////class rentRecord////////////////////////
class rentRecord
   {
   private:
   // set of pointers to rentRow objects (one per tenant)
   set<rentRow*, compareRows> setPtrsRR;
   set<rentRow*, compareRows>::iterator iter;

   public:
```

```
        ~rentRecord();
        void insertRent(int, int, float);
        void display();
        float getSumOfRents();          // sum all rents in record
        };  // end class rentRecord

//////////////////////////class rentInputScreen//////////////////
class rentInputScreen
    {
    private:
    tenantList* ptrTenantList;
    rentRecord* ptrRentRecord;

    string renterName;
    float rentPaid;
    int month;
    int aptNo;

    public:
    rentInputScreen(tenantList* ptrTL, rentRecord* ptrRR) :
                    ptrTenantList(ptrTL), ptrRentRecord(ptrRR)
        { /*empty*/ }
    void getRent();             //rent for one tenant and one month
    };  // end class rentInputScreen

//////////////////////////////class expense/////////////////////////
class expense
    {
    public:
    int month, day;
    string category, payee;
    float amount;
    expense()
        {  }
    expense(int m, int d, string c, string p, float a) :
          month(m), day(d), category(c), payee(p), amount(a)
      { /*empty */ }
    // needed for use in 'set'
    friend bool operator < (const expense&, const expense&);
    friend bool operator == (const expense&, const expense&);
    // needed for output
    friend ostream& operator << (ostream&, const expense&);
    };  // end class expense
/////////////////////////////////////////////////////////////////
class compareDates  //function object--compares expenses
    {
    public:
       bool operator () (expense*, expense*) const;
    };
/////////////////////////////////////////////////////////////////
class compareCategories  //function object--compares expenses
    {
    public:
```

```
      bool operator () (expense*, expense*) const;
   };


//////////////////////////class expenseRecord//////////////////////
class expenseRecord
   {
   private:
   // vector of pointers to expenses
   vector<expense*> vectPtrsExpenses;
   vector<expense*>::iterator iter;

   public:
   ~expenseRecord();
   void insertExp(expense*);
   void display();
   float displaySummary();         // used by annualReport
   };   // end class expenseRecord


//////////////////////class expenseInputScreen///////////////////////
class expenseInputScreen
   {
   private:
   expenseRecord* ptrExpenseRecord;

   public:
   expenseInputScreen(expenseRecord*);
   void getExpense();
   };   // end class expenseInputScreen


//////////////////////////class annualReport/////////////////////////
class annualReport
   {
   private:
   rentRecord* ptrRR;
   expenseRecord* ptrER;
   float expenses, rents;

   public:
   annualReport(rentRecord*, expenseRecord*);
   void display();
   };   // end class annualReport


//////////////////////////class userInterface////////////////////////
class userInterface
   {
   private:
   tenantList*          ptrTenantList;
   tenantInputScreen*   ptrTenantInputScreen;
   rentRecord*          ptrRentRecord;
   rentInputScreen*     ptrRentInputScreen;
   expenseRecord*       ptrExpenseRecord;
   expenseInputScreen*  ptrExpenseInputScreen;
   annualReport*        ptrAnnualReport;
```

```
    char ch;

    public:
    userInterface();
    ~userInterface();
    void interact();
    };  // end class userInterfac
/////////////////////////////end file landlord.h/////////////////////////
```

Classes Declarations

Declaring classes is the easy part. Most class declarations arise directly from the classes depicted on the CRC cards and on the class diagram. The names are changed from the multi-word English versions to single-word computerese, so that, for example, Tenant List becomes `tenantList`.

A few new classes have been added. We probably won't actually discover that we need classes until we start to write method bodies, but it will be clearer to mention them here.

First, when looking over the attributes of the Rent Record, you will probably realize that each line of the display consists of an address and 12 rent amounts. It seems reasonable to combine these quantities into a class called `rentRow`. A more experienced facilitator might have suggested this in the CRC phase, but no one gets everything right the first time.

Second, we'll find that we're storing pointers to objects in various kinds of STL containers. This means that we must define comparison objects for these containers, as described in Chapter 15, "The Standard Template Library." These comparison objects are actually classes named `compareTenants`, `compareRows`, `compareDates`, and `compareCategories`.

Attribute Declarations

Many of the attributes (member data) for each class can be determined from the Responsibilities part of the CRC cards. For example, the Tenant CRC card shows Name and Apartment Number as attributes. These translate into `name` and `aptNumber` in the `tenant` class declaration.

Other attributes are derived from the Collaborators field of the CRC cards. For example, the revised version of the Rent Input Screen, shown in Figure 16.20, shows that Tenant List and Rent Record are collaborators of this class. Collaborators on the CRC cards typically become attributes that are pointers or references to other classes. This is because you can't collaborate with someone if you can't find them. Thus the `rentInputScreen` class has the attributes `ptrTenantList` and `ptrRentRecord`, and pointers to `tenantList` and `rentRecord`.

Aggregate Declarations

Aggregates are shown on the class diagram and referred to as *lists* on the CRC cards. Usually, aggregates become containers that are attributes of the containing class (the whole).

Neither the CRC cards nor the class diagram suggest what sort of container should be used for these lists. As a programmer, you'll need to choose an appropriate container for each aggregate, whether it's a simple array, an STL container, or something else. In Landlord, we made the following choices:

- The `tenantList` class contains an STL `set` of pointers to `tenant` objects.

- The `rentRecord` class contains a `set` of pointers to `rentRow` objects.

- The `expenseRecord` class contains a `vector` of pointers to `expense` objects.

We used sets for `tenantList` and `rentRecord` to provide fast access. We used a vector for `expenseRecord` because we need to sort the `Expense` objects both by date and by category, and vectors (unlike sets) can be sorted efficiently.

In all the aggregations, we chose to store pointers, rather than actual objects, to avoid the copying that takes place every time an actual object is stored. Storing objects directly might be appropriate in situations where the objects are small and there aren't many of them. Of course, the performance penalty for storing objects isn't great in a small program like this, but for efficiency you should always consider storing pointers.

Method Declarations

Many methods (member functions) can be inferred from the use cases. For example, let's examine the first use case card, "User inputs an expense," shown in Figure 16.14.

The first statement on this card is "User tells the User Interface that she wants to input an expense." A single method in the `userInterface` class can take care of figuring out what the user wants to do, such as inputting a rent or displaying expenses. This method can then dispatch control to the appropriate object (`rentInputScreen` or `expenseReport`). We'll call this method `interact()`, because it interacts with the user.

The next three statements in the use case are "User Interface calls Expense Input Screen," "User types data into Expense Input Screen," and "Expense input screen creates a new expense object." These statements can all be handled by a method of the class `expenseInputScreen`. We can call this method `getExpense()`.

The last two statements are "Expense Input Screen passes new Expense object to Expense Record," and "Expense Record inserts new Expense object into list of Expenses." Again, these really describe the same method of the `expenseRecord` class, which we can call `insertExp()`. This function will take the new expense object as an argument and insert it into the container in `expenseRecord`.

Similar analysis of the other use cases will reveal most of the other methods.

The .CPP Files

The .CPP files contain the method bodies whose declarations were given in the .H file. Writing the code for these methods should be fairly straightforward at this point. You know the function name, what it's supposed to do, and probably the arguments passed to it.

We've separated the class method definitions from `main()`, which is in the short LORDAPP.CPP file. In `main()` a `userInterface` object is created and its `interact()` method is called. Here's the LORDAPP.CPP file:

```
// lordApp.cpp
// client file for apart program
#include "landlord.h"

int main()
   {
   userInterface theUserInterface;

   theUserInterface.interact();
   return 0;
   }
//////////////////////////end file lordApp.cpp//////////////////////
```

Finally, here's the LANDLORD.CPP file, which contains all the class method definitions.

```
//landlord.cpp
//models the finances for an apartment building
#include "landlord.h" //for class declarations, etc.

//////////////////////////global functions//////////////////////////
void getaLine(string& inStr)      // get line of text
   {
   char temp[21];
   cin.get(temp, 20, '\n');
   cin.ignore(20, '\n');
   inStr = temp;
   }
//------------------------------------------------------------
char getaChar()                    // get a character
   {
   char ch = cin.get();
   cin.ignore(80, '\n');
   return ch;
   }
//------------------------------------------------------------

//////////////////////////methods for class tenant//////////////////////////
tenant::tenant(string n, int aNo) : name(n), aptNumber(aNo)
   { /* empty */ }
//------------------------------------------------------------
tenant::~tenant()
   { /* empty */ }
//------------------------------------------------------------
int tenant::getAptNumber()
   { return aptNumber; }
//------------------------------------------------------------
bool operator < (const tenant& t1, const tenant& t2)
   { return t1.name < t2.name; }
//------------------------------------------------------------
bool operator == (const tenant& t1, const tenant& t2)
   { return t1.name == t2.name; }
```

```cpp
//··········································································
ostream& operator << (ostream& s, const tenant& t)
   { s << t.aptNumber << '\t' << t.name << endl;  return s; }
//--------------------------------------------------------------------

///////////////////method for class tenantInputScreen///////////////
void tenantInputScreen::getTenant()           //get tenant info
   {
   cout << "Enter tenant's name (George Smith): ";
   getaLine(tName);
   cout << "Enter tenant's apartment number (101): ";
   cin >> aptNo;
   cin.ignore(80, '\n');                       //make tenant
   tenant* ptrTenant = new tenant(tName, aptNo);
   ptrTenantList->insertTenant(ptrTenant); //send to tenant list
   }
///////////////////////////////////////////////////////////////////////
bool compareTenants::operator () (tenant* ptrT1,
                                  tenant* ptrT2) const
   { return *ptrT1 < *ptrT2; }
//--------------------------------------------------------------------

///////////////////////methods for class tenantList/////////////////
tenantList::~tenantList()                      //destructor
   {
   while( !setPtrsTens.empty() )               //delete all tenants,
      {                                        //remove ptrs from set
      iter = setPtrsTens.begin();
      delete *iter;
      setPtrsTens.erase(iter);
      }
   }  // end ~tenantList()
//--------------------------------------------------------------------
void tenantList::insertTenant(tenant* ptrT)
   {
   setPtrsTens.insert(ptrT);                   //insert
   }
//--------------------------------------------------------------------
 int tenantList::getAptNo(string tName) //name on list?
    {
    int aptNo;
    tenant dummy(tName, 0);
    iter = setPtrsTens.begin();
    while( iter != setPtrsTens.end() )
       {
       aptNo = (*iter)->getAptNumber(); //look for tenant
       if(dummy == **iter++)             //on the list?
          return aptNo;                  //yes
       }
    return -1;                          //no
    }
//--------------------------------------------------------------------
 void tenantList::display()                     //display tenant list
```

```
      {
      cout << "\nApt#\tTenant name\n-------------------\n";
      if( setPtrsTens.empty() )
         cout << "***No tenants***\n";
      else
         {
         iter = setPtrsTens.begin();
         while( iter != setPtrsTens.end() )
            cout << **iter++;
         }
      }  // end display()
//------------------------------------------------------------

///////////////////////methods for class rentRow///////////////////
rentRow::rentRow(int an) : aptNo(an)     // 1-arg constructor
   { fill( &rent[0], &rent[12], 0); }
//------------------------------------------------------------
void rentRow::setRent(int m, float am)
   { rent[m] = am; }
//------------------------------------------------------------
float rentRow::getSumOfRow()             // sum of rents in row
   { return accumulate( &rent[0], &rent[12], 0); }
//------------------------------------------------------------
bool operator < (const rentRow& t1, const rentRow& t2)
   { return t1.aptNo < t2.aptNo; }
//------------------------------------------------------------
bool operator == (const rentRow& t1, const rentRow& t2)
   { return t1.aptNo == t2.aptNo; }
//------------------------------------------------------------
ostream& operator << (ostream& s, const rentRow& an)
   {
   s << an.aptNo << '\t';                //print apartment number
   for(int j=0; j<12; j++)               //print 12 rents
      {
      if(an.rent[j] == 0)
         s << "  0  ";
      else
         s << an.rent[j] << "  ";
      }
   s << endl;
   return s;
   }


////////////////////////////////////////////////////////////////
bool compareRows::operator () (rentRow* ptrR1,
                               rentRow* ptrR2) const
   { return *ptrR1 < *ptrR2; }

///////////////////////methods for class rentRecord///////////////////
rentRecord::~rentRecord()                //destructor
   {
   while( !setPtrsRR.empty() )           //delete rent rows,
      {                                  //remove ptrs from set
```

```
            iter = setPtrsRR.begin();
            delete *iter;
            setPtrsRR.erase(iter);
            }
      }
//--------------------------------------------------------------
void rentRecord::insertRent(int aptNo, int month, float amount)
   {
   rentRow searchRow(aptNo);         //temp row with same aptNo
   iter = setPtrsRR.begin();                   //search setPtrsRR
   while( iter != setPtrsRR.end() )
      {
      if(searchRow==**iter)                    //rentRow found?
         {                                     //yes,
         (*iter)->setRent(month, amount); //put rent in row
         return;
         }
      else
         iter++;
      }                                        //didn't find it
   rentRow* ptrRow = new rentRow(aptNo);  //make new row
   ptrRow->setRent(month, amount);            //put rent in row
   setPtrsRR.insert(ptrRow);                  //put row in vector
   } // end insertRent()
//--------------------------------------------------------------
void rentRecord::display()
   {
   cout << "\nAptNo\tJan  Feb  Mar  Apr  May  Jun  "
        <<            "Jul  Aug  Sep  Oct  Nov  Dec\n"
        << "................................."
        << "------------------------------\n";
   if( setPtrsRR.empty() )
      cout << "***No rents***\n";
   else
      {
      iter = setPtrsRR.begin();
      while( iter != setPtrsRR.end() )
         cout << **iter++;
      }
   }
//--------------------------------------------------------------
float rentRecord::getSumOfRents()    // return sum of all rents
   {
   float sumRents = 0.0;
   iter = setPtrsRR.begin();
   while( iter != setPtrsRR.end() )
      {
      sumRents += (*iter)->getSumOfRow();
      iter++;
      }
   return sumRents;
   }
//--------------------------------------------------------------
```

```
/////////////////methods for class rentInputScreen//////////////
void rentInputScreen::getRent()
   {
   while(true)
      {
      cout << "Enter tenant's name: ";
      getaLine(renterName);
      aptNo = ptrTenantList->getAptNo(renterName);
      if(aptNo > 0)                       // if name found,
         break;                           // get rent amount
      else                                // ask again
         cout << "No tenant with that name.\n";
      }
   cout << "Enter amount paid (345.67): ";
   cin >> rentPaid;
   cin.ignore(80, '\n');
   cout << "Enter month rent is for (1-12): ";
   cin >> month;
   cin.ignore(80, '\n');
   month--;                              // internal is 0-11
   ptrRentRecord->insertRent(aptNo, month, rentPaid);
   }  // end getRent()
//-------------------------------------------------------------


///////////////////methods for class expense/////////////////////
bool operator < (const expense& e1, const expense& e2)
   {                                // compares dates
   if(e1.month == e2.month)         // if same month,
      return e1.day < e2.day;       // compare days
   else                             // otherwise,
      return e1.month < e2.month;   // compare months
   }
//-------------------------------------------------------------
bool operator == (const expense& e1, const expense& e2)
   { return e1.month == e2.month && e1.day == e2.day; }
//-------------------------------------------------------------
ostream& operator << (ostream& s, const expense& exp)
   {
   s << exp.month << '/' << exp.day << '\t' << exp.payee << '\t' ;
   s << exp.amount << '\t' << exp.category << endl;
   return s;
   }
//-------------------------------------------------------------


//////////////////////////////////////////////////////////////////
bool compareDates::operator () (expense* ptrE1,
                                expense* ptrE2) const
   { return *ptrE1 < *ptrE2; }
//-------------------------------------------------------------


//////////////////////////////////////////////////////////////////
bool compareCategories::operator () (expense* ptrE1,
                                     expense* ptrE2) const
```

```
      { return ptrE1->category < ptrE2->category; }
//-------------------------------------------------------------

///////////////////////methods for class expenseRecord////////////////
expenseRecord::~expenseRecord()            //destructor
   {
   while( !vectPtrsExpenses.empty() )      //delete expense objects,
      {                                    //remove ptrs from vector
      iter = vectPtrsExpenses.begin();
      delete *iter;
      vectPtrsExpenses.erase(iter);
      }
   }
//-------------------------------------------------------------
void expenseRecord::insertExp(expense* ptrExp)
   { vectPtrsExpenses.push_back(ptrExp); }
//-------------------------------------------------------------
void expenseRecord::display()
   {
   cout << "\nDate\tPayee\t\tAmount\tCategory\n"
        << "-------------------------------------\n";
   if( vectPtrsExpenses.size() == 0 )
      cout << "***No expenses***\n";
   else
      {
      sort( vectPtrsExpenses.begin(),         // sort by date
            vectPtrsExpenses.end(), compareDates() );
      iter = vectPtrsExpenses.begin();
      while( iter != vectPtrsExpenses.end() )
         cout << **iter++;
      }
   }
//-------------------------------------------------------------
float expenseRecord::displaySummary() // used by annualReport
   {
   float totalExpenses = 0;

   if( vectPtrsExpenses.size() == 0 )
      {
      cout << "\tAll categories\t0\n";
      return 0;
      }
   // sort by category
   sort( vectPtrsExpenses.begin(),
         vectPtrsExpenses.end(), compareCategories() );

   // for each category, sum the entries
   iter = vectPtrsExpenses.begin();
   string tempCat = (*iter)->category;
   float sum = 0.0;
   while( iter != vectPtrsExpenses.end() )
      {                                       //same category
      if(tempCat == (*iter)->category)
```

```
              sum += (*iter)->amount;
          else                              //different category
              {
              cout << '\t' << tempCat << '\t' << sum << endl;
              tempCat = (*iter)->category;
              sum = (*iter)->amount;        // add last entry
              }
          totalExpenses += sum;
          iter++;
          } // end while
      cout << '\t' << tempCat << '\t' << sum << endl;
      return totalExpenses;
      } // end displaySummary()
      //------------------------------------------------------------

//////////////methods for class expenseInputScreen//////////////
expenseInputScreen::expenseInputScreen(expenseRecord* per) :
                              ptrExpenseRecord(per)
      { /*empty*/ }
      //------------------------------------------------------------
void expenseInputScreen::getExpense()
      {
      int month, day;
      string category, payee;
      float amount;

      cout << "Enter month (1-12): ";
      cin >> month;
      cin.ignore(80, '\n');
      cout << "Enter day (1-31): ";
      cin >> day;
      cin.ignore(80, '\n');
      cout << "Enter expense category (Repairing, Utilities): ";
      getaLine(category);
      cout << "Enter payee "
          << "(Bob's Hardware, Big Electric Co): ";
      getaLine(payee);
      cout << "Enter amount (39.95): ";
      cin >> amount;
      cin.ignore(80, '\n');
      expense* ptrExpense = new
                  expense(month, day, category, payee, amount);
      ptrExpenseRecord->insertExp(ptrExpense);
      }
//----------------------------------------------------------------

//////////////////methods for class annualReport//////////////
annualReport::annualReport(rentRecord* pRR,
                          expenseRecord* pER) :
                                      ptrRR(pRR), ptrER(pER)
      { /* empty*/ }
      //------------------------------------------------------------
void annualReport::display()
```

```
   {
   cout << "Annual Summary\n--------------\n";
   cout << "Income\n";
   cout << "\tRent\t\t";
   rents = ptrRR->getSumOfRents();
   cout << rents << endl;

   cout << "Expenses\n";
   expenses = ptrER->displaySummary();
   cout << "\nBalance\t\t\t" << rents - expenses << endl;
   }
//------------------------------------------------------------

////////////////methods for class userInterface//////////////
userInterface::userInterface()
   {
   //reports exist for the life of the program
   ptrTenantList      = new tenantList;
   ptrRentRecord      = new rentRecord;
   ptrExpenseRecord   = new expenseRecord;
   ptrAnnualReport    = new annualReport(ptrRentRecord,
                                         ptrExpenseRecord);

   }
//------------------------------------------------------------
userInterface::~userInterface()
   {
   delete ptrTenantList;
   delete ptrRentRecord;
   delete ptrExpenseRecord;
   delete ptrAnnualReport;
   }
//------------------------------------------------------------
void userInterface::interact()
   {
   while(true)
      {
      cout << "Enter 'i' to input data, \n"
           << "        'd' to display a report, \n"
           << "        'q' to quit program: ";
      ch = getaChar();
      if(ch=='i')                               // enter data
         {
         cout << "Enter 't' to add tenant, \n"
              << "        'r' to record rent payment, \n"
              << "        'e' to record expense: ";
         ch = getaChar();
         switch(ch)
            {
            //input screens exist only while being used
            case 't': ptrTenantInputScreen =
               new tenantInputScreen(ptrTenantList);
               ptrTenantInputScreen->getTenant();
               delete ptrTenantInputScreen;
```

```
                        break;
              case 'r': ptrRentInputScreen =
                 new rentInputScreen(ptrTenantList, ptrRentRecord);
                 ptrRentInputScreen->getRent();
                 delete ptrRentInputScreen;
                 break;
              case 'e': ptrExpenseInputScreen =
                 new expenseInputScreen(ptrExpenseRecord);
                 ptrExpenseInputScreen->getExpense();
                 delete ptrExpenseInputScreen;
                 break;
              default: cout << "Unknown input option\n";
                 break;
              }  // end switch
           }  // end if
         else if(ch=='d')                          // display data
           {
           cout << "Enter 't' to display tenants, \n"
                << "      'r' to display rents\n"
                << "      'e' to display expenses, \n"
                << "      'a' to display annual report: ";
           ch = getaChar();
           switch(ch)
              {
              case 't': ptrTenantList->display();         break;
              case 'r': ptrRentRecord->display();         break;
              case 'e': ptrExpenseRecord->display();      break;
              case 'a': ptrAnnualReport->display();       break;
              default: cout << "Unknown display option\n";
              }  // end switch
           }  // end elseif
         else if(ch=='q')
           return;                                 // quit
         else
           cout << "Unknown option. Enter only 'i', 'd' or 'q'\n";
         }  // end while
      }  // end interact()
//////////////////////end of file apart.cpp//////////////////////
```

More Simplifications

The code we show for Landlord, while quite lengthy, still contains many simplifications. It uses a character-mode user interface, not the menus and windows of a modern Graphic User Interface. There's very little error-checking for the user's input. Only one year's worth of data can be handled.

Interacting with the Program

After going to the trouble to design and write the Landlord program, you may be interested in seeing some sample interaction with it. Here's how it looks when Beverly uses it to insert a new tenant's name and apartment number. First she enters **i** followed by **t**, for "insert tenant." Then she enters the relevant data at the prompts. (The prompts often show the proper format in parentheses.)

```
Enter 'i' to input data,
      'd' to display a report,
      'q' to quit program: i
Enter 't' to add a tenant,
      'r' to record a rent payment,
      'e' to record an expense: t
Enter tenant's name (George Smith): Harry Ellis
Enter tenant's apartment number: 101
```

After she's entered all the tenants, she can display the tenant list (for brevity we show only five of the twelve tenants):

```
Enter 'i' to input data,
      'd' to display a report,
      'q' to quit program: d
Enter 't' to display tenants,
      'r' to display rents,
      'e' to display expenses,
      'a' to display annual report: t
```

```
Apt#    Tenant name
-------------------
101     Harry Ellis
102     Wanda Brown
103     Peter Quan
104     Bill  Vasquez
201     Jane  Garth
```

To input a rent paid by a tenant, Beverly enters **i**, then **r**. (From now on we'll leave out the option lists displayed by the program.) The interaction looks like this:

```
Enter tenant's name: Wanda Brown
Enter amount paid (345.67): 595
Enter month rent is for (1-12): 5
```

Here Wanda Brown has sent a check for the May rent in the amount of $595. (The tenant's name must be typed exactly as it appears in the tenant list. A smarter program would be more flexible.)

To see the entire Rent Record, Beverly types **d** followed by **r**. Here's the result after the May rents have been received (for brevity we show the rents for only five of Beverly's 12 units):

```
AptNo  Jan  Feb  Mar  Apr  May  Jun  Jul  Aug  Sep  Oct  Nov  Dec
------------------------------------------------------------------
101    695  695  695  695  695   0    0    0    0    0    0    0
102    595  595  595  595  595   0    0    0    0    0    0    0
103    810  810  825  825  825   0    0    0    0    0    0    0
104    645  645  645  645  645   0    0    0    0    0    0    0
201    720  720  720  720  720   0    0    0    0    0    0    0
```

Notice that Beverly raised Peter Quan's rent in March.

To input an expense, Beverly types **i** followed by **e**. Here's some sample interaction:

```
Enter month: 1
Enter day: 15
Enter expense category (Repairing, Utilities): Utilities
Enter payee (Bob's Hardware, Big Electric Co): P. G. & E.
Enter amount: 427.23
```

To display the Expense Report, you type **d** and **e**. Here we show only the beginning of the report:

```
Date    Payee          Amount   Category
-------------------------------------------
1/3     First MegaBank  5187.30  Mortgage
1/8     City Water       963.10  Utilities
1/9     Steady State    4840.00  Insurance
1/15    P. G. & E.       727.23  Utilities
1/22    Sam's Hardware    54.81  Supplies
1/25    Ernie Glotz      150.00  Repairs
2/3     First MegaBank  5187.30  Mortgage
```

To display the annual report, Beverly enters **d** and **a**. Here's a partial version, covering the first five months of the year:

```
Annual Summary
--------------
Income
      Rents           42610.12
Expenses
      Advertising         95.10
      Insurance         4840.00
      Mortgage         25936.57
      Repairs           1554.90
      Supplies           887.22
      Utilities         7000.16
```

The expense categories are sorted in alphabetical order. In a real situation there would be many more budget categories, including legal fees, taxes, travel expenses, landscaping, cleaning and maintenance costs, and so on.

Prototyping

Prototyping is the creation of user interface screens that are non-functional but are visually similar to what will appear in the final program. Prototyping is especially important if you're programming for a target environment like Microsoft Windows, which uses a Graphic User Interface (GUI). User input screens can be quite elaborate in this environment, and their design has an important effect on user satisfaction.

In a GUI, designing user interface screens (actually Windows-style windows) must be approached with the same care as the rest of the design process. You create prototype user interface screens, and try them out on users and BDEs. If they're not satisfactory, you modify them. If they're still not satisfactory, you modify them again. Only when the BDEs and users are satisfied will you integrate the screens into the finished program.

Because our Landlord program uses a simple character-based interface, we haven't dealt with prototyping in this chapter. Even with such a simple interface, however, it would be a good idea to show the client how you intend the interface to look before finalizing the program.

Final Thoughts

In a real project of any size, the design process would probably not go as smoothly as we've portrayed it in this chapter. Several iterations of the CRC cards, use cases, and class diagram steps may be necessary. Programmers may find themselves confused about what the business domain experts intended, requiring a return to the design process while in the midst of programming. The BDEs may change their minds about what they want in the middle of the design or programming phases.

There are many other facets of object-oriented design that we haven't mentioned, such as interaction diagrams, state diagrams, and so on. We've really only scratched the surface of the complex and rapidly-evolving field of object-oriented design. The bibliography has suggestions for further reading.

Summary

Trial and error may be sufficient for simple OO programs. For more complex programs, a more organized approach is usually necessary. In this chapter, we've shown several design methodologies.

A problem summary statement defines what the user wants the program to do. From this statement, any noun is a candidate to become a class.

CRC cards are filing cards representing classes. The letters stand for class, responsibilities, collaborators. A class's responsibilities are what it must know (data or attributes) and what it must do (member functions or methods). A class's collaborators are other classes it must call on to carry out its responsibilities. A CRC modeling group, consisting of software specialists working with experts on the business, prepares the CRC cards. Each card may represent a class (or object) in the final program.

Use cases are detailed descriptions of program operations. Like CRC cards, they can help to identify classes.

The relationships among classes can be shown in a class diagram. There are five major kinds of class relationships.

> One class may be an attribute of another.
>
> In association, one class uses another.
>
> In Aggregation, one class is contained within another.

Composition is a stronger form of aggregation, in which the parts are more necessary to the whole.

In generalization, one class is derived from another using inheritance.

A class diagram represents all the classes and their relationships. Each kind of relationship is shown using a different notation. Using the class diagram, the programmer can start to write the code for the project.

Questions

Answers to questions can be found in Appendix G, "Answers to Questions and Exercises."

1. True or false: Object-oriented design is concerned with the syntax of C++ program statements.

2. CRC cards are used to (among other things)

   a. summarize problems encountered in program code.

   b. discover what constructors a class may have.

   c. enumerate return types for class methods.

   d. deduce what classes may be necessary in a program.

3. The letters CRC stand for c_____, r_____, and c_____.

4. True or false: after a set of CRC cards is created, new cards can be added at a later time.

5. Responsibilities are things a class must k_____ and things a class must d _____.

6. A facilitator

   a. is more concerned with the program than its users.

   b. should understand object-oriented design.

   c. should discourage BDEs from expressing their own ideas.

   d. does nothing but take notes.

7. If class A uses class B to help it carry out a task, then class B is called a _____ of class A.

8. The Problem Summary Statement

   a. is a short description of the real world problem a program is supposed to solve.

   b. describes the attributes of classes in a program.

    c. lists problems that have been found in the code.

    d. contains nouns that may become classes in the program.

9. True or false: at least some of the CRC cards must be completed before the Problem Summary Statement is written.

10. Classes in the program may correspond to

    a. verbs in the Problem Summary Statement.

    b. CRC cards.

    c. reports or input screens.

    d. names of famous programmers.

11. True or false: vague, general entities in the business domain are not good candidates for classes in the program.

12. True or false: entities with a single attribute and no other responsibilities (except perhaps displaying themselves) are good candidates for classes.

13. In the design process, which of the following may happen from time to time?

    a. A use case will be completed before some CRC cards.

    b. A class diagram will be drawn before some use cases are written.

    c. Some code will be written before the class diagram is complete.

    d. The header file will be changed while methods are still being coded.

14. Actors are _____ who interact with the _____.

15. A use case is

    a. one class using another to carry out a task.

    b. a detailed list of class attributes.

    c. a convenient container for programming documents.

    d. a description of the steps necessary for a class to carry out a responsibility.

16. Use cases may help to identify

    a. additional classes.

    b. additional responsibilities of existing classes.

    c. collaborators of existing classes.

    d. additional details of tasks performed by classes.

17. True or false: attributes are one of the major class relationships.

18. Assume there is an association between class **A** and class **B**. Also, **objA** is an object of class **A**, and **objB** is an object of class **B**. Which of the following applies?

    a. **objA** may send a message to **objB**.

    b. Class **B** must be a subclass of class **A**, or vice versa.

    c. **objB** must be an attribute of class **A**, or vice versa.

    d. **objB** may help **objA** carry out a task.

19. If class **B** is a collaborator of class **A**, then it's likely they are related by a(n) _____.

20. True or false: an association is a relationship between objects, as opposed to a relationship between classes.

21. Aggregation means that

    a. one class contains a number of other classes.

    b. an object of one class contains a number of objects of another class.

    c. one class is descended from another class.

    d. an object of one class is descended from an object of another class.

22. Composition is a _____ form of _____.

23. True or false: although we talk about classes being related by association and aggregation, we really mean that objects of these classes are so related.

24. The class relationship called generalization is the same as

    a. inheritance.

    b. aggregation.

    c. association.

    d. abstraction.

25. The direction of an association is called _____.

26. Multiplicity refers to the number of _____ a(n) _____ is related to.

27. The classes in a class diagram are represented by _____.

28. Prototyping refers to the creation of

    a. CRC cards.

    b. a class diagram.

   c. a preliminary user interface.

   d. the .H file.

29. The .H file contains class i_____s, while the .CPP file contains the class
     i_____s.

30. Classes should be _____ coupled but have _____ cohesion.

Projects

We don't have room in this book for exercises involving the kind of projects involved in this chapter. However, we list some suggestions for projects you may want to pursue on your own.

   1. Reread the explanation of the Horse program from Chapter 10, "Pointers," but do *not* look at the code. Create CRC cards, use cases, and make a class diagram for this program. Use the results to create a .H file, and compare your results with the program. There are many correct results.

   2. Reread the explanation of the Elev program from Chapter 13, "Multifile Programs," but do *not* look at the code. Create CRC cards, use cases, and make a class diagram for this program. Use the results to create appropriate .H files. Compare your results with the program.

   3. Create CRC cards, use cases, and make a class diagram for a business situation you're familiar with, whether it's horse trading, software consulting, or dealing rare comic books.

   4. Create CRC cards, use cases, and make a class diagram for a program you've always wanted to write, but haven't had time for. If you can't think of anything, try a simple word-processing program, a game, or a genealogical program that allows you to enter information about your ancestors and displays a family tree.

APPENDIX A

ASCII CHART

Table A.1 IBM Character Codes

DEC	HEX	Symbol	Key	Use in C
0	00	(NULL)	Ctrl 2	
1	01	☺	Ctr A	
2	02	☻	Ctrl B	
3	03	♥	Ctrl C	
4	04	♦	Ctrl D	
5	05	♣	Ctrl E	
6	06	♠	Ctrl F	
7	07	•	Ctrl G	Beep
8	08	◘	Backspace	Backspace
9	09	○	Tab	Tab
10	0A	◙	Ctrl J	Linefeed (new line)
11	0B	♂	Ctrl K	Vertical Tab
12	0C	♀	Ctrl L	Form Feed
13	0D	♪	Enter	Carriage Return
14	0E	♫	Ctrl N	
15	0F	☼	Ctrl O	
16	10	►	Ctrl P	
17	11	◄	Ctrl Q	
18	12	↕	Ctrl R	
19	13	‼	Ctrl S	

continued on next page

continued from previous page

DEC	HEX	Symbol	Key	Use in C
20	14	¶	Ctrl T	
21	15	§	Ctrl U	
22	16	_	Ctrl V	
23	17	↨	Ctrl W	
24	18	↑	Ctrl X	
25	19	↓	Ctrl Y	
26	1A	→	Ctrl Z	
27	1B	←	Escape	
28	1C	∟	Ctrl \	
29	1D	↔	Ctrl]	
30	1E	▲	Ctrl 6	
31	1F	▼	Ctrl -	
32	20		SPACE BAR	
33	21	!	!	
34	22	"	"	
35	23	#	#	
36	24	$	$	
37	25	%	%	
38	26	&	&	
39	27	'	'	
40	28	(	(	
41	29	)	)	
42	2A	*	*	
43	2B	+	+	
44	2C	,	,	
45	2D	–	–	
46	2E	.	.	
47	2F	/	/	

DEC	HEX	Symbol	Key	Use in C
48	30	0	0	
49	31	1	1	
50	32	2	2	
51	33	3	3	
52	34	4	4	
53	35	5	5	
54	36	6	6	
55	37	7	7	
56	38	8	8	
57	39	9	9	
58	3A	:	:	
59	3B	;	;	
60	3C	<	<	
61	3D	=	=	
62	3E	>	>	
63	3F	?	?	
64	40	@	@	
65	41	A	A	
66	42	B	B	
67	43	C	C	
68	44	D	D	
69	45	E	E	
70	46	F	F	
71	47	G	G	
72	48	H	H	
73	49	I	I	
74	4A	J	J	
75	4B	K	K	

continued on next page

continued from previous page

DEC	HEX	Symbol	Key	Use in C
76	4C	L	L	
77	4D	M	M	
78	4E	N	N	
79	4F	O	O	
80	50	P	P	
81	51	Q	Q	
82	52	R	R	
83	53	S	S	
84	54	T	T	
85	55	U	U	
86	56	V	V	
87	57	W	W	
88	58	X	X	
89	59	Y	Y	
90	5A	Z	Z	
91	5B	[	[	
92	5C	\	\	
93	5D	]	]	
94	5E	^	^	
95	5F	_	_	
96	60	'	'	
97	61	a	a	
98	62	b	b	
99	63	c	c	
100	64	d	d	
101	65	e	e	
102	66	f	f	
103	67	g	g	

DEC	HEX	Symbol	Key	Use in C
104	68	h	h	
105	69	i	i	
106	6A	j	j	
107	6B	k	k	
108	6C	l	l	
109	6D	m	m	
110	6E	n	n	
111	6F	o	o	
112	70	p	p	
113	71	q	q	
114	72	r	r	
115	73	s	s	
116	74	t	t	
117	75	u	u	
118	76	v	v	
119	77	w	w	
120	78	x	x	
121	79	y	y	
122	7A	z	z	
123	7B	{	{	
124	7C	¦	¦	
125	7D	}	}	
126	7E	~	~	
127	7F	Δ	Ctrl ←	
128	80	Ç	Alt 128	
129	81	ü	Alt 129	
130	82	é	Alt 130	
131	83	â	Alt 131	

continued on next page

continued from previous page

DEC	HEX	Symbol	Key	Use in C
132	84	ä	Alt 132	
133	85	à	Alt 133	
134	86	å	Alt 134	
135	87	ç	Alt 135	
136	88	ê	Alt 136	
137	89	ë	Alt 137	
138	8A	è	Alt 138	
139	8B	ï	Alt 139	
140	8C	î	Alt 140	
141	8D	ì	Alt 141	
142	8E	Ä	Alt 142	
143	8F	Å	Alt 143	
144	90	É	Alt 144	
145	91	æ	Alt 145	
146	92	Æ	Alt 146	
147	93	ô	Alt 147	
148	94	ö	Alt 148	
149	95	ò	Alt 149	
150	96	û	Alt 150	
151	97	ù	Alt 151	
152	98	ÿ	Alt 152	
153	99	Ö	Alt 153	
154	9A	Ü	Alt 154	
155	9B	¢	Alt 155	
156	9C	£	Alt 156	
157	9D	¥	Alt 157	
158	9E	₧	Alt 158	
159	9F	ƒ	Alt 159	
160	A0	á	Alt 160	

DEC	HEX	Symbol	Key	Use in C
161	A1	í	Alt 161	
162	A2	ó	Alt 162	
163	A3	ú	Alt 163	
164	A4	ñ	Alt 164	
165	A5	Ñ	Alt 165	
166	A6	a̲	Alt 166	
167	A7	o̲	Alt 167	
168	A8	¿	Alt 168	
169	A9	⌐	Alt 169	
170	AA	¬	Alt 170	
171	AB	½	Alt 171	
172	AC	¼	Alt 172	
173	AD	¡	Alt 173	
174	AE	«	Alt 174	
175	AF	»	Alt 175	
176	B0	▒	Alt 176	
177	B1	▓	Alt 177	
178	B2	█	Alt 178	
179	B3	│	Alt 179	
180	B4	┤	Alt 180	
181	B5	╡	Alt 181	
182	B6	╢	Alt 182	
183	B7	╖	Alt 183	
184	B8	╕	Alt 184	
185	B9	╣	Alt 185	
186	BA	║	Alt 186	
187	BB	╗	Alt 187	
188	BC	╝	Alt 188	

continued on next page

continued from previous page

DEC	HEX	Symbol	Key	Use in C
189	BD	╜	Alt 189	
190	BE	╛	Alt 190	
191	BF	┐	Alt 191	
192	C0	└	Alt 192	
193	C1	┴	Alt 193	
194	C2	┬	Alt 194	
195	C3	├	Alt 195	
196	C4	─	Alt 196	
197	C5	┼	Alt 197	
198	C6	╞	Alt 198	
199	C7	╟	Alt 199	
200	C8	╚	Alt 200	
201	C9	╔	Alt 201	
202	CA	╩	Alt 202	
203	CB	╦	Alt 203	
204	CC	╠	Alt 204	
205	CD	═	Alt 205	
206	CE	╬	Alt 206	
207	CF	╧	Alt 207	
208	D0	╨	Alt 208	
209	D1	╤	Alt 209	
210	D2	╥	Alt 210	
211	D3	╙	Alt 211	
212	D4	╘	Alt 212	
213	D5	╒	Alt 213	
214	D6	╓	Alt 214	
215	D7	╫	Alt 215	
216	D8	╪	Alt 216	

DEC	HEX	Symbol	Key	Use in C
217	D9	⌟	Alt 217	
218	DA	⌐	Alt 218	
219	DB	█	Alt 219	
220	DC	▬	Alt 220	
221	DD	▌	Alt 221	
222	DE	▐	Alt 222	
223	DF	▬	Alt 223	
224	E0	α	Alt 224	
225	E1	β	Alt 225	
226	E2	Γ	Alt 226	
227	E3	π	Alt 227	
228	E4	Σ	Alt 228	
229	E5	σ	Alt 229	
230	E6	μ	Alt 230	
231	E7	τ	Alt 231	
232	E8	Φ	Alt 232	
233	E9	Θ	Alt 233	
234	EA	Ω	Alt 234	
235	EB	δ	Alt 235	
236	EC	∞	Alt 236	
237	ED	φ	Alt 237	
238	EE	$\in$	Alt 238	
239	EF	$\cap$	Alt 239	
240	F0	$\equiv$	Alt 240	
241	F1	$\pm$	Alt 241	
242	F2	$\geq$	Alt 242	
243	F3	$\leq$	Alt 243	
244	F4	$\int$	Alt 244	

continued on next page

continued from previous page

DEC	HEX	Symbol	Key	Use in C
245	F5	⌡	Alt 245	
246	F6	÷	Alt 246	
247	F7	≈	Alt 247	
248	F8	°	Alt 248	
249	F9	•	Alt 249	
250	FA	·	Alt 250	
251	FB	✓	Alt 251	
252	FC	η	Alt 252	
253	FD	^{2}	Alt 253	
254	FE	■	Alt 254	
255	FF	(blank)	Alt 255	

Those key sequences consisting of "Ctrl" are typed by pressing the CTRL key, and while it is being held down, pressing the key indicated. These sequences are based on those defined for PC Personal Computer series keyboards. The key sequences may be defined differently on other keyboards.

IBM Extended ASCII characters can be displayed by pressing the Alt key and then typing the decimal code of the character on the keypad.

STANDARD C++ KEYWORDS

Keywords implement specific C++ language features. They cannot be used as names for variables or other user-defined program elements. Many of the keywords are common to both C and C++, while others are specific to C++. Some compilers may support additional keywords, which usually begin with one or two underscores, as in **_cdecl** or **__int16**.

A

```
asm
auto
```

B

```
bool
break
```

C

```
case
catch
char
class
const
const_cast
continue
```

D

```
default
delete
do
double
dynamic_cast
```

E

```
else
enum
explicit
export
extern
```

F

```
false
float
for
friend
```

G

```
goto
```

I

```
if
inline
int
```

L

```
long
```

M

```
main
mutable
```

N

```
namespace
new
```

O

operator

P

private
protected
public

R

register
reinterpret_cast
return

S

short
signed
sizeof
static
static_cast
struct
switch

T

template
this
throw
true
try
typedef
typeid
typename

U

union
unsigned
using

virtual
void
volatile

wchar_t
while

APPENDIX C

MICROSOFT VISUAL C++

This appendix tells you how to use Microsoft Visual C++ to create console-mode applications, which are the kind of applications used in this book. This discussion is based on Visual C++ version 5.0.

The present version of Visual C++ has good (although not perfect) adherence to Standard C++. It comes in various versions, including a student version for under $100.

We'll assume that Visual C++ is installed in your system, and that you know how to start it by using the Windows Start button and navigating to the appropriate menu item: Microsoft Visual C++.

You'll want to make sure you can see file extensions (like .CPP) when operating MVC++. In Windows Explorer, make sure that the option Hide MS-DOS File Extensions for File Types That are Registered is not checked.

Screen Elements

When you start Microsoft Visual C++ you'll see that the resulting application is actually called Microsoft Developer Studio. The studio can work with other languages besides C++, but we won't worry about that here.

The Developer Studio window is initially divided into three parts. On the left is the View Pane. This has three tabs, for ClassView, FileView, and InfoView. Once you have a project going, the ClassView tab will show you the class hierarchy of your program, and FileView will show you the files used in the project. InfoView allows you to navigate through the documentation and help file structure. Click the plus signs to expand the hierarchies, then double-click the document you want to read.

The largest part of the screen usually holds a document window. It can be used for various purposes, including displaying your source files. It can also display the contents of help files. At the bottom of the screen is a long window with more tabs: Build, Debug, and so on. This will display messages when you perform operations such as compiling your program.

Single-File Programs

It's easy to build and execute a single-file console program using Microsoft Visual C++. There are two possibilities: the file already exists or the file needs to be written.

In either case you should begin by making sure that no project is currently open. (We'll discuss projects in a moment.) Click the File menu. If the Close Workspace item is active (not grayed) click it to close the current workspace.

Building an Existing File

If the .CPP source file already exists, as it does for the example programs in this book, select Open from the File menu. (Note that this is not the same as Open Workspace.) Use the Open dialog box to navigate to the appropriate file, select it, and click the Open button. The file will appear in the document window. (If you're compiling an example program that uses Console Graphics Lite, such as the CIRCSTRC program in Chapter 5, "Functions," or the CIRCLES program in Chapter 6, "Objects and Classes," turn to the section "Building Console Graphics Lite Programs.")

To compile and link this file, select Build from the Build menu. A dialog box will appear asking if you want to create a Default Project Workspace. Click Yes. The file will be compiled and linked with any necessary library files.

To run the program, select Execute from the Project menu. If all goes well, a console window will appear with the program's output displayed in it.

When the program terminates, you'll see the phrase *Press any key to continue*. The compiler arranges for this to be inserted following the termination of any program. It keeps the console display on the screen long enough to see the program's output.

You can also run programs directly from MS-DOS. In Windows 95 and 98, you can obtain a box for MS-DOS by clicking the Start button, selecting Programs and then the MS-DOS Prompt item. In the resulting window you'll see what's called the *C-prompt*: the letter C, usually followed by the name of the current directory. You can navigate from one directory to another by typing **cd** (for Change Directory) and the name of the new directory. To execute a program, including any of the examples from this book, make sure you're in the same directory as the appropriate .EXE file, and type the name of the program (with no extension). You can find out more about MS-DOS using the Windows help system.

Writing a New File

To start writing your own .CPP file, select New from the File menu and click the Files tab. Select C++ Source File, and click OK. A blank document window will appear. Type in your program. Save the new file by selecting Save As from the File menu, navigating to the correct directory, and typing the file name with the .CPP extension (such as MYPROG.CPP). As before, select Build from the Build menu and click Yes to the default workspace question. Your program will be compiled and linked.

If there are errors, they will appear in the Build window at the bottom of the screen. (You may need to click the Build tab to make this window appear.) If you double-click the error line, an arrow will appear next to the line containing the error in the source file. Also, if you position the cursor on the error number in the Build window (such as C2143) and press the F1 key, an explanation of the error will appear in the document window. You can correct the errors and repeat the build process until the message reads "0 error(s), 0 warning(s)." To execute the program, select Execute from the Build menu.

Before working on a new program, don't forget to select Close Workspace from the File menu. This ensures that you begin with a clean workspace. To open a program you've already built, select Open Workspace from File menu, navigate to the right directory, and double-click the file with the appropriate name and the .DSW extension.

Run-Time Type Information (RTTI)

A few programs, such as EMPL_IO.CPP in Chapter 12, "Streams and Files," use RTTI. With Microsoft Visual C++ you need to enable a compiler option to make this feature work. Select Settings from the Project menu and click the C/C++ tab. From the Category list box, select C++ Language. Click the checkbox named Enable Run-Time Type Information. This will avoid various compiler and linker errors, some of which are misleading.

Multifile Programs

We've shown the quick and dirty approach to building programs. This approach works with one-file programs. When projects have more than one file things become slightly more complicated. We'll start by reviewing what's meant by the terms *workspace* and *project*.

Projects and Workspaces

Visual C++ uses a concept called a *workspace*, which is one level of abstraction higher than a project. A workspace can contain many projects. It consists of a directory and several configuration files. Within it, each project can have its own directory, or the files for all the projects can simply reside in the workspace directory.

Conceptually it's probably easiest, at least for the small programs in this book, to assume that every project has its own separate workspace. That's what we'll assume in this discussion.

A project corresponds to an application (program) that you're developing. It consists of all the files needed to create that application as well as information about how these files are to be combined. The result of building a project is usually a single .EXE file that a user can execute. (Other results are possible, such as .DLL files.)

Source Files Already Exist

Let's assume that the files you want to include in a new project already exist, and that they are in a particular directory. Select New from the File menu, and click the Projects tab in the New dialog box. Select Win32 Console Application from the list. First, in the Location box, type the path to the directory, but do *not* include the directory name itself. Next, type the name of the directory containing the files in the Project Name box. (By clicking the button to the right of the Location field you can navigate to the appropriate directory, but make sure to delete the directory name itself from the location field.) Make sure the Create New Workspace box is checked, and click OK.

For example, if the files are in `C:\Book\Ch13\Elev`, then you would first type `C:\Book\Ch13\` in the Location field and then **Elev** in the Project Name field. When you type the project name, it's automatically added to the location. (If it was there already it would be added again, resulting in a location of `C:\Book\Ch13\Elev\Elev`, which is not what you want.)

At this point various project-oriented files, with extension .DSP, .DSW, and so forth, have been added to the directory.

Now you need to add your source files to the project. This includes both .CPP and .H files. Select Add To Project from the Project menu, click Files, select the files you want to add, and click OK. You can review the files you've selected by clicking the FileView tab and then the plus sign for the project. You can also see the class structure, complete with member functions, by clicking the ClassView tab.

To open a file so you can see it and modify it, select Open from the File menu and select the file.

Sometimes a file (such as the MSOFTCON.H file necessary for console graphics programs) is not in the same directory as the other source files for your program. You can nevertheless add it to your project in the same way that you add other files. Select Add To Project from the Project menu, select Files, and then navigate to the file you want (or type in the complete pathname).

Saving, Closing, and Opening Projects

To save the project, select Save Workspace. To close the project, select Close Workspace. (Answer Yes to the query Close All Document Windows.) To open an existing project, select Open Workspace from the file menu, navigate to the proper directory, select the .DSW file, and click Open.

Compiling and Linking

As with one-file programs, the easiest way to compile, link, and run a multifile program is to select Execute from the Build menu. You can compile and link your project without running it by selecting Build from the Build menu.

Building Console Graphics Lite Programs

Building programs that use the Console Graphics Lite functions (described in Appendix E, "Console Graphics Lite") requires some steps in addition to those needed for ordinary example programs. Programs that use these functions should include the line `#include "msoftcon.h"`.

- Open the source file for the program as described earlier.

- Select Build from the Build menu. Answer Yes when asked if you want to create a default project workspace. A project will be created, but the compiler will complain it can't find MSOFTCON.H.

- To tell it where to find this file, select Options from the Tools menu. Click on the Directories tab. Select Include Files from the Show Directories For list. On the bottom line of the Directories list, type the complete pathname of the directory where MSOFTCON.H is stored. (This directory should be called MSOFTCON.) Click on OK.

- Now try building your file again. Now the compiler can find the header file, but there will be numerous linker errors because the linker doesn't know where to find the code for the graphics functions. This code is in MSOFTCON.CPP.

- Select Add To Project from the Project menu; then select Files. In the resulting dialog box (called Insert Files into Project), navigate to the MSOFTCON directory. Select the MSOFTCON.CPP file, Click OK.

Now your program should compile and link correctly. Select Execute from the Build menu to see it run.

Debugging

In Chapter 3, "Loops and Decisions," we suggest using the debugger to provide an insight into how loops work. Here's how to do that with Microsoft Visual C++. These same steps can help you debug your program if it behaves incorrectly. We'll be discussing one-file programs here, but the same approach applies, with appropriate variations, to larger multifile programs.

Start by building your program as you normally would. Fix any compiler and linker errors. Make sure your program listing is displayed in the Edit window.

Single Stepping

To start the debugger, simply press the F10 key. You'll see a yellow arrow appear in the margin of the listing, pointing to the opening brace following main.

If you want to start somewhere other than the beginning of the program, position the cursor on the line where you want to start debugging. Then, from the Build menu, select Start Debug, and then Run to Cursor. The yellow arrow will appear next to the statement selected.

Now press the F10 key. This causes the debugger to step to the next executable statement. The yellow arrow will show where you are. Each press of F10 moves it to the next statement. If you're in a loop, you'll see the yellow arrow move down through the statements in the loop and then jump back to the top of the loop.

Watching Variables

You'll see a Watch window in the bottom right corner of your screen. To observe the values of variables change as you step through the program, you'll need to place these variable's names in this Watch window. To do this, right-click a variable name in the source code. A pop-up menu will appear. Select QuickWatch from this menu. In the resulting QuickWatch dialog box, click Add Watch. The variable and its current value will appear in the Watch window. If a variable is out of scope, such as before it's been defined, the Watch window will show an error message instead of a value next to the variable name.

Stepping Into Functions

If your program uses functions, you can *step into* them (single-step through the statements within the function) by using the F11 key. By contrast, the F10 key *steps over* function calls (treats them as a single statement). If you use F11 to trace into library routines like `cout <<`, you can trace through the source code of the library routine. This can be a lengthy process, so avoid it unless you're really interested. You need to switch judiciously between F11 and F10, depending on whether you want to explore a particular function's inner workings or not.

Breakpoints

Breakpoints allow you to stop the program at any arbitrary location. Why are they useful? We've already shown that you can execute the program up to the cursor location by selecting Run to Cursor. However, there are times when you want to be able to stop the program in multiple locations. For example, you might want to stop it after an `if` and also after the corresponding `else`. Breakpoints solve this problem because you can insert as many as you need. (They also have advanced features we won't describe here.)

Here's how to insert a breakpoint in your listing. First, position the cursor on the line where you want the breakpoint. Then click the right mouse button, and from the resulting menu select Insert/Remove Breakpoint. You'll see a red circle appear in the left margin. Now whenever you run your program at full speed (by selecting Build/Start Debug/Go, for example) it will stop at the breakpoint. You can then examine variables, single-step through the code, or run to another breakpoint.

To remove a breakpoint, right-click it and select Remove Breakpoint from the menu.

There are many other features of the Debugger, but what we've discussed here will get you started.

APPENDIX D

BORLAND C++BUILDER

This appendix tells you how to use Borland C++Builder to create console-mode applications, which are the kind of applications used in this book.

C++Builder is Borland's most advanced development product, and, as of this writing, the C++ product that adheres most closely to Standard C++. It's available in a student version for under $100. This discussion is based on C++Builder 3.0.

We'll assume that C++Builder is installed on your system, and that you can start it by using the Windows Start button and navigating to the appropriate menu item: C++Builder.

You'll want to make sure you can see file extensions (like .CPP) when operating C++Builder. In Windows Explorer, make sure that the option Hide MS-DOS File Extensions for File Types That are Registered is not checked.

Running the Example Programs in C++Builder

The programs in this book require minor modifications to run under C++Builder. Here's a quick summary.

You can compile most of the example programs and run them without modification in Window's MS-DOS window (Start/Programs/MS-DOS Prompt). However, if you want to run them from within C++Builder, using the Run command from the Run menu, then you'll need to install a statement at the end of the program to keep the console window on the screen long enough to see. You can do this in two steps:

- Insert the statement `getch();` just before the final `return` statement in `main()`. This enables you to see the program's output.

- Insert the statement `#include <conio.h>` at the beginning of `main()`. This is necessary for `getch()`.

If you're creating a multifile program, (as in Chapters 13, "Multifile Programs," and 16, "Object-Oriented Design"), insert the statement `#include <condefs.h>` at the beginning of `main()`.

If the program you're building uses Console Graphics Lite functions (described in Appendix E, "Console Graphics Lite"), you'll need to take some additional steps. These are summarized later in this appendix.

In the balance of this appendix we'll cover these points in more detail and describe how to use C++Builder to edit, compile, link and execute console-mode programs.

Cleaning up the Screen

When it's first started, C++Builder shows you some screen objects you won't need for console-mode programs. You'll see a window on the right called Form1. Click on its close button (the X in the upper-right corner) to make it go away. Likewise, you won't need the Object Inspector, so click its close button too. You'll need to get rid of these two items every time you start C++Builder.

You may see a window titled UNIT1.CPP. with a source file in it. This means C++Builder has started a skeleton project for you. However, it's not the kind of project you want, so click Close All on the File menu to get rid of it.

You won't need the Component Palette. This is a toolbar with tabs labeled Standard, Additional, Win32, and so on. To get rid of it, click the Component Palette item near the bottom of the View menu. This unchecks the item, so the palette will no longer be displayed. (If you want it back, you can check this item again.)

If you need additional screen space, you can also turn off the standard toolbar. This toolbar contains buttons for opening, saving, and other common tasks. All these tasks can also be accessed from the menu bar, so if you don't mind doing without the marginal convenience of the buttons, you can remove the toolbar by clicking the Toolbar item near the bottom of the View menu.

Creating a New Project

C++Builder (as do other modern compilers) thinks in terms of *projects* when creating programs. A project consists of one or more source files. It can also contain many other kinds of files which we don't need to be concerned with here, such as resource files and definition files. The result of a project is usually a single .EXE file that a user can execute.

To begin a new project, select New... from the File menu. You'll see a dialog box called New Items. Click the New tab (if necessary). Then double-click the Console Wizard icon. In the resulting dialog box, make sure that the Window Type is Console and the Execution Type is .EXE. Click Finish and you'll see the following source file appear in the Project Source window:

```
#pragma hdrstop
#include <condefs.h>

//------------------------------------------------------------
#pragma argsused
int main(int argc, char **argv)
{
        return 0;
}
```

This is a skeleton version of a console-mode program. You don't need some of the lines in this program, and you will need to add some others. We'll make these changes, and add a statement to print some text so you can see if the program works. Here's the result:

```
//test1.cpp
//#include <condefs.h>   //not needed for one-file programs
#include <iostream>
#include <conio.h>
//#pragma hdrstop         //not needed


//-------------------------------------------------------------------
//#pragma argsused        //not needed
//int main(int argc, char **argv)    //arguments not needed
int main()
   {
   cout << "Happy are they whose programs "
        << "compile the first time.";
   getch();
   return 0;
   }
```

The CONDEFS.H file doesn't need to be included (unless your program has more than one file), and the two programs aren't necessary. Also you don't need the arguments to main().

If you run the original skeleton program you'll find that the console window doesn't remain visible long enough to see. As we noted, this can be fixed by inserting the statement

```
getch();
```

at the end of the program, just before return. This causes the program to wait for a keystroke, so the console window remains in view until you press any key. The getch() function requires the CONIO.H header file, so you'll need to include it at the beginning of your program.

If you're creating your own program, you can start with the skeleton program and type in your own lines. If your starting with an existing file, read the section "Starting with Existing Files."

Saving A Project

The text you see in the Project Source window is a source file, which has the extension .CPP. C++Builder (as do other modern compilers) thinks in terms of a project, which can consist of (potentially) many such source files. Information about a project is recorded in a file with the extension .BPR. Thus when you save a project, you're actually saving both the .CPP file (or files) and the .BPR file. When you first create it, the project is called Project1 (or a higher number).

To save the project and change its name, select Save Project As from the File menu, navigate to the directory where you want to store the file, type the name you want to give the project, followed by the .BPR extension, and click OK.

Starting with Existing Files

You may be starting a project with files that already exist, such as the ones in this book. If so, you'll need a little trick. You want the main file in your project, that is, the one containing `main()`, to have the same name as the project. However, C++Builder will automatically create a file with this name, the skeleton file. It will then try to override your file with the skeleton file when you try to save the project.

Here's how to avoid the problem. Suppose your project is called MYPROJ, and your main file is MYPROJ.CPP. Implement the following steps:

- Temporarily rename your main file (MYPROJ.CPP) to a name other than the project name, say XMYPROJ.CPP.

- Use Save Project As to save your project. Give the project the same name as the original file, but with the .BPR extension: MYPROJ.BPR. Click Save. The skeleton file that was created, MYPROJ.CPP, will be saved as well.

- Close the project with Close All.

- Delete the skeleton file (MYPROJ.CPP).

- Rename your source file (XMYPROJ.CPP)to the same name as the project(MYPROJ.CPP).

Now when you open the project again (using Open Project from the File menu), your source file will be the project's source file as well. You can then modify it or compile it.

Compiling, Linking, and Executing

To build an executable program, select Make or Build from the Project menu. This causes your .CPP file to be compiled into an .OBJ file, and the .OBJ file to be linked (with various library files) into an .EXE file. For example, if you're compiling MYPROG.CPP, the result will be MYPROG.EXE. If there are compiler or linker errors, they will be displayed. Edit your program until you've eliminated them.

Executing from C++Builder

If you've modified your program by inserting `getch()` as described earlier, then you can compile, link, and run your program directly in C++Builder by simply selecting Run from the Run menu. If there are no errors, the console window will appear, along with the output of the program.

Executing from MS-DOS

You can also run programs directly from MS-DOS. In Windows 95 and Windows 98, you can obtain a box for MS-DOS by clicking the Start button, selecting Programs and then the MS-DOS Prompt item. In the resulting window you'll see what's called the *C-prompt*: the letter C, usually followed by the name of the current directory. You can navigate from one directory to another by typing **cd** (for Change Directory) and the name of the new directory. To execute a program, including any of the examples from this book, make sure you're in the same directory as the appropriate .EXE file, and type the name of the program (with no extension). You can find out more about MS-DOS using the Windows help system.

Precompiled Header Files

You can speed up compilation times dramatically by selecting Options from the Project menu, selecting the Compiler tab, and clicking on Use Precompiled Headers. In a short program most of the compile time is spent compiling the C++ header files such as **iostream**. Using the Precompiled Headers option causes these header files to be compiled only once, instead of each time you compile your program.

Closing and Opening Projects

When you're done with a project, you can close it by selecting Close All from the File menu. To open a previously-saved project, select Open Project from the File menu, navigate to the appropriate .BPR file, and double-click it.

Adding a Header File to Your Project

Most C++ programs employ one more user-written header file (in addition to many library header files, like IOSTREAM and CONIO.H). Here's how to create a header file.

Creating a New Header File

Select New... from the File menu, make sure the New tab is selected, and double-click the Text icon. You'll see a source window titled FILE1.TXT. Type in the text of your file and save it using Save As on the File menu, with an appropriate name, followed by the .H file extension. Save it in the same file as your source (.CPP) files. The new filename will appear on a tab next to the other files in the project. You can switch from file to file by clicking the tabs.

Editing an Existing Header File

To open an existing header file, select Open from the File menu, and select Any File (*.*) from the Files Of Type list. You can then select the header file from the list.

When you write the include statement for the header file in your .CPP file, make sure you enclose the filename in quotes:

```
#include "myHeader.h"
```

The quotes tell the compiler to look for the header file in the same directory as your source files.

Telling C++Builder the Header File's Location

If you add a .H file, the compiler must know where to find it. If it's in the same directory as your other files, then you don't need to do anything.

However, if your .H file is in a different directory, you'll need to tell C++Builder where to find it. (This is true of the BORLACON.H file necessary for console-mode graphics.) Go to Options on the Project menu and select the Directories/Conditionals tab. In the Directories section, click the button with the three dots on the right of the Include Path list. A Directories dialog box will appear.

In the bottom field of the Directories dialog box, type the complete pathname of the directory where the .H file is located. Click the Add button to place the path in the list of include paths. Then click OK twice more to close the dialog boxes.

Don't try to add header files to the project with the Add To Project option in the Project menu.

Projects with Multiple Source Files

Real applications, and some of the example programs in this book, require multiple source (.CPP) files. Incidentally, in C++Builder, source files are often called *units*, a term specific to this product. In most C++ development environments, files are called files or *modules*.

If you use more than one source file in your project, you'll need to include the file CONDEFS.H:

```
#include <condefs.h>   //necessary for multifile programs
```

in the main source file; that is, the one containing `main()`. This is not necessary for one-file programs, as we mentioned earlier, but is essential for multifile programs.

Creating Additional Source Files

You make additional .CPP files the same way you make header files: Select File/New, and double-click the Text Icon in the New dialog box. Type in the source code, and use Save

As to save the file. When using Save As, make sure to select C++Builder Unit (.CPP) from the Save File As Type list. This will automatically supply the .CPP extension, so all you need to type is the name. If you fail to do this, and simply type the .CPP after the name, the file won't be recognized as a C++Builder unit.

Adding Additional Source Files to your Project

You may have created a new additional source file as just described, or one may already exist, such as BORLACON.CPP, which is used for Console Graphics Lite programs. To add a source file to the project, select Add To Project from the Project menu, navigate to the appropriate directory, and select the filename from the list. Then click Open. That tells C++Builder it's part of the project.

Multiple source files are displayed with tabs in the edit window (if they're in full-size windows), so you can quickly switch from one file to another. You can open and close these files individually so they don't all need to be on the screen at the same time.

The Project Manager

You can see what source files are part of the project by selecting Project Manager from the View menu. You'll see a diagram of file relationships, similar to that shown in the Windows Explorer. Clicking the plus sign next to the project icon will display all the project's source files. The file you just added to the project should be among them.

If you right-click a file in the Project Manager the context menu will show you choices that include Open, Save, Save As, and Compile. This is a handy way to perform these tasks on individual source files.

In a multifile program you can compile individual files separately by selecting Compile Unit from the Project menu. You can compile and link all the source files by selecting Make from the Project menu. This will cause only those source files that have been changed since the previous compile to be recompiled.

Weird New Lines in Your Program

When you compile a multifile program, C++Builder automatically inserts lines into the source code of your primary source file. These lines specify what the other source files are. For example, if you had a two-file program consisting of FILE1.CPP and FILE2.CPP, you might see the following in FILE1.CPP:

```
//------------------------------------------------------------
USEUNIT("file2.cpp");
//------------------------------------------------------------
```

This is a permanent change to your source file. It's not a very elegant approach to compiling multifile programs, but at least you don't have to add these lines yourself.

Console Graphics Lite Programs

Here's how to build programs that use the Console Graphics Lite package. This includes such programs as CIRCSTRC from Chapter 5, "Functions," and CIRCLES in Chapter 6, "Objects and Classes."

- Create a new project as described earlier, using the program name as the project name, but with the .BPR extension.

- In the source file, change `#include<msoftcon.h>` to `#include<borlacon.h>`

- Tell the compiler where this MSOFTCON.H header file is by following the instructions in the section earlier in this Appendix titled "Telling C++Builder the Header File's Location." (The header should be in a directory called BORLACON.)

- Add the source file BORLACON.CPP to your project by following the instructions in the section earlier in this Appendix titled "Adding Additional Source Files to your Project."

- Insert the line `#include <condefs.h>` at the beginning of your program. This is necessary for multifile programs.

- To keep the display on the screen, insert the line `getch();` just before the `return` statement at the end of `main()`.

- To support `getch()`, insert the line `#include <conio.h>` at the beginning of your program.

Debugging

In Chapter 3, "Loops and Decisions," we suggest using a debugger to provide an insight into how loops work. Here's how to do that with Visual C++. These same steps can help you debug your program if it behaves incorrectly. We'll be discussing one-file programs here, but the same approach applies, with appropriate variations, to large multifile programs.

Start by building your program as you normally would. Fix any compiler and linker errors. Make sure your program listing is displayed in the Edit window.

Single Stepping

To start the debugger, just press the F8 key. The program will be recompiled, and the first line in the program, usually the `main()` declarator, will be highlighted. Repeated presses of F8 will cause control to move to each statement of the program in turn. When you enter a loop, you'll see highlight move down through the loop, then return to the top of the loop for the next cycle.

Watching Variables

To see how the values of variables change as you single step through the program, select Add Watch from the Run menu. The Watch Properties dialog box will appear. Type the name of the variable you want to watch into the Expression field of this dialog box, and click OK. A window called Watch List will appear. By repeatedly using the Add Watch dialog box you can add as many variables as you want to the Watch List.

If you position the Edit Window and the Watch List so you can see them both at the same time, you can watch the value of the variables change as you single step through the program. If a variable is out of scope, such as before it's been defined, the Watch List will show an error message instead of a value next to the variable name.

In the particular case of the CUBELIST program, the watch mechanism doesn't recognize the validity of the `cube` variable when it's defined within the loop. Rewrite the program so it's defined before the loop; then its value will be displayed properly on the Watch List.

Tracing Into Functions

If your program uses functions, you can *trace* into them (single-step through the statements within the function) by using the F7 key. The F8 key *steps over* function calls (treats them as a single statement). If you use F7 to trace into library routines like `cout <<`, you can trace through the source code of the library routine. This can be a lengthy process, so avoid it unless you're really interested. You will need to switch judiciously between F7 and F8, depending on whether or not you want to explore a particular function's inner workings.

Breakpoints

Breakpoints allow you to stop the program at any arbitrary location. Why are they useful? We've already shown that you can execute the program up to the cursor location by selecting Run to Cursor from the Run menu. However, there are times when you want to be able to stop the program in multiple locations. For example, you might want to stop it after an `if` and also after the corresponding `else`. Breakpoints solve this problem because you can insert as many as you need. (They also have advanced features we won't describe here.)

Inserting a breakpoint in your listing is easy. Look at your program listing in the edit window. You'll see a dot in the left margin opposite each executable program line. Simply left-click the dot where you want to insert the breakpoint. You'll see a red circle appear in the left margin, and the program line will be highlighted. Now whenever you run your program at full speed (by selecting Run from the Run menu, for example) it will stop at the breakpoint. You can then examine variables, single-step through the code, or run to another breakpoint.

To remove the breakpoint, left-click it again. It will vanish.

There are many other features of the Debugger, but what we've described here will get you started.

APPENDIX E

CONSOLE GRAPHICS LITE

It's nice to be able to enliven example programs with graphics, so we've included many graphics-based examples. ANSI Standard C++ does not include graphics specifications, but it certainly doesn't prohibit graphics, and Windows supports various kinds of graphics.

Previous editions of this book were based on Borland C++, and used Borland graphics functions in many examples. In this edition, in keeping with making the book compliant with ANSI C++, we've attempted to make the examples less compiler-specific. However, every compiler handles graphics differently, so we've used two approaches to graphics, one for Microsoft Visual C++ and one for Borland C++. (It's possible the approach used for the Microsoft compiler will work with other compilers as well.)

In this edition we use console graphics. The console is a character-mode screen, typically arranged with 80 columns and 25 rows. Most of the non-graphics example programs in this book write text to the console window. A console program can run in its own window within Windows, or as a standalone MS-DOS program.

In console graphics, rectangles, circles, and so forth are made up of characters (such as the letter 'X' or a small character-size block) rather than pixels. The results are crude but work fine as demonstration programs.

The example programs use calls to a set of "generic" console functions created specifically for this book, which we call Console Graphics Lite. These functions translate function calls in the example programs into different actual functions, depending on which of two files is compiled and linked to your project. These files are MSOFTCON.CPP for Microsoft compilers, and BORLACON.CPP for Borland compilers.

In previous editions, some programs used pixel graphics ("real" graphics, in which individual screen pixels are manipulated) rather than character graphics. Unfortunately, it's no longer practical to accommodate pixel graphics. Microsoft's compilers have eliminated their support for pixel graphics, unless you want to write a full-scale Windows program, with all the complexity that that involves. So all the graphics examples in this edition use console-mode graphics.

Using the Console Graphics Routines

To build an example program that uses graphics, you must add several steps to the normal build procedure. These are as follows:

- Include the appropriate header file (MSOFTCON.H or BORLACON.H) in your source code and add it to your project if necessary.

- Add the appropriate source file (MSOFTCON.CPP or BORLACON.CPP) to your project.

- Make sure the compiler can find the appropriate header file and source file.

The header files contain declarations for the Console Graphics Lite functions. The source files contain the definitions (source code) for these functions. You need to compile the appropriate source file and link the resulting .OBJ file with the rest of your program. This happens automatically during the build process if you add the source file to your project.

To learn how to add a file to your project, read either Appendix C, "Microsoft Visual C++," or Appendix D, "Borland C++Builder." Then apply this process to the appropriate source file. MSOFTCON.CPP is located in the MSOFTCON directory, and BORLACON.CPP is in the BORLACON directory on the CD that accompanies this book.

To make sure your compiler can find the header file, you may need to add the pathname where it's located to the Directories option for your compiler. Again, refer to the appropriate appendix to see how this is done.

The Console Graphics Functions

The Console Graphics Lite functions assume a console screen with 80 columns and 25 rows. The upper-left corner is defined as the point (1,1) and the lower-right corner is the point (80,25).

These functions were designed specifically for the example programs in this book and are not particularly robust or sophisticated. If you use them in your own programs you should be careful to draw all shapes entirely within the confines of the 80-by-25 character screen. If you use invalid coordinates, their behavior is undefined. Table E.1 lists these functions.

Table E.1 Functions for Console Graphics Lite

Function Name	Purpose
init_graphics()	Initializes graphics system
set_color()	Sets background and foreground colors

Function Name	Purpose
set_cursor_pos()	Puts cursor at specific row and column
clear_screen()	Clears entire console screen
wait(n)	Pauses program for n milliseconds
clear_line()	Clears entire line
draw_rectangle()	Specify top, left, bottom, right
draw_circle()	Specify center (x, y) and radius
draw_line()	Specify end points (x1, y1) and (x2, y2)
draw_pyramid()	Specify top (x, y) and height
set_fill_style()	Specifies fill character

You must call **init_graphics()** before you use any other graphics functions. This function sets the fill character, and in the Microsoft version it also initializes other essential parts of the console graphics system.

The **set_color()** function can use either one or two arguments. The first sets the foreground color of characters displayed subsequently, and the second (if present) sets the background color of the character. Usually you want to keep the background black.

```
set_color(cRED);            //sets foreground to red
set_color(cWHITE, cBLUE);   //foreground white, background blue
```

Table E.2 shows the color constants that can be used for either foreground or background.

Table E.2 Color Constants for set_color()

cBLACK
cDARK_BLUE
cDARK_GREEN
cDARK_CYAN
cDARK_RED
cDARK_MAGENTA
cBROWN
cLIGHT_GRAY
cDARK_GRAY

continued on next page

continued from previous page

cBLUE
cGREEN
cCYAN
cRED
cMAGENTA
cYELLOW
cWHITE

The functions beginning with `draw_` create shapes or lines using a special character called the *fill character*. This character is set to a solid block by default, but can be modified using the `set_fill_style()` function. Besides the solid block, you can use uppercase 'X' or 'O' characters, or one of three shaded block characters. Table E.3 lists the fill constants:

Table E.3   Fill Constants for `set_fill_style()`

SOLID_FILL
X_FILL
O_FILL
LIGHT_FILL
MEDIUM_FILL
DARK_FILL

The `wait()` function takes an argument in milliseconds, and pauses for that amount of time.

```
wait(3000);   //pauses for 3 seconds
```

The other functions are largely self-explanatory. Their operation can be seen in those examples that use graphics.

Implementations of the Console Graphics Lite functions

These routines used for Console Graphics Lite aren't object-oriented, and could have been written in C instead of C++. Thus there's no real reason to study them, unless you're interested in a quick-and-dirty approach to graphics operations like drawing lines and circles.

The idea was to create the minimum routines that would do the job. You can examine the source files if you're curious.

Microsoft Compilers

The Microsoft compilers no longer include their own console graphics routines as they did several years ago. However, Windows itself provides a set of routines for simple console graphics operations, such as positioning the cursor and changing the text color. For the Microsoft compilers, the Console Graphics Lite functions access these built-in Windows console functions. (Thanks to AndrÈ LaMothe for suggesting this solution. His excellent game book is listed in Appendix H, "Bibliography.")

To use the console graphics functions you should use a project of type "Win32 Console Application," as described in Appendix C, "Microsoft Visual C++."

The Windows console functions won't work unless you initialize the console graphics system, so calling the `init_graphics()` function is essential if you're using the Microsoft compiler.

Borland Compilers

Borland C++ still has built-in graphics function, both for console-mode graphics and for pixel graphics. If you use the BORLACON.CPP file, the Console Graphics Lite functions are translated into Borland console functions, which they closely resemble.

You might wonder why you can't use the Borland compiler to access the console functions built into Windows. The problem is that to create a console-mode program in Borland C++, you must use either an EasyWin or a DOS target, both of which are 16-bit systems. The Windows console functions are 32-bit functions, and so can't be used in Borland's console mode.

When you use Borland C++, the `iostream` approach to I/O (`cout <<`) doesn't produce different colors. Thus some of the example programs, like HORSE.CPP, won't show up in color in the Borland version. If you want different colors, you'll need to revert to console-mode functions like `cputs()` and `putch()`, found in the CONIO.H file.

APPENDIX F

DEBUGGING

This appendix contains charts showing the algorithms and container member functions available in the Standard Template Library (STL). This information is based on *The Standard Template Library* by Alexander Stepanov and Ming Lee (1995), but we have extensively condensed and revised it, taking many liberties with their original formulation in the interest of quick understanding.

Algorithms

Table F.1 shows the algorithms available in the STL. The descriptions in this table offer a quick and condensed explanation of what the algorithms do; they are not intended to be serious mathematical definitions. For more information, including the exact data types to use for arguments and return values, consult one of the books listed in Appendix H, "Bibliography."

The first column gives the function name, the second explains the purpose of the algorithm, and the third specifies the arguments. Return values are not systematically specified. Some are mentioned in the Purpose column and many are either obvious or not vital to using the algorithm.

In the arguments column, the names `first`, `last`, `first1`, `last1`, `first2`, `last2`, `first3`, and `middle` represent iterators to specific places in a container. Names with numbers (like `first1`) are used to distinguish multiple containers. The names `first1`, `last1` delimits range 1, and `first2`, `last2` delimits range 2. The arguments `function`, `predicate`, `op`, and `comp` are function objects. The arguments `value`, `old`, `new`, `a`, `b`, and `init` are values of the objects stored in a container. These values are ordered or compared based on the < or == operators or the `comp` function object. The argument `n` is an integer.

In the Purpose column, moveable iterators are indicated by `iter`, `iter1`, and `iter2`. When `iter1` and `iter2` are used together, they are assumed to move together step-by-step through their respective containers (or possibly two different ranges in the same container).

Table F.1 Algorithms

Name	Purpose	Arguments
Non-mutating Sequence Operations		
for_each	Applies 'function' to each object.	first, last, function
find	Returns iterator to first object equal to 'value'.	first, last, value
find_if	Returns iterator to first object for which 'predicate' is true.	first, last, predicate
adjacent_find	Returns iterator to first adjacent pair of objects that are equal.	first, last
adjacent_find	Returns iterator to first adjacent pair of objects that satisfy 'predicate'.	first, last, predicate
count	Adds to 'n' the number of objects equal to 'value'.	first, last, value, n
count_if	Adds to 'n' the number of objects satisfying 'predicate'.	first, last, predicate, n
mismatch	Returns first non-equal pair of corresponding objects in two ranges.	first1, last1, first2
mismatch	Returns first pair of corresponding objects in two ranges that don't satisfy 'predicate'.	first1, last1, first2, predicate
equal	Returns true if corresponding objects in two ranges are all equal.	first1, last1, first2
equal	Returns true if corresponding objects in two ranges all satisfy 'predicate'.	first1, last1, first2, predicate
search	Checks if second range is contained within the first. Returns start of match, or last1 if no match.	first1, last1, first2, last2

Name	Purpose	Arguments
Non-mutating Sequence Operations		
search	Checks if second range is contained within the first, where equality is determined by 'predicate'. Returns start of match, or last1 if no match.	first1, last1, first2, last2, predicate
Mutating Sequence Operations		
copy	Copies objects from range 1 to range 2.	first1, last1, first2
copy_backward	Copies objects from range 1 to range 2, inserting them backwards, from last2 to first2.	first1, last1, first2
swap	Interchanges two objects.	a, b
iter_swap	Interchanges objects pointed to by two iterators.	iter1, iter2
swap_ranges	Interchanges corresponding elements in two ranges.	first1, last1, first2
transform	Transforms objects in range 1 into new objects in range 2 by applying 'operator'.	first1, last1, first2, operator
transform	Combines objects in range 1 and range 2 into new objects in range 3 by applying 'operator'.	first1, last1, first2, first3, operator
replace	Replaces all objects equal to 'old' with objects equal to 'new'.	first, last, old, new
replace_if	Replaces all objects that satisfy 'predicate' with objects equal to 'new'	first, last, predicate, new
replace_copy	Copies from range 1 to range 2, replacing all objects equal to 'old' with objects equal to 'new'.	first1, last1, first2, old, new

continued on next page

continued from previous page

Name	Purpose	Arguments
Mutating Sequence Operations		
replace_copy_if	Copies from range 1 to range 2, replacing all objects that satisfy 'predicate' with objects equal to 'new'.	first1, last1, first2, predicate, new
fill	Assigns 'value' to all objects in range.	first, last, value
fill_n	Assigns 'value' to all objects from first to first+n	first, n, value
generate	Fills range with values generated by successive calls to function 'gen'.	first, last, gen
generate_n	Fills from first to first+n with values generated by successive calls to function 'gen'.	first, n, gen
remove	Removes from range any objects equal to 'value'.	first, last, value
remove_if	Removes from range any objects that satisfy 'predicate'.	first, last, predicate
remove_copy	Copies objects, excepting those equal to 'value', from range 1 to range 2.	first1, last1, first2, value
remove_copy_if	Copies objects, excepting those satisfying 'pred', from range 1 to range 2.	first1, last1, first2, pred
unique	Eliminates all but the first object from any consecutive sequence of equal objects.	first, last
unique	Eliminates all but the first object from any consecutive sequence of objects satisfying 'predicate'.	first, last, predicate

Name	Purpose	Arguments
Mutating Sequence Operations		
unique_copy	Copies objects from range 1 to range 2, except only the first object from any consecutive sequence of equal objects is copied.	first1, last1, first2
unique_copy	Copies objects from range 1 to range 2, except only the first object from any consecutive sequence of objects satisfying 'predicate' is copied.	first1, last1, first2, predicate
reverse	Reverses the sequence of objects in range.	first, last
reverse_copy	Copies range 1 to range 2, reversing the sequence of objects.	first1, last1, first2
rotate	Rotates sequence of objects around iterator 'middle'.	first, last, middle
rotate_copy	Copies objects from range 1 to range 2, rotating the sequence around iterator 'middle'.	first1, middle1, last1, first2
random_shuffle	Randomly shuffles objects in range.	first, last
random_shuffle	Randomly shuffles objects in range, using random-number function 'rand'.	first, last, rand
partition	Moves all objects that satisfy 'predicate' so they precede those that do not satisfy it.	first, last, predicate

continued on next page

continued from previous page

Name	Purpose	Arguments
Mutating Sequence Operations		
stable_partition	Moves all objects that satisfy 'predicate' so they precede those that do not, and also preserves relative ordering in the two groups.	first, last, predicate
Sorting and Related Operations		
sort	Sorts objects in range.	first, last
sort	Sorts elements in range, using 'comp' as comparison function	first, last, comp
stable_sort	Sorts objects in range, maintains order of equal elements.	first, last
stable_sort	Sorts elements in range, using 'comp' as comparison function, maintains order of equal elements.	first, last, comp
partial_sort	Sorts all objects in range, places as many sorted values as will fit between first and middle. Order of objects between middle and last is undefined.	first, middle, last
partial_sort	Sorts all objects in range, places as many sorted values as will fit between first and middle. Order of objects between middle and last is undefined. Uses 'predicate' to define ordering.	first, middle, last, predicate
partial_sort_copy	Same as partial_sort(first, middle, last), but places resulting sequence in range 2.	first1, last1, first2, last2
partial_sort_copy	Same as partial_sort(first, middle, last, predicate), but places resulting sequence in range 2.	first1, last1, first2, last2, comp

Name	Purpose	Arguments
	Sorting and Related Operations	
nth_element	Places the nth object in the position it would occupy if the whole range were sorted.	first, nth, last
nth_element	Places the nth object in the position it would occupy if the whole range were sorted using 'comp' for comparisons.	first, nth, last, comp
lower_bound	Returns iterator to first position into which 'value' could be inserted without violating the ordering.	first, last, value
lower_bound	Returns iterator to first position into which 'value' could be inserted without violating an ordering based on 'comp'.	first, last, value, comp
upper_bound	Returns iterator to last position into which 'value' could be inserted without violating the ordering.	first, last, value
upper_bound	Returns iterator to last position into which 'value' could be inserted without violating an ordering based on 'comp'.	first, last, value, comp
equal_range	Returns a pair containing the lower bound and upper bound between which 'value' could be inserted without violating the ordering.	first, last, value
equal_range	Returns a pair containing the lower bound and upper bound between which 'value' could be inserted without violating an ordering based on 'comp'.	first, last, value, comp

continued on next page

continued from previous page

Name	Purpose	Arguments
	Sorting and Related Operations	
binary_search	Returns true if 'value' is in the range.	first, last, value
binary_search	Returns true if 'value' is in the range, where the ordering is determined by 'comp'.	first, last, value, comp
merge	Merges sorted ranges 1 and 2 into sorted range 3.	first1, last1, first2, last2, first3
merge	Merges sorted ranges 1 and 2 into sorted range 3, where the ordering is determined by 'comp'.	first1, last1, first2, last2, first3, comp
inplace_merge	Merges two consecutive sorted ranges, first, middle and middle, last into first, last.	first, middle, last
inplace_merge	Merges two consecutive sorted ranges, first, middle and middle, last into first-last, where the ordering is based on 'comp'.	first, middle, last, comp
includes	Returns true if every object in the range first2, last2 is also in the range first1, last. (Sets and multisets only.)	first1, last1, first2, last2
includes	Returns true if every object in the range first2-last2 is also in the range first1-last1, where ordering is based on 'comp'. (Sets and multisets only.)	first1, last1, first2, last2, comp
set_union	Constructs sorted union of elements of ranges 1 and 2. (Sets and multisets only.)	first1, last1, first2, last2, first3

Name	Purpose	Arguments
	Sorting and Related Operations	
set_union	Constructs sorted union of elements of ranges 1 and 2, where the ordering is based on 'comp'. (Sets and multisets only.)	first1, last1, first2, last2, first3, comp
set_intersection	Constructs sorted intersection of elements of ranges 1 and 2. (Sets and multisets only.)	first1, last1, first2, last2, first3
set_intersection	Constructs sorted intersection of elements of ranges 1 and 2, where the ordering is based on 'comp'. (Sets and multisets only.)	first1, last1, first2, last2, first3, comp
set_difference	Constructs sorted difference of elements of ranges 1 and 2. (Sets and multisets only.)	first1, last1, first2, last2, first3
set_difference	Constructs sorted difference of elements of ranges 1 and 2, where the ordering is based on 'comp'. (Sets and multisets only.)	first1, last1, first2, last2, first3, comp
set_symmetric_ difference	Constructs sorted symmetric difference of elements of ranges 1 and 2. (Sets and multisets only.)	first1, last1, first2, last2, first3
set_ symmetric_ difference	Constructs sorted difference of elements of ranges 1 and 2, where the ordering is based on 'comp'. (Sets and multisets only.)	first1, last1, first2, last2, first3, comp
push_heap	Places value from last-1 into resulting heap in range first, last.	first, last

continued on next page

Name	Purpose	Arguments
	Sorting and Related Operations	
push_heap	Places value from last-1 into resulting heap in range first, last, based on ordering determined by 'comp'.	first, last, comp
pop_heap	Swaps the values in first and last-1; makes range first, last-1 into a heap.	first, last
pop_heap	Swaps the values in first and last-1; makes range first, last-1 into a heap, based on ordering determined by 'comp'.	first, last, comp
make_heap	Constructs a heap out of the range first, last.	first, last
make_heap	Constructs a heap out of the range first, last, based on the ordering determined by 'comp'.	first, last, comp
sort_heap	Sorts the elements in the heap first, last.	first, last
sort_heap	Sorts the elements in the heap first, last, based on the ordering determined by 'comp'.	first, last, comp
min	Returns the smaller of two objects.	a, b
min	Returns the smaller of two objects, where the ordering is determined by 'comp'.	a, b, comp
max	Returns the larger of two objects.	a, b
max	Returns the larger of two objects, where the ordering is determined by 'comp'.	a, b, comp
max_element	Returns an iterator to the largest object in the range.	first, last

Name	Purpose	Arguments
	Sorting and Related Operations	
max_element	Returns an iterator to the largest object in the range, with an ordering determined by 'comp'.	first, last, comp
min_element	Returns an iterator to the smallest object in the range.	first, last
min_element	Returns an iterator to the smallest object in the range, with an ordering determined by 'comp'.	first, last, comp
lexicographical_ compare	Returns true of the sequence in range 1 comes before the sequence in range 2 alphabetically.	first1, last1, first2, last2
lexicographical_ compare	Returns true of the sequence in range 1 comes before the sequence in range 2 alphabetically, based on ordering determined by 'comp'.	first1, last1, first2, last2, comp
next_permutation	Performs one permutation on the sequence in the range.	first, last
next_permutation	Performs one permutation on the sequence in the range, where the ordering is determined by 'comp'.	first, last, comp
prev_permutation	Performs one reverse permutation on the sequence in the range.	first, last
prev_permutation	Performs one reverse permutation on the sequence in the range, where the ordering is determined by 'comp'.	first, last, comp

continued on next page

continued from previous page

Name	Purpose	Arguments
Generalized Numeric Operations		
accumulate	Sequentially applies init = init + *iter to each object. in the range	first, last, init
accumulate	Sequentially applies init = op(init, *iter) to each object in the range.	first, last, init, op
inner_product	Sequentially applies init=init+(*iter1)*(*iter2) to corresponding values from ranges 1 and 2.	first1, last1, first2, init
inner_product	Sequentially applies init=op1(init,op2(*iter1,*iter2)) to corresponding values from ranges 1 and 2.	first1, last1, first2, init, op1, op2
partial_sum	Adds values from start of range 1 to current iterator, and places the sums in corresponding iterator in range 2. *iter2 = sum(*first1, *(first1+1), *(first1+2), ..*iter1)	first1, last1, first2

partial_sum	Sequentially applies 'op' to
	objects between 'first1' and
	current iterator in range 1,
	and places results in
	corresponding iterator in
	range 2.
	answer = *first;
	for(iter=first+1; iter != iter1; iter++)
	    op(answer, *iter);
	*iter2 = answer;
		first1, last1,
		first2, op

adjacent_ difference	Subtracts adjacent objects in range 1 and places differences in range 2. *iter2 = * (iter1+1) - *iter1;	first1, last1, first2

Name	Purpose	Arguments
	Generalized Numeric Operations	
`adjacent_difference`	Sequentially applies `'op'` to adjacent objects in range 1 and places results in range 2. `*iter2 = op(*(iter1+1),*iter1);`	`first1, last1, first2, op`

Member Functions

The same names are used for member functions that have similar purposes in the different containers. However, no container class includes all the available member functions. Table F.2 is intended to show which member functions are available for each container. Explanations of the functions are not given, either because they are more-or-less self evident, or because they are explained in the text.

Table F.2 Member Functions

	Vector	List	Deque	Multi-Set	Set	Multi-Map	Map-	Stack	Queue	Priority Queue
`operator==`	X	X	X	X	X	X	X	X	X	
`operator!=`	X	X	X	X	X	X	X	X	X	
`operator<`	X	X	X	X	X	X	X	X	X	
`operator>`	X	X	X	X	X	X	X	X	X	
`operator<=`	X	X	X	X	X	X	X	X	X	
`operator>=`	X	X	X	X	X	X	X	X	X	
`operator =`	X	X	X							
`operator[]`	X		X			X				
`operator*`		X	X							
`operator->`		X	X							
`operator ()`				X	X	X				
`operator +`			X							
`operator -`			X							
`operator++`		X	X							

continued on next page

continued from previous page

	Vector	List	Deque	Multi-Set	Set	Multi-Map	Map-	Stack	Queue	Priority Queue
operator --		X	X							
operator +=			X							
operator -=			X							
begin	X	X	X	X	X	X	X			
end	X	X	X	X	X	X	X			
rbegin	X	X	X	X	X	X	X			
rend	X	X	X	X	X	X	X			
empty	X	X	X	X	X	X	X	X	X	X
size	X	X	X	X	X	X	X	X	X	X
max_size	X	X	X	X	X	X	X			
front	X	X	X						X	
back	X	X	X						X	
push_front		X	X							
push_back	X	X	X							
pop_front		X	X							
pop_back	X	X	X							
swap	X	X	X	X	X	X	X			
insert	X	X	X	X	X	X	X			
erase	X	X	X	X	X	X	X			
find				X	X	X	X			
count				X	X	X	X			
lower_bound				X	X	X	X			
upper_bound				X	X	X	X			
equal_range				X	X	X	X			
top								X		X
push								X	X	X
pop								X	X	X
capacity	X									

	Vector	List	Deque	Multi-Set	Set	Multi-Map	Map-	Stack	Queue	Priority Queue
reserve	X									
splice		X								
remove		X								
unique		X								
merge		X								
reverse		X								
sort		X								

Iterators

Table F.3 lists the type of iterator required by each algorithm.

Table F.3   Type of Iterator Required by Algorithm

	Input	Output	Forward	Bidirectional	Random Access
for_each	X				
find	X				
find_if	X				
adjacent_find	X				
count	X				
count_if	X				
mismatch	X				
equal	X				
search			X		
copy	X	X			
copy_backward	X	X			
iter_swap		X			
swap_ranges			X		

continued on next page

continued from previous page

	Input	Output	Forward	Bidirectional	Random Access
transform	X	X			
replace			X		
replace_if			X		
replace_copy	X	X			
fill			X		
fill_n		X			
generate			X		
generate_n		X			
remove			X		
remove_if			X		
remove_copy	X	X			
remove_copy_if	X	X			
unique			X		
unique_copy	X	X			
reverse				X	
reverse_copy		X			
rotate			X		
rotate_copy		X	X		
random_shuffle				X	
partition				X	
stable_partition				X	
sort					X
stable_sort					X
partial_sort					X
partial_sort_copy	X			X	
nth_element					X
lower_bound			X		

	Input	Output	Forward	Bidirectional	Random Access
upper_bound			x		
equal_range			x		
binary_search			x		
merge	x	x			
inplace_merge				x	
includes	x				
set_union	x	x			
set_intersection	x	x			
set_difference	x	x			
set_symmetric_difference	x	x			
push_heap					x
pop_heap					x
make_heap					x
sort_heap					x
max_element	x				
min_element	x				
lexicographical_comparison		x			
next_permutation				x	
prev_permutation				x	
accumulate	x				
inner_product	x				
partial_sum	x	x			
adjacent_difference	x	x			

ANSWERS TO QUESTIONS AND EXERCISES

Chapter 1

Answers to Questions

1. procedural, object-oriented
2. b
3. data, act on that data
4. a
5. data hiding
6. a, d
7. objects
8. False; the organizational principles are different.
9. encapsulation
10. d
11. False; most lines of code are the same in C and C++.
12. polymorphism
13. d
14. b

Chapter 2

Answers to Questions

1. b, c

2. parentheses

3. braces { }

4. It's the first function executed when the program starts

5. statement

6.
```
// this is a comment
/* this is a comment */
```

7. a, d

8. a. 4

   b. 10

   c. 4

   d. 4

9. False

10. a. integer constant

    b. character constant

    c. floating-point constant

    d. variable name or identifier

    e. function name

11. a. `cout << 'x';`

    b. `cout << "Jim";`

    c. `cout << 509;`

12. False; they're not equal until the statement is executed.

13. `cout << setw(10) << george;`

14. IOSTREAM

15. `cin >> temp;`

16. IOMANIP

17. string constants, preprocessor directives

18. true

19. 2

20. assignment (=) and arithmetic (like + and *)

21.
```
temp += 23;
temp = temp + 23;
```

22. 1

23. 2020

24. to provide declarations and other data for library functions, overloaded operators, and objects

25. library

Solutions to Exercises

1.
```cpp
// ex2_1.cpp
// converts gallons to cubic feet
#include <iostream>
using namespace std;

int main()
    {
    float gallons, cufeet;

    cout << "\nEnter quantity in gallons: ";
    cin >> gallons;
    cufeet = gallons / 7.481;
    cout << "Equivalent in cublic feet is " << cufeet << endl;
    return 0;
    }
```

2.
```cpp
// ex2_2.cpp
// generates table
#include <iostream>
#include <iomanip>
using namespace std;

int main()
    {
    cout << 1990 << setw(8) << 135 << endl
```

```
            << 1991 << setw(8) << 7290 << endl
            << 1992 << setw(8) << 11300 << endl
            << 1993 << setw(8) << 16200 << endl;
        return 0;
        }
```

3.
```
// ex2_3.cpp
// exercises arithmetic assignment and decrement
#include <iostream>
using namespace std;

int main()
    {
    int var = 10;

    cout << var << endl;        // var is 10
    var *= 2;                   // var becomes 20
    cout << var-- << endl;      // displays var, then decrements it
    cout << var << endl;        // var is 19
    return 0;
    }
```

Chapter 3

Answers to Questions

1. b, c

2. `george != sally`

3. −1 is true; only 0 is false.

4. The initialize expression initializes the loop variable, the test expression tests the loop variable, and the increment expression changes the loop variable.

5. c, d

6. True

7.
```
for(int j=100; j<=110; j++)
    cout << endl << j;
```

8. braces (curly brackets)

9. c

10.

```
int j = 100;
while( j <= 110 )
    cout << endl << j++;
```

11. False

12. At least once.

13.

```
int j = 100;
do
    cout << endl << j++;
while( j <= 110 );
```

14.

```
if(age > 21)
        cout << "Yes";
```

15. d

16.

```
if( age > 21 )
    cout << "Yes";
else
    cout << "No";
```

17. a, c

18. '\r'

19. preceding, surrounded by braces

20. reformatting

21.

```
switch(ch)
{
case 'y':
    cout << "Yes";
    break;
case 'n':
    cout << "No";
    break;
default:
    cout << "Unknown response";
}
```

22. ticket = (speed > 55) ? 1 : 0;

23. d

24. limit == 55 && speed > 55

25. unary, arithmetic, relational, logical, conditional, assignment

26. d

27. the top of the loop

28. b

Solutions to Exercises

1.
```cpp
// ex3_1.cpp
// displays multiples of a number
#include <iostream>
#include <iomanip>                    //for setw()
using namespace std;

int main()
   {
   unsigned long n;                   //number

   cout << "\nEnter a number: ";
   cin >> n;                          //get number
   for(int j=1; j<=200; j++)          //loop from 1 to 200
      {
      cout << setw(5) << j*n << "  "; //print multiple of n
      if( j%10 == 0 )                 //every 10 numbers,
         cout << endl;                //start new line
      }
   return 0;
   }
```

2.
```cpp
// ex3_2.cpp
// converts fahrenheit to centigrad, or
// centigrad to fahrenheit
#include <iostream>
using namespace std;

int main()
   {
   int response;
   double temper;

   cout << "\nType 1 to convert fahrenheit to celsius,"
        << "\n     2 to convert celsius to fahrenheit: ";
   cin >> response;
   if( response == 1 )
      {
      cout << "Enter temperature in fahrenheit: ";
      cin >> temper;
      cout << "In celsius that's " << 5.0/9.0*(temper-32.0);
```

```
            }
        else
            {
            cout << "Enter temperature in celsius: ";
            cin >> temper;
            cout << "In fahrenheit that's " << 9.0/5.0*temper + 32.0;
            }
        cout << endl;
        return 0;
        }
```

3.

```
    // ex3_3.cpp
    // makes a number out of digits
    #include <iostream>
    using namespace std;
    #include <conio.h>                       //for getche()

    int main()
        {
        char ch;
        unsigned long total = 0;             //this holds the number

        cout << "\nEnter a number: ";
        while( (ch=getche()) != '\r' )       //quit on Enter
            total = total*10 + ch-'0';       //add digit to total*10
        cout << "\nNumber is: " << total << endl;
        return 0;
        }
```

4.

```
    // ex3_4.cpp
    // models four-function calculator
    #include <iostream>
    using namespace std;

    int main()
        {
        double n1, n2, ans;
        char oper, ch;

        do {
            cout << "\nEnter first number, operator, second number: ";
            cin >> n1 >> oper >> n2;
            switch(oper)
                {
                case '+':  ans = n1 + n2;  break;
                case '-':  ans = n1 - n2;  break;
                case '*':  ans = n1 * n2;  break;
                case '/':  ans = n1 / n2;  break;
                default:   ans = 0;
                }
```

```
            cout << "Answer = " << ans;
            cout << "\nDo another (Enter 'y' or 'n')? ";
            cin >> ch;
            } while( ch != 'n' );
        return 0;
        }
```

Chapter 4

Answers to Questions

1. b, d

2. True

3. semicolon

4.
```
struct time
    {
    int hrs;
    int mins;
    int secs;
    };
```

5. False; only a variable definition creates space in memory.

6. c

7. `time2.hrs = 11;`

8. 18 in 16-bit systems (3 structures times 3 integers times 2 bytes), or 36 in 32-bit systems

9. `time time1 = { 11, 10, 59 };`

10. True

11. `temp = fido.dogs.paw;`

12. c

13. `enum players { B1, B2, SS, B3, RF, CF, LF, P, C };`

14.
```
players joe, tom;
joe = LF;
tom = P;
```

15. a. No

    b. Yes

    c. No

    d. Yes

16. 0, 1, 2

17. `enum speeds { obsolete=78, single=45, album=33 };`

18. Because false should be represented by 0.

Solutions to Exercises

1.

```cpp
// ex4_1.cpp
// uses structure to store phone number
#include <iostream>
using namespace std;
////////////////////////////////////////////////////////////
struct phone
    {
    int area;          //area code (3 digits)
    int exchange;      //exchange (3 digits)
    int number;        //number (4 digits)
    };
////////////////////////////////////////////////////////////
int main()
    {
    phone ph1 = { 212, 767, 8900 };  //initialize phone number
    phone ph2;                       //define phone number
                                     // get phone no from user
    cout << "\nEnter your area code, exchange, and number";
    cout << "\n(Don't use leading zeros): ";
    cin >> ph2.area >> ph2.exchange >> ph2.number;

    cout << "\nMy number is "        //display numbers
        << '(' << ph1.area << ") "
        << ph1.exchange << '-' << ph1.number;

    cout << "\nYour number is "
        << '(' << ph2.area << ") "
        << ph2.exchange << '-' << ph2.number << endl;
    return 0;
    }
```

2.

```cpp
// ex4_2.cpp
// structure models point on the plane
#include <iostream>
```

```cpp
using namespace std;
//////////////////////////////////////////////////////////////
struct point
   {
   int xCo;       //X coordinate
   int yCo;       //Y coordinate
   };
//////////////////////////////////////////////////////////////
int main()
   {
   point p1, p2, p3;                        //define 3 points

   cout << "\nEnter coordinates for p1: ";  //get 2 points
   cin >> p1.xCo >> p1.yCo;                 //from user
   cout << "Enter coordinates for p2: ";
   cin >> p2.xCo >> p2.yCo;

   p3.xCo = p1.xCo + p2.xCo;                //find sum of
   p3.yCo = p1.yCo + p2.yCo;                //p1 and p2

   cout << "Coordinates of p1+p2 are: "     //display the sum
        << p3.xCo << ", " << p3.yCo << endl;
   return 0;
   }
```

3.

```cpp
// ex4_3.cpp
// uses structure to model volume of room
#include <iostream>
using namespace std;
//////////////////////////////////////////////////////////////
struct Distance
   {
   int feet;
   float inches;
   };
//////////////////////////////////////////////////////////////
struct Volume
   {
   Distance length;
   Distance width;
   Distance height;
   };
//////////////////////////////////////////////////////////////
int main()
   {
   float l, w, h;
   Volume room1 = {  { 16, 3.5 }, { 12, 6.25 }, { 8, 1.75 } };

   l = room1.length.feet + room1.length.inches/12.0;
   w = room1.width.feet  + room1.width.inches /12.0;
   h = room1.height.feet + room1.height.inches/12.0;
```

```
cout << "Volume = " << l*w*h << " cubic feet\n";
return 0;
}
```

Chapter 5

Answers to Questions

1. d (half credit for b)

2. definition

3.
```
void foo()
    {
    cout << "foo";
    }
```

4. declaration, prototype

5. body

6. call

7. declarator

8. c

9. False

10. To clarify the purpose of the arguments.

11. a, b, c

12. Empty parentheses mean the function takes no arguments.

13. one

14. True

15. At the beginning of the declaration and declarator.

16. `void`

17.
```
main()
    {
    int times2(int);        // prototype
    int alpha = times2(37);    // function call
    }
```

18. d

19. To modify the original argument (or to avoid copying a large argument).

20. a, c

21.
```
int bar(char);
int bar(char, char);
```

22. faster, more

23. `inline float foobar(float fvar)`

24. a, b

25. `char blyth(int, float=3.14159);`

26. visibility, lifetime

27. Those functions defined following the variable definition.

28. The function in which it is defined.

29. b, d

30. On the left side of the equal sign.

Solutions to Exercises

1.
```
// ex5_1.cpp
// function finds area of circle
#include <instream>
using namespace std;
float circarea(float radius);

int main()
    {
    double rad;
    cout << "\nEnter radius of circle: ";
    cin >> rad;
    cout << "Area is " << circarea(rad) << endl;
    return 0;
    }
//-------------------------------------------------------------
float circarea(float r)
    {
    const float PI = 3.14159F;
    return r * r * PI;
    }
```

2.

```cpp
// ex5_2.cpp
// function raises number to a power
#include <iostream>
using namespace std;
double power( double n, int p=2);    //p has default value 2

int main()
   {
   double number, answer;
   int pow;
   char yeserno;

   cout << "\nEnter number: ";       //get number
   cin >> number;
   cout << "Want to enter a power (y/n)? ";
   cin >> yeserno;
   if( yeserno == 'y' )              //user wants a non-2 power?
      {
      cout << "Enter power: ";
      cin >> pow;
      answer = power(number, pow);  //raise number to pow
      }
   else
      answer = power(number);       //square the number
   cout << "Answer is " << answer << endl;
   return 0;
   }
//-----------------------------------------------------------
// power()
// returns number n raised to a power p
double power( double n, int p )
   {
   double result = 1.0;             //start with 1
   for(int j=0; j<p; j++)           //multiply by n
      result *= n;                  //p times
   return result;
   }
```

3.

```cpp
// ex5_3.cpp
// function sets smaller of two numbers to 0
#include <iostream>
using namespace std;

int main()
   {
   void zeroSmaller(int&, int&);
   int a=4, b=7, c=11, d=9;

   zeroSmaller(a, b);
   zeroSmaller(c, d);
   cout << "\na=" << a << " b=" << b
```

```
                           << " c=" << c << " d=" << d;
        return 0;
        }
//--------------------------------------------------------------
// zeroSmaller()
// sets the smaller of two numbers to 0
void zeroSmaller(int& first, int& second)
    {
    if( first < second )
        first = 0;
    else
        second = 0;
    }
```

4.
```
// ex5_4.cpp
// function returns larger of two distances
#include <iostream>
using namespace std;
//////////////////////////////////////////////////////////////
struct Distance                    // English distance
    {
    int feet;
    float inches;
    };
//////////////////////////////////////////////////////////////
Distance bigengl(Distance, Distance);  //declarations
void engldisp(Distance);

int main()
    {
    Distance d1, d2, d3;            //define three lengths
                                    //get length d1 from user
    cout << "\nEnter feet: ";  cin >> d1.feet;
    cout << "Enter inches: ";  cin >> d1.inches;
                                    //get length d2 from user
    cout << "\nEnter feet: ";  cin >> d2.feet;
    cout << "Enter inches: ";  cin >> d2.inches;

    d3 = bigengl(d1, d2);           //d3 is larger of d1 and d2
                                    //display all lengths
    cout << "\nd1="; engldisp(d1);
    cout << "\nd2="; engldisp(d2);
    cout << "\nlargest is "; engldisp(d3); cout << endl;
    return 0;
    }
//--------------------------------------------------------------
// bigengl()
// compares two structures of type Distance, returns the larger
Distance bigengl( Distance dd1, Distance dd2 )
    {
    if(dd1.feet > dd2.feet)         //if feet are different, return
        return dd1;                 //the one with the largest feet
```

```
        if(dd1.feet < dd2.feet)
            return dd2;
        if(dd1.inches > dd2.inches)    //if inches are different,
            return dd1;                //return one with largest
        else                           //inches, or dd2 if equal
            return dd2;
        }
//-------------------------------------------------------------
// engldisp()
// display structure of type Distance in feet and inches
void engldisp( Distance dd )
        {
        cout << dd.feet << "\'-" << dd.inches << "\"";
        }
```

Chapter 6

Answers to Questions

1. A class declaration describes how objects of a class will look when they are created.

2. class, object

3. c

4.
```
class leverage
    {
    private:
        int crowbar;
    public:
        void pry();
    };
```

5. False; both data and functions can be private or public.

6. `leverage lever1;`

7. d

8. `lever1.pry();`

9. `inline` (also `private`)

10.
```
int getcrow()
{ return crowbar; }
```

11. created (defined)

12. the class of which it is a member

13.
```
leverage()
   { crowbar = 0; }
```

14. True

15. a

16. `int getcrow();`

17.
```
int leverage::getcrow()
{ return crowbar; }
```

18. member functions and data are, by default, public in structures but private in classes

19. three, one

20. calling one of its member functions

21. b, c, d

22. False; trial and error may be necessary.

23. d

24. True

25. `void aFunc(const float jerry) const;`

Solutions to Exercises

1.
```cpp
// ex6_1.cpp
// uses a class to model an integer data type
#include <iostream>
using namespace std;
/////////////////////////////////////////////////////////////////
class Int                          //(not the same as int)
   {
   private:
      int i;
   public:
      Int()                        //create an Int
         { i = 0; }
      Int(int ii)                  //create and initialize an Int
         { i = ii; }
      void add(Int i2, Int i3)     //add two Ints
         { i = i2.i + i3.i; }
      void display()               //display an Int
```

```cpp
            { cout << i; }
      };
/////////////////////////////////////////////////////////////////
int main()
      {
      Int Int1(7);                    //create and initialize an Int
      Int Int2(11);                   //create and initialize an Int
      Int Int3;                       //create an Int

      Int3.add(Int1, Int2);                //add two Ints
      cout << "\nInt3 = "; Int3.display();  //display result
      cout << endl;
      return 0;
      }
```

2.

```cpp
// ex6_2.cpp
// uses class to model toll booth
#include <iostream>
using namespace std;
#include <conio.h>

const char ESC = 27;          //escape key ASCII code
const double TOLL = 0.5;       //toll is 50 cents
/////////////////////////////////////////////////////////////////
class tollBooth
      {
      private:
         unsigned int totalCars;  //total cars passed today
         double totalCash;        //total money collected today
      public:                     //constructor
         tollBooth() : totalCars(0), totalCash(0.0)
            { }
         void payingCar()                         //a car paid
            { totalCars++; totalCash += TOLL; }
         void nopayCar()                          //a car didn't pay
            { totalCars++; }
         void display() const                     //display totals
            { cout << "\nCars=" << totalCars
                   << ", cash=" << totalCash
                   << endl; }
      };
/////////////////////////////////////////////////////////////////
int main()
      {
      tollBooth booth1;            //create a toll booth
      char ch;

      cout << "\nPress 0 for each non-paying car,"
           << "\n      1 for each paying car,"
           << "\n      Esc to exit the program.\n";
      do {
         ch = getche();             //get character
```

```cpp
         if( ch == '0' )              //if it's 0, car didn't pay
            booth1.nopayCar();
         if( ch == '1' )              //if it's 1, car paid
            booth1.payingCar();
         } while( ch != ESC );        //exit loop on Esc key
      booth1.display();               //display totals
      return 0;
      }
```

3.

```cpp
// ex6_3.cpp
// uses class to model a time data type
#include <iostream>
using namespace std;
////////////////////////////////////////////////////////////////
class time
   {
   private:
      int hrs, mins, secs;
   public:
      time() : hrs(0), mins(0), secs(0) //no-arg constructor
         { }
                                          //3-arg constructor
      time(int h, int m, int s) : hrs(h), mins(m), secs(s)
         { }

      void display() const              //format 11:59:59
         { cout << hrs << ":" << mins << ":" << secs; }

      void add_time(time t1, time t2)    //add two times
         {
         secs = t1.secs + t2.secs;       //add seconds
         if( secs > 59 )                 //if overflow,
            { secs -= 60; mins++; }      //   carry a minute
         mins += t1.mins + t2.mins;      //add minutes
         if( mins > 59 )                 //if overflow,
            { mins -= 60; hrs++; }       //   carry an hour
         hrs += t1.hrs + t2.hrs;         //add hours
         }
   };
////////////////////////////////////////////////////////////////
int main()
   {
   const time time1(5, 59, 59);         //creates and initialze
   const time time2(4, 30, 30);         //   two times
   time time3;                          //create another time

   time3.add_time(time1, time2);        //add two times
   cout << "time3 = "; time3.display(); //display result
   cout << endl;
   return 0;
   }
```

Chapter 7

Answers to Questions

1. d

2. same

3. `double doubleArray[100];`

4. 0, 9

5. `cout << doubleArray[j];`

6. c

7. `int coins[] = { 1, 5, 10, 25, 50, 100 };`

8. d

9. `twoD[2][4]`

10. True

11. `float flarr[3][3] = { {52,27,83}, {94,73,49}, {3,6,1} };`

12. memory address

13. a, d

14. an array with 1000 elements of structure or class `employee`

15. `emplist[16].salary`

16. d

17. `bird manybirds[50];`

18. False

19. `manybirds[26].cheep();`

20. array, `char`

21. `char city[21]` (An extra byte is needed for the null character.)

22. `char dextrose[] = "C6H1206-H2O";`

23. True

24. d

25. `strcpy(blank, name);`

26.
```
class dog
    {
    private:
        char breed[80];
        int age;
    };
```

27. False

28. b, c

29. `int n = s1.find("cat");`

30. s1.insert(12, "cat");

Solutions to Exercises

1.
```cpp
// ex7_1.cpp
// reverses a C-string
#include <iostream>
#include <cstring>                    //for strlen()
using namespace std;

int main()
    {
    void reversit( char[] );          //prototype
    const int MAX = 80;               //array size
    char str[MAX];                    //string

    cout << "\nEnter a string: ";     //get string from user
    cin.get(str, MAX);

    reversit(str);                    //reverse the string

    cout << "Reversed string is: ";   //display it
    cout << str << endl;
    return 0;
    }
//----------------------------------------------------------------
//reversit()
//function to reverse a string passed to it as an argument
void reversit( char s[] )
    {
    int len = strlen(s);              //find length of string
    for(int j = 0; j < len/2; j++)    //swap each character
        {                             //   in first half
        char temp = s[j];             //   with character
        s[j] = s[len-j-1];            //   in second half
        s[len-j-1] = temp;
        }
```

```
    }

// reversit()
// function to reverse a string passed to it as an argument
void reversit( char s[] )
   {
   int len = strlen(s);               // find length of string
   for(int j = 0; j < len/2; j++)     // swap each character
      {                               //    in first half
      char temp = s[j];               //    with character
      s[j] = s[len-j-1];              //    in second half
      s[len-j-1] = temp;
      }
   }
```

2.

```
// ex7_2.cpp
// employee object uses a string as data
#include <iostream>
#include <string>
using namespace std;
///////////////////////////////////////////////////////////
class employee
   {
   private:
      string name;
      long number;
   public:
      void getdata()            //get data from user
         {
         cout << "\nEnter name: ";  cin >> name;
         cout << "Enter number: "; cin >> number;
         }
      void putdata()            //display data
         {
         cout << "\n   Name: " << name;
         cout << "\n   Number: " << number;
         }
   };
///////////////////////////////////////////////////////////
int main()
   {
   employee emparr[100];        //an array of employees
   int n = 0;                   //how many employees
   char ch;                     //user response

   do {                         //get data from user
      cout << "\nEnter data for employee number " << n+1;
      emparr[n++].getdata();
      cout << "Enter another (y/n)? "; cin >> ch;
      } while( ch != 'n' );
```

```
        for(int j=0; j<n; j++)        //display data in array
           {
           cout << "\nEmployee number " << j+1;
           emparr[j].putdata();
           }
     cout << endl;
     return 0;
     }
```

3.

```
// ex7_3.cpp
// averages an array of Distance objects input by user
#include <iostream>
using namespace std;
/////////////////////////////////////////////////////////////
class Distance                         // English Distance class
   {
   private:
      int feet;
      float inches;
   public:
      Distance()                       //constructor (no args)
         { feet = 0; inches = 0; }
      Distance(int ft, float in)  //constructor (two args)
         { feet = ft; inches = in; }

      void getdist()                   //get length from user
         {
         cout << "\nEnter feet: ";  cin >> feet;
         cout << "Enter inches: ";  cin >> inches;
         }

      void showdist()                  //display distance
         { oout << feet << "\'-" << inches << '\"'; }

      void add_dist( Distance, Distance );    //declarations
      void div_dist( Distance, int );
   };
//-------------------------------------------------------------
                                       //add Distances d2 and d3
void Distance::add_dist(Distance d2, Distance d3)
   {
   inches = d2.inches + d3.inches;  //add the inches
   feet = 0;                        //(for possible carry)
   if(inches >= 12.0)               //if total exceeds 12.0,
      {                             //then decrease inches
      inches -= 12.0;               //by 12.0 and
      feet++;                       //increase feet
      }                             //by 1
   feet += d2.feet + d3.feet;       //add the feet
   }
//-------------------------------------------------------------
                                       //divide Distance by int
```

```
void Distance::div_dist(Distance d2, int divisor)
   {
   float fltfeet = d2.feet + d2.inches/12.0;  //convert to float
   fltfeet /= divisor;                        //do division
   feet = int(fltfeet);                       //get feet part
   inches = (fltfeet-feet) * 12.0;            //get inches part
   }
/////////////////////////////////////////////////////////////////
int main()
   {
   Distance distarr[100];          //array of 100 Distances
   Distance total(0, 0.0), average;   //other Distances
   int count = 0;                  //counts Distances input
   char ch;                        //user response character

   do {
      cout << "\nEnter a Distance";          //get Distances
      distarr[count++].getdist();            //from user, put
      cout << "\nDo another (y/n)? ";        //in array
      cin >> ch;
      }while( ch != 'n' );

   for(int j=0; j<count; j++)               //add all Distances
      total.add_dist( total, distarr[j] );  //to total
   average.div_dist( total, count );        //divide by number

   cout << "\nThe average is: ";            //display average
   average.showdist();
   cout << endl;
   return 0;
   }
```

Chapter 8

Answers to Questions

1. a, c

2. `x3.subtract(x2, x1);`

3. `x3 = x2 - x1;`

4. True

5. `void operator -- () { count--; }`

6. None.

7. b, d

8.
```
void Distance::operator ++ ()
    {
    ++feet;
    }
```

9.
```
Distance Distance::operator ++ ()
    {
    int f = ++feet;
    float i = inches;
    return Distance(f, i);
    }
```

10. It increments the variable prior to use, the same as a non-overloaded ++operator.

11. c, e, b, a, d

12. True

13. b, c

14.
```
String String::operator ++ ()
    {
    int len = strlen(str);
    for(int j=0; j<len; j++)
        str[j] = toupper( str[j] )
    return String(str);
    }
```

15. d

16. False if there is a conversion routine; true otherwise.

17. b

18. True

19. constructor

20. True, but it will be hard for humans to understand.

Solutions to Exercises

1.
```
// ex8_1.cpp
// overloaded '-' operator subtracts two Distances
#include <iostream>
using namespace std;
//////////////////////////////////////////////////////////////////
```

```cpp
class Distance                         //English Distance class
   {
   private:
      int feet;
      float inches;
   public:                             //constructor (no args)
      Distance() : feet(0), inches(0.0)
         { }                           //constructor (two args)
      Distance(int ft, float in) : feet(ft), inches(in)
         { }
      void getdist()                   //get length from user
         {
         cout << "\nEnter feet: ";  cin >> feet;
         cout << "Enter inches: ";  cin >> inches;
         }
      void showdist()                  //display distance
         { cout << feet << "\'-" << inches << '\"'; }

      Distance operator + ( Distance ); //add two distances
      Distance operator - ( Distance ); //subtract two distances
   };
//------------------------------------------------------------
                                      //add d2 to this distance
Distance Distance::operator + (Distance d2)   //return the sum
   {
   int f = feet + d2.feet;           //add the feet
   float i = inches + d2.inches;     //add the inches
   if(i >= 12.0)                     //if total exceeds 12.0,
      {                              //then decrease inches
      i -= 12.0;                     //by 12.0 and
      f++;                           //increase feet by 1
      }                              //return a temporary Distance
   return Distance(f,i);             //initialized to sum
   }
//------------------------------------------------------------
                                      //subtract d2 from this dist
Distance Distance::operator - (Distance d2)   //return the diff
   {
   int f = feet - d2.feet;           //subtract the feet
   float i = inches - d2.inches;     //subtract the inches
   if(i < 0)                         //if inches less than 0,
      {                              //then increase inches
      i += 12.0;                     //by 12.0 and
      f--;                           //decrease foot by 1
      }                              //return a temporary Distance
   return Distance(f,i);             //initialized to difference
   }
////////////////////////////////////////////////////////////////
int main()
   {
   Distance dist1, dist3;            //define distances
   dist1.getdist();                  //get dist1 from user

   Distance dist2(3, 6.25);          //define, initialize dist2
```

```cpp
   dist3 = dist1 - dist2;              //subtract

                                       //display all lengths
   cout << "\ndist1 = ";  dist1.showdist();
   cout << "\ndist2 = ";  dist2.showdist();
   cout << "\ndist3 = ";  dist3.showdist();
   cout << endl;
   return 0;
   }
```

2.

```cpp
// ex8_2.cpp
// overloaded '+=' operator concatenates strings
#include <iostream>
#include <cstring>          //for strcpy(), strlen()
using namespace std;
#include <process.h>       //for exit()
/////////////////////////////////////////////////////////////
class String               //user-defined string type
   {
   private:
      enum { SZ = 80 };                //size of String objects
      char str[SZ];                    //holds a C-string
   public:
      String()                         //no-arg constructor
         { strcpy(str, ""); }
      String( char s[] )               //1-arg constructor
         { strcpy(str, s); }
      void display()                   //display the String
         { cout << str; }
      String operator += (String ss)   //add a String to this one
         {                             //result stays in this one
         if( strlen(str) + strlen(ss.str) >= SZ )
            { cout << "\nString overflow"; exit(1); }
         strcat(str, ss.str);          //add the argument string
         return String(str);           //return temp String
         }
   };
/////////////////////////////////////////////////////////////
int main()
   {
   String s1 = "Merry Christmas!  ";   //uses 1-arg ctor
   String s2 = "Happy new year!";      //uses 1-arg ctor
   String s3;                          //uses no-arg ctor

   s3 = s1 += s2;          //add s2 to s1, assign to s3

   cout << "\ns1="; s1.display();      //display s1
   cout << "\ns2="; s2.display();      //display s2
   cout << "\ns3="; s3.display();      //display s3
   cout << endl;
   return 0;
   }
```

3.
```cpp
// ex8_3.cpp
// overloaded '+' operator adds two times
#include <iostream>
using namespace std;
/////////////////////////////////////////////////////////////////
class time
    {
    private:
        int hrs, mins, secs;
    public:
        time() : hrs(0), mins(0), secs(0) //no-arg constructor
            { }                            //3-arg constructor
        time(int h, int m, int s) : hrs(h), mins(m), secs(s)
            { }
        void display()                    //format 11:59:59
            { cout << hrs << ":" << mins << ":" << secs; }

        time operator + (time t2)         //add two times
            {
            int s = secs + t2.secs;       //add seconds
            int m = mins + t2.mins;       //add minutes
            int h = hrs + t2.hrs;         //add hours
            if( s > 59 )                  //if secs overflow,
                { s -= 60; m++; }         //   carry a minute
            if( m > 59 )                  //if mins overflow,
                { m -= 60; h++; }         //   carry an hour
            return time(h, m, s);         //return temp value
            }
    };
/////////////////////////////////////////////////////////////////
int main()
    {
    time time1(5, 59, 59);               //create and initialze
    time time2(4, 30, 30);               //   two times
    time time3;                          //create another time

    time3 = time1 + time2;               //add two times
    cout << "\ntime3 = "; time3.display(); //display result
    cout << endl;
    return 0;
    }
```

4.
```cpp
// ex8_4.cpp
// overloaded arithmetic operators work with type Int
#include <iostream>
using namespace std;
#include <process.h>                      //for exit()
/////////////////////////////////////////////////////////////////
class Int
    {
    private:
```

```cpp
        int i;
    public:
        Int() : i(0)                        //no-arg constructor
            { }
        Int(int ii) : i(ii)                 //1-arg constructor
            { }                             //    (int to Int)
        void putInt()                       //display Int
            { cout << i; }
        void getInt()                       //read Int from kbd
            { cin >> i; }
        operator int()                      //conversion operator
            { return i; }                   //    (Int to int)
        Int operator + (Int i2)             //addition
            { return checkit( long double(i)+long double(i2) ); }
        Int operator - (Int i2)             //subtraction
            { return checkit( long double(i)-long double(i2) ); }
        Int operator * (Int i2)             //multiplication
            { return checkit( long double(i)*long double(i2) ); }
        Int operator / (Int i2)             //division
            { return checkit( long double(i)/long double(i2) ); }

        Int checkit(long double answer)             //check results
            {
            if( answer > 2147483647.0L || answer < -2147483647.0L )
                { cout << "\nOverflow Error\n"; exit(1); }
            return Int( int(answer) );
            }
    };
/////////////////////////////////////////////////////////////////
int main()
    {
    Int alpha = 20;
    Int beta = 7;
    Int delta, gamma;

    gamma = alpha + beta;                   //27
    cout << "\ngamma="; gamma.putInt();
    gamma = alpha - beta;                   //13
    cout << "\ngamma="; gamma.putInt();
    gamma = alpha * beta;                   //140
    cout << "\ngamma="; gamma.putInt();
    gamma = alpha / beta;                   //2
    cout << "\ngamma="; gamma.putInt();

    delta = 2147483647;
    gamma = delta + alpha;                  //overflow error
    delta = -2147483647;
    gamma = delta - alpha;                  //overflow error

    cout << endl;
    return 0;
    }
```

Chapter 9

1. a, c

2. derived

3. b, c, d

4. `class Bosworth : public Alphonso`

5. False

6. `protected`

7. yes (assuming **basefunc** is not private)

8. `BosworthObj.alfunc();`

9. True

10. the one in the derived class

11. `Bosworth() : Alphonso() { }`

12. c, d

13. True

14. `Derv(int arg) : Base(arg)`

15. a

16. True

17. c

18. `class Tire : public Wheel, public Rubber`

19. `Base::func();`

20. False

Solutions to Exercises

1.
```
// ex9_1.cpp
// publication class and derived classes
#include <iostream>
#include <string>
using namespace std;
/////////////////////////////////////////////////////////////
class publication                           // base class
   {
   private: protected:
```

```
        string title;
        float price;
    public:
        void getdata()
            {
            cout << "\nEnter title: "; cin >> title;
            cout << "Enter price: "; cin >> price;
            }
        void putdata() const
            {
            cout << "\nTitle: " << title;
            cout << "\nPrice: " << price;
            }
    };
//////////////////////////////////////////////////////////////
class book : private publication      // derived class
    {
    private:
        int pages;
    public:
        void getdata()
            {
            publication::getdata();
            cout << "Enter number of pages: "; cin >> pages;
            }
        void putdata() const
            {
            publication::putdata();
            cout << "\nPages: " << pages;
            }
    };
//////////////////////////////////////////////////////////////
class tape : private publication      // derived class
    {
    private:
        float time;
    public:
        void getdata()
            {
            publication::getdata();
            cout << "Enter playing time: "; cin >> time;
            }
        void putdata() const
            {
            publication::putdata();
            cout << "\nPlaying time: " << time;
            }
    };
//////////////////////////////////////////////////////////////
int main()
    {
    book book1;                           // define publications
    tape tape1;
```

```
        book1.getdata();                   // get data for them
        tape1.getdata();

        book1.putdata();                   // display their data
        tape1.putdata();
        cout << endl;
        return 0;
        }
```

2.

```cpp
// ex9_2.cpp
//inheritance from String class
#include <iostream>
#include <cstring>                 //for strcpy(), etc.
using namespace std;
/////////////////////////////////////////////////////////////////
class String                       //base class
    {
    protected:                     //Note: can't be private
        enum { SZ = 80 };          //size of all String objects
        char str[SZ];              //holds a C-string
    public:
        String()                   //constructor 0, no args
            { str[0] = '\0'; }
        String( char s[] )         //constructor 1, one arg
            { strcpy(str, s); }    //  convert string to String
        void display() const       //display the String
            { cout << str; }
        operator ohar*()           //conversion function
            { return str; }        //convert String to C-string
    };
/////////////////////////////////////////////////////////////////
class Pstring : public String      //derived class
    {
    public:
        Pstring( char s[] );       //constructor
    };
//-------------------------------------------------------------
Pstring::Pstring( char s[] )       //constructor for Pstring
    {
    if(strlen(s) > SZ-1)           //if too long,
        {
        for(int j=0; j<SZ-1; j++)  //copy the first SZ-1
            str[j] = s[j];         //characters "by hand"
        str[j] = '\0';             //add the null character
        }
    else                           //not too long,
        String(s);                 //so construct normally
    }
/////////////////////////////////////////////////////////////////
int main()
    {                                          //define String
    Pstring s1 = "This is a very long string which is probably "
```

```
                    "no, certainly--going to exceed the limit set by SZ.";
        cout << "\ns1="; s1.display();            //display String

        Pstring s2 = "This is a short string.";  //define String
        cout << "\ns2="; s2.display();            //display String
        cout << endl;
        return 0;
        }
```

3.
```
// ex9_3.cpp
// multiple inheritance with publication class
#include <iostream>
#include <string>
using namespace std;
/////////////////////////////////////////////////////////////////
class publication
    {
    private:
        string title;
        float price;
    public:
        void getdata()
            {
            cout << "\nEnter title: "; cin >> title;
            cout << "   Enter price: "; cin >> price;
            }
        void putdata() const
            {
            cout << "\nTitle: " << title;
            cout << "\n   Price: " << price;
            }
    };
/////////////////////////////////////////////////////////////////
class sales
    {
    private:
        enum { MONTHS = 3 };
        float salesArr[MONTHS];
    public:
        void getdata();
        void putdata() const;
    };
//-------------------------------------------------------------
void sales::getdata()
    {
    cout << "   Enter sales for 3 months\n";
    for(int j=0; j<MONTHS; j++)
        {
        cout << "      Month " << j+1 << ": ";
        cin >> salesArr[j];
        }
    }
```

```cpp
//-------------------------------------------------------------
void sales::putdata() const
   {
   for(int j=0; j<MONTHS; j++)
      {
      cout << "\n   Sales for month " << j+1 << ": ";
      cout << salesArr[j];
      }
   }
/////////////////////////////////////////////////////////////////
class book : private publication, private sales
   {
   private:
      int pages;
   public:
      void getdata()
         {
         publication::getdata();
         cout << "   Enter number of pages: "; cin >> pages;
         sales::getdata();
         }
      void putdata() const
         {
         publication::putdata();
         cout << "\n   Pages: " << pages;
         sales::putdata();
         }
   };
/////////////////////////////////////////////////////////////////
class tape : private publication, private sales
   {
   private:
      float time;
   public:
      void getdata()
         {
         publication::getdata();
         cout << "   Enter playing time: "; cin >> time;
         sales::getdata();
         }
      void putdata() const
         {
         publication::putdata();
         cout << "\n   Playing time: " << time;
         sales::putdata();
         }
   };
/////////////////////////////////////////////////////////////////
int main()
   {
   book book1;            // define publications
   tape tape1;
```

```
            book1.getdata();    // get data for publications
            tape1.getdata();

            book1.putdata();    // display data for publications
            tape1.putdata();
            cout << endl;
            return 0;
            }
```

Chapter 10

Answers to Questions

1. `cout << &testvar;`

2. 4 bytes

3. c

4. `&var, *var, var&, char*`

5. constant; variable

6. `float* ptrtofloat;`

7. name

8. `*testptr`

9. pointer to; contents of the variable pointed to by

10. b, c, d

11. No. The address `&intvar` must be placed in the pointer `intptr` before it can be accessed.

12. any data type

13. They both do the same thing.

14.
```
    for(int j=0; j<77; j++)
        cout << endl << *(intarr+j);
```

15. Because array names represent the address of the array, which is a constant and can't be changed.

16. reference; pointer

17. a, d

18. `void func(char*);`

19.
```
for(int j=0; j<80; j++)
   *s2++ = *s1++;
```

20. b

21. `char* revstr(char*);`

22. `char* numptrs[] = { "One", "Two", "Three" };`

23. a, c

24. wasted

25. memory that is no longer needed

26. `p->exclu();`

27. `objarr[7].exclu();`

28. a, c

29. `float* arr[8];`

30. b

Solutions to Exercises

1.
```cpp
// ex10_1.cpp
// finds average of numbers typed by user
#include <iostream>
using namespace std;

int main()
   {
   float flarr[100];               //array for numbers
   char ch;                        //user decision
   int num = 0;                    //counts numbers input
   do
      {
      cout << "Enter number: ";    //get numbers from user
      cin >> *(flarr+num++);       //until user answers 'n'
      cout << "  Enter another (y/n)? ";
      cin >> ch;
      }
   while(ch != 'n');

   float total = 0.0;              //total starts at 0
   for(int k=0; k<num; k++)        //add numbers to total
      total += *(flarr+k);
```

```cpp
   float average = total / num;        //find and display average
   cout << "Average is " << average << endl;
   return 0;
   }
```

2.

```cpp
// ex10_2.cpp
// member function converts String objects to upper case
#include <iostream>
#include <cstring>          //for strcpy(), etc
#include <cctype>           //for toupper()
using namespace std;
/////////////////////////////////////////////////////////////////
class String                //user-defined string type
   {
   private:
      char* str;                        //pointer to string
   public:
      String(char* s)                   //constructor, one arg
         {
         int length = strlen(s);        //length of string argument
         str = new char[length+1];      //get memory
         strcpy(str, s);                //copy argument to it
         }
      ~String()                         //destructor
         { delete str; }
      void display()                    //display the String
         { cout << str; }
      void upit();                      //uppercase the String
   };
//---------------------------------------------------------------
void String::upit()                     //uppercase each character
   {
   char* ptrch = str;                   //pointer to this string
   while( *ptrch )                      //until null,
      {
      *ptrch = toupper(*ptrch);         //uppercase each character
      ptrch++;                          //move to next character
      }
   }
/////////////////////////////////////////////////////////////////
int main()
   {
   String s1 = "He who laughs last laughs best.";

   cout << "\ns1=";        //display string
   s1.display();
   s1.upit();              //uppercase string
   cout << "\ns1=";        //display string
   s1.display();
   cout << endl;
   return 0;
   }
```

3.

```
// ex10_3.cpp
// sort an array of pointers to strings
#include <iostream>
#include <cstring>                  //for strcmp(), etc.
using namespace std;
const int DAYS = 7;                 //number of pointers in array

int main()
   {
   void bsort(char**, int);       //prototype
                                  //array of pointers to char
   char* arrptrs[DAYS] = { "Sunday", "Monday", "Tuesday",
                           "Wednesday", "Thursday",
                           "Friday", "Saturday"  };

   cout << "\nUnsorted:\n";
   for(int j=0; j<DAYS; j++)      //display unsorted strings
      cout << *(arrptrs+j) << endl;

   bsort(arrptrs, DAYS);          //sort the strings

   cout << "\nSorted:\n";
   for(j=0; j<DAYS; j++)          //display sorted strings
      cout << *(arrptrs+j) << endl;
   return 0;
   }
//-------------------------------------------------------------
void bsort(char** pp, int n)      //sort pointers to strings
   {
   void order(char**, char**);    //prototype
   int j, k;                      //indexes to array

   for(j=0; j<n-1; j++)           //outer loop
      for(k=j+1; k<n; k++)        //inner loop starts at outer
   order(pp+j, pp+k);             //order the pointer contents
   }
//-------------------------------------------------------------
void order(char** pp1, char** pp2)  //orders two pointers
   {                                //if string in 1st is
   if( strcmp(*pp1, *pp2) > 0)  //larger than in 2nd,
      {
      char* tempptr = *pp1;       //swap the pointers
      *pp1 = *pp2;
      *pp2 = tempptr;
      }
   }
```

4.

```
// ex10_4.cpp
// linked list includes destructor
#include <iostream>
using namespace std;
```

```cpp
/////////////////////////////////////////////////////////////////
struct link                        //one element of list
   {
   int data;                       //data item
   link* next;                     //pointer to next link
   };
/////////////////////////////////////////////////////////////////
class linklist                     //a list of links
   {
   private:
      link* first;                 //pointer to first link
   public:
      linklist()                   //no-argument constructor
         { first = NULL; }         //no first link
      ~linklist();                 //destructor
      void additem(int d);         //add data item (one link)
      void display();              //display all links
   };
//---------------------------------------------------------------
void linklist::additem(int d)      //add data item
   {
   link* newlink = new link;       //make a new link
   newlink->data = d;              //give it data
   newlink->next = first;          //it points to next link
   first = newlink;                //now first points to this
   }
//---------------------------------------------------------------
void linklist::display()           //display all links
   {
   link* current = first;          //set ptr to first link
   while( current != NULL )        //quit on last link
      {
      cout << endl << current->data; //print data
      current = current->next;     //move to next link
      }
   }
//---------------------------------------------------------------
linklist::~linklist()              //destructor
   {
   link* current = first;          //set ptr to first link
   while( current != NULL )        //quit on last link
      {
      link* temp = current;        //save ptr to this link
      current = current->next;     //get ptr to next link
      delete temp;                 //delete this link
      }
   }
/////////////////////////////////////////////////////////////////
int main()
   {
   linklist li;         //make linked list

   li.additem(25);      //add four items to list
   li.additem(36);
```

```
li.additem(49);
li.additem(64);

li.display();        //display entire list
cout << endl;
return 0;
}
```

Chapter 11

Answers to Questions

1. d

2. True

3. base

4. `virtual void dang(int);` or `void virtual dang(int);`

5. late binding or dynamic binding

6. derived

7. `virtual void aragorn()=0;` or `void virtual aragorn()=0;`

8. a, c

9. `dong* parr[10];`

10. c

11. True

12. c, d

13. `friend void harry(george);`

14. a, c, d

15. `friend class harry;` or `friend harry;`

16. c

17. It performs a member-by-member copy.

18. `zeta& operator = (zeta&);`

19. a, b, d

20. False; the compiler provides a default copy constructor.

21. a, d

22. `Bertha(Bertha&);`

23. True, if there was a reason to do so.

24. a, c

25. True; trouble occurs if it's returned by reference.

26. They operate identically.

27. a, b

28. The object of which the function using it is a member.

29. No; since `this` is a pointer, use `this->da=37;`.

30. `return *this;`

Solutions to Exercises

1.

```
// ex11_1.cpp
// publication class and derived classes
#include <iostream>
#include <string>
using namespace std;
////////////////////////////////////////////////////////////////
class publication
    {
    private:
        string title;
        float price;
    public:
        virtual void getdata()
            {
            cout << "\nEnter title: "; cin >> title;
            cout << "Enter price: "; cin >> price;
            }
        virtual void putdata()
            {
            cout << "\n\nTitle: " << title;
            cout << "\nPrice: " << price;
            }
    };
////////////////////////////////////////////////////////////////
class book : public publication
    {
    private:
        int pages;
    public:
        void getdata()
            {
```

```
               publication::getdata();
               cout << "Enter number of pages: "; cin >> pages;
               }
           void putdata()
               {
               publication::putdata();
               cout << "\nPages: " << pages;
               }
        };
////////////////////////////////////////////////////////////////
class tape : public publication
    {
    private:
        float time;
    public:
        void getdata()
            {
            publication::getdata();
            cout << "Enter playing time: "; cin >> time;
            }
        void putdata()
            {
            publication::putdata();
            cout << "\nPlaying time: " << time;
            }
    };
////////////////////////////////////////////////////////////////
int main()
    {
    publication* pubarr[100];          //array of ptrs to pubs
    int n = 0;                         //number of pubs in array
    char choice;                       //user's choice

    do {
       cout << "\nEnter data for book or tape (b/t)? ";
       cin >> choice;
       if( choice=='b' )               //make book object
          pubarr[n] = new book;        //   put in array
       else                            //make tape object
          pubarr[n] = new tape;        //   put in array
       pubarr[n++]->getdata();         //get data for object
       cout << "   Enter another (y/n)? ";  //another pub?
       cin >> choice;
       }
    while( choice =='y');              //cycle until not 'y'

    for(int j=0; j<n; j++)             //cycle thru all pubs
       pubarr[j]->putdata();           //print data for pub
    cout << endl;
    return 0;
    }
```

2.

```cpp
// ex11_2.cpp
// friend square() function for Distance
#include <iostream>
using namespace std;
/////////////////////////////////////////////////////////////
class Distance                        //English Distance class
   {
   private:
      int feet;
      float inches;
   public:
      Distance()                      //constructor (no args)
         { feet = 0; inches = 0.0; }
      Distance(float fltfeet)         //constructor (one arg)
         {                            //feet is integer part
         feet = static_cast<int>(fltfeet);
         inches = 12*(fltfeet-feet);  //inches is what's left
         }                            //constructor (two args)
      Distance(int ft, float in) : feet(ft), inches(in)
         {  }
      void showdist()                 //display distance
         { cout << feet << "\'-" << inches << '\"'; }
      friend Distance operator * (Distance, Distance); //friend
   };
//----------------------------------------------------------
                                      //multiply d1 by d2
Distance operator * (Distance d1, Distance d2)
   {
   float fltfeet1 = d1.feet + d1.inches/12;  //convert to float
   float fltfeet2 = d2.feet + d2.inches/12;
   float multfeet = fltfeet1 * fltfeet2;      //find the product
   return Distance(multfeet);        //return temp Distance
   }
/////////////////////////////////////////////////////////////
int main()
   {
   Distance dist1(3, 6.0);           //make some distances
   Distance dist2(2, 3.0);
   Distance dist3;

   dist3 = dist1 * dist2;            //multiplication

   dist3 = 10.0 * dist3;             //mult and conversion
                                     //display all distances
   cout << "\ndist1 = "; dist1.showdist();
   cout << "\ndist2 = "; dist2.showdist();
   cout << "\ndist3 = "; dist3.showdist();
   cout << endl;
   return 0;
   }
```

3.

```cpp
// ex11_3.cpp
// creates array class
// overloads assignment operator and copy constructor
#include <iostream>
using namespace std;
//////////////////////////////////////////////////////////////
class Array
    {
    private:
        int* ptr;                   //pointer to "array" contents
        int size;                   //size of array
    public:
        Array() : ptr(0), size(0)   //no-argument constructor
            { }
        Array(int s) : size(s)      //one-argument constructor
            { ptr = new int[s]; }
        Array(Array&);              //copy constructor
        ~Array()                    //destructor
            { delete[] ptr; }
        int& operator [] (int j)    //overloaded subscript op
            { return *(ptr+j); }
        Array& operator = (Array&);  //overloaded = operator
    };
//------------------------------------------------------------
Array::Array(Array& a)          //copy constructor
    {
    size = a.size;                  //new one is same size
    ptr = new int[size];            //get space for contents
    for(int j=0; j<size; j++)       //copy contents to new one
        *(ptr+j) = *(a.ptr+j);
    }
//------------------------------------------------------------
Array& Array::operator = (Array& a)  //overloaded = operator
    {
    delete[] ptr;                   //delete old contents (if any)
    size = a.size;                  //make this object same size
    ptr = new int[a.size];          //get space for new contents
    for(int j=0; j<a.size; j++)     //copy contents to this object
        *(ptr+j) = *(a.ptr+j);
    return *this;                   //return this object
    }
//////////////////////////////////////////////////////////////
int main()
    {
    const int ASIZE = 10;           //size of array
    Array arr1(ASIZE);              //make an array

    for(int j=0; j<ASIZE; j++)      //fill it with squares
        arr1[j] = j*j;

    Array arr2(arr1);               //use the copy constructor
    cout << "\narr2: ";
```

```
for(j=0; j<ASIZE; j++)        //check that it worked
    cout << arr2[j] << "  ";

Array arr3, arr4;             //make two empty Array objects
arr4 = arr3 = arr1;           //use the assignment operator
cout << "\narr3: ";
for(j=0; j<ASIZE; j++)        //check that it worked on arr3
    cout << arr3[j] << "  ";
cout << "\narr4: ";
for(j=0; j<ASIZE; j++)        //check that it worked on arr4
    cout << arr4[j] << "  ";
cout << endl;
return 0;
}
```

Chapter 12

Answers to Questions

1. b, c

2. `ios`

3. `ifstream`, `ofstream`, and `fstream`

4. `ofstream salefile ("SALES.JUN");`

5. True

6. `if(foobar)`

7. d

8. `fileOut.put(ch);` (where ch is the character)

9. c

10. `ifile.read( (char*)buff, sizeof(buff) );`

11. a, b, d

12. the byte location at which the next read or write operation will take place

13. False; file pointer can be a synonym for current position.

14. `f1.seekg(-13, ios::cur);`

15. b

16. b, c

17. `skipws` causes whitespace characters to be ignored on input so that `cin` will not assume the input has terminated.

18. `int main(int argc, char *argv[] )`

19. PRN, LPT1.

20. `istream& operator >> (istream&, Sample& )`

Solutions to Exercises

1.

```cpp
// ex12_1.cpp
// write array
#include <iostream>
#include <fstream>               // for file streams
using namespace std;
/////////////////////////////////////////////////////////////
class Distance                      // English Distance class
   {
   private:
      int feet;
      float inches;
   public:
      Distance() : feet(0), inches(0.0) // constructor (no args)
         { }                          // constructor (two args)
      Distance(int ft, float in) : feet(ft), inches(in)
         { }
      void getdist()                  // get length from user
         {
         cout << "\n   Enter feet: ";  cin >> feet;
         cout << "   Enter inches: ";  cin >> inches;
         }
      void showdist()               // display distance
         { cout << feet << "\'-" << inches << '\"'; }
   };
/////////////////////////////////////////////////////////////
int main()
   {
   char ch;
   Distance dist;                   // create a Distance object
   fstream file;                    // create input/output file
                                    // open it for append
   file.open("DIST.DAT", ios::binary | ios::app |
                         ios::out | ios::in );

   do                               // data from user to file
      {
      cout << "\nDistance";
      dist.getdist();               // get a distance
                                    // write to file
      file.write( (char*)&dist, sizeof(dist) );
```

```cpp
            cout << "Enter another distance (y/n)? ";
            cin >> ch;
            }
        while(ch=='y');                     // quit on 'n'

        file.seekg(0);                      // reset to start of file
                                            // read first distance
        file.read( (char*)&dist, sizeof(dist) );
        int count = 0;
        while( !file.eof() )                // quit on EOF
            {
            cout << "\nDistance " << ++count << ": "; // display dist
            dist.showdist();
            file.read( (char*)&dist, sizeof(dist) );  // read another
            }                                         // distance
        cout << endl;
        return 0;
        }
```

2.

```cpp
    // ex12_2.cpp
    // imitates COPY command
    #include <fstream>                  //for file functions
    #include <iostream>
    using namespace std;
    #include <process.h>                //for exit()

    int main(int argc, char* argv[] )
        {
        if( argc != 3 )
            { cerr << "\nFormat: ocopy srcfile destfile"; exit(-1); }
        char ch;                            //character to read

        ifstream infile;                    //create file for input
        infile.open( argv[1] );             //open file
        if( !infile )                       //check for errors
            { cerr << "\nCan't open " << argv[1]; exit(-1); }

        ofstream outfile;                   //create file for output
        outfile.open( argv[2] );            //open file
        if( !outfile )                      //check for errors
            { cerr << "\nCan't open " << argv[2]; exit(-1); }

        while( infile )                     //until EOF
            {
            infile.get(ch);                 //read a character
            outfile.put(ch);                //write the character
            }
        return 0;
        }
```

3.

```cpp
// ex12_3.cpp
// displays size of file
#include <fstream>                   //for file functions
#include <iostream>
using namespace std;
#include <process.h>                 //for exit()

int main(int argc, char* argv[] )
   {
   if( argc != 2 )
      { cerr << "\nFormat: filename\n"; exit(-1); }
   ifstream infile;                  //create file for input
   infile.open( argv[1] );           //open file
   if( !infile )                     //check for errors
      { cerr << "\nCan't open " << argv[1]; exit(-1); }
   infile.seekg(0, ios::end);        //go to end of file
                                     // report byte number
   cout << "Size of " << argv[1] << " is " << infile.tellg();
   cout << endl;
   return 0;
   }
```

Chapter 13

Answers to Questions

1. a, b, c, d

2. `#include` directive

3. the compiler to compile the .CPP file and the linker to link the resulting .OBJ files

4. a, b

5. class library

6. True

7. c, d

8. True

9. False

10. a, c, d

Chapter 14

Answers to Questions

1. b and c

2. class

3. False. Different functions are created at compile time.

4.
```
template<class T>
T times2(T arg)
    {
    return arg*2;
    }
```

5. b

6. True

7. instantiating

8. c

9. fixed data type, any data type

10. store data

11. c

12. `try`, `catch`, and `throw`

13. `throw BoundsError();`

14. False. They must be part of a try block.

15. d

16.
```
class X
    {
    public:
        int xnumber;
        char xname[MAX];
        X(int xd, char* xs)
            {
            xnumber = xd;
            strcpy(xname, xs);
            }
    };
```

17. False

18. a and d

19. d

20. True

Solutions to Exercises

1.
```cpp
// ex14_1.cpp
// template used for function that averages array
#include <iostream>
using namespace std;
//////////////////////////////////////////////////////////////
template <class atype>                    //function template
atype avg(atype* array, int size)
    {
    atype total = 0;
    for(int j=0; j<size; j++)             //average the array
        total += array[j];
    return (atype)total/size;
    }
//////////////////////////////////////////////////////////////
int intArray[]  =       {1, 3, 5, 9, 11, 13};
long longArray[] =      {1, 3, 5, 9, 11, 13};
double doubleArray[] = {1.0, 3.0, 5.0, 9.0, 11.0, 13.0};
char charArray[] =      {1, 3, 5, 9, 11, 13};

int main()
    {
    cout << "\navg(intArray)=" << avg(intArray, 6);
    cout << "\navg(longArray)=" << avg(longArray, 6);
    cout << "\navg(doubleArray)=" << avg(doubleArray, 6);
    cout << "\navg(charArray)=" << (int)avg(charArray, 6) << endl;
    return 0;
    }
```

2.
```cpp
// ex14_2.cpp
// implements queue class as a template
#include <iostream>
using namespace std;
const int MAX = 3;
//////////////////////////////////////////////////////////////
template <class Type>
class Queue
    {
    private:
        Type qu[MAX]; //array of any type
        int head;      //index of start of queue (remove item here)
```

```cpp
        int tail;        //index of end of queue (insert item here)
    public:
        Queue()                         //constructor
           { head = -1; tail = -1; }
        void put(Type var)              //insert item at queue tail
           {
           qu[++tail] = var;
           if(tail >=MAX-1)             //wrap around if past array end
              tail = -1;
           }
        Type get()                      //remove item from queue head
           {
           Type temp = qu[++head]; //store item
           if(head >= MAX-1)            //wrap around if past array end
              head = -1;
           return temp;                 //return item
           }
    };
//////////////////////////////////////////////////////////////////
int main()
    {
    Queue<float> q1;       //q1 is object of class Queue<float>

    q1.put(1111.1F);                             //put 3
    q1.put(2222.2F);
    q1.put(3333.3F);
    cout << "1: " << q1.get() << endl;    //get 2
    cout << "2: " << q1.get() << endl;
    q1.put(4444.4F);                             //put 2
    q1.put(5555.5F);
    cout << "3: " << q1.get() << endl;    //get 1
    q1.put(6666.6F);                             //put 1
    cout << "4: " << q1.get() << endl;    //get 3
    cout << "5: " << q1.get() << endl;
    cout << "6: " << q1.get() << endl;

    Queue<long> q2;        //q2 is object of class Queue<long>

    q2.put(123123123L);  //put 3 longs, get 3 longs
    q2.put(234234234L);
    q2.put(345345345L);
    cout << "1: " << q2.get() << endl;
    cout << "2: " << q2.get() << endl;
    cout << "3: " << q2.get() << endl;
    return 0;
    }
```

3.

```cpp
// ex14_3.cpp
// implements queue class as a template
// uses exceptions to handle errors in queue
#include <iostream>
using namespace std;
```

```cpp
const int MAX = 3;
//////////////////////////////////////////////////////////////
template <class Type>
class Queue
   {
   private:
      Type qu[MAX]; //array of any type
      int head;      //index of front of queue (remove old item)
      int tail;      //index of back of queue (insert new item)
      int count;     //number of items in queue
   public:
      class full  {  };         //exception classes
      class empty  {  };
//------------------------------------------------------------
      Queue()                   //constructor
         { head = -1; tail = -1; count = 0; }

      void put(Type var)        //insert item at queue tail
         {
         if(count >= MAX)        //if queue already full,
            throw full();        //   throw exception
         qu[++tail] = var;       //store item
         ++count;
         if(tail >=MAX-1)        //wrap around if past array end
            tail = -1;
         }
//------------------------------------------------------------
      Type get()                //remove item from queue head
         {
         if(count <= 0)          //if queue empty,
            throw empty();       //   throw exception
         Type temp = qu[++head]; //get item
         --count;
         if(head >= MAX-1)       //wrap around if past array end
            head = -1;
         return temp;            //return item
         }
   };
//////////////////////////////////////////////////////////////
int main()
   {
   Queue<float> q1;    //q1 is object of class Queue<float>
   float data;         //data item obtained from user
   char choice = 'p';  //'x', 'p' or 'g'

   do                  //do loop (enter 'x' to quit)
      {
      try              //try block
         {
         cout << "\nEnter 'x' to exit, 'p' for put, 'g' for get: ";
         cin >> choioe;
         if(choice=='p')
            {
```

```
            cout << "Enter data value: ";
            cin >> data;
            q1.put(data);
            }
        if(choice=='g')
            cout << "Data=" << q1.get() << endl;
        }  //end try
    catch(Queue<float>::full)
        {
        cout << "Error: queue is full." << endl;
        }
    catch(Queue<float>::empty)
        {
        cout << "Error: queue is empty." << endl;
        }
    } while(choice != 'x');
return 0;
}  //end main()
```

Chapter 15

Answers to Questions

1. a, b, d

2. vector, list, deque

3. set, map

4. a

5. True

6. c

7. False

8. iterator

9. a function object

10. c

11. False (it simply returns its value)

12. 3, 11

13. duplicate

14. b, c

15. points to

16. False

17. bidirectional

18. `*iter++`

19. d

20. c

21. True

22. iterators

23. It's a string used to separate the printed values.

24. b

25. the elements will be ordered

26. True

27. pairs (or associations)

28. False

29. a, d

30. constructor

Solutions to Exercises

1.
```cpp
// ex15_1.cpp
// type float stored in array, sorted by sort()
#include <iostream>
#include <algorithm>
using namespace std;

int main()
   {
   int j=0, k;
   char ch;
   float fpn, farr[100];

   do {
      cout << "Enter a floating point number: ";
      cin >> fpn;
      farr[j++] = fpn;
      cout << "Enter another ('y' or 'n'): ";
      cin >> ch;
      } while(ch == 'y');
   sort(farr, farr+j);
   for(k=0; k<j; k++)
```

```
        cout << farr[k] << ", ";
   cout << endl;
   return  0;
   }
```

2.

```
// ex15_2.cpp
// vector used with string objects, push_back(), and []
#include <iostream>
#include <string>
#pragma warning (disable:4786)   //Microsoft only
#include <vector>
#include <algorithm>
using namespace std;

int main()
   {
   vector<string> vectStrings;
   string word;
   char ch;

   do {
      cout << "Enter a word: ";
      cin >> word;
      vectStrings.push_back(word);
      cout << "Enter another ('y' or 'n'): ";
      cin >> ch;
      } while(ch == 'y');
   sort( vectStrings.begin(), vectStrings.end() );
   for(int k=0; k<vectStrings.size(); k++)
      cout << vectStrings[k] << endl;
   return 0;
   }
```

3.

```
// ex15_3.cpp
// home-made reverse() algorithm reverses a list
#include <iostream>
#include <list>
using namespace std;

int main()
   {
   int j;

   list<int> theList;
   list<int>::iterator iter1;
   list<int>::iterator iter2;

   for(j=2; j<16; j+=2)               //fill list with 2, 4, 6, ...
      theList.push_back(j);
```

```cpp
    cout << "Before reversal: ";    //display list
    for(iter1=theList.begin(); iter1 != theList.end(); iter1++)
       cout << *iter1 << " ";

    iter1 = theList.begin();      //set to first element
    iter2 = theList.end();        //set to one-past-last
    --iter2;                      //move to last

    while(iter1 != iter2)
       {
       swap(*iter1, *iter2);      //swap front and back
       ++iter1;                   //increment front
       if(iter1==iter2)           //if even number of elements
          break;
       --iter2;                   //decrement back
       }

    cout << "\nAfter reversal: ";  //display list
    for(iter1=theList.begin(); iter1 != theList.end(); iter1++)
       cout << *iter1 << " ";
    cout << endl;
    return 0;
    }
```

4.

```cpp
// ex15_4.cpp
// a multiset automatically sorts person objects stored by pointer
#include <iostream>
#include <set>
#pragma warning (disable:4786)
#include <string>
using namespace std;

class person
    {
    private:
       string lastName;
       string firstName;
       long phoneNumber;
    public:
       person() :              // default constructor
          lastName("blank"), firstName("blank"), phoneNumber(0L)
          { }
                               // 3-arg constructor
       person(string lana, string fina, long pho) :
             lastName(lana), firstName(fina), phoneNumber(pho)
          { }
       friend bool operator<(const person&, const person&);

       void display() const    // display person's data
          {
          cout << endl << lastName << ",\t" << firstName
```

```cpp
                        << "\t\tPhone: " << phoneNumber;
            }
        long get_phone() const // return phone number
            { return phoneNumber; }
    }; //end class person
//--------------------------------------------------------------
// overloaded < for person class
bool operator<(const person& p1, const person& p2)
    {
    if(p1.lastName == p2.lastName)
        return (p1.firstName < p2.firstName) ? true : false;
    return (p1.lastName < p2.lastName) ? true : false;
    }
//--------------------------------------------------------------
// function object to compare persons using pointers
class comparePersons
    {
    public:
    bool operator() (const person* ptrP1,
                     const person* ptrP2) const
        { return *ptrP1 < *ptrP2; }
    };
//////////////////////////////////////////////////////////////
int main()
    {                                 // a multiset of ptrs to persons
    multiset<person*, comparePersons> setPtrsPers;
    multiset<person*, comparePersons>::iterator iter;

                                    //make persons
    person* ptrP1 = new person("KuangThu", "Bruce", 4157300);
    person* ptrP2 = new person("McDonald", "Stacey", 3327563);
    person* ptrP3 = new person("Deauville", "William", 8435150);
    person* ptrP4 = new person("Wellington", "John", 9207404);
    person* ptrP5 = new person("Bartoski", "Peter", 6946473);
    person* ptrP6 = new person("McDonald", "Amanda", 8435150);
    person* ptrP7 = new person("Fredericks", "Roger", 7049982);
    person* ptrP8 = new person("McDonald", "Stacey", 7764987);

    setPtrsPers.insert(ptrP1);            //put persons in multiset
    setPtrsPers.insert(ptrP2);
    setPtrsPers.insert(ptrP3);
    setPtrsPers.insert(ptrP4);
    setPtrsPers.insert(ptrP5);
    setPtrsPers.insert(ptrP6);
    setPtrsPers.insert(ptrP7);
    setPtrsPers.insert(ptrP8);
                                            //display multiset
    cout << "\n\nSet sorted when created:";
    for(iter=setPtrsPers.begin(); iter != setPtrsPers.end(); iter++ )
        (**iter).display();

    iter = setPtrsPers.begin();          //delete all persons
    while( iter != setPtrsPers.end() )
```

```
        {
        delete *iter;                //delete person
        setPtrsPers.erase(iter++);   //remove pointer
        }
    cout << endl;
    return 0;
    }  // end main()
```

Chapter 16

Answers to Questions

1. False

2. d

3. class, responsibilities, collaborators

4. True

5. know, do

6. b

7. collaborator

8. a, d

9. False

10. b, c

11. True

12. Usually false

13. a, b, c, d

14. human beings, program

15. d

16. a, b, c, d

17. False

18. a, d

19. association

20. True

21. b

22. strong, aggregation

23. True

24. a

25. navigability

26. objects, object

27. rectangles

28. c

29. interfaces, implementations

30. loosely, tight

APPENDIX H

BIBLIOGRAPHY

This appendix lists some books that might prove useful or interesting to students of C++.

Books on Advanced C++

After you've mastered the fundamentals of C++, the next books you should probably buy are *Effective C++*, by Scott Meyers (Addison Wesley, 1997), and *More Effective C++*, also by Scott Meyers (Addison Wesley, 1996). These books contain, respectively, "50 specific ways to improve your programs and designs" and "35 new ways to improve your programs and designs." Each of the topics in these books is short but clearly presented. These books are a fund of important ideas and are widely read by C++ programmers.

Thinking in C++ by Bruce Eckel (Prentice Hall, 1995) is probably a little too fast for beginners, but it covers the fundamentals of the language and is excellent at explaining why things work the way they do.

C++ FAQs (Frequently Asked Questions) by Marshall Cline and Greg Lomow (Addison Wesley, 1995) contains hundreds of topics about C++ in short question-and-answer format. It's easy reading and will contribute to your understanding of C++.

Defining Documents

Because the author is the language's creator, the most definitive text on C++ is *The C++ Programming Language, Third Edition*, by Bjarne Stroustrup (Addison Wesley, 1997). Every serious C++ programmer should have a copy of this book. It assumes a certain level of sophistication, so it's not for beginners. However, it's clearly written, and once you've mastered the fundamentals it's an invaluable aid to the finer points of C++ usage.

You probably won't need the actual defining document for Standard C++ until you've progressed quite far in your study of C++. *The Final Draft Information Standard (FDIS) for the C++ Programming Language*, X3J16/97-14882, is available from the Information Technology Council (NSTIC), Washington, DC.

The previous defining document on C++ was *The Annotated C++ Reference Manual* by Margaret Ellis and Bjarne Stroustrup (Addison Wesley, 1990). This is fairly heavy going and filled with arcane explanations. It's also out of date.

Books on Specific Topics

C++ IOStreams Handbook, by Steve Teale (Addison Wesley, 1993) is a good explanation of the details of streams and files in C++. There's material here you won't find anywhere else.

The Standard Template Library, by Alexander Stepanov and Meng Lee, (Hewlett-Packard, 1994) is the defining document on the STL. You can learn all about the STL from it, but it doesn't have many examples, and there are books that are easier to read. One is *STL Tutorial and Reference Guide*, by David R Musser and Atul Saini (Addison Wesley, 1996).

Although it's nominally based on Java, *Object-Oriented Design in Java* by Stephen Gilbert and Bill McCarty (Waite Group Press, 1998) is a comprehensive, easy-to-read introduction to program design in any language.

C++ Distilled, by Ira Pohl (Addison Wesley, 1997) is a short summary of the important features of C++. It's great if you've forgotten a particular syntax and want to look it up in a hurry.

Books on the History of C++

The Design and Evolution of C++ by Bjarne Stroustrup (Addison Wesley, 1994) is a description by its creator of how C++ came to be the way it is. It's interesting in its own right, and knowing the history can even help you understand the language.

Ruminations on C++, by Andrew Koenig (Addison Wesley, 1997) is a rather informal discussion of various topics by one of the pioneers in C and C++. It's easy to read and will give you fresh insights.

Books on Other Topics

Windows Game Programming for Dummies" by AndrÈ LaMothe (IDG Books, 1998) is a fascinating look at the details of game programming. AndrÈ's book explains (among many other things) how to use the Windows console graphics routines, which form the basis of Console Graphics Lite routines discussed in Appendix E, "Console Graphics Lite," of this book. If you have any interest in writing game programs, buy this book.

The C Programming Language, by Brian Kernighan and Dennis Ritchie (Addison Wesley, 1978) is the definitive book about C, the language on which C++ was based. It's not a primer, but once you know some C it's the reference you'll want.

Learning C++ Online

Finally, if you want to learn C++ in an interactive Web-based environment where your exams are graded online and you can ask questions of online "mentors," try *C++ Interactive Course*, by Robert Lafore (Macmillan Computer Publishing, 1996).

INDEX

Symbols

& address-of operator, 391-392
&& AND logical operator, 103-104
+ arithmetic operator, 52
= assignment operators, 478-479
    arithmetic assignment operators, 53-54
    chaining, 481
    inheritance, 481
    overloading, 479-481, 484-491
    prohibiting copying, 485
    self-assignment, 497-498
? conditional operator, 100-103, 107, 326
. dot operator, 326
>> extraction operator, 39-40, 515, 529-530
    cascading, 39-40
    overloading, 557-561
-- decrement operator, 56, 292
/ division operator, 52
== equal to relational operator, 69
++ increment operator, 54-56, 292-293
    overloading, 292-293
    postfix, 55-56
    prefix, 55-56
<< insertion operator, 27, 46, 515
    cascading, 46
    overloading, 557-561
<= less than or equal to relational operator, 69
< less than relational operator, 69
* multiplication operator, 52
!= not equal to relational operator, 69
! NOT logical operator, 104, 106
|| OR logical operator, 104-105
% remainder operator, 52-53
:: scope resolution operator, 326, 349
[ ] subscript operator, 309-312
- subtraction operator, 52

A

abstract base classes, 356
abstract classes, 459
access specifiers
    default, 361
    private access specifier, 342-343, 361-362
    protected access specifier, 342-344
    public access specifier, 342-343, 362
    tips for selecting, 362
access violation error message, 443
accessibility and inheritance, 341-345
accessing
    array elements, 244
        structures, 254
        with pointers, 399-401
    base class members, 341-345
    characters in string objects, 281-282
    data with iterators, 683-684
    elements of arrays
        structures, 254
        with pointers, 399-401
    member function data with this pointer, 493-494
    members
        of static functions, 477-478
        of structures, 123-124
accumulate algorithm, 659, 824
adapters
    containers, 658-659
    iterators, 687
        insert iterator, 687-690
        raw storage iterator, 687
        reverse iterator, 687-688
addition (+) operator, 52
address-of (&) operator, 391-392
addresses (memory), pointers to, 390
    accessing variable pointed to, 395-397

address-of & operator, 391-392
constants, 394-395
variables, 392-393
adjacent difference algorithm, 824-825
adjacent find algorithm, 814
aggregates, declaring, 758-759
aggregation (classes), 744, 746-747
algorithms, 653
accumulate algorithm, 659, 824
adjacent difference algorithm, 824-825
adjacent find algorithm, 814
binary search algorithm, 820
containers, 680, 682-683
copy algorithm, 659, 815
copy backward algorithm, 815
count algorithm, 659, 662-663, 814
count if algorithm, 814
equal algorithm, 659, 814
equal range algorithm, 819
fill algorithm, 659, 816
fill n algorithm, 816
find algorithm, 659, 661-662, 814
header files, 662
ranges, 662
find if algorithm, 814
for each algorithm, 659, 667-668, 814
function objects, 665
generate algorithm, 816
generate n algorithm, 816
if algorithm, 666-667
includes algorithm, 820
inner product algorithm, 824
inplace merge algorithm, 820
iter swap algorithm, 659, 815
iterators, 681-682, 685-686, 827-829
lexicographical compare algorithm, 823
lower bound algorithm, 819
make heap algorithm, 822
max algorithm, 822
max element algorithm, 822-823
merge algorithm, 659, 664-665, 820
min algorithm, 822
min element algorithm, 823
mismatch algorithm, 814
next permutation algorithm, 823
nth element algorithm, 819
partial sort algorithm, 818
partial sort copy algorithm, 818

partial sum algorithm, 824
partition algorithm, 817
pop heap algorithm, 822
prev permutation algorithm, 823
push heap algorithm, 821-822
random shuffle algorithm, 817
remove algorithm, 816
remove copy algorithm, 816
remove copy if algorithm, 816
remove if algorithm, 816
replace algorithm, 815
replace copy algorithm, 815
replace copy if algorithm, 816
replace if algorithm, 815
reverse algorithm, 817
reverse copy algorithm, 817
rotate algorithm, 817
rotate copy algorithm, 817
search algorithm, 659, 663-664, 814-815
set difference algorithm, 821
set intersection algorithm, 821
set symmetric difference algorithm, 821
set union algorithm, 820-821
sort algorithm, 659, 663, 818
sort heap algorithm, 822
stable partition algorithm, 818
stable sort algorithm, 818
STL, 653-654, 659-669, 813-825
swap algorithm, 659, 815
swap ranges algorithm, 815
transform algorithm, 668-669, 815
unique algorithm, 816
unique copy algorithm, 817
upper bound algorithm, 819
user-written functions, 665-666
AND logical operator, 103-105
animation loops, 75
The Annotated C++ Reference Manual, 889
answers to questions
chapter 1, 831
chapter 2, 832-833
chapter 3, 834-836
chapter 4, 838-839
chapter 5, 841-842
chapter 6, 845-846
chapter 7, 849-850
chapter 8, 853-854
chapter 9, 859

chapter 10, 864-865
chapter 11, 869-870
chapter 12, 874-875
chapter 13, 877
chapter 14, 878-879
chapter 15, 882-883
chapter 16, 887-888
append() member function, 280
applications (console-mode)
    Borland C++Builder, 797-805
    Microsoft Visual C++, 791-796
arguments
    exceptions, 642-645
    functions, 24, 57
        arrays, 251-253, 404-406
        C-strings, 411-412
        constants, 153-154, 187-188, 230
        defaults, 178-179
        function templates, 619-621
        naming, 160
        objects, 214-215
        overloaded functions, 172-176
        parameters, 154
        passing, 152-160
        passing by pointers, 403-406
        passing by reference, 402
        references, 166-172
        structures, 155-160
        values, 155-156
        variables, 154-155
    manipulators, 517-518
    overloaded operators, 294
arithmetic assignment operators, 53-54, 307-308
arithmetic expressions, parsing, 434-438
arithmetic operators, 52
    addition (+) operator, 52
    division (/) operator, 52
    multiplication (×) operator, 52
    overloading, 299-303
    precedence, 107
    remainder (%) operator, 52-53
    subtraction (-) operator, 52
arrays, 241, 655
    bounds, 260
    buffers, 265-266
    C-strings, 270-272
    class members, 255-258
    data types, 241, 264-265

defining, 242-243, 248-249
elements, 243-244
    accessing, 244, 249, 399-401
    averaging, 244-245
    sorting, 406-410
examples, 242, 261-264
functions
    arguments, passing by pointers, 404-406
    calling, 252
    declarations, 252
    definitions, 252-253
    passing, 251
in other computer languages, 241
index, 244
index numbers, 241
initializing, 245-246, 250
memory management, 416
multidimensional arrays, 246-248
    accessing elements, 249
    defining, 248-249
    formatting numbers, 249
    initializing, 250
objects, 258-260
    accessing, 260-261
    bounds, 260
    examples, 261-264
passing to functions, 251
pointers, 399-402
    sorting array elements, 406-410
    to objects, 423-425
    to strings, 414-415
size, 242
structures, 253-255
    accessing elements, 254
    defining, 254
    similarities, 241
ASCII character set, 35, 109-110
asm keyword, 787
assigning string objects, 276-277
Assignment operator invoked message, 480
assignment operators, 478-479
    arithmetic assignment operators, 53-54
    chaining, 481
    inheritance, 481
    overloading, 479-481, 484-491
    prohibiting copying, 485
    self-assignment, 497-498
assignment statements
    integer variables, 33-34
    structures, 126

associations of classes, 744-746
associative containers, 655-656, 693-694
    keys, 656-657, 694
    maps, 656-657, 694, 697-700
    multimaps, 657, 694, 697-700
    multisets, 657, 694-697
    sets, 656-657, 694-697
associativity of operators, 406
at() member function, 281-282
atoi() library function, 525
attributes
    classes, 744-745, 758
    objects, 10-11
auto keyword, 180, 787
automatic variables, 180
    initialization, 181
    lifetime, 180
    scope, 181
    storage, 185
    visibility, 181
averaging array elements, 244-245

B

back() member function, 671
bad alloc class, 646
badbit flag, 523
base classes, 17-18, 337-341
    abstract base classes, 356
    accessing members, 341-345
    destructors, 465-466
    instantiating objects of, 459
    pure virtual functions, 459-460
    virtual base classes, 466-468
BDEs (business domain experts), 722
begin() member function, 658
behavior of objects, 11
bidirectional iterators, 660, 678-680
binary I/O, 533-534
binary operators, 106
    arithmetic assignment operators, 307-308
    arithmetic operators, 299-303
    comparison operators, 304-306
    overloading, 299
        arithmetic assignment operators, 307-308
        arithmetic operators, 299-303
        comparison operators, 304-306
binary search algorithm, 820

binding
    dynamic binding, 458
    early binding, 458
    late binding, 458
    static binding, 458
blanks in C-strings, 267-268
books about C++, 889-890
bool keyword, 787
bool variables, 43-44, 103
boolalpha flag, 516
Boole, George, 44
BORLACON.CPP, 807
Borland C++Builder, 797
    building existing files, 800
    closing projects, 801
    Console Graphics Lite, 804
    creating projects, 798-799
    debugging programs, 804
        breakpoints, 805
        single stepping, 804
        tracing into functions, 805
        watching variables, 805
    file extensions, 797
    header files, 801
        creating, 801
        editing, 802
        telling location of, 802
    multiple source file projects, 802-803
    opening projects, 801
    precompiled header files, 801
    running programs, 797-798, 800-801
    saving projects, 799
    screen elements, 798
Borland compilers, 23-24, 811
bounds of arrays, 260
braces in functions, 25
break keyword, 98, 787
break statement, 98, 107-109
bsort() function, 408-410
bubble sorts, 408-410
buffers
    arrays, 265-266
    C-strings, 265-266
bugs in pointers, 443
build process for multifile programs, 577
business domain experts, 722

C

C, 8
  C++, 19-20
  keywords, 787
The C Programming Language, 890
C++ and C, 19-20
C++ Distilled, 890
C++ FAQs, 889
C++ Interactive Course, 890
C++ IOStreams Handbook, 890
The C++ Programming Language, Third Edition, 889
C++Builder (Borland), 797
  building existing files, 800
  closing projects, 801
  Console Graphics Lite, 804
  creating projects, 798-799
  debugging programs, 804
    breakpoints, 805
    single stepping, 804
    tracing into functions, 805
    watching variables, 805
  file extensions, 797
  header files, 801
    creating, 801
    editing, 802
    telling location of, 802
  multiple source file projects, 802-803
  opening projects, 801
  precompiled header files, 801
  running programs, 797-798, 800-801
  saving projects, 799
  screen elements, 798
C-strings, 264-265
  arrays, 270-272
  blanks, 267-268
  buffers, 265-266
  class members, 272-273
  comparing, 306
  concatenating, 302
  constants, 267
  converting to string objects, 316-318
  copying, 269-270
  function arguments, 411-412
  multiple lines, 268-269
  pointers, 410-412
    copying, 412-413
    library functions, 413

  user-defined strings, 273-275
  variables, 265-266
calling functions, 148-150
  member functions, 200-202
  with array arguments, 252
capacity() member function
  deques, 675
  string class, 282
cascading operators
  extraction (>>) operator, 39-40
  insertion (<<) operator, 46
case keyword, 787
cast operators
  dynamic cast operator, 498-501
  reinterpret cast operator, 399, 535, 789
  typeid operator, 498, 501-502
casts, 50-52
catch blocks, 634, 638, 640
catch keyword, 634, 638, 787
cerr, 522
ch = fill() member function, 518
chaining assignment operators, 481
char character variable, 35-36
char data type, 264-265
char keyword, 787
char strings, 530-532
character constants, 36-37
character I/O, 532-533
character variables
  char character variable, 35-36
  character constants, 36-37
  switch statement, 99
  wchar t character variable, 35-36
checking for errors in streams, 525-527
child, *see* derived classes
cin, 38-39, 522
  get() member function, 267-268
  overloaded extraction and insertion operators, 557-559
class diagrams, 721-722, 750-753
class keyword, 197, 475, 787
class libraries
  exceptions, 647
  implementations, 574-575
  interfaces, 574
  multifile programs, 573-575

Class-Requirements-Collaborators (CRC) cards, 721-722
   classes section, 728-730
   collaborators section, 731
   creating, 727-728
   examples, 731-736, 739-741
   notes, 736
   responsibilities section, 729-731
Class-Requirements-Collaborators (CRC) modeling
  team, 725-727
classes, 15-16, 195
   abstract classes, 459
   arrays as class members, 255-258
   attributes, 758
   base classes, 17-18, 337-341
      abstract base classes, 356
      accessing members, 341-345
      destructors, 465-466
      instantiating objects of, 459
      pure virtual functions, 459-460
      virtual base classes, 466-468
   benefits of, 231-232
   C-strings as class members, 272-273
   container class libraries, 653
   containers, 376-380
   data hiding, 197-198
   data members, 198
      initialization, 208
      private, 197-198
      public, 197-198
      public versus private, 199-200
      static, 224-228
   declaring, 197, 199, 758
   derived classes, 17-18, 337-341, 345-347, 351-352
   dynamic type information, 498
      dynamic cast operator, 498-501
      typeid operator, 501-502
   exception classes
      bad alloc class, 646
      xalloc class, 646
   features of, 195-196
   friend classes, 475
   friend functions, 468-474
   hierarchies, 352-357
   inheritance, 16-18, 337-341
      code reusability, 337
      examples, 349-352
      graphic shapes, 357-359
      hierarchies, 352-357
      kind of relationship, 376

      levels of, 362-365
      multiple inheritance, 365-376
      private inheritance, 359-362
      program development, 380-381
      public inheritance, 359-362
istream iterator class, 692-693
key abstraction, 750
member functions, 198-199
   calling, 200-202
   const, 228-230
   constructors, 206-210, 212-213
   defining outside the classes, 213-214
   destructors, 210-211
   messages, 202
   public versus private, 199-200
   within class declarations, 199
members
   arrays, 255-258
   C-strings, 272-273
objects, 197
   as function arguments, 214-215
   benefits of, 231-232
   const, 230-231
   data types, 205-206
   defining, 200
   examples, 219-223
   examples of, 202-204
   initializing, 208, 216-217
   memory, 224-225
OOD, 721
   class diagrams, 721-722, 750-753
   CRC cards, 721-722, 727-736, 739-741
   CRC modeling team, 725-727
   example program, 722-725
   problem summary statements, 726-727
   use cases, 721-722, 737-740, 742-743
ostream iterator class, 690-691
relationships, 744
   aggregation, 744, 746-747
   association, 744-746
   attributes, 744-745
   cohesion, 750
   composition, 746-747
   coupling, 750
   generalization, 744, 749-750
   has a relationships, 744
   instance relationships, 744
   multiplicity, 748
   uses relationships, 744-746
reusability, 18

self-containing classes, 429
specifiers, 197
storage classes (variables), 179
    automatic variables, 180-181
    external variables, 182-183
    static variables, 183-185
    summary, 185
stream classes, 513
    advantages, 513-514
    copying, 521-522
    fstream class, 528, 539
    hierarchy, 514-515
    ifstream class, 513, 528
    ios class, 515-519
    iostream class, 515
    iostream withassign class, 515, 521-522
    istream class, 515, 519, 521
    istream withassign class, 515, 521-522
    istrstream class, 561
    ofstream class, 528
    ostream class, 515, 521
    ostream withassign class, 515, 521-522
    ostrstream class, 561-562
    predefined stream objects, 522
    strstream class, 561
string class, 275, 282
    accessing characters in string objects, 281-282
    append() member function, 280
    assigning objects, 276-277
    at() member function, 281-282
    capacity() member function, 282
    compare() member function, 280-281
    comparing objects, 280-281
    concatenation, 302-303
    converting to C-strings, 316-318
    copy() member function, 282
    defining objects, 276-277
    editing objects, 279-280
    erase() member function, 279-280
    find() member function, 278
    find first not of() member function, 279
    find first of() member function, 278
    find last not of() member function, 279
    find last of() member function, 279
    finding objects, 278-279
    getline() member function, 277-278
    input/output, 277-278
    insert() member function, 280

    length() member function, 282
    max size() member function, 282
    new operator, 419-420
    replace() member function, 279-280
    rfind() member function, 279
    size() member function, 282
    substr() member function, 281
    swap() member function, 276
structures, 134
subclasses, *see* derived classes
superclasses, *see* base classes
syntax, 195-196
templates, 622-625
    determining storage parameters, 633
    example, 628-630
    syntax, 625-628
    user-defined data types, 630-632
clear line() function, 809
clear screen() function, 809
clear() function, 523
Cline, Marshall, 889
clog, 522
close() member function, 535
closing
    files, 535
    streams, 535
code
    catch blocks, 634, 638, 640
    reusability, 337
    try blocks, 634, 638
cohesion of classes, 750
command-line arguments, 562-564
comments, 29
    syntax, 30-31
    uses of, 30
compare() member function, 280-281
comparing
    string objects, 280-281
    strings, 305-306, 433-434
comparison operators, overloading, 304-306
compilers, 23
    assignment operators, 478-481
    Borland compilers, 23-24, 811
    Console Graphics Lite, 807
    copy constructors, 479, 484
    function templates, 618-619
    graphics, 807
        console graphics, 807, 811
        pixel graphics, 807

Inprise compilers, 23-24
keywords, 787
Microsoft compilers, 23-24, 811
whitespace, 26-27
composition of classes, 746-747
concatenating strings
C-strings, 302
string class , 302-303
conditional operator, 100-103, 107, 326
console functions, 807-811
console graphics, 807
compilers, 807
Borland compilers, 811
Microsoft compilers, 811
inheritance, 357-359
routines, 808
Console Graphics Lite
C++Builder (Borland), 804
compilers, 807
functions, 807-811
inheritance, 357-359
passing structures to functions, 158-160
routines, 808
Visual C++, 794-795
console-mode applications
Borland C++Builder, 797
building existing files, 800
closing projects, 801
Console Graphics Lite, 804
creating projects, 798-799
debugging, 804-805
file extensions, 797
header files, 801-802
multiple source file projects, 802-803
opening projects, 801
precompiled header files, 801
running example programs in, 797-798
running programs, 800-801
saving projects, 799
screen elements, 798
Microsoft Visual C++, 791
building existing files, 792
Console Graphics Lite, 794-795
debugging, 795-796
multifile programs, 793-794
RTTI, 793
screen elements, 791
single-file programs, 792
writing files, 792-793

const, 228
arguments of member functions, 230
function arguments, 187-188
member functions, 228-230
objects, 230-231
const keyword, 43, 228, 787
const cast keyword, 787
const modifier, 413-414
const objects, 328-329
constants
#define directive, 43
C-strings, 267
character constants, 36-37
const keyword, 43, 228, 787
floating point constants, 42-43
integer constants, 34
passing to functions, 153-154
pointers, 394-395, 401-402
set color() function, 809-810
set fill style() function, 810
strings, 28
constructors, 206-207, 209
automatic initialization, 207
classes, 345-347, 351-352
conversion constructors, 315
copy constructors, 216-217, 479, 482
default, 216-217
invoking, 483
out of memory message, 484
overloading, 482-490, 492
prohibiting copying, 485
temporary objects, 484
examples, 209-210
initialization list, 208
multiple inheritance, 371-373
multi-argument constructors, 374
no-argument constructors, 373-374
names, 207-208
overloading, 212-213
syntax, 208-209
container class libraries, 653
containers, 376-380
adapters, 658-659
algorithms, 680, 682-683
associative containers, 655-656, 693-694
keys, 656-657, 694
maps, 656-657, 694, 697-700
multimaps, 657, 694, 697-700
multisets, 657, 694-697
sets, 656-657, 694-697

function objects, 714
iterators, 680-681
member functions, 657-658
priority queues, 658
queues, 658
sequence containers, 655-656
    arrays, 655
    deques, 655-656
    lists, 655-656
    vectors, 655-656
sequential containers, 669, 676
    deques, 675
    lists, 672-675
    vectors, 669-672
stacks, 658
STL, 653-659, 669-676, 693-700
contents of operator, 396
continue keyword, 787
continue statement, 110-111
control statements, 67
decisions, 84
    break statement, 98, 107-109
    continue statement, 110-111
    goto statement, 111
    if statement, 84-87
    if...else statement, 88-96, 100
    switch statement, 96-100
loops, 70, 90-91
    do loop, 81-83
    for loop, 70-77
    if statements, 87
    selecting which loop to use, 84
    while loop, 77-81
conversion constructors, 315
conversion operator, 315-316
conversions, 292, 312-313
C-strings and string objects, 316-318
data types, 48-49, 313-316
explicit keyword, 326-328
guidelines for using, 326
limitations, 325
objects of different classes, 318-324
preventing, 326-328
selecting best method of, 324
variables, 48-49
copy algorithm, 659, 815
copy backward algorithm, 815
copy constructors, 216-217, 479, 482
invoking, 483
out of memory message, 484

overloading, 482-490, 492
prohibiting copying, 485
temporary objects, 484
copy() member function, 282
copying
C-strings, 269-270, 412-413
prohibiting, 485
stream classes, 521-522
count = gcount() member function, 520
count algorithm, 659, 662-663, 814
count if algorithm, 814
coupling classes, 750
courses on C++, 890
cout, 27, 522, 557-559
.cpp filename extension, 23
.CPP files, 23, 759-768
CRC cards, 721-722
classes section, 728-730
collaborators section, 731
creating, 727-728
examples, 731-736, 739-741
notes, 736
responsibilities section, 729-731
CRC modeling team, 725-727
ctor, *see* constructors
curly brackets in functions, 23

D

DAGs (directed acyclic graphs), 340
data
access with iterators, 683-684
conversions, 292, 312-313
    C-strings and string objects, 316-318
    data types, 313-316
    explicit keyword, 326-328
    guidelines for using, 326
    limitations, 325
    objects of different classes, 318-324
    preventing, 326-328
    selecting best method of, 324
encapsulation, 11
flow, *see* streams
global data, 9-10
hiding, 11, 197-198
    friend functions, 469
    problems with, 468
local data, 9
streams, 27

data members (classes), 198
    initialization, 208
    member functions, 198-199
    public versus private, 199-200
    static, 224-227
        declaration, 227-228
        definition, 227-228
data structures, 653
data types
    arrays, 241, 264-265
    char data type, 264-265
    conversions
        basic types, 313
        user-defined types and basic types, 313-316
    creating, 18
    enumerations, 135-141
        integer values, 141
        limitations, 141
    extensibility, 11
    objects, 205-206
    structured programming languages, 11
    unsigned long data type, 577
    user-defined data types
        class templates, 630-632
        converting to basic types, 313-316
    variables, 46
        casts, 50-52
        conversions, 48-49
        type safety, 52
        unsigned data types, 47-48
debugging
    animation loops, 75
    C++Builder programs, 804
        breakpoints, 805
        single stepping, 804
        tracing into functions, 805
        watching variables, 805
    pointers, 443
    Visual C++ programs, 795
        breakpoints, 796
        single stepping, 795-796
        stepping into functions, 796
        watching variables, 796
dec flag, 516
dec manipulator, 517
decision trees, 94
decisions, 84
    break statement, 98, 107-109
    continue statement, 110-111

goto statement, 111
if statement, 84-86
    loops, 87
    multiple statements, 86
if...else statement, 88-89
    assignment expressions, 91-92
    construction, 95-96
    loops, 90-91
    matching the else, 94-95
    nesting, 92-94
    versus switch statement, 100
switch statement, 96-98
    character variables, 99
    default keyword, 99-100
    versus if...else statement, 100
declarator (functions), 150
declaring
    aggregates, 758-759
    attributes (classes), 758
    classes, 197, 758
        member functions, 199
    functions, 149-150
        library functions, 151
        using definition in place of, 152
        with array arguments, 252
    methods, 759
    static class data, 227-228
    structures, 120-121
        combining declaration and definition, 124-125
        syntax, 121
        use of, 121-122
    variables, 33
decrement (--) operator, 56, 292
default copy constructor, 216-217
default keyword, 99-100, 787
defaults
    access specifiers, 361
    arguments (functions), 178-179
defining
    arrays, 242-243
        multidimensional arrays, 248-249
        structures, 254
    functions, 150
        array arguments, 252-253
        body, 150
        declarator, 150
        library functions, 151
        using in place of declaration, 152

member functions outside classes, 213-214
objects, 200
pointers, 394
static class data, 227-228
string objects, 276-277
structures, 122-125
variables, 33
    at point of use, 39
    in for statements, 76
    integer variables, 31-33
    multiple definitions, 46
#define preprocessor directive, 43
delete keyword, 787
delete operator, 418-419
deques, 655-656, 675
dereferencing pointers, 397, 421
derived classes, 17-18, 337-341, 345-347, 351-352
design (OOD), 721
    class diagrams, 721-722, 750-753
    CRC cards, 721-722, 727-736, 739-741
    CRC modeling team, 725-727
    example program, 722-725
    problem summary statements, 726-727
    use cases, 721-722, 737-740, 742-743
The Design and Evolution of C++, 890
destructors, 210-211, 476-478
    base classes, 465-466
    exceptions, 647
    virtual destructors, 465-466
    warnings about, 484
Developer Studio (Microsoft), 791
development of programs, 380-381
diagrams of classes, 721-722, 750-753
directed acyclic graphs, 340
directives, 28
    #define preprocessor directive, 43
    #include preprocessor directive, 28, 59-60
    preprocessor directives, 28, 43, 59-60
    using directive, 29
directories for multifile programs, 576
disk file I/O
    binary I/O, 533-534
    char strings with embedded blanks, 530-532
    character I/O, 532-533
    error handling, 544
        analyzing errors, 545-546
        reacting to errors, 544-545
    formatted file I/O, 528-530

member functions, 546-557
object I/O, 535-539
overloaded extraction and insertion operators, 559-561
streams, 528
diskCount() member function, 547
diskIn() member function, 546-549
diskOut() member function, 546-549
display() function, 252, 428-429
displaying linked list contents, 428-429
Divide Error error message, 110
division (/) operator, 52
do keyword, 787
do loop, 81-83
    test expression, 81
    uses, 84
documentation, 889
    books, 889-890
    online course, 890
dot (.) operator
    accesssing structure members, 123-124
    overloading, 326
double floating point variable, 42
double keyword, 787
draw circle() function, 809
draw line() function, 809
draw pyramid() function, 809
draw rectangle() function, 809
dynamic binding, 458
dynamic cast operator, 498-501
dynamic keyword, 787
dynamic type information (classes), 498
    dynamic cast operator, 498-501
    typeid operator, 501-502

E

early binding, 458
Eckel, Bruce, 889
editing
    data
        const objects, 328-329
        global data, 9-10
    string objects, 279-280
educational resources, 890
Effective C++, 889
elements (arrays), 243-244
    accessing, 244, 399-401
    averaging, 244-245

multidimensional arrays, 249
pointers, 399-401
sorting, 406-410
structures, 254
Ellis, Margaret, 889
else keyword, 788
empty() member function, 658
encapsulation, 11, 468
end() member function, 658
endl manipulator, 34, 517
ends manipulator, 517
enum keyword, 137, 788
enumerations, 135-141
        integer values, 141
        limitations, 141
eofbit flag, 523, 532
equal algorithm, 659, 814
equal range algorithm, 819
equal to (==) relational operator, 69
erase() member function
        lists, 673
        string class, 279-280
        vectors, 671-672
error flag functions
        clear(), 523
        int = bad(), 523
        int = eof(), 523
        int = fail(), 523
        int = good(), 523
error handling
        disk file I/O, 544
                analyzing errors, 545-546
                reacting to errors, 544-545
        exceptions, 615, 633
                arguments, 642-645
                catch blocks, 634, 638
                class libraries, 647
                destructors, 647
                examples, 636-638, 641-642
                extracting data from exception objects, 645
                function nesting, 646
                handling, 647-648
                multiple exceptions, 639-641
                purpose of, 633-634
                sequence of events, 638-639
                syntax, 634-635
                throwing, 634, 637
                try blocks, 634, 638
                when not to use, 647

functions
        longjmp() function, 634
        setjmp() function, 634
error messages
        access violation error message, 443
        Divide Error error message, 110
        null pointer assignment error message, 443
        page fault error message, 443
        stack is empty error message, 349
        unidentifed identifier error message, 58
        unknown variable error message, 181
error-status flags, 522-523, 531-532
errors
        cerr, 522
        streams, 522
                checking, 525-527
                error-status flags, 522-523, 531-532
                inputting numbers, 523-524
                inputting strings and characters, 525
                no-input input, 524-525
                too many characters, 524
escape sequences, 28, 37-38
exception classes
        bad alloc class, 646
        xalloc class, 646
exceptions, 615, 633
        arguments, 642-645
        catch blocks, 634, 638, 640
        class libraries, 647
        destructors, 647
        examples, 636-638, 641-642
        extracting data from exception objects, 645
        function nesting, 646
        handling, 647-648
        multiple exceptions, 639-641
        purpose of, 633-634
        sequence of events, 638-639
        syntax, 634-635
        throwing, 634, 637
        tips for when not to use, 647
        try blocks, 634, 638
.exe filename extension, 23
executable files, 23
exercise solutions
        chapter 2, 833-834
        chapter 3, 836-838
        chapter 4, 839-841
        chapter 5, 842-845

chapter 6, 846-848
chapter 7, 850-853
chapter 8, 854-858
chapter 9, 859-864
chapter 10, 865-869
chapter 11, 870-874
chapter 12, 875-877
chapter 14, 879-882
chapter 15, 883-887
exit() library function, 88
explicit keyword, 326-328, 788
exponential notation, 42-43
export keyword, 788
expressions, 40
extensibility, 11
extensions (filenames)
    C++Builder, 797
    .cpp, 23
    .exe, 23
    .H, 29
    Visual C++, 791
extern keyword, 788
external variables, 182-183
    initialization, 183
    lifetime, 183
    purpose of, 183
    scope, 183
    storage, 185
    visibility, 183
extraction (>>) operator, 39-40, 515, 529-530
    cascading, 39-40
    overloading, 557-561

F

failbit flag, 523
false keyword, 788
Fibonacci series, 80-81
file pointers, 540-541
    specifying the offset, 542
    specifying the position, 541
files, 513
    closing, 535
    disk file I/O
        binary I/O , 533-534
        char strings with embedded blanks,
            530-532
        character I/O , 532-533
        error handling, 544-546

formatted file I/O, 528-530
member functions, 546-557
object I/O, 535-539
overloaded extraction and insertion opera-
    tors, 559-561
streams, 528
executable files, 23
extensions (filenames)
    C++Builder, 797
    .cpp, 23
    .exe, 23
    .H, 29
    Visual C++, 791
formatted file I/O, 528
header files, 28-29
    library functions, 58
    manipulators, 46
library files, 58
opening, 539-540
source files, 23
fill algorithm, 659, 816
fill() member function, 518
fill n algorithm, 816
*The Final Draft Information Standard (FDIS) for the C++
    Programming Language*, 889
find algorithm, 659, 661-662, 814
    header files, 662
    ranges, 662
find() member function, 278
find first not of() member function, 279
find first of() member function, 278
find if algorithm, 814
find last not of() member function, 279
find last of() member function, 279
finding string objects, 278-279
fixed flag, 516
flags
    error-status flags, 522-523, 531-532
    formatting flags, 516-518
    ios flags, 249
        fixed flag, 249
        showpoint flag, 249
float floating point variable, 41-42
float keyword, 788
floating point constants, 42-43
floating point variables, 40
    constants, 42-43
    double, 42

float, 41-42
    long double, 42
flow of data, *see* streams
flush manipulator, 517
flush() member function, 521
for each algorithm, 659, 667-668, 814
for keyword, 788
for loop, 70-71
    animation, 75
    blocks, 74
    defining variables in for statement, 76
    increment expression, 72
    indentation, 74-75
    initialization expressions, 71, 77
    iterations, 73
    multiple statements in body, 73-74
    style, 74-75
    test expressions, 72, 77
    uses, 84
    variations, 76
    visibility of variables, 74
foreign languages and wchar t character variable, 35-36
formatted file I/O, 528-530
formatting numbers in arrays, 249
formatting flags, 516-518
FORTRAN, 8
forward iterators, 660, 678-680
fread() member function, 528
friend classes, 475
friend functions, 468-469
    controversies surrounding, 469
    examples, 469-472
    functional notation, 472-474
friend keyword, 469, 472, 788
front() member function, 673, 675
fstream class, 528, 539
function libraries, 574
function objects, 665, 707
    modifying container behavior, 714
    predefined function objects, 707-710
    writing, 710-714
functions
    arguments, 24, 57
        arrays, 251-253, 404-406
        C-strings, 411-412
        constants, 153-154, 187-188, 230
        default arguments, 178-179
        naming, 160

objects, 214-215
overloaded functions, 172-176
parameters, 154
passing, 152-160
passing by pointers, 403-406
passing by reference, 402
references, 166-172
structures, 155-160
values, 155-156
variables, 154-155
braces, 25
bsort() function, 408-410
calling, 148-150, 252
console functions, 807-811
curly brackets, 25
declaring, 149-150
    library functions, 151
    using definition in place of, 152
    with array arguments, 252
defining, 150
    array arguments, 252-253
    body, 150
    declarator, 150
    library functions, 151
    using in place of declaration, 152
definition of, 24, 147
display() function, 252, 428-429
error flag functions
    clear(), 523
    int = bad(), 523
    int = eof(), 523
    int = fail(), 523
    int = good(), 523
examples, 148-149
friend functions, 468-469
    controversies surrounding, 469
    examples, 469-472
    functional notation, 472-474
history of, 8
illustration, 151
inline functions, 176-178, 188
invoking, 147-150
ios functions, 518-519
library functions, 56-57, 151
    atoi(), 525
    exit(), 88
    getche(), 90-91
    header files, 58

library files, 58
malloc(), 417
pointers, 413
rand(), 264
sqrt(), 56-57
srand(), 264
strcat(), 275
strcmp(), 306, 433-434
strcpy(), 270, 413
strlen(), 269-270
longjmp() function, 634
macros, 622
main() function, 25, 152
member functions, 24, 198-199, 352
append(), 280
at(), 281-282
back(), 671
begin(), 658
calling, 200-202
capacity(), 282, 675
ch = fill(), 518
class declarations, 199
close(), 535
compare(), 280-281
const, 228-230
constructors, 206-210, 212-213
containers, 657-658
copy(), 282
count = gcount(), 520
defining outside the classes, 213-214
definition of, 11
destructors, 210-211
disk file I/O, 546-557
diskCount(), 547
diskIn(), 546-549
diskOut(), 546-549
empty(), 658
end(), 658
erase(), 279-280, 671-673
fill(), 518
find(), 278
find first not of(), 279
find first of(), 278
find last not of(), 279
find last of(), 279
flush(), 521
fread(), 528
front(), 673, 675

fwrite(), 528
get(), 267-268, 519-520, 532-533
getline(), 277-278, 520, 530
ignore(), 520
insert(), 280, 671-673
length(), 282
lower bound(), 696-697
max size(), 282, 658, 670
merge(), 674
messages, 202
multiple inheritance, 366-370
open(), 539-540
overriding, 347-348
p = precision(), 518
parse(), 435
peek(), 520
pop(), 257, 348-349
pop back(), 671
pop front(), 673, 675
pos = tellg(), 520
pos = tellp(), 521
precision(), 518
public versus private, 199-200
push(), 257-258, 348-349
push back(), 670
push front(), 673
put(), 521, 532
putback(), 520
rbegin(), 658
rdbuf(), 533
read(), 520, 536
rend(), 658
replace(), 279-280
reverse(), 674
rfind(), 279
seekg(), 520, 541-543
seekp(), 521, 541
setdata(), 199
setf(), 516, 518-519
setjmp(), 634
showdata(), 199
size(), 282, 658, 670
solve(), 435
STL, 825-827
substr(), 281
swap(), 276, 671
tellg(), 541, 543-544
tellp(), 541

this pointer, 492-497
typeid(), 550-555
unique(), 674
unsetf(), 516, 518
upper bound(), 696-697
w = width(), 518
width(), 518
write(), 521, 536
names, 24
nesting exceptions, 646
operator=() function, 480
    passing arguments by reference, 480-481
    returning values, 481
order() function, 407-408
overloaded functions, 172-176, 188
passing arrays to, 251
pointers, 402
    normal functions, 454-456
    passing arguments with, 403-406
    virtual functions, 456-458
prototypes, 149
purpose of, 147
returning objects, 217-220
static functions, 476-477
    accessing members, 477-478
    numbering members, 478
structures
    passing by reference, 170-171
    returning, 164-166
templates, 615-618
    arguments, 619-621
    blueprints, 619
    compilers, 618-619
    determining what works, 622
    syntax, 618, 621
    tips for simplifying, 619
values, 161-164, 185-187
virtual functions, 453-454
    examples, 460-465
    pointers, 456-458
    pure virtual functions, 459-460
fwrite() member function, 528

G

game for horse-racing, 438-443
generalization (classes), 744, 749-750
generate algorithm, 816

generate n algorithm, 816
get from (>>) operator, 39-40, 515, 529-530
    cascading, 39-40
    overloading, 557-561
get pointer, 540-541
    specifying the offset, 541-543
    specifying the position, 541
get() member function, 267-268, 519-520, 532-533
getche() library function, 90-91
getline() member function, 277-278, 520, 530
Gilbert, Stephen, 890
global data, 9-10
global variables, *see* external variables
golden ratio, 80
goodbit flag, 523
goto keyword, 788
goto statement, 111
graphic shapes and inheritance, 357-359
graphics, 807
    compilers, 807
    console graphics, 807
        compilers, 807, 811
        inheritance, 357-359
        routines, 808
    Console Graphics Lite, 158-160
    pixel graphics, 807
greater than (>) relational operator, 69
greater than or equal to (>=) relational operator, 69

H

H file, 29, 753-758
.H filename extension, 29
handling exceptions, 647-648
hardfail flag, 523
has a relationships, 376-380, 744
header files, 28-29, 753-758
    C++Builder projects, 801
        creating, 801
        editing, 802
        telling location of, 802
    library functions, 58
    manipulators, 46
    multifile programs, 576
hex flag, 516
hex manipulator, 517
hiding data, 11, 197-198
hierarchies of classes, 352-357, 514-515
horse-racing game, 438-443

I

I/O, *see* input/ouput
identifiers, 33
if algorithms, 666-667
if keyword, 85, 788
if statement, 84-86
    loops, 87
    multiple statements, 86
if...else statement, 88-89
    assignment expressions, 91-92
    construction, 95-96
    loops, 90-91
    matching the else, 94-95
    nesting, 92-94
    versus switch statement, 100
ifstream class, 513, 528
ignore() member function, 520
implementations of class libraries, 574-575
include files, *see* header files
#include preprocessor directive, 28, 59-60
includes algorithm, 820
increment ++ operator, 54-56
    overloading, 292-293
    postfix, 55-56
    prefix, 55-56
indentation in for loops, 74-75
indexes (arrays), 241, 244
indirect addressing pointers, 397
indirection operator, 396-397
inheritance, 16-18, 337-341
    accessibility, 341-345
    assignment operators, 481
    code reusability, 337
    examples, 349-352
    graphic shapes, 357-359
    hierarchies, 352-357
    kind of relationship, 376
    levels of, 362-365
    multiple inheritance, 365-366
        ambiguity, 374-376
        constructors, 371-374
        disambiguation, 375
        member functions, 366-370
        private derivation, 371
        virtual base classes, 466-468
    private inheritance, 359-362
    program development, 380-381
    public inheritance, 359-362

inheritance trees, 340
init graphics() function, 808-809, 811
initializing
    arrays, 245-246
        multidimensional arrays, 250
    members of structures, 125-126
    nested structures, 131-132
    objects, 208, 216-217
    variables, 37
        automatic variables, 181
        external variables, 183
        static variables, 185
inline functions, 176-178, 188
inline keyword, 178, 788
inner product algorithm, 824
inplace merge algorithm, 820
Inprise compilers, 23-24
input iterators, 660, 678-679
input/output
    cin, 38-39
    disk file I/O
        binary I/O, 533-534
        char strings with embedded blanks, 530-532
        character I/O, 532-533
        error handling, 544-546
        formatted file I/O, 528-530
        member functions, 546-557
        object I/O, 535-539
        overloaded extraction and insertion opera-
            tors, 559-561
        streams, 528
    streams, 513-514
    string objects, 277-278
insert iterators, 687-690
insert() member function
    lists, 673
    string class, 280
    vectors, 671-672
inserting
    data with iterators, 684
    items in linked lists, 427-428
insertion (<<) operator, 27, 46, 515
    cascading, 46
    overloading, 557-561
instance relationships of classes, 744
instance variables, *see* objects
instantiating
    objects, 200
    objects of a base class, 459

int = bad() function, 523
int = eof() function, 523
int = fail() function, 523
int = good() function, 523
int integer variable, 31-33
int keyword, 788
integer constants, 34
integer variables, 31
    assignment statements, 33-34
    defining, 31-33
    int integer variable, 31-33
    integer constants, 34
    long integer variables, 35
    output variations, 34
    short integer variables, 35
    true/false values, 106
interacting with programs, 768-770
interfaces
    class libraries, 574
    iterators, 678-680
internal flag, 516
invoking
    copy constructors, 483
    functions, 147-150
ios class, 515
    formatting flags, 516-517
    functions, 518-519
    manipulators, 517-518
ios flags, 249
iostream class, 515
iostream withassign class, 515, 521-522
istream class, 515, 519, 521
istream iterator class, 692-693
istream withassign class, 515, 521-522
istrstream class, 561
iter swap algorithm, 659, 815
iterators
    adapters, 687
        insert iterator, 687-690
        raw storage iterator, 687
        reverse iterator, 687-688
    algorithms, 681-682, 685-686, 827-829
    bidirectional iterators, 660, 678-680
    containers, 680-681
    data access, 683-684
    data insertion, 684
    forward iterators, 660, 678-680
    input iterators, 660, 678-679

    interfaces, 678-680
    output iterators, 660, 678-680
    random access iterators, 660, 678-679
    smart pointers, 677-678
    STL, 654, 660, 676-693
    stream iterators, 690
        istream iterator class, 692-693
        ostream iterator class, 690-691

J-K

Kernighan, Brian, 890
key
    to exercises
        chapter 2, 833-834
        chapter 3, 836-838
        chapter 4, 839-841
        chapter 5, 842-845
        chapter 6, 846-848
        chapter 7, 850-853
        chapter 8, 854-858
        chapter 9, 859-864
        chapter 10, 865-869
        chapter 11, 870-874
        chapter 12, 875-877
        chapter 14, 879-882
        chapter 15, 883-887
    to questions
        chapter 1, 831
        chapter 2, 832-833
        chapter 3, 834-836
        chapter 4, 838-839
        chapter 5, 841-842
        chapter 6, 845-846
        chapter 7, 849-850
        chapter 8, 853-854
        chapter 9, 859
        chapter 10, 864-865
        chapter 11, 869-870
        chapter 12, 874-875
        chapter 13, 877
        chapter 14, 878-879
        chapter 15, 882-883
        chapter 16, 887-888
key abstraction of classes, 750
keys of associative containers, 656-657, 694
keywords
    asm, 787
    auto, 180, 787

bool, 787
break, 98, 787
C, 787
C++, 787
case, 787
catch, 634, 638, 787
char, 787
class, 197, 475, 787
compilers, 787
const, 43, 228, 787
const cast, 787
continue, 787
default, 99-100, 787
definition of, 33
delete, 787
do, 787
double, 787
dynamic, 787
else, 788
enum, 137, 788
explicit, 326-328, 788
export, 788
extern, 788
false, 788
float, 788
for, 788
friend, 469, 472, 788
goto, 788
if, 85, 788
inline, 178, 788
int, 788
long, 788
main, 788
mutable, 326, 328-329, 788
namespace, 788
new, 788
operator, 293, 789
private, 197-198, 360, 789
protected, 789
public, 197-198, 360, 789
purpose of, 787
register, 789
reinterpret cast, 789
return, 789
short, 789
signed, 789
sizeof, 789
static, 789

static cast, 789
struct, 121, 789
switch, 96, 789
template, 618, 621, 624, 789
this, 789
throw, 634, 789
true, 789
try, 634, 638, 789
typedef, 789
typeid, 789
typename, 789
union, 789
unsigned, 789
using, 789
variable names, 33
virtual, 456, 468, 790
void, 149, 163, 790
volatile, 790
wchar t, 790
kind of relationships, 376
Koenig, Andrew, 890

L

Lafore, Robert, 890
LaMothe, André, 890
late binding, 458
Lee, Meng, 653, 890
left flag, 516
length() member function, 282
less than (<) relational operator, 69
less than or equal to (<=) relational operator, 69
lexicographical compare algorithm, 823
libraries
    class libraries
        exceptions, 647
        implementations, 574-575
        interfaces, 574
        multifile programs, 573-575
    container classes, 653
    function libraries, 574
    Standard Template Library (STL), 653
        algorithms, 653-654, 659-669, 680-683,
            685-686, 813-825, 827-829
        containers, 653-659, 669-676, 680-683,
            693-700
        function objects, 707-714
        iterators, 654, 660, 676-693

member functions, 825-827
problems with, 661
storing user-defined objects, 700-706
library files, 58
library functions, 56-57, 151
atoi(), 525
exit(), 88
getche(), 90-91
header files, 58
library files, 58
malloc(), 417
pointers, 413
rand(), 264
sqrt(), 56-57
srand(), 264
strcat(), 275
strcmp(), 306, 433-434
strcpy(), 270, 413
strlen(), 269-270
linked lists
displaying contents, 428-429
inserting items, 427-428
pointers, 425-429
lists, 655-656, 672-675
erase(), 673
front(), 673, 675
insert(), 673
merge(), 674
pop front(), 673, 675
push front(), 673
reverse(), 674
unique(), 674
local data, 9
local variables, *see* automatic variables
lock manipulator, 517
logical operators, 103
AND, 103-105
NOT, 104, 106
OR, 104-105
precedence, 107
XOR, 105
Lomow, Greg, 889
long double floating point variable, 42
long integer variables, 35
long keyword, 788
longjmp() function, 634

loops, 70
do loop, 81-83
for loop, 70-71
animation, 75
blocks, 74
defining variables in for statement, 76
increment expressions, 72
indentation, 74-75
initialization expression, 71, 77
iterations, 73
multiple statements in body, 73-74
style, 74-75
test expressions, 72, 77
variations, 76
visibility of variables, 74
if statements, 87
if...else statements, 90-91
selecting which loop to use, 84
while loop, 77-79
multiple statements, 79-80
precedence of operators, 80-81
test expressions, 78
lower bound algorithm, 819
lower bound() member function, 696-697

M

macros, 622
main keyword, 788
main() function, 25, 152
make heap algorithm, 822
malloc() libary function, 417
manipulators, 34, 517
arguments, 517-518
dec manipulator, 517
endl manipulator, 34, 517
ends manipulator, 517
flush manipulator, 517
header files, 46
hex manipulator, 517
lock manipulator, 517
oct manipulator, 517
resetiosflags manipulator, 249, 518
setfill manipulator, 518
setiosflags manipulator, 249, 517-518
setprecision manipulator, 249, 518
setw manipulator, 44-45, 266, 518
unlock manipulator, 517
ws manipulator, 517

maps, 656-657, 694, 697-700
max algorithm, 822
max element algorithm, 822-823
max size() member function, 658
    string class, 282
    vectors, 670
McCarty, Bill, 890
member access operator, 123
member functions, 24, 198-199, 352
    >>, 519
    <<, 521
    append(), 280
    arguments, 230
    at(), 281-282
    back(), 671
    begin(), 658
    calling, 200-202
    capacity(), 282, 675
    ch = fill(), 518
    class declarations, 199
    close(), 535
    compare(), 280-281
    const, 228-230
    constructors, 206-207, 209
        automatic initialization, 207
        copy constructor, 216-217
        default copy constructor, 216-217
        example, 209-210
        initialization list, 208
        names, 207-208
        overloading, 212-213
        syntax, 208-209
    containers, 657-658
    copy(), 282
    count = gcount(), 520
    defining outside classes, 213-214
    definition of, 11
    destructors, 210-211
    disk file I/O, 546-557
    diskCount(), 547
    diskIn(), 546-549
    diskOut(), 546-549
    empty(), 658
    end(), 658
    erase()
        lists, 673
        vectors, 671-672
        string class, 279-280

fill(), 518
find(), 278
find first not of(), 279
find first of(), 278
find last not of(), 279
find last of(), 279
flush(), 521
fread(), 528
front(), 673, 675
fwrite(), 528
get(), 267-268, 519-520, 532-533
getline(), 277-278, 520, 530
ignore(), 520
insert()
    lists, 673
    vectors, 671-672
    string class, 280
length(), 282
lower bound(), 696-697
max size(), 658
    string class, 282
    vectors, 670
merge(), 674
messages, 202
multiple inheritance, 366-370
open(), 539-540
overriding, 347-348
p = precision(), 518
parse(), 435
peek(), 520
pop(), 257
pop back(), 671
pop front(), 673, 675
pos = tellg(), 520
pos = tellp(), 521
precision(), 518
public versus private, 199-200
push(), 257-258
push back(), 670
push front(), 673
put(), 521, 532
putback(), 520
rbegin(), 658
rdbuf(), 533
read(), 520, 536
rend(), 658
replace(), 279-280

reverse(), 674
rfind(), 279
seekg(), 520, 541-543
seekp(), 521, 541
setdata(), 199
setf(), 516, 518-519
showdata(), 199
size(), 658
    string class, 282
    vectors, 670
solve(), 435
STL, 825-827
substr(), 281
swap()
    string class, 276
    vectors, 671
tellg(), 541, 543-544
tellp(), 541
this pointer, 492-493
    accessing member function data, 493-494
    returning values, 494-497
typeid(), 550-555
unique(), 674
unsetf(), 516, 518
upper bound(), 696-697
w = width(), 518
width(), 518
write(), 521, 536
members of classes
    arrays, 255-258
    C-strings, 272-273
memory
    addresses, pointers to, 390-397
    considerations when programming, 224-225
    management
        arrays, 416
        delete operator, 418-419
        new operator, 416-420, 422-423
    streams, 561-562
merge algorithm, 659, 664-665, 820
merge() member function, 674
messages
    Assignment operator invoked message, 480
    error messages
        access violation, 443
        Divide Error, 110
        null pointer assignment, 443
        page fault, 443

        stack is empty, 349
        unidentifed identifier, 58
        unknown variable, 181
    member functions, 202
methods, 11, 759
Meyers, Scott, 889
Microsoft compilers, 23-24, 811
Microsoft Developer Studio, 791
Microsoft Visual C++, 791
    building existing files, 792
    Console Graphics Lite, 794-795
    debugging programs, 795
        breakpoints, 796
        single stepping, 795-796
        stepping into functions, 796
        watching variables, 796
    file extensions, 791
    multifile programs, 793-794
        closing, 794
        compiling, 794
        linking, 794
        opening, 794
        saving, 794
    projects, 793
    RTTI, 793
    screen elements, 791
    single-file programs, 792
    source files, 793-794
    workspaces, 793
    writing files, 792-793
min algorithm, 822
min element algorithm, 823
mismatch algorithm, 814
modifier const, 413-414
modules, history of, 8
More Effective C++, 889
MS-DOS
    C++Builder programs, 801
    Visual C++ programs, 792
MSOFTCON.CPP, 807
multidimensional arrays, 246-248
    accessing elements, 249
    defining, 248-249
    formatting numbers, 249
    initializing, 250
multifile programs, 573
    build process, 577
    class libraries, 573-574
        implementations, 574-575
        interfaces, 574

conceptualization, 576
creating, 576-577
directories, 576
examples
    high-rise elevator simulation example,
      583-598
    very long number class example, 577-582
    water-distribution system example, 598-611
header files, 576
organization, 576
projects, 576-577
multimaps, 657, 694, 697-700
multiple exceptions, 639-641
multiple inheritance, 365-366
  ambiguity, 374-376
  constructors, 371-373
    multi-argument constructors, 374
    no-argument constructors, 373-374
  disambiguation, 375
  member functions, 366-370
  private derivation, 371
  virtual base classes, 466-468
multiple lines in C-strings, 268-269
multiplication (*) operator, 52
multisets, 657, 694-697
Musser, David R, 890
mutable keyword, 326, 328-329, 788
The Mythical Man-Month, 8

N

names
  constructors, 207-208
  functions, 24
  structures, 121
  variables, 33
    conventions, 33
    keywords, 33
namespace keyword, 788
namespaces, 29
naming arguments (functions), 160
nesting
  functions, 646
  if statements in loops, 87
  if...else statements, 92-94
  structures, 129
    accessing members, 130-131
    depth of, 132
    initialization, 131-132
    user-defined type conversions, 131

new keyword, 788
new operator and memory management, 416-420,
  422-423
next permutation algorithm, 823
not equal to (!=) relational operator, 69
NOT logical operator, 104, 106
nth element algorithm, 819
null pointer assignment error message, 443
numbering members of static functions, 478
numbers
  arrays, formatting, 249
  random numbers, generating, 264

O

object I/O, 535-539
object-oriented design (OOD), 721
  class diagrams, 721-722, 750-753
  CRC cards, 721-722
    classes section, 728-730
    collaborators section, 731
    creating, 727-728
    examples, 731-736, 739-741
    notes, 736
    responsibilities section, 729-731
  CRC modeling team, 725-727
  example program, 722-725
  problem summary statements, 726-727
  use cases, 721-722, 737-740, 742-743
Object-Oriented Design in Java, 890
object-oriented programming, 7
  analogy, 12-13
  basics of, 11
  classes, 15-16
  data types, 18
  inheritance, 16-18
  need for, 7
  objects, 14-15
  organization, 13
  overloading, 19
  polymorphism, 19
  reusability, 18
objects, 14-15, 195, 197
  arguments (functions), 214-215
  arrays, 258-260
    accessing, 260-261
    bounds, 260
    examples, 261-264
  attributes, 10

base classes, 459
behavior, 11
benefits of, 231-232
const, 230-231, 328-329
cout, 27
data types, 18, 205-206
defining, 200
examples, 202-204. 219-223
initializing, 208, 216-217
memory, 224-225
persistence, 744
pointers, 420-421
    arrays of pointers, 423-425
    new operator, 422-423
    referring to member functions, 421-422
predefined stream objects, 522
returning from functions, 217-220
user-defined objects, 700-706
oct flag, 516
oct manipulator, 517
ofstream class, 528
OOD (object-oriented design), 721
class diagrams, 721-722, 750-753
CRC cards, 721-722
    classes section, 728-730
    collaborators section, 731
    creating, 727-728
    examples, 731-736, 739-741
    notes, 736
    responsibilities section, 729-731
CRC modeling team, 725-727
example program, 722-725
problem summary statements, 726-727
use cases, 721-722, 737-740, 742-743
OOP (object-oriented programming), 7
analogy, 12-13
basics of, 11
classes, 15-16
data types, 18
inheritance, 16-18
need for, 7
objects, 14-15
organization, 13
overloading, 19
polymorphism, 19
reusability, 18
open() member function, 539-540
opening files, 539-540
operator keyword, 293, 789

operator=() function, 480
passing arguments by reference, 480-481
returning values, 481
operators
address-of & operator, 391-392
arithmetic operators, 52
    addition (+) operator, 52
    division (/) operator, 52
    multiplication (*) operator, 52
    precedence, 107
    remainder (%) operator, 52-53
    subtraction (-) operator, 52
assignment operators, 478-479
    arithmetic assignment operators, 53-54
    chaining, 481
    inheritance, 481
    overloading, 479-481, 484-491
    prohibiting copying, 485
    self-assignment, 497-498
associativity, 406
binary operators, 106, 299-308
cast operators
    dynamic cast operator, 498-501
    reinterpret cast operator, 399, 535, 789
    typeid operator, 498, 501-502
conditional operator, 100-103, 107, 326
contents of operator, 396
conversion operator, 315-316
decrement operator, 56
delete operator, 418-419
dot operator, 123-124
dynamic cast operator, 498-501
extraction (>>) operator, 39, 515, 529-530
    cascading, 39-40
    overloading, 557-561
get from (>>) operator, *see* extraction (>>) operator
increment (++) operator, 54
    postfix, 55-56
    prefix, 55-56
indirection operator, 396-397
insertion (<<) operator, 27, 515
    cascading, 46
    overloading, 557-561
logical operators, 103
    AND, 103-105
    NOT, 104, 106
    OR, 104-105
    precedence, 107
    XOR, 105

manipulators
    endl manipulator, 34
    header files, 46
    setw manipulator, 44-45
member access operator, 123
new operator, 416-420, 422-423
overloading, 19, 291-292
    arguments, 294
    assignment operators, 479-481, 484-491, 497-498
    binary operators, 299-308
    conditional (?) operator, 326
    dot (.) operator, 326
    extraction operator, 557-561
    guidelines for using, 325-326
    insertion operator, 557-561
    limitations, 325
    multiple overloading, 304
    operator keyword, 293
    pointer-to-member operator, 326
    return values, 294-295
    scope resolution (::) operator, 326
    subscript [ ] operator, 309-312
    temporary objects, 296-297
    unary operators, 292-298
parsing, 435
polymorphism, 19
precedence, 40, 80-81, 107
put to (<<) operator, *see* insertion (<<) operator
reinterpret cast operator, 399, 535, 789
relational operators, 67-69
    equal to (==) relational operator, 69
    greater than (>) relational operator, 69
    greater than or equal to (=) relational operator, 69
    less than (<) relational operator, 69
    less than or equal to (<=) relational operator, 69
    not equal to (!=) relational operator, 69
    precedence, 107
scope resolution (::) operator, 326, 349
subscript [ ] operator, 309-312
typeid operator, 498, 501-502
unary operators, 106
    overloading, 292-298
    precedence, 107
OR logical operator, 104-105
order() function, 407-408

ostream class, 515, 521, 690-691
ostream withassign class, 515, 521-522
ostrstream class, 561-562
output, 27
output iterators, 660, 678-680
overloaded functions, 172-176, 188
overloading, 19
    constructors, 212-213, 482-490, 492
    operators, 291-292
        arguments, 294
        assignment operators, 479-481, 484-491, 497-498
        binary operators, 299-308
        conditional (?) operator, 326
        dot (.) operator, 326
        extraction operator, 557-561
        guidelines for using, 325-326
        insertion operator, 557-561
        limitations, 325
        multiple overloading, 304
        operator keyword, 293
        return values, 294-295
        scope resolution (::) operator, 326
        subscript [ ] operator, 309-312
        temporary objects, 296-297
        unary operators, 292-298
overriding member functions, 347-348

P

p = precision() member function, 518
page fault error message, 443
parameters of functions, 154
parent, *see* base classes
parse() member function, 435
parsing, 434
    arithmetic expressions, 434-438
    operators, 435
partial sort algorithm, 818
partial sort copy algorithm, 818
partial sum algorithm, 824
partition algorithm, 817
Pascal, 8
passing
    arguments to functions, 152
        by pointers, 403-406
        by reference, 166-172, 402
        by value, 155-156

constants, 153-154
structures, 155-160
variables, 154-155
arrays to functions, 251
peek() member function, 520
persistence, 744
pixel graphics, 807
Pohl, Ira, 890
pointers, 389
addresses in memory, 390
accessing variable pointed to, 395-397
address-of & operator, 391-392
constants, 394-395
variables, 392-393
arrays, 399-402
sorting array elements, 406-410
to objects, 423-425
to strings, 414-415
C-strings, 410-412
copying, 412-413
library functions, 413
changing types with dynamic cast operator,
499-501
const modifier, 413-414
constants, 401-402
debugging, 443
defining, 394
dereferencing, 397, 421
examples
horse-racing game, 438-443
parsing, 434-438
file pointers, 540-541
specifying the offset, 542
specifying the position, 541
functions, 402
normal functions, 454-456
passing arguments with, 403-406
virtual functions, 456-458
indirect addressing, 397
iterators as smart pointers, 677-678
linked lists, 425-429
objects, 420-421
arrays of pointers, 423-425
new operator, 422-423
referring to member functions, 421-422
pointers, 429-434
reinterpret cast, 399
smart pointers, 677-678

sorting, 431-432
syntax, 394
this pointer, 492-493
accessing member function data, 493-494
returning values, 494-497
to void, 398
uses of, 389-390
variables, 401-402
polymorphism, 19, 454
pop() member function, 257. 348-349
pop back() member function, 671
pop front() member function, 673, 675
pop heap algorithm, 822
popping items in stacks, 257-258
pos = tellg() member function, 520
pos = tellp() member function, 521
precedence of operators, 40, 80-81, 107
precision() member function, 518
predefined stream objects, 522
preprocessor directives, 28
#define, 43
#include, 28, 59-60
prev permutation algorithm, 823
preventing conversions, 326-328
printer output, 565-566
priority queues, 658
private access specifier, 342-343, 361-362
private inheritance, 359-362
private keyword, 197-198, 360, 789
problem summary statements, 726-727
procedural languages, 8
data types, 11
lack of real-world modeling, 10-11
unrestricted access, 9-10
program development and inheritance, 380-381
programming
object-oriented programming, 7
analogy, 12-13
basics of, 11
classes, 15-16
data types, 18
inheritance, 16-18
need for, 7
objects, 14-15
organization, 13
overloading, 19
polymorphism, 19
reusability, 18
structured programming, 8-11

programs
    construction of, 24
        comments, 29-31
        directives, 28-29
        expressions, 40
        functions, 24-25
        header files, 29
        input, 38-39
        namespaces, 29
        output, 27-28
        statements, 26
        variables, 31-37, 40-44
        whitespace, 26-27
    interacting, 768-770
    multifile programs, 573
        build process, 577
        class libraries, 573-575
        conceptualization, 576
        creating, 576-577
        directories, 576
        header files, 576
        high-rise elevator simulation example,
          583-598
        organization, 576
        projects, 576-577
        very long number class example, 577-582
        water-distribution system example, 598-611
    prototyping, 770-771
    writing, 753
        aggregate declarations, 758-759
        attribute declarations, 758
        class declarations, 758
        CPP files, 759-768
        header file, 753-758
        method declarations, 759
prohibiting copying, 485
projects
    C++Builder
        closing, 801
        creating, 798-799
        opening, 801
        saving, 799
    multifile programs, 576-577
    Visual C++, 793
protected access specifier, 342-344
protected keyword, 789
prototypes, 149
prototyping, 770-771

public access specifier, 342-343, 362
public inheritance, 359-362
public keyword, 197-198, 360, 789
pure virtual functions, 459-460
push back() member function, 670
push front() member function, 673
push heap algorithm, 821-822
push() member function, 257-258, 348-349
pushing items in stacks, 257-258
put pointer, 540-541
put to (<<) operator, 27, 46, 515
    cascading, 46
    overloading, 557-561
put() member function, 521, 532
putback() member function, 520

Q

questions, answers to
    chapter 1, 831
    chapter 2, 832-833
    chapter 3, 834-836
    chapter 4, 838-839
    chapter 5, 841-842
    chapter 6, 845-846
    chapter 7, 849-850
    chapter 8, 853-854
    chapter 9, 859
    chapter 10, 864-865
    chapter 11, 869-870
    chapter 12, 874-875
    chapter 13, 877
    chapter 14, 878-879
    chapter 15, 882-883
    chapter 16, 887-888
queues, 658

R

rand() library function, 264
random access iterators, 660, 678-679
random numbers, generating, 264
random shuffle algorithm, 817
raw storage iterators, 687
rbegin() member function, 658
rdbuf() member function, 533
read() member function, 520, 536

reading
    C-strings
        embedded blanks, 267-268
        multiple lines, 268-269
    data in formatted files, 529-530
    objects from a disk, 536-537
reference sources of C++ information, 889
    books, 889-890
    online course, 890
references to arguments (functions), 166-172
register keyword, 789
reinterpret cast keyword, 789
reinterpret cast operator, 399, 535, 789
reinterpret cast pointers, 399
relational operators, 67-69
    equal to (==) relational operator, 69
    greater than (>) relational operator, 69
    greater than or equal to (=) relational operator, 69
    less than (<) relational operator, 69
    less than or equal to (<=) relational operator, 69
    not equal to (!=) relational operator, 69
    precedence, 107
relationships of classes, 744
    aggregation, 744, 746-747
    associations, 744-746
    attributes, 744-745
    cohesion, 750
    composition, 746-747
    coupling, 750
    generalization, 744, 749-750
    has a relationships, 376, 744
    instance relationships, 744
    kind of relationships, 376
    multiplicity, 748
    uses relationships, 744-746
remainder (%) operator, 52-53
remove algorithm, 816
remove copy algorithm, 816
remove copy if algorithm, 816
remove if algorithm, 816
rend() member function, 658
replace algorithm, 815
replace copy algorithm, 815
replace copy if algorithm, 816
replace if algorithm, 815
replace() member function, 279-280
resetiosflags manipulator, 249, 518
return keyword, 789

returning
    structure variables from functions, 164-166
    values
        by reference, 185-187
        from functions, 161-164
        overloaded operators, 294-295
reusability, 18, 337
reverse algorithm, 817
reverse copy algorithm, 817
reverse iterators, 687-688
reverse() member function, 674
rfind() member function, 279
right flag, 516
Ritchie, Dennis, 890
rotate algorithm, 817
rotate copy algorithm, 817
routines (console graphics), 808
RTTI (Run-Time Type Information) and Visual C++, 793
Ruminations on C++, 890
Run-Time Type Information (RTTI) and Visual C++, 793

S

Saini, Atul, 890
scientific flag, 516
scope of variables
    automatic variables, 181
    external variables, 183
scope resolution (::) operator, 326, 349
search algorithm, 659, 663-664, 814-815
seekg() member function, 520, 541-543
seekp() member function, 521, 541
self-assignment, 497-498
self-containing classes, 429
sequence containers, 655-656, 669, 676
    arrays, 655
    deques, 655-656, 675
    lists, 655-656, 672-675
    vectors, 655-656, 669-672
sequences for escape, 28, 37-38
set color() function, 808-810
set cursor pos() function, 809
set difference algorithm, 821
set fill style() function, 809-810
set intersection algorithm, 821
set symmetric difference algorithm, 821
set union algorithm, 820-821
setdata() member function, 199

setf() member function, 516, 518-519
setfill manipulator, 518
setiosflags manipulator, 249, 517-518
setjmp() function, 634
setprecision manipulator, 249, 518
sets, 656-657, 694-697
setw manipulator, 44-45, 266, 518
short integer variables, 35
short keyword, 789
showbase flag, 516
showdata() member function, 199
showpoint flag, 516
showpos flag, 516
signed keyword, 789
single-stepping for loops, 75
size of arrays, 242
size() member function, 658
    string class, 282
    vectors, 670
sizeof keyword, 789
skipws flag, 516, 525
Smalltalk, 11, 198
smart pointers, 677-678
solutions to exercises
    chapter 2, 833-834
    chapter 3, 836-838
    chapter 4, 839-841
    chapter 5, 842-845
    chapter 6, 846-848
    chapter 7, 850-853
    chapter 8, 854-858
    chapter 9, 859-864
    chapter 10, 865-869
    chapter 11, 870-874
    chapter 12, 875-877
    chapter 14, 879-882
    chapter 15, 883-887
solve() member function, 435
sort algorithm, 659, 663, 818
sort heap algorithm, 822
sorting
    array elements, 406-410
    elements of arrays, 406-410
    pointers, 431-432
source files, 23
specifiers (classes), 197
sqrt() library function, 56-57
srand() library function, 264

stable partition algorithm, 818
stable sort algorithm, 818
stack is empty error message, 349
stacks, 255-257, 658
    popping items, 257-258
    pushing items, 257-258
Standard Template Library (STL), 653
    algorithms, 653-654, 659-661, 813-825
        containers, 680, 682-683
        count, 662-663
        find, 661-662
        for each, 667-668
        function objects, 665
        if, 666-667
        iterators, 681-682, 685-686, 827-829
        merge, 664-665
        search, 663-664
        sort, 663
        transform, 668-669
        user-written functions, 665-666
    containers, 653-655
        adapters, 658-659
        algorithms, 680, 682-683
        associative containers, 656-657, 693-700
        iterators, 680-681
        member functions, 657-658
        sequence containers, 655-656, 669-676
    function objects, 707
        modifying container behavior, 714
        predefined function objects, 707-710
        writing, 710-714
    iterators, 654, 660, 676, 683
        adapters, 687-690
        algorithms, 681-682, 685-686
        containers, 680-681
        data access, 683-684
        data insertion, 684
        interfaces, 678-680
        smart pointers, 677-678
        stream iterators, 690-693
    member functions, 825-827
    problems with, 661
    storing user-defined objects, 700-706
The Standard Template Library, 890
statements, 26
    assignment statements
        integer variables, 33-34
        structures, 126

control statements, 67
    decisions, 84-100, 107-111
    loops, 70-84, 87, 90-91
decision statements
    break statement, 98, 107-109
    continue statement, 110-111
    goto statement, 111
    if statement, 84-87
    if...else statement, 88-96, 100
    switch statement, 96-100
syntax, 26
static binding, 458
static cast keyword, 789
static class data, 224-227
    declaration, 227-228
    definition, 227-228
static functions, 476-477
    accessing members, 477-478
    numbering members, 478
static keyword, 789
static variables, 183-184
    initialization, 185
    storage, 185
stdio flag, 516
Stepanov, Alexander, 653, 890
STL (Standard Template Library), 653
    algorithms, 653-654, 659-661, 813-825
        containers, 680, 682-683
        count, 662-663
        find, 661-662
        for each, 667-668
        function objects, 665
        if, 666-667
        iterators, 681-682, 685-686, 827-829
        merge, 664-665
        search, 663-664
        sort, 663
        transform, 668-669
        user-written functions, 665-666
    containers, 653-655
        adapters, 658-659
        algorithms, 680, 682-683
        associative containers, 656-657, 693-700
        iterators, 680-681
        member functions, 657-658
        sequence containers, 655-656, 669-676

function objects, 707
    modifying container behavior, 714
    predefined function objects, 707-710
    writing, 710-714
iterators, 654, 660, 676, 683
    adapters, 687-690
    algorithms, 681-682, 685-686
    containers, 680-681
    data access, 683-684
    data insertion, 684
    interfaces, 678-680
    smart pointers, 677-678
    stream iterators, 690-693
member functions, 825-827
problems with, 661
storing user-defined objects, 700-706
STL Tutorial and Reference Guide, 890
storage classes (variables), 179
    automatic variables, 180-181
    external variables, 182-183
    static variables, 183-185
    summary, 185
storing user-defined objects, 700-706
strcat() library function, 275
strcmp() library function, 306, 433-434
strcpy() library function, 270, 413
stream classes, 513
    advantages, 513-514
    copying, 521-522
    fstream class, 528, 539
    hierarchy, 514-515
    ifstream class, 513, 528
    ios class, 515
        formatting flags, 516-517
        functions, 518-519
        manipulators, 517-518
    iostream class, 515
    iostream withassign class, 515, 521-522
    istream class, 515, 519, 521
    istream withassign class, 515, 521-522
    istrstream class, 561
    ofstream class, 528
    ostream class, 515, 521
    ostream withassign class, 515, 521-522
    ostrstream class, 561-562
    predefined stream objects, 522
    strstream class, 561

stream iterators, 690
  istream iterator class, 692-693
  ostream iterator class, 690-691
streams, 27, 513
  advantages, 513-514
  closing, 535
  command-line arguments, 562-564
  definition of, 513
  disk file I/O, 528
      binary I/O, 533-534
      char strings with embedded blanks, 530-532
      character I/O, 532-533
      formatted file I/O, 528-530
      object I/O, 535-539
  errors, 522
      checking, 525-527
      error-status flags, 522-523, 531-532
      inputting numbers, 523-524
      inputting strings and characters, 525
      no-input input, 524-525
      too many characters, 524
  input/output, 513-514
  memory, 561-562
  overloaded extraction and insertion operators,
      557-561
  printer output, 565-566
string class, 275, 282
  accessing characters in string objects, 281-282
  assigning objects, 276-277
  comparing objects, 280-281
  concatenation, 302-303
  converting to C-strings, 316-318
  defining objects, 276-277
  editing objects, 279-280
  finding objects, 278-279
  input/output, 277-278
  member functions
      append(), 280
      at(), 281-282
      capacity(), 282
      compare(), 280-281
      copy(), 282
      erase(), 279-280
      find(), 278
      find first not of(), 279
      find first of(), 278
      find last not of(), 279
      find last of(), 279

      getline(), 277-278
      insert(), 280
      length(), 282
      max size(), 282
      replace(), 279-280
      rfind(), 279
      size(), 282
      substr(), 281
      swap(), 276
  new operator, 419-420
strings, 28, 241
  arrays of pointers, 414-415
  C-strings, 264-265
      arrays, 270-272
      blanks, 267-268
      buffers, 265-266
      class members, 272-273
      concatenating, 302
      constants, 267
      converting to string objects, 316-318
      copying, 269-270
      multiple lines, 268-269
      pointers, 410-413
      user-defined strings, 273-275
      variables, 265-266
  comparing, 305-306, 433-434
  disk file I/O, 530-532
  string class, 275, 282
      accessing characters in string objects,
          281-282
      assigning objects, 276-277
      comparing objects, 280-281
      concatenation, 302-303
      converting to C-strings, 316-318
      defining objects, 276-277
      editing objects, 279-280
      finding objects, 278-279
      input/output, 277-278
      new operator, 419-420
strlen() library function, 269-270
Stroustrup, Bjarne, 889-890
strstream class, 561
struct keyword, 121, 789
structured programming, 8
  problems with, 8
      data types, 11
      lack of real-world modeling, 10-11
      unrestricted access, 9-10

structures, 119, 223-224, 653
    arrays, 253-255
        accessing elements, 254
        defining, 254
        similarities to, 241
    assignment statements, 126
    classes, 134
    combining declaration and definition, 124-125
    declaration, 120-121
        syntax, 121
        use of, 121-122
    defining, 122-123
    definition of, 119
    examples
        card game, 132-134
        measurements, 127-128
    members, 119-120
        accessing, 123-124
        accessing in nested structures, 130-131
        initializing, 125-126
    names, 121
    nesting, 129
        accessing members, 130-131
        depth of, 132
        initialization, 131-132
        user-defined type conversions, 131
    passing to functions, 155-160, 170-171
    returning structure variables from functions, 164-166
    syntax, 119-120
    tags, 121
style of loops, 74-75
subclasses, *see* derived classes
subscript [ ] operator, overloading, 309-312
substr() member function, 281
subtraction (-) operator, 52
superclasses, *see* base classes
swap algorithm, 659, 815
swap() member function
    string class, 276
    vectors, 671
swap ranges algorithm, 815
switch keyword, 96, 789
switch statement, 96-98
    character variables, 99
    default keyword, 99-100
    versus if...else statement, 100
syntax
    class templates, 625-628
    classes, 195-196

comments, 30-31
constructors, 208-209
exceptions, 634-635
function templates, 618, 621
pointers, 394
statements, 26
structures, 119-121

T

tags (structures), 121
Teale, Steve, 890
tellg() member function, 541, 543-544
tellp() member function, 541
template keyword, 618, 621, 624, 789
templates, 615
    classes, 622-625
        determining storage parameters, 633
        example, 628-630
        syntax, 625-628
        user-defined data types, 630-632
    functions, 615-618
        arguments, 619-621
        blueprints, 619
        compilers, 618-619
        determining what works, 622
        syntax, 618, 621
        tips for simplifying, 619
text in strings, 241
Thinking in C++, 889
this keyword, 789
this pointer, 492-493
    accessing member function data, 493-494
    returning values, 494-497
throw keyword, 634, 789
throwing exceptions, 634, 637
to void pointers, 398
transform algorithm, 668-669, 815
trees, 656
    decision trees, 94
    inheritance trees, 340
true keyword, 789
try blocks, 634, 638
try keyword, 634, 638, 789
type casts, 50-52
type information (classes), 498
    dynamic cast operator, 498-501
    typeid operator, 501-502
type safety, 52
typedef keyword, 789

typeid keyword, 789
typeid operator, 498, 501-502
typeid() member function, 550-557
typename keyword, 789
types
    data types
        unsigned long data type, 577
        user-defined data types, 630-632
    enumerations, 135-141
        integer values, 141
        limitations, 141

U

UML (Universal Modeling Language)
    class diagrams, 722
        aggregation, 746-747
        associations, 745
        composition, 747
        creating, 750-753
        generalization, 749-750
        multiplicity, 748-749
        navigability of associations, 746
    multiplicity symbols, 748
unary operators, 106
    overloading, 292-295
        arguments, 294
        postfix notation, 297-298
        prefix notation, 298
        temporary objects, 296-297
    precedence, 107
unidentifed identifier error message, 58
union keyword, 789
unique algorithm, 816
unique copy algorithm, 817
unique() member function, 674
unitbuf flag, 516
Universal Modeling Language (UML)
    class diagrams, 722
        aggregation, 746-747
        associations, 745
        composition, 747
        creating, 750-753
        generalization, 749-750
        multiplicity, 748-749
        navigability of associations, 746
    multiplicity symbols, 748
unknown variable error message, 181
unlock manipulator, 517

unsetf() member function, 516, 518
unsigned data types, 47-48
unsigned keyword, 789
unsigned long data type, 577
upper bound algorithm, 819
upper bound() member function, 696-697
uppercase flag, 516
use cases, 721-722, 737-740, 742-743
user interface screens, 770-771
user-defined data types
    class templates, 630-632
    converting
        from basic type to user-defined type, 315
        to basic types, 313-316
user-defined objects, storing, 700-706
uses relationships (classes), 744-746
using directive, 29
using keyword, 789

V

values
    passing to functions, 153-156
    returning
        by reference, 185-187
        from functions, 161-164
variables
    automatic variables, 180
        initialization, 181
        lifetime, 180
        scope, 181
        storage, 185
        visibility, 181
    bool variables, 43-44, 103
    C-strings, 265-266
    character variables
        char character variable, 35-36
        character constants, 36-37
        switch statement, 99
        wchar t character variable, 35-36
    data types, 46
        casts, 50-52
        conversions, 48-49
        type safety, 52
        unsigned data types, 47-48
    declarations, 33
    defining, 33
        at point of use, 39
        in for statements, 76
        multiple definitions, 46

external variables, 182-183
 initialization, 183
 lifetime, 183
 purpose of, 183
 scope, 183
 storage, 185
 visibility, 183
floating point variables, 40
 constants, 42-43
 double, 42
 float, 41-42
 long double, 42
global variables, *see* external variables
identifiers, 33
initialization, 37
instance variables, 11
integer variables, 31
 assignment statements, 33-34
 defining, 31-33
 int integer variable, 31-33
 integer constants, 34
 long integer variables, 35
 output variations, 34
 short integer variables, 35
 true/false values, 106
local variables, *see* automatic variables
names, 33
 conventions, 33
 keywords, 33
passing to functions, 154-155
pointers, 392-393, 395-397, 401-402
static variables, 183-184
 initialization, 185
 storage, 185
storage classes, 179
 automatic variables, 180-181
 external variables, 182-183
 static variables, 183-185
 summary, 185
structures, 119
 accessing members, 123-124, 130-131
 assignment statements, 126
 classes, 134
 combining declaration and definition, 124-125
 declaration, 120-122
 defining, 122-123
 definition of, 119
 examples, 127-128, 132-134

initializing members, 125-126
 members, 119-120, 123
 names, 121
 nesting, 129-132
 syntax, 119-120
 tags, 121
vectors, 655-656, 669-672
 back(), 671
 erase(), 671-672
 insert(), 671-672
 max size(), 670
 pop back(), 671
 push back(), 670
 size(), 670
 swap(), 671
virtual base classes, 466-468
virtual destructors, 465-466
virtual functions, 453-454
 examples, 460-465
 pointers, 456-458
 pure virtual functions, 459-460
virtual keyword, 456, 468, 790
visibility of variables
 automatic variables, 181
 external variables, 183
Visual C++, 791
 building existing files, 792
 Console Graphics Lite, 794-795
 debugging programs, 795
  breakpoints, 796
  single stepping, 795-796
  stepping into functions, 796
  watching variables, 796
 file extensions, 791
 multifile programs, 793-794
  closing, 794
  compiling, 794
  linking, 794
  opening, 794
  saving, 794
 projects, 793
 RTTI, 793
 screen elements, 791
 single-file programs, 792
 source files, 793-794
 workspaces, 793
 writing files, 792-793
void keyword, 149, 163, 790
void pointers, 398
volatile keyword, 790

W-Z

w = width() member function, 518
wait() function, 809-810
wchar t character variable, 35-36
wchar t keyword, 790
while loop, 77-79
    multiple statements, 79-80
    precedence of operators, 80-81
    test expressions, 78
    uses, 84
whitespace, 26-27
width() member function, 518
Windows Game Programming for Dummies, 890
workspaces (Visual C++), 793
write() member function, 521, 536
writing
    data to formatted files, 528-529
    function objects, 710-714
    objects to a disk, 535-536
    programs, 753
        aggregates declarations, 758-759
        attribute declarations, 758
        class declarations, 758
        CPP files, 759-768
        header file, 753-758
        method declarations, 759
ws manipulator, 517

xalloc class, 646
XOR logical operator, 105

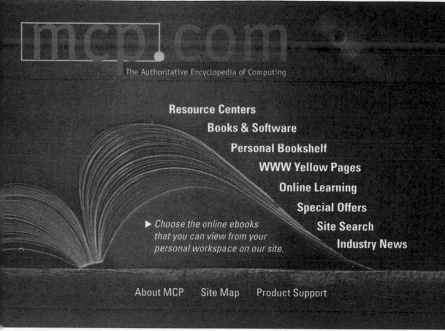

mcp.com
The Authoritative Encyclopedia of Computing

Resource Centers
Books & Software
Personal Bookshelf
WWW Yellow Pages
Online Learning
Special Offers
Site Search
Industry News

▶ *Choose the online ebooks that you can view from your personal workspace on our site.*

About MCP   Site Map   Product Support

Get the best information and learn about latest developments in:

- Design

- Graphics and Multimedia

- Enterprise Computing and DBMS

- General Internet Information

- Operating Systems

- Networking and Hardware

- PC and Video Gaming

- Productivity Applications

- Programming

- Web Programming and Administration

- Web Publishing

Turn to the *Authoritative* Encyclopedia of Computing

You'll find over 150 full text books online, hundreds of shareware/freeware applications, online computing classes and 10 computing resource centers full of expert advice from the editors and publishers of:

- Adobe Press
- BradyGAMES
- Cisco Press
- Hayden Books
- Lycos Press
- New Riders

- Que
- Que Education & Training
- Sams Publishing
- Waite Group Press
- Ziff-Davis Press

mcp.com
The Authoritative Encyclopedia of Computing

When you're looking for computing information, consult the authority.
The Authoritative Encyclopedia of Computing at mcp.com.

Other Related Titles

Using C++
Rob McGregor
ISBN: 0-8979-1997-4
$29.99 US/$42.95 CAN

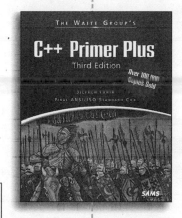

**C++ Primer Plus,
Third Edition**
Stephen Prata
ISBN: 1-57169-162-9
$35.00 US/$50.95 CAN

C++ Unleashed
Jesse Liberty
ISBN: 0-627-31239-5
$39.99 USA/$57.95 CAN

C++ How-To
Jan Walter
ISBN: 1-57169-159-6
$39.99 US/$57.95 CAN

**Sams Teach Yourself
C++ in 21 Days, Second
Edition**
Jesse Liberty
ISBN: 0-672-31080-8
$29.99 US/$42.95 CAN

**Sams Teach Yourself
C++ in 24 Hours**
Jesse Liberty
ISBN: 0-672-31067-8
$24.99 US/$35.95 CAN

**ActiveX Programming
with Visual C++**
Jerry Anderson
ISBN: 0-7897-1030-7
$49.95 US/$71.95 CAN

SAMS
www.samspublishing.com

**Complete Idiot's Guide
to C++**
Paul Snaith
ISBN: 0-7897-1816-2
$16.99 US/$24.95 CAN